Tomart's Value Guide to Disney
ANIMATION ART

An Easy-To-Use Compilation of Over 40 Animation Art Auctions Organized by Film, Character and Art Type

by Tom Tumbusch and Bob Welbaum

TOMART PUBLICATIONS
division of Tomart Corporation
Dayton, Ohio

DEDICATION

To Harold Tumbusch and Robert Morris Welbaum — Our Guiding Lights, Our Inspirations,

Our Fathers

ACKNOWLEDGEMENTS

The authors are deeply indebted to all the many people who contributed to this book:

The list must begin with the press and public relations offices at Sotheby's, Christie's East, Christie's Los Angeles, Howard Lowery, and S/R Laboratories. Names have changed over the course of forty-plus auctions and five years, but without them there would have been no auction results to list or artwork to show. Kudos can start with the current incumbents, Vredy Lytsman (Christie's East), Kate Drury (Sotheby's), Beth Shepherd (Christie's Los Angeles), their colleagues and assistants, as well as their immediate predecessors. Also thanks to the entire staff of Howard Lowery beginning with Howard himself, and Ron Stark of S/R Laboratories. They are consummate professionals all.

Next come the technical experts: Richard Taylor of Gifted Images Gallery, Paula Sigman-Lowery and Howard Lowery, and Ron Stark. Their inputs kept the information technically accurate and provided essential detail. We're convinced this is a much more useful book because of them.

A special mention must go to the production staff at Tomart Publications. There was Marijke Smith (photo processing), Kelly McLees (photography), Nathan Hanneman (production assistance), Jeremy Boggs (production assistance), and Anthony Taylor (production assistance). And without Kerrie Cela, Rebecca Snyder, Dan Lawson, Angela Lindsay, and Rebecca Sue Trissel, no orders would have been fulfilled. Also a heart-felt thank you to Denise Tudor, called in for page layout and final production.

Finally, thanks to everyone who has spent hard-earned money to purchase animation magic. This book is the summation of your marketplace decisions. We sincerely hope you find it useful.

Prices listed are based on the cash purchase price which includes the hammer price and usually includes a 10 to 15% buyer's premium. (The exception is S/R Laboratories, whose prices do not include the buyer's premium.) They are presented as a guide for information purposes only. No one is obligated in any way to buy, sell or trade according to these prices. Condition, rarity, demand and the reader's desire to own determine the actual price paid. No offer to buy or sell at the prices listed is intended or made. Buying and selling is conducted at the consumer's risk. Neither the authors nor the publisher assumes any liability for any losses suffered for use of, or any typographic errors contained in, this book. All value estimates are presented in U.S. dollars. The dollar sign is omitted to avoid needless repetition.

Published by Tomart Publications, Dayton, Ohio, 45439

Library of Congress Catalog Card Number: 98-60585

ISBN: 0-914293-41-9   Manufactured in the United States of America

1 2 3 4 5 6 7 8 9 0   0 9 8 7 6 5 4 3 2 1

FOREWORD

There is always difficulty in determining the approximate value of "animation art." Each piece is unique and there are many different types of art which get lumped into this rather broad category. This book is designed to educate the novice while providing a value guide indispensable to experts. The prices listed herein are not estimates. They are up-to-the-press-deadline prices paid at leading auction houses conducting sales of animation art.

The auction results reported were first published in *Tomart's DISNEYANA Update* magazine soon after each sale was completed. The information has been reorganized in this volume so comparables can easily be located to provide guidance to the reader. The introduction is must reading for the novice because this market is full of "terms" which can easily cause confusion and/or costly mistakes. This is compounded by the media which persists in reporting "a cel sold for $25,000" when, in fact, the sale was comprised of a cel from a prominent animator's key drawing with a unique matching original painted pan background. The media doesn't feel those extra words are important, but if the same cel sold alone, the price would have been more like $3,000. The above describes all the elements of a cel set-up as it was filmed for one or two frames of a Disney animated film. Animation art for feature films, cartoons, TV shows, TV in-and-outs, training films, industrial films, and TV commercials is all floating around out there in the world somewhere. In addition, there are many other types of "cels" never actually used in the production of a film which are created for promotion or the fan and collector market. These fan or collector cels range from "hand-inked and -painted or gallery cels" to silkscreened limited-edition re-creation "sericels" to mass-produced press-printed cels which get bound into books, magazines, and movie programs. There are also many fake cels in circulation.

Animation art was first sold commercially by the Courvoisier Gallery of San Francisco, but became available many other ways as described in "History of Disney Animation Art Sales" on page 8.

Production cels are actually transfers of the creative work performed by the animator. But they are the normally preferred type of animation art because the cel set-up comprises the actual material photographed for some of the most acclaimed animation ever done.

If each frame is animated, it takes 1440 drawings and 1440 cels per character for each minute of film. So even after the great museums of the world add new film set-ups to their collections, plenty of material is left for collectors and fans. The Disney brothers started their first animated film production facility in 1923 and subsequent activities have resulted in art used in thousands of films, TV projects, theme park attractions, and for other special uses. The introductory material on the following pages provides the background needed to help readers match animation art pieces in the auction-result descriptions to come up with a comparable value. If this search is somehow not productive, a list of other resources is also provided.

TABLE OF CONTENTS

INTRODUCTION

Basic animation art knowledge comes from a good understanding of the process. The following narrative is an oversimplification of animation, but serves to begin to bring all the elements into focus.

The first step after a story is chosen is to design the look of the characters. Next comes the storyboard, the art of communicating the entire story with key drawings. When the storyboards are approved, the project goes into production. The supervising director must get the soundtrack recorded. He then assigns scenes to the artist who will bring life to the characters. These animators do the key drawings or "extremes" – only about a tenth of the drawings which create the illusion of movement when the finished film is projected. The remaining drawings needed to make the movement flow smoothly are completed by the assistant animator and "inbetweeners" (apprentice animators learning the craft). Assignments usually consist of an exposure sheet for charting animation drawings and sometimes a layout drawing showing how the camera will zoom in or out or pan right or left as the assigned scene unfolds. The animator adds a timing sheet to guide his assistant and the inbetweeners. The director assigns backgrounds and special effects to other artists on the production team.

Once the animators, background painters, and special-effects artists have done their jobs, the work is checked for smoothness of movement and error detection before the drawings are transferred to cels and painted. This step is called the "pencil test" and saves a lot of wasted work should the drawings need to be revised. If the character(s) interact with the background, a sketchy line tracing of the painted background may be prepared for the pencil-test process. Examples of this have been sold through the Disney Art Program.

Publicity photo of Walt Disney demonstrating a Zeotrope on TV's "Disneyland The Story of Animated Drawing". The Zeotrope is one of the early devices used in creating the illusion of animation.

Once the pencil test is approved, the drawings go to the ink and paint department for cel production. The finished cels are then checked and organized with backgrounds and exposure sheets by the pre-production staff and sent to the camera to be shot for the final production.

This method describes the original Disney process which was used from when the studio was founded until a new method was tested on *Goliath II* in 1960. *101 Dalmatians* was the first feature using this new process. At this point, drawings were cleaned up more to define a single line and transferred to the cel, not by tracing the drawing, but by a flat plate Haloid-Xerox process. This method was used for most features while the studio experimented with other methods. *The Black Cauldron* used a photographic process to transfer the drawings. The large film transparency then became the cel when developed and painted on the reverse. The major problem with this process was increased cel opacity. When three or four cels were photographed on a background, the thicknesses of cel on top of cel caused unsatisfactory image clarity and color shifts. Animator drawings, depending on films up through *The Little Mermaid*, were hand-traced, Xeroxed, or photographed to a cel. These cels were then hand-painted on the reverse. Starting with *Beauty and the Beast*, drawings were transferred frame by frame to video where they were colorized, composited with the backgrounds and computer effects before being outputted to film. For films using this video-to-film process, hand-painted cels have been created after the fact for sale with the original backgrounds. Even though there are many different types of animation art, the dominate focus when discussing the subject seems to center on cels and cel set-ups because these are the elements filmed a frame at a time to make the animated film. They are also the most abundant type of animation art in circulation.

Cels

A cel – short for celluloid – is actually the blank clear plastic sheet to which animation drawings are traced, machine transferred, or photographed. Prior to 1940, cels were made of nitrocellulose, an unstable and flammable material. The change to safety cels, made of cellulose acetate, began with Disney's *Fantasia*.

Originally cels were traced onto the front of clear celluloid sheets using pen or brush and ink, then painted on the reverse with specially prepared gum-based paints. Cels were never intended to withstand the test of time. They only needed to last long enough to meet production schedules. The paints and inks were designed for easy removal. During the Great Depression and periods during World War II, cels were washed off and reused because the supply of new ones was slim. These reused cels have pen scratches from the original use still in evi-

dence. Thus, it is a gift of fortune when old cels remain intact today. The paint dehydrates and flakes easily, especially on older cels. So care is recommended during handling and framing.

Cel material, sizes, punching, and paints have all changed over the years. A "12-field" drawing area was used by Disney up until work began on *Snow White and The Seven Dwarfs*. During this first animated feature, much of the work was done on "16-field"-size cels. The 12-field cel continued to be used on cartoons, shorts, and selected feature scenes done at the Hyperion Avenue Studio. When the new Burbank Studio was completed in 1940, all animators switched to the 16-field size. Some cels are punched with only two holes at the bottom. Other early standard cels have three or five holes. Films produced in 70mm or Cinemascope formats may have wider cels, but many for *Lady and the Tramp* were cut down to a more convenient size for sale at Disneyland. Today's standard-size cel is 12-1/2" x 15-1/2". Back in the 1930s, 10" x 12-1/4" was more standard.

There have always been special sizes of cels and backgrounds to accommodate special movements right or left, up or down, or characters moving at rapid speed. Normally, each major character in the scene is on a separate cel, except for parade or crowd scenes where groups of images are animated together. The larger and more complete the character appears, generally the greater the value. The expression captured on the single cel is also very important. Collectors also consider such things as the eyes being open, the direction the character is facing, and many other factors to determine the price they wish to pay. The more famous the character, the greater the demand and higher the price. The same goes for the film or cartoon. The early classics are in demand from a historic perspective, while *The Little Mermaid*, *Beauty and the Beast*, *Aladdin*, and *The Lion King* have more contemporary appeal. *Winnie the Pooh* and *101 Dalmatians* have a large following unique to these works.

Backgrounds

Painted production backgrounds have been rendered in every type of artist paints ranging from watercolors to fine oil paint to modern acrylics. The most often used were opaque water-based tempera or poster paints commonly referred to in auction listings as "gouache paintings." Thin illustration board suitable for water-based paints was the most often used "canvas" for background paintings. Backgrounds for the multiplane camera were normally rendered with oil-based paints on glass ... rather thick glass. This camera could utilize up to six background layers which could be adjusted to different levels. All cels created for this camera were 12-field cels. The purpose of the multiplane camera was to get more depth into animation, which is particularly exciting when the characters are moving. Backgrounds could be moved north, south, east, or west. Most of these bulky glass set-ups were cleaned off and reused. Very few authentic multiplane camera backgrounds on glass survived outside the studio.

The most important point to understand is the real value in a cel set-up is in the background, not in the cel. There can be hundreds of cels for a single background.

Effects Cels

Special effects like rain, snow, fire, water drops in a pond, and other similar phenomenon are the work of special-effects animators who are charged with all sorts of mood-creating or effects detailing. This method of adding realism was developed by Disney, but copied by the competition. These special effects are usually done on separate cels except in an case where a drop splashes off a character's nose, for example. Special-effects cels were not often saved, nor are they a major factor in value or collecting. They are mentioned here for reference in case such cels are seen.

The Cel Set-Up

Set-ups include a background, character cel (or cels if multiple characters appear in the scene), and possibly a special-effects cel. These are combined and photographed as a single frame of film. There are 24 frames per second for film productions; 30 frames per second for made-for-TV productions. If a character moves or talks rapidly, all 24 frames of Disney films are usually animated with a slightly different drawing for each frame. If action is normal, each set-up is usually shot twice. The eye can't normally detect lack of movement in less than six frames ... about one fourth of a second. The original background is the key value element in the set-up. The number of cels, as mentioned earlier, can be many times greater. Demand for the complete picture is stronger than for the cels alone. A special-effects cel adds little to the value, but is a nice touch if it is still available.

Since only one set-up can incorporate the original, a variety of other non-production backgrounds have been used over the years to complete the finished look of the frame for all the other cels.

Stencils, printed full-color copies of the original, and color photographic copies of the original have all been used as "stand-ins." Some may enhance value because a complete picture is better than an incomplete one. But none of the substitutes come close to matching the value of the original background.

A Cel or Not a Cel

A substitute background has a place in completing the picture. A hand-inked and -painted limited-edition gallery cel produced from the original animation art using the color guide prepared by the credited art director provides a modern-day duplicate of the cel used to put together a classic film. Silkscreened sericels are like a picture print on mylar and allow just about anyone to own classic Disney images. Press-printed cels seem to be pushing things a bit much, but the effect can be rather striking when these imitations are nicely framed. However, none of these quite compare to ownership of production cels from the actual filming along with the original background.

Now that animation art has entered the fine-art arena and values have climbed, counterfeit cels and backgrounds are more common. It requires a trained eye to recognize a fake. In a single case in 1982, Walt Disney Productions prosecuted an artist for the creation of over 18,000 bogus cels. A supply of equally fake labels was confiscated as well. So collectors should be aware it is possible to get an education the hard way.

In 1988, Time Inc. and The Walt Disney Company collaborated on *Mickey Is Sixty!*, a special commemorative magazine for Mickey Mouse's sixtieth birthday. Included was "free exclusive Disney animation art" as proclaimed on the cover. This "exclusive" was nothing more than a thin sheet of mylar printed with a publicity image of Mickey as the Sorcerer's Apprentice. Occasionally a framed copy appears on the secondary market as a genuine cel from *Fantasia*.

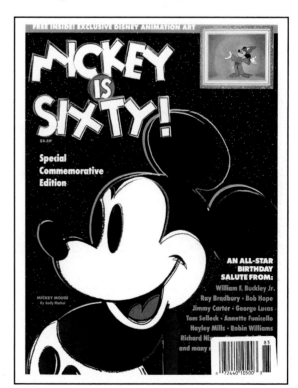

Design art for a character proposed for *Fantasia*.

Other Types of Disney Animation Art

Cels and cel set-ups certainly dominate Disney animation art availability, but there is also a good selection of other types of art available to the fan and collector market. Such material comes from all the steps in the animation process.

> Character design
> Model sheets
> Maquettes
> Storyboards
> Camera direction layout art
> Concept art
> Backgrounds only
> Animation drawings
> Promotional cels
> 3-D and stop motion
> Example multiplane camera set-ups

In addition to animation done for cartoons, shorts, and features, there is a wide variety of other animation art done for commercial clients, the government, television, theme parks, and special events. Included in this category are all types of art for:

Industrial films
Government training films
Television commercials for films, theme parks,
    TV shows, and licensees
TV in-and-outs
Theme park attractions
Special events

Character Design Art

Disney has a long history of putting a unique touch on even the most classic characters, such as Snow White, the Seven Dwarfs, Peter Pan, even Winnie the Pooh. Each film has dozens of characters. Every one goes through a design process which may see many different versions before being finalized. This work is done on sketch pads or plain sheets of paper. In tough times, characters have been designed on interleaf cel protector sheets. Much of the work is destroyed when designs are set, but designers and animators have been known to keep favorites which may have been rejected or revised. Most dealers with good connections with former or retired animators can find this type of material.

The Hunchback of Notre Dame: Quasimodo maquette, 10-1/8"
high, #45/45, S/Jun 21/97 (2000-3000)   3450

Model Sheets

Once the character design was approved, sketches were done from all sides and in different positions. These were then composited on a large sheet and "statted" for use by the animation team. Originals are mostly gone, but many of the statted composites remains.

Maquettes

A maquette is a three-dimensional figure produced from the model sheets to aid in the animation process. They can be painted or unpainted. These figures can be turned to any angle to guide the animator as he plans what the camera will see and how the character will move. The detail of the maquette also serves as a constant reminder of all the elements which need to be in each and every drawing. Maquettes are usually created for every major character in the film. They have been used for many animated features. It is rare to find them on the collector's market. The exceptions are certain maquettes created alongside the original animation art models for sale as art pieces. These are characters from *Beauty and the Beast*, *Aladdin*, *The Lion King*, *Pocahontas*, and *The Hunchback of Notre Dame*.

Mickey Mouse model sheet

ZIP A DEE DOO DAH -- ZIP A DEE YEA

MY OH MY - WHAT A WONDERFUL DAY

----- HEADING MY WAY --

ZIP A DEE DOO DAH-- ZIP A DEE YEA

THERE-S A BLUE BIRD OVER MY SHOULDER

IT-S THE TRUTH -- IT-S ACTUAL

EVERYTHING IS SATISFACTUAL.....

ZIP A DEE DOO DAH -- ZIP A DEE YEA

WONDERFUL FEELING -- WONDERFUL DAY

MUSIC.....

MUSIC......

PLENTY OF SUNSHINE HEADING MY WAY

ZIP A DEE DOO DAH -- ZIP A DEE YEA

Storyboard panels for the song "Zip-A-Dee Doo Dah" as originally laid out by Ken Anderson. When changes in lyrics and concept were made, the song storyboard was redone. Kay Kamen Ltd. Art Director Lou Lispi salvaged these storyboard drawings from Ken's wastebasket during a studio visit to serve as character reference for merchandise planning back in New York.

Publicity photo for *Bambi*. The release caption read: "Hollywood, California. Walt Disney, famed producer of animated cartoons here weeds out some of the 4,000,000 drawings made for his new feature "Bambi" now completed." Note concept art and model sheets in the array of art.

Storyboards

Here is one of the great Disney contributions to the animation process. A surviving script for *Steamboat Willie*, the first Mickey Mouse cartoon released, shows the story drawings were originally done right on the script. Somewhere along the line the drawings were separated and pinned on large boards so they could be revised to insert a gag, change the action or improve a character. Storyboard drawings were normally simple black-and-white pencil sketches, but many were colored as part of showing the look of the film during story review. The story art seems to increase in popularity as more of it becomes available. Most was done by the art directors in the story department of the studio as represented by the likes of Ken Anderson, Bill Peet, Ted Sears, Roy Williams, and Jack Kinney.

Camera Direction Layout Art

This is probably the rarest of all the art steps in the animation process to find. Most were either destroyed or kept by the studio. Two or three different colored pencils were used for line drawings. A large rectangle in red would show where the shot was to begin. Then a smaller one in blue showed how far the camera would zoom in and where the zoom action would stop. Many examples of camera direction art are shown in *The Art of Walt Disney* by Christopher Finch and many other books, but examples weren't kept by animators or others. Little material of this type from the early cartoons or animated classics has ever reached the secondary market.

Concept Art

This type art is done in conjunction with story development to help define the look, mood, emotional goals, settings, style, and other values which need clear understanding before the animation team can begin work. These drawings help in the development process and get all the artists on the same page once these details have been finalized.

Walt Disney occasionally hired outside artists and illustrators to do drawings and paintings to inspire his staff. Some worked full-time stints. Others were employed for certain projects. Gustaf Tenggren's work strongly influenced *Snow White and the Seven Dwarfs* and *Pinocchio*. Salvador Dali worked at the studio for a few months on an unproduced project called *Destino*.

Over the years *Pogo* artist Walt Kelly, Ferdinand Horvath, Eyvind Earle, *Dennis the Menace* creator Hank Ketcham, Mary Blair, and many others all worked on various Disney concepts, art direction, and even some animation.

One of the earliest known Disney backgrounds in circulation is from the *Alice Comedy* series.

Backgrounds Only

Looking at an animation art collection, it is easy to get the impression the cels are always kept with backgrounds. In fact, most older set-ups were matched up after the fact. Cels are usually wrapped by scene or scene segment. Backgrounds are filed on large racks which allow them to dry thoroughly, but not overlap or lay on top of each other. These racks are on wheels for easy movement from the background department to the checking department where all final materials are verified and organized for shooting before going into the camera department for filming. After filming, the material is stored until no longer needed for production.

Many backgrounds were saved by artists. Like animators, background artists saved examples of work by fellow artists. Some were saved for inspiration; others for admiration. Sometimes the background department saved some pieces for reuse or future reference. Many backgrounds have been auctioned as stand-alone art. A look at these results quickly confirms which is the most valuable element in the cel set-up. Even though good backgrounds command high prices when sold alone, many remain in the files of animation art dealers who continue to search for a matching cel. Completing the set-up offers a potentially higher price for the cel – particularly when a dealer knows a collector who would pay a premium for the complete scene.

Animation Drawings

The real creative work from the animator's point of view, these drawings create life and personality on the screen. This is the art the studio kept, the drawings from which the cels were created. Most of the great scenes are preserved in the studio animation archives. They are referred to when similar scenes occur in more modern films. These drawings and exposure sheets save thousands of man-hours because they provide frame-by-frame guides even though the character may look totally different.

Animators work in different ways – some very rough or sketchy, others with strong prominent lines, most produced drawings somewhere in between. Still, this "rough" animation all requires some clean-up work. A cleaned-up animation drawing, usually the job of assistant animators, eliminates guidelines and other marks made in working out the key drawings in the scene. Once "cleaned-up," the line-drawing image left no doubt what lines were to be transferred to the cel. Normally, only cleaned-up drawings were kept and remain available for collectors.

When scenes were cut or changed, many of the drawings were retained by the animators. However they were exchanged, these drawings were the animation art most kept by the animators themselves. Most of them are amazed by the cel set-up prices realized at auctions. Usually the only ones they ever kept were nice framed

Animation drawing of the Old Hag from *Snow White and the Seven Dwarfs.*

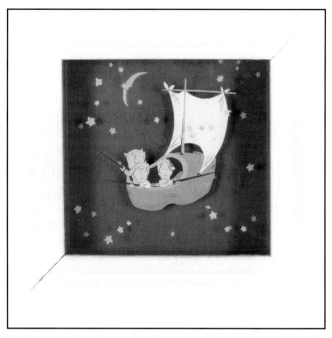

Courvoisier *Wyken, Blynken, Nod* multi plane camera demonstration set-up.

set-ups to decorate their kid's rooms ... or to send to relatives for much the same purpose. Nearly all the animators interviewed by the authors have kept several folders full of animation and other drawings by friends whom they admired. The Dwarfs were all popular. Most kept examples of Norm Ferguson's Pluto flypaper sequence from *Playful Pluto*, Wolfgang Reitherman's Monstro the Whale from *Pinocchio*, and the list goes on and on. The animators who pioneered the craft kept thousands of momentos. Much of this material has been made available over the years, but lacking the color of the cel set-up, these original drawings have never achieved values anywhere close to color tracings transferred to a cel and painted.

Promotional Cels

During the 1930s and '40s, cels were created for a variety of promotional purposes. Title cels incorporating leading characters were often done as gifts to theater-chain owners. In more recent times, California Institute of the Arts, or CalArts, the school Walt and Roy Disney helped found to train animators, did Disney cels as a fund-raising project. Artists in training at the Disney/MGM Studios n Florida have done souvenir cels for purchase by guests visiting the theme park. The images for these cels are usually transferred using the flat photo Haloid-Xerox process and hand-painted on the reverse.

3-D and Stop Motion

The process for normal 3-D is nearly the same as regular animation production. The camera and lens provide most of the technology needed. Enhanced 3-D seen in theme park productions like "Captain Eo," "Honey, I Shrunk the Audience," and "It's Tough to be a Bug!" require additional animation.

Stop-motion films like *Tim Burton's The Nightmare Before Christmas* and *James and the Giant Peach* require full three-dimensional sets and figures. Sets and the stop-motion figures from *Nightmare* and *James* were prominently featured in Sotheby's auctions, and other materials from older stop-motion and the 3-D cartoons *Adventures in Music: Melody* and *Working for Peanuts* could be in circulation.

Example Multiplane Camera Set-Ups

The Courvoisier Gallery did approximately 15 different examples of multiplane camera set-ups during the 1940s when this revolutionary new technique to provide more realistic depth to two-dimensional images received a tremendous amount of publicity. None of the components in these examples were actual animation art, but merely a demonstration on how the technique worked. The Courvoisier pieces were about 6" square and 2" thick. The window-glass panels inside were much thinner than the glass used in the real multiplane camera set-up which averaged about six to eight feet from the top glass foreground panel to the painted background. The various layers in the Courvoisier examples are also silkscreened rather than painted.

Industrial Films

During World War II, the Disney Studio lost the entire European film market which had previously provided almost half of its revenue. Most materials used to make toys were also rationed, costing Walt Disney Productions a major portion of its licensing income. So the studio

Multiplane Camera

looked to other sources. It set up a division to go into the business world to solicit animated film production for commercial clients. For example, the studio made films on dental health for the American Dental Association in the 1920s, 1930s, and revised in 1940, *Jet Propulsion* (1946) for General Electric Co. and *How To Catch a Cold* (1951) for International Cellucotton Co. (Kleenex).

The effort did not provide the return anticipated and the division was eliminated, even though the studio did *Steel and America* as late as 1965 for the American Iron & Steel Institute. Cels from many of these films were distributed to executives, customers, and friends. Few contained classic Disney characters or surface for resale on the collector's market.

Government Training Films

Very little, if any, of this art has reached the secondary market. Most of the films were probably classified at the time with much of the work done under military guard. Storyboard scenes have been featured in national and specialized magazines ... and the single issue of *Dispatch from Disney* published by the Disney studio for mailing to studio employees serving in the military.

Donald Duck and the Seven Dwarfs were used in theatrical trailers to drum up support for the war effort by getting those at home to file their income-tax returns early and to buy war bonds and war bond-saving stamps. The authors have not seen any cels from these trailers up for sale, but who knows what might turn up ... or what might have already been sold as cels from the feature film.

Television Commercials

Television commercials for films, theme parks, TV program promotional announcements, licensed manufacturers, fast-food chains, and others normally utilize clips

Pan background and cel set-up from a *Gargoyle's* TV episode.

from the films or programs along with new animation to cement everything together. The cels for older spots have appeared on the secondary market. The outlining on hand-inked cels is often all-black ink instead of a combination of colored inks. Cels done in the early 1950s have very thick black lines approaching an eighth of an inch wide. Set-ups were often done with a plain color background to save money. Since the characters are often from an animated classic, there are cases where this type of cel has been represented as being from the film. The reason is simple. TV commercial cels are worth far less – only 10% to 20% of what a film cel would bring.

TV Programming

Disney maintains animation studios all around the world. These studios employ many talented animators and have worked on various animated features, but most were established to produce TV programs like "DuckTales," "Darkwing Duck," "Gargoyles," "The Wuzzles" and many more, including animated-feature characters like Ariel and Aladdin. These cels are sold through the Walt Disney Art Classics program dealers and theme parks for around $350 to $700 each with backgrounds.

Cels of Tinker Bell, Jiminy Cricket, Mickey Mouse in various costumes, and other characters were done from 1955 through the early 1970s in conjunction with the

Theme park animation set-ups from the *Carnium Comman* attraction.

This cel setup from *The Mad Doctor* (1933) set a new record for black & white animation art when it sold at Christie's East auction on June 8, 1988 for $63,800.

"Disneyland" and "Mickey Mouse Club" programs. Brief animation to provide introducing or concluding 'thoughts' to existing live-action or cartoon footage are called TV "in-and-outs." Thousands of these were sold at The Art Corner at Disneyland and are prolific on the secondary market. These are not always complete-figure cels. Sometimes the legs, feet, and other parts of the body were out of the shot or painted on the background.

The "Mickey Mouse Club March" opening to the popular afternoon kids' show was staged against a plain colored background, as were introductions to special days and events on the programs.

The value of older cels or set-ups depends more on the importance of the character, segment, or place in Disney TV history than factors normally used to calculate the value of art from animated features.

Theme Park Animation

The amount of animated magic at Disney theme parks is mind-boggling. Seeing things fly, drawings move, robots seem life-like, and stop-motion flowers bloom in a matter of seconds becomes so commonplace it is easy for the visitor to suspend reality. Not all these animation techniques result in collectible art. However, shows like Cranium Command featured at Epcot's Wonders of Life pavilion provide a nice selection of modestly priced cels and a unique addition to a Disney animation art collection. Conversely, all the animation done for the various scanners in the Disneyland TWA Rocket to the Moon attraction isn't nearly as varied or interesting, but holds historical significance for collectors of Disneyland memorabilia.

Special-Events Cels

Mickey Mouse helped present an Oscar on Academy Awards night the year he celebrated his 60th Birthday. Naturally this was carefully worked out in advance and produced with art and cels done by a team headed by animator Mark Henn. Many of these cels were distributed to members of the Academy of Motion Picture Arts and Sciences as well as being sold through theme parks and Disney original art dealers. Disney does special tributes and presentations internally for employees and customer groups, the press, and the financial community. Large conventions can have stock footage tailored with special inserts or tags mentioning specific names in an animated-character welcoming or departing message. Major theme park openings or events have utilized short animated sequences similar to TV in-and-outs for short promotional films to be seen by select audiences such as Magic Kingdom Club directors or members.

The *Wicked Witch on her Peacock Throne,* sold at Christie's East June 8, 1988, was the first color cel set-up to sell for as much as $52,800.

These are the sources of animation art witnessed by The authors in reviewing auctions, catalogs, collectors' convention dealer rooms, and art found in private collections since 1972. There are probably others not mentioned because Disney makes animation magic so many different ways.

History of Disney Animation Art Sales

Disney animation art was traded privately ever since the films were completed and the art was no longer needed. Tens of thousands of cels were washed off or trashed. The same fate befell many backgrounds. Artists sometimes salvaged samples of their work or pieces they felt would be useful for future guidance. Museum requests for samples were often granted as were many requests from exhibitors and fans.

Cels first became commercially available in 1937 as a result of a licensing agreement between San Francisco art dealer Guthrie Courvoisier and the Disney brothers. Art first offered through the Courvoisier Gallery was from *Snow White.* Special set-ups were prepared by a 20-artist unit at the Disney Studios using original and stenciled backgrounds on a variety of art boards and wood-veneer. Characters in studio-prepared set-ups were usually cut out of the original cel and adhered directly to the background. Set-ups had two small labels: a copyright/"handle with care" notice and a label noting the title of the film. Backs were sealed using a special colored paper and a white label was added stating the art's provenance. Because Courvoisier distributed animation art to many other galleries, it is not unusual to see labels from local framers and galleries in addition to those placed by the studio. *Pinocchio* was the last film prepared by the studio unit for Courvoisier.

Kay Kamen did a cel test market with Stix, Baer and Fuller, a St. Louis department store, in 1938. However, Walt and Roy Disney preferred the fine-art distribution through galleries and museums set up by the Courvoisier Gallery of San Francisco. Courvoisier was licensed as Disney's sole representative in the sale of backgrounds, story sketches, animation drawings, and cels. While he prided himself for obtaining top dollar from his upscale clientele, the record shows his vision was limited. The first 63 *Snow White* cels sold for a total of $1,345, or about $21.35 each. A newspaper article about Courvoisier mentioned Disney animation art priced from $5 to $35. Disney's share was much less.

By 1938-39, cels from other Disney films were offered through Courvoisier, but the cost of preparing the art at the studio was getting out of balance with the revenue the program was yielding. Roy Disney suggested Courvoisier begin preparing the set-ups themselves. Working out of a warehouse in San Francisco, Courvoisier hired artists from nearby colleges to put

Band Concert cel set-up sold at Christie's East on December 4, 1985 at the same auction as this book's cover photo. *The Brave Little Tailor* cel set-up (cover) commanded $20,900 and the above cel set-up sold later at the same auction for $24,000.

The Organ Background from the Seven Dwarfs' cottage sold for $28,600 at the November 10, 1988 Christie's East auction, the highest price paid for an individual background up to that time.

Pinnochio Searching for Monstro Under Water cel set-up brought $39,600 at the June 8, 1988 auction at Christie's East.

Mickey and *Lonesome Ghost* cel set-up established the highest price for a Mickey Mouse set-up when it sold for $49,500 at the November 10, 1988 Christie's East auction.

ELEMENTS OF A CEL SET-UP

THIS PICTURE IS FRAGILE AND SHOULD BE FRAMED UNDER GLASS. THIS STICKER CAN BE REMOVED AND USED ON THE EXTERIOR OF THE NEW BACK.

This is an original painting actually used in Walt Disney Productions'

THE BLACK CAULDRON

For each movement in the action of a character in a Walt Disney Productions' animated film, a cel painting must be made. These cel paintings are then photographed in succession over master backgrounds producing, on the motion picture film, numerous pictures, each with its change in movement. These, when projected on the screen in rapid succession, create the illusion of motion.

Cel paintings are the final step in the creation of a Walt Disney Productions' animated film. With story sketches the artists express their first creative ideas, then with animation drawings they give life and movement to the characters.

Walt Disney Productions' originals are included in many important Museums and private collections. Notable among these are: The Metropolitan Museum of Art, New York; Museum of Modern Art, New York; Cleveland Museum of Art; Toledo Museum of Art; William Rockhill Nelson Gallery, Kansas City, Mo.; Phillips Memorial Gallery, Washington, D.C.; San Francisco Museum of Art; Honolulu Academy of Arts; etc.

WALT DISNEY PRODUCTIONS
Burbank, California

© Walt Disney Productions

WDP-1572

Studio authenticating label   Pencil outline background

Taran cel   Apple cel   Gurgi cel

The Black Cauldron, full set-up with pencil outline background

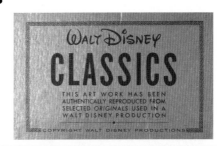

A cel set-up from *The Sword and the Stone* sold at Disneyland for $3.49 around 1963. It is comprised of two full cels and a printed background. The authenticating label is identical to the one accompanying the Aristocats cel at the lower right.

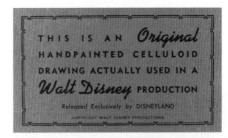

Walt Disney Classics are prints with a clear overlay sold at Disneyland. They have authenticating labels similar to cels, but printed in green. They are not cels and are worth only a fraction of a cel's value.

Studio authentication   Courvoisier authentication

Courvoisier cel set-up from *Snow White and Seven Dwarfs* with four trimmed cels on a stenciled background. Both authenticating labels pictured above.

Aristocats cel set-up with printed background sold at Disneyland with proper authenticating label above.

Snow White and the Seven Dwarfs animation action layout drawing

Courvoisier cutout cel mounted on wood veneer background

Pinocchio concept art by Gustav Tenggren

Rat's house background from *Adventures of Ichabod & Mr. Toad*

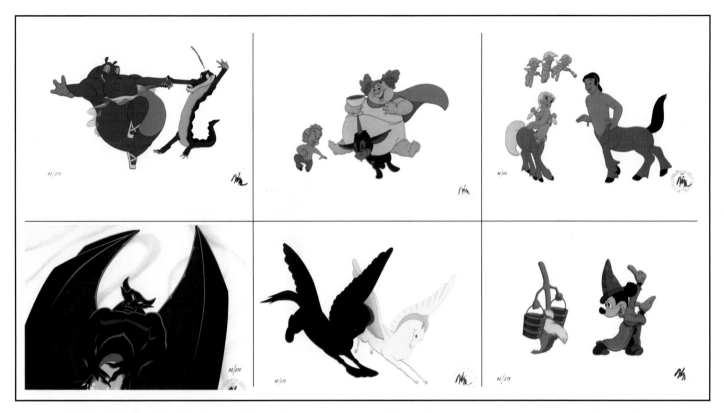

A set of six "Gallery Cels" were hand-inked and painted by Disney ink and paint artist from the original animation drawings and sold as a set of six.

Disney MGM Studio Theme Park Souvenir Cel. The image is transferred from the original drawing using a flatplate Xerox process and painted on the reverse by apprentice artists. Mickey at the Drawing Board was the first of several produced for sale at the Studio's Animation Gallery.

Sericel of Pluto entitled "Sticky Situation". Sericels are silk-screened from stencils cut from the original animation drawings and produced in limited editions.

James and the Giant Peach: Fully armatured production James puppet (9 x 3"); w/18 sets of eyes; photocopy model sheet (21 x 24"); 2 "Guardianship Decree" copies; "Map to America"; original Lane Smith "Map to America"; miniature bed; 2 pieces of artwork presenting James' peach-pit home; (decrees, map & pits 11 x 17"); (4000-6000)   14,950

Tim Burton's The Nightmare Before Christmas: Set for the interior of Jack's tower, S/Dec 16/93 (1500-2000)   17,250

Peter Pan: Peter (5"), Wendy (7-1/2"), Michael & John (4-3/4" ea.) in Peter's hideout, watercolor vertical pan production background, CE/Dec 16/94 (28,000-35,000)   27,600

Record Breaking Cels

Working out of a warehouse in San Francisco, Courvoisier hired artists from nearby colleges to put together the Disney art. The elaborate wood-veneer and stenciled backgrounds were no longer produced. In their place were chalk-and-pencil concepts of what a background might look like. These artists, in most cases, never saw the films. The Courvoisier-prepared backgrounds may usually be distinguished from those prepared at the Disney Studios by a tiny "WDP" symbol placed in the lower right corner of the art. It seems ironic Courvoisier would place a studio-like symbol on their own art in order to make it seem as though it came from the Disney Studios. There were no paints to repair the cels in Courvoisier's warehouse so they began laminating the cels in a rigid high-heat plastic envelope.

The cost of preparing art for sale became a growing problem and Courvoisier turned unsuccessfully to prints lithographed by Whitman and silkscreened demonstration multiplane camera set-ups.

As America entered World War II, sales of animation art began to decrease and Courvoisier ceased the preparation of new Disney cels in 1942 after *Bambi*. The company remained a licensee until 1946 by selling existing art, prints and imitation multiplane camera set-ups screen-printed on glass and cardboard. These multiplane decorative units had no factual relationship with actual multiplane cels or backgrounds. About 15 different ones were produced.

The Disney Studio continued to prepare cel set-ups as decorative items, internal use and as gifts for special visitors. Fan letters to the studio were sometimes rewarded with a cel set-up in the mail. Walt Disney gave them away when he traveled. Others were given to important theater owners and/or managers. Most are identifiable by a "Walt Disney Productions" label with copy very much like the one used by Courvoisier. No animation art marketing effort was in effect from 1946 to 1954. Set-ups from films produced during those years are scarce and now command high prices.

Cels reappeared commercially at The Art Corner shop in Disneyland's Tomorrowland beginning in 1955. A profuse supply of *Lady and the Tramp* art was sold for as little as 99¢. Cels in the $1.47 and $3.95 price ranges were also sold. The Art Corner sold cels from the "Disneyland" TV show, *Sleeping Beauty*, TV commercials, *101 Dalmatians*, and other films up through *The Aristocats*. A distinctive metallic gold label authenticates the art as having been sold at Disneyland. Over the years, five different versions of the label were used. The cels sold in the theme park had inexpensive paperboard mats and no backgrounds. As the program continued, the studio mass produced litho backgrounds from

Record Breaking Cels

Sleeping Beauty, *101 Dalmatians*, *The Sword in the Stone*, *Mary Poppins*, and *The Aristocats* for use in these souvenir set-ups. In addition, for a limited time, the studio produced Disney Classics – high-grade photographic prints of memorable cel set-ups especially made for this purpose. An embossed mat was used for the Classics and a gold metallic label with green ink noted the "art's" authenticity.

101 Dalmatians, released in 1961, was Disney's first feature-length film using the Xerographic process. The animation drawings were "copied" directly onto the cel by machine instead of being traced by hand, giving the characters an all-black outline, sketchier look. Gone was the intricate colored hand-inking. And in 1966 The Art Corner was gone as well to make way for a new Tomorrowland. The remaining Art Corner cels were sold at the Emporium on Main Street, U.S.A. until the supply ran out. Cels were not offered again at Disneyland until 1973 when the Disney Original Art Program was organized under the Consumer Products Division. Cels from *Robin Hood* and later films were sold at the Bernard Danenberg Galleries in New York and the Circle Gallery in Los Angeles starting at $75 framed. Set-ups from *Robin Hood* up through *Oliver and Company* were laminated. Selected art has been sold at private galleries ever since. Most new pieces were being sold in the $200

to $600 range by 1985.

Except for some recently produced serigraphed (screen-printed) cels, limited-edition "gallery" cels and souvenir cels from the Animation Studio Tour in Florida, each cel is a one-of-a-kind piece of art.

Instead of offering cels in trimmed sizes as before, the Walt Disney Art Classics program offered the art in full size with better mats and featuring a special embossed seal. Later the seal would be changed to a hot-stamp version about the size of a silver dollar, and in 1988 the seal was again changed to dime size.

This original art program has set up a group of authorized dealers throughout the world. It also manages the art sold at Disney Stores and Walt Disney Gallery stores.

In recent years the studio has begun to issue "Limited Edition cels" along with cels from current film releases. For a list of dealers offering original Disney art, write to: Walt Disney Art Classics, The Walt Disney Company, 500 S. Buena Vista Street, Burbank, CA 91521.

Many outstanding cels were never sold commercially and have no labels or seals. Animator Ward Kimball recalls giving out cels and drawings to the children in his neighborhood. Very often a cel or original drawing was sent to a young would-be animator just for writing a letter to Walt and many pieces were sent to relatives or friends of employees as examples of the studio's work. One of the greatest preservers of Disney animation art was John Basmajian.

He was a long-time inbetweener for the studio, having begun work there in the early 1930s. He loved animation art and saved many classic cel set-ups, pan backgrounds, and other early works from the studio trash bins. Shortly before his death, Basmajian began to sell selected pieces from his vast collection ... enough to stock an entire auction at Christie's East in 1984. None of the cels from the Basmajian Collection, Walt Disney's gift cels, and others salvaged by other employees have any kind of authenticity sticker, seal, or mark. The Disney paints, however, were all custom made by the studio and can be positively identified by spectrographic analysis. Since many cels have been repaired with newer paints, an expert opinion can be helpful in resolving any concerns. Caution is always wise when buying animation art. Newcomers to the hobby will best be served by making their purchases from reputable dealers, galleries, and auctioneers.

Auctions of older pieces became more popular in the later 1970s and growing interest fueled demand among the general public. Collecting up until 1985 was mainly a hobby conducted among animation enthusiasts. Few people not familiar with the process even knew such art existed. Rarely was a piece passed from one collector to another for over $1000. More often a nice set-up was simply traded for one with greater appeal. The first Disneyana book published in 1972 dedicated several pages to the subject and perhaps helped trigger interest.

Things began to change around 1979 as more people found out what cels were all about. Restoration processes for damaged cels were more widely publicized. Retired animators began appearing at collectors' conventions. Those who didn't make such appearances were sought out by collectors or dealers. Estate or family pieces were relinquished as prices grew higher.

In late 1984, the big Basmajian sale blew the lid off. The auction couldn't have been timed better. The material was all of exceptional quality and the market was primed. A Mickey Mouse cel from the 1938 short *Brave Little Tailor* was estimated to bring up to $2,500 in the December 8 auction at Christie's East in New York City. It actually sold for $20,900. A year later a cel from *The Band Concert* went for $24,000. A new record was set in 1986 when a cel set-up of the Old Hag preparing the poison apple from *Snow White and the Seven Dwarfs* realized $30,800. A cel set-up of *Pinocchio* searching for Monstro underwater brought $39,600 in the summer of 1988 and a Mickey Mouse set-up from *Lonesome Ghosts* hammered down for $49,500 in November bidding. Meanwhile, the organ background for the Seven Dwarfs' cottage and one of the scary woods, without any cels, brought $28,600 and $37,400 respectively. The Wicked Queen on her peacock throne established the highest record for a color cel set-up, going for $52,800.

Black-and-white Mickey Mouse cartoon cel set-ups then became the rage among animation art buyers. A 1933 Mickey cartoon piece started the action at $63,800. Mickey shouting from the wings in the original *Orphan's Benefit* sold for $121,000, while another from the same film void of any major characters nailed an amazing $148,500.

Heads seemed to cool as fast as Disneyana prices in 1989. Values realized have become less volatile as the market has matured. Disney has also increased the supply by introducing limited-edition hand-painted cels with and without photographed backgrounds; sericels; and more art distributed through The Disney Stores, The Walt Disney Gallery locations, and theme park stores. Still, a rare complete storyboard for the 1929 Mickey Mouse short *The Plow Boy* sold for $101,500 in 1995 – a record for animation drawings.

This book provides a good picture of the market for a wide variety of Disney animation art as the market has existed since stabilizing in 1993. It is organized to help the reader find pieces similar to ones they are likely to find in a search of secondary market sources.

Care of Animation Art

All animation art should be treated with the same care and respect as any fine artwork.

Cels are especially delicate. Please remember cels were originally considered an intermediate step in production. They were only expected to last a relatively short time until the film was completed. The fact that so many cels and set-ups from the 1930s and '40s have somehow survived to the present in collectible condition is nothing short of miraculous. If a cel is damaged, it can be restored. This work should only be done by a reputable professional.

What Affects Value

Each piece must be evaluated individually. Major factors affecting collector desirability include the artist, type of drawing, character, the film, and the artistic nature of the work. Character size can be important. Prominent characters are generally more desirable. The character's eyes generally should be open. Dramatic pose, completeness of subject, condition, and uniqueness can be other factors.

Because of their age and fragility, it is not unusual to find damaged cels and backgrounds. S/R Laboratories animation art conservation center in Westlake Village, CA is one recognized authority on Disney animation art and they are glad to answer the needs of collectors, galleries, museums and dealers. Call the lab at 818-991-9955 for further information and assistance. Most prominent galleries know other experts and restorers in the reader's area.

Where to Find More Information
Auction Houses

Christie's East, 219 East 67th Street, New York, NY 10021, telephone 212-606-0430, fax 212-452-2063, web site www.christies.com.

Christie's Los Angeles, 360 North Camden Drive, Beverly Hills, CA 90210, telephone 310-385-2600, web site www.christies.com.

Howard Lowery, 3812 W. Magnolia Blvd., Burbank, CA 91505, telephone 818-972-9080, fax 818-972-3910

Sotheby's, 1334 York Avenue, New York, NY 10021, telephone 212-606-7000, web site www.sothebys.com

S/R Laboratories, 31200 Via Colinas, Suite 210, Westlake Village, CA 91362; 818-991-9955; fax 818-

991-5418; web site www.srlabs.com

Reference Books

The Art of Hercules: The Chaos of Creation by Stephen Rebello and Jane Healey (Hyperion, 1997)

The Art of Pocahontas by Stephen Rebello (Hyperion, 1995)

The Art of The Hunchback of Notre Dame by Stephen Rebello (Hyperion, 1996)

The Art of The Lion King by Christopher Finch (Hyperion, 1994)

The Art of The Little Mermaid by Jeff Kurtti (miniature edition, Hyperion, 1997)

The Art of Walt Disney by Robert D. Feild (Macmillan, 1942; Collins, 1945 & 1947)

The Art of Walt Disney: From Mickey Mouse to The Magic Kingdoms by Christopher Finch (Abrams, multiple editions)

Before the Animation Begins: The Art and Lives of Disney Inspirational Sketch Artists by John Canemaker (Hyperion, 1996)

Cel Magic: Collecting Animation Art by R. Scott Edwards & Bob Stobener (Laughs Unlimited Inc., 1991)

Disney Animation: The Illusion of Life by Frank Thomas & Ollie Johnston (Abbeville, 1981; also published as *The Illusion of Life: Disney Animation* by Hyperion, 1995)

Disney A to Z: The Official Encyclopedia by Dave Smith (Hyperion, 1996)

The Disney Films by Leonard Maltin (Hyperion, multiple editions)

Disney's Animation Magic by Don Hahn (Disney Press, 1996)

Disney's Art of Animation by Bob Thomas (Hyperion, multiple editions)

The Disney That Never Was: The Stories and Art from Five Decades of Unproduced Animation by Charles Solomon (Hyperion, 1995)

The Disney Villain by Frank Thomas & Ollie Johnston (Hyperion, 1993)

Encyclopedia of Walt Disney's Animated Characters by John Grant (Hyperion, multiple editions)

Too Funny For Words: Disney's Greatest Sight Gags by Frank Thomas & Ollie Johnston (Abbeville, 1987)

Treasures of Disney Animation Art (Abbeville, 1982)

Walt Disney's Bambi: The Story and The Film by Frank Thomas & Ollie Johnston, with flip book (Stewart, Tabori & Chang, 1990)

Walt Disney's Fantasia by John Culhane (Abrams, 1983)

Walt in Wonderland: The Silent Films of Walt Disney by Russell Merritt and J.B. Kaufman (Johns Hopkins Press, 1994)

The Wonderful World of Disney Television: A Complete History by Bill Cotter (Hyperion, 1997)

Clubs

Metropolitan Cartoon Art & Collectibles Club, P.O. Box 414, Manhasset, NY 11030; Grace Parks 516-627-2123, fax 516-627-0443; e-mail tooncB@ibm.net

NFFC: The Club For Disneyana Enthusiasts, P.O. Box 19212, Irvine, CA 92623-9212; 714-731-4705; www.nffc.org

Dealers

Cel-ebration! Animation Gallery, P.O. Box 123, Little Silver, NJ 07739; voice/fax 732-842-8489; www.cel-ebration.com

Cohen Books and Collectibles, P.O. Box 810310, Boca Raton, FL 33481; voice 561-487-7888, fax 561-487-3117; e-mail cohendisney@prodigy.net

Collector's Paradise Gallery, P.O. Box 1540, Studio City, CA 91614; 818-785-4080

Gifted Images Gallery, 7A North Park Avenue, Rockville Centre, NY 11570; 800-726-6708

Rena Siegel, P.O. Box 565073, Miami, FL 33256-5073; 305-661-4368; e-mail rena@netrox.net

Santa Ana Coins & Collectibles, 12862 Garden Grove Blvd., Ste. "E", Garden Grove, CA 92843; voice 800-842-3865, fax 714-741-9180; e-mail SACC.JJ@worldnet.att.net

Restoration

S/R Labs, 31200 Via Colinas, Suite 210, Westlake Village, CA 91362; 818-991-9955; e-mail srlabs@earthlink.net; web site www.srlabs.com

Stillway Restorations, Judy Stillway, 8817 Queen Elizabeth Blvd., Annandale, BA 22003-4247; 703-764-0490

About This Book

The listings in this guide are summaries of actual lots sold by major auction houses in the U.S.A. since 1985 as reported in Tomart's books and *Tomart's DISNEYANA Update* magazine. In addition, a section of "Other Collectible Art" has been included. Lots are listed as identified in the auction catalogs.

Basically, each section lists productions by title or type, then chronologically by auction. These listings provide a data base with a minimum of organization. They include both production and special-purpose artwork.

Some lots contain artwork from multiple productions. Generally, placement of the listing is determined by cel origin. Lots with cels from more than one production are either listed under "Combinations" or are duplicated under both productions.

Many characters have appeared in multiple productions and formats. The more significant cross references have been included as practicable.

Descriptions have been compiled from auction catalogs and have been condensed to save space. In general, framing/matting information, minor condition descriptions, and miscellaneous details have been deleted. Items not specifically identified are cels or combinations of cels (gouache on celluloid, trimmed celluloid, or partial celluloid). Cels may be laminated. Unless otherwise identified, drawings are black and/or colored pencil on paper/animation sheet. Drawings may also be trimmed. Undefined left-right directions are from the viewer's perspective. Unless otherwise specified, dimensions are the sizes of visible images (usually character cel images) in inches, height followed by width. The exception is S/R Laboratories, whose dimensions are width followed by height; S/R character dimensions are vertical. Background information (if any) is given immediately following the artwork description. Information in brackets does not appear on the art, but helps clarify the description. Estimated values are in parentheses.

The only auction house that consistently rates lots by condition is Howard Lowery. These condition ratings have been included as space permits. Key: VF - Very Fine; F - Fine; VG - Very Good; G – Good.

FEATURE FILMS

This section is organized alphabetically by title and art type, then chronologically by auction.

THE ADVENTURES OF ICHABOD AND MR. TOAD (1949)

Also see TELEVISION: ANTHOLOGY SERIES
Segments were *The Wind in the Willows* (Mr. Toad), and *The Legend of Sleepy Hollow*.

ANIMATION DRAWINGS
2 matching key colored pencil drawings: Mr. Toad in nightgown & Moley; 3 x 4-1/2", 3 x 2-1/2", animators notes, VF, HL/Feb 26-27/94 (300-400) 385
2 matched full-figure drawings: reclining Toad (supported by 2 hands) w/eyes closed, waving left hand in "tut, tut" gesture; shy Moley standing; 3-1/2 x 5-1/2", 3 x 2-1/2", HL/May 31/97 (300-400) 230
Near-full-figure drawing of exuberant Toad standing w/left hand on knee, right arm above head & index finger up, 5 x 3", HL/May 31/97 (150-225) 316
2 full-figure drawings: hatless Rat standing looking right, 5-1/8"; front view of Mole bent at waist, looking & pointing right, 3-5/8"; 12-field sheets; SR/Fall/97 (300-500) 300
2 drawings: Toad (eyes closed, all but heels) makes a point as he's held in reclining position; full figure of shy Moley standing looking left; 4-1/4 x 4-1/2", 3 x 2-1/2"; VF; HL/Apr 25/98 (200-300) 259
5 lively drawings of Toad from 3 different scenes, 3 x 3-1/2" to 4-1/2 x 4-1/2", VF, HL/Apr 25/98 (500-700) 920
2 near-full-figure drawings in sequence of smiling Toad standing with arms out, 4 x 5" each, VF, HL/Apr 25/98 (300-500) 316

BACKGROUNDS
Donald & Goofy walking with clubs from *How To Play Golf*, watercolor production background from *The Adventures of Ichabod & Mr. Toad*, 3-1/2 & 5-1/2", inscribed "... Walt Disney", CE/Dec 16/94 (2500-3500) 6900
Sleepy Hollow schoolhouse master background (exterior w/view inside), 11 x 14-1/2", tempera on background sheet, VF+, HL/Aug 6/95 (2000-2500) 2128
Master background of Van Tassel home interior, 11 x 15", tempera on background sheet, VF, HL/Nov 19/95 (2000-2500) 2185
Original master background painting of Van Tassel home interior, tempera on background sheet, 11-1/2 x 14-1/2", VF+, HL/Apr 28/96 (1800-2200) 1955
Master background of picnic site w/basket on grass & cake, covered dish, & plate on corner of blanket, 11-1/2 x 15", tempera on background sheet, HL/Oct 6/96 (1500-2000) 1955
Master background of Van Tassel house interior decorated for Halloween, tempera on background sheet, 11-1/2 x 15", HL/May 3/97 (1800-2000) 2300
Master background of country road at sunset with stone wall & trees in autumn colors, tempera on background sheet, 11 x 14-1/2", HL/May 3/97 (1500-2000) 3450
Master background of Rat's home on the river, 11 x 22-1/2", tempera on background sheet, VF, HL/Nov 16/97 (1800-2400) 6440

CEL SET-UPS
Full figure of Ichabod Crane reading in bed, 6", hand-prepared background, S/Jun 10/95 (900-1200) 1495
Full figure of wide-eyed Ichabod & sleepy horse riding to left thru dark woods, 4-7/8", 16-field, display background, ct, SR/Fall/95 (500-900) 830
Full figure of Headless Horseman riding horse & waving sword, 3-1/2", printed background of forest at night, S/Dec 14/96 (1000-1500) 1495
Katrina (7") smiles coquettishly as Ichabod (7") examines horseshoe, pan watercolor production background of picnic scene, needs restoration, S/Dec 14/96 (3000-5000) 3737
Smiling Ichabod (7") holds Katrina's hand (5"), airbrushed Courvoisier background of

outdoors, signed "Walt Disney" probably by Hank Porter, S/Dec 14/96 (1200-1800) 1725
2 items: full figure of determined Ichabod & scared horse racing thru forest with bridge in background, 4 x 6", printed background; photostat model sheet depicting multiple characters, S/Dec 14/96 (800-1200) 805
Side view of alert Mole, Rat, Toad, & MacBadger in boat (in foreground) gliding by bridge at night, 8 x 7", gouache master background, mat signed by Marc Davis, SR/Spring/97 (2000-4000) 2040
Near-full figure of worried Ichabod sitting on stool, looking left while pouring tea, 5-1/4", Art Props watercolor background, shadow & steam effects, SR/Spring/97 (800-1400) 810
Full figure of panicked, reclined Toad, head raised to stare at ball & chain on foot, 7-1/4 x 3-1/2", master background of dirt road & sky, SR/Fall/97 (3000-5000) 2200
Full figure of terrified Ichabod in midair eye-to-eye with terrified horse, 10 x 14", matching original master background (tempera on background sheet), VF, HL/Nov 16/97 (3000-4000) 4945

CELS – FULL FIGURE
Ichabod on horse, color model or publicity cel, 6-1/2 x 7", VF, HL/Apr 10/94 (800-1200) 1008
Prancing Ichabod w/bowl of greens & napkin, 9 x 6-1/2", F+, HL/Apr 10/94 (800-1200) 784
Mr. Toad (3/4") rides carefree Cyril Proudbottom prancing to left, (5-1/2 x 5-1/2"), CE/Jun 18/94 (1500-2000) 920
Mole launching paper airplane, copyright stamp, 4-1/2 x 5", VF, HL/Aug 21/94 (700-900) 448
2 full-figure cels of Toad: as lawyer & excited, 4-1/2 x 3-1/2" & 5 x 4-1/2", HL/Nov 13/94 (700-900) 1008
Ichabod bows chivalrously, 6-1/2 x 5", HL/Apr 23/95 (900-1200) 784
2 full-figure cels: Ichabod doffs hat & bows, Katrina walking; 6-1/2 x 5", 6 x 4-1/2", VF, HL/Nov 19/95 (1800-2400) 1725
Front view of happy Toad standing with hands full of paper airplanes, 5-1/2", SR/Spring/96 (800-1200) 970
Front view of sitting Mole holding deed above head (all but corner of deed), looking up, 7-1/4", SR/Spring/96 (600-900) 450
Front view of Ichabod & horse sitting together laughing hysterically, 7-1/8", 12-field cel, SR/Fall/96 (800-1200) 1300
3 full-figure cels: well-dressed confident Toad; panicked Moley holding paper, facing to right; panicked MacBadger jumping to left; 3-1/4 x 4", 4-1/4 x 3-1/2", 4-1/2 x 3", VF+, HL/Oct 6/96 (1800-2400) 1610
Brom Bones standing laughing (with hand over mouth) with 2 cronies (one partial figure), 4-1/2 x 6", HL/May 31/97 (200-250) 230
Headless Horseman galloping to right, sword upraised, 3-1/2 x 4-1/2", VF, HL/Nov 16/97 (600-900) 1840

CELS – PARTIAL FIGURE
Flirtatious Katrina Van Tassel w/umbrella facing left, 7 x 6", F+, HL/Apr 10/94 (600-900) 476
Profile portrait of Ichabod Crane reading book, 7-1/2 x 9", F-VF, HL/Aug 21/94 (800-1000) 728
Large image of apprehensive Ichabod sitting holding reins, 4-1/2 x 4-1/2", F+, HL/Aug 21/94 (900-1200) 672
Color model cel of front half of gypsy cart pulled by full figure of smiling Cyril with Mr. Toad riding, 5-1/2", horizontal crease, matched w/key color model drawing of ducks; plus knees-up cel of Rat, Mole & Badger standing together toasting, 4-1/2"; all 12-field, SR/Spring/95 (400-800) 850
Portrait of Ichabod Crane, napkin around neck, holding bones & staring into space, 4-1/2 x 4-1/2", HL/Apr 28/96 (700-900) 805
Tiny Toad clings to smiling Cyril's collar as Cyril pulls gypsy cart, 5-1/2 x 5-1/2", F, HL/Apr 28/96 (500-800) 633
Ichabod dances with Katrina Von Tassel, 7-1/2 x 6-1/2", VF, HL/Oct 6/96 (700-1000) 805
Ankles-up view of shocked Ichabod sitting, looking left & pouring tea, 4-1/2 x 4", HL/Feb 23/97 (700-1000) 633
Waist-up of smiling Ichabod facing right w/book in one hand, pie in other, 8-1/4", WDP stamp, "To Bob Mochrie...Walt Disney"

on mat, S/Dec 19/97 (600-900) 2300

LAYOUT ART
Toad on Cyril in detailed layout sketch, 6-1/2 x 8", studio notes, F+, HL/Apr 10/94 (500-700) 840

MODEL ART (also see CEL SET-UPS, CELS – PARTIAL FIGURE)
3 color model drawings: full-figure front view of intoxicated Mr. Toad, rear half of motor car, exhaust fumes; 4-1/4 x 2", 8-1/2 x 8-1/2", 2 x 6-1/2", HL/May 31/97 (200-250) 173

STORY ART
Story drawing of Toad & Cyril racing with gypsy cart, 6 x 8", conté crayon on story sheet, HL/Aug 6/95 (300-500) 504
Story sketch of Toad in court dress, 4-1/2 x 4-1/2", conté crayon on story sheet, HL/Nov 19/95 (150-200) 431
4 separate story sheets in sequence of Toad's wagon smashing into pieman, 5-1/2 x 4" to 6 x 8", conté crayon on story sheets, VF, HL/Nov 16/97 (400-600) 345
Story drawing of Toad, Cyril & gypsy cart speeding to right, conté crayon & charcoal on story sheet, 6 x 8", VF, HL/Apr 25/98 (300-400) 403

TITLE ART
Title card: silhouette of Headless Horseman galloping across landscape in front of full moon, with original hand-lettered overlay "Ichabod" from Oct. 26, 1955 "Disneyland" TV show, 11 x 8", SR/Spring/95 (1200-1800) 1540

ALADDIN (1992)

Also see TELEVISION: ALADDIN
CEL SET-UPS
Jafar on throne w/Iago on shoulder, 8-1/2", non-production cel w/production overlay & key watercolor production background with notes, CE/Dec 16/94 (10,000-15,000) 11,500
Full figure of Iago flying to right toward palace pillar, 4", watercolor production background, CE/Dec 18/97 (1500-2000) 1150
"Magic Carpet Ride," 1994: full-figure limited-edition pan cel & color print of matching background of Prince Ali & Jasmine riding carpet, #23/500, seal & certificate, 10 x 23-1/2", VF+, HL/Apr 25/98 (800-1200) 920

SERICELS
"Magic Carpet Ride" sericel, limited to 2500, 7 x 8-1/2", autographed by Eric Goldberg, Andreas Deja, Randy Cartwright, Glen Keane, HL/Apr 23/95 (400-600) 616

ALICE IN WONDERLAND (1951)

Also see SHORTS & FEATURETTES: ALICE IN COMMUNICATIONLAND; TELEVISION: ANTHOLOGY SERIES
ANIMATION DRAWINGS (also see CELS-FULL FIGURE)
3 polished rough pencil drawings in sequence of Alice (may be from edited scene), 8-1/2 x 6-1/2", F, HL/Feb 26-27/94 (600-900) 1100
Rough drawing of Alice, 8", CE/Dec 16/94 (600-800) 633
20 finished "rough" drawings, 1-1/2 x 1-1/2" to 10 x 8", HL/Apr 23/95 (3000-4000) 5936
2 drawings: ankles-up front view of wary Alice standing with arms up in 'stop' pose, 6-1/2", timer's chart; hips-up of worried Queen of Hearts standing looking toward right, left index finger up, 4-3/4", 12-field, SR/Fall/95 (400-800) 660
Hem-up front-view drawing of curious Alice, 5-5/8", 12-field sheet, SR/Spring/96 (300-600) 410
21 polished "rough" drawings (10 of Alice), 4 x 3" to 9-1/2 x 8", HL/Apr 28/96 (3000-4000) 6038
Hem-up front-view drawing of surprised Alice with arms out, 5-3/4", 12-field sheet, SR/Spring/97 (300-600) 310
Two hips-up front-view drawings of Queen of Hearts: angry & startled; 5-1/2" & 4-3/4", 12-field sheets; SR/Spring/97 (400-800) 490
Close-up front-view drawing of relaxed Cheshire Cat, right hand on hip, pointing right with his left thumb, 8", 16-field sheet, timer's chart, in triple-opening mat with print of croquet game signed by Ward Kimball & descriptive caption, SR/Spring/97 (900-1400) 1280
18 detailed "rough" drawings, 3 x 3-1/2" to 9 x 7", HL/May 3/97 (3000-4000) 4830

Full-figure drawing of smiling Alice standing, 8-1/4"; drawing of Alice bending down with eyes closed, 4"; study of Alice from neck up, 5 & 3"; CLA/Jun 7/97 (800-1200)   978

Portrait drawing of skeptical Alice, hands crossed in lap, looking up, 7-5/8", 16-field sheet, outer portions show considerable wear & shallow pieces missing at right edge & upper right corner, SR/Fall/97 (500-900)   380

Full-figure drawing of wide-eyed Alice standing facing toward right with arms straight out, 7-1/8", 12-field sheet, SR/Spring/98 (300-600)   310

Publication drawing & matched unpainted cel of March Hare, Alice, & Mad Hatter pouring tea [at table], both 16-field, SR/Spring/98 (300-600)   730

Hips-up front-view drawing of shocked Queen leaning forward at waist, 4-5/8", 12-field sheet, inker's notation, SR/Spring/98 (300-600)   300

BACKGROUNDS

Large tree w/"Discard" & numbers written in margin, 11 x 15", tempera on background board, VF, HL/Nov 16/97 (800-1000)   1495

CEL SET-UPS

Queen of Hearts swings flamingo as Alice & King watch, watercolor production background, 10-1/2 x 13-1/4", CE/Dec 15/93 (12,000-15,000)   11,500

Tweedledee & Tweedledum, printed background, 8-1/2 x 11-1/2", CE/Dec 15/93 (800-1200)   920

Alice's sister glances up while holding her book, publication background, 8-1/4", S/Dec 16/93 (400-600)   460

White Rabbit washes ashore in umbrella, hand-prepared non-studio background, 3-1/2", S/Dec 16/93 (1200-1800)   1380

White Rabbit falling in umbrella, blue sky tempera master background from *Sky Trooper*, 8 x 6", studio notes, stamps & signatures of Herwig & Mique Nelson, mat inscribed "From 'Alice in Wonderland'" & "original WDP", WDP label, VF, HL/Apr 10/94 (900-1200)   896

Alice (7") watches upset White Rabbit (w/watch & umbrella, 4-1/2"), watercolor production background, S/Jun 17/94 (5000-7000)   4887

Alice (3-1/2") & March Hare (5") at table enjoying tea as Dormouse (1-1/2") floats between them w/umbrella, gouache production background, inscribed "To Jim Lawlor, Best Wishes, Walt Disney" on mat, S/Jun 17/94 (8000-10,000)   10,925

Alice (7") & Dinah (3") run after White Rabbit, watercolor production background, inscribed "To Jack Sharp, Best Wishes, Walt Disney" on mat, S/Jun 17/94 (4000-6000)   4600

Alice looks inquisitive, DL print background, 7", S/Jun 17/94 (1800-2200)   1610

Alice stands in defendant's box of courtroom surrounded by Heart guards, watercolor production background, inscribed "To Raul Apold with Best Wishes Walt Disney" on mat, 6", S/Jun 17/94 (5000-8000)   4600

Alice (6-1/2") with Dogerpillar, watercolor production background, CE/Jun 18/94 (4000-5000)   3220

Face & arms of Cheshire Cat in tree, left thumb pointing right, 5-1/2", full pan cel on 10-1/8 x 32-5/8" gouache master background, paint restoration, SR/Fall/94 (5000-9000)   5100

Hips-up front view of Alice looking up to left, Hanna-Barbera production gouache background of foliage, 6", 12-field, slight discoloration, light lifting paint, some ink wear, SR/Fall/94 (1000-1600)   1480

Full figure of reclining Cheshire Cat, 3-1/2 x 6-1/2", complementary color print background, HL/Nov 13/94 (2500-3500)   3136

Alice in Garden of Talking Flowers w/6 Bread-&-Butterflies (3 mounted on mat), 10 x 11-1/2", master background (tempera on background sheet), VF, HL/Apr 23/95 (7000-9000)   12,320

Alice (5-1/2") in garden watches Bread & Butterflies (2"), watercolor production background, 3 butterflies on mat, CE/Jun 9/95 (12,000-15,000)   17,250

Queen of Hearts smiles as she holds heart-shaped fan in right hand & reaches with left, 6", hand-prepared background, S/Jun 10/95 (800-1200)   1150

Tweedledum & Tweedledee stand on log, each with hands on hips, & frown at each other,
4-1/2" each, watercolor production background, S/Jun 10/95 (2500-3500)   4312

Waist-up view of Alice (1-3/4") sitting in spoon from King Stefan's castle as caterpillar-as-butterfly (3") hovers against tapestry background, characters from Jell-O commercial, 1955, DL Art Corner label, SR/Fall/95 (300-600)   660

Mad Hatter, March Hare & Dormouse singing at tea party, 1970s educational filmstrip *The Glad Tea Party*, matching master background (tempera on background sheet), 9 x 11", HL/Mar 16-17/96 (600-900)   748

Chest-up portrait of Walrus looking at left hand, 6-1/2", master gouache background from *Aqua-mania*, SR/Spring/96 (600-1000)   600

3 shocked cards holding paint brushes, complementary color print background of hedge, 4-1/2 x 6-1/2", HL/Apr 28/96 (900-1200)   920

Full figures of Alice sitting on head of Toucan bird & White Rabbit running with open umbrella [from Dodo's Caucus Race]; master background from that sequence (tempera on background sheet); 8-3/4 x 11-1/2", HL/Oct 6/96 (4000-5000)   3220

Expectant Jury seated in Jury Box, 8-1/2", key watercolor production background, CE/Dec 12/96 (4000-6000)   8625

Smiling Alice stands in front of tea party table looking up, 8", printed background, S/Dec 14/96 (1200-1800)   1840

Alice talks with red rose as tulip & blue foxglove look on, 6-1/2", trimmed watercolor production background, signed "To...Walt Disney", S/Dec 14/96 (8000-10,000)   35,650

Full figure of curious Alice standing on path facing left, 6-1/4", 16-field cel, color print background of Tulgy Wood, SR/Spring/97 (1100-1900)   1210

Full figure of endearing Queen of Hearts standing holding heart scepter, facing right, looking back over right shoulder, 7"; color print background of royal croquet court, ct, SR/Spring/97 (700-1100)   1180

Full figures of Alice (4-1/2") sitting under tree amid flowers holding Dinah & watching butterfly (1-1/2"), trimmed watercolor production back-ground, signed "To...Walt Disney" in Bob Moore's hand, S/Jun 21/97 (12,000-18,000)   16,100

Pair of matching cels of Dodo sailing on sea of tears with aid of two birds as boat & rudder, background unidentified, 7-1/2 x 11-1/2", VF+, HL/Nov 16/97 (700-1000)   920

Full figure of enlarged Alice sitting in house staring at cookie in her hand, 6 x 10", printed back-ground, S/Dec 19/97 (1800-2200)   2070

Full-figure front view of Walrus (7-1/2") & Carpenter (5") walking side by side, hand-prepared back-ground, S/Dec 19/97 (800-1200)   805

CELS – FULL FIGURE

Carpenter carrying ladder, 8-1/4 x 11-3/4", CE/Dec 15/93 (700-900)   575

Tweedledee & Tweedledum, 7 x 11", CE/Dec 15/93 (800-1200)   1092

Shouting Mad Hatter holds open pocket watch, 7-1/2 x 9-1/2", CE/Dec 15/93 (800-1200)   1380

Cheshire Cat grins, 5-1/2 x 8-1/2", CE/Dec 15/93 (800-1200)   1840

Alice talks to Caterpillar, 9-1/2 x 12", CE/Dec 15/93 (2500-3000)   3220

2 singing flowers, 7-3/4", S/Dec 16/93 (2000-2500)   2875

March Hare & Mad Hatter shaking hands, 7-1/4", S/Dec 16/93 (2000-3000)   2875

3 cels framed together: 4-1/2" White Rabbit racing w/watch; 2-cel set-up: 8-1/2" Alice leaning over 7" White Rose; 4 x 5" cater-pillar holding hookah tube; S/Dec 16/93 (4000-6000)   4888

Mama & baby horn creatures, 1-1/2 x 5-1/2", VF, HL/Feb 26-27/94 (500-700)   935

Pencil bird, 4 x 2-1/2", VF, HL/Apr 10/94 (300-400)   840

Shocked White Rabbit listens to oversized watch, 4 x 4", VF+, HL/Apr 10/94 (1500-2000)   2128

Front view of Tweedledum & Tweedledee, 7 x 7-1/2", VF, HL/Apr 10/94 (900-1200)   840

Bread-and-butterflies landing on leaf, 6 x 9-1/2", VF, HL/Apr 10/94 (800-1000)   1064

Cheshire Cat, 7", CE/Jun 18/94 (1500-2000)   2185

Bread-&-butterflies flying in front of plant, CE/Jun 18/94 (500-700)   1093

Reclining Cheshire Cat pointing, 4-3/4 x 7", CE/Jun 18/94 (1500-2000)   5750

Caterpillar laying on leaf while smoking, 6-1/2", CE/Jun 18/94 (1200-1500)   1725

Front view of Walrus with cane, 6-1/2 x 4-1/2", CE/Jun 18/94 (600-800)   690

Alice kneeling facing right, 6 x 9", CE/Jun 18/94 (800-1200)   1380

5 members of the Jury standing, 6-1/2 x 7", CE/Jun 18/94 (1000-1500)   805

2 tulips, 6-1/2" & similar, CE/Jun 18/94 (300-500)   1265

Gauntlet of playing cards, 9-3/4 x 1-1/2" & smaller, CE/Jun 18/94 (500-700)   805

Front view of 6 pansies, 3" & smaller, CE/Jun 18/94 (800-1200)   2185

Surprised Dinah sitting, 5 x 5", VF+, HL/Aug 21/94 (600-800)   728

Chimney sweep Bill the Lizard walking with ladder, 8 x 14", VF+, HL/Aug 21/94 (600-800)   1008

4 cels of Wonderland creatures: trumpet flower, 3 pansies from Garden of Talking Flowers, two of Bread-&-Butterflies; 5 x 3", 9 x 5-1/2", 2 x 3-1/2", 2 x 4-1/2", F-VF, HL/Aug 21/94 (600-800)   952

Accordion owl flying left, 5 x 3", 16-field, some ink wear, SR/Fall/94 (400-700)   410

Alice stands looking straight up & to left, 7", 16-field, SR/Fall/94 (1000-1600)   1070

Front views of smug Walrus (eyes closed) & suspicious Carpenter (holding hammer up) walking together, 6-3/4", SR/Fall/94 (800-1400)   830

Happy Carpenter with condiments, 10-1/2 x 6", VF, HL/Nov 13/94 (500-700)   560

Smug Queen of Hearts shows ankle, 7 x 5-1/2", VF, HL/Nov 13/94 (500-700)   1064

Wide-eyed Alice on hands & knees, 6 x 7-1/2", F+, HL/Nov 13/94 (1200-1600)   1680

Caterpillar on leaf smokes hookah, 7-1/2", CE/Dec 16/94 (1000-1500)   1265

White Rabbit runs toward camera, 4-1/2", CE/Dec 16/94 (800-1200)   690

Alice (5-1/2") & Dinah (1-1/2") walking, CE/Dec 16/94 (1200-1500)   1610

Dodo (4-1/2") & Caterpillar (5"), CE/Dec 16/94 (1000-1500)   1150

Tweedledee & Tweedledum walking toward camera, 5", CE/Dec 16/94 (1000-1500)   920

Surprised Dinah sitting, 5", CE/Dec 16/94 (600-800)   518

Alice looks up, 6-1/2", CE/Dec 16/94 (1200-1500)   2070

Owl sits on branch, 3-1/2", CE/Dec 16/94 (500-700)   322

Brush Dog, 5", CE/Dec 16/94 (300-500)   633

Delighted King of Hearts, 4-1/2", CE/Dec 16/94 (500-700)   253

Daisy gesturing to daffodil, 6-1/2" & similar, CE/Dec 16/94 (800-1200)   978

Bubble-blowing Walrus (4", bend forward at waist) & baby Oyster (4-1/2"), CE/Dec 16/94 (600-800)   690

Mad Hatter sits cross-legged & explains tea etiquette, 7", S/Dec 17/94 (1000-1500)   1955

Worried White Rabbit runs w/large pocket watch, 4 x 6", S/Dec 17/94 (1200-1800)   1150

King (4") & Queen of Hearts (7") looking back at each other, S/Dec 17/94 (2000-2500)   2070

Tweedledum & Tweedledee stand side-by-side w/arms raised, each 5", S/Dec 17/94 (800-1200)   977

Pelican, bird & whale of jury stand together; + 3 graphite-on-paper drawings from 1953 educational production *Mr. Dermis' Holiday*: White Rabbit in conductor's uniform; Tweedledee & Tweedledum talk to White Rabbit; Tweedledee & Tweedledum talk to Owl; S/Dec 17/94 (700-900)   632

Curious Dinah stands facing right, looking up, 4-1/4", 12-field, SR/Spring/95 (200-400)   390

Curious Alice stands looking left, 6-1/4", 16-field, ct, SR/Spring/95 (900-1400)   1740

Thoughtful Alice sits facing toward left, 4-3/4", 16-field, with shadow painting, SR/Spring/95 (900-1400)   1270

Alice disdainfully executing seated curtsy, 7 x 8-1/2", F+, HL/Apr 23/95 (1000-1500)   1456

Angry mob of characters moves toward camera, 5-1/2 x 5-1/2", F+, HL/Apr 23/95 (900-1200)   1456

2 mirror images of Caterpillar as butterfly, 4-3/4", CE/Jun 9/95 (500-700) — 345

Reclined Cheshire Cat pointing, 4-3/4", CE/Jun 9/95 (1500-2000) — 2875

Alice sitting & contemplating flowers in her hands, 5", CE/Jun 9/95 (1000-1500) — 1955

Cautious Alice standing, 7", CE/Jun 9/95 (1500-2000) — 2070

Running Ace of Hearts, 6", CE/Jun 9/95 (400-600) — 460

White Rabbit lying on back studying watch, 2-1/2 x 3", CE/Jun 9/95 (700-900) — 1150

Publicity cel:of frantic White Rabbit running with blur lines, circa 1980s, 3-1/4", CE/Jun 9/95 (400-600) — 230

3 dandelions, 5", CE/Jun 9/95 (600-800) — 633

Flowers, 8" & smaller, CE/Jun 9/95 (600-800) — 690

Dodo (2") oversees caucus race, Pelican 1-1/2", Parrot 2", S/Jun 10/95 (700-900) — 690

Irritated White Rabbit lying on back holding watch, 2-1/2 x 3", VF+, HL/Aug 6/95 (600-800) — 1120

Alice wrestles with flamingo, 4-1/2 x 6-1/2", DL gold label, VF, HL/Aug 6/95 (1200-1600) — 2688

Alice walking bent forward at waist, 7 x 4", VF, HL/Aug 6/95 (1000-1500) — 2016

Door w/Door Knob looking up, 4-1/2 x 3-1/2", F+, HL/Aug 6/95 (500-700) — 1456

White Rabbit (dressed as page & holding trumpet) pointing up, 4 x 4", VF+, HL/Aug 6/95 (700-900) — 1064

3 tooting tea pots facing right, 5-1/2 x 5", VF, HL/Aug 6/95 (300-500) — 448

Hookah-smoking Caterpillar, complementary cel of smoke, 8 x 5-1/2", VF+, HL/Nov 19/95 (1800-2400) — 1610

Tweedledee & Tweedledum fighting, 7-1/2 x 5", VF, HL/Nov 19/95 (900-1200) — 805

Wary Alice standing, 6-1/2 x 3-1/2", VF, HL/Nov 19/95 (1200-1600) — 2070

2 full-figure cels: cheerful Carpenter stands looking right with two fingers in mouth, 4-3/4"; Walrus stands facing left smoking cigar with eyes closed, 6-1/2"; together in double-opening mat with brass plaque, SR/Spring/96 (600-1000) — 600

Front view of pencil bird looking straight down, 3", 16-field, SR/Spring/96 (500-900) — 1130

Intent Alice on hands & knees, 5-1/2 x 7-1/2", HL/Apr 28/96 (1200-1600) — 2300

Smiling Queen of Hearts holding "croquet mallet," 7 x 6", HL/Apr 28/96 (900-1200) — 1725

Worried White Rabbit (dressed as page) running, 3 x 2-3/4", HL/Apr 28/96 (700-900) — 1035

King of Hearts tips crown (5-1/2") as amused Queen watches (7"), CE/Jun 20/96 (700-900) — 2760

Smiling Cheshire Cat lying on right side, pointing to left, 5", CE/Jun 20/96 (1500-2000) — 2760

Alice sitting, 5", CE/Jun 20/96 (1000-1500) — 2185

2 cels of flowers, 6" & 4", CE/Jun 20/96 (400-600) — 920

Smug Walrus & suspicious Carpenter walk together, 8 x 10", HL/Oct 6/96 (900-1200) — 920

Dodo blithely rides toucan across sea of tears, 5-1/4 x 9", HL/Oct 6/96 (600-900) — 546

Teapot, 4-1/4 x 4", HL/Oct 6/96 (300-400) — 138

Caterpillar on leaf holds hookah mouthpiece, over cel of inky smoke from another film, 6-1/2 x 6-1/2", HL/Oct 6/96 (800-1000) — 2070

Ace (paint bucket on head), Two (paint bucket on left foot), & Three of Clubs being dragged away by other cards, 5-1/2 x 12-1/2", HL/Oct 6/96 (700-1000) — 1725

Air & sea creatures running in circle directed by Dodo in Caucus Race, 4-1/2 x 8-1/2", HL/Oct 6/96 (800-1000) — 805

Sad Alice walks to left with head down, 7 x 4", HL/Oct 6/96 (1000-1500) — 2530

Befuddled Tweedledee & Tweedledum standing outdoors staring at each other, 5-1/2 x 5-1/4" cel image, HL/Oct 6/96 (600-900) — 1610

View down canopy of lances formed by Hearts playing cards, 10-1/2 x 14-1/4", VF, HL/Oct 6/96 (500-700) — 920

Grim White Rabbit runs left holding trumpet behind him, 2-1/4", CE/Dec 12/96 (800-1000) — 633

Alice stands admiring 4 bread-&-butterflies, 6-1/2", CE/Dec 12/96 (1500-2000) — 2300

Carefree Dodo surfs on upside-down toucan while being pushed by irritated parrot,

3", CE/Dec 12/96 (800-1200) — 575

Haughty Caterpillar lying on leaf holding hookah mouthpiece, 8-1/2", CE/Dec 12/96 (800-1200) — 1380

2 circa 1955 cels from TV productions: full figure of Alice looking up, 4-1/2"; waist-up of Alice facing forward, looking left, 4"; S/Dec 14/96 (700-900) — 575

Walrus gestures, 6-1/2 x 5", HL/Feb 23/97 (400-500) — 575

Two Clubs standing with paint & brushes, 4-1/2 x 6", HL/Feb 23/97 (500-700) — 518

King of Hearts holds scepter, looks back & up; 4 x 4", HL/Feb 23/97 (700-1000) — 748

Shovel bird, 5 x 5-1/2", HL/Feb 23/97 (300-500) — 863

Tweedledee & Tweedledum holding hands & dancing, 6-1/2", ct, SR/Spring/97 (600-1000) — 1100

Front view of confident Walrus (eyes closed) & discouraged Carpenter with hammer raised walking together, 11-1/2 x 9-3/4", 16-field cel, dry brush effects, ct, SR/Spring/97 (600-1000) — 1740

Somber Alice walks w/head down, 7 x 4", HL/May 3/97 (1000-1500) — 1265

Startled Alice lying on ground, looking up, paint brush in left hand, 7-1/2" length, CLA/Jun 7/97 (1000-1500) — 1610

Worried White Rabbit looks left while running right, holding watch up, 4-1/2", CLA/Jun 7/97 (1000-1500) — 1725

Publicity cel of White Rabbit, circa 1980s, 3-1/4", CLA/Jun 7/97 (300-500) — 46

Wide-eyed Alice faces right, looking to side, 5-1/2", S/Jun 21/97 (1000-1500) — 1495

Tweedledum & Tweedledee mirror each other as they block Alice's departure from their company, 5" each, S/Jun 21/97 (800-1200) — 690

Mother Oyster watches young oysters frolic, sight 8-1/2 x 11-1/2", S/Jun 21/97 (600-800) — 690

3 Dandylions as vocal trio, 4-1/4" & 5", S/Jun 21/97 (800-1200) — 690

Front view of smiling Walrus stepping left, looking back to right, 7", 16-field cel, SR/Fall/97 (600-900) — 700

Haughty Red Rose in conducting pose, 7-3/4 x 6-1/2", VF, HL/Nov 16/97 (700-1000) — 805

White Rabbit running, 4-1/4 x 3-1/2", VF+, HL/Nov 16/97 (600-900) — 575

2 cels: full-figure large image of kneeling Alice facing right, door w/Door Knob & open curtains; 6-1/2 x 14-1/4", VF, HL/Nov 16/97 (2000-3000) — 3680

Front view of grinning Cheshire Cat standing, left arm holding lever, 2-1/2 x 2-3/4", VF+, HL/Nov 16/97 (1500-2000) — 2990

Approx. 22 quivering Mome Raths, 8-3/4 x 11", VF+, HL/Nov 16/97 (500-700) — 1093

Tweedledee & Tweedledum fight (one jumping in air), 6-1/4 x 5-1/4", VF, HL/Nov 16/97 (600-800) — 1035

Dinah crawls to right, 3-3/4 x 5-1/2", VF, HL/Nov 16/97 (300-500) — 316

Dodo sails on flood with aid of 2 birds, 5" overall, S/Dec 19/97 (900-1200) — 1035

Six pansies, restored, 7-1/4 x 7-3/4", VF, HL/Apr 25/98 (700-1000) — 1380

Blissful White Rabbit in court garb looking up & to right, 5 x 4", VF, HL/Apr 25/98 (600-900) 1035

Curious Dinah facing right, 4 x 5", VF, HL/Apr 25/98 (500-700) — 633

Flight of five Umbrella Birds, 4 x 6", VF+, HL/Apr 25/98 (500-700) — 690

Alice stands facing toward left, looking down; restored; 7 x 4"; VF; HL/Apr 25/98 (1000-1500) — 1265

Color model cel: 2 slightly different full figures of Caterpillar as butterfly, 5 x 7-1/2", F+, HL/Apr 25/98 (700-1000) — 460

Matched cel and publication drawing of Alice bending down [to look thru keyhole which shows in drawing], 4 3/8", both 12-field, SR/Spring/98 (900-1500) — 1010

White Rabbit runs right with hand to head, eyes closed, holding huge watch up; 5"; 12-field cel; SR/Spring/98 (800-1200) — 1070

CELS – PARTIAL FIGURE (also see ANIMATION DRAWINGS)

Scene from "The Caucus Race", 10-1/4 x 15-1/4", CE/Dec 15/93 (400-600) — 575

Portrait of surprised White Rabbit, 5-3/4 x 6-1/2", CE/Dec 15/93 (800-1200) — 1265

Walrus bows, 7-1/2 x 9", CE/Dec 15/93 (400-600) — 345

Determined Alice from waist up, 7", CE/Jun 18/94 (1200-1500) — 1495

Alice peeks thru reeds to right, 4-1/2", CE/Jun 18/94 (1200-1500) — 1380

Worried White Rabbit, 6-1/2 x 6", CE/Jun 18/94 (1000-1500) — 748

Alice (2") parts grass to view rocking horsefly, CE/Jun 18/94 (700-900) — 1380

March Hare (5-1/2") holds Dormouse (3") by hair, CE/Jun 18/94 (800-1200) — 1495

Alice in Garden of Talking Flowers, 11-1/2 x 14", VF, HL/Aug 21/94 (3000-4000) — 4480

Hem-up image of demure Alice standing looking down & toward left, 7", 16-field, SR/Fall/94 (1000-1600) — 1240

Portrait of wide-eyed Alice with hands together, 6 x 4", VF, HL/Nov 13/94 (700-1000) — 1680

Inquisitive Alice facing right (knees up), 6-1/2 x 4-1/2", VF+, HL/Nov 13/94 (1000-1500) — 1904

Alice wearing eyeglasses creature looks back, 8" (knees up), CE/Dec 16/94 (1000-1500) — 920

Apprehensive Alice stares at cake she's holding, 7", CE/Dec 16/94 (1500-2000) — 1725

Alice faces toward right & gestures, 6-1/4", CE/Dec 16/94 (1200-1500) — 1840

Alice stands facing right w/hands in pockets looking down, 8-1/2", CE/Dec 16/94 (1000-1500) 1840

Waist-up of Walrus leaning over & looking down with right hand up in 'stop' pose, 5-1/2", full figures of 3 blanketed oysters to left, 12-field, SR/Spring/95 (400-700) — 650

Near-full-figure close-up of grinning Cheshire Cat, 8-1/2 x 6-1/2", VF, HL/Apr 23/95 (2000-3000) — 4256

Portrait of Alice, 4 x 5-1/2", VF, HL/Apr 23/95 (1000-1500) — 1288

Alice standing & examining object in her hands, 9-1/4", CE/Jun 9/95 (1000-1500) — 1725

Close-up of Mad Hatter examining cup, 6", CE/Jun 9/95 (600-800) — 518

Ankles-up view of standing Alice looking up & to left, 8-1/2", S/Jun 10/95 (800-1200) — 1840

White Rabbit reading scroll; Dodo being borne across waters on feet of mynah bird, gold DL label, S/Jun 10/95 (800-1200) — 1265

Mad Hatter holding teapot to mouth, 5-1/2 x 6", VF, HL/Aug 6/95 (600-900) — 728

Front view of 2 pair of pansies facing each other, 7 x 10", VF, HL/Aug 6/95 (600-800) — 616

Shoulders-up of sleepy Alice with bird's nest & bird on top of her head, 4-3/4", 16-field, SR/Fall/95 (500-900) — 610

Waist-up images of angry Walrus looking right to see Carpenter hanging upside down underwater, 7-3/8", water & dry-brush effects, SR/Fall/95 (600-1000) — 810

Front view of smiling March Hare extending tea cup, 6 x 4", VF, HL/Nov 19/95 (600-900) — 805

Close-up front view of head (eyes closed) & arms (left thumb pointing to right) of Cheshire Cat, 5", SR/Spring/96 (400-800) — 300

Near-full figures of puzzled Tweedledee & Tweedledum, 5-1/2 x 5-1/2", HL/Apr 28/96 (900-1200) 805

Mad Hatter (from mid-thigh up) holds 3-spouted tea pot horizontally with one hand, 8", CE/Jun 20/96 (700-900) — 1955

Overhead view of Mad Hatter peering inside White Rabbit's watch, 6-1/2 x 4-1/2", VF+, HL/Oct 6/96 (800-1200) — 1380

Near-full figure of Alice sitting looking right in anticipation, 6-1/2", CE/Dec 12/96 (1000-1500) — 920

Knees-up image of Alice wearing eyeglasses creature, 7-1/2 x 4-3/4", HL/Feb 23/97 (1500-2000) — 2070

March Hare cracks a teapot open like an egg, 5 x 5-1/4", VF, HL/Nov 16/97 (700-900) 977

Near-full figure of Alice walking toward left, 3-3/4 x 2-1/4", VF+, HL/Apr 25/98 (500-800) — 863

CONCEPT AND INSPIRATIONAL ART

4 inspirational studies by Horvath, 3 x 7" to 5-1/2 x 5-1/2", HL/Nov 19/95 (700-1000) — 863

Signed rendering by David Hall of Alice meeting 3 Clubs (as men in costume) who are painting roses red, pencil on paper mounted to animation board, 6-1/4 x 8" including signature, HL/Feb 23/97 (1500-2000) — 1840

Signed rendering by David Hall of Alice meeting

Queen of Hearts & courtiers, pencil on paper mounted to animation board, 6-1/2 x 8" including signature, HL/Feb 23/97 (1500-2000) 2300
Rendering by Mary Blair of Caterpillar talking to Alice, tempera on board, 5-1/4 x 6-3/4", HL/Feb 23/97 (1200-1600) 6038
Inspirational sketch by Bill Peet: Alice walks on forest path holding basket, accompanied by 2 birds, 5-1/2", CE/Dec 18/97 (800-1200) 460
Concept drawing of Cheshire cat's smile by David Hall, sight 5-1/2 x 7-1/2", CE/Dec 18/97 (700-900) 1725
Full-figure character study of Alice by Mary Blair, tempera on board, 6 x 4", VF, HL/Apr 25/98 (900-1200) 1093

DYE-TRANSFER PRINTS

Knees-up front view of Alice in field of daisies, 9-7/8 x 8", Disney label, SR/Fall/96 (300-600) 330

LAYOUT ART

5 atmospheric layout drawings of Queen's courtroom, 11 x 14", 20 x 10", F, HL/Apr 23/95 (1000-1500) 896
7 finished layout drawings, one with layout chart, 5 x 4" to 7-1/2 x 3", F, HL/Apr 23/95 (1200-1600) 1008
5 polished layout drawings of Alice "wearing" outgrown cottage, pencil & conté crayon on animation sheets, 9 x 11" to 11 x 21", HL/Apr 28/96 (1000-1500) 1610

MODEL ART (also see CELS – FULL FIGURE)

13 photostat model sheets, 11 x 14", F, HL/Apr 10/94 (1000-1500) 2912

STORY ART

Story painting of talking flowers, CE/Jun 20/96 (1500-2000) 1725
Story painting of talking flowers & bread-&-butterflies, CE/Jun 20/96 (1500-2000) 2185

THE ARISTOCATS (1970)

ANIMATION DRAWINGS

Full-figure rough drawing of shocked Duchess & three kittens looking down, 6 x 8-1/2", HL/Aug 6/95 (200-300) 476

CEL SET-UPS

Full figures of O'Malley & Duchess talking on street, 3-1/3" & similar, key watercolor production background, CE/Dec 16/94 (6000-8000) 8050
Waist-up front view of surprised Georges Hautecourt about to put papers into briefcase, 8", Hanna-Barbera production background of library, 12-field, SR/Spring/95 (200-400) 200
Full figure of carefree O'Malley introducing himself, 6-1/4", DL litho background of countryside & gold Art Corner label, original price sticker, SR/Spring/96 (300-500) 510
Half-image portraits of wary O'Malley & charming Duchess sitting together, 6" & 5-1/2", DL outdoor litho background, gold Art Corner label & price sticker, SR/Spring/96 (400-600) 810
Full-figure front view of angry Edgar standing putting on trousers, 8", DL litho background of living room, gold Art Corner label & price sticker, SR/Spring/96 (200-400) 200
Full figures of Italian & English Cats dancing together, 10-1/8 x 6-1/4", 16-field cel, contemporary background, Disney Art Program seal, SR/Fall/96 (300-600) 310
Limited-edition family portrait of O'Malley, Duchess, & kittens sitting on sofa, #148/500, color print of background painting, 11 x 14", HL/Oct 6/96 (1000-1500) 805
O'Malley lounges contentedly in branches of tree, painted india ink & watercolor Studio Art Props background, 9 x 12-1/2", HL/Oct 6/96 (900-1200) 748
Portrait of Duchess, Marie (both full figure, 6-1/2" & 3"), O'Malley (8"), Berlioz (3") & Toulouse (3") seated on chair, watercolor production background, CE/Dec 12/96 (3500-4500) 7475
Close-up of Duchess sitting in alley, 7", full 16-field original watercolor production background, S/Dec 14/96 (1500-2000) 1725
Close-up half images of O'Malley (5-5/8") & Duchess (5-1/4") sitting together, litho background of snowy outdoors, DL Art Corner label, SR/Spring/97 (500-900) 500
Hips-up of Madame Bonfamille, eyes closed, facing right, extending left arm while holding Duchess on shoulder, 6-3/4", litho background of home interior, gold DL Art Corner label, SR/Spring/97 (400-700) 400
Smiling O'Malley & fierce Toulouse (full figure) face off, 4-1/4 x 9-1/2", color print background of outdoors, HL/May 31/97 (300-400) 316
Full figure of smug Marie sitting by log, 6 x 3-1/2", color print background, HL/May 31/97 (200-400) 230
Family portrait of Duchess (6"), O'Malley (7") & 3 kittens (2-1/2" each) sitting proudly on chair, printed background, S/Jun 21/97 (1500-2000) 3162
Full figure of eager Roquefort looking left, holding half-eaten cracker, 4-3/4", DL litho background of snowy forest, gold Art Corner label, original price sticker, SR/Fall/97 (300-500) 200
Half image of O'Malley lying across log to flirt with sitting Duchess, 5" & 5-5/8", DL litho background & gold Art Corner label, SR/Fall/97 (600-900) 440
Cels of O'Malley, Duchess, Toulouse, Berlioz, Scat Cat & Italian buddy over 3 color print backgrounds & labels as sold at DL; 5-1/2 x 8", 6-1/2 x 7", 5 x 5-1/2"; F overall, HL/Nov 16/97 (700-1000) 863

CELS – FULL FIGURE

O'Malley & Duchess dance, 4 x 13", VF, HL/Feb 26-27/94 (300-400) 825
3 cels: Edgar stepping holding fishing rod, M. Hautecourt walking, Madame Bonfamille leaning on bed; 6-1/2 x 7", 6 x 5", 10 x 4"; VF+, HL/Feb 26-27/94 (400-500) 715
O'Malley & Duchess dancing apart, 4 x 13", VF+, HL/Nov 13/94 (400-600) 560
Roquefort yawns, 6-3/4", CE/Dec 16/94 (400-600) 115
O'Malley & Scat Cat dancing, 5-1/2 x 4-1/2", HL/Aug 6/95 (300-500) 588
O'Malley sits with Toulouse & Berlioz, 6-1/2 x 6-1/2", HL/Oct 6/96 (700-1000) 489
Sad Duchess stands facing left, 3-1/2 x 3-1/2", HL/May 31/97 (150-200) 184
Uncle Waldo (minus tail feathers) stands facing left & adjusts battered hat, 5-1/2 x 3-1/4", HL/May 31/97 (100-150) 184
2 cels: full-figure of O'Malley bowing to right, 3-3/8"; portrait of Dutchess looking down & to left, 4-3/8"; SR/Spring/98 (300-500) 590

CELS – PARTIAL FIGURE

Matched set of 2 portrait cels of Duchess & O'Malley meowing a duet; 5 x 4", 5 x 5"; matted; VF, HL/Feb 26-27/94 (400-600) 880
2 portraits: lovely Duchess, suave O'Malley; 6-1/2 x 5-1/2", 5-1/2 x 4-1/2", HL/Apr 28/96 (600-800) 633
Gabble sisters in swimming poses looking down, 4 x 7-1/2", HL/May 31/97 (100-200) 92
Portrait of dainty Duchess w/head down, mouth open & eyes closed, 5 x 4-1/2", HL/May 31/97 (150-250) 127
Chest-up of Amelia, Abigail & Uncle Waldo, 6 x 1-1/2" ea., WDP seal, CE/Jun 18/94 (300-500) 253
3 cels: Marie singing w/eyes closed, 3"; Duchess holding Marie, 2 x 5"; Chinese Cat playing piano w/chopsticks, 5-1/2"; latter two w/gold DL label, S/Jun 19/96 (600-800) 920
Portrait of Mme. Bonfamille sitting holding Duchess on her lap, 8-1/4 x 7", VF, HL/Apr 25/98 (150-200) 489

DYE-TRANSFER PRINTS

O'Malley, Duchess, & kittens posing on sofa, 10 x 8", SR/Fall/94 (200-500) 310

STORY ART

Story drawing of O'Malley looking thru windshield at startled milkman, 6-1/2 x 9-1/2", HL/May 31/97 (75-100) 81
Cartoony story drawing of M. Hautecourt (in dark glasses) reading document with 3 kittens crawling on him, 4-1/2 x 7-1/2", HL/May 31/97 (200-300) 288
3 early story drawings of servants; colored marker on paper; 8 x 5-1/2", 4-1/2 x 11", 5-1/2 x 10-1/2"; F; HL/Apr 25/98 (800-1200) 230

BAMBI (1942)

Also see TELEVISION: ANTHOLOGY SERIES

ANIMATION DRAWINGS (also see MODEL ART)

Bambi & Thumper talk to Flower, publicity drawing, 9-1/2 x 11", S/Dec 16/93 (300-500) 345
2 drawings of newly-antlered Bambi, 5 x 6" & 6 x 3", VF, HL/Apr 10/94 (400-600) 504
Full-figure drawing of young Bambi standing, 5-3/4", 16-field sheet, edge discoloration & wear, SR/Fall/94 (250-500) 720
2 full-figure drawings: animation drawing of Thumper with notes; model drawing of Bambi with notes & autographed by Ollie Johnston, 2-1/2 x 2" & 4 x 3", HL/Nov 13/94 (700-1000) 1120
Full-figure drawing of Bambi's father, 8", CE/Dec 16/94 (300-400) 322
Drawing of young Bambi (full figure) being licked on top of head by his mother (head & neck), 4-3/4", 12-field sheet, SR/Spring/95 (300-600) 310
3 full-figure drawings: flirtatious Miss Bunny, 2 of twitterpated Thumper; 3-1/2" to 5-1/4", some edge wear, SR/Spring/95 (900-1200) 1540
2 side-view full-figure animation drawings: Bambi's mother & young Bambi, 5-1/2 x 6" & 1-1/2 x 1-1/4", HL/Apr 23/95 (400-600) 476
Drawing of young Bambi (near-full figure) being nuzzled by his mother (neck up), 4-3/4", 12-field sheet, SR/Fall/96 (250-450) 280
Near-full-figure drawing of young Bambi standing facing right, looking back left & down, 4-3/4", 16-field sheet, some wear & discoloration, SR/Spring/97 (300-700) 330
Full-figure side-view drawing of young Bambi looking back as legs go in four directions, 4-1/4", 12-field sheet, signed by Marc Davis, SR/Fall/97 (900-1200) 970
2 full-figure front-view rough animation drawings of Bambi as young buck, 7-1/2 x 4" & 7 x 4", F, HL/Nov 16/97 (500-700) 403
Publicity drawing of young Bambi (4-1/2") smiling at Flower (2-1/2") in meadow as Thumper (3") rolls on his back in the flowers, CE/Dec 18/97 (2000-3000) 1955

CEL SET-UPS (also see MODEL ART)

Bambi looks into forest, watercolor preparation background, 8-1/2 x 11", CE/Dec 15/93 (2500-3500) 8280
Bambi talks to Thumper, circa 1980s, watercolor background, 10-1/2 x 12-1/5", CE/Dec 15/93 (700-900) 1265
Thumper as young rabbit, airbrushed background, WDP stamp, Courvoisier Galleries label, 2", S/Dec 16/93 (1000-1500) 1380
2 x 3" Bambi & 2" Thumper on ice, airbrushed background, WDP stamp, Courvoisier label, S/Dec 16/93 (2000-3000) 3163
Bambi watching leaves, airbrushed background, 4-1/2", S/Dec 16/93 (2500-3500) 3450
4-3/4" Bambi & 2-1/4" Thumper smiling at each other, studio-prepared background, WDP stamp, S/Dec 16/93 (2000-3000) 3163
Full-figures of young Bambi & squirrel, 7 x 7", Courvoisier label, complementary airbrush background in mat inscribed "Bambi" & stamped "original WDP," F+, HL/Apr 10/94 (2200-2800) 4256
Bambi (3" x 3") & Thumper (2") slide on ice, airbrushed Courvoisier background, S/Jun 17/94 (2500-3500) 3737
Bambi (4-1/2 x 4-1/2") talks to Thumper (3 x 2", w/paper roll), 1980s educational series, watercolor production background, CE/Jun 18/94 (700-900) 690
Bambi (3"), Thumper (2-1/2"), Friend Owl (3") & baby rabbit by water in winter, 1980s educational series, key watercolor production background, CE/Jun 18/94 (700-900) 518
Bambi & Flower talk in meadow, circa 1980s, educational series, watercolor production background, CE/Jun 18/94 (300-400) 1610
Bambi (4 x 4") with butterfly on tail as Thumper (1-3/4 x 1-1/2") & 2 sisters laugh, Walt Disney Studios watercolor & gouache preliminary background, WDP label, original WDP stamp, "To Jason-Best Wishes, Walt Disney" on mat, CE/Jun 18/94 (5000-7000) 9775
Full figures of standing Thumper (1-1/2") & young Bambi (dry brush accents, 3-3/4") eyeing each other, original master oil-paint background of forest, prepared by Courvoisier, label, SR/Fall/94 (4000-6000) 6,500
Full figures of young Bambi (4-3/4") standing in flowers as 2 bunnies (2-1/2") watch, original overlay of

flowers, watercolor display background, paint restoration, SR/Fall/94 (2200-3200) 5400

"Say Bird" limited-edition cel of Bambi surrounded by friends, 11 x 15", print background, #340/500, Disney seal & certificate, HL/Nov 13/94 (1800-2400) 5376

Bambi (6") w/2 rabbits (2"), Courvoisier airbrush & watercolor background, CE/Dec 16/94 (2500-3500) 6900

Full figures of Bambi (4") & Thumper (1-1/2"), Courvoisier background, CE/Dec 16/94 (800-1200) 2530

Full figure of Bambi (1") & Mother (1-1/2") walking in forest, Courvoisier airbrush background, CE/Dec 16/94 (1200-1500) 3450

Full figure of Owl in tree gesturing, Courvoisier airbrush background, 4", CE/Dec 16/94 (1000-1500) 1035

Thumper (2-3/4") standing on log & Flower (2-3/4") in flowers look up, watercolor preliminary production background, CE/Dec 16/94 (4000-5000) 5750

Full-figure publicity cel of Thumper, 6-3/4", watercolor background from unknown production, CE/Dec 16/94 (4000-6000) 14,950

Full figures of flirtatious Miss Bunny (4") & twitterpated Thumper (5") in meadow, Courvoisier watercolor background, CE/Dec 16/94 (4000-6000) 5175

Full figure of Flower's girlfriend w/flower, 3", publication background, CE/Dec 16/94 (1500-2000) 1610

Full figure of young Bambi, 5-1/2", illustration background, CE/Dec 16/94 (3000-4000) 4370

Publicity cel of young Bambi from TV promotion for 1988 theatrical re-release, 7 x 6", print of key background, S/Dec 17/94 (1000-1500) 1150

Full figure of Bambi (4-1/2 x 4") meeting Flower (3"), airbrushed Courvoisier background & label, S/Dec 17/94 (2000-3000) 4600

Publicity set-up of Bambi looking at butterfly, 5 x 4", from 1988 TV promotion of theatrical re-release, print of key background, S/Dec 17/94 (1000-1500) 1150

Bambi (4") with eyes closed laughs with Thumper (1"), airbrushed veneer Courvoisier background & label, S/Dec 17/94 (2000-3000) 2875

Full figures of curious young Bambi & friendly Thumper walking side by side to right, 7", watercolor background of meadow, original key overlay, 12-field, 1981 educational filmstrip, SR/Spring/95 (400-700) 640

Full-figure front view of smiling Thumper standing on hind legs, 4-5/8", Courvoisier oil-on-wood-veneer background, SR/Spring/95 (1800-2400) 1980

Full figures of young Bambi (5-1/4") & Flower (2-1/2") standing facing each other on path as 4 birds watch, gouache display background, rippling, 12-field, ct, SR/Spring/95 (3000-5000) 5100

Full figures of Thumper (3") & Miss Bunny (3-1/2"), Courvoisier watercolor & airbrush background, CE/Jun 9/95 (2000-2500) 3450

Full figure of young Bambi in meadow watching butterfly, 5", watercolor & airbrush background, inscribed "...Walt Disney", CE/Jun 9/95 (3000-4000) 4370

Field mouse reaches for raindrop, 2", key oil production background, CE/Jun 9/95 (2500-3500) 5175

Full figure of eager Thumper ready to run, 2-1/2", Courvoisier airbrush & watercolor background, CE/Jun 9/95 (1500-2000) 2300

Full figures of young Bambi (4") & Thumper (2") meeting in forest clearing, watercolor production background with overlay, CE/Jun 9/95 (10,000-15,000) 21,850

Full figures of young Bambi (3-1/2") & smiling Thumper (1-1/2"), Courvoisier watercolor & airbrush background, CE/Jun 9/95 (1500-2000) 3220

Full figure of Friend Owl spreading wings in tree, 6" long, Courvoisier watercolor background, CE/Jun 9/95 (700-900) 1150

Full figures of Bambi (7") & Thumper (3") in forest, circa 1980s, watercolor production background, CE/Jun 9/95 (600-800) 690

Full figures of young Bambi facing Flower (on hind legs), 9 x 10", complementary painted background as prepared by Courvoisier, HL/Aug 6/95 (3000-3500) 5824

Full figure of wide-eyed young Bambi sitting in meadow amid birds & bees, 7-1/2 x 8", painted background as prepared by Courvoisier, HL/Aug 6/95 (1800-2400) 4480

Full figure of young stag standing facing left in red meadow, turning in alarm, 6-1/4", 16-field, watercolor display background, SR/Fall/95 (800-1200) 800

Full figure of Flower staring at alluring eyes (on 2nd cel) within bunch of flowers, 3 x 3" cel image, newly created background painting, HL/Nov 19/95 (1500-2000) 2070

Near-full figure of inquisitive young Bambi standing in forest, 5-1/2 x 4-1/2", color print background, HL/Nov 19/95 (2000-3000) 3450

Full figure of young Bambi standing in forest facing right, 5-1/4", Courvoisier watercolor background, ct, SR/Spring/96 (1200-1600) 4180

Young Bambi (full figure, 3-3/4") listens to Mother (three-quarter figure, 7-1/2"), new Courvoisier-style forest background with overlay, some stabilized fissuring, ct, SR/Spring/96 (1000-1600) 1100

Full figures of happy young Bambi jumping as 5 bunnies sit watching, 4-1/2", Courvoisier watercolor outdoor background & label, some color shift & paint separation, ct, SR/Spring/96 (4000-5000) 4400

DAE: Bambi & Thumper meet Flower amid wildflowers, color print background as issued, #129/500, 11 x 15", HL/Apr 28/96 (1600-2000) 1380

Full figure of Flower & 2 bunnies in meadow, complementary Courvoisier background painting, 5-1/2 x 7", HL/Apr 28/96 (1000-1200) 1035

Full figure of Thumper standing in grass watching butterfly, wood-veneer Courvoisier background, mat inscribed "...Walt Disney", 3", S/Jun 19/96 (2500-3500) 3450

Full figure of Thumper (2") looking up at 2 birds in tree, Courvoisier background, S/Jun 19/96 (1000-1500) 2185

Full figures of Bambi (2-1/2 x 1-1/2") & Thumper (2") standing on ice, airbrushed Courvoisier background, S/Jun 19/96 (2000-3000) 3737

Full figures of young Bambi & Faline playing in forest, Courvoisier background, approx. 3" each, S/Jun 19/96 (2500-3500) 3737

Full figures of young Bambi & Mother standing in snow amid bare trees, Courvoisier watercolor background, 2", CE/Jun 20/96 (700-900) 1380

Full figures of happy young Bambi standing (4-1/2") & smiling Thumper sitting (2"), Courvoisier watercolor & airbrush background, partial overlay, mat signed by Walt Disney, CE/Jun 20/96 (5000-7000) 9430

Full figures of smiling young Bambi (4") standing in forest amid Thumper (2-1/2") & other bunnies (2" & smaller), Courvoisier watercolor & airbrush background, CE/Jun 20/96 (5000-7000) 6670

Full figure of young Bambi (3-7/8") & Flower (partly behind log, 2-1/4") touching noses in clearing, airbrush enhanced, watercolor background, prepared at studio with Courvoisier background layouts & templates, studio label, Courvoisier monogram stamp, SR/Fall/96 (3000-5000) 5400

Full-figure front view of Thumper standing looking right, 2-1/2", pre-production watercolor background of forest, studio stamps, ct, SR/Fall/96 (2500-3500) 2530

Full-figure front view of young Bambi looking to right, 5 x 2-1/2" cel, over watercolor painting (watercolor on heavyweight paper), HL/Oct 6/96 (1200-1600) 2990

Full figures of Thumper laughing as confused Bambi sits on ice, 5-1/4 x 6-1/2" cel image, complementary painted background as prepared by Courvoisier, HL/Oct 6/96 (3000-5000) 4888

Full figures of Bambi (4-1/2") & Thumper (2") in snow near bare tree, Courvoisier watercolor background & half a label, CE/Dec 12/96 (3000-5000) 4600

Near-full figure overhead view of young Bambi standing in forest watching two butterflies circling above him, 3-1/2", Courvoisier watercolor background & label, CE/Dec 12/96 (2500-3500) 3220

Squirrels, 2-1/2" & smaller, Courvoisier watercolor background & label, CE/Dec 12/96 (600-800) 748

Full figure of young Bambi (3 x 3-1/3") & Thumper (2")

walking on ice, airbrushed Courvoisier background, S/Dec 14/96 (2500-3500) 4025

Near-full figures of young Bambi (5-1/2 x 4-1/4") smiling at bunny (2 x 1") hiding at right, full 16-field original preliminary watercolor background of forest, S/Dec 14/96 (7000-9000) 8050

Full figures of wobbly baby Bambi (3-1/4 x 3") & attentive Thumper (1-1/2 x 1-1/4") on ice, pan oil production background, S/Dec 14/96 (15,000-20,000) 12,650

Full figures of baby Bambi (4-3/4 x 4") standing on forest trail looking down & smiling at Miss Bunny (1-3/4 x 1-1/2"), original preliminary watercolor background signed by Maurice Nobel, S/Dec 14/96 (7000-9000) 13,800

Full figures of baby Bambi (7-3/4") & Thumper (4") standing smiling at each other, circa 1980s educational series, airbrushed key production background, S/Dec 14/96 (1000-1500) 1495

Near-full figure of young Bambi standing in grass on hill turning to look back at two bunnies, painted background w/overlay of grass as prepared by Courvoisier, 5-1/2 x 6-1/2", HL/Feb 23/97 (3000-3500) 3795

Full figures of smiling young Bambi & Thumper standing on ice, complementary painted winter background as prepared by Courvoisier, 7 x 8" overall, HL/Feb 23/97 (3500-4000) 4370

Young Bambi (5-1/2") & Flower (2-1/2") meet amid carpet of blossoms, two full hand-inked overlays, watercolor & gouache background, SR/Spring/97 (3000-6000) 4400

Near-full figure of young Bambi inspecting forest, portion of woodland background (watercolor on background sheet) from another film, 9 x 7", HL/May 3/97 (4000-5000) 3680

Thumper (3"), Miss Bunny (2-1/2"), & friends in forest (1-1/2" & similar) stare intently; Courvoisier forest background & label, CLA/Jun 7/97 (2000-3000) 2415

Full-figure publicity cel of smiling Thumper standing, 1940, 6-1/2", Courvoisier watercolor circle background, mat signed by Walt Disney, CLA/Jun 7/97 (2000-3000) 2760

Full figures of Thumper (2-1/2") standing beside tree smiling at brother (1-1/4"), airbrushed Courvoisier background, S/Jun 21/97 (1200-1800) 2875

Young Bambi chases 6 rabbits thru forest (some deterioration), sight 8 x 11", preliminary watercolor background, S/Jun 21/97 (1500-2000) 1725

Full-figure rear view of young Bambi (5") turning to look at back legs as 5 rabbits (1-1/2" each) watch, airbrushed Courvoisier background, signed "Best wishes ... Walt Disney" in unknown hand, needs restoration, S/Jun 21/97 (2500-3500) 3162

Young Bambi looks up at butterfly, 4 x 3", airbrushed Courvoisier background of leaves, S/Jun 21/97 (2500-3500) 4025

Production set-up: full figure of Thumper (2-1/2") eyeing Miss Bunny (3") by hollow log, watercolor production background, signed by Walt Disney on mat, Courvoisier label, S/Jun 21/97 (10,000-12,000) 16,100

Young Bambi meets Flower, 5 x 4-1/4" & 2-1/4 x 4", Studio Art Props background of flower-filled meadow (tempera on background board), F+, HL/Nov 16/97 (3000-4000) 6325

"Bambi in the Flowers" limited-edition cel of young Bambi, Flower, & Thumper amid flowers, #319/500, 11 x 15" overall, matching color print background, VF+, HL/Nov 16/97 (1400-1800) 1840

Full figure of spindly young Bambi standing facing left, 3-3/4 x 3-1/2", over impressionistic study for a background (watercolor on heavyweight paper), F, HL/Nov 16/97 (1200-1600) 1840

Full figures of young Bambi following Great Stag thru snow, 6-1/2 x 6-1/4", complementary painted background, "WDP" monogram stamp as prepared by Courvoisier, F, HL/Nov 16/97 (3000-4000) 3910

Full figures of wide-eyed young Bambi (4-1/2") standing in front of six bunnies (backs turned, 1-1/2"), Courvoisier watercolor production background of meadow & separately framed label, CE/Dec 18/97 (5000-7000) 4600

Full figures of surprised young Bambi (4") standing in front of six bunnies (backs turned, 5"), Courvoisier watercolor production background of meadow, CE/Dec 18/97 (4000-6000) 3680

Bambi walks away thru forest, 3", printed background; Woody Woodpecker walking to right w/hand outstretched, 3", gouache production background, Walter Lantz stamp; S/Dec 19/97 (500-700) 517

Full figure of Flower sitting in forest rubbing eyes, 3", hand-prepared background, S/Dec 19/97 (800-1200) 690

Full figures of happy Thumper sitting watching butterfly, 2-1/2", airbrushed Courvoisier background, WDP label, S/Dec 19/97 (1000-1500) 3162

Full figures of young Bambi (3 x 2") & mother (5 x 4") walking thru forest, production set-up w/watercolor or production background, "To Bob Mochrie ... Walt Disney" on mat, S/Dec 19/97 (8000-12,000) 9200

Near-full figure of young adult Bambi facing left, complementary color print background of meadow, restored, 7-1/2 x 6-1/2", VF, HL/Apr 25/98 (1000-1500) 1150

"Bambi in the Flowers": Xerographic-line, hand-painted limited-edition cel of Bambi, Thumper & Flower in sea of flowers, #202/500, matching color print background, seal & certificate, 11 x 15" overall, VF+, HL/Apr 25/98 (1200-1600) 1725

Matching set: bird standing on tree limb, 3 birds' heads sticking out of holes in trunk, master background of forest (oil on background sheet), stamps, restored, 8-1/2 x 11", VF, HL/Apr 25/98 (2000-3000) 2760

Flower partially submerged in meadow flowers inhaling fragrance with eyes closed, complementary painted background, restored, 2 x 2-1/2" cel, VF, HL/Apr 25/98 (700-1000) 1093

Rabbit family in meadow amid clover blossoms, complementary painted background, signed by Marc Davis, restored, 3-1/2 x 6-1/4" cel, VF, HL/Apr 25/98 (1200-1600) 1610

CELS – FULL FIGURE (also see MODEL ART)

Bambi & 2 bunnies, publicity release, 5-1/2 x 7-1/2", CE/Dec 15/93 (700-900) 632

Bambi & 2 bunnies, circa 1940s publicity release, 5-1/2 x 7", CE/Dec 15/93 (800-1200) 690

Attentive Bunny family facing right (watching off-camera Bambi), 4-1/2 x 2-1/2", restored, VF, HL/Apr 10/94 (400-600) 896

Flower walking with nose in air, eyes closed, 3-1/4", paint cracks, SR/Fall/94 (500-900) 550

Shy Flower stands facing right, 3-5/8", 12-field, ct, SR/Spring/95 (1200-1800) 1400

Full-face view of awed young Bambi, 3-1/2 x 2-1/2", HL/Apr 23/95 (1500-2000) 2912

Young Bambi in classic pose, 5 x 5", HL/Apr 23/95 (2500-3500) 4032

Side view of happy young Bambi high stepping, 4 x 2-1/2", HL/Apr 23/95 (1800-2000) 2464

Publicity cel: three-quarter rear view of Flower looking into distance from hill, circa 1940s, 3-1/2", CE/Jun 9/95 (600-800) 230

Embarrassed Flower stands facing left, waving, 1950s TV, 3-5/8", 16-field, ct, SR/Fall/95 (600-900) 600

Profile of young Bambi prancing, 4 x 3", HL/Apr 28/96 (1800-2600) 2530

Happy Thumper sitting up, 3-1/2 x 2-1/4", HL/Apr 28/96 (1200-1600) 1955

Baby Bambi meeting 4 birds with overlay of windblown flowers & grass, 6 x 9-1/2", F, HL/Apr 28/96 (3000-4000) 5175

Eager fawn Faline standing facing toward left, 7-1/4", CE/Dec 12/96 (1000-1500) 1380

Awed Flower sitting looking up, 3-1/2", CE/Dec 12/96 (1000-1500) 1495

Happy Thumper standing looking up & to left, 3", CE/Dec 12/96 (1000-1500) 2415

Young Bambi happily prancing to left, 3-1/2 x 2-1/2", HL/May 3/97 (1800-2000) 2300

Young Bambi standing facing right & laughing, eyes closed, 4 x 2-1/4", VF, HL/Nov 16/97 (900-1200) 1495

CELS – PARTIAL FIGURE

Near-full figure of alert young Bambi standing, 4 x 3", HL/Aug 6/95 (1500-2000) 4032

3/4 rear view of Flower (head, shoulders & tail) looking amid daisies, 2-1/2 x 3", HL/Nov 19/95 (900-1200) 1610

Near-full figure of baby Bambi struggling to walk,

4-1/2 x 4", HL/Apr 28/96 (1200-1600) 1725

2 large cels of Bambi, possibly from commercial use, circa 1980s, 9" each, S/Dec 14/96 (300-500) 460

CONCEPT AND INSPIRATIONAL ART

Drawing of Owl, pastel on paper, 5", S/Dec 16/93 (700-900) 690

Character-design drawing of Friend Owl, 5 x 3-1/2", signed & dated "1940" by Clair Weeks, VF, HL/Feb 26-27/94 (300-400) 495

2 frightened birds (3 x 3"), inspirational Marc Davis sketch, black & white pastel on full animation paper, studio stamp; inspirational sketch of Bambi & mother, 3-1/2 x 3", CE/Jun 18/94 (500-700) 633

Atmospheric inspirational painting of 2 deer walking thru fire-lit forest, 7 x 9", watercolor on paper, HL/Nov 13/94 (500-700) 672

Watercolor concept painting of deer moving thru autumn forest, 12-1/2 x 5-5/16", SR/Spring/95 (1800-2600) 2060

Concept sketch of doe & rabbit watching fawn walk in forest, black with red pencil on 8-1/2 x 6-1/2" sheet, SR/Spring/95 (1800-2600) 1340

Concept painting of forest, oil on paper, 1942, 10-1/8 x 7-5/8", SR/Spring/95 (2000-4000) 2040

Impressionistic atmosphere painting of Bambi & mother silhouetted against night sky in forest, 7-1/2 x 10", black, purple & blue watercolor on paper, HL/Apr 23/95 (300-400) 952

Full-figure concept drawing of young Bambi, 4-1/2", graphite & watercolor on partial paper, CE/Jun 9/95 (400-600) 633

Concept watercolor painting of young Bambi (2-1/2") walking in forest with Mother (3-1/2"), CE/Jun 9/95 (800-1200) 1725

Concept sketch of mother licking young deer as rabbit watches, charcoal on 10-3/4 x 9" sheet, SR/Fall/95 (1800-3200) 2180

14 study drawings of deer bounding thru forest & 3 layout drawings of forest scenery, 2 x 6" to 11 x 24", pencil & conté crayon on animation sheets, HL/Nov 19/95 (1500-2000) 1265

A herd of deer passes through forest, watercolor concept painting by Maurice Noble, 11-3/4 x 4-3/4" on heavy watercolor board, SR/Spring/96 (1800-2600) 1800

Impressionistic background study of windblown grasses, oil on background sheet, 11-1/2 x 16", HL/Apr 28/96 (500-700) 460

2 background studies of forest, pencil & conté crayon on animation sheets, 8-1/2 x 11", HL/Apr 28/96 (700-900) 345

Aerial-view concept sketch of deer standing in forest at edge of meadow, 9-3/4 x 7-1/4" charcoal image on 12-1/2 x 10-1/2" sheet, SR/Fall/96 (1000-1500) 1000

Pencil concept sketch by Tyrus Wong of animals in forest, 6-1/4 x 4 11/16" image within frame line on 9-5/8 x 6-5/8" sheet, glue residue beyond image area, SR/Fall/96 (1000-1500) 1630

Inspirational drawing of 3 birds in hollowed-out tree during storm, conté crayon & white pastel on animation sheet, 6 x 8", HL/Oct 6/96 (500-700) 518

Full-figure concept sketch of Flower, conté crayon on animation sheet, 7 x 9", HL/Oct 6/96 (400-600) 345

Concept painting of Bambi & mother walking thru forest, watercolor on paper, 7-1/2 x 10-1/4", HL/Oct 6/96 (1200-1600) 1495

Concept piece: rear view thru trees of stag (2") standing in forest, overall 4-1/2 x 6", watercolor on paper mounted to cardboard, S/Dec 14/96 (300-500) 805

Atmospheric concept painting of forest, 6 x 12-1/2", HL/Feb 23/97 (800-1000) 1265

Atmospheric painting of young Bambi & mother in thicket in evening, watercolor on paper, 7 x 9-1/4", HL/May 3/97 (1200-1600) 1495

Full-color concept art of red-breasted bluebird & nest, colored pastel on animation sheet, 8-1/2 x 11", HL/May 31/97 (300-400) 403

Character study of doe's head & fawn lying down, 6 x 5", HL/May 31/97 (600-900) 374

Full-figure study drawing of deer running right, likely by Bernard Garbutt, 4-1/2 x 3-1/2", HL/May 31/97 (100-200) 144

Inspirational art of devastation after forest fire;

ink, conté crayon & charcoal on animation sheet; 5 x 6-1/2", HL/May 31/97 (400-600) 259

Concept art of young Bambi frightened by lightning, sight 7 x 9-1/4", white & blue pastel on black paper, S/Jun 21/97 (500-700) 805

"Little April Shower" concept art: animals take shelter from rain amid toadstools; sight 6 x 14-1/2"; grey, black & white pastel on paper, S/Jun 21/97 (2000-3000) 3162

Concept art of young Bambi inspecting grasshopper, 4-1/2 x 4", signed by Marc Davis, S/Jun 21/97 (2000-3000) 2587

Concept sketch of Bambi attacking two dogs by Retta Scott, charcoal, 12 x 11", general wear & discoloration, two repaired edge tears, SR/Fall/97 (600-900) 660

Inspirational painting of forest, watercolor on animation sheets (2 sheets taped together & cut down), 9 x 12", VG, HL/Nov 16/97 (300-500) 259

Impressionistic inspirational study of mushrooms for background, by Dick Anthony, 6-1/2 x 9", oil on board, signed, VF, HL/Nov 16/97 (600-900) 1093

Pastel-on-paper concept of a partridge sitting in forest, 7-1/2 x 9-1/2", S/Dec 19/97 (600-800) 747

5 concepts of Owl by Marc Davis, avg. 4", two initialed "MD", ink & crayon on paper, all trimmed & applied to one large sheet, S/Dec 19/97 (1000-1500) 1150

Inspirational sketch of adult male deer running, 2", charcoal on paper; pan layout drawing of animals playing in forest; 2 animation drawings of Faline, 3"; 9 drawings of animals; animation drawing of Flower, 4"; animation drawing of Thumper, 4"; animals 3" & smaller, CE/Dec 18/97 (600-800) 978

Watercolor concept painting of bare branches etched against winter sky & snowy landscape, 10-1/8 x 7-3/4" on 12-field board, SR/Spring/98 (800-1400) 830

Inspirational painting of young Bambi exploring stream, pencil & watercolor on animation sheet, 11 x 14-1/4", F+, HL/Apr 25/98 (800-1000) 1495

DYE-TRANSFER PRINTS

Full figures of Bambi, Thumper, & Flower watching butterfly on Bambi's tail, 10-3/8 x 8-1/4", SR/Fall/95 (300-600) 325

Young Bambi turns to watch butterfly on tail as Thumper & Flower look on, 10 x 8", SR/Spring/96 (300-600) 300

Full figures of Thumper, Flower, & young Bambi watching butterfly on his tail in forest, signed by Walt Disney on mat, sight 7-1/2 x 9-1/2", WDP label, S/Dec 19/97 (1200-1800) 1840

Full figures of Thumper, Flower, & young Bambi watching butterfly on his tail in forest, 1950s, mat inscribed & signed by Walt Disney, 12 x 13", F, HL/Apr 25/98 (2000-2500) 2760

LAYOUT ART

Layout drawing: Bambi falling on reed as field mouse watches, production stamp & notes, full margins, 10 x 12", S/Dec 16/93 (300-500) 920

Layout drawing of baby Bambi startling 4 bunnies, 5-1/2 x 7", HL/Mar 11/95 (300-500) 770

6 background & overlay layout drawings plus special-effects drawing of multiple Bambis, 9 x 13" to 12 x 14", VG-F overall, HL/Nov 19/95 (700-1000) 748

Detailed layout drawing of quail family peeking out from their home, sight 6 x 7", S/Dec 14/96 (600-800) 1035

Pencil layout drawing of young Bambi chasing butterfly, 4-1/2 x 10-1/2", S/Dec 19/97 (1000-1500) 1265

MODEL ART (also see ANIMATION DRAWINGS)

Model sheet of young Bambi, 4" & smaller, CE/Dec 16/94 (500-700) 1380

Full-figure model or publicity cel of flirtatious Miss Bunny & flustered Thumper, 5 x 5-1/2" cel image, color print background, HL/Nov 19/95 (2000-2500) 2530

Model cel of Thumper & Miss Bunny, 4-1/2 x 5-1/2", HL/Apr 28/96 (2000-3000) 1725

Original photostat model sheet "Bambi at Infant Age," 13-7/8 x 11", some wear, vertical crease, SR/Fall/96 (100-300) 370

2 items: model sheet (approx. 4") of Bambi; front-view shoulders-up animation drawing of Bambi (5"), CE/Dec 12/96 (1500-2000) 2070

Color model cel of Great Prince (10-1/4 x 7")
approaching Bambi (full figure, 6-1/4 x 5-1/4")
who's standing with head turned as forest fire
nears, pan oil production background, S/Dec
14/96 (15,000-20,000)   10,350
23 photostat model sheets, S/Dec 14/96
(800-1200)   1035
1950s model sheet of young Bambi's head, signed
"O'Malley," 11 x 13", HL/May 31/97
(200-300)   288
2 model sheets: Bambi & action suggestions; sight 12-
1/2 x 15-1/2", CLA/Jun 7/97 (800-1200)   863
2 animator's model sheets: Bambi; Thumper;
circa 1950s; sight 12-1/2 x 15-1/2",
CLA/Jun 7/97 (800-1200)   483
2 animator's model sheets: Bambi; Flower; circa 1950s;
sight 12-1/2 x 15-1/2", CLA/Jun 7/97 (800-
1200)   518
2 early model sheets of baby skunk dated October
1938, 13-7/8 x 11", vintage studio photostats,
some waviness, SR/Fall/97 (150-300)   100
Animation study of Bambi; animator training model
sheet; 7" & smaller, CE/Dec 18/97 (
600-800)   575
Original sheet of studies of infant Bambi's head, avg.
2" to 2-1/2", 16-field sheet, SR/Spring/98
(600-900)   660

SILKSCREEN ART
5 special multiplane scenes of silkscreen images
on glass in box frames, each w/original label
on back numbered 1-5, made by Courvoisier,
6-1/2 x 6-1/2 x 1", 8 x 8 x 1-1/2", F,
HL/Apr 10/94 (2000-3000)   1904
Bambi meets Flower in meadow, 1-1/2" & smaller,
multiplane painting, silkscreening on 2 pieces
of glass, Courvoisier label, CE/Dec 16/94
(700-900)   1725
Happy Thumper & butterflies amid windflowers,
silkscreened image on 2 levels of glass in box
frame to simulate multiplane process, photocopy
of original Courvoisier label, 8 x 8-3/4 x 1-3/4",
HL/Mar 16-17/96 (300-500)   690
Full figure of Thumper skating on ice as two chipmunks
sit on log watching, multiplane painting, silkscreen
on 2 pieces of glass, 3", Courvoisier label,
CLA/Jun 7/97 (700-900)   805
Full figure of Thumper with eyes closed sitting amid
flowers & butterfly, 3-5/8 x 3-5/8", Courvoisier
shadow box, silkscreen on 2 glass levels over 3rd
background level to recreate 3-D look of multiplane camera, hand-prepared crayon background,
partial Courvoisier label, restored frame,
SR/Fall/97 (600-900)   600
Full figure of Thumper skating on ice as two chipmunks
sit on log watching, Courvoisier shadow box,
silkscreen on 2 sheets of glass set off by 3rd background level to approximate 3-D effect of multiplane camera, 5-1/2 x 5", SR/Spring/98 (600-
900)   680
Young Bambi & Flower meet in flower-filled meadow, 6
x 5-1/8", Courvoisier shadow box, silkscreen on 2
glass levels over 3rd background level to recreate
3-D look of multiplane camera, SR/Spring/98
(700-1000)   770

STORY ART
Bambi & bunnies study anthill, red pencil & black
conté crayon drawing on story sheet by Bernard
Garbutt, 3-1/2 x 6", VF, HL/Feb 26-27/94
(500-800)   605
Story sketch of young Bambi, conté crayon on anima-
tion sheet, 4 x 5-1/2", VF+, HL/Apr 10/94
(500-700)   504
Story drawing of deer moving thru forest in fall, water-
color on paper mounted to illustration board, 4-
1/2 x 19", HL/Aug 21/94 (3500-4000)   4144
Drawing of Bambi turning to stare at startled
Flower & Thumper, charcoal & conté
crayon on animation sheet, initialed
"MD" (Marc Davis), 8 x 10-1/2", VF,
HL/Aug 21/94 (1000-1200)   1232
Story drawing of eager Thumper hopping after
Miss Bunny, 7-1/2 x 8-1/2", brown, gray
& black conté crayon, signed by Marc Davis,
HL/Nov 13/94 (1000-1500)   2128
Story drawing of laughing Flower on his back,
holding feet, 8-1/2 x 10-1/2", charcoal
& conté crayon on animation sheet,
HL/Apr 23/95 (600-900)   560
Story painting of young Bambi & mother walking

thru forest, 7-1/2 x 10", watercolor on
paper (deer are on separate sheet),
HL/Aug 6/95 (900-1200)   1680
Story drawing by Felix Salten of squirrel at base
of tree, 11-1/2 x 11", conté crayon on
animation sheet, HL/Aug 6/95 (300-500)   476
Story drawing of Bambi leading Thumper & Flower
away on road to twitterpation, 9 x 11-1/2",
conté crayon on animation sheet,
HL/Aug 6/95 (600-900)   1064
Full-figure story drawing of Thumper, 6 x 8",
conté crayon on animation sheet,
HL/Nov 19/95 (600-800)   1093
Drawing of Miss Bunny amid grass & flowers,
signed by Marc Davis, red & black conté
crayon on animation sheet, 6-1/4 x 8"
total, VF, HL/Oct 6/96 (1000-1500)   1610
Full-figure sketch of young Bambi (4 x 3") walking
with 4 bunnies (approx. 2" ea) by Marc
Davis, S/Dec 14/96 (800-1200)   4312
Story sketch of playful encounter between young
Bambi & Faline, 7 x 8-1/2", HL/May 31/97
(200-250)   230
Story drawing of Thumper & Miss Bunny flirting,
initialed & signed by Marc Davis, 6-1/4 x 8"
including signature, grey, brown & black
conté crayon on animation sheet, VF,
HL/Nov 16/97 (1800-2400)   2300
Story drawing of Bambi, Flower, Thumper & Owl from
"Twitterpated" scene, 6-1/2 x 11-1/4", grey &
black conté crayon on animation sheet, VF,
HL/Nov 16/97 (600-800)   978
Story painting of young Bambi & Mother sitting
nestled in thicket, 8 x 10-1/2", watercolor &
india ink on animation sheet, 8 deer studies
in margin, VF, HL/Nov 16/97 (1800-2200) 1725
Story painting of Bambi & mother sitting in thicket
with sunlight filtering thru trees, watercolor
on animation sheet, 6-1/2 x 9", VF,
HL/Nov 16/97 (600-900)   978
Story drawing of 2 deer in silhouette walking thru
charred forest, india ink & conté crayon on
animation sheet, 5 x 6-1/2", VF,
HL/Apr 25/98 (300-400)   431
Story sketch signed by Marc Davis of partially prostrate
Bambi being charged by Ronno, charcoal with
red frame line on 7-1/2 x 5-3/4" sheet,
SR/Spring/98 (500-900)   500

TITLE ART
Title treatment in browns, reds, & moss greens by Dick
Anthony, opaque watercolor on heavyweight
paper, 8-1/4 x 10-3/4", VF, HL/Apr 25/98
(1200-1600)   2185

BEAUTY AND THE BEAST (1991)
CEL SET-UPS
2 limited-edition cel paintings: *On the Terrace* &
At the Window, #258/500, color print
backgrounds, seals & certificates, 11 x 15",
HL/Aug 21/94 (4000-5000)   4480
Top-of-stairs view of scissors poised to save Lumiere
from torch-wielding Le Fou, 17 x 24-1/2", large
tempera-on-background-sheet master background,
notes, HL/Apr 23/95 (2500-3500)   2688
Waist-up frontal of insane asylum's D'Arque, 9 x 12-
1/2", tempera-on-background-sheet master
background of woods, HL/Apr 23/95 (1800-
2200)   1680
Frightened Maurice in woods, 8-1/2 x 12-1/2",
tempera-on-background-sheet master
background, HL/Apr 23/95 (1400-1800)   1120
Waist-up front view of snarling beast with arms up, 9",
watercolor production background of window &
curtains, seal, CE/Dec 18/97 (1500-2000) 2070

BEDKNOBS & BROOMSTICKS (1971)
CEL SET-UPS
Sad Fisherman Bear stands on island beach, 10 x 14"
overall, Studio Art Props background painting
(tempera on board), VF, HL/Nov 16/97 (500-
700)   316
Matching production set-up of 2 fish (4" each) & octopus (6") playing cards under water, matching
watercolor production background, S/Dec 19/97
(2500-3500)   6037
CELS
Fish dancing; full figures of King Leonidas with
2 soccer players; 6 x 14" & 7-1/2 x 14",

HL/Apr 23/95 (400-600)   420
Near-full figure of King Leonidas standing, casually leaning to right & blowing, 7-5/8", ct, SR/Fall/95
(300-500)   330

THE BLACK CAULDRON (1985)
BACKGROUNDS
Gouache pre-production background by Jim Coleman
of early morning mists in forest, 32 x 10-1/4",
SR/Fall/94 (1200-1800)   1480
Gouache pre-production background by Jim Coleman
of mists swirling around Horned King's castle,
12-1/8 x 15-3/4" on 12-1/2 x 16" board,
SR/Fall/97 (1500-2000)   1000

CEL SET-UPS/MODEL ART
Hen Wen being dragged by Creeper, line-print back-
ground; pan multi-cel set of Taran, Eilonwy,
Fflewddur Fflam & Gurgi as magical explosion
engulfs them; 9 x 13" & 11 x 21"; Disney seals
& labels; VF+; HL/Nov 13/94 (600-800)   560
Fflewddur Fflam, Princess Eilonwy, Hen Wen,
Taran & Gurgi; Hen Wen threatened by
Creeper; 9 x 13" & 10 x 14"; Disney seals
& labels, matching line-print backgrounds,
VF+, HL/Nov 13/94 (600-800)   672
Color model cels of Taran & 3 Witches of Morva,
master background when young warrior
trades enchanted sword for Cauldron (tempera
on pan background sheet), 11 x 21", HL/Apr
28/96 (1000-2000)   2760
Full figure of Gurgi in forest about to acquire some
"munchings & crunchings," line-print
background, 3 x 6" cel image, HL/May 31/97
(300-400)   184
Side view of towering Horned King with Creeper clinging to bottom of his cloak, 10-3/4", color print
background featuring cauldron, SR/Fall/97 (600-
900)   400
Full figures of Gurgi and sword-wielding Taran
confronting Horned King, 11 x 18" overall,
color print background of evil one's castle
with cauldron, gwythaints & guards, VF+,
HL/Nov 16/97 (300-500)   1150
Front-view color model cel of 9 undead warriors
emerging from cauldron, 29-1/2 x 11-1/2" on
ten 30 x 12-1/2" pan cels with special effects,
airbrush phosphorescence trailing, watercolor
display background, SR/Spring/98
(400-800)   1200

CELS – FULL FIGURE/MODEL ART
2 front-view cels: close-up of Horned King, full
figures of 6 Cauldron Born walking toward
camera; 9-1/2 x 18" & 7-1/2 x 15": each
with Disney seal & Walt Disney Co. label,
VF+, HL/Apr 10/94 (600-900)   952
Publicity cel of Taran & Gurgi confronting Horned
King, 8-1/2 x 10-1/2", VF+, HL/Nov 13/94
(400-600)   616
2 full-figure cels of lively Gurgi, 3-1/2 x 3" &
5 x 3-1/2", HL/Apr 23/95 (300-500)   308
Kneeling Taran offers sword to eager Orddu, Orgoch,
& Orwen (all standing), 7 x 11-1/2", HL/Oct
6/96 (400-600)   920
Full figures of angry Taran & surprised Eilonwy standing
together arguing, both 6-1/4", 16-field cel,
SR/Fall/97 (600-900)   400
Color model cel of Horned King with clawed hands outstretched & crazed eyes blazing red, 9-3/4", 16-
field cel, SR/Spring/98 (300-600)   300

CELS – PARTIAL FIGURE/MODEL ART
2 cels: hips-up of Guard holding Taran (full figure) off

ground by back of neck & sword in his stomach, 11"; waist-up front view of shocked Eilonwy, 8"; both 16-field, SR/Fall/94 (500-900) 500

Knees-up view of Taran, Eilonwy & Fflewddur Fflam with Fair Folk, Fflam looking thru harp at Fair Folk; 8-1/2 x 14-1/2" & 7-1/2 x 9"; Disney seals & one Walt Disney Co.label; VF+; HL/Nov 13/94 (500-900) 784

Front-view close-up of Horned King yelling, 11 x 18-1/2", VF+, HL/Feb 23/97 (500-700) 920

2 color model cels: hips-up of Dallben looking at camera with arms crossed, 6-1/2"; knees-up front image of happy Fflewddur Fflam, 8-5/8"; both 16-field cels, SR/Fall/97 (600-900) 400

Waist-up of smiling Taran holding happy Gurgi (full figure), 7-1/2 x 10", WDP seal & certificate, VF+, HL/Apr 25/98 (300-500) 575

Matched set of 3 cels: Orwen eavesdropping on Orgoch & Orddu, 6-1/2 x 11-1/2", seal & certificate, VF+, HL/Apr 25/98 (400-600) 374

Waist-up side view of grinning Orddu nose to nose with shocked Taran with her left hand supporting his chin, 4-1/4 x 10-1/4", seal & certificate, 4-1/4 x 10-1/4", VF, HL/Apr 25/98 (300-400) 431

CONCEPT AND INSPIRATIONAL ART

Gouache atmosphere study by Jim Coleman of mist rising off river, 13-1/2 x 6 3/8" board, SR/Spring/95 (300-700) 430

Atmospheric concept painting of Horned King's castle, tempera on board, 7 x 12", HL/May 3/97 (500-700) 1265

Atmospheric background design for labyrinthine depths of Horned King's castle, tempera on background board, 11-1/2 x 16", HL/May 3/97 (500-800) 1495

Jim Coleman's signed concept sketch of the Horned King's castle, half fortress, half mountain, rising from water-filled crater, 12-1/2 x 15-1/2" sheet, SR/Spring/98 (300-600) 350

CINDERELLA (1950)

Also see TELEVISION: ANTHOLOGY SERIES
ANIMATION DRAWINGS

14 rough drawings, 4 x 2-1/2" to 8 x 6-1/2", HL/Apr 23/95 (2000-3000) 5376

Cinderella in serving clothes examining invitation, 7", CE/Jun 9/95 (400-600) 633

15 polished rough drawings, 4 x 2-1/2" to 8 x 6-1/4", HL/Apr 28/96 (2000-3000) 6900

14 polished "rough" drawings, 4 x 3-1/4" to 7-1/2 x 6", HL/May 3/97 (2000-3000) 4600

Hips-up drawing of somber Cinderella standing in work clothes, 7", S/Jun 21/97 (600-800) 460

Hips-up drawing of shocked Cinderella in torn dress looking left, right hand up, 7-5/8", 16-field sheet, timer's chart, SR/Fall/97 (600-900) 660

BACKGROUNDS

Master background of Tremaine kitchen with Dutch door open, 11 x 14", tempera on background sheet, HL/Aug 6/95 (2000-3000) 4704

CEL SET-UPS

Suzy Mouse curtsies, publication background, 4", S/Dec 16/93 (700-900) 690

Cinderella (waist-up) stands in stepmother's house, watercolor production background, 6-1/2", S/Dec 16/93 (7000-9000) 6325

Gus & Mert[?] in castle dress throwing rice, complementary print background, 4 x 5-1/2", VF, HL/Apr 10/94 (1200-1600) 1680

Grand Duke sleeps with pillow & glass slipper in his lap, photographic color print background, 9 x 12", F+, HL/Apr 10/94 (800-1200) 896

Jaq (3 x 2-1/2") & Gus (2-1/2 x 1-1/2") talk to friends (3 x 3" & smaller), key watercolor production background, mat inscribed "Cinderella", stamped "original WDP" & signed "Walt Disney" by studio artist, CE/Jun 18/94 (8000-12,000) 16,100

Lucifer ready to strike, 8-3/4 x 9-1/2", key watercolor production background, CE/Jun 18/94 (2000-3000) 2070

Cinderella at ball, 6-3/4 x 3-1/2", Mary Blair watercolor concept background, mat signed "Walt Disney" & stamped "WDP", CE/Jun 18/94 (2000-3000) 7130

Orchestra leader begins music, matching master background, notes, Ken O'Connor's initials, 7-1/2 x 10", HL/Aug 21/94 (2000-3000) 2240

Publicity cel of Gus, Jaq, & 2 other mice from 1988 TV promotion for video release, 2-1/2 to 3",

---

matching pan watercolor production background, S/Dec 17/94 (1200-1800) 1380

Full figure of startled Lucifer, 8-1/2 x 21-1/2", matching master background (tempera on background sheet), note, HL/Mar 11/95 (3000-4000) 4400

Key production set-up of mice looking at ball gown pictured in book, each mouse approx. 2", book 6-1/4" x 8", watercolor production background, label & stamp, signature attributed to Walt Disney on mat, S/Jun 10/95 (8000-12,000) 14,950

Full figures of surprised Cinderella (7-1/2") in ball gown & smiling Fairy Godmother (6-1/2") w/wand, watercolor production background, inscribed "To ... Walt Disney", Courvoisier label, S/Jun 10/95 (8000-10,000) 29,900

Full figure of Cinderella looking down examining ball gown by pool, 7-1/2", display watercolor background & sparkling overlay effects cel, SR/Fall/95 (3500-4500) 6200

Full figure of Grand Duke sitting on floor amid armor, lifting visor of knight's helmet he's wearing, 8-7/8" matching gouache key master background, 16-field, ct, SR/Fall/95 (2500-5000) 2500

Full figure of serious Gus picking necklace up off floor, 8 x 4-3/4", color print display background, SR/Fall/95 (600-1000) 1570

Full-figure rear view of Cinderella walking out wide door into courtyard balancing three breakfast trays (one on head), 5", pre-production background, SR/Spring/96 (1800-2600) 1800

Publicity cel: Cinderella in rags sitting on rock (4"), Major (6-1/2"), Bruno sitting (2-1/2") & mice (1") in field amid pumpkin debris, watercolor production background, CE/Jun 20/96 (6000-8000) 6900

Full figures of Fairy Godmother (7") & Cinderella in ball gown (7-1/2"), watercolor production background from same scene, mat signed by Walt Disney, CE/Jun 20/96 (10,000-15,000) 36,800

Full figure of nervous Jaq standing on tile floor and looking back, watercolor production background, 4-1/4", CE/Jun 20/96 (7000-8000) 6900

Front view of uncertain Cinderella standing in ball gown, 6-1/2", hand-prepared background of ballroom, Walt Disney signature by Bob Moore, S/Dec 14/96 (3000-5000) 8625

Full figures of Jaq stringing beads on Gus' tail as he fills bag, complementary color print background, 5 x 6-3/4", HL/May 3/97 (1400-1800) 2300

Smiling Cinderella in ball gown (facing left) in palace, 8-1/2", watercolor production background, Courvoisier label, mat inscribed & signed by Walt Disney, CLA/Jun 7/97 (10,000-15,000) 9775

Full figures of King (in nightclothes, 6") rushing past Grand Duke (7") toward chair, watercolor pan production background, S/Jun 21/97 (5000-7000) 3450

Front view of Drizella (8-1/2") & Anastasia (curtsying, 5-1/2") at ball, printed background, S/Jun 21/97 (700-900) 1035

Frantic Cinderella looks out of coach (8 x 11"), hand-prepared background, S/Jun 21/97 (10,000-15,000) 8050

Lucifer gleefully paws through pile of clothes, 5-1/2" on three cel levels, key master background, SR/Fall/97 (5000-9000) 5700

2 limited-edition cels: "Preparing for the Ball" & "The Royal Ball", both #442/500, 11-1/4 x 15-1/4", color print backgrounds, VF+, HL/Nov 16/97 (1000-2000) 1380

"Cinderella's Reflection": limited-edition cel of Cinderel-

la in ball gown by fountain, #172/500, 11 x 15", color print of matching background, VF+, HL/Nov 16/97 (500-1000) 1725

Cinderella in gown made by friends stands staring at large magical pumpkin, 6-3/4", hand-prepared background w/hand-prepared overlay, S/Dec 19/97 (1000-1500) 2300

Waist-up front view of Cinderella as scullery maid looking right, 5-1/2", hand-prepared background of bedroom, S/Dec 19/97 (1000-1500) 1380

Ankles-up front view of suspicious Lady Tremaine standing by open door, 7-1/4", matching gouache background painting of chateau interior, 16-field, SR/Spring/98 (1800-2800) 2010

CELS – FULL FIGURE (also see MODEL ART)

Cinderella glancing back while fleeing, 4 x 3", restored, VF, HL/Apr 10/94 (1200-1600) 2240

Jaq, 4-1/2 x 5", VF+, HL/Apr 10/94 (700-1000) 952

Kneeling Cinderella (facing right) reads, 7", CE/Jun 18/94 (1500-2000) 1495

Gus (3-1/2 x 2-1/2") points left & up for shocked Jaq (4-1/4 x 3-1/2"), CE/Jun 18/94 (800-1200) 2530

Cinderella in serving clothes with broom, 7-1/2 x 3", CE/Jun 18/94 (1000-1500) 1380

Cinderella at door holding broom & ball invitation, 10 x 4", VF, HL/Aug 21/94 (1500-2000) 1568

Surprised Cinderella in ball gown, 8-1/2 x 5-1/2", VF+, HL/Aug 21/94 (2000-3000) 4144

Angry Jaq gesturing, 5 x 4-1/2", VF, HL/Aug 21/94 (700-1000) 1064

Large image of laughing Gus facing left, 6 x 6-1/2", VF, HL/Aug 21/94 (1000-1500) 1120

Set of 4 hand-inked & -painted cels: Cinderella in rags & Fairy Godmother; Gus & Jaq; Lucifer (head only) & Jaq w/armload of corn kernels; Cinderella & Prince; created by Studio artists from original animation drawings, in portfolio, laminated, seal, #107/275, certificates of authenticity; 4-1/2 x 9", 7 x 7", 7-1/2 x 12"; VF+; HL/Aug 21/94 (3500-4500) 2688

Lucifer stands facing left, 5", 12-field, paint restoration, SR/Fall/94 (500-800) 550

Gus bends down, holding hat [gathering beads], 3-1/4" image, 12-field, SR/Fall/94 (500-900) 850

Gus trying to eat stack of corn kernels, 4-1/2 x 5", HL/Nov 13/94 (600-800) 896

Feisty Jaq, 3 x 4-1/2", HL/Nov 13/94 (600-800) 896

Cinderella & Prince meet at ball, 4-1/2 x 3-1/2", notes, HL/Nov 13/94 (2000-2500) 2912

2 full-figure cels: energetic Jaq; blue-frocked girl mouse kneeling with tape measure; 4-1/2 x 5" & 4 x 6", HL/Nov 13/94 (1000-1500) 1904

2 full figures of Jaq, 3-1/2" & similar, CE/Dec 16/94 (800-1200) 1725

Pumpkin (2 x 2", with vines 2 x 8") begins transformation into coach, S/Dec 17/94 (600-800) 805

Gus (full figure, 4") is grabbed by Jaq's arm, from 1988 TV promotion of video release, S/Dec 17/94 (400-600) 460

2 cels: hips-up of Gus looking straight up with both arms out & one foot up, 5-1/8"; full-figure front view of irritated Lucifer sitting, looking left, 4"; SR/Spring/95 (700-1100) 990

3 full-figure cels of Cinderella, 3-1/4 x 1" to 3-1/4 x 2", F-VF, HL/Apr 23/95 (1000-1500) 1456

4 hand-inked & -painted limited-edition cels: Cinderella w/Prince Charming, Cinderella w/Fairy Godmother, Gus & Jaq, Lucifer confronts Gus; 4-1/2 x 9", 7 x 7", 7-1/2 x 12"; #218/275, VF+, HL/Apr 23/95 (3000-5000) 4088

Eager Footman holds pillow with glass slipper, 4-3/4", CE/Jun 9/95 (400-600) 518

Contented female mouse & 2 child mice, 3 x 3-1/2", CE/Jun 9/95 (600-800) 633

Female mouse with ribbon, 5", CE/Jun 9/95 (600-800) 460

Gus & Jaq stand together looking up, 2-1/2", CE/Jun 9/95 (400-600) 460

Traveling Coach & horses, 10-1/2", CE/Jun 9/95 (1000-1500) 2530

Cinderella carries dirty laundry, 6-1/2", S/Jun 10/95 (1000-1500) 1955

Cinderella standing in serving clothes looking down, 7 x 4", HL/Aug 6/95 (1200-1600) 2240

Smiling Mert (or Bert) with tape measure around neck, 7-1/2 x 3", HL/Aug 6/95 (500-700) 952

2 prancing coach horses facing left, 9-1/2", 16-field, ct, SR/Fall/95 (500-1000) 500

Front overhead view of Cinderella looking up as she & Prince Charming stand together w/him holding her hand, 2-1/2", 16-field (actually a sheet

of film), SR/Fall/95 (200-500) 1180
Footman stands facing left with *eyes closed*, holding
 pillow with glass slipper, 4-3/4", SR/Fall/95
 (400-700) 490
Happy Cinderella stands in ball gown facing left,
 7-3/8", overlay effects display cel of fairy dust,
 SR/Fall/95 (2500-3500) 4050
Cinderella kneels to pick up pitcher, 6-1/2",
 SR/Fall/95 (800-1200) 1740
4 hand-inked & -painted limited-edition cels: Cinderella
 w/Prince Charming, Cinderella w/Fairy Godmother, Gus & Jaq, Lucifer confronts Gus;
 #165/275; 4-1/2 x 9", 7 x 7", 7-1/2 x 12";
 VF+, HL/Nov 19/95 (2500-3500) 3220
2 full-figure cels of dressed-up, smug stepsisters: front
 view of Anastasia, Drizella facing right; both 7"
 with eyes closed, SR/Spring/96 (800-1200) 800
Cinderella stands in wedding gown facing right,
 bending down, 8", 16-field, SR/Spring/96
 (1400-1800) 1400
Lady Tremaine (near-full, 8-1/2"), Drizella (6"), & Duke
 (7") standing together, 16-field, SR/Spring/96
 (700-1200) 770
Medium-long side view of pumpkin coach and
 horses, 5", CE/Jun 20/96 (700-900) 2990
Medium-long front view of Prince & Cinderella in
 wedding dress with King and Grand Duke
 holding train high, 3", CE/Jun 20/96
 (800-1200) 2760
Cinderella stands in ball gown looking down,
 6-1/2 x 5", HL/Oct 6/96 (2000-2500) 4025
Jaq looking up as he rides scissors being hoisted on
 strings, 7 x 7-1/2", HL/Oct 6/96 (700-900) 1035
Complete magic coach moving to left, 3 x
 10-1/4", HL/Oct 6/96 (1000-1500) 2530
Smiling bird pointing to left, 3 x 3", HL/Oct 6/96
 (300-500) 345
Cinderella (5-1/4") fleeing from startled Prince
 (full figure, 6-1/2") with bushes between
 them, CE/Dec 12/96 (2000-2500) 4025
Surprised Gus (3") & smiling Jaq (3-1/2") stand looking
 to left, CE/Dec 12/96 (1500-2000) 1610
Thoughtful Cinderella kneeling & studying open dress
 book [on floor] with 5 mice & 2 birds, 8",
 CE/Dec 12/96 (2500-3500) 3220
Gus, 2", CE/Dec 12/96 (600-800) 690
Cinderella stands in ball gown looking down,
 6-1/2", CE/Dec 12/96 (1500-2000) 3680
Front view of smug Drizella beginning to curtsy,
 5-1/2 x 5", HL/Feb 23/97 (400-600) 403
Smiling Cinderella facing right, looking down &
 lifting hem of wedding gown, 8-1/4 x
 4-1/4", HL/May 3/97 (2000-3000) 2300
Profile view of King, eyes open, feet missing, 8";
 full figure of Duke, eyes closed, holding
 cigar, 6", CLA/Jun 7/97 (700-900) 345
Sneering Lucifer sits, 3-1/2" with 2" tail, needs
 restoration, S/Jun 21/97 (700-900) 920
Kind Cinderella kneeling, 5-3/4 x 4-1/2", VF+,
 HL/Nov 16/97 (1500-2000) 2128
Smiling Cinderella in ball gown walking right, 8 x
 5-3/4", VF, HL/Nov 16/97 (2000-2800) 3680
Large image of pumpkin coach w/Cinderella inside,
 8 x 13", VF, HL/Nov 16/97 (2400-2800) 2760
Panicked footman (transformed Bruno) runs to right,
 4-1/4 x 4", VF, HL/Nov 16/97 (400-600) 345
Suzy(?) Mouse with back turned prepares ribbon,
 5 x 6", VF+, HL/Apr 25/98 (500-700) 748
Front view of snarling Lucifer, 4 x 6", VF, HL/Apr
 25/98 (500-700) 1150
Front view of Cinderella in serving clothes standing
 looking down, 7", SR/Spring/98
 (1200-1800) 1200
Smiling Gus & Jaq (both 2-3/8") standing, being
 watched by suspicious Lucifer (5-1/8"), 16-field
 cels, SR/Spring/98 (1200-1600) 1840

CELS – PARTIAL FIGURE (also see CELS-FULL FIGURE)
Portrait of lady mouse, 3-1/2 x 3", F-VF,
 HL/Feb 26-27/94 (300-400) 550
Knees-up view of Prince Charming looking up,
 6 x 3", VF, HL/Apr 10/94 (600-900) 728
Front view of Cinderella holding mice-made
 dress & looking right, 8 x 4-1/2", VF+,
 HL/Apr 10/94 (1200-1600) 3808
Gus lying on back with hand to forehead, 9",
 S/Jun 17/94 (400-600) 1035
Sleeping Grand Duke w/glass slipper on pillow,
 7", CE/Jun 18/94 (500-700) 863
2 smiling girl mice (from skirt hem up, eyes closed),

4" & similar, CE/Jun 18/94 (300-500) 1495
Front view of thankful Cinderella wearing dress made
 by mice, 8", CE/Jun 18/94 (1000-1500) 2415
Jaq covers eyes & holds unbraided tail, 5-1/2",
 CE/Jun 18/94 (400-600) 2530
Angry Anastasia & Drizella, 7" & similar,
 CE/Jun 18/94 (400-600) 230
Half image of innocent Bruno sitting to right, looking
 up, 5", 12-field, SR/Fall/94 (300-600) 390
Portrait of Cinderella holding tiny garment, 6 x
 3-1/2", F+, HL/Apr 23/95 (1000-1500) 1792
Near-full figure of startled Grand Duke in mid-
 stride, 7-1/2", CE/Jun 9/95 (500-700) 230
Portrait of smiling Jaq, 5", CE/Jun 9/95
 (600-800) 1265
Waist-up close-up of thoughtful Gus looking up,
 5", CE/Jun 9/95 (600-800) 1093
Knees-up image of smiling Lady Tremaine looking
 down, 6", CE/Jun 9/95 (600-800) 805
Medium close-up of smiling Fairy Godmother,
 5-3/4", CE/Jun 9/95 (700-900) 1093
Lady Tremaine reads ball invitation, 6 x 4", VF,
 HL/Aug 6/95 (900-1200) 784
Large image of stalking Lucifer, 10 x 10-1/2",
 VF, HL/Aug 6/95 (1000-1500) 1064
2 front-view cels: ankles-up of King sitting, 6-5/8";
 knees-up of Grand Duke standing holding hat
 & monocle, looking left, 8", SR/Fall/95 (700-
 1100) 700
Waist-up front view of smiling Fairy Godmother
 holding wand up, 8", SR/Fall/95
 (1200-1800) 1200
Anastasia & Drizella destroy Cinderella's (rear view)
 pink outfit, 14-1/4 x 10", SR/Fall/95
 (700-1100) 1400
Large portrait of Fairy Godmother clapping hands,
 7-1/2 x 6", HL/Nov 19/95 (800-1200) 1093
Portrait of Cinderella holding Gus' jacket, 6 x
 3-1/2", HL/Apr 28/96 (1000-1500) 1955
Portrait of dithery Fairy Godmother, 6 x 4",
 HL/Apr 28/96 (800-1200) 805
Portrait of smiling Fairy Godmother w/wand upraised,
 8 x 6", HL/Apr 28/96 (1200-1500) 1208
Jubilant King waving monocle of reserved Duke,
 5-1/2 x 7", VF, HL/Apr 28/96 (600-800) 575
Near-full-figure front view of Cinderella admiring
 wedding dress she's wearing, 6",
 CE/Jun 20/96 (800-1200) 3680
Right profile (from hips up) of Cinderella in
 serving clothes, with broom handle,
 6-1/2", CE/Jun 20/96 (800-1200) 1265
Eager Lucifer licking chops with paws clasped together
 in front of him, 4-1/2 x 6", HL/Oct 6/96 (800-
 1000) 978
2 items: Grand Duke sits sleeping w/glass slipper
 on pillow in lap, 7"; Lady Tremaine, 6-1/2";
 CE/Dec 12/96 (1500-2000) 1150
Knees-up view of Prince Charming bowing at waist,
 4-1/2 x 3-1/2", HL/Feb 23/97 (600-900) 575
Knees-up profile view of Prince, eyes open, 8";
 neck-up view of Samson, eyes closed, 7",
 CLA/Jun 7/97 (600-900) 575
11 cels: King, Bruno, Anastasia in nightclothes,
 Grand Duke, orchestra leader, Lady Tremaine,
 3 of Bruno as footman; from *Sleeping Beauty*:
 Kings Hubert & Stefan toasting, forest animals
 in Prince Phillip's clothing; S/Jun 21/97 (700-
 900) 1725
Cinderella (7") turns away from Prince (rear view,
 8-1/2"), S/Jun 21/97 (2500-3500) 4025
Hem-up view of Cinderella standing facing right with
 arms out, 5-5/8", 12-field cel, SR/Fall/97
 (1200-1800) 1070
Portrait of Fairy Godmother w/right arm extended
 forward, 7 x 4-1/2", VF+, HL/Nov 16/97
 (800-1200) 633
Knees-up front view of Lady Tremaine looking
 & gesturing to right, 7 x 7-1/4", VF+,
 HL/Nov 16/97 (800-1200) 1150
Cinderella turns away as she holds hands w/Prince,
 7-1/4 x 7-1/2", F+, HL/Nov 16/97
 (2000-2500) 2990
Thoughtful Cinderella in bed undoes a hair braid,
 6-1/2 x 9-1/2", F, HL/Nov 16/97
 (1800-2200) 1725
5 birds flying w/cloth panel & thread in their beaks,
 6-1/2 x 10", VF, HL/Feb 23/97 (600-900) 633
Profile of Cinderella in ball gown facing left, 9",
 applied to blue painted cardboard,

CE/Dec 18/97 (2000-3000) 3680
Side view of Grand Duke sitting asleep holding glass
 slipper on pillow on his knees, 6-1/2 x 6-3/4",
 16-field cel, SR/Spring/98 (400-700) 440
Hips-up medium close-up of Lady Tremaine (eyes
 closed) facing toward left & holding invitation,
 7-1/4 x 4", VF, HL/Apr 25/98 (400-600) 431

CONCEPT AND INSPIRATIONAL ART
4 items of illustration art: Cinderella & Prince dancing
 in ballroom; Gus & Jaq look at glass slipper on
 Cinderella's foot; Anastasia & Drizella bowing
 before Prince at ball; Lady Tremaine & daughters
 turning to look at Cinderella who's overheard
 invitation to ball; each watercolor on heavy
 paper, S/Jun 10/95 (1000-1500) 3162
38 animation sheets featuring one or two detailed
 designs for storybook, including watercolor
 painting of King & Duke (watercolor on
 heavyweight paper), 4-1/2 x 4" to 6-1/2
 x 9", HL/Mar 3/97 (800-1200) 2760
Inspiration painting by Mary Blair of Cinderella
 & Prince dancing on balcony, 10 x 12",
 tempera on paper mounted to board, VF,
 HL/Nov 16/97 (2000-3000) 7245
Concept painting of boudoir with ornate fireplace,
 draped balcony, & Lady Tremaine in curtained
 bed, mixed media on 15-1/2 x 12-1/2" board,
 SR/Spring/98 (1100-1600) 920

DYE-TRANSFER PRINTS
Full-figure close-up of four mice standing together
 in moonlight, 10 x 8", SR/Spring/95
 (300-600) 310
Cinderella stands in ball gown by fountain as birds
 watch, 11 x 8-1/2", SR/Spring/96
 (300-600) 440

LAYOUT ART
Layout drawing of Lady Tremaine sitting up in
 bed in richly rendered bedroom, colored
 conté crayon on 16-field animation sheet,
 11-1/2 x 15", HL/Feb 23/97 (400-600) 805

MODEL ART
Model cel of curious Jaq, 4 x 5-1/2",
 HL/Nov 19/95 (600-900) 690
Color model cel of Lady Tremaine, 7-1/2 x 5",
 HL/Oct 6/96 (600-900) 805
5 color model drawings of Cinderella in coach,
 coachman, horses & reins; 2 x 4" to 11 x
 13-1/2", HL/Feb 23/97 (500-700) 1035
Color model drawing of Cinderella in tattered
 dress picking up glass slipper, 7-1/2 x
 6-1/2", HL/May 31/97 (200-300) 978

STORY ART
Story painting by Mary Blair of Cinderella weeping
 in lap of Fairy Godmother, tempera on paper
 mounted to board, 8 x 9", HL/Oct 6/96
 (1500-2000) 2300

DUMBO (1941)
**Also see TELEVISION: THE MICKEY MOUSE
CLUB, UNIDENTIFIED TV**
ANIMATION DRAWINGS
Colored pencil drawing of laughing Timothy Mouse
 holding hat with peanut inside, 4-1/2 x 5",
 VF, HL/Feb 26-27/94 (300-400) 550
Colored pencil drawing of Glasses Crow singing,
 3-1/2 x 3", VF, HL/Feb 26-27/94 (200-400) 550
Full-figure drawing of feisty Timothy Mouse,
 5 x 4-1/2", HL/Nov 13/94 (300-400) 364
Full-figure drawing of Timothy Mouse putting peanut
 in hat, 4 x 4-1/2", HL/Nov 13/94 (300-400) 420
2 matched drawings of Timothy & his hat, 7 x 6"
 & 2 x 2", HL/Aug 6/95 (300-500) 420
Full-standing-figure drawings of Jim (facing toward right,
 5-1/4") & Glasses Crow (rear view, looking left,
 4-1/4"), 12-field, SR/Fall/95 (400-700) 400
Full-figure drawings of Jim & Glasses Crow dancing in
 circle, black grease pencil with red frame line on
 8-1/4 x 8 3/4" sheet with five-hole punch, four-
 opening double mat, Ward Kimball signature,
 originally released by Courvoisier Galleries,
 SR/Spring/96 (300-600) 330
Full-figure drawing of Timothy gingerly offering
 peanut, 4-1/2 x 4-1/2", HL/Apr 28/96
 (300-500) 460
Full-figure extreme drawing of smiling Jim Crow tipping
 hat, 5 x 4-1/2", HL/Oct 6/96 (400-500) 460
Full-figure drawing of Timothy Mouse looking and
 pointing up while holding feather behind his
 back, 4-1/2 x 6", HL/Oct 6/96 (400-500) 489

Full-figure extreme drawing of sad Dumbo, head down & holding pennant in trunk; 5-1/2 x 6", HL/Oct 6/96 (1200-1600) 1955

2 matching full-figure drawings: 5 excited crows in circle, jubilant Timothy holding feather [for circle's center]; 6-1/2 x 8-1/2" & 3 x 3-1/2", HL/Oct 6/96 (500-700) 690

Full-figure front-view drawing of happy Timothy standing holding hat with peanut inside, 4-1/2 x 4", HL/Feb 23/97 (200-300) 345

Full-figure drawing of determined hatless Timothy Mouse standing facing right, 3-1/2 x 4", HL/May 31/97 (200-300) 173

5 drawings (3 full-figure rough) of Timothy Mouse, 5 x 4-1/2" to 5 x 6-1/4", F, HL/Nov 16/97 (1000-1500) 863

Full-figure drawing of angry hatless Timothy falling thru air, separate drawing of his crushed hat; 5-1/4 x 5-1/4" & 1-1/4 x 2-1/4"; VF, HL/Nov 16/97 (300-400) 374

Waist-up drawing of tipsy Dumbo sitting, 5-1/2 x 6", HL/Nov 16/97 (500-1200) 863

Full-figure drawing of Timothy Mouse standing holding hat in left hand, peanut out in right, 4-3/4 x 4-3/4", VF, HL/Apr 25/98 (300-400) 431

Full-figure front-view drawing of Dumbo walking holding flag in trunk, 5-1/4", 12-field sheet, areas of discoloration, SR/Spring/98 (500-1000) 1420

3 full-figure drawings of clowns on 12-field sheets: clown diving into barrel, 6-5/8"; front view of clown standing with eyedropper, 5-1/2", fully rendered with gouache; clown standing spraying gas with hose from gas pump, 6-5/8"; some darkening, paint smear on back of diving clown; SR/Spring/98 (800-1200) 820

BACKGROUNDS

Watercolor master background of padlocked circus wagon at night, 8-1/2 x 11", studio stamps & notes, VF+, HL/Apr 10/94 (2000-2500) 5264

Watercolor pre-production background: aerial view from inside big top, 14-3/4 x 11-1/5"; cleaned, stabilized & restored; mounted on heavy board; SR/Spring/97 (1200-1800) 1380

CEL SET-UPS

Dumbo in front of circus tent, 1940s publicity cel, preliminary watercolor background, 8-1/2 x 11-1/2", CE/Dec 15/93 (4000-6000) 4025

4" Dumbo cradled in mother's trunk, airbrushed background, Courvoisier label, S/Dec 16/93 (2000-3000) 3163

Baby Dumbo grasps Timothy's tail, 8-1/2 x 11", laminated, complementary watercolor & airbrush background by Courvoisier, WDP & Disney copyright stamps, original mat & label, 1 of 48 released, restored, VF, HL/Apr 10/94 (3000-5000) 4256

Dumbo (4-1/2 x 6") holding happy Timothy Mouse's tail (1-1/2") w/trunk, airbrushed Courvoisier background & label; Walt Disney's Dumbo of the Circus book (poor condition), S/Jun 17/94 (3000-4000) 3737

Dumbo unfurls ears, airbrushed Courvoisier background, inscribed "To Alice Patterson, my Best Wishes, Walt Disney" on mat, Courvoisier label, 3 x 6", S/Jun 17/94 (3000-3500) 4887

Happy Dumbo sits in tub, 4-1/2 x 3", airbrush & watercolor Courvoisier background, CE/Jun 18/94 (2500-3500) 7475

Full figure of ringmaster Timothy Mouse, complementary Courvoisier airbrush background stamped "WDP", 7 x 4", HL/Aug 21/94 (1500-2000) 1456

Happy Dumbo plays in bath, complementary Courvoisier airbrush background & label, WDP stamp, 7-1/2 x 8-1/2", HL/Aug 21/94 (2500-3500) 4704

Dumbo perched on telephone wires with four crows, complementary Courvoisier airbrush background & label, inscribed, stamped "original WDP", 8 x 10", HL/Aug 21/94 (5000-6000) 4480

Crows push Dumbo w/magic feather & Timothy to edge of cliff, Courvoisier complementary background, stamp & notes, 8 x 10", HL/Aug 21/94 (5000-7000) 5488

Full figures of Timothy examining Dumbo's ears, complementary Courvoisier airbrush background, 7-1/2 x 10-1/2", HL/Aug 21/94 (2000-3000) 5600

Full figure of happy Dumbo stepping to right, looking up, 4-1/2", Art Props gouache background of circus grounds, SR/Fall/94 (2200-3200) 4330

Dumbo sitting w/tent pole by train, 3", watercolor production background, CE/Dec 16/94 (4000-6000) 6900

Giraffe & camels, 6" & smaller, Courvoisier airbrush background, CE/Dec 16/94 (500-700) 518

Timothy Mouse (1-1/2") paces in front of concerned Dumbo (4 x 5"), airbrushed Courvoisier background, S/Dec 17/94 (2000-3000) 4025

Mother Kangaroo happily cradles joey in her arms, 7", wood-veneer Courvoisier background, S/Dec 17/94 (900-1100) 1035

Happy Dumbo flies down [to greet Mom], 4" (4-1/2" ear span), airbrushed Courvoisier background & label, WDP stamp, S/Dec 17/94 (2000-3000) 3737

3 elephants precariously balanced atop ball, 7"; 3 tigers lounging in their cage, 9"; both over airbrushed Courvoisier backgrounds, S/Dec 17/94 (800-1200) 1265

Timothy Mouse (1-1/2") addresses 2 elephants (5-1/2") cowering on top of perches, airbrushed Courvoisier background, S/Dec 17/94 (800-1200) 1495

Full figure of confident Dumbo (eyes closed) flying overhead with Timothy in hat, 4-3/4", 12-field, gouache display background of sky, ct, SR/Spring/95 (2500-3500) 2940

Mrs. Jumbo lovingly holds Dumbo, 4-1/2 x 5", complementary airbrush background monogrammed "WDP," copyright stamps, Courvoisier & Arthur Ackermann & Son labels, HL/Apr 23/95 (3000-4000) 4704

Full figure of excited Dumbo standing on bench, 5", Courvoisier airbrush background, CE/Jun 9/95 (2000-3000) 2990

Happy Mrs. Jumbo holding aviator Dumbo on trunk, 6-1/2", Courvoisier airbrush background, CE/Jun 9/95 (2500-3500) 4140

2 elephants struggling on high wire, 9", Courvoisier airbrush background, CE/Jun 9/95 (600-800) 805

Portrait of Mrs. Jumbo holding baby Dumbo in trunk, 4-3/4", Courvoisier airbrush background, CE/Jun 9/95 (1500-2000) 3450

Dumbo splashing ears in bath, 7", Courvoisier airbrush & watercolor background with overlay, CE/Jun 9/95 (4000-6000) 6900

Dumbo (3-1/4") w/Timothy (1/2") flies over crows (2") perched on electric pole, watercolor production background, CE/Jun 9/95 (5000-7000) 6900

Large full figure of Dumbo w/Timothy in hat, 5", unfinished Courvoisier background, CE/Jun 9/95 (1000-1500) 2875

Full figures of Dumbo and Timothy walking dejectedly, 7-1/4 x 9-1/2", complementary airbrush background as prepared by Courvoisier, HL/Aug 6/95 (3000-5000) 4368

Full figures of 3 elephants struggling atop ball under big top, 10-1/2 x 8-1/2", complementary painted background as prepared by Courvoisier, HL/Aug 6/95 (1000-1500) 1064

Full figure of Casey Junior crossing bridge to left, 7-3/4", Courvoisier watercolor background & label, ct, SR/Spring/96 (1600-2400) 1760

Full figures of 6 storks flying in formation w/bundles against full moon, 9-1/4" wide, Courvoisier watercolor background & original label, SR/Spring/96 (900-1400) 990

Full figure of stork flying to right w/bundle amid clouds, 6-1/2 x 3-1/2", 16-field, Art Props background, ct, SR/Spring/96 (2000-4000) 2000

Full figure of happy baby Giraffe floating down (head & neck outside bundle) under two parachutes, 4-1/2", 16-field cel, display background of starry sky, ct, SR/Spring/96 (700-1000) 940

Full figure of smiling Timothy standing looking right, 5-1/2", Courvoisier watercolor background of circus tent, stamp & original label, some lifting paint, SR/Spring/96 (1400-2000) 1400

Full figures of Timothy (1-1/2") standing in front of sad Dumbo (sitting, 5-1/2"), both facing left, Courvoisier watercolor background of circus grounds, stamp & label, SR/Spring/96 (2600-3400) 4060

Full-figure front view of tiny Timothy leading sad Dumbo amid circus tents, complementary Cour-

voisier airbrush background, 9-1/2 x 9", VF, HL/Apr 28/96 (2500-3000) 2760

Full figure of clowns riding fire engine, complementary Courvoisier airbrush background, 6-1/2 x 9", HL/Apr 28/96 (1200-1600) 1495

Contented mother kangaroo & full figure of jumping baby as seen thru window, Courvoisier airbrush background, 5" & smaller, CE/Jun 20/96 (600-800) 633

Full figure of Timothy standing looking up, holding left arm out & feather behind his back in right hand, Courvoisier watercolor & airbrush background, 6-1/2", CE/Jun 20/96 (800-1200) 1495

6 storks flying in line with bundles, Courvoisier airbrush background, 2-1/4", CE/Jun 20/96 (800-1200) 920

Full figures of Timothy talking to Dumbo (head & front legs on ground) outside tent, Courvoisier watercolor background, 9", CE/Jun 20/96 (4000-6000) 8050

Publicity cel: full figures of happy Timothy (2") w/arms spread & Dumbo (6") w/one foot off ground standing outside by tent, Courvoisier watercolor & airbrush background, CE/Jun 20/96 (3000-4000) 4600

Full figure of Casey Jr. (without train) poised to move, Courvoisier airbrush & watercolor background, 4-1/2", CE/Jun 20/96 (800-1200) 2760

Full figures of Dumbo (Timothy in hat, 4") with feather in trunk pausing in flight to look back at five crows (1/2" ea.), Courvoisier airbrush background, CE/Jun 20/96 (2500-3500) 5175

Full figures of sad Timothy (5/8") & Dumbo (3-3/4") walking to left by circus tent, master watercolor background, originally released by Courvoisier, monogram stamp, SR/Fall/96 (3500-5000) 4430

Full figure of Dumbo clinging precariously to mother's tail as she leads him out of circus wagon, complementary Courvoisier painted background, 7-1/2 x 10", HL/Oct 6/96 (2000-2500) 3680

Large image of sleepy Dumbo looking up & to right w/Timothy peering out from under his hat, 10", Courvoisier airbrush background & label, CE/Dec 12/96 (4000-6000) 7475

Full figures of Dumbo sitting on sagging phone wires, feather in trunk, eyes closed, with Timothy & 5 crows on his head, 5 x 5-1/2", airbrushed Courvoisier background, S/Dec 14/96 (4000-6000) 4025

Full-figure rear view of Dumbo standing with head turned to left, 3-1/2", watercolor background of outdoors, S/Dec 14/96 (2000-3000) 3162

Full figure of Baby Dumbo sitting looking straight up, 4-1/4", airbrushed Courvoisier background & label, S/Dec 14/96 (600-800) 3162

Dumbo (near-full figure, 5 x 8") takes Timothy's (full figure, 1-1/4") tail in his trunk & follows, walking to left, airbrushed Courvoisier background of circus tent exterior, S/Dec 14/96 (2500-3500) 4600

Full-figure rear view of worried Dumbo standing looking left, 3-1/2", 12-field cel, 8 x 9-1/8" Courvoisier watercolor background with WDP stamp, SR/Spring/97 (3000-6000) 3000

Full-figure front view of Dumbo sitting on ground in front of tent blowing bubbles, 7", key bubble effects, Courvoisier watercolor background, WDP stamp, SR/Spring/97 (3000-5000) 3730

Pink elephant, 4-1/2", Courvoisier airbrush background & label, CLA/Jun 7/97 (700-900) 345

Full figures of downcast Timothy (1") & Dumbo (6") walking to left, watercolor production background of outdoors, Courvoisier label, CLA/Jun 7/97 (4000-6000) 5175

Full figures of Dumbo flying (3", ear span 4-1/2"), feather in trunk, Timothy in hat, amid 6 crows (each approx. 1"), airbrushed Courvoisier background, S/Jun 21/97 (4000-6000) 6900

Full figure of happy Mrs. Jumbo (5-1/2 x 8") lying cradling Dumbo (3") between legs, airbrushed Courvoisier background, S/Jun 21/97 (3000-5000) 4312

Full figures of Dumbo in clown hat & happy Timothy standing on grass in front of circus tent by Art Props Dept., 6-1/2", watercolor background painting, Courvoisier label, hand-lettered mat with "Original WDP" stamp, SR/Fall/97 (6000-9000) 4500

Limited-edition cel of Dumbo, Timothy & Crows on

edge of cliff, #267/275, color print background, VF+, HL/Nov 16/97 (500-1000) 1093

Dumbo's mother cradles him in her trunk, 6" overall, airbrushed Courvoisier background & label, S/Dec 19/97 (2500-3500) 6325

Large full-figure promotional cel of smiling Dumbo sitting, looking up & to right, 6 x 6", printed background, S/Dec 19/97 (1200-1800) 1265

Full figures of happy Dumbo & Timothy walking right in front of circus tent, for publicity, complementary painted background, WDP stamp, restored, 7-3/4 x 9-3/4", F+, HL/Apr 25/98 (2000-3000) 4025

Full figures of Dumbo flying with Timothy in his hat (1-1/2") & 5 crows in V-formation (3"), Courvoisier watercolor background & label, ct, SR/Spring/98 (2000-3000) 2480

Hips-up of hatless Timothy with right arm out, 3-1/2", round presentation with custom watercolor background, SR/Spring/98 (800-1400) 810

CELS – FULL FIGURE
Straw Hat Crow & Preacher Crow dance, 10-1/4 x 12", CE/Dec 15/93 (500-700) 862

Happy Dumbo (2-1/4 x 5-1/2") flying with Timothy (1/2 x 1/4") in his hat, CE/Jun 18/94 (2500-3500) 2760

Publicity cel of Dumbo sitting, 6 x 6", CE/Jun 18/94 (1500-2500) 3220

Dumbo holding onto tail with trunk & carrying doll on back, 3 x 5-1/2", CE/Jun 18/94 (2000-3000) 3220

Dumbo (2-1/2") flying with eyes closed w/Timothy in hat & crows (1/2" each) flying between ears, "WDP" stamp, S/Dec 17/94 (1500-2000) 2875

Baby Dumbo sits with ears tucked behind his back, looking up, 3", S/Dec 14/96 (2000-3000) 3162

Glasses Crow stands facing right with beak open, eyes closed, 4 x 3-1/2", HL/May 31/97 (200-250) 150

CELS – PARTIAL FIGURE
Two elephants gossip, 9-1/2 x 3-1/4", ct, SR/Spring/96 (600-1000) 800

CONCEPT AND INSPIRATIONAL ART
3 concept drawings: Dumbo falling after losing feather; 2 circus elephants colliding; chaos among circus elephants; S/Dec 16/93 (800-1200) 1610

2 concept drawings: circus hand reaching for Dumbo hiding behind mother; row of circus elephants on balls before ringmaster; graphite, black pastel & crayon on paper, S/Dec 16/93 (600-800) 920

Concept drawing of Dumbo high on window ledge in spotlight with feather in trunk, notes, 3" x 4", S/Jun 17/94 (300-500) 690

Ring Master inspirational sketch, 8 x 4-1/4", color crayon on animation paper, CE/Jun 18/94 (400-600) 230

Concept drawing of Dumbo (2 x 4") peering from under fallen tent, waving American flag, WDP stamp, image 5-1/2 x 7", S/Dec 17/94 (300-500) 747

Concept drawing of Dumbo (5") walking away, wearing clown hat & crying, image 5-1/2 x 7", WDP stamp, S/Dec 17/94 (300-500) 920

Overhead view of 4 clowns with net, inspirational sketch, watercolor on paper, CE/Jun 9/95 (300-500) 748

3 large concept drawings of Dumbo & bird: 2 with bird sitting on trunk; one of tears showering bird as he cries; 1st pastel on paper, 2nd & 3rd graphite & red pencil on paper, S/Jun 10/95 (700-900) 1092

2 watercolor concepts: Dumbo sitting on box marked 'Jumbo' (3-1/2 x 5") while 2 boys (about 4" each) laugh at 3rd who holds out pair of earmuffs; Dumbo (6 x 6") sitting down wearing large pink ruff; both graphite & watercolor on paper, plus photostat (6-1/2 x 6") of Dumbo in baby's outfit examining bird perched on his trunk; S/Jun 10/95 (700-900) 977

3 concept pieces: Dumbo weeping in corner of circus train car, 6", pastel on paper; 2 graphite-&-red-pencil-on-paper drawings of Dumbo happily spouting water, 5", & having near miss with plane, 3", S/Jun 10/95 (600-800) 690

3 concept pieces: pastel & drawing of Dumbo soaring w/bird; drawing of Dumbo crying as clowns torment him; Dumbo approx. 3-1/2" in each (not including trunk), pastel on paper/graphite & red pencil on paper, S/Jun 10/95 (700-900) 1150

3 drawings: acrobats grab Dumbo by ears as they swing from trapeze, then watch amazed as he flies away; Dumbo approx. 3" in each; graphite, red pencil & watercolor on paper, S/Jun 10/95 (700-900) 1150

4 concept pieces: clown whacking Dumbo's behind with board, pastel on paper; drawing of Ringmaster; 2 drawings of unstable tower of elephants; drawings graphite on paper, S/Jun 10/95 (700-900) 1610

4 studies of clown antics, 5 x 5" to 8 x 8-1/2", HL/Apr 28/96 (200-300) 460

2 pages of studies of Dumbo on animation paper by Bill Tytla, S/Jun 19/96 (1000-1500) 1495

Sheet of drawings titled "Dumbo/Doodlings" depicts sketches for Pink Elephant sequence, pencil & conté crayon on animation sheet, 8-1/2 x 10", HL/May 31/97 (100-200) 138

Concept artwork for circus parade: heralds ride giraffes, graphite & white pastel on paper, sight 5-1/2 x 7", S/Jun 21/97 (700-900) 1035

Concept art of Timothy (4-1/4") being blown back by blast from elephant trunk, S/Jun 21/97 (700-900) 920

LAYOUT ART
Full-figure front-view layout drawing of Dumbo stepping forward & looking up, 4", CE/Dec 18/97 (1000-1500) 1495

10 layouts for the credits, 3 x 4-1/2" to 8 x 10-1/4", overall F, HL/Apr 25/98 (500-700) 1265

MODEL ART
2 stat model sheets: Casey Jones (from *The Brave Engineer*) & Casey Jones Jr.; both 14 x 11", some wrinkling SR/Spring/95 (200-400) 240

SPECIAL-EFFECTS ART
Exploding plaid elephants fill 10-7/8 x 7-7/8" cel, SR/Spring/97 (300-700) 300

STORY ART
Timothy, story sketch released by Courvoisier, 8-3/4 x 8-1/2", CE/Dec 15/93 (300-500) 368

2 story sketches of crows dancing, 5-3/4 x 7-1/2" & similar, CE/Dec 15/93 (700-900) 575

8 story originals from sketchy to polished; 7 x 5-1/2" to 9 x 9-1/2"; pencil, watercolor & conté crayon on animation sheets, HL/Apr 23/95 (1000-1500) 1120

Story painting of Timothy bring Dumbo to wagon containing his mother, 5-1/2 x 7-1/2", watercolor on story sheet, HL/Nov 19/95 (1000-1500) 1150

2 story paintings on same sheet: happy Ringmaster hanging onto side of railroad car, expectant Mrs. Jumbo looking upward; watercolor & conté crayon on paper, 4-1/4 x 6-1/4", HL/Feb 23/97 (1000-1500) 920

Story sketch of angry Mrs. Jumbo pulling her baby back with her trunk, captioned "31 Jumbo?... You mean, Dumbo!..." 6 x 4-3/8", SR/Fall/97 (900-1200) 1070

FANTASIA (1940)
Also see TELEVISION: ACADEMY AWARDS, UNIDENTIFIED TV; UNIDENTIFIED/ MISCELLANEOUS: MICKEY MOUSE

Segments were *Toccata and Fugue in D Minor*, *The Nutcracker Suite*, *The Sorcerer's Apprentice*, *Rite of Spring*, *Pastoral*, *Dance of the Hours*, *Night on Bald Mountain*, and *Ave Maria*.

ANIMATION DRAWINGS
Chernabog raises hands, 8 x 10-3/4", CE/Dec 15/93 (1000-1500) 1495

Twirling Blossom, 15 x 12-1/2", CE/Dec 15/93 (300-400) 345

Colored pencil drawing of 10 of Chernabog's demonic spirits, VF, HL/Feb 26-27/94 (500-700) 825

Rough colored drawing of Yen Sid practicing, 7 x 5", VG, HL/Apr 10/94 (700-1000) 672

Full-figure pencil drawing of Sorcerer Mickey on cut-down animation sheet, 4 x 2-1/2", F, HL/Apr 10/94 (500-700) 616

Colored pencil drawing of Chernabog, 9 x 11-1/2", studio notes, VF, HL/Apr 10/94 (2000-3000) 1680

Full figure of contrite Sorcerer Mickey w/broom, 4 x 5", CE/Jun 18/94 (1000-1500) 1495

Drawing of towering Chernabog recoiling in pain, 10", 16-field sheet, SR/Fall/94 (1600-2200) 2640

Full-figure drawing of Sorcerer Mickey walking right, looking back left, 6-1/2", shadows, 16-field, SR/Fall/94 (1800-2800) 1820

Full-figure drawing of zebra centaurette pouring wine vessel into cup, shadow, 6-3/4", 16-field sheet, production stamp, SR/Fall/94 (500-900) 500

Close-up drawing of towering Chernabog's head, 8-1/2", 12-field sheet, with inker's notations, production stamp, SR/Fall/94 (1400-1800) 1560

Chest-up front-view drawing of Zeus looking down with arms across chest, 5-3/4", 12-field sheet, inker's notation, SR/Fall/94 (300-500) 480

Full-figure drawing of centaurette Sunflower standing facing left, 6-1/2", 12-field, inker's notations, production stamp, SR/Fall/94 (500-900) 460

2 full-figure drawings of abashed, hatless Sorcerer Mickey standing facing right, 4", 12-field sheets, inker's notations, SR/Fall/94 (2200-2800) 2040

Hyacinth Hippo dancing, 7-1/2 x 10", initialed by Howard Swift, HL/Nov 13/94 (600-800) 784

4 sequential drawings: medium close-up of Chernabog gesturing, 9 x 14" to 9-1/2 x 15", HL/Nov 13/94 (6000-9000) 8064

Full-figure drawing of Sorcerer Mickey, 4", CE/Dec 16/94 (800-1200) 1093

2 Pegasi flying, 7" ea., CE/Dec 16/94 (600-800) 460

4 cupids holding flower blossoms as trumpets, 2" ea., CE/Dec 16/94 (200-300) 173

Full-figure drawing of Mickey, 4", CE/Dec 16/94 (600-800) 748

Extreme drawing of Sorcerer Mickey with arms raised preparing to conduct, 4-1/2", S/Dec 17/94 (1000-1500) 2587

Close-up drawing of towering Chernabog's head, 12-field sheet, production stamp, SR/Spring/95 (1400-1800) 1380

Full-figure drawing of excited Sorcerer Mickey standing facing left, arms extended, 4-1/2", 12-field sheet, inker's notation, production stamp, SR/Spring/95 (1400-1800) 1680

Hips-up front-view drawing of calm Chernabog, arms in front of chest, 8-1/2", 12-field sheet, some fading, SR/Spring/95 (1200-1600) 1630

Full-figure drawing of happy Sorcerer Mickey walking to right, looking back over shoulder, 6-3/4", 16-field sheet, SR/Spring/95 (1800-2800) 2450

Drawing of angry Chernabog; matching 2nd-level drawing of swirling smoke; 3rd drawing of cavorting demons; 8 x 5-1/2", 8 x 9-1/2", 8 x 12", HL/Apr 23/95 (1000-1500) 2912

3 full-figure drawings of sprites: 3-1/2 x 2-1/2", 4-1/2 x 2-1/2", 6 x 4-1/2"; HL/Apr 23/95 (600-800) 952

Full-figure drawing of running Sorcerer Mickey, 4 x 6-1/2", HL/Apr 23/95 (1000-1500) 2688

Full-figure drawing of apprehensive Sorcerer Mickey, 4-1/2 x 8", HL/Apr 23/95 (1200-1600) 2464

4 detailed rough drawings in sequence of Sorcerer Mickey, 3-1/2 x 3-1/4", HL/Apr 23/95 (1600-2400) 5152

Apprehensive Sorcerer Mickey holding bucket, 4-1/4", CE/Jun 9/95 (1500-2000) 1955

Full-figure drawing of surprised Sorcerer Mickey standing, 6", CE/Jun 9/95 (1500-2000) 1840

Full-figure drawing of chastened Mickey Mouse holding sorcerer's hat, 4 x 3-1/2", HL/Aug 6/95 (1500-2000) 1904

Smiling Sorcerer Mickey w/left arm raised, 5-1/2 x 5-1/2", HL/Aug 6/95 (1200-1600) 3360

Full-figure drawing of happy Centaurette Sunflower kneeling, polishing hoof with cattail, 5-1/4", 16-field, SR/Fall/95 (400-800) 400

Frame-filling front close-up drawing Chernabog's face looking down, 12-field sheet, SR/Fall/95 (1200-1600) 1780

Waist-up close-up drawing of towering Chernabog w/left arm up as shield, 12 x 10-1/2", 16-field, production stamp, SR/Fall/95 (1400-2000) 2060

Full-figure drawing of smiling zebra centaurette pouring from wine vessel, 6-1/2", 16-field sheet, production stamp, SR/Fall/95 (500-900) 500

Front view of hatless Sorcerer w/hands up, 9-1/2 x 6-1/2", HL/Nov 19/95 (1000-1500) 1725

Close-up drawing of laughing Chernabog (head & neck), 7-1/2 x 9-1/2", HL/Nov 19/95 (1500-2000) 1725

Full-figure drawing of relieved Sorcerer Mickey sitting, 6 x 4", HL/Nov 19/95 (1500-2000) 5750

Full-figure drawing of awed Sorcerer Mickey (w/o hat), 3-1/2 x 3", HL/Nov 19/95 (1000-1500) 1610

Rough drawings signed by Preston Blair of Hyacinth Hippo, and Hyacinth & Ben Ali Gator; 4-1/2 x 5-1/2" & 6 x 12", HL/Nov 19/95 (700-900) 863

Full-figure drawing of authoritative Sorcerer Mickey facing left with arms extended, 7-5/8", 16-field, some edge wear & discoloration, repaired shallow tears, SR/Spring/96 (1500-2200) 1700

Full-page near-full-figure drawing of towering Chernabog, 16-field, production stamp & effects notation, some edge wear, SR/Spring/96 (1200-1800) 1920

Full-figure drawing of Sorcerer Mickey standing facing left in coaxing pose, 4-1/4", 16-field, production stamp, SR/Spring/96 (1200-1800) 1940

Large-image full-figure drawing of apprehensive, hatless Sorcerer Mickey looking down & to his left, 6 x 4-1/2", HL/Apr 28/96 (1500-2000) 1955

Full-figure drawing of zebra centaurette pouring wine into cup, 7 x 5", HL/Apr 28/96 (600-900) 575

Full-figure drawing of eager "pickaninny" centaurette holding cattail brush & another centaurette's hoof, 5-1/2 x 5", HL/Apr 28/96 (600-800) 575

Full-figure drawing of graceful Hyacinth Hippo dancing, 9-1/2 x 7", HL/Apr 28/96 (500-700) 460

Full-figure drawing of bare-headed, forlorn Sorcerer Mickey crouching & looking upward, 4-1/2 x 5-1/2", HL/Apr 28/96 (700-1000) 1150

Near-full-figure extreme drawing of Sorcerer Mickey bent at waist w/arms up, looking behind him, 5 x 4", HL/Apr 28/96 (1200-1600) 2990

Rough drawing of large image of Chernabog's head by Bill Tytla, 5 x 8", S/Jun 19/96 (800-1200) 690

2 rough drawings of Chernabog by Bill Tytla: within folded wings; towering atop mountain; S/Jun 19/96 (1000-1500) 1092

Full-figure drawing of hatless Sorcerer Mickey smiling sheepishly with hands behind back, 6", CE/Jun 20/96 (1000-1500) 1495

Close-up drawing of Chernabog's head, 11-1/4 x 8-3/4", 12-field sheet, inker's call-outs, production stamp. SR/Fall/96 (1200-1600) 1630

Full-figure drawing of suspicious Sorcerer Mickey walking right, looking back, 6-1/4", 16-field sheet, inker's note, production stamp, SR/Fall/96 (1800-2800) 1820

Large-image drawing: looking up at grimacing Chernabog shielding face w/left arm, 10-3/4 x 8-1/2", 16-field sheet, production stamp, SR/Fall/96 (1400-2000) 1900

Full-figure drawing of smiling pickaninny centaurette Sunflower sitting facing right, holding cattail brush, 5-1/4", 16-field sheet, inker's notation, SR/Fall/96 (400-800) 300

Full-figure drawing of eager Sorcerer Mickey crouching to left, looking up, 3-1/2", 16-field sheet, inker's notation, production stamp, SR/Fall/96 (1400-1800) 1580

Full-figure drawing of Zebra Centaurette pouring wine vessel into cup, shadow, 6-1/2", 16-field sheet, inker's notation, production stamp, wear & repaired shallow tear, SR/Fall/96 (500-900) 500

Knees-up drawing of chastened hatless Sorcerer Mickey facing right, 3", 12-field sheet, inker's notations, SR/Fall/96 (700-1400) 800

Shaded full-figure extreme drawing of gesturing Sorcerer Mickey looking back, 6 x 5", HL/Oct 6/96 (1800-2200) 2530

Near-full-figure drawing of hatless Sorcerer Mickey facing left, looking up in fear with left hand raised, 6-1/2 x 5", HL/Oct 6/96 (900-1200) 1150

Front-view drawing of grinning Chernabog reaching down, 9 x 11", HL/Oct 6/96 (2000-3000) 3220

Full-figure extreme drawing of chastened hatless Sorcerer Mickey, left hand on cheek, facing right & looking up, 6 x 4-1/2", HL/Oct 6/96 (1500-2000) 1955

2 full-figure drawings: centaurette Melinda walking right with arms extended & eyes closed; hopeful centaur Brudus facing left with arms extended; 8 x 9" & 6-1/2 x 8", HL/Oct 6/96 (1000-1500) 1495

Portrait drawing: looking up at grinning Chernabog, 7-1/2 x 10", HL/Oct 6/96 (1200-1600) 2760

3 animation drawings: key drawing of 2 cupids,

3"; full figure of cupid holding grapes, 4"; full figure of centaurette Melinda, 8-1/4", CE/Dec 12/96 (600-800) 690

Full-figure drawing of chastened Sorcerer Mickey facing right, tip of hat drooping, 5", CE/Dec 12/96 (1200-1500) 1955

Drawing of hatless Sorcerer Mickey looking up to left, attempting to ward off some threat, 6-1/2", S/Dec 14/96 (800-1200) 1380

Drawing of hatless Sorcerer Mickey looking downward w/surprised expression, 5", S/Dec 14/96 (800-1200) 1380

3 rough drawings of Chernabog, 7" ea., S/Dec 14/96 (800-1200) 1610

2 rough drawings of Chernabog, each sheet 12-1/2 x 15-1/2", S/Dec 14/96 (1000-1500) 1495

Full-figure polished extreme drawing of happy Mickey placing Sorcerer's hat on his head, 6 x 3-1/2", HL/Feb 23/97 (1200-1600) 3335

Rough drawing: Hyacinth Hippo coyly powders her nose, with matching special-effects drawing of powder, 7-1/2 x 8", HL/Feb 23/97 (400-600) 863

Front-view drawing of 3 sinister hooded gators looking down, 9-1/2 x 10", HL/Feb 23/97 (300-400) 575

Front-view drawing of Sorcerer looking down [into camera], hands in front of chest, palms out & overlapping; 5-1/2 x 5"; plus 2 matching effects drawings, HL/Feb 23/97 (700-900) 1093

Full-figure rough drawing of apprehensive hatless Sorcerer Mickey standing facing right & looking up, 5-1/2 x 4", HL/Feb 23/97 (500-700) 1265

3 drawings of Night on Bald Mountain souls cavorting: single figure, quartet, 9 demons; 3 x 4-1/4", 6-1/2 x 3", 8 x 12", HL/Feb 23/97 (600-900) 863

Full-figure drawing of happy Sorcerer Mickey facing right & looking back in dancing pose, 4-1/2", 16-field sheet, production stamp, SR/Spring/97 (1500-1900) 2970

Drawing of towering Chernabog w/clinched fists, 16-field sheet, production stamp, inker's notation, SR/Spring/97 (1400-2000) 1940

Full-figure drawing of awed, hatless Sorcerer Mickey facing left, 6-1/4", 12-field sheet, production stamp, inker's notation, SR/Spring/97 (1700-2500) 1940

Waist-up drawing of Chernabog with clinched fists, 8 x 11", HL/May 3/97 (1500-2000) 2185

Full-figure drawing of smiling hatless Sorcerer Mickey standing looking back to right, 4-1/2", CLA/Jun 7/97 (1500-2000) 2070

Rough full-figure drawing of frantic Sorcerer Mickey running, 5", signed by Preston Blair, CLA/Jun 7/97 (1500-2000) 1150

2 full-figure drawings of centaurs: flirtatious Melinda looking right, 4-1/2 x 4"; eager Brudus facing left, 6-1/2 x 8", S/Jun 21/97 (1200-1800) 1265

4 drawings of Chernabog: with large wingspan pointing down from atop Bald Mt; 2 of head; torso & wings; each 12-1/2 x 15-1/2", S/Jun 21/97 (1000-1500) 1955

Portrait drawing: looking up at grinning Chernabog, 7-1/2", 12-field sheet, production stamp, SR/Fall/97 (1400-1800) 1460

Full-figure rough drawing of dancing Sorcerer Mickey, 4 7/8", 16-field sheet, production stamp, SR/Fall/97 (2200-2800) 1980

Front-view drawing of towering Chernabog with arms & wings outstretched, 10-1/2 x 14-1/2", VF+, HL/Nov 16/97 (2000-2500) 2760

Waist-up drawing of Hyacinth Hippo holding powder puff, 7 x 11-1/2", VF, HL/Nov 16/97 (600-800) 1035

Full-figure drawing of flirtatious centaurette parading to right, 8-1/4 x 6", VF, HL/Nov 16/97 (600-900) 978

Full-figure drawing of Chernabog, wings half spread, arms extended downward, looking down, matching special-effects drawing of flames, 11 x 9-1/4", VF+, HL/Nov 16/97 (3000-3500) 3220

Full-figure drawing of Ben Ali Gator pulling Hyacinth Hippo by arm off couch by James Bodrero, signed "Jim", 6 x 10-1/2", VF, HL/Nov 16/97 (600-900) 1380

Full-figure drawing of chastened Mickey facing right, looking up, holding up two buckets, 4",

CE/Dec 18/97 (1500-2000) 2070

Study drawing of flamboyant Chernabog, 14", CE/Dec 18/97 (1500-2000) 1725

Full-figure drawing of chastened hatless Sorcerer Mickey facing right & looking up, 4", S/Dec 19/97 (800-1200) 1725

Full-figure drawing of Sorcerer Mickey standing facing right in coaxing pose, 7", S/Dec 19/97 (1800-2200) 3162

Full-figure drawing of apprehensive Sorcerer Mickey facing right, looking back over right shoulder, 6-1/4", 16-field sheet, studio production stamp, SR/Spring/98 (1800-2400) 2220

Close-up drawing of towering, grimacing Chernabog shielding eyes, 9-1/4", 16-field sheet, studio production stamp, SR/Spring/98 (1600-2200) 1650

Detailed pencil study of cupids escorting parading centaurette; pencil, conté crayon & white tempera on animation sheet; 6 x 8"; VF; HL/Apr 25/98 (600-800) 805

Waist-up front-view drawing of stern hatless Yen Sid with arms up, 8-1/2 x 9-1/4"; +2 drawings of highlight effect; VF; HL/Apr 25/98 (700-900) 1380

Full-figure drawing of hatless Sorcerer Mickey walking purposefully to right, 4 x 7-1/4", VF, HL/Apr 25/98 (1000-1200) 1150

Waist-up front-view drawing of Hyacinth Hippo holding powder puff at mouth level, 8-1/4 x 10-1/2", VF, HL/Apr 25/98 (600-800) 1150

Full-figure drawing of awed hatless Sorcerer Mickey standing facing right, crouching & looking up; 3-1/2 x 3"; VF+; HL/Apr 25/98 (700-900) 1610

BACKGROUNDS

Rite of Spring master background of desert-like land, 11-1/2 x 15", watercolor on background sheet, HL/Aug 6/95 (2000-3000) 2688

Pan master background painting for never-used Clair De Lune, 11 x 43-1/2", watercolor on pan background sheet, HL/Nov 19/95 (2000-3000) 6325

Master background of countryside for Pastoral Symphony, watercolor on background sheet, stamps, 11 x 14-3/4", VF, HL/Apr 25/98 (4000-5000) 7763

CEL SET-UPS

Defiant Sorcerer Mickey, Courvoisier airbrush background, 8-1/2 x 9-1/2", CE/Dec 15/93 (5500-6500) 8970

Pilgrims with candles by lake, Courvoisier airbrush background, 8-1/2 x 12-1/4", CE/Dec 15/93 (2500-3500) 2990

Frost Fairies, hand-prepared background, 7-1/2 x 7-1/4", CE/Dec 15/93 (3000-3500) 4370

Centaur & Centaurette hold hands & wave as sun pierces clouds, hand-prepared background, 7 x 11", CE/Dec 15/93 (1800-2500) 1495

3 cupids blowing horns & flying over flower garland, airbrushed background, stamped WDP, S/Dec 16/93 (1800-2200) 2588

Baby Pegasus under mother's wing, airbrushed background, WDP stamp, 4", S/Dec 16/93 (2500-3000) 3450

5" Mother Pegasus lands in water with three 2" ponies behind her, airbrushed background, WDP stamp, S/Dec 16/93 (2500-3500) 3738

5" diameter portrait of Mlle. Upanova, airbrush background, WDP monogram stamp, Courvoisier label, VF, HL/Apr 10/94 (1000-1200) 1680

Pegasus family flying, watercolor master background, 10 x 13-1/2", checker Al Woolery's "OK" & signature, date "7-24-1940", Disney copyright stamp, VF, HL/Apr 10/94 (6000-9000) 7280

Ave Maria: pilgrims marching, 8-1/2 x 12", complementary airbrush background, Courvoisier label, VF, HL/Apr 10/94 (4000-5000) 3920

Hop Low waddles between 2 rows of mushroom dancers, airbrushed Courvoisier background, "WDP" stamp to lower right, Courvoisier label, avg. image 2", S/Jun 17/94 (2500-3500) 2875

3 cherubs in tree branches, airbrushed Courvoisier background, avg. size 2-1/2", S/Jun 17/94 (2000-2500) 2070

Pegasus family swimming, airbrushed background, WDP stamp & copyright; adult 2" length, S/Jun 17/94 (2000-3000) 3162

101 Dalmatians: Full figure of angry Nanny sitting in attic, 4", matching production set-up with watercolor pan production background & Xerox line-on-cel overlay, S/Dec 19/97 (6000-8000) 4025

101 Dalmatians: Near-full figure of Pongo with paws on seat cushions looking around apartment, 11 x 15", master background of apartment's bay window (tempera on background sheet), VF, HL/Oct 6/96 (1500-2000) 5720

101 Dalmatians: Angry Cruella sitting in bed talking on phone, 7", watercolor w/Xerographic line-on-celluloid background, S/Dec 14/96 (4000-6000) 8625

Aladdin: Jafar on throne w/Iago on shoulder, 8-1/2", non-production cel w/production overlay & key watercolor production background with notes, CE/Dec 16/94 (10,000-15,000) 11,500

The Adventures of Ichabod and Mr. Toad: Full figure of terrified Ichabod in midair eye-to-eye with terrified horse, 10 x 14", matching original master background (tempera on background sheet), VF, HL/Nov 16/97 (3000-4000) 4945

The Adventures of Ichabod and Mr. Toad: Full figure of wide-eyed Ichabod & sleepy horse riding to left thru dark woods, 4-7/8", 16-field, display background, ct, SR/Fall/95 (500-900) 830

Alice in Wonderland: Alice in Garden of Talking Flowers w/6 Bread-&-Butterflies (3 mounted on mat), 10 x 11-1/2", master background (tempera on background sheet), VF, HL/Apr 23/95 (7000-9000) 12,320

Alice in Wonderland: Queen of Hearts swings flamingo as Alice & King watch, watercolor production background, 10-1/2 x 13-1/4", CE/Dec 15/93 (12,000-15,000) 11,500

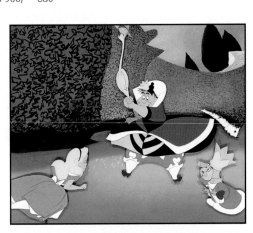

Alice in Wonderland: Alice talks with red rose as tulip & blue foxglove look on, 6-1/2", trimmed watercolor production background, signed "To...Walt Disney", S/Dec 14/96 (8000-10,000)   35,650

Alice in Wonderland: Expectant Jury seated in Jury Box, 8-1/2", key watercolor production background, CE/Dec 12/96 (4000-6000)   8625

Alice in Wonderland: Alice (7") & Dinah (3") run after White Rabbit, watercolor production background, inscribed "To Jack Sharp, Best Wishes, Walt Disney" on mat, S/Jun 17/94 (4000-6000)   4600

Alice in Wonderland: Full figure of endearing Queen of Hearts standing holding heart scepter, facing right, looking back over right shoulder, 7"; color print background of the royal croquet court, ct, SR/Spring/97 (700-1100)   1180

The Aristocats: Full figures of O'Malley & Duchess talking on street, 3-1/3" & similar, key watercolor production background, CE/Dec 16/94 (6000-8000)   8050

Bambi: Young Bambi meets Flower, 5 x 4-1/4" & 2-1/4 x 4", Studio Art Props background of flower-filled meadow (tempera on background board), F+, HL/Nov 16/97 (3000-4000)   6325

Bambi: Bambi looks into forest, watercolor preparation background, 8-1/2 x 11", CE/Dec 15/93 (2500-3500)   8280

Bambi: Full figures of young Bambi (4") & Thumper (2") meeting in forest clearing, watercolor production background with overlay, CE/Jun 9/95 (10,000-15,000) 21,850

Bambi: Full figures of smiling young Bambi & Thumper standing on ice, complementary painted winter background as prepared by Courvoisier, 7 x 8" overall, HL/Feb 23/97 (3500-4000)   4370

Bambi: Full figures of young Bambi (5-1/4") & Flower (2-1/2") standing facing each other on path as 4 birds watch, gouache display background, rippling, 12-field, ct, SR/Spring/95 (3000-5000)   5100

Bambi: Color model cel of Great Prince (10-1/4 x 7") approaching Bambi (full figure, 6-1/4 x 5-1/4") who's standing with head turned as forest fire nears, pan oil production back-ground, S/Dec 14/96 (15,000-20,000)   10,350

Bambi: Full figures of Thumper laughing as confused Bambi sits on ice, 5-1/4 x 6-1/2" cel image, complementary painted background as prepared by Courvoisier, HL/Oct 6/96 (3000-5000)   4888

Bambi: Full figures of young Bambi (3 x 2") & mother (5 x 4") walking thru forest, production set-up w/watercolor production background, "To Bob Mochrie ... Walt Disney" on mat, S/Dec 19/97 (8000-12,000)   9200

Bambi: Production set-up: full figure of Thumper (2-1/2") eyeing Miss Bunny (3") by hollow log, watercolor production background, signed by Walt Disney on mat, Courvoisier label, S/Jun 21/97 (10,000-12,000)   16,100

Bambi: Full-figure publicity cel of Thumper, 6-3/4", watercolor background from unknown production, CE/Dec 16/94 (4000-6000)   14,950

Bambi: Full figures of happy young Bambi jumping as 5 bunnies sit watching, 4-1/2", Courvoisier watercolor outdoor background & label, some color shift & paint separation, ct, SR/Spring/96 (4000-6000)   4400

Bambi: Full figure of standing Thumper (1-1/2") & young Bambi (dry brush accents, 3-3/4") eyeing each other, original master oil-paint background of forest, prepared by Courvoisier, label, SR/Fall/94 (4000-6000)   6,500

Cinderella: Jaq (3 x 2-1/2") & Gus (2-1/2 x 1-1/2") talk to friends (3 x 3" & smaller), key watercolor production background, mat inscribed "Cinderella", stamped "original WDP" & signed "Walt Disney" by studio artist, CE/Jun 18/94 (8000-12,000) 16,100

Cinderella: Full figures of Fairy Godmother (7") & Cinderella in ball gown (7-1/2"), watercolor production background from same scene, mat signed by Walt Disney, CE/Jun 20/96 (10,000-15,000) 36,800

Cinderella: Story painting by Mary Blair of Cinderella weeping in lap of Fairy Godmother, tempera on paper mounted to board, 8 x 9", HL/Oct 6/96 (1500-2000) 2300

Cinderella: Full figure of startled Lucifer, 8-1/2 x 21-1/2", matching master background (tempera on background sheet), note, HL/Mar 11/95 (3000-4000) 4400

Cinderella: Knees-up of smiling Cinderella facing left, 9", gouache master background of ballroom, inscribed & signed by Walt Disney as gift to President Aleman of Mexico, original mat (general staining), label, restored, SR/Spring/98 (10,000-15,000) did not sell

Cinderella: Inspiration painting by Mary Blair of Cinderella & Prince dancing on balcony, 10 x 12", tempera on paper mounted to board, VF, HL/Nov 16/97 (2000-3000) 7245

Dumbo: Full figures of Dumbo flying with Timothy in his hat (1 1/2") & 5 crows in V-formation (3"), Courvoisier watercolor background & label, ct, SR/Spring/98 (2000-3000)   2480

Dumbo: Full figures of sad Timothy (5/8") & Dumbo (3-3/4") walking to left by circus tent, master watercolor background, originally released by Courvoisier, monogram stamp, SR/Fall/96 (3500-5000)   4430

Dumbo: Full figures of Timothy (1-1/2") standing in front of sad Dumbo (sitting, 5-1/2"), both facing left, Courvoisier watercolor background of circus grounds, stamp & label, SR/Spring/96 (2600-3400)   4060

Dumbo: Happy Dumbo sits in tub, 4-1/2 x 3", airbrush & watercolor Courvoisier background, CE/Jun 18/94 (2500-3500)   7475

Fantasia: Unicorns & fawn over master background, 9-1/2 x 11", watercolor & airbrush on background sheet, mat inscribed & signed by Walt Disney, HL/Nov 13/94 (3000-4000)   4704

Fantasia: Full figures of smiling Sorcerer Mickey pointing to cistern as broom climbs steps, 8 x 9", preliminary background painting (water-color on heavyweight paper), HL/Oct 6/96 (6000-9000)   12,075

Fantasia: Full figures of 2 cupids (3" each) combing hair of lovely centaurette (5 x 5" w/o hair), watercolor production background, S/Dec 14/96 (10,000-15,000) 20,700

Fantasia: Full figure of zebra centaurette carrying jug at head level, 6", plain Courvoisier airbrush background & label, SR/Fall/97 (1800-3000)   1460

Fantasia: Pegasus parents & 3 offspring swim on lake, complementary painted background as prepared by Courvoisier, 9-1/2 x 14" overall, HL/Feb 23/97 (3000-5000)   4830

Fantasia: One of 4 sequential drawings: medium close-up of Chernabog gesturing, 9 x 14" to 9-1/2 x 15", HL/Nov 13/94 (6000-9000)   8064

Fantasia: Frost Fairies, hand-prepared background, 7-1/2 x 7-1/4", CE/Dec 15/93 (3000-3500)   4370

Fantasia: Pegasus family flying, watercolor master background, 10 x 13-1/2", checker Al Woolery's "OK" & signature, date "7-24-1940", Disney copyright stamp, VF, HL/Apr 10/94 (6000-9000)   7280

Fantasia: Mushroom Dance, 2" avg. size, airbrushed Courvoisier background & label, S/Jun 10/95 (2000-3000)   4312

Fantasia: Defiant Sorcerer Mickey, Courvoisier airbrush background, 8-1/2 x 9-1/2", CE/Dec 15/93 (5500-6500)   8970

Fantasia: Full figure of happy Sorcerer Mickey leading bucket-carrying broom to cistern, complementary painted background as prepared by Courvoisier, 6-3/4 x 8-1/2" overall, HL/Feb 23/97 (10,000-12,000)   11,500

Fantasia: Surprised Sorcerer Mickey (5") w/broom (5") climbing steps in background, watercolor production background, partial stamp, mat inscribed "Walt Disney", CE/Jun 9/95 (15,000-20,000)   19,550

The Hunchback of Notre Dame: Frollo talks to Phoebus on parapet w/Notre Dame in background, 12-1/2 x 17", S/Jun 21/97 (2500-3500)   9200

Fantasia: Flirtatious pink Centaurette stands facing right, 7-3/4", paint crack in hair, SR/Spring/95 (800-1200)   1400

Fantasia: Made-up Blue Centaurette holds apple, 6-3/8", ct, SR/Spring/98 (1000-1500)   1240

The Hunchback of Notre Dame: Smiling Esmerelda & Djali peek around corner of stone wall, 12-1/2 x 17", S/Jun 21/97 (2500-3500)   11,500

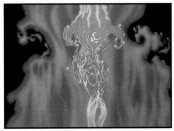

The Hunchback of Notre Dame: 2 set-ups: front view of Esmerelda's apparition in flames; not shown: Frollo clutches chest & recoils; 12-1/2 x 17" each; S/Jun 21/97 (2500-3500)   3450

The Hunchback of Notre Dame: Full-figure side view of little girl standing before Quasimodo on Cathedral steps as Esmerelda, Phoebus, & crowd watch, 12-1/2 x 17", S/Jun 21/97 (3000-4000)   5750

The Hunchback of Notre Dame: Frollo confronts angry Quasimodo, Phoebus, & Esmerelda as 3 soldiers watch, 14-1/2 x 26-1/2", S/Jun 21/97 (2500-3500)   8625

The Hunchback of Notre Dame: Quasimodo holds baby bird in palms of his hands at edge of parapet, 12-1/2 x 17", S/Jun 21/97 (2000-3000)   6900

The Hunchback of Notre Dame: Ground-level view of falling Frollo clutching demonized gargoyle, 15-1/2 x 37-1/2" (2000-3000)   2587

2 dewdrop fairies, Courvoisier airbrushed background, WDP stamp & label, 2" & 1", S/Jun 17/94 (1200-1800) 2185

Madame Upanova in 3rd position holding up cornucopia, airbrushed Courvoisier background, 7", S/Jun 17/94 (1000-1500) 3450

Baby black Pegasus lands in water among 4 siblings, airbrushed Courvoisier background & label, avg. size 2", S/Jun 17/94 (2500-3500) 2875

Milkweed Ballet performing *Waltz of the Flowers*, airbrushed background, Courvoisier label, WDP copyright stamp, avg. size 1", S/Jun 17/94 (1500-2000) 2875

Sorcerer Mickey (3") leads bucket-laden broom (4"), airbrushed Courvoisier background & label, S/Jun 17/94 (8000-10,000) 13,800

Chinese Mushrooms, 2-3/4 x 1-3/4" and smaller, airbrush Courvoisier background, CE/Jun 18/94 (2000-3000) 2185

Mother Pegasus (4 x 8-3/4") & baby (1-3/4 x 1-1/2") in nest, watercolor & airbrush Courvoisier background, CE/Jun 18/94 (2000-3000) 2760

Chinese Mushrooms, Courvoisier multiplane painting, Courvoisier label on back, paint on glass, CE/Jun 18/94 (1000-1500) 920

Milkweed Ballet, 1", Courvoisier label & airbrush background, CE/Jun 18/94 (800-1200) 1725

3 Cupids watching from tree, 3" & smaller, Courvoisier label & airbrush background, WDP stamp, CE/Jun 18/94 (2000-2500) 1725

Blue baby Pegasus, 3-1/2 x 3", Courvoisier airbrush background, CE/Jun 18/94 (1500-2000) 1265

Determined Sorcerer Mickey ready to cast spell, 7-1/4 x 4-1/2", hand-prepared background, CE/Jun 18/94 (8000-12,000) 10,350

Chinese Mushroom dancers, complementary Courvoisier airbrush background & label, stamped "WDP", 6 x 7", HL/Aug 21/94 (2500-3500) 2240

Full figure of determined Sorcerer Mickey facing left in spell-casting pose, 7-1/2", watercolor display background, paint restoration, SR/Fall/94 (6000-10,000) 9000

Unicorns & fawn over master background, 9-1/2 x 11", watercolor & airbrush on background sheet, mat inscribed & signed by Walt Disney, HL/Nov 13/94 (3000-4000) 4704

Full figure of Autumn Fairy, 4-1/2", Courvoisier airbrush background & label, CE/Dec 16/94 (1500-2000) 1725

Elephant blows bubble with fish inside, 5", Courvoisier background, CE/Dec 16/94 (1200-1500) 1380

Full figure of baby Black Pegasus flying, 2-1/4", Courvoisier airbrush background, CE/Dec 16/94 (600-800) 978

Mother Pegasus (4 x 9") looks lovingly down at Baby Black Pegasus (2") who has head buried in nest, airbrushed Courvoisier background & label, S/Dec 17/94 (2000-3000) 3162

Sorcerer Mickey (2-1/2") happily leads broom (near-full figure, 3"), airbrushed Courvoisier background, WDP stamp, S/Dec 17/94 (5000-7000) 6612

Elephant ballerina happily dances, airbrushed Courvoisier background, 5", S/Dec 17/94 (700-900) 1610

Mother Pegasus soars over water, 5" with 10" wingspan, airbrushed Courvoisier background, WDP stamp, S/Dec 17/94 (2000-3000) 2070

Front view of smiling Baby Black Pegasus standing in water with head up & eyes closed, 2-1/2", Courvoisier watercolor background, mat, stamp & label, SR/Spring/95 (1600-2200) 1740

Sorcerer Mickey (3") leads broom w/full buckets (5"), Courvoisier airbrush & watercolor background, CE/Jun 9/95 (8000-10,000) 10,925

Full figures of Bacchus (2") riding Jacchus (1/2"), w/2 attending Centaurettes (1/2") & 4 Cupids holding canopy, Courvoisier airbrush & watercolor background, CE/Jun 9/95 (2000-3000) 3450

Pegasus family swimming, 6", Courvoisier airbrush background, CE/Jun 9/95 (2000-3000) 2760

Full figures of sleeping Hyacinth Hippo on couch (5") & menacing Ben Ali Gator (3"), Courvoisier airbrush background, CE/Jun 9/95 (3500-4500) 5520

Publicity cel: smiling Sorcerer Mickey on pedestal amid stars & comets, 6", presentation

background, CE/Jun 9/95 (4000-6000) 4830

Mlle. Upanova doing splits (9" long) as Elephant (4-1/4") looks thru curtain, Courvoisier airbrush background, CE/Jun 9/95 (2500-3500) 3220

Surprised Sorcerer Mickey (5") w/broom (5") climbing steps in background, watercolor production background, partial stamp, mat inscribed "Walt Disney", CE/Jun 9/95 (15,000-20,000) 19,550

Mushroom Dance, 2" avg. size, airbrushed Courvoisier background & label, S/Jun 10/95 (2000-3000) 4312

4 milkweed ballerinas, 8-1/2 x 9-1/2", complementary painted background as prepared by Courvoisier, HL/Aug 6/95 (1800-2200) 2128

Set of cels of Autumn Fairy & *Blossom Ballet* flowers over complementary painted background as prepared by Courvoisier, 9 x 18", HL/Nov 19/95 (2400-3000) 2530

Autumn Fairy (2-3/4") & falling leaves, two cel levels, Courvoisier watercolor background of plants w/airbrushing & special effects, original label, SR/Spring/96 (2200-3200) 1500

Full-figure rear view of baby blue Pegasus sitting on tree branch, 3-1/2", Courvoisier watercolor background & label, ct, SR/Spring/96 (1600-2400) 1760

Hyacinth Hippo reclined with mouth open, 8-3/4 x 6"; Courvoisier watercolor background of pillow-strewn lounge, stamp & label; some discolored & lifting paint, SR/Spring/96 (1400-2000) 1400

Publicity cel & background (tempera on heavyweight paper) of Sorcerer Mickey water-carrying broom down steps, for 1960s re-release, 7 x 10", HL/Apr 28/96 (700-1000) 3910

2 frost fairies, complementary color print background, 4-1/2 x 5", HL/Apr 28/96 (2500-3500) 2760

Pegasus family swimming on lake, complementary Courvoisier airbrush background, 6-1/2 x 8-1/2", HL/Apr 28/96 (3500-4500) 3795

4 dewdrop fairies w/wings outspread fly above 6 flower blossoms floating on water, elaborate complementary Courvoisier airbrush background, 12-1/2 x 10-1/2", HL/Apr 28/96 (2500-3000) 3910

Full figure of baby black Pegasus flying among clouds, silk-screened on glass in box frame to simulate multiplane camera technique, by Courvoisier, 8 x 8-1/2 x 1-1/2", HL/Mar 16-17/96 (400-600) 1093

Full figures of mushrooms dancing in circle; airbrushed Courvoisier background; inscribed "To ... Walt Disney"; 1-1/2", 2" & 3", S/Jun 19/96 (2500-3500) 4025

Full figures of 4 milk blossoms dancing, airbrushed background of pine branch, Courvoisier label, 9-1/2 x 10-1/2", S/Jun 19/96 (1500-2000) 1840

Nutcracker Suite's Blossom & Autumn Fairies, Courvoisier watercolor & airbrush background of floating blossoms, 2" ea., CE/Jun 20/96 (2500-3000) 2300

Full figure of cautious apprentice Mickey carrying two buckets of water, Courvoisier airbrush background, 5", CE/Jun 20/96 14, 950

Full figures of 5 dewdrop fairies (approx. 1-3/4") flitting across surface of stream, airbrush effects, blossoms float downstream in ripples, tree fronds, watercolor Courvoisier background, monogram stamp, SR/Fall/96 (2500-3000) 3850

Publicity set-up: full figure of Sorcerer Mickey standing in classic pose with comet running overhead between hands, 12-3/4", two effects levels, background precipice in gouache & airbrush on third cel level, SR/Fall/96 (2000-4000) 2250

3 cupids on tree branch conversing, 8 x 8", Courvoisier background, HL/Oct 6/96 (2000-3000) 1955

Rite of Spring: head of hungry dinosaur over water hole w/lighting effect on overlay cel, 3-3/4 x 7" cel image, complementary non-Studio background, HL/Oct 6/96 (900-1200) 1093

Full figures of smiling Sorcerer Mickey pointing to cistern as broom climbs steps, 8 x 9", preliminary background painting (watercolor on heavyweight paper), HL/Oct 6/96 (6000-9000) 12,075

Full figures of 3 cupids playing pipes [toward ground], 4-1/2 x 7-1/2" cel image, complementary painted sky background, HL/Oct 6/96 (2000-2500) 1955

Full figure of blue baby Pegasus looking down while fly-

ing, 3", Courvoisier airbrush background & label, CE/Dec 12/96 (1000-1500) 1035

Blue unicorn (3-1/4"), pink unicorn & faun (3-1/2") frolic in field, Courvoisier watercolor & airbrush background and label, CE/Dec 12/96 (1500-2000) 1265

Full figures of 3 flying cupids playing their pipes downward, 7-1/2" long, Courvoisier airbrush background of sky & label, CE/Dec 12/96 (1500-2000) 1725

Full figures of yellow and blue baby pegasi cavorting, 3" each, Courvoisier airbrush background & label, CE/Dec 12/96 (1500-2000) 1495

Full figure of Snowflake Fairy amid leaves, 5", Courvoisier airbrush background & label, CE/Dec 12/96 (1500-2000) 1955

Full figure of sad centaurette Melinda sitting under tree, 3-3/4", Courvoisier airbrush & watercolor background & label, CE/Dec 12/96 (1500-2000) 1840

Full figures of dancing mushrooms, 4" & smaller, airbrushed Courvoisier background, CE/Dec 12/96 (3000-4000) 3220

Pegasus family swimming together, parents 2 x 4", airbrushed Courvoisier background of lake & trees, with label, S/Dec 14/96 (2500-3500) 3450

Full figure of stern Sorcerer Mickey standing looking left w/arms folded across chest, 7", airbrushed Courvoisier background w/corner of table & chair, S/Dec 14/96 (8000-10,000) 10,925

Full figures of stern Sorcerer Mickey (7") staring at broom (6") standing upright in corner, airbrushed Courvoisier background, S/Dec 14/96 (8000-10,000) 12,650

Large-image ballet chorus line of hippos, 7-1/2" each, airbrushed Courvoisier background & label, S/Dec 14/96 (4000-6000) 4025

Full figures of pink (2 x 2") & blue (3 x 4") baby Pegasi flying over foliage, airbrushed Courvoisier background & label, S/Dec 14/96 (1000-1500) 1150

Circa 1940s publicity cel: full figures of Sorcerer Mickey (5") directing broom (4-3/4") carrying 2 buckets of water down steps, preliminary production background, S/Dec 14/96 (6000-8000) 7475

Full figures of 2 cupids (3" each) combing hair of lovely centaurette (5 x 5" w/o hair), watercolor production background, S/Dec 14/96 (10,000-15,000) 20,700

Full figures of smiling Sorcerer Mickey (5") leading broom (4-1/2") carrying 2 buckets of water at bottom of steps, watercolor production background, S/Dec 14/96 (10,000-15,000) 27,600

Full figure of Frost Fairy poised over flower amid blue & white sparkles, complementary airbrush background as prepared by Courvoisier, 7-1/4 x 9-1/4", HL/Feb 23/97 (2400-2800) 2415

Full figure of young pink pegasus struggling to fly in storm, complementary painted background as prepared by Courvoisier, 4-3/4 x 6" overall, HL/Feb 23/97 (1200-1600) 1035

Full figure of happy Sorcerer Mickey leading bucket-carrying broom to cistern, complementary painted background as prepared by Courvoisier, 6-3/4 x 8-1/2" overall, HL/Feb 23/97 (10,000-12,000) 11,500

Pegasus parents & 3 offspring swim on lake, complementary painted background as prepared by Courvoisier, 9-1/2 x 14" overall, HL/Feb 23/97 (3000-5000) 4830

Full figures of 2 frost fairies (3-1/4" & 3-3/8") flashing across ice, single level with detailed dry brush & ink effects, key matching watercolor background, SR/Spring/97 (3000-6000) 4400

Full figure of Mother & Father Pegasus in flight, complementary airbrush background as prepared by Courvoisier, 5-1/2 x 5-1/2" overall, HL/May 3/97 (2500-3500) 2185

Close-up of Bacchus holding inverted goblet over Jacchus' tongue, complementary airbrush background, signed by Ward Kimball, 6 x 4-1/2" overall inc. signature, HL/May 3/97 (2500-3500) 1725

Full-figure front view of Madame Upanova, portion of master background (watercolor on background sheet), 10 x 6" overall, HL/May 3/97 (3000-4000) 2185

Unicorns & fauns frolic in field, watercolor production background, mat signed by Walt Disney, Courvoisier label; side view of black pegasus flying, Courvoisier airbrush background & label, CLA/Jun 7/97 (5000-7000) 8625

Centaurette Melinda 4", Courvoisier airbrush background & label, CLA/Jun 7/97 (800-1200) 978

Full figure of *Nutcracker Suite* Frost Fairy (1-1/2") skating design in ice, airbrushed Courvoisier background, S/Jun 21/97 (1500-2000) 1955

Full figures of 3 *Night on Bald Mt.* flame dancers (each 2-1/2") w/demons cavorting behind them, airbrushed Courvoisier background, S/Jun 21/97 (1800-2200) 2587

Full figures of black Father Pegasus (3" w/3-1/2" wingspan) hovering over 5 flying foals (approx. 1" each), airbrushed Courvoisier background of sea & sky, S/Jun 21/97 (2000-3000) 6900

Side view of *Ave Maria* candlelight procession thru bare hills at sunrise, sight 7-1/2 x 9", airbrushed Courvoisier background & label, S/Jun 21/97 (1800-2200) 1725

Hatless Sorcerer Mickey looking back & up as he carries buckets of water, 6", round airbrushed Courvoisier background & label, S/Jun 21/97 (7000-9000) 8050

5 blue demons dance (4 full figure), full image 11-1/2 x 5", 12-field cel, master title background of flames from *The Secrets of Life*, 1956, SR/Fall/97 (900-1500) 1090

Full figure of zebra centaurette carrying jug at head level, 6", plain Courvoisier airbrush background & label, SR/Fall/97 (1800-3000) 1460

Full figure of sad centaurette Melinda sitting under tree, 4 x 4-1/4", complementary painted background & label as prepared by Courvoisier, F+, HL/Nov 16/97 (1800-2200) 1725

Large-field cel of milkweed blossoms, 9 x 14-1/4", tan-colored background, stamp & label as prepared by Courvoisier, VF, HL/Nov 16/97 (1800-2400) 1955

Full figures of dancing mushrooms, 3 x 6", painted background of naturalistic setting with flowers suggesting Chinese lanterns overhead, Courvoisier label, F, HL/Nov 16/97 (2000-2500) 2300

Full figures of 3 cupids blowing horns in unison, 4 x 7-1/2", complementary painted background of sky, as prepared by Courvoisier, VF, HL/Nov 16/97 (1800-2400) 2300

Full figure of Sorcerer Mickey standing in cloud w/sky & stars behind him gesturing to left, 7.14", studio airbrush background, CE/Dec 18/97 (12,000-15,000) 12,650

Full figure of determined Sorcerer Mickey on flat mountaintop rearing back to cast spell to right, The Disney Channel 1983, 6", studio production background, CE/Dec 18/97 (1500-2000) 2070

Full figures of two Dewdrop Fairies (2" each) fluttering amid flowing blossoms, airbrushed Courvoisier background & label, WDP stamp, S/Dec 19/97 (1000-1500) 1035

Baby black Pegasus stands proudly in nest, 3", airbrushed Courvoisier background & label, WDP stamp, S/Dec 19/97 (1200-1800) 1150

Full-figure front view of Nubian zebra centaurette carrying carafe at head level w/both hands, 6-1/2", airbrushed Courvoisier background & label, WDP stamp, S/Dec 19/97 (1200-1800) 1495

Mother Pegasus places wing over black fowl in nest, 4 x 8-1/2" overall, airbrushed background, S/Dec 19/97 (1500-2500) 2875

Full figures of Chinese mushroom dancers, 3", styled Courvoisier watercolor airbrush background, ct, SR/Spring/98 (2000-3000) 2550

Full figures of Pegasus babies flying in arc in watercolor sky, each approx. 1-3/4", Courvoisier label, SR/Spring/98 (1200-1800) 2910

Full-figure front view of Yen Sid coolly standing holding broom, looking down & to right, 8-3/4", watercolor display background, ct, SR/Spring/98 (5000-9000) 8100

Full figure of hatless Sorcerer Mickey turning to right in surprise to see broom carrying two buckets away from him, both 3-3/4", custom watercolor display background, SR/Spring/98 (9000-15,000) 8000

Full-figure rear view of Autumn Fairy (2-3/4") amid leaves, added wings, Courvoisier background w/airbrushing & special effects, original label, SR/Spring/98 (1800-2400) 1820

Full-figure front view of Mlle. Upanova standing looking down, portion of master background (watercolor on background sheet), WDP stamps, 10 x 6" overall, F, HL/Apr 25/98 (1500-2500) 2070

CELS – FULL FIGURE (also see MODEL ART)

Happy Sorcerer Mickey prancing to left, WDP seal, unknown production, circa 1970s, 10-1/2 x 13-1/2", CE/Dec 15/93 (2000-2500) 2300

Centaur & Centaurette carry containers of grapes, 8 x 11", CE/Dec 15/93 (1300-1500) 1380

Pastoral: limited-edition cel of Melinda, Brudus & 3 cupids, #48/275, 9 x 11", Disney seal, VF+, HL/Apr 10/94 (400-600) 616

Nutcracker Suite: Thistle Boys, 6-1/2 x 10", G, HL/Apr 10/94 (800-1200) 672

Smiling Mickey Mouse as Sorcerer's Apprentice, 1950s publicity cel, 5-1/2", sight 10" diameter, CE/Jun 18/94 (3000-4000) 2990

Full-figure front-view of two hippo ballerinas on tiptoes carrying mirror, 6-3/4 x 6-1/2", 12-field, paint restoration, SR/Fall/94 (1200-1800) 2470

Golden-haired centaurette facing right, 4 x 3", HL/Nov 13/94 (1200-1800) 1008

Apollo drives chariot across sun, 6", CE/Dec 16/94 (2000-2500) 2300

2 fairies, 3" & smaller, CE/Dec 16/94 (800-1200) 920

Blue centaurette poses with eyes closed, 8-1/2" high, 7" tail, S/Dec 17/94 (1000-1500) 1495

Blonde centaurette sits demurely with eyes closed, 4-1/2" x 4-1/2", S/Dec 17/94 (800-1200) 977

Flirtatious pink Centaurette stands facing right, 7-3/4", paint crack in hair, SR/Spring/95 (800-1200) 1400

Centaur couples dancing, 7-1/2 x 12", VF, HL/Apr 23/95 (2200-2800) 2128

6 limited-edition cels of scenes from *Dance of the Hours*, *Pastoral Symphony*, *Night on Bald Mountain*, *The Sorcerer's Apprentice*, #35/275, 5-1/2 x 8-1/2" to 10-1/2 x 14", VF+, HL/Nov 19/95 (3000-5000) 4370

2 promenading centaurettes, 5-1/2 x 7", VG, HL/Nov 19/95 (2000-2500) 1725

Pink baby Pegasus, 2-1/2 x 2-1/2", HL/Apr 28/96 (1200-1600) 1725

Little blue unicorn looking to his right, 2-3/4 x 2", HL/Apr 28/96 (1200-1600) 1150

3 cels from DAE: Sorcerer Mickey & broom, Melinda & Brudus with 3 cupids, Bacchus & Jacchus with faun #163/275, 6 x 9", 8-1/2 x 11", 8 x 6", VF+, HL/Apr 28/96 (1200-1600) 1840

2 hippo ballerinas dancing toward camera carrying mirror, 4" & 5", S/Jun 19/96 (2000-3000) 6325

Front view of stern Yen Sid holding broom & glancing to right, 9", CE/Jun 20/96 (5000-7000) 7820

Panicked Sorcerer Mickey (7") running amid water-carrying brooms, illustration book cel, 2 full cels, CE/Jun 20/96 (5000-7000) 12,650

2 baby Pegasi facing each other, 3" each, CE/Jun 20/96 (1500-2000) 1150

3 full-figure hand-inked & -painted limited-edition cels from DAE: Ben Ali Gator & Hyacinth Hippo dance, Bacchus rides Jacchus as faun watches, centaurs Brudus & Melinda meet as 3 cupids watch; each #189/275; 6 x 9", 8-1/2 x 11-1/2", 7 x 10-1/2", HL/Oct 6/96 (1200-1600) 1150

Apollo driving flaming chariot across sky amid clouds, 3 x 5", applied to black paper, S/Dec 14/96 (2000-3000) 1495

Black centaurette Sunflower polishing hoof of platinum-blonde centaurette (partial figure) [from deleted scene], 7 x 8", HL/May 3/97 (3000-3500) 2760

Demure Hyacinth Hippo & smiling Ben Ali Gator dancing, limited edition #193/275, 7-1/4 x 10-1/2", HL/May 31/97 (500-700) 374

Sorcerer Mickey stepping to left, arms up, looking up, 7-1/2", CE/Dec 18/97 (10,000-15,000) 11,500

Two Centaurettes carry baskets of grapes as they circle with right hands raised together, 6-3/4", ct, some rippling, SR/Spring/98 (1100-1500) 1210

Faun plays pipes & dances to left, 4", ct, SR/Spring/98 (200-400) 220

Made-up Blue Centaurette holds apple, 6-3/8", ct, SR/Spring/98 (1000-1500) 1240

Front view of centaurette, centaur & 3 fauns sleeping together; gouache & oil on celluloid; minor restoration; 3 x 7-1/4"; VF; HL/Apr 25/98 (800-1200) 1380

Front view of surprised Sorcerer Mickey in mid

gesture, restored, 2-1/4 x 2", VF, HL/Apr 25/98 (3000-4000) 4370

CELS – PARTIAL FIGURE (also see MODEL ART)

Mother Pegasus (4") noses cherry blossoms as smiling foal (1-1/4") pops head up, WDP stamp, Courvoisier label, S/Jun 17/94 (2000-3000) 2300

Sorcerer Mickey (facing left) points upward w/right hand, 1-3/4 x 2-1/4", VF, HL/Apr 23/95 (2500-3500) 3136

Chest-up portrait of lovely palomino Centaurette looking left & up, 5-1/2", 12-field, SR/Fall/95 (900-1400) 900

Sorcerer Mickey (facing left) points upward with right hand, 1-3/4 x 2-1/4", F, HL/Nov 19/95 (2500-3500) 3910

Near-full-figure three-quarter rear view of broom carrying 2 buckets of water, 4", CE/Jun 20/96 (2000-3000) 3680

Matching original set: colored model drawing and cel of eager Zeus (waist-up) leaning forward and looking down, 5 x 9-1/2", VF, HL/Nov 16/97 (1800-2200) 2070

Waist-up profile of hatless Sorcerer facing right, looking down, right hand on point of hat, 4-1/4", CE/Dec 18/97 (3000-5000) 3220

CONCEPT AND INSPIRATIONAL ART

Mushroom dancers, inspirational sketch, pastel on black paper, 10 x 12", CE/Dec 15/93 (800-1200) 1725

Yellow thistle men, inspirational sketch, pastel on black paper, 10 x 12", CE/Dec 15/93 (800-1200) 1380

Mushroom scene, inspirational sketch, pastel on black paper, 9-1/4 x 12", CE/Dec 15/93 (800-1200) 977

Pilgrims walk thru field, inspirational sketch, pastel on paper, 10 x 12-1/4", CE/Dec 15/93 (800-1000) 862

Blossoms dancing on water, 7 inspirational sketches, pastel on black paper, 8 x 10" & similar, CE/Dec 15/93 (5000-6500) 4025

Mushrooms look up, inspirational sketch, 7-3/4 x 10-1/4", CE/Dec 15/93 (400-600) 690

Hyacinth Hippo tiptoes, inspirational sketch, watercolor on paper, 11 x 8-3/4", CE/Dec 15/93 (500-700) 402

Pegasus family flying, inspirational sketch, pastel on paper, 5-1/2 x 7", CE/Dec 15/93 (800-1200) 862

Sketch of candlelight procession thru cathedral arches, white pastel on black paper, Concert Feature stamp & production info on verso, 5-1/2 x 7", S/Dec 16/93 (1000-1500) 1150

Atmospheric sketch of town besieged by demons; pen, pencil & pastel on black paper; production notes along bottom margin; Concert Feature label marked "Seq. No. 11.0" "Artist Bill Wallett" "Date 10-26-39"; S/Dec 16/93 (3000-5000) 3450

4 pastels from *Blossom Ballet*: 3 of Thistle Boys dancing; one close-up of thistle in explosion of color, each pastel on black paper, S/Dec 16/93 (1800-2200) 4313

Concept sketch of dancing ostriches, stamped WDP, Courvoisier label, 6" length, S/Dec 16/93 (400-600) 920

4 concepts from *Blossom Ballet*: 2 of Thistle Boys; one of single Thistle; one of row of Orchid Girls dancing before row of Thistle Boys; all pastel on black paper, S/Dec 16/93 (1800-2200) 5463

4 concept drawings: 3 of Ben Al E. Gator & Hyacinth Hippo; Ben creeping down fountain; each w/Concert Feature stamp & production notes on verso, S/Dec 16/93 (1800-2200) 2300

Concept of spectral green female floating above orange flames, pastel on black paper, S/Dec 16/93 (800-1200) 920

2 pastels of candlelight procession thru forest, pastel on paper, S/Dec 16/93 (600-800) 1150

Nutcracker Suite: Blossom Ballet dancers emerging from darkness, pastel on black animation sheet, 8 x 10-1/2", VF, HL/Apr 10/94 (700-900) 672

Ostrich ballerina character study, 7 x 4; Concert Feature, Disney monogram & copyright stamps, F+, HL/Apr 10/94 (400-600) 560

2 concepts: laughing hippo, watercolor on paper, 7"; 3 baby Pegasi & unicorn foal, ink & pastel on paper, approx. 4" each, S/Jun 17/94

(600-800) 690

5 colorful concept pastels on black paper from
Blossom Ballet, S/Jun 17/94 (2000-3000) 2185

Concept sketch of Centaur wooing reluctant Centaurette, 4" each, S/Jun 17/94
(800-1000) 920

Concept sketch of dancing ostriches, stamped
WDP, Courvoisier label, 6" length,
S/Jun 17/94 (400-600) 920

3 concept drawings for Dance of the Hours,
S/Jun 17/94 (1200-1800) 1955

5 pastel concepts from Blossom Ballet, all pastel
on black paper, S/Jun 17/94 (2000-3000) 3450

Full-figure watercolor concept painting of Madame
Upanova (11-1/2"), watercolor on construction
paper applied to paper; watercolor concept of 3
high-kicking ostriches (7-1/2"), watercolor on
paper; both with Concert Feature stamp,
S/Jun 17/94 (600-800) 575

Ave Maria inspirational sketch, pastel on black
paper, CE/Jun 18/94 (700-900) 690

Elephanchine, inspirational sketch by Preston Blair,
10-1/4 x 7-1/4", ink & color pencil over
graphite, studio stamp & notes, CE/Jun 18/94
(500-700) 978

Chinese Mushrooms inspirational sketch, 4 x
2-1/4" & smaller, pastel on black paper,
CE/Jun 18/94 (800-1200) 2070

Night on Bald Mountain inspirational drawing,
pastel on black paper, CE/Jun 18/94
(3000-4000) 2760

Pastoral Symphony color sketch by Claude Coats,
identification stamped & numbered, notes,
watercolor on paper, CE/Jun 18/94
(800-1200) 1610

Russian Dance inspirational sketch, pastel on
black paper, CE/Jun 18/94 (800-1200) 748

2 fauns (4-3/4 x 3-1/2" & smaller) & a centaurette
(7-1/2 x 7-1/2") run together, concept drawing,
color pastel on paper, stamps, numbered "243",
CE/Jun 18/94 (2000-3000) 748

3 inspirational sketches from The Nutcracker Suite,
pastel on paper, CE/Jun 18/94 (800-1200) 1495

Hippopotamus inspirational sketch, 5-1/2 x 4" &
smaller, stamps & notes, CE/Jun 18/94
(400-600) 403

Drawing of 6 thistle Cossack dancers, colored
pastel on black animation sheet, 8 x
10-1/2", HL/Aug 21/94 (1800-2200) 1680

Concept sketch of flowers falling into stream, pastel
on black paper, Courvoisier stamp, 10-3/4 x
8-1/8", SR/Fall/94 (900-1400) 2040

Impressionistic painting of Vulcan at his anvil,
18 x 19", tempera & pastel on board,
HL/Nov 13/94 (900-1200) 2128

3 inspirational sketches for The Arab Dance, pastel
on black paper, CE/Dec 16/94 (800-1200) 1035

4 inspirational sketches for Dance of the
Reed Flutes, pastel on black paper,
CE/Dec 16/94 (1500-2000) 1150

4 inspirational sketches of Chinese Mushrooms,
pastel on black paper, CE/Dec 16/94
(1200-1500) 2185

8 inspirational sketches for the Russian Dance,
pastel on black paper, CE/Dec 16/94
(800-1200) 4600

Night on Bald Mountain inspirational sketch,
CE/Dec 16/94 (800-1200) 690

3 inspirational sketches of Chinese Mushrooms,
pastel on black paper, CE/Dec 16/94
(1000-1500) 2530

Russian Dance inspirational sketch, pastel on
brown paper, CE/Dec 16/94 (800-1200) 978

5 inspirational watercolor sketches for Ave Maria,
CE/Dec 16/94 (1000-1500) 575

2 inspirational sketches for Dance of the Reed
Flutes, pastel on black paper,
CE/Dec 16/94 (600-800) 1035

6 inspirational sketches of Chinese Mushrooms,
pastel on black paper, CE/Dec 16/94
(1000-1500) 4600

Pastel of stained glass window in different hues of
purple as viewed from below from Ave Maria,
pastel on black paper, Concert Feature stamp,
8 x 10-1/2", S/Dec 17/94 (500-700) 632

Concept painting from The Nutcracker Suite:
royal frog (3") sitting on lily pad as subject
(2") bows, watercolor & gouache on paper,
S/Dec 17/94 (2500-3500) 2875

5 pastel concept drawings from The Nutcracker Suite:
two drawings of 5 pink blossoms swirling around
white blossom; 3 rows of blossoms; row of
dancing blue orchid girls; 2 pink orchid girls
dancing in front of row of thistle boys; all pastel
on black paper, S/Dec 17/94 (2000-3000) 2587

Concept sketch of Morpheus, 7-1/2" overall, pastel
on blue paper, "Property of Walt Disney Productions" stamp, S/Dec 17/94
(800-1200) 1725

Concept drawing of Bacchus, 8" overall, pastel
on black paper, S/Dec 17/94 (700-900) 1150

Concept drawing of 9 yellow-capped mushrooms
from The Nutcracker Suite, pastel on black
paper, 1 to 2", S/Dec 17/94 (800-1200) 920

Concept painting of Mother Pegasus (6-1/2")
lifting Baby (4") out of cherry blossoms by
tail, graphite & watercolor on heavy paper, "Property of Walt Disney Productions"
stamp, S/Dec 17/94 (800-1200) 1725

Concept sketch of Bacchus & Jacchus frolicking
happily in spilled wine, each 4", graphite &
watercolor on heavy paper, "Property of Walt Disney Productions" stamp, S/Dec 17/94
(700-900) 1380

3 concept drawings of swirling, floating, & dancing
blossoms from The Nutcracker Suite, pastel
on black paper, S/Dec 17/94 (1500-2000) 1150

Concept painting: Mlle. Upanova stands in 3rd
position, ink & watercolor on heavy paper,
8", WDP stamp, S/Dec 17/94 (700-900) 920

Concept painting of alluring goldfish from The
Arabian Dance, 7-1/2", graphite & watercolor on heavy
paper, "Property of Walt Disney Productions"
stamp, S/Dec 17/94 (700-900) 1725

4 inspirational drawings from The Dance of the
Hours: elephant in tutu; row of ostriches in
tutus performing the can-can; 2 of Hyacinth
Hippo & Ben Al E. Gator dancing; first ink
& graphite on paper by Preston Blair, others
graphite & colored pencil on paper by
James Bodrero, S/Dec 17/94 (1200-1800) 3162

Pastel concept of stained glass window with candlelight
below from Ave Maria, 8", pastel on black paper
mounted on illustration board, Concert Feature
stamp, S/Dec 17/94 (800-1200) 805

Concept painting of 3 cherubs playing in clouds,
2-1/2" to 3", graphite & watercolor on
heavy paper, "Property of Walt Disney Productions" stamp, S/Dec 17/94 (700-900) 805

Inspirational sketch of Rite of Spring dinosaurs, 3
to 7", pastel on green paper, S/Dec 17/94
(600-800) 805

Concept painting of Baby Pegasus triumphantly
flying into air, 5", watercolor on heavy paper,
"Property of Walt Disney Productions"
stamp, S/Dec 17/94 (700-900) 1610

Concept drawing of Baby Pegasus (3") looking
happily out of nest with mother (4 x 5")
lying contentedly next to him, WDP stamp,
S/Dec 17/94 (400-600) 805

Watercolor concept sketch by M. Ahrens of Madame
Upanova on her toes, 8-5/8 x 11-3/4",
SR/Spring/95 (400-800) 680

Watercolor concept painting for Pastoral of sunlight
streaming thru trees, 26-1/8 x 10-3/4", cut
in half & rejoined, SR/Spring/95
(1800-3000) 1710

Watercolor concept sketch: chorus line of 3 high-
kicking ostriches, 8-7/8", 12-field sheet, Courvoisier & studio stamps, SR/Spring/95
(500-900) 720

Concept painting: close-up of 4 sleepy baby unicorns
in nest, watercolor on 11-1/2 x 9-1/2" board,
SR/Spring/95 (2500-4000) 4620

Drawing of 3 Appatasauri from Rite of Spring, 7 x 9",
pastel on green paper, HL/Apr 23/95 (1000-
1500) 1008

The Russian Dance: inspirational sketch, pastel
on brown paper, CE/Jun 9/95 (500-700) 748

Inspirational sketch of Ben Ali Gator in tutu, 5",
watercolor on paper, CE/Jun 9/95 (400-600) 345

2 inspirational sketches of The Russian Dance, pastel
on brown paper, CE/Jun 9/95 (500-700) 1093

3 drawings of swirling blossoms from Nutcracker
Suite, pastel on black paper, S/Jun 10/95
(1000-1500) 1495

Atmospheric concept sketch of demons dancing
in dark caverns, graphite & white paint on

paper, S/Jun 10/95 (600-800) 1380

4 concept drawings: Baby Pegasus landing in water;
Baby Pegasus sitting on tree branch; 6 apprecia-
tive centaurs standing in row; centaur tipping
hat to centaurette; S/Jun 10/95 (800-1200) 690

3 early inspirational drawings for Chinese Dance;
7-1/2 x 9-1/2", 6-1/2 x 17", 8 x 14";
HL/Nov 19/95 (900-1200) 748

4 concept sketches [for Ave Maria?]; 5 x 7", 5-1/2
x 7"; pastel on paper, HL/Nov 19/95 (600-
800) 1265

Study of violin-playing bugs on toadstools plus
sketches of bug horn player; 7 x 9-1/2"
& 8-1/2 x 8-1/2"; pencil, ink, watercolor
& conté crayon on paper & animation
sheet, HL/Nov 19/95 (800-1200) 1150

21 pieces for Rite of Spring & The Nutcracker
Suite focusing on special-effects work: drawings,
3 renderings of Earth in volcanic period, 3
"Process Lab Model Cels" & 2 photostats of
live-action footage of volcanic activity; 3 x 4"
to 11 x 14", HL/Nov 19/95 (1200-1600) 1380

Concept pastel of "Nutcracker Suite" snowflake
fairies, 10-1/2 x 7 3/4", 12-field sheet,
Concert Feature stamp, SR/Spring/96
(1000-1600) 1210

Concept painting by Kay Nielson of Chernabog amid
flames & miniature dancing demons, pastel on
black paper, 7 x 5-1/2", 12-field sheet,
SR/Spring/96 (3000-5000) 3000

Centaurette caught in rising storm, concept pastel on
black 14 x 4-1/4" paper, SR/Spring/96 (1600-
2600) 1940

Watercolor concept painting of autumn leaves for
"Waltz of the Flowers," 10-1/2 x 7-3/4" on 12-
field sheet of watercolor paper, Concert Feature
stamp, SR/Spring/96 (1400-2200) 2270

Concept of fairy looping threads of dew, 9-7/8 x
7-3/8" pastel on 12-3/4 x 8-3/4" black
punched paper, SR/Spring/96
(1200-1800) 2160

2 concept drawings: orchid girl & whirling Russian
dancers, pastel on black animation sheets,
8 x 10-1/2", HL/Apr 28/96 (900-1200) 978

2 concept drawings: water bubbles rise past leafy
forms, greenish specks; both for Nutcracker
Suite effects; pastel on black animation sheets;
8 x 10-1/2", HL/Apr 28/96 (300-500) 748

4 sheets of study sketches for Dance of the Hours, 6
x 6" to 9 x 12", HL/Apr 28/96 (800-1200) 633

4 Ave Maria concept pastels: 2 matted together
of light shining down thru forest; procession
of lights; figure lighting candle in church;
S/Jun 19/96 (1000-1500) 1092

14 pastel abstract concepts from Toccata &
Fugue in D Minor, 3 on construction
paper, 11 on 8-1/2 x 8-1/2" storyboard
paper, S/Jun 19/96 (1000-1500) 1092

Night on Bald Mountain atmospheric concept piece
of shadows falling over town by Bill Wallett, colored pastel on black paper, S/Jun 19/96 (800-
1200) 1150

Moody inspirational piece of Bald Mountain
transforming from place of demons to place
of goodness, pastel on black paper,
S/Jun 19/96 (1500-2500) 1495

2 concept pencil sketches by Kay Nielson: 3 female
nudes amidst ring of fire; demon dancing in
flames, S/Jun 19/96 (1000-1500) 920

Inspirational piece for never-produced Clair De
Lune segment of sunrays on trees, pastel
on black paper mounted on heavy
cardboard, S/Jun 19/96 (500-700) 690

3 concept drawings from Ave Maria sequence, pastel
on paper, CE/Jun 20/96 (1000-1500) 1150

Watercolor concept painting by Claude Coats of
demons prowling against landscape of rooftops,
8-1/8 x 6-1/4" sheet of heavy stock affixed to
10 x 8" sheet, background department &
"Concert Feature" stamps, SR/Fall/96
(1800-2400) 2450

Concept sketch of Thistle Dancers, pastel on black
paper, green frame line, 10-3/8 x 7-5/8",
12-field sheet Courvoisier monogram stamp,
three corners missing outside frame line,
SR/Fall/96 (700-1100) 1740

Dewdrop fairy concept pastel, 9-5/8 x 7-1/4" on 12-
field sheet of black paper, SR/Fall/96 (1200-
1800) 2380

Oil concept painting of spiral stairway in Sorcerer's chambers, 12-1/4 x 9-5/8" on artist's board, SR/Fall/96 (1000-4000) 3240

Concept sketch of mother Pegasus protecting nest, pencil in velvety Art Deco style on 7-1/4 x 8-7/8" sheet, SR/Fall/96 (400-800) 1270

Concept sketch for Blossom Ballet, 10-3/8 x 7-3/4", pastel on 12 x 10" black paper, edge wear, SR/Fall/96 (900-1400) 990

Watercolor concept painting for underwater "Arabian Dance," 9-1/8 x 7-7/8" on 9-7/8 x 9-1/4" heavy paper, SR/Fall/96 (1200-1800) 1960

2 concept sketches: happy Baby Pegasus flying left, 3-1/2", second study of head in lower left corner; centaur lovers play hide & seek, 6-1/8"; 12-field sheets, SR/Fall/96 (400-800) 630

Inspirational drawing of Bacchus riding Jacchus as Centaurette refills his goblet & two fauns push him upright, 7-1/4 x 9", HL/Oct 6/96 (1000-1500) 2645

5 concept drawings for *Toccata & Fugue*, colored pastel on colored story sheets: 5-1/4 x 7", 7 x 9", HL/Oct 6/96 (1000-1500) 978

Nutcracker Suite winter sequence inspirational study: Frost Fairies trace ice & snow over landscape, watercolor on heavyweight paper, signed on back by artist Curt Perkins, 8 x 11", HL/Oct 6/96 (1000-1500) 1380

2 concept drawings: Bacchus w/eyes open sitting & laughing w/feet up on barrel, 5"; Russian thistle dancers; sight 10 x 12" each, CE/Dec 12/96 (600-800) 633

Inspirational sketch of Sorcerer Mickey in silhouette on peak amid celestial bodies and clouds, drawn and signed by Ken Anderson, 1", CE/Dec 12/96 (1000-1500) 2300

Watercolor concept painting of *Ave Maria* pilgrims walking to right in distance thru mist-shrouded forest, CE/Dec 12/96 (1500-2000) 1725

Concept drawing of *Pastoral* centaurettes, unicorns & fauns on hillside looking & gesturing skyward, 2" & smaller, marked "22", CE/Dec 12/96 (2000-2500) 1725

Watercolor concept piece of forest, sight 10-1/2 x 14", S/Dec 14/96 (800-1200) 920

Moody inspirational piece depicting Bald Mountain transitioning from demonic bastion to holy symbol, 10 x 13", pastel on black paper, S/Dec 14/96 (1200-1800) 2587

Watercolor concept piece, probably for *Pastoral Symphony*, 10 x 12", S/Dec 14/96 (800-1200) 1150

3 concepts of floating blossoms for *Nutcracker Suite*, each 10 x 12", pastel on black paper, S/Dec 14/96 (1000-1500) 1150

2 items: set of 6 detailed thumbnail *Night on Bald Mountain* sketches of mountain unfolding into Chernabog & spirits rising from town below, watercolor & pastel on blue-grey paper; cel of vulture flying above noose, 3"; S/Dec 14/96 (2500-3500) 3162

Inspirational painting of swirling stars & pillar of light upon sea for *Sorcerer's Apprentice*, transparent & opaque watercolor on heavyweight paper, 5-1/4 x 7", HL/Feb 23/97 (1500-2000) 3220

Color study of Russian girl dancers from *Nutcracker Suite*, pastel on black animation sheet, 6-1/2 x 7", HL/Feb 23/97 (200-300) 633

Concept sketch for Blossom Ballet, 10-1/4 x 7-3/4", pastel on 12 x 10" black paper, lower left corner missing, SR/Spring/97 (900-1500) 920

Sheet of study drawings of eight centaurette heads, 3" to 4-3/4", 12-field sheet, moderate wear & discoloration, SR/Spring/97 (700-1200) 610

Full-figure concept sketch of adult Pegasus, 4 x 7", graphite & watercolor on heavy paper, S/Jun 21/97 (700-900) 1035

Concept artwork of Elephanchine from *Dance of the Hours*, 6-1/2", colored pencil & pastel on heavy paper, S/Jun 21/97 (800-1200) 1150

Full-figure concept drawing of Hyacinth Hippo, 7", watercolor on heavy paper, S/Jun 21/97 (800-1200) 1725

Concept art of 2 dinosaur heads amid foliage from *Rite of Spring*, 7 x 9", charcoal & graphite on paper, S/Jun 21/97 (400-600) 690

Concept art of *Nutcracker Suite* mushrooms, sight 8 x 10", pastel on construction paper, S/Jun 21/97 (1500-2000) 1725

Concept art of two satyrs (4" & 5") teasing a centaurette (7"), pastel on paper, S/Jun 21/97 (800-1200) 805

Watercolor concept art of insect string orchestra section for unproduced segment, by Lloyd Hastings, sight 5-1/4 x 7", S/Jun 21/97 (800-1200) 1150

Early concept painting signed by Sylvia Holland of fauns about to shoot arrow & slingshot at backs of 2 Percheron centaurettes, 9-1/2 x 12", watercolor & india ink on animation sheet, VF, HL/Nov 16/97 (400-600) 1380

Full-figure rear view of elephant ballerina standing, concept drawing, 7-1/4 x 3-3/4", originally sold thru Courvoisier, F+, HL/Nov 16/97 (500-700) 546

Inspirational art of thistle dancers, 8 x 11", colored pastel on black animation sheet, VF, HL/Nov 16/97 (1200-1600) 1898

Portrait of Bacchus, pastel sketch by James Bodrero (pastel on brown animation sheet), 8 x 9-3/4", F+, HL/Nov 16/97 (900-1200) 2530

Inspirational painting by Sylvia Holland for *Pastoral Symphony*, watercolor on animation sheet, 9 x 11-1/2", VF, HL/Nov 16/97 (600-900) 978

Inspirational drawing of blossom ballet dancers, white pastel on black animation sheet, 8 x 10-1/2", VF+, HL/Nov 16/97 (600-900) 805

Inspirational painting for Pastoral: Pegasus family swimming by foliage & Greek columns, gouache on paper, sight 4-1/4 x 5-1/4", CE/Dec 18/97 (1500-2000) 1093

Watercolor concept painting on paper of chorus line of 3 dancing ostriches, 11-1/2", copyright stamp, CE/Dec 18/97 (1500-2000) 1150

Concept drawing of winged female ghosts, sight 5-1/2 x 2-1/2", graphite on paper, CE/Dec 18/97 (1000-1500) 1725

Clair de Lune: concept painting of crane in bamboo-flanked waters, 9-1/2 x 11-1/2", watercolor on paper, S/Dec 19/97 (800-1200) 920

Inspirational sketch of Cossack flower dancers, pastel on black animation sheet, 8 x 10-1/2", F, HL/Apr 25/98 (700-1000) 1725

Inspirational painting of mother Pegasus soaring to nest as storm approaches; watercolor, pencil & blue conté crayon on animation sheet; 8 x 11"; F; HL/Apr 25/98 (1000-1500) 1035

Color study sketch of dewdrop fairy transforming flowers, pastel on heavyweight black paper, 7-1/4 x 9-1/4", VF, HL/Apr 25/98 (300-500) 978

Painting by Claude Coats of Chernabog's shadow blanketing village, pencil & watercolor on heavyweight paper, stamps, 6 x 8", VF, HL/Apr 25/98 (1200-1600) 2070

Inspirational painting by Claude Coats of owl & animal eyes in tree watching Bald Mt. in distance, watercolor on heavyweight paper, stamps, 5-3/4 x 7-3/4", VF, HL/Apr 25/98 (1200-1600) 1150

Inspirational art by Kay Nielsen of vulture perched atop gallows in village, pencil & white tempera on paper, stamp, 3-1/2 x 4-1/2", F, HL/Apr 25/98 (1200-1600) 2760

3 concept drawings by Thor Putnam: 2 of demons & spirits answering call, 5 cloaked demons atop Bald Mt.; colored pastel on black paper; labels signed by artist; 5-1/4 x 7-1/4", 5-3/4 x 7-3/4", 5-3/4 x 18-1/2"; VG-VF; HL/Apr 25/98 (1800-2200) 1955

Haunting erotic drawing of merwoman (inspiration for Arab Dance?) with cel overlay, colored pastel on black paper, 9-1/2 x 4-1/4", VF, HL/Apr 25/98 (900-1200) 1955

Ave Maria inspirational sketch of pilgrims walking thru forest, pastel on brown animation sheet, 8 x 10-1/2", F+, HL/Apr 25/98 (1000-1500) 920

Inspirational portrait of redheaded centaurette in hat made from lily pad leaves, pastel on green paper, 8-1/4 x 9", VF, HL/Apr 25/98 (1000-1200) 920

Inspirational art by Gustav Tenggren of gnome lying against fence at dusk with village in valley behind him & mountain in distance, watercolor & india ink on heavyweight paper, 7-3/4 x 10-1/2", VF, HL/Apr 25/98 (1200-1600) 3565

Inspirational landscape study by Mel Shaw, watercolor on animation sheet, 7-1/4 x 9-3/4", VF, HL/Apr 25/98 (900-1200) 920

Concept painting: rear view of mythical creatures gathered to wave farewell to sun at dusk, tempera on paper, 6-1/4 x 8-1/2", VF, HL/Apr 25/98 (1200-1600) 2185

Inspirational painting or background study for *Night on Bald Mountain*: wind-swept landscape of rocks & gnarled trees under menacing sky, watercolor on heavyweight paper, 6 x 8", F, HL/Apr 25/98 (500-700) 748

LAYOUT ART

2 layout drawings of Cupids (2 x 1" & smaller) playing with Unicorns (2-1/2 x 1-1/2"), CE/Jun 18/94 (800-1200) 805

26 background & overlay layout drawings plus 2 character studies, 7-1/2 x 6-1/2" to 10-1/2 x 26", pencil & conté crayon on animation sheets, HL/Nov 19/95 (1800-2400) 1725

Pencil layout drawing for season change in "Waltz of the Flowers," 48 x 11-1/2" panoramic on single sheet with 3 vertical folds, plus original exposure sheet, SR/Spring/96 (800-1200) 1580

2 signed background layout drawings of Bald Mountain by Thor Putnam; black pencil & white tempera on animation sheet; 7-3/4 x 10-1/2", 8 x 10-1/2"; VF; HL/Apr 25/98 (1500-2000) 3450

Layout breakdown sketch for *Ave Maria*: front view of two rows massive parallel columns, pencil & conté crayon on animation sheet, 10-3/4 x 14", VG+, HL/Apr 25/98 (500-700) 489

MODEL ART

Original model-sheet drawing of unicorn & faun, colored pastel on paper, 8-1/2 x 11-1/2", HL/Aug 21/94 (800-1200) 784

5 photostats of model sheets, CE/Dec 16/94 (200-300) 575

Model sketches of a fairy from *Nutcracker Suite* in 4 different poses, 5-1/2" to 2-1/2", graphite & watercolor on heavy paper, "Property of Walt Disney Productions" stamp, S/Dec 17/94 (800-1200) 977

Les Clark's version of Sorcerer Mickey model sheet, 11-1/2 x 14-1/2", certificate of authenticity, HL/Apr 23/95 (2500-3000) 4928

Close-up of smiling Sorcerer Mickey w/left arm outstretched, model cel w/notes, 2-1/2 x 2-1/2", VF, HL/Apr 23/95 (2500-3500) 2912

Color model drawing of Centaurette, 6", CE/Jun 9/95 (600-800) 690

Full-figure model cel of apprehensive Sorcerer Mickey standing in plain tan hat, red robe, blue shorts & brown shoes, plus overlay cel of robe outline in lighter color, from private collection of Walt Kelly, 6-1/4 x 3-1/4", HL/Oct 6/96 (4000-5000) 4715

Full-figure model cel: side view of apprehensive Sorcerer Mickey standing in plain light blue hat, from private collection of Walt Kelly, 7 x 4", HL/Oct 6/96 (4000-5000) 4255

Model cel of tan & brown dappled unicorn, 4 x 5-1/4", HL/Oct 6/96 (700-1000) 690

Detailed color model drawing: full figure of surprised Sorcerer Mickey facing right standing next to whirlpool with floating chair, 3-1/2", S/Dec 14/96 (1500-2000) 2300

2 original full-figure Studio model-sheet drawings: rear view of Hyacinth Hippo sleeping, elephant ballerina dancing; pencil, india ink & pastel on paper; 9 x 6" & 4 x 8", VG, HL/Feb 23/97 (400-600) 345

SPECIAL ART

Contemporary drawing drawn & signed by Ken Anderson of wickedly grinning Sorcerer Mickey (all but top of hat) in spell-casting pose in front of startled broom with face and two arms holding buckets, sight 7-1/2 x 8-1/2", CE/Dec 18/97 (700-900) 690

STORY ART

Centaurette, story sketch, 5-3/4 x 7-3/4", CE/Dec 15/93 (400-600) 460

Centaurettes dance, story sketch, 5-3/4 x 7-3/4", CE/Dec 15/93 (500-700) 632

Centaurette, story sketch released by Courvoisier, 4-1/2 x 5-1/2", CE/Dec 15/93 (400-600) 690

Waltz of the Flowers story sketch, pastel on black paper, 9 x 12", CE/Dec 15/93 (800-1200) 1725

Story sketch of establishing shot for *Night on Bald Mountain*, pastel on paper, 9-1/2 x 13-1/2", CE/Dec 15/93 (3500-4500) 3680

HL/Apr 25/98 (900-1200) 920

Pastoral: story painting signed by artist Sylvia Holland, watercolor on animation sheet, 9 x 12", Concert Feature label, VF, HL/Apr 10/94 (700-1000)　　560

Night on Bald Mountain: conté-crayon story drawing of demon raised by Chernabog, 5-1/2 x 7-1/2", F, HL/Apr 10/94 (500-700)　504

Story art of 3 Orchid Girls, pastel on black animation sheet, 8 x 10-1/2", VF, HL/Apr 10/94 (600-900)　　784

Story painting by Sylvia Holland of Centaurettes frolicking, watercolor on heavy paper, 10-1/2 x 13", Concert Feature stamp, VF, HL/Apr 10/94 (700-1000)　　1120

2 story drawings of flowers in breeze, pastel on black animation sheets, 5 x 5-1/2", 3 x 10-1/2", VF, HL/Apr 10/94 (600-900)　　532

Story sketch of 2 ostriches, 6 x 6", CE/Jun 18/94 (400-600)　　575

Storyboard sketch of alligators & ostriches dancing ballet by James Bodrero, 5-1/2 x 1" & similar, graphite & crayon on full animation paper, stamp, CE/Jun 18/94 (400-600)　　805

Story drawing of Hop Low, colored pastel on black story sheet, 6 x 8", HL/Aug 21/94 (700-1000)　　1568

2 story drawings for "Dance of the Reed Flutes", colored pastel on black animation sheets, 8 x 10-1/2", HL/Aug 21/94 (1000-1500)　896

Story art of Chinese mushrooms, 8 x 10-1/2", colored pastel on black animation sheet, HL/Nov 13/94 (1000-1500)　　1064

Atmospheric story drawing from *Night on Bald Mountain*, 4 x 5", black-&-white conté crayon on tan paper, stamped, HL/Nov 13/94 (1000-1500)　　1512

Polished story/layout drawing of 4 pipe-playing fauns dancing thru wine puddles w/overlay of bunches of grapes, 12 x 15", conté crayon & colored & black pencil on animation sheet, HL/Apr 23/95 (800-1200)　　1008

Story drawing of thistle boys, 7-1/2 x 10-1/2", colored pastel on black animation sheet, HL/Apr 23/95 (1800-2200)　　1680

3 original story drawings from *Pastoral Symphony*, 7 x 9", 9 x 7-1/2", watercolor & conté crayon on animation sheets, HL/Apr 23/95 (1200-1600)　　1344

Story drawing for *Waltz of the Flowers*, 6 x 10", colored pastel on black animation sheet, HL/Apr 23/95 (800-1200)　　896

Storyboard drawing by James Bodrero of two ostrich ballerinas chatting, approx. 4" ea., S/Jun 10/95 (300-500)　　460

Story painting of bug orchestra's violin section that was cut from film, 8-1/2 x 9", ink & watercolor on medium-weight paper, HL/Nov 19/95 (800-1200)　　2990

Story drawing of Chernabog atop mountain at height of his power, 3-1/4 x 4-1/4", pencil & conté crayon on story sheet, HL/Nov 19/95 (2000-2500)　　3680

Story Dept. original of Thistle Boys & Orchid Girls, 8 x 10-1/2", pastel on black animation sheet, HL/Nov 19/95 (700-1000)　　1093

Story drawing of chastened Sorcerer Mickey offering broom, 3-1/2 x 4-1/2", HL/Nov 19/95 (2000-2500)　　3393

9 story drawings of primordial Earth, 3-1/2 x 4-1/2" to 5-1/2 x 7", pencil & conté crayon on story sheets, HL/Nov 19/95 (1200-1600)　　1150

2 story drawings for *The Russian Dance*, 7-1/2 x 10", pastel on black animation sheets, HL/Nov 19/95 (1000-1500)　　1955

Full-figure story drawing of Mushroom Dancers, 4-1/2 x 7", HL/Mar 16-17/96 (150-200)　　690

Story drawing of "cartoony" broom pouring bucket of water into cistern as Mickey's shadow supervises, brown conté crayon on story sheet, 4-1/2 x 6", HL/Apr 28/96 (1000-1500)　　1840

Story drawing of *Russian Dance*, pastel on black animation sheet, 8 x 10-1/2", HL/Apr 28/96 (1000-1500)　　920

Story painting of Centaurettes, india ink & watercolor on animation sheet, signed & annotated by Sylvia Holland, 9-1/2 x 12", HL/May 3/97 (2000-2500)　　2990

Story drawing of 10 Cossack dancers from *Nutcracker Suite*, 6 x 10-1/2",

HL/May 31/97 (300-400)　　178

Story sketch of baby Pegasus in nest with mother, 6 x 8", black & grey conté crayon on paper, released thru Courvoisier, VF, HL/Nov 16/97 (800-1200)　　978

Story drawing of 2 cupids stripping birch bark off tree; white, gray & black tempura on green animation sheet; 6 x 8"; F+; HL/Apr 25/98 (1000-1500)　　1035

Story painting of Pegasus nest high in sunlit tree, watercolor on heavyweight paper, 4-1/2 x 7-1/2", VF, HL/Apr 25/98 (1000-1500)　　900

Story painting of multitude of brooms pouring buckets into flood, watercolor on paper mounted to board, 4-3/4 x 6-1/4", F+, HL/Apr 25/98 (2000-2500)　　5750

Full-figure front-view story drawing of anthropomorphic dancing flower, colored pencil on paper trimmed to outline & mounted to black velvet paper for sale thru Courvoisier, WDP monogram stamp, 5-1/2 x 3", VF, HL/Apr 25/98 (200-400)　　460

Story painting by Mel Shaw of fauns in silhouette dancing against backdrop of lake & rocky island, watercolor on animation sheet, 7-1/4 x 9-3/4", F, HL/Apr 25/98 (900-1200)　　800

Story art of mushroom dancers, pastel on black animation sheet, WDP monogram stamp, 7-3/4 x 10-1/4", F+, HL/Apr 25/98 (1200-1600)　　1495

2 atmospheric story paints for *Ave Maria*: gathering of pilgrims at cathedral, watercolor & conté crayon on board, signed "A. Heath", stamp, 3-1/2 x 4-1/2", VF, HL/Apr 25/98 (1000-1500)　　1265

Story painting of Centaurettes frolicking under waterfall; watercolor, pencil & conté crayon on animation sheet; 6 x 8"; VF; HL/Apr 25/98 (600-800)　　863

3 story drawings of cupids preparing centaurettes; red & black pencil, conté crayon & white tempera on paper; 4-3/4 x 6", 4-3/4 x 6-1/2"; F; HL/Apr 25/98 (1200-1600)　　2185

Story drawing of cupids bedecking centaurettes with flowers, pencil & conté crayon on animation sheet, 6-1/2 x 8-1/4", VF, HL/Apr 25/98 (600-800)　　575

Story painting of haughty blonde centaurette against green background, watercolor & pencil on paper, 7-3/4 x 9-3/4", F, HL/Apr 25/98 (500-700)　　690

2 full-figure humorous story drawings of centaur-centaurette courtship; pencil & conté crayon on animation sheets; 7 x 5-1/2", 7 x 8-1/2"; F; HL/Apr 25/98 (600-800)　　575

THE FOX AND THE HOUND (1981)

ANIMATION DRAWINGS

4 drawings of Tod & Vixey: 2 together, one of each alone, sitting in similar facing poses, approx. 6", 16-field sheets, SR/Spring/96 (300-600)　　400

51 polished "rough" drawings, 2 x 3-1/2" to 7 x 8", HL/Apr 28/96 (1000-2000)　　633

Seven animation drawings: Slade, two of Chief, two of Copper (one as a pup), two of Tod, images 3-3/8" to 7-3/4", 16-field sheets, some with notations, SR/Fall/96 (300-600)　　310

Near-front-view rough drawing of frisky young Copper leaping, signed by Frank Thomas, 7 x 5" inc. signature, VF, HL/Feb 23/97 (150-200)　　489

Full-figure rough drawing of young Copper standing looking up, signed by Frank Thomas, 4 x 5" inc. signature, HL/May 31/97 (200-250)　　288

CEL SET-UPS

Young Tod & Copper, tempera master background of woodlands, 9 x 12", VF+, HL/Apr 10/94 (2000-3000)　　3584

Portrait of sitting Copper, 8-1/2", gouache pre-production outdoor background by Jim Coleman, 16-field, SR/Fall/94 (1000-2000) 1020

Full figures of young Copper sitting in hollow log looking up at Tod sitting on top, both 2-1/2", 16-field, photocopy of background layout, SR/Fall/94 (600-1200)　　680

Publicity cel of young Tod (4") & Copper (3") frolicking at swimming hole, TV promotion for 1988 theatrical re-release, print copy of matching production background, S/Dec 17/94 (300-500)　　402

Full figure of somber adult Copper standing in stream over prostrate, scared Tod, 10 x 4-1/2", reflec-

tions, original water effects, key photographic reproduction background, Disney Art Program seal & label, SR/Fall/95 (900-1300)　　900

Full figures of angry Slade (7-1/2") standing w/hands on hips & Chief (4") sitting facing right, 16-field, color print background w/2 barrels & large tree, Disney Art Program seal, SR/Fall/95 (400-800)　　400

Angry rooster chases Tod by startled Widow Tweed & Abigail, 10-1/2 x 15", master background (tempera on background sheet), VF+, HL/Nov 19/95 (2500-3500)　2300

Full-figure front view of lovely vixey sitting on stream bank, 8-1/8", key color print background, Disney Art Program seal, SR/Spring/96 (250-500)　　650

Limited-edition set-up of young Tod & Copper playing together, key litho background, Disney Art Program seal & certificate, 16-field, #276/500, SR/Fall/96 (500-900)　　500

Portrait of smiling Vixey sitting looking up & to right, 7-1/2", key color print background of forest, Disney Art Program seal & certificate, SR/Fall/96 (300-600)　　310

Near-full-figure of ruffled Tod sitting in meadow, 4-3/4 x 6" cel image, color print of matching background, Disney seal and certificate, VF+, HL/Oct 6/96 (300-400)　　288

Full-figure front view of coy Vixey sitting by stream looking down & to right; 8 x 4" cel image, matching color print background, Disney seal & certificate, VF+, HL/Oct 6/96 (300-400)　690

Large image of Vixey sitting looking up, color print background, 8-1/2 x 12" overall, Disney seal & certificate, VF+, HL/Feb 23/97 (200-400) 299

Full figure of young Tod sitting among fallen leaves facing left, 5-3/8", key master background (watercolor & pastel) by Jim Coleman, SR/Fall/97 (1800-2400)　　2670

2 cels of Vixey: full figure sitting looking up & to right, close-up portrait; 7-1/2 x 6" & 7-1/2 x 3-1/2"; each with color print background from film, VF+, HL/Nov 16/97 (400-600)　　460

Full figures of young Copper (standing, 5") & Tod (eyes closed, 6-1/2") facing right, watercolor production background of house door, S/Dec 19/97 (1500-2000)　　1150

Full figures of Boomer (5-1/2") & shocked Squeeks (1-3/4") standing on tree branch, facing left & looking down; signed pre-production watercolor, gouache, & pastel background by Jim Coleman; SR/Spring/98 (500-1000)　　750

CELS – FULL FIGURE

Ground-level front view of growling adult Copper, 7-1/2", 16-field, some lifting paint, paint stuck to backing, SR/Fall/94 (200-500)　　200

Big Mama advises baby Tod; baby Copper being held by neck; 8 x 6-1/2" & 6 x 9-1/2", Disney seal, VF+, HL/Nov 13/94 (500-700) 560

Close-up of baby Tod lying on back (partial figure); baby Tod & Copper rolling around laughing; 4 x 9" & 6 x 7-1/2", Disney seals & one WDP label, VF+, HL/Nov 13/94 (400-600) 448

2 large-image cels: Widow Tweed (ankles up) with Boomer, and with rambunctious Abigail & Tod (partial figure); 11 x 16" & 9 x 13-1/2", Disney seal & one WDP label, VF+, HL/Nov 13/94 (500-700)　　336

Tod, Vixey (all but tip of tail), log, & fish, 6-1/2 x 13", Disney seal, WDP label, Disneyana Shop certificate, VF+, HL/Apr 23/95 (400-500)　784

Big Mama lectures young Tod, 7-1/2 x 10", HL/Nov 19/95 (400-600)　　489

Tod stands on floating log, 3-5/16", full image with water effects is 6-1/2" on 3 16-field cel levels, Disney Art Program seal, SR/Fall/97 (450-650)　　800

CELS – PARTIAL FIGURE

Set of 3 matched cels of Tod with flower in mouth & finicky Vixey, 7-1/2 x 9", seal & certificate, VF+, HL/Nov 13/94 (400-600)　　504

Vixey (eyes closed) snuggles up to Tod, 6-1/2 x 4-1/2", Disney seal & certificate, VF+, HL/Nov 13/94 (400-600)　　532

Large close-up of head of ferocious bear, 10 x 11", dry brush & special effects, 16-field, Disney Art Program seal, SR/Spring/95 (150-300)　　250

Close-up of baby Tod lying on his back, 6 x 7-1/2", Disney seal, WDP label, Disneyana Shop certificate, VF+, HL/Apr 23/95 (300-500) 364

Portrait of young Copper smiling, 6-1/2 x 5", Disney seal, VF+, HL/Feb 23/97 (250-350) 345

Matched set of 2 cels of Tod nestled in Widow Tweed's lap to drink his milk, 9 x 12", Disney seal & certificate, VF+, HL/May 31/97 (300-400) 259

CONCEPT AND INSPIRATIONAL ART

2 pages of character studies of adult Copper, 8 x 10" & 8 x 10-1/2", india ink & watercolor on paper, F+, HL/Nov 13/94 (200-400) 336

4 original paintings: background design, concept painting, hunting scene by Don Bluth, story painting of Tod & Big Mama; 8-1/2 x 11" to 11-1/2 x 16"; pastel & tempera on background sheets & board, VF, HL/Nov 19/95 (900-1200) 1725

2 conceptual drawings by Mel Shaw: Tod sitting amid birds, Copper riding alongside Amos Slade (signed by Shaw), pastel on colored paper, 6-1/2 x 9-1/2" & 7-1/2 x 9-1/2", VF, HL/Feb 23/97 (500-700) 546

SPECIAL ART

Special drawing of Tod & Copper by Glen Keane at 1981 ASIFA-Hollywood event, inscribed & signed, 6 x 9-1/2" inc. signature, VF, HL/Apr 25/98 (300-400) 219

FUN AND FANCY FREE (1947)

Segments are Bongo and Mickey and the Beanstalk.

ANIMATION DRAWINGS

Full-figure drawing of sheepish Mickey looking up, 4-1/2 x 4", HL/Mar 16-17/96 (400-600) 1035

Full-figure drawing of cheerful Mickey looking up, 4-1/2 x 3-1/2", HL/Apr 28/96 (500-700) 920

Chest-up front-view drawing of ferocious Willie in boxing pose, 7-1/2", 12-field sheet, with timer's chart, SR/Fall/97 (400-700) 270

Full-figure front-view drawing of grinning Mickey standing, 5 x 3-3/4", VF, HL/Apr 25/98 (400-600) 546

Full-figure front-view drawing of smiling Mickey standing looking up, twirling tail; 5 x 3"; VF; HL/Apr 25/98 (400-600) 431

BACKGROUNDS

Master background painting of dawn at promontory, 8-1/2 x 10-1/2", tempera on background sheet, stamps & notes, VF+, HL/Apr 23/95 (1000-1500) 1456

Production background: close-up of table with knife handle, portion of bowl & base of goblet, sight 10 x 12", watercolor on paper, CE/Dec 12/96 (1500-2500) 1265

Master background painting of Happy Valley, tempera on background sheet, 11-1/4 x 14-3/4", VF+, HL/Apr 25/98 (3000-4000) 3910

CEL SET-UPS

Worried Goofy (4-1/2"), Donald (3-1/2"), & Mickey (3-1/2") tread cautiously in castle, watercolor production background, CE/Jun 18/94 (10,000-15,000) 21,850

Knees-to-head view of enraged Willy standing at castle moat, 11", key master watercolor background, SR/Fall/94 (3000-7000) 3000

Bongo cavorts w/5 friends, 5-1/2 x 7" & 3 x 6", complementary painted background, stamped, inscribed & signed by Walt Disney, VF, HL/Nov 13/94 (2000-2500) 2912

Bongo on unicycle offers bouquet of daisies to Lulubelle, ea. 4-1/2", airbrushed Courvoisier background & label, S/Dec 17/94 (1800-2200) 2185

Full figures of smiling Bongo on unicycle holding handkerchief for flirtatious Lulubelle, watercolor production background of forest, 4-1/2" each, CE/Jun 20/96 (3000-4000) 4025

Full figures of coy Bongo on unicycle (5-1/8") & admiring Lulubelle (4-1/4") facing each other, Art Props master gouache background of outdoors, Courvoisier label & hand-lettered mat w/"Original WDP" stamp, SR/Fall/97 (3000-4000) 2850

CELS – FULL FIGURE

Smiling Lulubelle stands facing left, looking back right, 6", 12-field, SR/Fall/94 (175-375) 300

Flirtatious Bongo leans forward on unicycle to left, 3-1/2", 16-field, SR/Spring/95 (300-600) 440

Smiling Mickey stands at shack door holding box aloft, 7 x 5", F+, HL/Aug 6/95 (1800-2400) 5824

Smiling Goofy sneaks up on hat, 4 x 6", HL/Nov 19/95 (500-800) 863

Large-image model cel of smiling Mickey with open arms, 8-1/2 x 5", HL/Apr 28/96 (2000-2500) 2530

Large-image of smiling Bongo looking up as he rides unicycle, 8 x 3-1/2", HL/Apr 28/96 (700-1000) 805

Mickey, Donald & Goofy in pea pod boat being saved from dragonfly by hungry fish, 9 x 15", VF, HL/Oct 6/96 (2000-2500) 3220

Mickey shushes Donald as they tiptoe along, 3-1/2 x 5-1/2", F, HL/Feb 23/97 (1500-2500) 2415

Mickey & Donald crossing water in pea pod boat as giant fish soars overhead (5 cels from different scenes), 9 x 12" overall, F, HL/Nov 16/97 (1000-1500) 1265

CELS – PARTIAL FIGURE

Willie the Giant (6-1/2 x 10"), reaches forward to grab Mickey Mouse (back to camera, 3/4"), S/Jun 19/96 (800-1200) 1265

CONCEPT AND INSPIRATIONAL ART

2 promotional watercolors of Bongo: on stomach happily sniffing flower; greeting crowd of forest friends; approx. 2-1/2" ea., watercolor on board, S/Jun 10/95 (600-800) 517

Full-figure character study of spiffy Jiminy Cricket standing looking left, conté crayon on story sheet, VF+, 4-1/2 x 2-3/4", HL/Oct 6/96 (300-400) 460

ILLUSTRATION ART

Front view of Mickey, Donald (both 4-3/4") & Goofy (6-1/2") walking thru oversized plants, ink & gouache on board, CE/Dec 16/94 (8000-12,000) 8050

STORY ART

Captioned story sketch of Mickey, Donald, & Goofy standing outside, colored pencil & watercolor on a 9 x 8" five-hole sheet, center fold & some discoloration, SR/Spring/96 (600-1000) 730

Full-figure storyboard drawing of Donald (3"), Mickey (3-1/2") & Goofy (4") walking cautiously to left, CE/Jun 20/96 (800-1200) 1265

3 story sketches: Bongo seeks shelter in cave, is chased away by hedgehog, beds down under pine bough; 7-7/8 x 6", charcoal on 9 x 8" 5-hole punched paper, SR/Fall/96 (200-500) 200

THE GREAT MOUSE DETECTIVE (1986)

ANIMATION DRAWINGS

56 rough drawings, 2 x 2" to 7 x 10-1/2", HL/Apr 28/96 (1000-2000) 2185

CEL SET-UPS

Grinning Ratigan in royal dress leans from balcony, 10 x 15", matching photoprint background, Disney seal & label, VF+, HL/Feb 26-27/94 (300-400) 303

In waterfront bar: Basil & Dawson being served; contented Dawson lying on piano as irate pianist winds up with club; Disney seals & color print backgrounds, 9-1/2 x 11-1/2" & 9 x 13-1/2", HL/Aug 21/94 (600-800) 896

3 cels: sophisticated Basil playing violin, color print background; full figure of happy Olivia sitting; full figure of surprised Toby (others on his back), color print background; 6 x 4-1/2", 8 x 11-1/2", 10 x 13"; all with seals, two with certificates; VF+; HL/Nov 13/94 (900-1200) 1232

Basil burns note in lab; startled Ratigan w/full figure of frightened Olivia falling; 11 x 15" & 10 x 15", w/Disney seals & matching line-print backgrounds, one label, VF+, HL/Nov 13/94 (600-800) 840

Disguised Dr. Dawson with show mouse on each arm, 7-1/4 x 11-1/2", original background study from never-completed *Oliver Twist* (tempera on background sheet), VF+, HL/Nov 16/97 (700-1000) 230

CELS – FULL FIGURE

Front view of disguised Dawson in cancan line with 2 identical showgirl mice, 9 x 6", 12-field, Disney Art Program seal & certificate, SR/Spring/95 (200-400) 220

Ratigan takes bow with eyes closed, 5" tall, silver WDC seal, S/Jun 10/95 (300-500) 402

4 cels: 2 of Ratigan in top hat & cape; Ratigan w/o top hat (Ratigans avg. 4-1/2"); Basil (5") gesturing dramatically w/eyes closed; S/Dec 14/96 (600-800) 460

Front view of Ratigan standing in spotlight spreading

---

cape & grinning at camera as 5 admiring henchmice look on, 9-1/2 x 14-1/2", VF+, HL/Apr 25/98 (300-400) 489

CELS – PARTIAL FIGURE

Basil measures formula, WDP seal, 10-1/2 x 12-1/2", CE/Dec 15/93 (800-1200) 747

Hips-up of Basil standing facing right, speaking with arms crossed, 6", 12-field, Disney Art Program seal, SR/Fall/94 (300-600) 300

Waist-up front view of charming Ratigan gesturing, 7", 12-field, SR/Fall/94 (300-700) 300

Set of 3 cels of Ratigan & cohorts celebrating, 9-1/2 x 16", VF+, HL/Nov 13/94 (400-500) 448

Basil (full figure) urges eager Toby to catch scent of villain; hopefully expectant Ratigan; 4 x 11" & 9 x 9"; VF+, HL/Nov 13/94 (600-800) 784

2 cels of charming Ratigan, 6-1/2 x 8" & 8-1/2 x 7-1/2", Disney seals, VF+, HL/Apr 23/95 (500-700) 784

Thigh-up view of smiling Ratigan gesturing, 6 x 7", Disney seal, VF+, HL/Aug 6/95 (300-400) 252

Portrait of charming Ratigan in royal robes wearing glasses & holding list, 7-1/2 x 10", HL/Apr 28/96 (250-350) 403

Waist-up portrait of grinning Ratigan, 9-3/4", 16-field, Disney Art Program seal, SR/Fall/96 (200-400) 350

"Watch the birdie!" Front view of grinning Basil holding startled Dawson & Olivia, 6-1/4 x 9", Disney seal & certificate, VF+, HL/Oct 6/96 (300-500) 748

Portrait of Ratigan as King reading from scroll, matted w/small sheet w/inscribed profile self-portrait by Vincent Price, 6-1/2 x 10", Disney seal & certificate, VF+, HL/Feb 23/97 (300-500) 690

Ratigan as King lands painfully on top of clockwork Queen Moustoria, 9 x 14", Disney seal & certificate, VF+, HL/Feb 23/97 (300-400) 288

Stomach-up view of pompous Ratigan facing right, eyes closed, holding up open pocket watch; seal & certificate; 10-1/4 x 13"; VF+; HL/Apr 25/98 (300-500) 316

CONCEPT AND INSPIRATIONAL ART

Concept painting of riverside pub The Rat Trap by Jim Coleman, watercolor on 12 1/4 x 9" board, signed, SR/Spring/98 (500-900) 920

MODEL ART

From estate of Vincent Price: Ratigan character model statue, unpainted resin, inscribed, 10" high w/o base; Ratigan publicity cel inscribed to Vincent Price; Ratigan pen drawing with personalized note from Glen Keane, CE/Jun 18/94 (1000-1500) 2990

HERCULES (1998)

CEL SET-UPS

All items in this section were auctioned at Sotheby's, June 20, 1998.

These include original art actually used in the making of the film. Each set-up features characters and, in many cases, effects cels specially created by artists in the Ink & Paint Dept. at the Walt Disney Studios in Burbank, California. The cels are then accompanied by either a production background with one of more production elements, or a non-production background with one or more production elements. The basis for the cels are original animation drawings rendered by Disney animators and used in the production of the film. Each set-up was matted and framed.

4 Muses descend stairway from vase with Hercules' likeness (with Muse Thalia perched on his shoulder) to vase with likeness of Titans, 19-1/2 x 25" (1500-2000) 1150

Full-figure front view of Muses singing about "Gospel Truth," 12-1/2 x 17" (1000-1500) 805

Full figure of Baby Hercules lying in crib with Zeus' hand & index finger pointing at him, 12-1/2 x 17" (1200-1800) 1035

"He's so tiny!" Zeus holds Baby Hercules as smiling Hera & Baby Pegasus watch, 19-1/2 x 30-3/4" (2500-3500) 2990

"A little dark, a little gloomy," Chest-up front view of Hades speaking with arms up, 19-1/2 x 25" (1200-1800) 1092

Hades stands over Baby Hercules' crib, 12-1/4 x 23-1/4" (2000-3000) 1610

"Memo to me," Chest-up front view of Hades speaking with one hand up, 12-1/2 x 17" (1200-1800) 3737

Full figures of Pain and Panic (holding eyeball) standing, 12-1/2 x 17" (1500-2000) 3105

Full figures of Baby Hercules & Baby Pegasus sleeping together in crib, 12-1/2 x 17" (2000-3000) 2300

Full-figure front view of Baby Hercules & Baby Pegasus sleeping together in crib, 12-1/2 x 17" (2000-3000) 2990

Full figures of flying Pain & Panic pulling Baby Hercules thru air, 12-1/2 x 17" (1500-2000) 1150

Full figures of Pain & Panic feeding potion to Baby Hercules, 12-1/2 x 17" (1500-2000) 1265

Full figures of sitting Baby Hercules playing with Pain & Panic as snakes, 12-1/2 x 35" (1500-2000) 2070

Aerial view of hay cart moving thru marketplace, 19-1/2 x 25" (1200-1800) 4312

Young Hercules looks upward as Amphitryon examines Penelope's (sitting on cart) ankle, 12-1/2 x 17" (1200-1800) 1380

2 set-ups: Amphitryon & Alcmene stand in front of house waving; Young Hercules with bag slung over shoulder waves; 12-1/2 x 22-1/2", 12-1/2 x 17"; (1000-1500) 805

"My boy," Looking up at smiling statue of Zeus in temple, 19-1/2 x 25" (1000-1500) 805

Full figures of Young Hercules hugging adult Pegasus, 12-1/2 x 26", (1500-2500) 1380

Young Hercules riding Pegasus poised on Zeus' finger, 12-1/2 x 34" (2500-3500) 2530

Full figures of Hercules singing as he flies astride Pegasus, 19-1/2 x 24" (1500-2000) 1150

Hercules and Pegasus search for Phil on misty island amid ruins, 12-1/2 x 38" (2500-3500) 1955

Full figure of Phil bursting out of bushes as Hercules watches, 12-1/2 x 17" (1200-1800) 1955

Full figure of angry Phil sitting in grass rubbing sore spots, 12-1/2 x 17" (1000-1500) 805

Long shot of Hercules & Pegasus following Phil to his home, 12-1/2 x 17" (1000-1500) 1610

Full figures of Phil & Hercules standing admiring statue of Achilles, 12-1/2 x 17" (2000-3000) 1840

2 set-ups: full figures of Phil standing on column before & after being struck by lightning, each 12-1/2 x 17" (2000-3000) 2070

Full-figure long shot of Pegasus & Hercules watching lightning bolt strike Phil as he stands atop column, 12-1/2 x 17" (1200-1800) 1092

Happy Hercules & Pegasus flank charred Phil standing on column, 13-1/2 x 19-3/4" (1000-1500) 1265

Phil pushes aside foliage to find his box of old training equipment, 12-1/2 x 17" (1200-1800) 977

Chest-up of distressed Hercules (holding broken sword) & angry Phil (olives on horns) standing in tree foliage, 12-1/2 x 17" (1200-1800) 977

Full figures of stern Phil standing on pedestal in front of full moon as Hercules does push-ups & Pegasus (all but wing tip) counts, 12-1/2 x 17" (1500-2000) 1150

Waist-up of hopeful Hercules & smiling Pegasus [after having thrown swords], 12-1/2 x 24-3/4" (1200-1800) 977

Full figures of Phil, Hercules, & Pegasus (all but wing tip) balancing on one leg on pedestals in front of sunset [ala The Karate Kid], 12-1/2 x 17" (2000-3000) 3450

Full figures of Phil turning wooden wheels & holding green flag, Hercules in sprinter's stance, shocked Pegasus (near-full figure) watching, 12-1/2 x 17" (1500-2000) 1150

Full figure of Hercules standing in ring holding damsel dummy surrounded by pop-up monsters, 12-1/2 x 17" (1200-1800) 977

Hercules catches arrows w/wooden shield while holding damsel dummy, 12-1/2 x 17" (1200-1800) 1150

"I'm ready!" Full figures of proud Hercules & Pegasus above him standing in ring amid remains of pop-up monsters, 19-1/2 x 33" (1500-2000) 1150

"...Come on, Phil!" Hips-up of pleading Hercules & Pegasus, 12-1/2 x 17" (1500-2000) 2415

"Not so fast, sweetheart!" Full-figure long shot of Nessus holding Meg up in one hand next to tree & in front of waterfall, 12-3/4 x 33-3/4" (2000-3000) 1725

Close-up of Nessus staring down Hercules as he holds struggling Meg, 12-1/2 x 17" (1500-2000) 1840

Hercules gets an idea as he picks himself off large rock, 12-1/2 x 17" (1200-1800) 1265

Long shot of Hercules about to ram Nessus as he stands in water struggling with Meg, 12-1/2 x 40" (2500-3500) 2070

"...by the way, Sweetcheeks," Knees-up of flirtatious Phil, 12-1/2 x 17" (1200-1800) 920

Knees-up of Meg glancing back as she fixes her hair, 12-1/2 x 17" (1200-1800) 4312

Irritated Phil & Pegasus strike identical arms-crossed poses, 12-1/2 x 17" (1200-1800) 1265

"Did they give you a name..." Meg talks as she bends down by water, 12-1/2 x 17" (1200-1800) 1955

Tongue-tied Hercules tries to talk to Meg, 12-1/2 x 17" (2000-3000) 1955

Full figures of smiling Meg sitting under tree as smiling Hercules and angry Phil & Pegasus stand facing her, 19-1/2 x 25" (2500-3500) 12, 650

"...you know how men are..." Endearing Meg talks to Hercules as he stands back-to-back w/skeptical Pegasus, 12-1/2 x 17" (2000-3000) 2875

Full figure of Pegasus lying in apple tree whistling innocently, 15-1/2 x 25" (1200-1800) 1265

Full figures of Phil climbing up smitten Hercules & tweaking his ear, 19-1/2 x 25" (1500-2000) 1840

Hips-up of Meg leaning against tree & staring into space, 12-1/2 x 17" (1000-1500) 1380

Full figures of Pain & Panic posing after transformation from bunny & gopher, 12-1/2 x 17" (1500-2000) 1610

2 set-ups: ankles-up front view of black marketeer with cloak open revealing sundials; hips-up side view of burnt man holding charred cat; each 12-1/2 x 17" (1000-1500) 920

"The end is coming!" Full figures of deranged man standing on steps with arms wrapped around Pegasus' head as shocked Hercules & Phil watch, background has apocalyptic graffiti on steps & wall, 19-1/2 x 33-1/2" (1800-2200) 1610

"...what you folks need..." Full figures of smiling Hercules standing with arms spread as Phil & Pegasus watch, 12-1/2 x 17" (2000-3000) 2300

Waist-up front view of Hercules holding enraged Phil, 19-1/2 x 25" (1500-2000) 1955

Full figures of surprised Hercules & Phil looking up as they sit/stand by wall, 12-1/2 x 17" (1200-1800) 1150

"Phil, this is great!" Ankles-up of excited Hercules holding Phil at eye level by cheeks as Pegasus watches, 12-1/2 x 17" (1500-2000) 1150

Waist-up of Hercules looking ahead as he holds disheveled Meg & Pegasus smiles wickedly, 13-1/2 x 18-3/4" (1200-1800) 977

Near-full figure of determined Hercules sliding down hill, 19-1/2 x 34" (1200-1800) 5750

Near-full figure of Hades sitting in stone chair snacking on worms, 16-3/4 x 24" (1500-2000) 1725

Smiling Hades in stone chair holds two flaming thumbs up, 12-1/2 x 17" (1500-2000) 4312

Full-figure long shot of Phil & Hercules standing in rain before 3-headed Hydra, 19-1/2 x 25" (2500-3500) 1955

Hades in stone chair prepares to light cigar w/flaming thumb, 19-1/2 x 25" (1500-2000) 3105

Close-up portrait of enraged Hades smoking cigar, 12-1/2 x 17" (1500-2000) 1610

Full figures of panicked townsperson & Hercules standing before huge open-mouthed wild boar, 12-1/2 x 17" (1500-2000) 1725

Full figure of grim Hercules standing facing right & drawing back arrow, 12-1/2 x 38" (1200-1800) 3450

Hips-up front view of smiling Hercules standing with arms out in shower of gold coins, 12-1/2 x 17" (1500-2000) 1265

Full-figure front views of Muses standing in blue dresses singing with hands clasped, 13-1/4 x 18-3/4" (1200-1800) 977

Enraged Hades (facing left) stares at sea serpent game piece in his hand, 12-1/2 x 17" (1500-2000) 1610

Phil, Hercules, & Pegasus sit in theater box applauding performance, 12-1/2 x 34-1/2" (2500-3500) 2645

Full figures of Muses standing posing in yellow outfits, top & bottom border, 19-1/2 x 25" (1200-1800) 3105

Full figures of smiling Hercules & Pegasus kneeling

after imprinting wet cement, 14-1/2 x 25" (1800-2200) 2645

Aerial view of Hades on balcony flinging fireball upward, 19-1/2 x 25" (1500-2000) 1150

Full figure of smiling Pain standing in front of wall wearing Hercules sandals, 12-1/2 x 17" (1200-1800) 977

Angry Hades with arms raised above terrified Pain, looking to his left, 12-1/2 x 17" (1500-2000) 3335

Full figures of Hercules & Pegasus kneeling in coliseum before crowd as column sections displace & mushroom cloud of black smoke rises in distance, 13 x 22" (1800-2200) 5175

"He's gotta have a weakness," Hades w/arm around suspicious Meg at sunset, 12-3/4 x 25" (1800-2200) 1840

Ankles-up of frustrated Hercules turning around while posing in lion's skin, 12-1/2 x 17" (1500-2000) 1840

"There is nothin' you can't do, Kid!" Phil (full figure) stands on table to give pep talk to sitting Hercules (ankles up), 12-1/2 x 17" (1500-2000) 1495

"Phil! Help!" Close-up of Hercules' head & shoulders flat on floor with girl's feet on his face & Phil lying beside him, 12-1/2 x 17" (1200-1500) 920

"I'm no hero." Hips-up front view of modest Hercules gesturing, 12-1/2 x 17" (1200-1800) 920

Knees-up of Hercules & Meg standing in garden talking, 12-1/2 x 17" (2000-3000) 1610

Full figures of Hercules holding Meg up after she tripped on stairs, 19-1/2 x 25" (1500-2000) 4887

Full figure of Meg reclined on bench holding her ankle under surprised Hercules' (knees up) nose, 12-1/2 x 20" (1500-2000) 3220

Ankles-up of lovestruck Meg sitting on bench holding flower & singing, 14-1/4 x 25" (1200-1800) 1610

Full-figure long shot of Meg walking in garden as Hades talks while sitting on melted statue, 19-1/2 x 45-1/2" (2000-3000) 2990

Full-figure elevated view of Hercules playfully sparring with serious Phil, 12-1/2 x 17" (1200-1800) 1035

Full figure of Hades lying across goal post crossbar, 12-1/2 x 17" (1500-2000) 1150

Knees-up of Hades standing in stadium w/arm around Hercules, 12-1/2 x 27-1/2" (1500-2000) 2300

"We dance, we kiss, we schmooze," Hips-up front view of smiling Hades standing with arms out, 12-1/2 x 17" (1500-2000) 2070

Full figure of stunned Hercules sitting on ground with huge barbell across knees, 12-1/2 x 17" (1200-1800) 977

"...is she not, like, a fabulous little actress?" Ankles-up of Hades putting Meg on display, 12-1/2 x 17" (1500-2000) 1495

Waist-up front view of Hades with his arm around sad Meg's shoulder, 12-1/2 x 17" (1500-2000) 1840

Hades, Pain, & Panic hover in chariot under cloud-covered sky as dawn breaks, 19-1/2 x 35-1/2" (1800-2200) 1840

"Let her go." Close-up of angry Hercules face to face with Hades, 12-1/2 x 17" (1800-2200) 3450

Full figure of Hercules swan diving as Hades stands watching from pinnacle, 12-1/2 x 17" (1800-2200) 1380

Waist-up front view of delighted Zeus with his arm around happy Hercules as god, 12-1/2 x 17" (1800-2200) 2645

Muses stand on cloud singing in front of sun rays, 12-1/2 x 17" (1200-1800) 1955

Close-up group scene of happy Meg, Hercules, Phil and Pegasus, 12-1/2 x 17" (2500-3500) 5462

MODEL ART

All items in this section were auctioned at Sotheby's, June 20, 1998.

Lots 118-125 are animators maquettes used during production. They were specially hand painted for the auction by the Ink & Paint Dept. at the Walt Disney Studios, Burbank, California. All are full figure. Dimensions are the heights in inches.

Zeus, #36/40, 20-1/2" (1500-2000) 2875

Hercules, #19/49, 18" (2000-3000) 4887

Meg, #25/44, 13" (1200-1800) 2875

Phil, #7/46, 9" (1500-2000) 4312

Pegasus, #12/43, 13-1/2" (1500-2000) 2185

Pain, #30/37, 7-1/2" (1200-1800) 2760
Panic, #30/37, 8" (1200-1800) 2415
Hades, #16/42, 17-1/2" (2000-3000) 4887

THE HUNCHBACK OF NOTRE DAME (1996)

CEL SET-UPS

All items in this section were auctioned at Sotheby's, June 21, 1997.

These include original art actually used in the making of the film. Each set-up featured a production background accompanied by character and effects cels specially created by artists in the Ink & Paint Dept. at the Walt Disney Studios, Burbank, CA. In many cases set-ups included original production overlays/underlays. The basis for the cels were original animation drawings rendered by Disney animators and used in the production of the film. Each set-up was matted and framed.

Full figure of Frollo on horseback dangling bundle
    over well, 19-1/2 x 25" (1500-2000) 1955
Overhead view of cathedral statues gazing down
    disapprovingly at full figure of Frollo on
    horseback, 12-1/2 x 17" (1500-2000) 1955
Quasimodo holds baby bird in palms of his hands at
    edge of parapet, 12-1/2 x 17" (2000-3000) 6900
"Here, get away from me!" Full figure of Laverne
    with 8 pigeons, 12-1/2 x 17" (1500-2000) 2587
Rear view of Gargoyles watching Quasimodo hunched
    over toy table, 12-1/2 x 17" (2500-3500) 2587
Laverne speaks as she places finger on model
    Parisian 12-1/2 x 17" (1500-2000) 1150
2 set-ups: "E?", "Eternal Damnation." Suspicious
    Frollo holds goblet as he quizzes Quasimodo. Qua-
    simodo responds w/upraised finger.
    12-1/2 x 18-1/2" & 12-1/2 x 17"
    (2000-3000) 4600
"And stay in here." Angry Frollo lectures Quasimodo
    at toy table, 12-1/2 x 17" (2000-3000) 7475
Upward shot of Quasimodo singing as he swings
    from column, 12-1/2 x 35" (2000-3000) 6325
Quasimodo sings as he walks amid columns,
    12-1/2 x 17" (2000-3000) 6325
Close-up front shot of Quasimodo singing in front
    of columns, 12-1/2 x 17" (1500-2000) 1840
Full figures of smiling Phoebus & Achilles standing
    watching Djali dance as piper plays & purple
    hat sits in foreground, 12-1/2 x 17"
    (2000-3000) 1610
Esmerelda smiles as she holds tambourine,
    12-1/2 x 17" (2000-3000) 3737
Full figure of Djali picking up hat as coins fly,
    12-1/2 x 30" (1500-2000) 1840
Full figure of Phoebus pulling Achilles into
    soldiers' path, 12-1/2 x 25" (1500-2500) 2300
Smiling Esmerelda & Djali peek around corner
    of stone wall, 12-1/2 x 17" (2500-3500) 11,500
Phoebus holds handful of coins as he & Achilles
    approach disguised Esmerelda & Djali
    sitting in street, 12-1/2 x 17" (1500-2500) 2185
Closeup of Djali w/pipe & Esmerelda peeking
    around wall, 12-1/2 x 17" (2500-3500) 3737
"Reporting for duty..." Phoebus & Frollo talk in
    hallway, 12-1/2 x 35-1/2" (1500-2500) 1840
Frollo talks to Phoebus on parapet w/Notre Dame
    in background, 12-1/2 x 17" (2500-3500) 9200
Clopin sings on knees in front of procession of
    townspeople, 12-1/2 x 17" (2000-3000) 2587
Cloaked Quasimodo cowers as Clopin reaches
    for him in front of townspeople, 12-1/2
    x 23-1/2" (3000-4000) 8625
Clopin sees Quasimodo in background as he
    sings to bowing crowd amid confetti,
    12-1/2 x 17" (2500-3500) 3450
Full figures of mischievous Clopin cutting strings
    to balloons Quasimodo is hiding behind,
    12-1/2 x 18-1/2" (2500-3500) 3737
Full figures of Esmerelda coming to aid Quasimodo
    who's fallen in dressing tent, 12-1/2 x 17"
    (2500-3500) 4600
2 set-ups: close-ups of startled Djali & sympathetic
    Esmerelda inside tent, each 12-1/2 x 17"
    (2000-3000) 1840
"By the way, great mask!" Esmerelda gestures
    before disappearing in tent, 12-1/2 x 17"
    (2000-3000) 3450
Clopin sings to horrified Frollo who's seated in
    reviewing chair, 12-1/2 x 17" (2500-3500) 2300
"Dance La Esmerelda..." Close-up frontal of
    grinning Clopin, 12-1/2 x 17" (1500-2000) 1840

Flirtatious Esmerelda wraps scarf around neck of
    horrified Frollo, 12-1/2 x 17" (2500-3500) 4312
Close-up of alluring Esmerelda, 10-1/2 x 13"
    (2000-3000) 4312
Esmerelda reaches from stage & grabs spear of
    admiring soldier, 12-1/2 x 17" (2000-3000) 5175
2 set-ups: full-figure long shot of Esmerelda holding
    spear overhead; close-up of Quasimodo
    applauding in crowd; 12-1/2 x 17" each
    (2500-3500) 4312
Smiling Esmerelda extends hand to Quasimodo
    from stage, 13-3/4 x 21" (2500-3500) 6900
Djali butts 2nd contestant off stage & into crowd,
    19-1/2 x 25" (2500-3500) 5175
2 set-ups: close-ups of enraged Frollo & happy Quasi-
    modo as King of Fools, 12-1/2 x 17"
    each (2000-3000) 5175
Front view of Frollo glaring while sitting in
    reviewing chair, 19-1/2 x 25" (2500-3500) 3737
Worried Esmerelda holds untied scarf, 12-1/2
    x 17" (2000-3000) 6325
Full figures of determined Esmerelda standing over
    bound Quasimodo w/knife in hand as crowd
    watches, 12-1/2 x 17-1/2" (2500-3500) 6900
Full figure of Djali standing in crowd with tongue
    out, 12-1/2 x 17" (1500-2000) 1380
Worried Esmerelda looks around, 12-1/2 x 17"
    (2000-3000) 3162
Full figure of Esmerelda standing in street by
    caged prisoner as crowd watches from
    distance, 12-1/2 x 34" (2500-3500) 4312
Close-up of happy Esmerelda, Djali, & man
    looking back to right as crowd watches,
    12-1/2 x 17" (3000-4000) 2587
Full figures of Esmerelda bowing on top of platform
    with Djali, 12-1/2 x 17" (2500-3500) 3162
2 set-ups: closeups in rain of suspicious Phoebus atop
    Achilles, 12-1/2 x 17"; cloaked pipe-smoking
    Djali next to Achilles, with Esmerelda's hand
    holding cane 11-1/4 x 13" (2500-3500) 2012
Djali (pipe in mouth) looks up as he & Esmerelda
    uncloak inside cathedral, 12-1/2 x 17"
    (2000-3000) 2300
Full figure of smiling Esmerelda standing w/hand
    on candelabra, 12-1/2 x 17" (2500-3500) 2587
Full figures of angry Djali & sword-wielding
    Esmerelda pinning Phoebus to floor,
    12-1/2 x 23-1/2" (3000-4000) 3737
Full figure of horrified Djali standing at Esmerelda's
    feet, 12-1/2 x 17" (1500-2000) 1150
Waist-up of Esmerelda looking around inside
    cathedral, 14 x 18-1/2" (1500-2000) 1955
Full-figure long view of Archdeacon confronting
    Frollo as Phoebus, Esmerelda, Djali, & 3
    soldiers watch, 12-1/2 x 17" (3000-4000) 3162
Full figures of dejected Esmerelda sitting against
    door as somber Djali stands at her side,
    12-1/2 x 17" (2000-3000) 1610
Archdeacon lights candles as he talks to Djali & Esmerel-
    da, 14-1/2 x 33-1/2" (2500-3500) 2012
Close-up of awed Esmerelda as she touches column
    & looks up, 12-1/2 x 17" (1500-2000) 1150
Close-up of sad Esmerelda looking up, 13-1/2 x
    18" (2000-3000) 2875
Full figures of Esmerelda (eyes closed) & Djali
    standing bathed in pool of light rays,
    12-1/2 x 20-3/4" (2500-3500) 2300
Shy Quasimodo stands between columns & smiles
    warmly, 12-1/2 x 17" (2000-3000) 2875
3 Gargoyles watch from above, 12-3/4 x 17"
    (2500-3500) 2587
Quasimodo leads Esmerelda in bell tower past 2
    (stone) Gargoyles, 12 x 21" (3000-4000) 2300
Close-up of Djali examining toy village & sheep,
    12-1/2 x 17" (2500-3500) 2875
"That's Little Sophia, and..." Quasimodo climbs
    among bells, 19-1/2 x 25" (2000-3000) 3737
Esmerelda holds Big Marie's clapper as Quasimodo
    talks, 12-1/2 x 17" (2500-3500) 3737
"Give me your hand." Full figures of Esmerelda & Qua-
    simodo sitting together on roof with city behind
    them, 12-1/2 x 17" (2500-3500) 2875
Gargoyles climb on each other to eavesdrop,
    12-1/2 x 17" (2500-3500) 2012
"You mean climb down?" Esmerelda & Djali look
    down as Quasimodo stands on railing and
    gestures, 12-1/2 x 17" (2500-3500) 2012
Esmerelda holds worried Djali as she pulls out
    scarf, 12-1/2 x 17" (2500-3500) 1610

Confident Quasimodo runs along crockets on
    cathedral's side as petrified Esmerelda & Djali
    cling to his back, 14 x 21-1/2" (2500-3500) 2875
"You're quite an acrobat." Full figures of Esmerelda
    holding Djali & clinging to smiling Quasimodo
    on roof, 12-1/2 x 17" (2500-3500) 2012
Close-up from below of sparks flying as Quasimodo,
    Esmerelda, & Djali slide down roof on panel,
    12-1/2 x 17" (2500-3500) 2875
Esmerelda, Djali, & Quasimodo blend in w/cathedral
    statue, 19-1/2 x 17-1/2" (3000-4000) 3737
Close-up of puzzled Quasimodo studying amulet,
    12-1/2 x 17" (2000-3000) 1610
Smitten Quasimodo crouches at base of statue,
    12-1/2 x 17" (2000-3000) 1610
Smiling Phoebus takes hand of startled Quasimodo
    as he climbs over parapet with river & city in
    background, 12-1/2 x 17" (2000-3000) 1610
Angry Quasimodo holds torch & stares at Phoebus
    in stairway, 12-1/2 x 17" (2000-3000) 1725
Gargoyles cheer from railing as glum Quasimodo
    walks along top of Cathedral, 12 x 26"
    (2500-3500) 3162
"Way to go, Loverboy..." Full figures of Laverne
    & Hugo cheering on walkway, 12-1/2 x 17"
    (1500-2000) 1495
"Don't be so modest." Laverne gestures as she
    & Hugo climb steps, 12-1/2 x 17"
    (1500-2000) 1380
Full-figure front view of smiling Gargoyles standing
    in front of bell, 12-1/2 x 17" (2500-3500) 2300
Grinning Hugo watches determined Victor lying on
    floor drawing, 12-1/2 x 27" (1800-2200) 1495
2 set-ups: front view of Esmerelda's apparition
    in flames; Frollo clutches chest & recoils;
    12-1/2 x 17" each (2500-3500) 3450
Full figure of tormented Frollo standing in empty
    hall fondling veil, 12-1/2 x 17" (1500-2000) 1495
"It's not my fault..." Frollo gestures to rows of red-
    robed judges, 12-1/2 x 17" (2000-3000) 1610
Full-figure side view of Frollo reaching toward
    fireplace & smoke image of Esmerelda,
    19-1/2 x 25" (2000-3000) 4887
Front view of scarf-clutching Frollo framed by 2
    pillars of fire, 19-1/2 x 25" (2000-3000) 1610
Frollo on horse in city holding silver coins in out-
    stretched palm, 12-1/2 x 17" (1500-2000) 1380
Full-figure side view of miller on knees inside house
    in front of Frollo as wife, child, & Phoebus
    watch, 14-3/4 x 20" (2000-3000) 1840
Esmerelda wades into river by bridge support,
    14 x 18-1/2" (1500-2000) 2587
"...I'm losing to a bird!" Frustrated Hugo plays
    cards w/pigeon, 12-1/2 x 17" (2500-3500) 2012
Hugo reaches for plate w/cheese & bread &
    bottle of wine, 12-1/2 x 17" (1500-2000) 1495
"Knights in shining armor..." Smiling Victor
    gestures, 12-1/2 x 17" (1500-2000) 1150
Hugo sings as he holds flaming hot dog, 12-1/2
    x 17" (1500-2000) 1150
Heart-shaped smoke ring encircles Quasimodo's
    face as he holds ace of hearts, 12-1/2 x 17"
    (2000-3000) 1610
3 Gargoyles in close harmony, 12-1/2 x 17"
    (2500-3500) 2300
Full figures of proud Gargoyles as barbers with
    barber pole & wigged Quasimodo in
    barber's chair, 12-1/2 x 17" (3000-4000) 2587
Pigeon-draped Laverne encircles eyes w/fingers
    as she sings, 12-1/2 x 17" (1500-2000) 1150
Laverne lies on piano in jewels & feather boa
    with hand on Quasimodo's head as she
    sings, 12-1/2 x 17" (2500-3500) 2012
Full figure of Hugo dressed as Esmerelda, 14 x
    29" (2500-3500) 2012
"You're the bell ringer!" Gargoyles rock inside
    bell tops, 12-1/2 x 17" (3000-4000) 2300
Full figures of smiling Quasimodo, Laverne, &
    Hugo standing amid flowers & romantic
    statuary, 12-1/2 x 17" (3000-4000) 2300
"You've done so much..." Esmerelda & Quasi
    hold hands, 12-1/2 x 17" (2500-3500) 2012
Full figure of Quasi dragging wounded Phoebus
    in bell tower, 12-1/2 x 17" (1500-2000) 1265
Frollo notices Esmerelda doll as he & Quasimodo
    sit at toy table, 12-1/2 x 17" (1800-2200) 1380
Full figures of Gargoyles standing & staring disapprov-
    ingly, 12-1/2 x 18-1/2" (2000-3000) 1610
Phoebus (holding torch) & hooded Quasimodo

walk down corridor of skeletons, 12-1/2
x 18-1/2" (2000-3000) 2587
"Hello, you're there!" Clopin confronts bound &
gagged Phoebus & Quasimodo with skulls,
12-1/2 x 17" (2000-3000) 2587
Full figures of Clopin mimicking Quasimodo as
bound & gagged Quasi & Phoebus stand
on gallows, 13-3/4 x 17-3/4" (2000-3000) 2070
Esmeralda & Phoebus stand talking in background
as Quasimodo climbs down ladder, 19-1/2
x 25" (2000-3000) 2070
Esmeralda thanks Phoebus with her arm on his
shoulder, 12-1/2 x 17" (2500-3500) 2012
Frollo confronts angry Quasimodo, Phoebus, &
Esmeralda as 3 soldiers watch, 14-1/2 x
26-1/2" (2500-3500) 8625
Frollo taunts angry Phoebus as Esmeralda watches,
15-1/2 x 17-1/2" (2000-3000) 2875
"The prisoner Esmerelda..." Frollo reads from
scroll by firelight, 10-1/2 x 13" (1500-2000) 1150
"Choose me or the fire." Frollo leers at frightened
Esmerelda, 12-1/2 x 17" (2000-3000) 1610
2 set-ups: close-up of determined Quasimodo
holding onto rope against wall, 12-1/2 x 17";
Esmerelda (bound to stake) coughs amid
smoke, 10-1/2 x 13-1/2"; (2000-3000) 1955
Angry Quasimodo turns from unconscious
Esmerelda lying on bed as Gargoyles peek
thru door, 12-1/2 x 17" (2500-3500) 2300
Full figure of grinning Hugo removing candles
from candelabra, 12-1/2 x 17" (1500-2000) 1955
Full figures of grinning Hugo loading catapult as
Victor finishes construction, 16-1/4 x 26-1/2"
(1800-2200) 1955
"Fly, my pretties!" Full-figure rear view of Laverne
launching pigeons from top of Cathedral,
12-1/2 x 20-3/4" (2000-3000) 1840
Close-up of Quasimodo offering spoonful of water
to unconscious Esmeralda, 12-1/2 x 17"
(2000-3000) 1610
Ground-level view of Frollo dangling from gargoyle
as Esmeralda holds on to Quasimodo who's
dangling next to him, 15 x 25" (2500-3500) 2587
Ground-level view of falling Frollo clutching
demonized gargoyle, 15-1/2 x 37-1/2"
(2000-3000) 2587
Close-up of smiling Quasimodo & Esmeralda
looking left after embracing, 12-1/2 x 17"
(2500-3500) 2587
Full-figure side view of little girl standing before
Quasimodo on Cathedral steps as Esmerelda,
Phoebus, & crowd watch, 12-1/2 x 17"
(3000-4000) 5750
"Three cheers for Quasimodo!" Clopin shouts from
halfway up pole, 14 x 20" (1500-2000) 2587
Esmerelda stands with & smiles admiringly at wry Phoe-
bus, 19-1/2 x 25" (2500-3500) 2587
Smiling Esmerelda & Phoebus hold Djali in front of
Cathedral door, 12-1/2 x 17" (3000-4000) 4025
MODEL ART
All items in this section were auctioned at Sotheby's,
June 21, 1997.
These are animators maquettes used during produc-
tion. All are full figure unless noted.

Clopin, 14-3/8" high, #21/21 (1000-1500) 1380
Djali, 7-7/8" high, #33/34 (1500-2000) 1380
Victor, 9" high, #2/39 (1500-2000) 1150
Laverne, 6-3/4" high, #2/37 (1500-2000) 1840
Hugo, 7" high, #2/39 (1500-2000) 1610
Frollo, torso length, 12-5/8" high, #31/37
(2000-3000) 1610
Esmeralda, 13-1/4" high, #34/48 (2000-3000) 2875
Quasimodo, 10-1/8" high, #45/45 (2000-3000) 3450

ICHABOD AND MR. TOAD
See THE ADVENTURES OF ICHABOD & MR. TOAD

JAMES & THE GIANT PEACH (1996)
All items in this section were auctioned at Sotheby's,
June 21, 1997.
CONCEPT & INSPIRATIONAL ART/STORY ART
26 pieces of concept art relating to Spiker & Sponge,
different mediums, all on paper, sheet
sizes range 8 x 9" to 29 x 24" (3000-5000) 2587
The next three items are concept artwork by Production Designer Harley Jessup.
2 Spiker & Sponge nightmare designs; peach floating

in ocean; peach flying; James on beach being
threatened by rhinoceros; image sizes vary
(1500-2000) 2185
Live-action designs: 2 of Spiker & Sponge's house;
their sitting room; James' attic room; James'
peach-pit house; New York City skyline;
animation designs for James' dreams of New
York using real postcards; image sizes vary
(1200-1800) 2185
3 peach pit interior designs, 5-1/4 x
10-1/8"each (800-1200) 1380
6 b&w story drawings & 3 color concepts; india ink,
colored pencil, pastel & ink marker on paper;
4 x 5-1/2" to 9-1/2 x 13"; VF; HL/Apr 25/98
(500-800) 489
ILLUSTRATION ART
These items are signed Lane Smith original illustration art (oil or oil & ink on board), image size 9 x 14",
from *James and The Giant Peach* by Roald Dahl, Disney Press, 1996.

Plate 6: Earthworm being used as bait to
lure sea gulls (700-900) 2587
Plate 7: Shark attacking peach (700-900) 2587
Plate 9: James sleeping in cocoon Spider
has spun for him (800-1200) 2300
Plate 10: James caught up in nightmare
about Spiker & Sponge (800-1200) 2070
Plate 12: James is haunted by ship's
figurehead resembling Spiker & Sponge
as he & Spider dive into ocean to rescue
Centipede (1500-2000) 4025
Plate 15: fierce, angry Cloud-Men encircle peach
(700-900) 1955
Plate 16: wicked Cloud-Men blow peach thru sky
(700-900) 2070
PROP ART
Peach pit interior 3-dimensional mock-up in two
pieces, painted & sculpted styrofoam,
12 x 12 x 5" (1000-1500) 805
48 items from sequence in which James has nightmare
about being a caterpillar who is sprayed by Spiker
& Sponge, then chased over a branch & thru
soup can by rhinoceros. Includes soup can; 2
mock-ups of Spiker & 1 of Sponge; 2 versions
of rhino; full storyboarding (41 sheets); photostat
copy of storyboards laid out (2000-3000) 1610
72 items from sequence in which Centipede emerges
victorious from battling pirates & attaches
compass to peach stem. Includes full-scale
peach stem w/compass attached (20 x 10");
9 pieces of concept art & designs for compass;
complete set of storyboards (61 sheets);
photostat copy of storyboards laid out in
sequence (1500-2000) 2070
130 items from sequence in which Peach arrives over
New York City only to be attacked by rhinoceros.
Includes fiberfill mock-up of rhino head (12 x 8")
w/red eyes & hinged mouth; 4 pieces of rhino
concept art; 2 drawings of cloud people;
complete set of storyboards (121 sheets); 2
photostat copies of storyboards laid out in
sequence (2000-3000) 2760
Spiker & Sponge's patio furniture: 2 wrought-iron
filigreed patio chairs (54 x 26" each); marble-
topped round table (27 x 24" diameter); (1000-
1500) 805
1/4 scale peach w/handle attached (19 x 19");
portion of miniature scale fence (8 x 11")
erected around peach for exhibition; miniature
prop car (6 x 13") when Spiker & Sponge
attempt to escape rolling peach (2000-3000) 3737
1/4 scale peach w/hole in its side, 19 x 19"
(1500-2500) 1840
1/4 scale peach w/snow-covered fence wrapped
around it, 19 x 19" (2000-3000) 1725
Pre-production collage w/corresponding props from
Capt. Jack's sunken pirate ship. Includes anchor;
chandelier; gibbet cage; globe; map box w/maps;
books; 3 sconces; canon base; bust of Capt. Jack
(2000-3000) 1610
Capt. Jack's desk & chair, pirate's trunk, concept
artwork of Jack at desk (2000-3000) 1840
Ship's Spiker & Sponge figure head, made of
painted styrofoam, 14 x 28" (1500-2500) 1150
Fully armatured production Earthworm puppet
with 17 pairs of glasses, 2-1/2 x 20-1/2"
(1500-2000) 3737
Fully armatured production Centipede puppet (14-1/2

x 4-1/2") w/14 eyelids, 3 photocopy model
sheets (2 are 24 x 27"), prop matchbook chair
(5 x 5-3/4") w/2 collage boards from which the
chair was designed (3000-5000) 8625
Fully armatured production Grasshopper puppet (16
x 8") w/30 mouths, 16 eyebrows, 2 photocopy
model sheets (19 x 24"), giant tea bag (4-1/2 x
5-3/4") used as pillow w/collage board from
which it was designed (3000-5000) 8625
Fully armatured production Glowworm puppet
(12-1/2 x 5") w/2 photocopy model sheets
(19 x 24") & 2 prop lanterns (one 12 x
17-1/2") 3000-5000) 2587
Fully armatured production Ladybug puppet (11 x 7-
1/2") w/8 eyelids, 54 mouths, 2 photocopy
model sheets, 3 giant gardening gloves with
collage boards from which they were designed
(3000-5000) 5175
Fully armatured production Spider puppet (7 x 10")
w/15 faces, sheet featuring various spider
designs (24 x 26-3/4"), replica of spider's
web nailed onto board (9-3/4 x 18-1/2";
(4000-6000) 10,350
Fully armatured production James puppet (9 x 3")
w/18 sets of eyes; photocopy model sheet (21 x
24"); 2 "Guardianship Decree" copies; "Map to
America"; original Lane Smith "Map to America";
miniature bed; 2 pieces of artwork presenting
James' peach-pit home; (decrees, map & pits
11 x 17"); (4000-6000) 14,950

THE JUNGLE BOOK (1967)
ANIMATION DRAWINGS (also see CEL SET-UPS)
Detailed rough drawing of stunned Baloo signed by
Frank Thomas, 8-1/2 x 5", HL/Aug 6/95
(300-400) 504
Near-full-figure drawing of suspended King Louie
gesturing with left arm & talking while his
left feet hold Mowgli around chin, 9 x 9",
HL/Mar 16-17/96 (150-200) 978
Rough drawing of perplexed Baloo, signed by Frank
Thomas, 8 x 5", HL/Apr 28/96 (400-600) 748
Smiling Baloo with eyes closed facing to right,
signed by Ollie Johnston, 8 x 10" inc.
signature, VF, HL/Oct 6/96 (300-500) 690
Rough drawing of Baloo (stomach up) facing left &
looking up with mouth open, signed by Frank
Thomas, 8 x 8", VF+, HL/Oct 6/96
(500-700) 1035
Wide-eyed, stunned Baloo (from stomach up)
signed by Frank Thomas; 8 x 5-1/2"
inc. signature, HL/Feb 23/97 (400-500) 633
Waist-up drawing of sad Baloo facing left & looking
up, signed by Frank Thomas & Dale Oliver,
8 x 7" including signatures, HL/Feb 23/97
(400-500) 748
Full-figure rough drawing of Baloo walking away to
right, signed by Frank Thomas, 8-1/2 x 4-1/2"
inc. signature, HL/May 31/97 (150-250) 403
Col. Hathi trumpeting, 11-1/2 x 9-1/2",
HL/May 31/97 (100-200) 138
Waist-up drawing of smiling Baloo facing left,
looking up, signed by Frank Thomas, 8-1/2
x 7-1/2", VF, HL/Nov 16/97 (300-400) 575
Waist-up rough drawing of smiling Baloo facing
left & looking up, signed by Frank Thomas
& Dale Oliver, 8-1/2 x 8" w/signature, VF,
HL/Nov 16/97 (300-500) 920
Waist-up rough drawing of bewildered Baloo, signed
by Frank Thomas, 8 x 5" inc. signature, VF,
HL/Apr 25/98 (300-400) 690
Full-figure rough drawing of happy Baloo standing,
signed by Ollie Johnston, 7 x 10-1/2" inc.
signature, VF, HL/Apr 25/98 (400-600) 690
Stomach-up portrait drawing of smiling Baloo facing
left & looking up, signed by Frank Thomas &
Dale Oliver, 8-1/2 x 7-1/2" inc. signatures, VF,
HL/Apr 25/98 (400-600) 805
BACKGROUNDS
Original pan background (tempera on background
sheet) with pre-production cels of Bagheera,
Mowgli, foreground vegetation, 11 x 39-1/2",
signed by Walt Peregoy, HL/Nov 13/94
(1200-1600) 3584
Background study (tempera on background sheet)
with overlay cel of Mowgli in 8 key poses,
12-1/2 x 30", signed by Walt Peregoy,
HL/Nov 13/94 (1200-1600) 2240
Preliminary background of jungle, watercolor on

board, CE/Dec 16/94 (2000-3000) 4140

CEL SET-UPS

Shere Kahn runs from fire attached to tail, hand-painted non-studio background, "Best wishes-Ken Anderson", 12" long, S/Dec 16/93 (2000-3000) 1725

Studio publicity cel of Baloo holding Mowgli, jungle master tempera background, 11 x 15", studio notes, w/matching animation drawing, VF+, HL/Apr 10/94 (4000-6000) 5600

Mowgli balancing water jug, jungle master tempera background, 12 x 16", studio notes, VF+, HL/Apr 10/94 (3500-4500) 4144

Full figure of King Louie swinging thru trees, tempera master background, 10-1/2 x 15", studio notes, VF+, HL/Apr 10/94 (3500-4500) 4704

Mowgli trying to be an elephant under watchful eye of Baby Elephant; Shere Kahn approaching happy Mowgli; each w/printed DL background, latter w/gold DL label (both need restoration), S/Jun 17/94 (1000-1500) 1380

Shere Kahn (6 x 12-1/2") & (Kaa (7-3/4 x 1-1/2"), watercolor production background, CE/Jun 18/94 (3000-4000) 5175

Shere Kahn (5-1/2 x 7") scratches Kaa's chin (4-1/2 x 5"), watercolor production background, CE/Jun 18/94 (3000-4000) 6325

Mowgli (3") plays w/laughing Baloo (lying down, 6-1/2"), key pan watercolor production background, CE/Jun 18/94 (8000-12,000) 21,850

Argumentative Baloo (chest up, 4 x 7-1/2"), watercolor production background, CE/Jun 18/94 (2000-3000) 4025

Full figure of King Louie; Kaa & Mowgli; color print backgrounds w/DL mats & labels, 8 x 10", HL/Aug 21/94 (1200-1600) 2240

Matching full-figure cel & master background of lively King Louie, 8 x 10", watercolor on background sheet, stamp, label, HL/Nov 13/94 (2500-3000) 4032

Somber Baloo (7") w/paws on Mowgli's shoulders (4-1/2"), DL background & label, CE/Dec 16/94 (700-900) 1725

Defensive King Louie w/stick, 7", watercolor production background, CE/Dec 16/94 (2500-3500) 2070

Baloo (7") lying at foot of standing Mowgli (5-1/2"), DL printed background, Walt Disney Studios seal, CE/Dec 16/94 (1000-1500) 2070

Close-up of smiling Shere Khan, 6-1/2", DL background & label, CE/Dec 16/94 (1000-1500) 2760

Close-up of Shere Khan speaking, 7", DL printed winter background, CE/Dec 16/94 (700-900) 1495

Full figures of Baloo (6-1/2") & monkey (3"), DL background & label, CE/Dec 16/94 (700-900) 1840

Head of angry Bagheera amid temple ruins, 5", key watercolor production background, CE/Dec 16/94 (3000-4000) 5175

Mowgli (5") watches King Louie dance (with eyes closed, 5-1/2"), printed background, gold DL label, S/Dec 17/94 (1000-1500) 1150

Suspicious Shere Kahn, 6" (chest up); King Louie 'going ape', 5"; each w/printed background & gold DL label, S/Dec 17/94 (1500-2500) 2300

Mesmerized Mowgli (6") trying to balance jug (8") on head; buzzards singing merrily, 3 to 4"; both with printed background & gold DL label, S/Dec 17/94 (1000-1500) 1495

Pan production set-up of Baloo (6") picking Mowgli (4") up from scene where Baloo 'comes back to life', with pan watercolor production background from scene where Rama examines bundle in front of den, S/Dec 17/94 (8000-10,000) 9775

2-cel set-up of Baloo (7-1/2") talking to Mowgli (5") who holds village girl's water pot; Col. Hathi (8"), eyes closed, standing imperiously; each with printed background & DL label, S/Dec 17/94 (1200-1800) 2185

Hips-up of smiling Baloo standing facing left with Mowgli (eyes closed) riding on his shoulders, 6", gouache pre-production background of jungle temple, Disney Art Program seal, SR/Spring/95 (1800-2800) 2220

Knees-up front view of Mowgli stretching, 6-1/4", photographic color print background with large rock, SR/Spring/95 (500-900) 550

Full figures of angry Baloo (7-3/4") sitting facing right,

holding squirming Mowgli off ground around waist, photographic color print jungle background, SR/Spring/95 (1100-1600) 1340

Full figures of disguised Baloo & King Louie dancing together, 7-1/2 x 8-1/2", color print background, clipped signatures of Ollie Johnston & Milt Kahl, HL/Apr 23/95 (1000-1500) 2912

"Mowgli, come back!" Sad Baloo watches from jungle, 9-1/2 x 15-1/2", matching cel & master background (tempera on background sheet), w/overlay cel autographed by Frank Thomas, Ollie Johnston & Ken Anderson, HL/Apr 23/95 (4000-5000) 4928

Full figure of horrified Bagheera sitting on log, 4-1/2", watercolor production background; plus matching layout drawing with notes, CE/Jun 9/95 (3000-4000) 5175

Full figures of 2 vultures holding sad Mowgli, 6-1/2", DL printed background & label, CE/Jun 9/95 (600-800) 920

Close-up of vulture, 6", DL printed background & label, CE/Jun 9/95 (300-500) 207

Large portrait of smiling Mowgli, 6-1/2", printed background, S/Jun 10/95 (800-1200) 1265

Mowgli's wolf brothers happily greet him, 5", watercolor production background, S/Jun 10/95 (2500-3500) 4025

Waist-up front view of worried Baloo standing w/paws up, looking down, 8-1/2", matching gouache key master background w/filtered jungle light, 16-field, SR/Fall/95 (2500-4500) 3680

Full-figure of King Louie sitting facing left, holding Mowgli up by shoulders, 5-3/4", color print background of jungle ruins, SR/Fall/95 (600-1000) 900

Full figures of determined Mowgli walking as monkey attendant follows with fan, 9 x 10", DL color print background, HL/Nov 19/95 (600-900) 690

Half image of shocked Bagheera (6") facing right toward hypnotic Kaa (head & neck), color print display background of jungle, 16-field, Disney Art Program seal, ct, SR/Spring/96 (500-900) 850

Full figure of Shere Kahn prowling jungle, 5-1/8", 16-field, color print display background, Disney Art Program seal, SR/Spring/96 (1000-1500) 1340

Love-struck Mowgli w/pot on head; Village Girl singing; w/color print backgrounds & gold DL labels; 8 x 10", VF+, HL/Apr 28/96 (900-1200) 1725

Close-up portrait of surprised Baloo, color print jungle background, gold DL label, 6 x 8", HL/Apr 28/96 (500-700) 1725

Wide-eyed Mowgli eating bananas w/banana peel on head, color print background & gold DL label, 7 x 11", VF, HL/Apr 28/96 (500-700) 489

Smiling Mowgli (3 x 7") singing with eyes closed as stern Mowgli (5") walks by; Baloo (7") dancing w/eyes closed as Kaa (6") watches; each on printed DL background, S/Jun 19/96 (800-1200) 1610

Full figure of cunning Shere Kahn prowling, 4-1/2 x 7-1/2"; Flaps the buzzard, 6-1/2"; each on printed DL background; S/Jun 19/96 (1200-1800) 1380

Baloo (waist-up; 7-1/2") looking at Kaa (5"), printed DL background, S/Jun 19/96 (600-800) 977

Full-figure side view of alert Bagheera sitting on tree limb facing left, 5", color print background. SR/Fall/96 (600-1000) 750

Waist-up of Baloo holding tiger's tail, 6-1/2", color print background, SR/Fall/96 (600-1000) 920

Pleading Baloo w/paws up in 'stop' motion, 10 x 15-1/2", matching master background of jungle, VF+, HL/Oct 6/96 (4000-4500) 6038

Full figures of Baloo & King Louie dancing, 8-1/2 x 11", color print background as sold at DL, VF, HL/Oct 6/96 (900-1200) 863

Stunned Baloo rubs back of neck as laughing monkey hangs by tail behind him, 5", printed DL background of outdoors, mat signed by Frank Thomas & Ollie Johnston, CE/Dec 12/96 (1000-1500) 2070

Worried Baloo (9-1/2") holds angry Shere Khan's tail (full figure, 4 x 9-1/2") as Khan circles back, watercolor production background, silver WDP seal, S/Dec 14/96 (7000-9000) 6900

Full figures of happy King Louie sitting as angry Mowgli walks alongside, color print background,

ground, 8-1/2 x 10" overall, HL/Feb 23/97 (800-1000) 920

Baloo dances (full figure) as Kaa watches, color print of Jungle Book background with color print of 101 Dalmatians background underneath, 10 x 9" overall, HL/Feb 23/97 (800-1000) 920

Full figure of happy King Louie on all fours facing right, 3", color print background of jungle & ruins, SR/Spring/97 (400-700) 520

Full figure of Shere Khan (eyes closed, 5-3/4") lying on ground talking to suspended Kaa (half image, 4-5/8"), 16-field 2-cel set-up w/color print jungle background, SR/Spring/97 (1200-1600) 1430

Full figure of surprised Bagheera, walking left on tree limb, looking into camera, 8-1/4" x 4-1/2", 16-field cel; color print background; ct; SR/Spring/97 (600-1000) 680

Shoulders-up close-up of coy village girl, 9-3/4", 16-field cel, color print background of village, SR/Spring/97 (700-1100) 920

Happy Baloo (5-1/2") crouches to look at irritated Mowgli (full figure, 4-3/4") sitting against rock, 16-field cels, all-matching set-up with key gouache master background of jungle clearing, SR/Spring/97 (6000-10,000) 8000

Scheming Shere Khan walks to left thru jungle; 7-1/2", all but hind legs; DL set-up with litho background; SR/Spring/97 (1100-1500) 1100

Portrait of Shere Khan sitting & looking up, color print background as released by Disney Art Program, 7 x 9" cel image, HL/May 3/97 (1000-1500) 1725

Alarmed Bagheera (at left edge) facing right, 6 x 7", preliminary pan watercolor background of jungle (11 x 27-1/2"), S/Jun 21/97 (5000-7000) 4025

Full figure of King Louie dancing in jungle, 5", printed background, S/Jun 21/97 (700-900) 1150

Full figures of smiling Mowgli (3") sitting in leaves under tree looks up as Baloo (7") stands watching, matching watercolor production background, S/Jun 21/97 (7000-9000) 23,000

Close-up of Shere Khan (6") tickling Kaa's chin with a claw, gouache pre-production background, SR/Fall/97 (6000-10,000) 4000

Full figure of King Louie hanging in sitting position from tree branch by both hands, facing left, looking down; 6-1/8"; color print background of jungle; SR/Fall/97 (600-900) 510

Full figures of Mowgli (4") standing on rock promontory facing right with arms up next to tower of 4 vultures (7-1/2"), original concept-piece background, SR/Fall/97 (6000-10,000) 4000

Friendly Kaa with coil around reluctant Mowgli's shoulders, 7 x 9", color print background & label as sold at DL, VF, HL/Nov 16/97 (900-1200) 1265

Smiling Shere Khan looks behind him, 6 x 8-1/2", color print background & label as sold at DL, VF+, HL/Nov 16/97 (800-1000) 978

Limited-edition cel of relaxed King Louie on throne & Mowgli wearing banana-peel hat, #89/500, 11-1/4 x 15-1/4", color print background, VF+, HL/Nov 16/97 (700-1000) 690

2 cels: chest-up of Mowgli examining ant crawling on arm, 6"; hips-up front view of Girl fixing her hair, 7"; each w/print background & gold DL Art Corner label, S/Dec 19/97 (1000-1500) 920

Full figures of angry Mowgli (5-1/2") beating monkey (4") who's holding him around waist, key production set-up w/matching watercolor & pastel trimmed production background of jungle ruins, S/Dec 19/97 (7000-9000) 5750

Publicity cel of Baloo picking up surprised Mowgli, 7 x 4", watercolor production background of jungle, framed together with matching drawing, S/Dec 19/97 (2500-3500) 4887

Full figures of Mowgli (5-3/8") standing facing sitting Shere Khan (6-1/8", mouth open), master gouache background painting, 16-field, SR/Spring/98 (3600-4200) 3630

Full figures of Mowgli & Bagheera sleeping together on tree branch, 6-1/2 x 3-3/4" on two cel levels, tree painted on paper & applied to cel over matching sky background, 16-field, SR/Spring/98 (4000-7000) 4430

"Floating Down River": limited-edition cel of Baloo floating in river w/Mowgli on his stomach, #248 of 500, color print of master background, seal & certificate, 10-1/2 x 14-3/4", VF+,

HL/Apr 25/98 (900-1200) 1035

Full figures of Bagheera sitting on tree branch as Mowgli (back turned) grabs his face, discarded background (tempera on background sheet), restored, 10-1/2 x 14-1/2", VF, HL/Apr 25/98 (1000-1500) 1725

CELS – FULL FIGURE (also see MODEL ART)

King Louie screams w/laughter, WDC seal, 8-3/4 x 11-1/2", CE/Dec 15/93 (600-800) 517

Shere Khan stands facing left, WDP seal, 12-1/4 x 15-3/4", CE/Dec 15/93 (1000-1200) 1495

3-1/2" King Louie in profile; 5" Kaa smiling; both w/gold DL labels, S/Dec 16/93 (1000-1500) 1380

2 full-figure cels of vultures, 4-1/2 x 3-1/2", 4 x 3-1/2", VF+, HL/Feb 26-27/94 (400-600) 220

Mowgli (full figure) & King Louie (hanging by hands; from wrists down) w/blue paper backing in mat, DL gold label, 5-1/2 x 4-1/2", F+, HL/Feb 26-27/94 (700-900) 1100

Disguised Baloo & King Louie dance, 7 x 12", Disney seal, VF+, HL/Apr 10/94 (900-1200) 1232

Floating Baloo, Mowgli on stomach, bee and water effects in 3 cels, 5-1/2 x 12", VF+, HL/Apr 10/94 (2000-2500) 3360

Bagheera (8" length) looking over his shoulder; Akela (11-1/2"; all but edge of tail) with pup climbing on her back, silver Walt Disney seal, S/Jun 17/94 (800-1200) 1035

Front view of stern Colonel Hathi standing holding stick in trunk, 7-1/2 x 5-1/2", CE/Jun 18/94 (700-900) 368

Shere Khan prowling to left, 5-1/2 x 8", CE/Jun 18/94 (700-900) 1495

King Louie (4") & Baloo (6") dance back to back, CE/Jun 18/94 (1200-1500) 2990

Mowgli (4-3/4 x 1-3/4") steps up on seated Baloo's stomach (7 x 7-1/4"), CE/Jun 18/94 (1000-1500) 5980

Bagheera & Mowgli sleeping together, 16-field, SR/Fall/94 (600-900) 810

2 cels: chest-up of Baloo facing right, looking down, 6"; full figure of Mowgli standing toward right, pointing up, 7-1/4"; both 16-field, SR/Fall/94 (800-1200) 1000

Happy Baloo lying down facing left, raising up on one paw, 6-3/4", 16-field, SR/Fall/94 (400-700) 800

Apprehensive Baloo (chest up); full-figure frontal of Col Hathi; 7-1/2 x 4-1/2" & 6-1/2 x 9", as sold at DL, VF, HL/Nov 13/94 (500-700) 840

Eager King Louie, 4 x 7-1/2", CE/Dec 16/94 (1000-1500) 4830

Happy Baby Elephant, 4-1/2", CE/Dec 16/94 (700-900) 1840

Startled Bagheera sitting, 3-1/2", CE/Dec 16/94 (700-900) 863

Surprised Mowgli reclined in water (hands & 1 foot submerged), 4", CE/Dec 16/94 (700-900) 978

Baloo in cautionary position, 8", silver WDP seal; 2 drawings of Baloo, 7 & 8", one signed by Frank Thomas, S/Dec 17/94 (1000-1500) 1265

Apprehensive Mowgli holds stick & walks, 6 x 1-1/2", HL/Mar 11/95 (400-500) 825

Panicked Shere Kahn runs to right w/flaming branch tied to tail, 11-3/4 x 7-3/4", two 16-field cels, SR/Spring/95 (1200-1800) 1800

Happy Baloo sits facing left, leaning back on left paw, 7", 16-field, SR/Spring/95 (400-700) 900

Smug Bagheera sits beside a bewildered Baloo, 7 x 7", HL/Apr 23/95 (700-1000) 1456

Shere Khan walking, 5 x 8-1/2", HL/Apr 23/95 (1000-1500) 2128

Mowgli crawls on contented Baloo's back, 6 x 10", HL/Apr 23/95 (900-1200) 1456

King Louie (4") and disguised Baloo (7-1/2") dancing together, CE/Jun 9/95 (800-1200) 920

Frightened Mowgli (4") & sad Baloo (7") stand together, CE/Jun 9/95 (700-900) 805

Startled Bagheera in mid-step, 9", CE/Jun 9/95 (600-800) 748

Skeptical Mowgli kneels with ant in hand, 4-1/2", DL label, CE/Jun 9/95 (700-900) 483

Laughing Baloo lying on his back, 4-1/2", CE/Jun 9/95 (700-900) 518

Large full figure of happy King Louie w/arms out, 4-1/2", DL label, CE/Jun 9/95 (600-800) 575

Baloo prepares to hoist Mowgli into air, 5-1/2 x 6-1/2"; with drawing traced from original

animation drawing for display purposes; F-VF, HL/Aug 6/95 (900-1200) 1344

Kaa stares into walking Mowgli's (full figure) eyes as tail knots around boy's left wrist, 7 x 9", DL label, VF, HL/Aug 6/95 (700-1000) 1792

Mowgli stands on sitting Baloo's stomach, 7 x 7", HL/Nov 19/95 (1000-1500) 863

Baloo lying on back with eyes closed & monkey on stomach, 6-1/2 x 12", VF+, HL/Mar 16-17/96 (700-1000) 1150

2 cels of King Louie dancing, in sun & shadow colors, 5-3/4" & 6-3/4", SR/Spring/96 (600-1000) 900

Angry Col. Hathi (7-1/4") stands with anxious Winifred, 16-field, Disney Art Program seal, SR/Spring/96 (400-800) 490

Bewildered Mowgli sits on wings of 2 vultures, 6 x 8-1/2", F, HL/Apr 28/96 (700-1000) 863

Angry Baloo (sitting) holds up grimacing Mowgli, 7 x 5", VF+, HL/Apr 28/96 (1000-1500) 1380

Baloo tutors Mowgli, 5 x 6", VF, HL/Apr 28/96 (900-1200) 1610

2 cels of monkeys swinging Mowgli; 6 x 15", 7-1/2 x 11", VF, HL/Apr 28/96 (700-1000) 633

2 full-figure cels: profile of Mowgli standing looking right, rear view of Baloo with food balanced on right paw; 7-1/2 x 2", 6-1/2 x 4-1/2", VF+, HL/Apr 28/96 (700-1000) 978

Mowgli rides on & scratches Baloo's (on all fours) back, 7 x 8", VF+, HL/Oct 6/96 (1000-1500) 1438

Happy Baloo stands holding surprised Mowgli at eye level, 7 x 4-1/2", VF, HL/Oct 6/96 (750-1000) 1495

Matched full figures of two vultures, 4-1/2 x 6", HL/Feb 23/97 (300-500) 357

Front view of worried Bagheera walking, eyes downcast; 5-1/2 x 2-1/2", HL/Feb 23/97 (400-600) 403

Sitting Baloo hoists Mowgli over his head, 7 x 4-1/2", HL/Feb 23/97 (700-1000) 1610

Grim Shere Khan prowling, 4-1/2 x 7", HL/May 3/97 (1200-1600) 1495

Mowgli & Bagheera walking together to right, 3-1/2 x 6", S/Jun 21/97 (1000-1500) 920

Happy Baloo standing holding surprised Mowgli at eye level, 7 x 4-1/4", VF+, HL/Nov 16/97 (800-1200) 1495

Grinning King Louie sits, knuckles on ground, looking down, 6 x 8-1/4", VF+, HL/Nov 16/97 (600-900) 863

Shocked Bagheera sits facing left, 4-1/4 x 5-1/2", VF+, HL/Nov 16/97 (400-500) 920

Baloo floats on river, head & feet up, 5-1/4 x 8", VF+, HL/Nov 16/97 (500-700) 920

Happy Baby Elephant marches to left, eyes closed, 4 x 4-3/4", VF+, HL/Nov 16/97 (300-400) 547

Sitting Baloo looks away as he holds Mowgli at eye level, 6 x 4-1/4", VF+, HL/Apr 25/98 (800-1000) 1093

Baby Elephant sits facing toward left, 4-1/4 x 4", blue backing board as prepared for sale at DL, VF, HL/Apr 25/98 (300-400) 489

Happy King Louie stands with arms up, 6-1/2 x 5-1/4", VF+, HL/Apr 25/98 (600-800) 690

CELS – PARTIAL FIGURE (also see CELS – FULL FIGURE, MODEL ART)

Baloo w/crossed eyes pats head, gold DL label, restoration needed, 6" (chest up), S/Dec 16/93 (100-150) 345

Fearsome Shere Khan leaps to left, 4 x 4-1/2", VF, HL/Feb 26-27/94 (500-700) 330

Portrait of Baloo floating in water, 7 x 8", Disney seal, WDP label & certificate from DL's Disneyana shop, VF, HL/Apr 10/94 (700-900) 1008

Kaa with Mowgli sitting in his coils, 5 x 7-1/2", mat with gold DL label, VF, HL/Apr 10/94 (900-1200) 1232

Baloo (facing right) holds Mowgli above eye level, 7 x 6", VF, HL/Apr 10/94 (700-900) 1120

Portrait of glaring Shere Khan, 5-1/2 x 7-1/2", backing board & DL label, restored, VF, HL/Apr 10/94 (700-1000) 1064

Shere Kahn crouching intently, 7-1/2"; Baloo (head & shoulders) smiling, 6"; Baby Elephant happily sitting up, 5"; each with gold DL label, S/Jun 17/94 (1200-1800) 2185

Close-up of sad Baloo (7 x 8-1/2") with paws on Mowgli's shoulders (4-3/4 x 2"),

CE/Jun 18/94 (1000-1500) 1265

Sad Bagheera sitting (stomach up), 7-3/4 x 4", WDP seal, CE/Jun 18/94 (700-900) 575

Portrait of smiling Shere Khan, 8 x 6", Disney seal & label, VF+, HL/Nov 13/94 (800-1200) 1232

Large-image portrait of smiling Baloo looking down, 7 x 8-1/2", VF+, HL/Nov 13/94 (400-600) 840

2 portrait cels: laughing Baloo (eyes closed) & angry Col. Hathi, 7 x 8" & 6 x 9", Disney seals & labels, VF+, HL/Nov 13/94 (700-1000) 672

Determined Mowgli (ankles up) walks away to right from Kaa, 6 x 7", Disney label, VF+, HL/Nov 13/94 (800-1200) 1120

Front view of Col. Hathi holding broken cane, WDP seal, 7", CE/Dec 16/94 (800-1200) 1265

Thighs-up view of smiling Mowgli holding up coconut, 5-1/2", CE/Dec 16/94 (700-900) 1035

Shoulders-up portrait of alluring man-village girl, 8", 16-field, SR/Spring/95 (400-800) 660

2 portraits of Kaa, 4-1/2 x 4" & 6-1/2 x 5-1/2", VF, HL/Apr 23/95 (600-900) 896

Close-up of irritated Baloo, 5-1/2", DL label, CE/Jun 9/95 (600-800) 345

Happy Baloo (6-1/2") holding up smiling Mowgli (5-1/2"), CE/Jun 9/95 (1000-1500) 1035

4 elephants in line, CE/Jun 9/95 (600-800) 633

Baloo stands trance-like & stares straight ahead, 5-1/2", gold DL label, mat signed by Frank Thomas & Ollie Johnston, S/Jun 10/95 (800-1200) 1610

Standing Shere Kahn speaks humbly with eyes closed, 8", silver WDP stamp, S/Jun 10/95 (800-1200) 920

Expressive portrait of Baloo, 6 x 9", as sold at DL, HL/Aug 6/95 (300-500) 560

2 large-image cels of coy village girl (one color model), 7 x 5-1/2" & 7-1/2 x 6", VF+, HL/Aug 6/95 (600-900) 672

Portrait of Baloo looking upward, right palm up, 6 x 9-1/2", HL/Nov 19/95 (600-800) 863

Enthusiastic Baloo (disguised as ape) dancing, 6 x 4-1/2", VF+, HL/Mar 16-17/96 (300-400) 690

Horizontal view from the shoulders up of Baloo looking ill, 6 x 6-1/2", VF+, HL/Mar 16-17/96 (300-500) 633

Near-full figure of surprised Bagheera walking left, looking into camera, 8-1/2 x 4-1/4", 16-field, SR/Spring/96 (300-700) 570

Portrait of bewildered Baloo with left arm extended to side, 8 x 9-1/2", Disney seal & label, VF+, HL/Apr 28/96 (500-700) 748

Large near-full figure of disdainful Shere Khan lying down, 8 x 13", Disney seal, WDP label, VF+, HL/Apr 28/96 (1000-1200) 1840

Shere Khan talks to Kaa (hanging from above), 9-1/2 x 13", Disney seal, VF, HL/Apr 28/96 (1200-1600) 1725

Portrait of grimacing Shere Khan, 6-1/4 x 6", VF, HL/Oct 6/96 (700-900) 863

Waist-up portrait of cheerful Baloo looking down & toward left, arm up, mouth open, 6-1/2 x 9-1/2", VF+, HL/Oct 6/96 (600-900) 1035

Portrait of suspicious Shere Khan, 6", mat signed by Frank Thomas & Ollie Johnston, CE/Dec 12/96 (1000-1500) 1840

Sad Baloo (7") with paws on Mowgli's shoulders (3") as he speaks, S/Dec 14/96 (1000-1500) 1610

Near-full-figure large image of determined Kaa coiled vertically, 8-3/4 x 6-1/4", HL/Feb 23/97 (400-600) 1150

Hips-up view of growling Baloo with arms in fighting pose, 5-1/2 x 7-1/2", HL/Feb 23/97 (700-900) 633

One-quarter body image of Kaa looking left with interest, 3-1/2 x 5-1/2", HL/May 31/97 (200-400) 748

Shoulders-up portrait of chagrined Baloo looking into camera while lying horizontally, 5-3/4 x 6-1/4", VF+, HL/Nov 16/97 (400-500) 633

Close-up of angry Shere Khan leaping with claws extended, 7 x 7", VF, HL/Nov 16/97 (900-1500) 863

Portrait of Baloo disguised as monkey, 8 x 8-1/4", F, HL/Nov 16/97 (500-700) 690

Stomach-up portrait of upset Baloo with paw over left eye, 6-1/2 x 6", VF+, HL/Apr 25/98 (500-700) 748

Shere Khan & Kaa face each other, blue backing board, 6-1/4 x 9-1/4", VF, HL/Apr 25/98

(900-1200) 1093
Stomach-up side view of Baloo holding Mowgli at eye level, 6-1/2 x 5", VF+, HL/Apr 25/98 (1000-1200) 1495
Charming Kaa faces panicked Baloo, blue paper backing as sold at DL, 5-3/4 x 8-1/4", F+, HL/Apr 25/98 (600-900) 863

CONCEPT AND INSPIRATIONAL ART
Concept painting by Ken Anderson of King Louie on jungle throne, signed "Ken Anderson—to my friend Fred from Ken," mixed media on 15-1/2 x 11-3/4" board, SR/Fall/94 (1000-1500) 1160
Pan watercolor concept painting of 2 monkeys carrying Mowgli (5") off, signed by Walter Peregoy, S/Dec 17/94 (2000-3000) 2875
Sheet of Ken Anderson concept sketches of Mowgli's encounter w/village girl, black ink on 13-15/16 x 9-1/8" sheet, SR/Fall/96 (300-500) 310

LAYOUT ART (also see CEL SET-UPS)
Layout concept painting of jungle, watercolor on cardboard, CE/Jun 18/94 (1000-1500) 1610

MODEL ART
Shere Khan (full figure, lying down) talks to Kaa (overhead), color model cels with stamps & notes, 9 x 12-1/2", VF, HL/Aug 21/94 (1200-1600) 2016
Thighs-up model cel of expressive Baloo, 9-1/2 x 6-1/2", VF, HL/Aug 6/95 (500-700) 616
Full-figure front-view color model cel of stern Col. Hathi standing holding 'baton', looking left & down, 7-1/2", 16-field, SR/Fall/96 (300-600) 310
4 model sheets: Baloo, Bagheera, Kaa, Shere Khan; 14 x 11" original studio photostatic print sheets; 1st 3 show originals were signed "OK Woolie" by Woolie Reitherman; SR/Fall/97 (400-600) 1040

STORY ART
Story drawing of Col. Hathi whispering to subordinate, conté crayon on paper, 6 x 8-1/2", VF, HL/Apr 10/94 (300-400) 840
Polished story drawing of Bagheera, Shere Khan & Col Hathi, 6 x 8-1/2", orange and black conté crayon on story sheet, HL/Nov 13/94 (300-400) 672

LADY AND THE TRAMP (1955)

ANIMATION DRAWINGS
14 finished "rough" colored pencil drawings, 2 x 3" to 10 x 6", F-VF, HL/Apr 10/94 (2000-3000) 2912
Full-figure drawing of Lady, 5-1/2", CE/Dec 16/94 (500-700) 518
Chest-up drawing of contented Tramp sitting, 8-1/2", CE/Dec 16/94 (400-600) 230
22 assorted drawings, 3 x 3-1/2" to 4 x 10-1/2", F+, HL/Apr 23/95 (3000-4000) 6440
"Rough" drawing of Lady about to be fitted with muzzle, 12-1/2 x 15-1/2", VF, HL/Apr 23/95 (600-800) 672
Full-figure drawing of Peg sitting facing left, eyes closed, 7", 16-field sheet, SR/Fall/95 (400-700) 400
Full-figure drawing of Tramp standing looking down, 4-1/2", 16-field sheet, light stain, SR/Spring/96 (200-500) 430
Full-figure drawing of flirtatious Peg standing facing toward left, looking into camera, 7-1/2", 16-field sheet, some edge wear & surface soil, SR/Spring/96 (200-400) 200
3 full & 2 near-full-figure polished drawings in sequence of demure Lady walking, 3 x 3-1/4", HL/Apr 28/96 (700-1000) 1265
22 polished "rough" drawings, 3 x 3-1/2" to 7 x 11-1/2", HL/Apr 28/96 (3000-4000) 6325
Sheet of brush-&-ink drawings of Tramp, 16-field sheet, faint vertical crease, SR/Fall/96 (300-600) 310
Rough drawing of smiling Tony playing accordion, 10-1/2 x 9-1/2", VF, HL/Oct 6/96 (200-300) 575
Full-figure drawing of smiling Tramp standing facing left with right front paw up, 5-1/2 x 5", F+, HL/Oct 6/96 (300-400) 489
Full-figure drawings of Tramp & Jock standing, 4-1/2 x 8-1/2", HL/Feb 23/97 (300-400) 403
Rough drawing (3-1/2 x 6") paired with full-figure cel (3-1/4 x 6-1/2") from same scene: Lady picking up leash w/nose, HL/Feb 23/97

(2000-2500) 1840
20 detailed "rough" drawings: Lady (9), Tramp (5), Lady & Tramp, Trusty (2), Bull, Jock, Beaver; 2 x 2-1/4" to 6-1/2 x 10", F-VF, HL/May 3/97 (3000-4000) 4485
Full-figure drawing of quizzical Lady standing facing left & looking up, 3-1/2 x 4", HL/May 31/97 (150-200) 196
6 pencil drawings (5 roughs) of Lady, S/Dec 19/97 (600-800) 460
6 rough animation drawings of Tony by John Lounsbery, 11" & similar, CE/Dec 18/97 (700-900) 483

BACKGROUNDS (also see LAYOUT ART)
Background design painting of 3 houses, 9 x 24", india ink, conté crayon & watercolor on board, HL/Aug 6/95 (1500-2000) 2016
Gouache master background by Eyvind Earle of park with gnarled tree & bridge at night, 38-1/2 x 11-3/8", SR/Spring/96 (18,000-26,000) 15,000
Gouache master background: looking into nursery (with overturned crib) from closet, 19-3/8 x 9-1/4", SR/Fall/96 (3000-7000) 4840
Pan preliminary art of Trusty's, Lady's & Jock's homes, 12 x 37", watercolor on heavy paper applied to board, S/Jun 21/97 (2000-3000) 5175
Original master pan background of Lady's street, 11-1/2 x 24", tempera on background sheet, VF+, HL/Nov 16/97 (6000-9000) 6900

CEL SET-UPS
Lady & Tramp walk with pups, watercolor preliminary illustration background (probably for children's book), 10 x 14", CE/Dec 15/93 (4000-6000) 3680
Tramp walking, watercolor background, 4-1/2 x 4", S/Dec 16/93 (500-700) 460
Lady seated, gouache production background from unknown feature, 4", S/Dec 16/93 (2000-3000) 2300
4-1/2" Tramp & 3" Lady sitting in park, studio prepared background, WDP stamp & label, S/Dec 16/93 (5000-7000) 8050
Tempera original background of family home with two complementary cels of Lady & Tramp trimmed to outline & mounted on overlay cel, 10 x 23", restored, VF, HL/Apr 10/94 (8000-12,000) 15,120
Tony (7-1/2") w/hands on hips as Joe (8-1/2") serves spoonful of spaghetti, publication background, S/Jun 17/94 (1200-1500) 1955
Lady (4-1/2") & Tramp (6"), each on different preliminary background, framed together, S/Jun 17/94 (3000-4000) 3737
Lady (4-1/4" length) w/muzzle, Tramp (4-1/2" length) running to right, printed background, S/Jun 17/94 (1800-2200) 1725
Long pan watercolor production background of zoo w/cel of Lady (3") & key cel of Tramp (4"), S/Jun 17/94 (20,000-25,000) 23,000
Full figure of Tramp lapping up water, printed background, 5", S/Jun 17/94 (800-1200) 920
Peg, DL printed background & label, 7", CE/Jun 18/94 (600-800) 690
Toughy, Boris, Pedro & Bull singing in pound, 5-1/2" & smaller, key watercolor production background, CE/Jun 18/94 (7000-9000) 5750
Publicity cel of happy Lady, 7-1/2 x 4-1/2", hand-prepared background, CE/Jun 18/94 (1500-2000) 1150
Tramp with book in mouth meets professor (bent at waist), master background of Lady's front yard, studio notes, 10 x 14", VF, HL/Aug 21/94 (6000-8000) 6720
Bull & Toughy (3-1/2") sit in pound cage, 39-1/2 x 12" key gouache master background, SR/Fall/94 (4000-8000) 6,000
Full-figure ground view of growling Lady, 5", gouache matching key master background of yard, SR/Fall/94 (6000-12,000) 6000
Full figure of curious Lady standing facing left, looking up, 5", gouache master background of parlor, SR/Fall/94 (5000-10,000) 7300
Trusty (4-3/4") & Jock (4") at front door of house, watercolor production background, CE/Dec 16/94 (4000-6000) 5175
Lady (2-1/4"), Tramp (3-1/4"), puppies, baby, bandaged Trusty all sitting/playing on carpet; watercolor production background; WDP label, CE/Dec 16/94 (8000-12,000) 16,100

Bull (3-1/2"), Toughy (4"), Pedro (3"), & Boris (4") singing, publication background, S/Dec 17/94 (800-1200) 1725
Hips-up of curious Lady standing on hind legs inspecting table of gifts, 6", key gouache master background, crease across lower body, ct, SR/Spring/95 (7000-12,000) 9600
Full figure of Mrs. Darling standing facing left, holding baby wrapped in blanket in front of window, 8-1/2", key pan master background of bedroom, SR/Spring/95 (10,000-16,000) 15,800
Full figures of Si & Am scratching carpet by piano, 10-1/4 x 6-1/4", gouache master background of parlor, SR/Spring/95 (2500-5000) 5500
Full figures of Lady, Tramp (4-1/4"), & 2 puppies walking/running to right, display background of room with Christmas tree, SR/Spring/95 (2500-3500) 3460
Full figure of Tramp walking right, 5-1/2 x 6", complementary background painting, VF, HL/Apr 23/95 (900-1200) 1680
Full figure of Tramp in front of Rinaldi's Barber Shop, 10-1/2 x 13", master background (tempera on background sheet), F-VF, HL/Apr 23/95 (4000-5000) 5488
Near-full figures of Lady (3") in mid-stride and Tramp (4-1/2") standing on sidewalk, watercolor production background from 1950s short, CE/Jun 9/95 (4000-6000) 6325
Plotting Si & Am facing right & staring straight ahead, 4" each, printed background, S/Jun 10/95 (800-1200) 1610
Full figures of sitting Toughy laughing as Jock watches, 8 x 10", color print background of outdoors as sold at DL, HL/Aug 6/95 (600-900) 532
Full-figure front view of Lady (2-3/4") lying on carpet as Mrs. Darling (5-5/8") sits knitting in background, 27-1/4 x 11" master background, SR/Fall/95 (10,000-16,000) 16,500
Full figure of Jim Dear pushing door shut as snow blows into house, 5-1/2", 3 cel levels, key master background, SR/Fall/95 (3000-7000) 4840
Full figure of Peg standing facing right, looking into camera, 6", 12-field, photocopy layout background, signed "To Raymond ... Peggy Lee," SR/Fall/95 (900-1200) 990
Tramp & muzzled Lady look into pond at zoo, 10-1/4 x 20-1/2", matching master background (tempera on background sheet), HL/Nov 19/95 (7000-10,000) 8050
Full figure of excited Lady wearing muzzle, master background of zoo exterior (tempera on background sheet), 1-3/4 x 10", HL/Nov 19/95 (2500-3500) 3565
Full figure of muzzled Lady standing on path, 4 x 4", complementary color print background, HL/Nov 19/95 (1000-1500) 1150
Chest-down of Jim Dear in slippers carrying puppy Lady thru house, 9-1/2", key gouache master background, SR/Spring/96 (3000-7000) 6400
Full figure of coy Lady (5") & happy Tramp (behind Lady, 7") sitting outside gate to Dear's house, watercolor production background, S/Jun 19/96 (7000-9000) 8050
Full figures of Lady (3-1/2"), Tramp (5"), & Jock (3-1/2") sitting in yard, watercolor preliminary background, mat inscribed "...Walt Disney", CE/Jun 20/96 (4000-6000) 6900
Tramp (5") eats spaghetti as Lady (3-1/2") watches admiringly, watercolor production background, mat signed "Walt Disney", Courvoisier label, CE/Jun 20/96 (25,000-35,000) 57,500
Full figure of smiling Lady standing at base of stairs looking up, watercolor pan production background, 3", CE/Jun 20/96 (12,000-15,000) 10,925
Full figure of howling Baby Lady sitting on floor, 3-1/2", signed by Frank Thomas & Ollie Johnston, color print display background, Art Corner stamp, gold label, SR/Fall/96 (600-1000) 610
Full figure of Lady w/leash in mouth standing with Jim Dear (from chest down), 7-1/2 x 15-1/2", master background of house walkway (tempera on background sheet), HL/Oct 6/96 (4000-5000) 6038
Lady & Tramp seated at table facing each other with plate of spaghetti, 6-1/2 x 9-1/2" cel, non-Studio painted background,

HL/Oct 6/96 (4000-5000) 6325

Near-full figures of Tramp chasing 4 chickens, 11 x 22", CinemaScope master background of hen house (tempera on background sheet), HL/Oct 6/96 6613

DAE limited-edition cel of Lady & Tramp eating spaghetti, 11 x 15", issued color print background, #297/500, HL/Oct 6/96 (3500-4500) 4255

Large-image 2-part portrait cel of sultry Lady sitting, 6 x 6", color print background, HL/Oct 6/96 (1000-1500) 1265

Lady, Tramp, Jock, bandaged Trusty, Baby Dear & puppies on living room floor from film's finale, sight 8 x 26-1/2", pan watercolor production background, S/Dec 14/96 (10,000-15,000) 16,100

Full figures of Lady (5 x 3-1/2") & Tramp (5-1/2 x 5") standing on street looking affectionately at each other, pan watercolor production background, S/Dec 14/96 (18,000-22,000) 13,800

Full figure of smiling Tramp (3-1/2 x 5") lying down watching Lady walk by w/ball in her mouth (half figure, 3-1/2 x 3"), airbrushed background, S/Dec 14/96 (2000-3000) 2185

Full figures of Lady sitting up w/ball in her mouth (5"), happy Tramp lying down (4 x 5"), Trusty (near-full figure rear view, 6" w/o tail) sitting; Jock (4") in sweater standing; watercolor production background of porch, S/Dec 14/96 (12,000-15,000) 23,000

Full figure of Tramp pulling on coattail of grimacing bystander who's being accosted by policeman, 9-1/2 x 7-5/16", litho background of forest, gold DL Art Corner label, SR/Spring/97 (1000-1500) 1050

Full-figure side view of Darling standing by open door, 7-1/8", gouache master background (23-1/2 x 12") of room interior, SR/Spring/97 (4000-8000) 5330

Full figure of Jim Dear (7-3/8") photographing Jim Junior (1-1/2") & puppies near Christmas tree as Darling (6-3/4") holds their attention, key master layout drawing on 24-1/4 x 12" sheet, Art Props stamp, SR/Spring/97 (2000-5000) 2790

Full figure of curious Lady standing, facing left, 4-3/8", color print background of indoors, SR/Spring/97 (1200-1600) 1340

Full figures of sitting Lady (6-1/4") watching Tramp puppy (4-1/4") pull on the rear of Baby's sleeper (7"), watercolor pan production background of house interior, CLA/Jun 7/97 (7000-9000) 7475

Full figures of Lady (4-1/2" long) & Tramp (5") meeting, watercolor pan production background of backyard w/horse trough, pump, & buggy, CLA/Jun 7/97 (12,000-15,000) 13,800

Tramp (4") puts left front paw on delighted Tony (6") as Lady (4" long) & Joe (behind dutch door, 3-3/4") watch, hand-prepared background by a gallery, CLA/Jun 7/97 (4000-6000) 3680

Near-full figure of eager Lady rounding corner of house, 2-1/2", matching pan watercolor production background, S/Jun 21/97 (12,000-15,000) 11,500

Pan production set-up of Tramp (4 x 6"), Pedro (2"), Boris (5-1/2"), Peg (6 x 7-1/2"), & shocked Lady (6-1/2") in pound, pan watercolor production background, S/Jun 21/97 (12,000-15,000) 11,500

Full figures of proud Tramp (5") in collar sitting by Christmas tree watching worried Baby (4") sitting w/rattle, printed background, S/Jun 21/97 (1500-2000) 1955

Full figure of feisty Jock standing on walkway, 4 x 5", printed background, S/Jun 21/97 (600-800) 920

Torso-up image of sultry Peg looking over shoulder, 5 x 7-1/2", printed background of dog pound, S/Jun 21/97 (700-900) 805

Full-figure side view of eager Lady (4-1/2") & Tramp (6-1/2") sitting at candlelit table, printed background, S/Jun 21/97 (2000-2500) 2587

Smiling Joe (apron up, 7") holds plate of bones up to Tramp (sitting full figure, 5") printed background w/wooden fence, S/Jun 21/97 (1500-2000) 2587

Full figure of happy puppy Lady sitting in middle of room, 2-5/8", 16-field cel, color print background. SR/Fall/97 (1200-1800) 1200

Full figure of somber Lady standing in doorway facing left, looking up, 4-3/8", detailed gouache key master background of kitchen, set-up is 20-3/4 x 9-3/4", SR/Fall/97 (7000-11,000) 11,100

Limited-edition cel "Prelude to a Kiss", #254/350, 12-1/2 x 32-1/2", color print of matching background, VF+, HL/Nov 16/97 (2000-3000) 3450

"Bella Notte" limited-edition cel of Lady & Tramp eating same strand of spaghetti, #408/500, 11-1/4 x 15-1/2", color print background, VF+, HL/Nov 16/97 (1500-2000) 3680

Full figure of happy Tramp walking right, 8-1/4 x 10-1/2", unused background of walkway & fence (tempera on background sheet), VF+, HL/Nov 16/97 (2000-3000) 3220

Peg (3") steps along board as Toughy (4-1/3"), Pedro (2") & Boris (5-1/2") harmonize, printed background, S/Dec 19/97 (1200-1500) 1725

Lady (near-full figure standing, 4-1/2 x 6") admires Tramp's new collar (full figure sitting, 8"), printed background of house interior, S/Dec 19/97 (2500-3500) 3162

Full-figure side view of muzzled Lady standing looking thru railing at Ape House, 5-3/4", key master gouache background painting, SR/Spring/98 (4000-7000) 4000

Full figure of puppy Lady jumping to left, 3-3/8", color print indoor background, SR/Spring/98 (800-1200) 850

"Prelude to a Kiss": hand-inked & -painted limited-edition cel of Lady & Tramp eating spaghetti while being serenaded by Joe & Tony, #254/350, color print background, seal & certificate, 12-1/2 x 32-1/2", VF+, HL/Apr 25/98 (3000-4000) 4600

CELS – FULL FIGURE (also see MODEL ART)

Happy Tramp stands facing right, 6 x 7-1/4", CE/Dec 15/93 (700-900) 1035

Carefree Peg walks to right, 6-1/4 x 7", CE/Dec 15/93 (1200-1600) 1610

5" Lady walking by seated 4-1/2" Tramp, gold DL label, S/Dec 16/93 (1800-2200) 2300

4 puppies frolic, gold DL label, 2", S/Dec 16/93 (400-600) 690

Profile of happy Tramp, 4 x 3-1/2", VF, HL/Feb 26-27/94 (700-1000) 935

Profile of Lady, 3 x 3", VF, HL/Feb 26-27/94 (900-1200) 1210

Si (or Am) running, 2-1/2 x 5-1/2", VF+, HL/Apr 10/94 (600-800) 448

Peg, 4 x 5", backing board w/DL label, original tissue paper & envelope, VF, HL/Apr 10/94 (600-800) 784

Quizzical Tramp lying down looking right, 3 x 5", VF+, HL/Apr 10/94 (900-1200) 1232

Angry barking Tramp (full figure) in professor's arms (knees up), 6 x 5", backing board, DL label, tissue & envelope, VF, HL/Apr 10/94 (900-1400) 1120

Tony & Joe (eyes closed) standing singing & playing instruments, 7 x 6", backing board, DL label, illustrated tissue overlay, VF, HL/Apr 10/94 (1000-1500) 1792

Bandaged Trusty, 4 puppies, & Jock in sweater; 5 x 10", backing board, gold DL label & illustrated tissue-paper protector, VF, HL/Apr 10/94 (1400-1800) 2016

Complementary full figures of Lady & Tramp, 4-1/2 x 5" & 4 x 4", VF, HL/Apr 10/94 (2000-2500) 2688

Tramp (half figure, walking right) & Toughy (sitting), 5-1/2 x 8", mat w/DL label, restored, VF, HL/Apr 10/94 (900-1200) 1064

Lady as puppy trying to walk to left , 3 x 3-1/2", VF+, HL/Apr 10/94 (600-900) 896

2 full-figure cels of Jock, 3 x 3-1/2" & 2-1/2 x 4", VG, HL/Apr 10/94 (900-1200) 1120

Lady (3" length) & Tramp (3-1/2" x 3") walk happily side by side, S/Jun 17/94 (1200-1800) 2587

Lady (3-1/4 x 3-1/2") stares at proud Tramp (5 x 2"), both night, CE/Jun 18/94 (2000-3000) 2530

Wistful Lady standing looks up, 6-1/2 x 5", CE/Jun 18/94 (1500-2000) 2185

Side view of muzzled Lady (5 x 4-3/4") & Tramp standing facing each other (5-3/4 x 7"), CE/Jun 18/94 (2000-3000) 2185

Tony & Joe play instruments (eyes closed, 6-1/2 x 6-1/2"), CE/Jun 18/94 (600-800) 1495

Lady runs with ball of yarn in mouth, 4-1/2 x 5", CE/Jun 18/94 (1000-1500) 1495

Large image of Peg, DL backing & label, 7 x 8-1/2", VF, HL/Aug 21/94 (800-1000) 1008

Scamp pulling on string, 2 x 8", F+, HL/Aug 21/94 (400-600) 728

Confident Tramp & wide-eyed Lady (behind table) sitting by table set with wine & breadsticks, 6 x 8", VF+, HL/Aug 21/94 (4000-6000) 7280

Smiling Lady holds toy in mouth, Darling's arm in upper right, 6-1/2 x 9", VF, HL/Aug 21/94 (1000-1500) 1568

Quizzical Lady (evening colors) standing facing right, DL label, "Art Corner" stamp, 4 x 4", VF, HL/Aug 21/94 (1000-1500) 1456

Tramp & Lady (bone in mouth) walk together, gold label & tissue as sold at DL, 3-1/2 x 5-1/2", F+, HL/Aug 21/94 (1500-2000) 1680

Sad Lady walking left & looking back, blue backing board with gold label as sold at DL, illustrated protective tissue, 3-1/2 x 5", VF+, HL/Aug 21/94 (1200-1600) 1232

Peg stands with Lady facing right & looking up, 5 x 5", VF, HL/Aug 21/94 (1800-2200) 1796

Wide-eyed Lady gasps in surprise while wearing muzzle, 4-1/2 x 5-1/2", VF+, HL/Aug 21/94 (1000-1500) 1120

Peg stands looking up, backing board & label as sold at Disneyland, 7 x 5-1/2", VF, HL/Aug 21/94 (800-1000) 896

Dreamy Lady stands looking back, 3-1/2 x 4-1/2", F, HL/Aug 21/94 (1000-1500) 1456

Apprehensive Lady stands facing right, mat w/label & "Art Corner" stamp as sold at DL, 4 x 5-1/2", F, HL/Aug 21/94 (900-1200) 1344

2 full-figure cels: determined-looking Lady walks right, 4-3/4"; suspicious Tramp stands facing left, looking back, 5-1/2", lifting & missing paint, cel tear; DL Art Corner labels, SR/Fall/94 (1600-2200) 2500

Jock stands in red plaid sweater facing left, 4-1/4", SR/Fall/94 (700-1100) 850

Strutting Peg walking to right, 5 x 6", VF, HL/Nov 13/94 (800-1000) 616

Lady & Tramp walk together, 5 x 6", DL label, VF+, HL/Nov 13/94 (2000-2500) 3584

Uneasy Lady sits facing left, looking down, 5 x 3-1/2", VF, HL/Nov 13/94 (1000-1500) 1456

Jock (2-1/2") & Tramp (4-1/2"), CE/Dec 16/94 (800-1200) 1840

Tramp (4") & Jock (3"), DL label, CE/Dec 16/94 (700-900) 1495

Tramp walking, 5", CE/Dec 16/94 (800-1200) 1725

Si & Am (4" each) triumphantly shake tails while Aunt Sarah's (8", all but right foot) back while being carried away, S/Dec 17/94 (600-800) 1265

Tramp (5-1/2 x 3-1/2") sits smiling as Lady (3-1/2 x 3-1/2") looks inquisitively to left, S/Dec 17/94 (2000-3000) 5750

Smiling Lady stands on hind legs, 5"; grinning Tramp faces forward, 5"; happy Bull, 3-1/2 x 6"; S/Dec 17/94 (1800-2200) 2185

Dachsie digging out of pound, 6", S/Dec 17/94 (300-500) 172

Seven somewhat sequential cels of Lady lowering herself from hind legs to all fours, 2" to 4", S/Dec 17/94 (2000-2500) 5175

Jock, 4-1/2"; Dachsie, 5" length; 2 cels of Bull (one with eyes closed), 3-1/2" x 6" each; S/Dec 17/94 (800-1200) 1610

Lady and Tramp running, 3-1/2 x 4", HL/Mar 11/95 (700-1000) 880

Bull (3-5/8") & Toughy (5-3/8") sit singing, 16-field, SR/Spring/95 (500-900) 990

Jock & Trusty overturn pound wagon with Tramp inside, 13 x 9-3/4", 16-field, SR/Spring/95 (2500-3500) 3460

Sad, muzzled Lady stands facing left, 4", SR/Spring/95 (700-1200) 990

2 full-figure cels: front view of alert Tramp sitting, looking right, 5"; panicked, muzzled Lady running forward & looking up, 3-1/2"; 16-field; SR/Spring/95 (800-2600) 2010

Lady & Jock sit facing each other, both 3", SR/Spring/95 (800-1200) 1700

Tramp walks toward left with bone in mouth, looking into camera, 4-1/2", gold Art Corner label, some lifting paint. SR/Spring/95 (900-1200) 1000

Somber Lady (3-1/4") & Tramp (4-3/4") sit side

by side toward left, looking back right,
SR/Spring/95 (1400-1800) 3130

Sitting Lady facing left, looking up in wonderment,
3-3/4 x 3-1/4", VF+, HL/Apr 23/95
(1000-1500) 2016

Lady as puppy lying down head first to left, 2-1/2
x 3-1/2", VF, HL/Apr 23/95 (700-1000) 1232

Alert Tramp sitting, 8 x 4-1/2", VF+,
HL/Apr 23/95 (900-1200) 2128

Friendly Peg stands facing right, tongue out,
3 x 3", VF+, HL/Apr 23/95 (500-700) 728

Smiling Tony playing accordion, 6-1/2 x 5", VF,
HL/Apr 23/95 (1000-1500) 1792

Sad Lady stands & looks down, 6", CE/Jun 9/95
(1000-1500) 978

Combative Jock, 7-1/2" long, CE/Jun 9/95
(800-1200) 1610

Side view of Lady (4") & Tramp (6") sitting
together, CE/Jun 9/95 (1000-1500) 2530

Hopeful Lady stands with leash in mouth,
4-1/2", CE/Jun 9/95 (1000-1500) 1955

Trusty (back turned) & Toughy sit together,
5-1/2", CE/Jun 9/95 (400-600) 633

Close-up of Bull, 4 x 4", CE/Jun 9/95 (300-500) 690

Tired Tramp walking, 3-1/2", CE/Jun 9/95
(800-1200) 863

Tramp walks to left, 4", CE/Jun 9/95 (800-1200) 920

Lady, 5-1/2" long; full figures of 2 sitting puppies,
2" & similar, CE/Jun 9/95 (1000-1500) 1840

Lion looks up as he lies with bone, 5",
CE/Jun 9/95 (400-600) 345

Happy Bull, 6" long, CE/Jun 9/95 (400-600) 460

Eager Lady standing, 3" x 3", S/Jun 10/95
(800-1200) 1610

Happy Lady sitting, 4 x 4-1/2", as sold at DL,
HL/Aug 6/95 (900-1200) 1232

Chastened Tramp cowers, evening colors, 2 x 6",
as sold at DL, HL/Aug 6/95 (700-1000) 896

Expectant Lady sitting up, 5 x 3", HL/Aug 6/95
(1200-1600) 2016

3 Lady puppies play, 3-1/2 x 6", HL/Aug 6/95
(600-900) 1064

Jock & Trusty (leg bandaged, partial figure) are
greeted by one of Lady's pups, 3 x 6", VF,
HL/Aug 6/95 (1000-1500) 1456

Sad Lady walking, 3 x 4-1/2", as sold at DL,
HL/Aug 6/95 (900-1200) 1344

Sitting Tramp, Tony, & Joe; 5 x 3", 7 x 5", 9-1/2
x 3-1/2", HL/Aug 6/95 (2000-2500) 4032

Mischievous Si & Am, 7-1/2 x 7", HL/Aug 6/95
(1200-1600) 2688

Tramp walking to right, 5-1/2 x 7", HL/Aug 6/95
(900-1200) 1344

Lady & Tramp running, 3 x 4-1/2", as sold at DL,
HL/Aug 6/95 (800-1200) 840

Jock stands facing right, 4-3/4" image, 16-field,
SR/Fall/95 (700-1200) 850

Happy Tramp (4") & Tony (6-3/4") stand facing each
other, SR/Fall/95 (1600-2200) 4640

Curious Lady sits, 4-1/2 x 3-1/2", HL/Nov 19/95
(1500-2000) 1955

Large full figure of alert Tramp (wearing collar)
sitting, 8 x 5", HL/Nov 19/95 (1200-1600) 2070

Tramp & muzzled Lady (trailing leash) run together,
4-1/2 x 8", released thru DL, HL/Nov 19/95
(1500-2000) 1725

Peg walks away, looking over left shoulder, 5-1/2 x 6",
as sold at DL, HL/Nov 19/95 (900-1200) 1035

Puppy Lady sits & howls, 3 x 3", HL/Nov 19/95
(800-1200) 690

Trusty & Jock standing, 6-1/2 x 8-1/2",
HL/Nov 19/95 (800-1000) 1093

Profile of sleepy beaver resting on tail, 5-1/2
x 4-1/2", HL/Nov 19/95 (200-300) 288

Alert Jock sitting, 4-1/4 x 3-1/4", HL/Mar 16-17/96
(500-700) 978

Chained Lady stands facing left & looking expectantly,
7-1/2 x 5-1/4", HL/Mar 16-17/96
(1000-1500) 1610

2 cels: near-full figure of demure Lady sitting facing
right, looking back & down, 4-5/8"; full figure
of happy Tramp walking right, looking back,
5-1/2"; SR/Spring/96 (1800-2600) 2550

Rear view of Policeman standing looking left, 8-1/2",
16-field, SR/Spring/96 (800-1200) 800

Trusty stands facing right, 5-1/4", gold DL Art Corner
label & stamp, SR/Spring/96 (800-1200) 820

Front view of Jock sitting looking left, 4-1/4",
SR/Spring/96 (700-1000) 940

Happy Tramp walking, mat signed by Frank Thomas,
5-1/2 x 4", HL/Apr 28/96 (1000-1500) 1725

Happy Lady playing with ball, 3 x 4", HL/Apr 28/96
(1000-1500) 1725

Profiles of confident Tramp leading demure Lady,
colored paper background, gold label as sold at
DL, 3-1/2 x 4", VG-F, HL/Apr 28/96 (1200-
1600) 1093

Peg struts, 7-1/2 x 8-1/2", VF, HL/Apr 28/96
(900-1200) 978

Friendly Tramp standing, 5-1/2 x 5", HL/Apr 28/96
(900-1200) 1840

Large-image publicity cel of friendly Tramp,
muzzled Lady & curious Beaver, 7-1/2
x 16", HL/Apr 28/96 (1200-1600) 1955

Profile of baby Lady crawling to left, 2-1/4 x
3-1/2", HL/Apr 28/96 (800-1200) 690

Surprised Lady sits w/head turned, 3-1/4 x 4",
HL/Apr 28/96 (1500-2000) 1610

Persuasive Tramp sits w/front paws in air, 6-1/2
x 5-1/2", HL/Apr 28/96 (1500-2000) 1725

Eager Tramp stands facing right, 3 x 4",
HL/Apr 28/96 (700-1000) 748

Full figures of Tramp (3 x 4") walking away from &
Lady (3") walking toward camera; Boris & Peg
nose-to-nose (6" each); Pedro scratching behind
his ear; 1st two with gold labels, all need restoration, 4-1/2"; S/Jun 19/96 (1500-2000) 1840

Tramp (4") sits watching muzzled Lady (3 x 2-1/2")
standing, gold DL label, needs restoration, S/Jun
19/96 (1500-2000) 1380

Puppy Scamp (4") tugs on back of unaware Baby
Dear's pajamas (6"), S/Jun 19/96 (800-1200) 920

Front view of angry Jock standing looking right,
2-7/8", 16-field cel, SR/Fall/96 (600-900) 660

Muzzled Lady sits facing left, 4", 16-field cel,
SR/Fall/96 (900-1200) 900

2 cels: near-full-figure front view of curious Lady sitting
looking right, 5"; full figure of charming Tramp
standing facing left, 5-3/4"; SR/Fall/96 (1800-
2600) 3720

Alert Tramp walking right with head turned away,
3-1/4 x 4", HL/Oct 6/96 (700-1000) 863

Pair of full-figure cels of Si & Am walking
identically, 6-1/4 x 3-3/4" each, VF+,
HL/Oct 6/96 (1200-1600) 1955

Set of 4 limited-edition cels, made from original
drawings: 2 of Lady & Tramp, Tramp licking
Tony, Si & Am being carried by Aunt Sarah;
6-1/2 x 6-1/2" to 9 x 12-1/2", VF+,
HL/Oct 6/96 (3000-4000) 2760

Dogcatcher (from shoulders down) inspects
Lady (full figure sitting), 6-1/2 x 10",
HL/Oct 6/96 (1200-1600) 1035

2 full-figure cels of combative Jock: standing
facing right & lying down to right, 3 x
3-1/2", 2-1/2 x 4", HL/Oct 6/96
(700-1000) 1380

Nonchalant Tramp walks to left, 4 x 3-3/4",
HL/Oct 6/96 (800-1200) 978

Tramp being attacked by 3 dogs, 6 x 7-1/4",
HL/Oct 6/96 (800-1200) 1265

Weary Tramp stands facing left with head down
and eyes closed, 4-1/2 x 5-1/2",
HL/Oct 6/96 (700-1000) 690

Publicity cels: Lady (full figure, 5") & Tramp
(behind her, 7") sit together & look at
each other admiringly, CE/Dec 12/96
(1500-2000) 2185

Rear view of Aunt Sarah carrying Si & Am as they
intertwine tails behind her back in "handshake,"
9", CE/Dec 12/96 (1500-2000) 1150

Concerned Lady sits & looks left, 5", CE/Dec 12/96
(1000-1500) 1495

Surprised Lady sitting facing left, looking back
& up over left shoulder, 3-1/2",
CE/Dec 12/96 (1000-1500) 1380

Smiling Tramp walks right, 5", CE/Dec 12/96
(1000-1500) 1265

Curious Lady stands on hind legs facing right,
6", S/Dec 14/96 (1000-1500) 1265

Inquisitive Tramp standing facing toward right,
4 x 4", S/Dec 14/96 (1000-1500) 1725

Jock sitting down & looking up, eyebrows obscuring
his eyes, 3-1/3"; large drawing of Tony playing
accordion, 10", S/Dec 14/96 (400-600) 920

Worried Lady pulls against taut chain & talks to
Tramp, 8 x 5", HL/Feb 23/97 (1200-1600) 1840

Front view of serious Jock with head & eyes

down [as if sniffing], 4-1/4 x 3-1/2",
HL/Feb 23/97 (400-600) 575

Profile of wide-eyed Lady standing facing right
with bone in mouth, 3-1/2 x 4",
HL/Feb 23/97 (1000-1500) 1150

Snarling Tramp walks left, 4-1/2 x 6",
HL/Feb 23/97 (900-1200) 978

Confused Lady (w/ears dragging) walking left next
to quizzical Jock (in plaid sweater), 4-1/2 x 7",
HL/Feb 23/97 (1400-1800) 1610

Tramp standing w/head turned & eyes closed with
a Lady puppy standing beside, 5-1/2 x 5",
HL/Feb 23/97 (700-1000) 805

Wary Jock sits facing left, 2-1/2 x 2-1/2",
HL/Feb 23/97 (700-1000) 633

Publicity cel of coy Lady & admiring Tramp (behind
her) sitting together, 7", 16-field cel, restored,
SR/Spring/97 (3000-4000) 3410

2 cels: happy Lady stands toward right, looking up,
3-1/4"; coy Tramp stands facing left, 5-1/8";
SR/Spring/97 (2200-2800) 2670

2 full figures: Lady running to right, smiling Tramp
looking back while walking right; 3-1/2 x 4",
3 x 4-1/4", HL/May 3/97 (1200-1600) 1955

Lady seated at table (5"), Tramp (5-1/2") sitting behind
her, Tony (7") playing accordion, Joe (6") playing
mandolin, CLA/Jun 7/97 (4000-6000) 9200

Tramp (bone in mouth, 5-1/4") & Lady (3-1/4")
walks together, CLA/Jun 7/97 (1500-2000) 1610

Stoic Lady (4-1/2") & eager Tramp (3-1/4")
stand facing right, cut signature of Walt
Disney, CLA/Jun 7/97 (2000-3000) 2185

Lady lies down & studies ground between paws,
7-1/2" long, CLA/Jun 7/97 (1500-2000) 1955

Happy Tramp stands, 8 x 4-1/2", S/Jun 21/97
(1000-1500) 1495

Smiling Lady stands facing left & looking up,
4 x 5", S/Jun 21/97 (1000-1500) 1725

Smiling Tramp (5-1/2") lies next to worried Lady
(4") sitting wearing muzzle, S/Jun 21/97
(1500-2000) 1725

Front views: eager Tramp (full-figure elevated, 3-1/4")
looking right; Lady (2") lying down, looking left
& speaking with eyes closed; original color card
background, mat, & gold DL Art Corner label;
SR/Fall/97 (1600-2000) 1100

Front view of Toughy (full figure), Boris, & Pedro
harmonizing, 6-3/4", SR/Fall/97
(900-1200) 600

Bull standing with mouth open, 5", SR/Fall/97
(600-900) 440

Smiling Tramp walking, DL label, 3-3/4 x 2", F+,
HL/Nov 16/97 (700-900) 920

Irritated puppy Scamp hangs from nape of neck as
thread lies beside him, 3-1/2 x 7-3/4" including
thread, VF+, HL/Nov 16/97 (300-400) 518

Tramp walks right & looks back, 4-1/4",
VF+, HL/Nov 16/97 (800-1200) 920

Proud Lady sits facing right with eyes closed,
wearing collar, 5-1/4 x 4-1/2", VF,
HL/Nov 16/97 (600-900) 633

Tony & Joe sings & play instruments, 6-1/2 x
7-1/4", VF+, HL/Nov 16/97 (700-1000) 2760

Happy Tramp walks right & looks into camera,
4-1/2 x 4-3/4", F, HL/Nov 16/97
(700-1000) 978

Happy Peg walks right, 3 x 3-1/4", VF+,
HL/Nov 16/97 (500-700) 518

Neck-down image of Jim Dear standing at open
door with 3 Lady puppies at his feet, 8-1/2
x 4-1/2", VF, HL/Nov 16/97 (700-1000) 518

Jock stands facing right, 3-3/4", SR/Spring/98
(600-900) 610

Trusty stands facing right with head down, 10 x 5-
5/16", SR/Spring/98 (700-1200) 700

Lady & Tramp (eyes closed, behind Lady) stand facing
right, 4 1/4 x 3 5/8", DL gold Art Corner label,
signed by Frank Thomas & Ollie Johnston,
SR/Spring/98 (1800-2600) 1760

Sad Lady stands facing left with leash in her mouth,
4-1/2", 12-field cel, SR/Spring/98
(1000-1600) 1240

Si & Am face each other: one sitting, one walking;
restored; 3-1/2 x 8-1/2"; VF; HL/Apr 25/98
(700-1000) 1265

Smiling Lady sits facing right, 5-1/2 x 4-3/4", VF,
HL/Apr 25/98 (900-1200) 1725

Happy Tramp stands facing right, looking back, 4-1/2
x 5-1/4", VF+, HL/Apr 25/98 (700-900) 1380

Lady stands on hind legs facing right, 3-3/4 x 2-3/4",
VF, HL/Apr 25/98 (800-1000) 1093
Lady puppy stands facing left & looking up in front of
Tramp who's standing w/eyes closed & head
cocked; backing board w/label & stamp as sold
at DL; 5-1/2 x 5"; F; HL/Apr 25/98 863

**CELS – PARTIAL FIGURE (also see CELS - FULL
FIGURE, MODEL ART)**
Portrait of 4-1/4" Lady & 6" Tramp, S/Dec 16/93
(2000-3000) 2588
Portrait of puzzled Lady sitting facing left, 6 x
5-1/2", VF+, HL/Apr 10/94 (900-1200) 3808
Flirtatious Tramp & happy Lady, 6-1/2 x 5-1/2" &
6-1/2 x 5", gold DL Art Corner labels, restored,
VF, HL/Apr 10/94 (2000-2500) 2128
Admiring Tramp looking up with spaghetti strand
in mouth, 6-1/2 x 3", VF+, HL/Apr 10/94
(900-1200) 3248
Portrait of Lady (4-1/2") & Tramp (5-1/4"); Jock (4"
x 4") wearing unraveling Christmas sweater;
zoo lion (6-1/2" length) holding bone; each
w/gold DL label, S/Jun 17/94
(1800-2200) 4312
Portrait of Lady looking surprised, 9", S/Jun 17/94
(2000-3000) 2300
Torso-up side view of Peg, 5-1/2 x 7",
CE/Jun 18/94 (700-900) 460
Grinning Joe (eyes closed) strums mandolin as
Tramp admires his technique, 9 x 10",
VF+, HL/Aug 21/94 (1400-1800) 2464
Near-full-figure side view of bright-eyed Tramp
standing facing right, 6 x 6-1/2", VF+,
HL/Aug 21/94 (900-1200) 1344
Joe gesturing (chest up); contented Tony (knees up,
eyes closed) playing accordion; 5 x 3-1/2",
4-1/2 x 4", VF, HL/Aug 21/94
(1000-1500) 1680
2 cels: sitting Tramp eating spaghetti, 5-1/2"; ears-up
portrait of Lady, 4"; both 12-field, SR/Fall/94
(1500-2200) 3240
Toughy (full figure), Boris, & Pedro harmonize, 6-1/2",
16-field, SR/Fall/94 (600-900) 900
Half image of sitting Lady facing right, 6-1/4",
SR/Fall/94 (900-1400) 1400
"Knees-up" of happy Tramp standing facing right, eyes
looking into camera, 6", 16-field, SR/Fall/94
(900-1400) 1040
Portrait of Lady looking up, label & DL Art Corner
stamp on backing board, 2-1/2 x 2-1/2", VF+,
HL/Nov 13/94 (400-600) 672
Near-full figure of sitting Lady facing right & looking
down, 4-1/2 x 4", VF, HL/Nov 13/94 (1000-
1500) 1792
Portrait of alert Tramp sitting facing right, 7 x 4",
VF, HL/Nov 13/94 (900-1200) 1344
Angry Lady from front paws up, 3", DL label & enve-
lope, CE/Dec 16/94 (1200-1500) 1150
Darling happily holds new puppy, 6-1/2 x 10";
Darling sitting in rocking chair knitting, 7";
S/Dec 17/94 (1800-2200) 1150
Near-full figure of Trusty facing right, scratching,
8 x 7-7/8", SR/Spring/95 (500-900) 1320
Shoulders-up of quizzical muzzled Lady sitting looking
left, 5-1/4", SR/Spring/95 (800-1200) 830
Portrait of Tramp looking down lovingly with
spaghetti hanging out of mouth; shy Lady
[sitting at table]; 6-1/2 x 3-1/2", 6-1/2 x
4"; VF+; HL/Apr 23/95 (4000-5000) 4592
Lady about to be fitted with muzzle, 8-1/2 x 11",
F+, HL/Apr 23/95 (1500-2000) 3360
Toughy, 5-1/2"; torso-up of Peg in classic pose,
6-1/2"; CE/Jun 9/95 (800-1200) 460
Apron-up side view of smiling Joe carrying tray
of bones to left, 7-3/4", CE/Jun 9/95
(500-700) 1495
Large-image portrait of Jock with eyes closed, 7-1/2
x 5", as sold at DL, HL/Aug 6/95 (600-900) 532
Profile portrait of Peg, 5 x 6", as sold at DL,
HL/Aug 6/95 (400-600) 672
Lady (head & front paws) smiles w/eyes closed, 4-1/2
x 6", as sold at DL, restored, VF, HL/Aug 6/95
(700-1000) 1568
Near-full figure of surprised Trusty sitting looking
up to left, 8-1/4", 16-field, ct, SR/Fall/95
(700-1200) 850
Near-full figures of Tramp & Lady standing in line
facing right, smiling Tramp (4") looks back as
mud flies by Lady (3-1/8"), SR/Fall/95

(1400-2200) 1700
Portrait of wide-eyed Jock, 7 x 7", HL/Nov 19/95
(900-1200) 863
Toughy, Pedro & Boris harmonize, 10-7/8 x 8",
16-field cel, SR/Spring/96 (700-1000) 700
Close-up of woeful pound dog sitting up (2-part cel),
4-1/2 x 3-1/2", VF+, HL/Apr 28/96
(500-700) 460
Portrait of delighted Tony, 5 x 5", VF,
HL/Apr 28/96 (600-800) 1093
Close-up portrait of startled Lady, gold label as
sold at DL, 5 x 6", F+, HL/Apr 28/96
(1000-1500) 1610
Close-up portrait of mischievous Tramp, gold label as
sold at DL, 5 x 4-1/2", F+, HL/Apr 28/96
(1000-1500) 1610
Large-image portrait of proud Tramp, 9 x 5",
HL/Apr 28/96 (1200-1600) 1265
Portrait of attentive Tramp, 7 x 3", HL/Apr 28/96
(700-1000) 1265
2 portrait cels: happy Tramp looking over left
shoulder, 7-1/2"; quizzical Lady, 4",
S/Jun 19/96 (1500-2500) 4025
Coy Lady w/paws perched on edge [of unseen cradle],
4 x 6"; Si (4" w/o tail) & Am (2") running away;
both w/gold DL labels, S/Jun 19/96
(1000-1500) 1380
Portrait of sleepy Lady looking back to left, gold DL
label, 5", S/Jun 19/96 (1000-1500) 920
Portrait of shocked Lady looking to right, 5-1/2
x 4-1/2", HL/Oct 6/96 (1200-1600) 1725
Toughy (full figure), Boris & Pedro harmonizing,
7 x 8-1/2", VF, HL/Oct 6/96 (700-1000) 978
Portrait of happy Trusty, 5-1/4 x 3", HL/Feb 23/97
(300-500) 805
Apron-up front view of smiling Tony singing &
playing accordion, 5-1/2 x 4",
HL/Feb 23/97 (500-700) 1495
Apron-up front view of quizzical Joe looking left,
arms out, palms up, fork with spaghetti in
his right hand; 8 x 6-3/4", HL/Feb 23/97
(500-700) 2990
Neck-up portrait of sad Lady looking down,
3-1/2 x 4-1/2", HL/Feb 23/97 (600-800) 850
Portrait of Tramp looking back with agonized expression, 6-1/2 x 3", HL/Feb 23/97 (600-800) 575
Near-full-figure rear view of strutting Peg turning
to smile back at camera, 6 x 7",
HL/Feb 23/97 (700-900) 805
Near-full-figure front view of jaunty Tramp sitting,
5-3/4", SR/Spring/97 (1400-1800) 1000
Sitting Tramp & Lady share an affectionate
look [behind table], 8 x 10" overall,
VF+, HL/May 3/97 (4000-5000) 7475
Darling (9") holds up puppy Lady (full figure, 6")
with bow around neck, CLA/Jun 7/97
(1500-2000) 1725
2 partial-figure cels: sitting Tramp (6-1/4") with
head facing forward & eyes peeking right,
expectant Lady (5-1/2") sitting facing right
& looking up, S/Jun 21/97 (2000-3000) 1955
Portrait of Jock with eyes looking down, 6-3/4",
SR/Fall/97 (1200-1600) 800
Large-image portrait of demure Lady, 6 x
4-1/2", F, HL/Nov 16/97 (800-1200) 1265
Large-image portrait of Jock looking left, 7-3/4
x 5", VF+, HL/Nov 16/97 (600-900) 748
Cel of table setting with wine jug & breadsticks,
6 x 5-1/2", F, HL/Nov 16/97 (300-400) 1265
Near-full figure of Lady standing facing right, 4-1/2
x 5-1/4", gold DL label, F, HL/Nov 16/97
(1000-1500) 1265
Near-full figure of smiling Tramp standing facing left,
looking down, 5-1/4 x 6", gold DL label, F,
HL/Nov 16/97 (900-1200) 1150
Toughy (full figure, 5"), Boris (5-1/2") & Pedro (2")
singing together, S/Dec 19/97 (1800-2200) 1380
Chest-up portrait of smiling Tramp looking down
& to right, 6-1/2", SR/Spring/98
(1000-1600) 1280
Lady seated behind set table w/Tramp (near-full figure)
sitting behind her, 6-1/4 x 8-1/2", VF, HL/Apr
25/98 (4000-6000) 6325
Portrait of Jock, 5-1/2 x 4", VF, HL/Apr 25/98
(500-700) 748
Apron-up front view of Tony singing & playing
accordion, 5-1/2 x 4", VF+, HL/Apr 25/98
(600-900) 1150
Apron-up front view of quizzical Joe looking left, right

arm holding spoonful of spaghetti, left arm out;
8 x 6-3/4"; VF; HL/Apr 25/98 (600-900) 1093

CONCEPT AND INSPIRATIONAL ART
Three portrait studies of Lady, 6 x 8", F,
HL/Apr 10/94 (200-300) 364
Four early character sketches of Lady, Tramp &
Trusty (1940s?), 3-3/4 x 6" to 7 x 9", water-
color & conté crayon on animation sheets,
Fair - Fine, HL/Apr 23/95 (500-700) 532
Four pieces of concept art: afghan holding rose in
mouth; early version of Si & Am together; two
drawings, each of single Siamese cat - watercolor
& colored pencil on paper, S/Dec 19/97 (200-
400) 230

DYE-TRANSFER PRINTS
Lady, Tramp, Jock, Trusty sit together, 11 x 8-1/4",
SR/Spring/95 (300-600) 350
Full figures of Lady & Tramp sitting together in
clearing, 3-1/2 x 9", SR/Fall/95 (300-600) 330

LAYOUT/TITLE ART
Background layout drawing of parlor, 25-1/4 x 11";
charcoal & pencil with background, camera, &
production notations in red; with original layout
end sheets for 2 scenes; 3 vertical folds;
SR/Fall/97 (1200-1800) 1480
15 title layout drawings for standard screen: 7 character
drawings & 8 hand-lettered 16-field pencil renderings for title overlays, in charcoal & taped to 16-
field sheets, SR/Fall/97 (1500-2500) 3210

MODEL ART
Full-figure color model cel of confused Lady looking
up, 3-1/2 x 3", F+, HL/Aug 21/94
(1200-1600) 1456
Color model drawing of happy Tramp, 7 x 4", studio
stamps & notes, HL/Nov 13/94 (200-300) 728
Large-image near-full-figure color model cel
of Tramp, 8 x 7", studio notes, VF,
HL/Nov 13/94 (900-1200) 1232
3 separate studio color model drawings of leashed
Lady being walked by pound official, with
notes, 2-1/2 x 4-1/2", 5 x 8-1/2", 10 x 10",
HL/Mar 16-17/96 (150-250) 633
Close-up color model cel of Trusty sitting and
talking, 6-1/2 x 6-1/2", HL/Apr 28/96
(500-800) 690
Full-figure color model cel of proud Lady walking to
right w/eyes closed & head up to display new
collar, 3 x 3-1/4", HL/Oct 6/96 (800-1200) 1495
Full-figure color model drawings of easy-going
Trusty & feisty Jock, 3-1/4 x 3-1/2" &
4-1/4 x 6", HL/May 31/97 (200-300) 403
Color model half figure of attentive Lady (3") sitting
watching full figure of Tramp (5-1/4") standing
facing left & pointing with right front paw,
CLA/Jun 7/97 (2000-3000) 1725

STORY ART
Evening-scene story painting: Lady (chained to
dog house) talks to Tramp, 9 x 10-1/2",
blue & purple watercolor & conté crayon,
VF, HL/Apr 23/95 (500-700) 784
Story painting of Lady getting first glimpse of
new baby, conté crayon & watercolor on
board, 8-1/2 x 10-1/2", HL/Apr 28/96
(700-1000) 1610
Story painting of Lady & Tramp standing outside
Tony's, watercolor & conté crayon on
illustration board, 8-1/2 x 11",
HL/Oct 6/96 (700-900) 3680
Atmospheric story drawing of tearful Lady chained
outside with head out of dog house as rat
emerges from wood pile, conté crayon
& blue watercolor on illustration board,
8 x 21-1/2", HL/Feb 23/97 (800-1200) 2530
Story art of Trusty & Jock attacking tipping Pound
wagon as horses rear, blue watercolor and
black conté crayon on board, 9 x 10-1/2",
VF, HL/May 3/97 (800-1200) 2185
Story painting of Aunt Sarah muzzling Lady, 8-1/2
x 10-1/2", watercolor & conté crayon on
illustration board, VF, HL/Nov 16/97
(600-900) 863
Story drawing of dog pound wagon w/Tramp pulling
away as Lady appeals to Jock & Trusty, conté
crayon & yellow & blue watercolor on board,
8-1/2 x 23-1/2", VF, HL/Apr 25/98
(800-1200) 2990

THE LION KING (1994)
CEL SET-UPS

"Circle of Life": hand-painted cel, #346/500, 11-1/2 x 15-1/2", color print background, HL/Apr 23/95 (3000-3500) 3584

Scar looks upward helplessly: "It's the lionesses job to do the hunting," 7-7/8" close-up, matching gouache key master background, [lot #161, S/Feb 11/95], SR/Spring/98 (2000-3000) 2070

All other items in this section were auctioned at Sotheby's, February 11, 1995.

These include original art actually used in the making of *The Lion King*. Each cel setup featured either a production background or a production overlay accompanied by a non-production background. The character and effects cels were specially created by artists in the Ink & Paint department at the Walt Disney Studios in Burbank, California. The basis for the cels were original animation drawings rendered by Disney animators and used in the production of the film. No original production cels were created in the making of *The Lion King*.

Rhinoceros lifts face to sun (1500-2000) 4312
Cheetah stands atop hill (1500-2000) 4312
Flock of birds fly in front of waterfall (2000-2500) 10,350
Gazelles leap across grassy plain, trees & mountain in background (1500-2000) 5750
Zebras splash thru river (2500-3000) 9775
Rafiki shakes walking staff (2000-3000) 10,350
Close-up of Rafiki putting thumb into melon half (2000-3000) 7475
Close-up of Rafiki presenting infant Simba on Pride Rock (3000-5000) 19,550
Monkeys cheer presentation of Simba (1000-1500) 2185
Zebras rear & stamp hooves for Simba (1500-2000) 4600
Giraffes, elephants & zebras bow to Simba (3000-4000) 5462
Close-up of disapproving Zazu: "Didn't your mother ever tell you not to play with your food?" (1800-2200) 4887
Close-up of Zazu as he reprimands Scar for missing Simba's presentation (1800-2200) 4887
Scar scrapes stone wall with claws in mock sincerity (2500-3500) 4887
Close-up of Zazu gesturing: "...As the King's brother you should have been first in line." (1800-2200) 5175
Mufasa confronts Scar about his disrespect for the monarchy (2500-3500) 4887
Scar responds: "Oh, I shall practice my curtsy." (2500-3500) 4600
Mufasa warns Scar: "Don't turn your back on me, Scar!" (3500-4500) 5462
Arrogant Scar explains to Zazu why he wouldn't dream of challenging Mufasa as Mufasa watches (3500-4500) 5462
Scar leaves cave after confrontation (2500-3500) 4600
Mufasa & Zazu (on shoulder) discuss Scar: "What am I going to do with him?" "He'd make a very handsome throw rug." (3500-4500) 14,950
Exterior of Rafiki's tree house lit by lightning in midst of storm (1500-2000) 10,925
Rafiki draws picture of Simba in his home (3000-4000) 9200
Smiling young Simba stands at edge of Pride Rock at dawn (3000-4000) 16,100
Eager young Simba awakens Mufasa & Sarabi (4000-6000) 9775
Simba trying to rouse Mufasa from sleep (3500-4500) 6900
Simba starts to succeed in waking his father: "You promised!" (3500-4500) 8625
Close-up of determined Simba staring at Mufasa (3000-4000) 13,800
Happy Simba with awakened Mufasa as Sarabi sleeps (4000-6000) 9775
Simba runs happily between his parents as they leave cave (3500-4500) 6900
Sarabi proudly watches (2000-3000) 4312
Mufasa warns Simba he must never go to shadowy area (3500-4500) 17,250
Mufasa teaches pouncing as determined Simba crouches in grass (3500-4500) 14,950
Smiling Simba after successful pounce on mortified Zazu (3500-4500) 21,850
Simba asks about forbidden land: "...What's out there?" (3000-4000) 8625
Scar's paw resting on Simba's head: "Yeah, right. I'm

your only nephew." 3000-4000) 5750
Scar 'mistakenly' tells Simba about elephant graveyard (3500-4500) 7475
Simba's dying to tell Nala about graveyard, but it's bath time with Sarabi & Sarafina (4000-6000) 18,400
Frustrated Simba gets bath from Sarabi (3000-4000) 7475
Simba tries to tell Nala about graveyard as she gets bath from Sarafina, but Sarabi overhears (4000-6000) 17,250
Smiling Simba tells Sarabi he's referring to the waterhole as Sarafina finishes Nala's bath (4000-6000) 11,500
Simba lets Nala know they're not going to the waterhole (3500-4500) 10,925
Simba & Nala smile broadly as they ask permission to leave (3500-4500) 9775
Simba & Nala whisper plans as they walk away & Zazu flies ahead (3500-4500) 8625
Zazu (walking) informs Nala & Simba they are betrothed (3500-4500) 26,450
Simba brags about the future to Nala: "Well, when I'm king, that'll be the first thing to go." (3500-4500) 7475
Close-up of Simba looking over shoulder during debate with Zazu (3000-4000) 7475
Zazu disdainfully examines Simba's mane: "Well, I've never seen a king of beasts with quite so little hair." (3500-4500) 17,250
Zazu wipes face & blows beak on elephant ear (2000-3000) 4887
Simba & Nala ride ostriches as Zazu flies into back of rhinoceros (3500-4500) 17,250
Angry Zazu on perch: "If this is where the monarchy is headed count me out!" (2000-3000) 6325
Simba rides on top of giraffe's head (3000-4000) 9200
Close-up of terrified Zazu (1000-1500) 4600
Chorus of alligators & birds (1000-1500) 4025
Simba & Nala singing atop tower of animals (6000-8000) 11,500
Oryx's horns pierce elephant's backside (1000-1500) 2070
Close-up of elephant's head reacting violently to Oryx's horns (1000-1500) 2070
Close-up of Simba gesturing to take credit for having 'ditched the dodo' (3000-4000) 7475
Close-up of shocked Simba on back after being pinned by Nala (2500-3500) 6325
Nala pins Simba again at edge of shadowy area (3000-4000) 18,400
Side view of Simba & Nala approaching elephant's skull (3000-4000) 8050
Front view of Simba & Nala approaching elephant's skull (3000-4000) 9200
Front view of angry Zazu hovering with left wing raised (2000-2500) 5175
Zazu confronts Simba by elephant tusk (2500-3500) 9200
Simba, Nala & Zazu are frightened by ominous laughter (2500-3500) 8265
Close-up of Zazu spreading wings to protect terrified Simba & Nala (2500-3500) 9200
Shenzi, Banzai & Ed approach Zazu, Simba & Nala by elephant tusk (4000-6000) 13,800
Shenzi cuts off running Simba, Nala & Zazu (4000-6000) 11,500
Front close-up of grinning Banzai: "We could have whatever' lion around." (1500-2000) 4600
Long shot of bewildered Simba & Nala among elephant bones (3000-4000) 9775
Close-up of terrified Simba's & Nala's faces framed by red smoke (3000-4000) 8050
Snarling Shenzi chasing terrified Simba thru elephant graveyard (3000-4000) 6900
Terrified Simba & Nala running on hind legs down elephant backbone (2500-3500) 6900
Long view down elephant backbone (1500-2000) 3737
Close-up of terrified Simba & Nala sliding down backbone (2500-3500) 8625
Simba scrambles to top of bone pile, leaving 3 hyenas below (3000-4000) 7475
Simba races down bone pile (3000-4000) 5750
Simba leaps over Nala to confront snarling Shenzi (3000-4000) 6900
Mufasa fights off 3 hyenas (3000-4000) 8625
Angry Mufasa traps Shenzi, Banzai & Ed on their backs (3000-4000) 8050
Close-up of angry Mufasa's head: "If you ever come near my son again..." (2000-3000) 5750

Shenzi & Banzai pretend they didn't know Simba is Mufasa's son (2000-3000) 3450
Ed nods head, revealing hyenas knew Simba's identity (1500-2000) 4025
Shenzi, Banzai & Ed cower together in fear (2500-3500) 3450
Angry Mufasa looks over shoulder: "You deliberately disobeyed me!" (2000-3000) 5750
Distraught Simba: "Dad, I'm...I'm sorry." (2500-3500) 6900
Long shot of Mufasa, Simba, Nala & Zazu walking across field for home (3000-4000) 9775
Uneasy Simba & Nala sit in grass: "I've got to teach my son a lesson." (3000-4000) 10,925
Mufasa lies in grass with Simba lying in mane: "We're pals, right?" (4000-6000) 34,500
Shenzi (on rock) tells Banzai & Ed to stop fighting (2500-3500) 3450
Disgusted Shenzi sits on rock (1500-2000) 4025
Disdainful Scar lying on ledge (3000-4000) 8050
Scar watches three hyenas from ledge above (3000-4000) 5175
Close-up of disdainful Scar (2000-3000) 4312
Scar holds up zebra leg (2000-3000) 4600
Scar walks thru steam clouds (3000-4000) 7475
Scar walks by saluting Ed: "It's clear from your vacant expressions..." (3000-4000) 7475
Scar leaps in front of startled Shenzi & Banzai (3000-4000) 5462
Scar smiles wickedly (2500-3500) 4025
Scar grabs Shenzi's cheek (3500-4500) 6900
Maniacal Scar sings: "Be prepared..." (2000-3000) 4025
Banzai with front paws on ledge & wearing bone mask (1500-2000) 3162
Threatening Scar approaches hyenas: "...You won't get a sniff without me." (2500-3500) 6325
Shenzi, Banzai & Ed smile diabolically thru red steam (2500-3500) 4887
Shenzi, Banzai & Ed stand ready to start wildebeest stampede (3000-4000) 5175
Shenzi nips at wildebeest in midst of stampede (2000-3000) 4312
Wildebeests stampede over ledge into the gorge (1500-2000) 3737
Scar yells to Mufasa & Zazu on ledge: "Simba's down there!" (3000-4000) 9200
Front view of terrified Simba fleeing stampede (2500-3500) 9775
Top view of terrified Simba fleeing just ahead of stampede (2500-3500) 5750
Mufasa & Scar on ledge watching flying Zazu point: "...on that tree." (3000-5000) 14,950
Close-up of terrified Mufasa's head: "Hold on, Simba!" (2500-3500) 7475
Simba clings desperately to branch amid dust (2000-3000) 5462
Side view of Mufasa running to rescue (3000-5000) 7475
Mufasa frantically looks for Simba after being trampled (2500-3500) 6900
Simba dangles from tree branch as stampede continues below him (2500-3500) 4025
Scared Simba stands amid wildebeest & dust (2500-3500) 5750
Mufasa about to grab Simba in jaws amid wildebeest & dust (3000-4000) 8625
Mufasa climbs rocks with Simba in mouth as stampede continues (3000-4000) 3737
Close-up of Mufasa depositing Simba onto ledge (2500-3500) 4600
Determined Mufasa starts to leap amid dust (2500-3500) 4887
Roaring Mufasa leaps with sun behind him (2000-3000) 4600
Simba watches Mufasa struggle up cliff (2500-3500) 5462
Scar disdainfully watches from ledge above (2500-3500) 5750
Mufasa hangs on cliff below Scar: "Help me!" (2500-3500) 5175
Close-up of snarling Scar bearing claws (2500-3500) 8625
Long shot of Simba watching from ledge: "Nooooo!!" (2000-3000) 4600
Close-up of anxious Simba in gorge: "Dad? Dad?" (2500-3500) 8625
Lone wildebeest runs thru dusty gorge (1000-1500) 3162

Long shot of Simba in gorge (2500-3500) 5750
Close-up of sad Simba under Mufasa's arm (2500-3500) 4887
Scar shows mock sympathy: "What will your mother think?" (3000-4000) 6325
Shocked Simba looking up: "Run away, Simba. Run!" (2000-3000) 6325
Long shot of Simba looking into dead-end canyon (2500-3500) 4025
Terrified Simba standing in rock crevasse (2000-3000) 7475
Close-up of Simba clamoring over rock in crevasse (2500-3500) 6325
Snarling Shenzi & Banzai watch from ledge (3000-4000) 3162
Ed laughs as Banzai removes thorns (2000-3000) 4887
Zazu & lion pride in mourning (2000-3000) 4312
Horrified lion pride looks up (2000-3000) 4312
Timon & Pumbaa charge buzzards clustered around Simba (3000-4000) 4887
Timon & Pumbaa inspect Simba: "Alrighty, what do we got here?" (3000-4000) 5175
Close-up of Pumbaa's face (2000-3000) 4312
Timon & Pumbaa in contemplation: "Gee, he looks blue." (3500-4500) 6900
Circle of Life Continues: Rafiki presents cub as adult Simba, Nala, Pumbaa, Timon & Zazu look on, specially created art (6000-8000) 37,375
Grinning Timon files one of Simba's claws (3500-4000) 5175
Pumbaa's tail cuts thru grass as he approaches watering hole (2500-3500) 2875
Rear view of Pumbaa at watering hole as grass bends away (2000-2500) 3162
Close-up of sad Pumbaa drinking alone (2500-3500) 6325
Kneeling Timon dramatizes song as sad Simba watches (3000-4000) 13,800
Timon closes Pumbaa's mouth: "Not in front of the kids!" (3500-4500) 14,950
Close-up of Simba admiring new jungle home: "It's beautiful!" (3000-3500) 11,500
Under-the-log view: Pumbaa lifting log & Timon showing bugs to Simba (4000-5000) 9200
Surprised Simba looking down: "What's that?" (2000-3000) 7475
Close-up of Timon holding grub among colorful bugs (2500-3500) 7475
Timon offers leaf tray of bugs to uneasy Simba as Pumbaa watches (4000-5000) 39,100
Top view of Timon lifting leaf tray of bugs: "Well, Kid?" (3000-4000) 5175
Uneasy Simba selects bug from tray: "Oh well... Hakuna Matata..." (2500-3500) 13,800
Close-up of Zazu sitting in bone prison: "Yes sire. You are the King..." (1500-2000) 6900
Shenzi, Banzai & Ed enter cave: "...We've got a bone to pick with you..." (2000-3000) 4312
Scar looks upward helplessly: "It's the lionesses' job to do the hunting" (2000-3000) 4312
Zazu in bone prison (1500-2000) 5750
Shenzi elbows Banzai: "...I said Que Pasa." (2000-3000) 3450
Scar orders three hungry hyenas out of cave (2500-3500) 4312
Trees & starry sky (1500-2000) 4600
Pumbaa lying on back in grass staring at sky (2500-3500) 8625
Adult Simba lying on back in grass looking up (2500-3500) 8050
Timon lying on back in grass looking up (2500-3500) 5175
Happy Rafiki repaints Simba's picture (2500-3500) 6900
Determined Pumbaa pursuing blue bug (1500-2000) 6900
Pumbaa straddling log & looking back (2500-3500) 5750
Close-up of concerned Timon turning around: "Pumbaa?" (2500-3500) 5750
Snarling Nala leaps at terrified Pumbaa (3000-4000) 8050
Panic-stricken Pumbaa stuck under root yelling at Timon (3000-4000) 6900
Terrified Timon pressing against Pumbaa: "Why do I always have to save..." (2000-3000) 8625
Close-up of ferocious Nala charging (2000-3000) 9200
Timon calms Pumbaa: "See, I told you he'd come in handy." (3000-4000) 10,350

Close-up of ferocious Nala pinning surprised Simba (3000-4000) 9200
Delighted Pumbaa standing in clearing (2500-3500) 6900
Confused Timon: "Time out! Let me get this straight..." (3000-4000) 11,500
Disbelieving Timon: "King? Pfff! Lady, have you got your lions crossed!" (2500-3500) 7475
Awe-struck Pumbaa standing on path: "Your majesty!" (2500-3500) 8625
Nala looks up as she drinks (2500-3500) 18,400
Nala & Simba roll in grass (3000-4000) 8050
Nala lays on her back in the grass & looks lovingly at Simba (2500-3500) 4600
Close-up of Simba looking down lovingly (2500-3500) 9200
Nala stands on hind legs & explains about Pride Lands to Simba in hammock (2000-3000) 4600
Overhead view of walking Nala looking up: "I left to find help & I found you." (2000-3000) 4600
Medium close-up portrait of disappointed Nala (2000-3000) 5175
Side view of frustrated Simba walking: "I can't go back..." (2500-3500) 6325
Medium close-up of annoyed Simba sitting & looking over shoulder (2000-3000) 6900
Smiling Rafiki sits on tree branch & leans forward (2000-3000) 6900
Simba confronts Rafiki in grass: "Creepy little monkey." (2500-3500) 12,650
Close-up of quizzical Rafiki (2000-3000) 7475
Saddened Simba sits in grass (2000-3000) 6325
Rafiki stands in clearing & gestures broadly (2000-3000) 9200
Medium close-up of perplexed Simba crawling under foliage (2000-3000) 5750
Confused Simba struggles thru jungle (2000-3000) 8625
Long shot of Rafiki swinging on vine thru jungle (2500-3500) 8625
Fearful Simba in jungle (2000-3000) 5175
Rafiki & Simba standing at parted reeds (3000-4000) 8625
Reflection of amazed Simba in pool (2000-3000) 6325
Simba looks down intently: "Look harder." (2000-3000) 4312
Mufasa's stern reflection in pool: "He lives in you." (1500-2000) 4600
Long shot of Simba watching Mufasa's mystic form in sky (3000-4000) 12,650
Mufasa's form radiates gold light: "You have forgotten who you are..." (2000-3000) 4312
Awed Simba looking up at sky (2500-3500) 7475
Close-up of awed Simba's windblown face (2000-3000) 6325
Simba runs across grass (2000-3000) 4887
Simba & Rafiki: "The weather...very peculiar, don't you think?" (3000-4000) 27,600
Smiling Timon awakens (2000-3000) 4887
Frightened Timon & Pumbaa reprimand Nala: "Don't ever do that again!" (3000-4000) 10,925
Confused Timon gestures: "The monkey's his uncle?" (2500-3500) 6325
Nala clarifies situation to Pumbaa & Timon (3000-4000) 10,350
Nala catches up with Simba (3000-4000) 12,650
Sitting Nala & Simba turn & look down: "Timon? Pumbaa?" (3000-4000) 10,350
Pumbaa bows respectfully (2000-3000) 4312
Close-up of Simba staring ahead under dark clouds (2500-3500) 11,500
Simba, Timon, Pumbaa, & Nala stand on rock ledge with clouds overhead (4000-6000) 8625
Nana, Simba, Timon, & Pumbaa peer over log (3500-4500) 9200
Scar stands on rock & calls: "Sarabi!" (2000-3000) 5750
Proud Sarabi walks thru growling hyenas (1500-2000) 4312
Sarabi reports to Scar (2500-3500) 5175
Scar growls at startled Sarabi (2500-3500) 5750
Simba nuzzles Sarabi (2500-3500) 6900
Close-up of Simba: "...Step down, Scar." (2000-3000) 4600
Wide-eyed Scar smiles at Simba & gestures: "They think I'm king." (2500-3500) 5175
Scar snarls as lightning flashes: "He admits it! Murderer." (2000-3000) 9775
Head shot of Simba against the rocks: "No! I'm not a

murderer!" (2000-3000) 3450
Scar & hyenas approach Simba threateningly (2500-3500) 7475
Simba & Scar face off: "...But this time Daddy isn't here to save you..." (2500-3500) 5462
Portrait of Scar against dark sky (2000-3000) 6325
Desperate Simba clings to edge of cliff with claws, flames in background (1500-2000) 8050
Simba's paw on Scar's throat (2000-3000) 3737
Pumbaa & Timon charge mass of fighting lions & hyenas (2500-3500) 4025
Close-up of hyena viciously attacking Simba (1500-2000) 4025
Rafiki yells & holds walking stick high on top of cliff (2500-3500) 4600
Rafiki in Ninja pose (2500-3500) 8625
Shenzi eyes Zazu & Timon in rib cage (3000-4000) 4887
Scar at edge of cliff (2000-3000) 6325
Stunned Shenzi, Banzai & Ed look thru flames: "It was all their fault." (1500-2000) 11,500
Apologetic Scar is cornered: "Ah, my friends." (2000-3000) 11,500
Nala & Sarabi looking up admiringly in rain (2000-3000) 5175
Determined Simba ascends Pride Rock in rain (2500-3500) 5175
Simba roars atop Pride Rock (3000-4000) 17,250
Close-up of Simba roaring (2000-3000) 8050

MODEL ART

All items in this section were auctioned at Sotheby's, February 11, 1995.

These are full-figure animation maquettes specially hand-painted for the auction by The Walt Disney Studios.

Young Simba, #4/20 (2500-3500) 5750
Rafiki, #3/12 (2500-3500) 8050
Mufasa, #8/18 (3000-4000) 5175
Zazu, #4/14 (2000-2500) 4887
Scar, #16/19 (2500-3500) 4600
Ed, #6/19 (2000-2500) 2300
Pumbaa, #6/17 (2500-3500) 5175
Timon, #5/15 (3000-4000) 4600
Adult Nala, #3/13 (2000-3000) 4600
Adult Simba, #4/17 (3000-4000) 4887

THE LITTLE MERMAID (1989)
Also see TELEVISION: THE LITTLE MERMAID CEL SET-UPS

4-cel pan set-up: Ursula ordering Flotsam & Jetsam after Eric, watercolor production background, 8", S/Dec 16/93 (7000-9000) 10,350
5 cels of Ariel, 4 of her sisters & effects w/color print of matching background, 8 x 15", WDC seal & certificate, VF+, HL/Apr 10/94 (2500-3500) 3640
Ariel & Flounder with color print background of mermaid's grotto, 10 x 15", Disney seal, VF+, HL/Apr 10/94 (1800-2400) 2128
Ariel and Scuttle spy thru ship's railing, color photographic background, Disney seal, 9 x 11", HL/Aug 21/94 (1000-1500) 1008
Prince Eric greets human Ariel at water's edge, color print background, Disney seal & label, 9 x 14-1/2", HL/Aug 21/94 (2000-2500) 2128
Expressive Ursula holding bottle containing "poor unfortunate soul", color print background, Disney seal, 8-1/2 x 12-1/2", HL/Aug 21/94 (1500-2000) 1456
Sebastian & friend as steel-drum section of "hot crustacean band," color print background, seal, 10 x 15", HL/Aug 21/94 (1000-1500) 896
Chef Louis (waist up) working at counter, 7", key watercolor production background, w/notes & Disney stamp, CE/Dec 16/94 (3000-4000) 2300
4-cel setup of Flounder tugging Ariel & barrel (2 x 2") out to Prince Eric's ship, matching watercolor background, certificate of authenticity, S/Dec 17/94 (2500-3500) 2587
2-cel set-up of Ariel (6-1/2 x 9") telling Flounder (3-1/2 x 4") to be quiet, matching watercolor background, certificate of authenticity, S/Dec 17/94 (8,000-10,000) 12,650
3-cel set-up of Flounder pulling on rope with all his might, 3-1/2" x 4-1/2", matching watercolor production background, certificate of authenticity, S/Dec 17/94 (2000-3000) 1955
Smiling Ariel in wedding dress stands on ship's deck,

reaching to Scuttle & Flounder, 7", key photographic reproduction background, Disney Art Program seal, SR/Spring/95 (1800-2400) 1850

Expressive cel of Ursula with two souls in jars, 7-1/2 x 10", color print background, HL/Apr 23/95 (1400-1800) 2016

Grimsby w/soot-covered face, 6", matching watercolor background, S/Jun 10/95 (1000-1500) 920

Sebastian & lobster play clam shells, 10-1/2 x 14-1/2", color print of master background, HL/Aug 6/95 (1000-1500) 1120

Waist-up view of surprised Ariel looking down, 8 x 12", color print of matching master background, HL/Aug 6/95 (2000-2500) 2688

Shoulders-up front-view close-up of somber Ariel with right hand on chest & mouth open, 5", key photographic reproduction background of rocks, Disney Art Program seal, SR/Fall/95 (900-1400) 1090

Jubilant Ariel snatches up Sebastian in Prince Eric's palace, 8 x 12-1/2", matching color print background, HL/Nov 19/95 (1000-1500) 1610

Full figure of Ariel trying to stand w/encouragement of Flounder, Scuttle & Sebastian, 10 x 16-1/2", matching color print background, HL/Nov 19/95 (1800-2400) 3450

Sebastian orchestrates 3 ducks playing turtle shells, 11 x 4-3/4", water effects cel level, key color print background, Disney Art Program seal, SR/Spring/96 (1200-1800) 1320

Full figures of Ariel (holding book, all but tip of fin) & Flounder in underwater library, 8-1/4", key color print background & Disney Art Program seal, SR/Spring/96 (1000-1600) 2640

Close-up of wistful Ariel singing "Part of Your World," matching color print background of her secret grotto, 10 x 13", HL/Apr 28/96 (1400-1800) 1150

Close-up portrait of sad Ariel, matching color photoprint of secret grotto, 9 x 13", HL/Apr 28/96 (1200-1600) 1495

Smiling Ariel sits on rock as she & Prince Eric try to communicate thru gestures, color print of matching background, 9 x 15", HL/Apr 28/96 (1500-2000) 1955

Full figures of King Triton chastising Ariel as Flounder watches, matching color print background, 8 x 13", HL/Apr 28/96 (2000-2500) 2300

Ariel examines book as Flounder watches, matching color print background of secret grotto, 9 x 14", HL/Apr 28/96 (1800-2200) 2760

Full figures of Sebastian conducting duck-&-turtle rhythm section, matching color print background, 10 x 14", HL/Apr 28/96 (1200-1600) 1265

Full figure of Ariel exploring sunken ship, matching color print background, 9 x 12", HL/Apr 28/96 (1200-1600) 1035

Curious Ariel peers over mast of sunken ship, matching color print background, 9 x 13", HL/Apr 28/96 (1200-1600) 920

Eric (chest-up side view, 6-5/8") & Ariel (sitting on rock, 9-1/8") trying to communicate, key color print background, Disney Art Program seal & certificate, SR/Fall/96 (1400-1800) 1400

Close-up of grinning Triton getting close to nervous Sebastian, original bubble effects, 8-1/2", key color print background, Disney Art Program seal & certificate, SR/Fall/96 (1000-1400) 700

Wide-eyed Ariel peers over sunken ship's mast, 4-7/8", bubble effects, key color print background, Disney Art Program seal & certificate, SR/Fall/96 (1200-1800) 1210

Waist-up front view of Ursula in dramatic pose, 5", key color print background of lair, bubble effects, Disney Art Program seal & certificate, SR/Fall/96 (1000-1600) 700

Portrait of shy Ariel seated at dining table, 5-1/2 x 3-1/2" cel image, background: view of seacoast out window behind her, HL/Oct 6/96 (900-1200) 863

Full figures of seahorse messenger summoning dejected Sebastian, 6 x 9" cel image, color print of matching background, HL/Oct 6/96 (700-1000) 489

Large-image close-up of maniacal Chef Louis & severed fish head, 8-1/2 x 13-3/4", color print of master background, HL/Oct 6/96 (500-700) 575

Ariel swimming around Triton, 7-1/4 x 10-1/4" cel image, color print of film background, mat signed by Andreas Deja, HL/Oct 6/96 (1800-2200) 2760

Close-up of smiling King Triton speaking to apprehensive Sebastian, 8-1/2 x 11", color print of matching master background, HL/Oct 6/96 (1000-1500) 1150

Ariel & Scuttle spying thru port on Prince Eric's ship, 2-3/4 x 3-3/4" cel image, color print of matching background, HL/Oct 6/96 (900-1200) 1610

Smiling King Triton speaking very close to reluctant Sebastian, 8-1/2 x 11", color print of master background, HL/Oct 6/96 (900-1200) 690

Happy Eric & Ariel move toward each other at ship's railing as sun sets, 6 x 10-1/2" cel image, color print of matching background, HL/Oct 6/96 (900-1200) 575

Overhead view of Ursula in her lair, 4 x 8" cel image, color print of matching master background, HL/Oct 6/96 (900-1200) 863

Chef Louis in kitchen triumphantly holding up Sebastian, 6-1/2 x 8-1/2" cel image, color print of matching master background, HL/Oct 6/96 (400-600) 431

Profile of angry Ariel swimming behind sunken ship's mast, 5-3/4 x 4" cel image, color print of matching master background, HL/Oct 6/96 (800-1000) 805

4 cels: Sebastian smiling & gesturing, 4", printed background; Scuttle demonstrating a dinglehopper, 5 x 6"; Scuttle attempting to tell Sebastian Vanessa is Ursula in disguise, 6-1/2 x 10"; head-&-shoulders of Ariel discovering Ursula's fee is her voice, 5"; S/Dec 14/96 (2500-3500) 1725

Full figure of Ursula (5 x 4") slithering out of conch-shell chamber, color print of matching background, 9-1/2 x 15" overall, Disney seal, VF+, HL/Feb 23/97 (700-1000) 805

Human Ariel bending over in water as Flounder, Scuttle & Sebastian watch, color print of matching background, 9-1/2 x 15" overall, Disney seal, VF+, HL/Feb 23/97 (1500-2000) 1955

"He's very handsome…" Ariel & Scuttle peer thru ship's railing, color print of matching background, 8 x 11" overall, Disney seal, VF+, HL/Feb 23/97 (800-1000) 633

King Triton (back turned) talks to Ariel (in wedding gown) at ship's railing, color print of matching background, 8-1/2 x 11-1/2" overall, Disney seal, VF+, HL/Feb 23/97 (800-1200) 1840

Ariel swims behind mast of sunken ship, color print of matching background, 9 x 14" overall, Disney seal, VF+, HL/Feb 23/97 (700-1000) 690

Large-image portrait of smiling King Triton looking down, color print of matching background, 9-1/2 x 14" overall, Disney seal, VF+, HL/Feb 23/97 (700-900) 518

Ursula swimming upside down w/arms raised, color print of matching background, 10 x 14" overall, Disney seal, VF+, HL/Feb 23/97 (700-900) 805

Full figures of smiling Prince Eric lifting Ariel on beach, color print of matching background, 8 x 14" overall, Disney seal, VF+, HL/Feb 23/97 (500-700) 748

Full figure of sad Sebastian standing on ocean floor, 3", key watercolor production background, CLA/Jun 7/97 (2000-3000) 1725

Close-up of smiling sea slug embracing Sebastian from "Under the Sea" sequence, 7 x 9", color print of matching background, VF+, HL/Nov 16/97 (600-800) 920

King Triton sits on throne, 9 x 10", color print of matching background, VF+, HL/Nov 16/97 (500-700) 690

Full figure of Ariel on lying sea floor amid human wreckage, 4 x 6-1/2", color print of matching background, VF+, HL/Nov 16/97 (900-1200) 1093

Sheet-clad Ariel seated on rock leans toward shocked Prince Eric, 8 x 15", color print of matching background, Disney seal, VF+, HL/Nov 16/97 (800-1000) 978

Full figure of Ursula slithering out of her conch cave, 3-1/4 x 4", color print of matching background, VF+, HL/Nov 16/97 (500-700) 518

Dreamy-eyed Ariel lying on undersea rock plucking sea-petals as agitated Sebastian scuttles back & forth below, 5-1/4 x 6" & 1 x 1-1/2", color print of matching background, VF+, HL/Nov 16/97 (1500-2000) 3450

Defiant Ariel facing left behind mast of sunken ship, 5-1/4 x 4", color print of matching background, VF+, HL/Nov 16/97 (600-800) 460

Vibrant Chef Louis holding up floured Sebastian, 6-1/2 x 6-1/2", color print of matching background of kitchen, VF+, HL/Nov 16/97 (500-700) 748

Angry Ursula (8") points an order to Flotsam & Jetsam (10"), matching pan watercolor production background, S/Dec 19/97 (8000-10,000) 8050

Waist-up front view of frazzled Chef Louie, 5-1/2", matching watercolor production background of kitchen, S/Dec 19/97 (4000-6000) 4025

Close-up of sad King Triton (6") hugging Ariel (back to camera, 7") in wedding dress, matching production set-up w/matching watercolor production background, S/Dec 19/97 (4000-6000) 4025

"Isn't it obvious, Daddy? Ariel's in love!" Hips-up front views of one of Ariel's sisters in lovestruck pose & stunned King Triton, unidentified background, seal, 7 x 7-1/2" cel, VF+, HL/Apr 25/98 (600-900) 575

Hips-up view of Ariel in her grotto with statue of Eric, color print of matching background, seal, 6-1/2 x 6-1/4" cel, VF+, HL/Apr 25/98 (1200-1600) 1265

Newly married Ariel bends at waist with hands & feet in water as Flounder & Scuttle watch, unidentified background, 9-1/2 x 13-1/2" cel, seal & certificate, VF+, HL/Apr 25/98 (1500-2000) 978

CELS – FULL FIGURE

Front view of Smiling Ariel swimming w/2 gadgets & bubbles in 3-cel set, 8-1/2 x 12", Disney seal, VF+, HL/Apr 10/94 (2000-3000) 2632

Sebastian lectures, 5 x 5", Disney seal, VF+, HL/Nov 13/94 (700-1000) 1120

Color model cel of Ariel, 7-1/2 x 6", HL/Mar 11/95 (600-900) 2035

Ursula sitting, matching water-effects cel, 6-1/2 x 7", HL/Apr 23/95 (700-1000) 1232

Smiling Ariel holding 2 "gizmos," 9 x 10-1/2", HL/Nov 19/95 (1800-2400) 2070

Matched full-figure images of smiling Ariel & Flounder, McDonald's TV commercial, 6 x 6-3/4", VF+, HL/Nov 16/97 (300-400) 690

CELS – PARTIAL FIGURE

Ariel close-up portrait signed by Glen Keane, 7 x 11, Disney seal, VF+, HL/Apr 10/94 (2000-2500) 2128

Portrait of Ariel gazing upward, 7-1/2 x 6-1/2", VF+, HL/Apr 10/94 (1500-2000) 2016

Wedding kiss of Prince Eric & Ariel, 6-1/2 x 12", WDC seal, VF+, HL/Apr 10/94 (2000-2500) 2688

Chest-up front-view of Ariel looking up with mouth open, 9", 16-field, Disney Art Program seal, SR/Fall/94 (1600-2400) 1600

Ariel & Prince Eric sitting [in boat] as he tries to guess her name, 5 x 8", Disney seal, VF+, HL/Nov 13/94 (1000-1500) 1456

Shoulders-up of happy Eric lifting delighted Ariel up by her waist, 4-3/4", 12-field, Disney Art Program seal, SR/Spring/95 (1400-2000) 1430

Portrait of gleeful Ursula with hands folded, 7 x 11-1/2", HL/Apr 28/96 (1000-1500) 2300

Promotional cel w/Ariel, Flounder (both full figure), Triton, Ursula, Scuttle & Sebastian, sight 12-1/2 x 16", S/Dec 14/96 (1200-1800) 1495

Angry Ariel being restrained by Flotsam & Jetsam, 6 x 8", VF+, HL/Feb 23/97 (1000-1500) 1725

Front view of Max squeezing between bride Ariel & Eric, 8 x 15", VF+, HL/Nov 16/97 (1000-1500) 1380

Large-image portrait of Ariel, hair swirling, looking up & singing, 7-1/2 x 10-1/4", VF+, HL/Nov 16/97 (1000-1500) 1265

MAKE MINE MUSIC (1946)

Also see TELEVISION: ANTHOLOGY SERIES

Segments were *The Martins and the Coys, Blue Bayou, All the Cats Join In, Without You, Casey at the Bat, Two Silhouettes, Peter and the Wolf, After You've Gone, Johnny Fedora and Alice Bluebonnet,* and *The Whale Who Wanted to Sing at the Met.*

ANIMATION DRAWINGS
All the Cats Join In: 4 drawings of bobbysoxer drying off & jumping into her clothes, 6 x 2" to 5-1/2 x 4-1/2", HL/Nov 13/94 (400-600) 728
Full-figure drawing of jitterbugging teenage girl, 5-1/2 x 2", VF, HL/Feb 23/97 (150-200) 316
Partial figure of Willie the Whale as Mephistopheles, 7-1/2 x 8-1/2", VF, HL/Feb 23/97 (900-1200) 978
Full-figure rear view of teenage girl drying w/towel, 5-1/2 x 4", VF, HL/Feb 23/97 (150-200) 259
3 drawings of teenage girl drying off; 5-1/4 x 4", 5-1/2 x 3", 5-1/2 x 3-1/2"; VF; HL/Apr 25/98 (400-600) 633

BACKGROUNDS
Preliminary watercolor background painting for establishing shot of *The Martins and the Coys*, 8-1/2 x 11-1/2", studio notes, VG, HL/Apr 10/94 (1500-2000) 2128

CEL SET-UPS (also see TITLE ART)
Full-figure front view of 2 sets of dancing fingers on frame-wide keyboard, 3", production background, 12-field, SR/Spring/95 (500-900) 550
Johnnie Fedora & Alice Bluebonnet together in dept. store window, 7-1/2 x 7-1/2", complementary painted background, Courvoisier label, inscribed "...Walt Disney" by Studio artist, HL/Apr 23/95 (1800-2200) 2912
Inquisitive Peter holding Ivan by nap of neck and Sasha in palm, 8 x 10-1/2", with master background (tempera on board), HL/Nov 19/95 (3500-4500) 3450
Full figures of Johnny Fedora & Alice Bluebonnet snuggling in dept. store window, 8 x 8-1/2", complementary Courvoisier airbrush background, HL/Nov 19/95 (2000-2500) 2070
Full figures of determined hunters Mischa (6", blunderbuss muzzle out of frame), Yascha (3-1/4"), & Vladimir (6") stalking thru snow, airbrushed Courvoisier background & label, S/Dec 14/96 (1000-1500) 1035
Full-figure front view of confident Casey standing with eyes closed & hand on hip, 4-1/4", color print background of baseball, bat, baseball cap, & diamond, SR/Spring/97 (400-700) 520
Peter & the Wolf: smiling Peter (near-full figure, 6-1/2") talks to Sonia (full figure, 4"), printed background of outdoors in winter, S/Dec 19/97 (1200-1800) 1035

CELS – FULL FIGURE
Willie standing in costume leaning toward left, 8", 16-field, SR/Fall/94 (1600-2400) 1740
3 full-figure cels: Ivan lying on back on 4 paws, facing right, looking up, 3-1/4"; angry Sasha standing facing right w/wings out in fighting pose, 1-1/8"; innocent Sonia standing facing left w/hands behind back, 4"; SR/Spring/95 (900-1500) 940
Peter & the Wolf: menacing wolf, 6-1/2 x 11", HL/Apr 23/95 (700-1000) 784
All the Cats Join In: rear view of 2 dancers, 6-1/2 x 4-1/2", HL/Aug 6/95 (500-700) 504
Waist-up view of somber Peter facing left, holding smiling Ivan up by back of neck in right hand & Sasha in palm of left hand, 7-1/2", color print display background of sky, ct, SR/Fall/95 (1200-1800) 1320
4 bobbysoxer couples dance, 8-1/2 x 5-3/8" on four 12-field cel levels, SR/Fall/96 (1000-2000) 1000
Curious Sonia the Duck facing left, 2-1/2 x 4-1/2", F, HL/Feb 23/97 (300-500) 431
Two full-figure cels: front view of Alice Bluebonnet atop lady's head, 5-2/3"; Johnnie Fedora on dept. store stand facing toward left, 4-1/2"; framed together; ct; SR/Spring/97 (1200-1800) 1210
Two *All the Cats Join In* cels: full figure of a couple dancing in each, 5-3/8" & 5", 12-field cels, SR/Spring/97 (800-1200) 820
Front view of 4 somber ballplayers sitting on sagging bench, 9-3/4 x 5", 12-field cel, ct, SR/Spring/97 (300-600) 480
All the Cats Join In: bobbysoxer & dance partner, 5-1/2 x 4-1/4", F+, HL/Nov 16/97 (600-900) 518

CELS – PARTIAL FIGURE/MODEL ART
Near-full figure of Willie singing *Pagliacci*, 10-1/2 x 7", VF, HL/Apr 10/94 (2000-3000) 3136
Color model of Willie "standing" in water singing to pelican on buoy & 3 seals on ice floe, 8-3/4"

water effects, folds, tear below punch, paint restoration, SR/Fall/94 (2000-3000) 1820
Confident Casey leans to his left & eavesdrops, 6-1/2 x 6-1/2", F, HL/Nov 19/95 (600-900) 690

CONCEPT AND INSPIRATIONAL ART
Two Fred Moore full-figure drawings of Grace Martin, 7-1/2" & 8-1/4", ink & watercolor on 15-1/2 x 12" sheet, fold covered by matting with double opening, SR/Spring/96 (800-1400) 4670

STORY ART
2 story sketches of teens dancing from *All the Cats Join In*, conté crayon on story sheets, 4-1/4 x 4-1/4" & 4-1/2 x 3", HL/May 31/97 (75-100) 546

TITLE ART
Title set-up for "Johnnie Fedora and Alice Bluebonnet Sung by the Andrew Sisters," 6-1/8", four 16-field cel levels, watercolor background, SR/Spring/97 (300-600) 220

MARY POPPINS (1964)

BACKGROUNDS
Background layout painting of the Park, pastel on cardboard, CE/Jun 18/94 (800-1200) 1610
Background layout painting of the Park, watercolor & pastel on cardboard, CE/Dec 16/94 (700-900) 1150
Production background of Park, pastel & watercolor on paper, with notes, CE/Dec 16/94 (800-1200) 1725
Production background of Park, pastel & watercolor on paper, CE/Dec 16/94 (800-1200) 2530
Landscape production background, 12-1/2 x 21", pastel & watercolor on cardboard, CE/Jun 9/95 (1500-2000) 1955
Landscape production background, 12-1/2 x 30", pastel & watercolor on cardboard, extensive notes, CE/Jun 9/95 (1500-2000) 1380
Landscape production background, 12 x 30-1/2", pastel & watercolor on cardboard, notes, CE/Jun 9/95 (1500-2000) 1840
Landscape production background, 12 x 31", pastel & watercolor on cardboard, notes, CE/Jun 9/95 (1500-2000) 1495
Master pan background painting of outdoors from *Jolly Holiday* sequence, 11 x 30", pastel & tempera on pan background sheet, HL/Nov 19/95 (2500-3000) 3910
Pair of gouache-&-pastel production backgrounds, one from scenes 4 & 7, one from scene 138, sight: 12-1/2 x 23" & 12-1/2 x 21", CE/Dec 12/96 (1200-1800) 1840
Gouache-&-pastel production background of woods, scene 116, sight 19 x 30", CE/Dec 12/96 (800-1200) 1265

CEL SET-UPS
4 penguins in row with separate cel of snowball, 8 x 10", color print background, as sold at DL, HL/Nov 13/94 (900-1200) 896
Pearly Band marching & playing, 4-1/2" x 9", pan gouache & pastel production background, S/Jun 10/95 (3000-5000) 3450
Close-up of upper crust monocled English horse & rider, 8 x 10", color print background as sold at DL, HL/Aug 6/95 (300-400) 224
Close-up of Master of the Hounds facing right, 7", DL litho background of countryside, gold Art Corner label, SR/Fall/95 (600-1200) 600
Full figures of 4 dancing penguin waiters matched to color publicity photo of Dick Van Dyke, background grass cut out & set over sheet of blue paper as sky, 7-1/2 x 12", HL/Apr 28/96 (2000-3000) 748
Mary & Bert stand on picturesque footbridge as swan family swims in stream; matching cels w/master background (tempera & pastel on background sheet) & color photos of Dick Van Dyke & Julie Andrews; 9 x 14", HL/Oct 6/96 (2000-3000) 2300
Full figures of 2 turtles looking up as they swim to right, pastel & watercolor background, 8-1/2 x 4-1/4", SR/Spring/97 (1400-2200) 1410
Front view of fox hunter & mount, both w/hand/hoof shielding eyes; 7-1/2" on two cel levels, litho background of forest, gold DL Art Corner label, SR/Spring/97 (1200-1600) 510
Front view of rider & mount, both with hand/hoof shielding eyes, looking into distance, color print background as sold at DL, 7 x 8-1/2" cel, VF,

HL/Apr 25/98 (200-400) 633

CELS – FULL FIGURE
Horse racers from Jolly Holiday sequence, 4-1/2 x 13", VF, HL/Feb 26-27/94 (200-300) 523
Angry penguin head waiter arranges flowers on penguin waiter's tray, 6-1/2 x 6", F+, HL/Aug 21/94 (1000-2000) 1008
3 penguin waiters, 5-1/2 x 6-1/2", as sold at DL, HL/Nov 13/94 (800-1000) 1344
Two penguins dance about a water splash, 7-1/2 x 9", VF+, HL/Mar 11/95 (400-600) 825
Front view of Pearly Band, 8 x 5-3/4", 16-field, SR/Spring/96 (500-900) 550
Three members of Pearly Band playing & dancing, 7-1/2 x 12-1/2", HL/Apr 28/96 (400-600) 460
2 fox hunters & 3 hounds running to right, 10 x 2-7/8", paint partially adhered to DL color background, some lifting, gold Art Corner label, SR/Fall/96 (300-600) 300
High-stepping dancing penguin, 4-1/4 x 3-1/4", HL/Oct 6/96 (300-400) 805
Penguin waiter facing left in dancing pose, 2-1/4 x 1-1/2", HL/May 31/97 (200-300) 288
Barnyard chorus singing, 13-3/4 x 7" on three 16-field levels, SR/Fall/97 (1500-2000) 1500
Combative Fox stands facing left, 5-1/2", 16-field cel, SR/Fall/97 (450-700) 300
4 eager penguins stand facing left, 3-1/3", 16-field cel, SR/Fall/97 (900-1400) 650

CELS – PARTIAL FIGURE
Husband-&-wife team in Pearly Band, 9-1/2 x 13", VF+, HL/Apr 23/95 (600-800) 504
Five horses & riders racing together to right, 12-1/4 x 5", SR/Fall/95 (300-600) 410
Waist-up front view of full Pearly Band, 8-1/2 x 15-1/2", VF+, HL/Nov 19/95 (900-1200) 805

MELODY TIME (1948)
Segments were *Once Upon a Wintertime, Bumble Boogie, Johnny Appleseed, Little Toot, Trees, Blame It on the Samba,* and *Pecos Bill.*

ANIMATION DRAWINGS
Four drawings of Pecos Bill riding Widowmaker, 6-1/2 x 4-1/2" to 6-1/2 x 7", HL/Mar 16-17/96 (600-900) 690
Portrait drawing & 3 photostats (enhanced with pencil) of drawing of progressive close-ups of Slue Foot Sue's face, all 12-field, shallow vertical folds & some wear, SR/Spring/96 (300-600) 570
Full-figure extreme drawing of flirtatious Slue Foot Sue standing in dress, 6 x 3", HL/May 31/97 (300-500) 288
Full-figure drawing of confident Pecos Bill twirling six-guns as he rides happy Widowmaker to left, 6-1/4 x 7", HL/May 31/97 (300-500) 288
Full-figure drawing of Pecos Bill firing six-guns as he rides Widowmaker to left, 5-5/8", 12-field sheet, SR/Spring/98 (250-500) 250

BACKGROUNDS
Master background of outdoors with Johnny Appleseed's wheelbarrow, shovel & trees, 8-1/2 x 11", tempera on background sheet, HL/Aug 6/95 (1400-1800) 2240
Master background of Pecos Bill's desert with river in foreground, 11 x 14-1/2", tempera on background sheet, HL/Nov 19/95 (1800-2200) 1725
Master background painting of bench, apple trees, baskets & wagon full of apples, tempera on background sheet, 8-1/2 x 11", HL/Apr 28/96 (1400-1800) 2760

CEL SET-UPS
Johnny Appleseed, simple complementary Courvoisier-style background, encapsulated in heavy plastic, G, HL/Feb 26-27/94 (300-400) 330
Color model or publicity cel of Pecos Bill riding Widowmaker in clouds & twirling lariat around both, 9 x 10-1/2", complementary painted background, inscribed, stamped, labeled, HL/Nov 13/94 (1200-1600) 2912
Full figure of Slue Foot Sue riding Widowmaker, 9-1/2 x 10-1/2", background of desert (tempera on background sheet), inscribed mat, stamped, HL/Apr 23/95 (2000-2500) 2240
Full-figure overhead view of happy Little Toot (1") looking up while towing paper boats, water & smoke effects, watercolor display background, SR/Spring/96 (400-800) 990

Full figure of Pecos Bill lying on Widowmaker's back in middle of ocean twirling lasso w/toes, airbrushed Courvoisier background, WDP label, 4 x 5" not including lasso, S/Jun 19/96 (800-1200)   1265

Guardian Angel (7") holds up apple to young Johnny Appleseed (6"), printed background of outdoors, S/Dec 14/96 (1500-2000)   1610

Full figures of Donald Duck and José Carioca dancing as Aracuan Bird (leaning on guitar) watches, festive painted background, 7-3/4 x 10-1/2" overall, HL/May 3/97 (2000-2500)   1955

Full figures of angry Widowmaker bucking Slue Foot Sue, overall 8 x 7", airbrushed studio-prepared background of desert, S/Jun 21/97 (2000-3000)   6325

Slue Foot Sue check her make-up in her compact, 7", hand-prepared background of Western scene, S/Dec 19/97 (1200-1800)   2070

Full figure of Johnny Appleseed kicking apples over his head into basket he's holding, master background of forest clearing & full apple basket (trimmed, tempera on background sheet), WDP label, 7-3/4 x 10-1/2", VF+, HL/Apr 25/98 (1000-1500)   1955

Full figure of Pecos Bill firing six-guns as he rides determined Widowmaker to left, 3-7/8", matching brightly colored gouache background painting of West enhanced w/special effects as prepared by Art Props Department, original Disney label, mat signed by Walt Disney, SR/Spring/98 (5000-9000)   5600

CELS – FULL FIGURE/MODEL ART

Once Upon A Wintertime: Joe & Jenny skate, 4-1/4", S/Dec 16/93 (400-600)   460

Slue Foot Sue on angry Widowmaker as six cowboys restrain him with ropes, 5 x 9-1/2", VF, HL/Apr 10/94 (800-1200)   644

Happy Little Toot in water, 4", CE/Dec 16/94 (600-800)   805

Blame It On The Samba: side view of Donald Duck & José Carioca riding musical note to left, 3-3/4 x 3", VF, HL/Apr 23/95 (700-900)   672

Young Johnny Appleseed, pot on head, walking with staff, carrying Bible, squirrel on pot, chipmunk on shoulder, 6 x 3", VF, HL/Nov 19/95 (1000-1500)   1150

Johnny's Angel stands looking left, 5-3/4", SR/Spring/96 (400-700)   400

Pecos Bill tipping hat as he sits astride Widowmaker, 6"; Slue Foot Sue sitting w/arm outstretched [to hold compact], 6-1/2"; plus glossy b&w photo of Bill & Widowmaker in same pose & photostat model sheet of Pecos Bill, S/Jun 19/96 (700-900)   1725

5 items from Johnny Appleseed: 3 cels of Johnny: imagining himself striking out to new frontier; later in life resting beneath tree surrounded by forest friends; befriending mountain lion to amazement of other animals. Model drawings of Johnny's Guardian Angel & photostat model sheet w/23 images of Johnny, S/Dec 14/96 (600-800)   2587

Blame It on the Samba: full figure of woozy blue Donald sitting, 3-1/2 x 3-1/2", HL/Feb 23/97 (400-500)   546

Pecos Bill on Widowmaker facing left, front hooves off ground, Pecos leaning on horse's head, both looking straight down, 3-1/4 x 5-1/2", VF, HL/Nov 16/97 (700-1000)   575

Young Johnny Appleseed kneeling, right arm extended horizontally, looking down, 5-3/4 x 6-1/4", VF, HL/Nov 16/97 (500-700)   575

Color model cel of Johnny Appleseed (4-1/8") standing facing left watching determined Guardian Angel (4-3/8") sitting in mid-air peeling apple, SR/Spring/98 (400-800)   490

CELS – PARTIAL FIGURE/MODEL ART

Knees-up model cel of demure Slue Foot Sue (eyes closed) holding open compact, 7-1/2 x 5", F+, HL/Nov 19/95 (700-1000)   863

Knees-up of Johnny Appleseed admiring apple, 6-1/4", 12-field, SR/Spring/96 (400-700)   730

Medium full-image of Little Toot's smiling father, 7", CE/Jun 20/96 (400-600)   1093

Knees-up view of Slue Foot Sue (eyes closed) holding powder puff & open compact, 7 x 4-1/2", VF, HL/Nov 16/97 (800-1000)   748

CONCEPT AND INSPIRATIONAL ART

Once Upon A Wintertime: boy & girl skate in park inspirational sketch, pastel on paper,

---

9-1/2 x 10-1/2", CE/Dec 15/93 (600-800)   690

Trees: 2 inspirational studies, 6 x 8" each, colored pastel on black paper, VF, HL/Nov 16/97 (400-600)   460

STORY ART

2 storyboard drawings of Little Toot with father, ink & pastel on 8-3/16 x 5 15'/16" storyboard sheets by Nick George, SR/Spring/96 (200-400)   970

Trees: 4 Richmond Kelsey story drawings, pastel & watercolor on paper stapled to black paper, 5-1/2 x 7", HL/Feb 23/97 (1000-1500)   1035

THE NIGHTMARE BEFORE CHRISTMAS (1993)

See **TIM BURTON'S THE NIGHTMARE BEFORE CHRISTMAS**

OLIVER AND COMPANY (1988)

CEL SET-UPS

Full figures of Jenny, Oliver & Georgette in kitchen, color photoprint background, 9-1/2 x 15", Disney seal & label, VF+, HL/Feb 26-27/94 (600-900)   550

3-cel set-up includes determined Tito at wheel & frightened Georgette riding [Fagin's cart], 8-1/2 x 13", color photoprint background of bridge cables, Disney seal & label, VF+, HL/Feb 26-27/94 (300-400)   286

Tito stands w/front paws on loot box, color print background; cast riding Fagin's cart; Tito, Dodger, Francis, Einstein, Rita stand together w/Rita growling; all w/Disney seal & labels; 8 x 12", 8 x 11", 7 x 10-1/2"; VF+, HL/Aug 21/94 (700-1000)   840

Oliver with front paws on hot dog stand; full figure of Rita; Fagin lying on floor with Dodger, Einstein, Rita & Francis; 10-1/2 x 16", 8 x 12", 9-1/2 x 13-1/2", each with color print background & seal, 2 with certificates, VF+, HL/Nov 13/94 (900-1200)   896

Full figure of cool Dodger (6 x 4") sitting on trash can, color print of matching background, matted with page w/Billy Joel's autograph, HL/Feb 23/97 (300-400)   863

Full figure of Oliver standing on paper in corner, facing left, looking back; color print of background; seal & certificate; 4 x 7 cel; VF+; HL/Apr 25/98 (300-400)   633

CELS – FULL FIGURE

Francis, Tito, Dodger & Rita (partial figure facing away in foreground) standing, 7-1/2 x 12-1/2", Disney seal & label, VF+, HL/Feb 26-27/94 (300-500)   303

Rita, Tito, Dodger (5"), Oliver, Francis, & Einstein (partial) sitting/standing together, 16-field, Disney Art Program seal, SR/Fall/94 (300-600)   390

Long shot of Fagin's gang disdainfully watching Roscoe & DeSoto walk away (most full figure) with back of Oliver's head in foreground, 7 x 12", VF+, HL/May 31/97 (300-500)   230

Enthusiastic Georgette & bewildered Tito standing together as Rita & Dodger (partial figures) leave to right, 6 x 11", VF+, HL/May 31/97 (300-400)   230

CELS – PARTIAL FIGURE

Smiling Georgette inside 8-bird circle from musical number, 9 x 12-1/2", VF, HL/Aug 6/95 (400-500)   224

Portrait of smiling Tito, 7 x 9-1/2", HL/Nov 19/95 (400-500)   403

CONCEPT AND INSPIRATIONAL ART

44 concept thumbnail drawings, 2-3/4" & smaller; 7 layout drawings, 35" & smaller, CE/Jun 9/95 (600-800)   633

101 DALMATIANS (1961)

ANIMATION DRAWINGS

Close-up rough drawing of Pongo, 8", CE/Jun 18/94 (400-600)   403

Waist-up drawing of angry Cruella de Vil looking left, 6-3/4", 16-field sheet, SR/Spring/96 (900-1500)   1200

Waist-up drawing of smiling Cruella facing right, leaning forward with right arm out, 9 x 6-1/4", 16-field sheet, timer's chart, SR/Fall/96

(900-1500)   1100

Profile drawing of determined Cruella de Vil facing right, bending down & looking up, 5-3/4 x 7-1/2", HL/Feb 23/97 (1000-1200)   1093

Waist-up drawing of intense, red-lipped Cruella de Vil facing left, pointing with right hand, 7-3/4", 16-field sheet, SR/Spring/97 (2000-2400)   1930

Portrait detailed rough drawing of stern Danny the Great Dane by John Lounsbery, 8 x 6", HL/May 31/97 (100-200)   374

Key drawing by Marc Davis of smiling Cruella standing facing left, 10-1/2", CLA/Jun 7/97 (800-1200)   575

Near-full-figure front-view drawing of Cruella de Vil by Marc Davis, 10", CLA/Jun 7/97 (800-1200)   1495

Half-image front-view drawing of Cruella de Vil looking right, 7-5/8", signed by Marc Davis, 16-field sheet, SR/Fall/97 (1200-1500)   800

Waist-up drawing by Marc Davis of smiling red-lipped Cruella de Vil facing right, looking back, 7", 16-field sheet, signed, SR/Spring/98 (1100-1600)   1090

CEL SET-UPS

6 cels: Nanny; Sgt. Tibs; Captain; Lucy (3); 1st with photographic copy of original background, S/Dec 16/93 (500-700)   460

5 cels: Pongo, Roger, Nanny, Anita (2), one of Anita with photographic copy of original background, S/Dec 16/93 (700-900)   920

4 cels: 7-1/2" Anita, 3-1/2" Nanny on knees, 6" Horace, 4" Jasper; 1st w/photographic copy of original background; S/Dec 16/93 (500-700)   345

Pepper watching Thunderbolt from top of Pongo's head, photographic copy of original background, 6", S/Dec 16/93 (800-1200)   1610

Full figure of Pongo seated, color print background of park, 8 x 10", DL label, VF, HL/Apr 10/94 (1000-1500)   1344

Pup on Pongo's head, 8 x 10", color print background of living room, DL label, VF+, HL/Apr 10/94 (2000-2500)   3136

Publicity cel of concerned Pongo & Perdita, watercolor production background, 6 x 7", S/Jun 17/94 (4000-6000)   4312

Pongo walks in park with nose & tail in air, color print background, DL label, 8 x 10", HL/Aug 21/94 (700-1000)   1008

3 cels: 2 of Anita; Roger & Anita; each w/color print background & label as sold at DL, 8 x 10", 10 x 8", HL/Aug 21/94 (600-900)   672

Concerned Pongo looks left, 8-1/2 x 10", color print background of interior of Radcliff house, as sold at DL, VF, HL/Nov 13/94 (800-1200)   1232

Cruella in bed reads newspaper, 7", key watercolor production background, CE/Dec 16/94 (5000-7000)   4600

Atmospheric set-up of lone puppy (3/4") running through snow as Badun's truck, Cruella's car, & delivery van approach, watercolor preliminary background with Xerox on cel lines, S/Dec 17/94 (1800-2200)   5462

Full figure of eager Pongo running right, 3-1/2 x 6-1/2", complementary background print, VF+, HL/Apr 23/95 (800-1200)   1344

"Mother, I'm hungry." Full figure of Rolly lying in front of TV, 4 x 4" cel image, color print background, VF, HL/Apr 23/95 (600-900)   2128

Roger wipes soot off Pongo, 7-1/2 x 9-1/2", print of line drawing for background of Radcliff home, VF, HL/Apr 23/95 (1200-1600)   1792

Cruella in bed reading paper, 7", studio-prepared background, CE/Jun 9/95 (1500-2000)   1840

Full figures of Pongo & 4 puppies as Labradors inside barn on hay, 4", cel overlay and watercolor production background, CE/Jun 9/95 (1500-2000)   2760

Near-full figure of angry Cruella standing in Darlings' house, 7-3/4", publication background, CE/Jun 9/95 (2000-3000)   3450

Full figure of Pongo sweeping snow with branch, 4 x 8", matching pan gouache production background w/xerographic lined cel overlay, S/Jun 10/95 (6000-8000)   6900

Classic scene of Pongo, Perdita & pups watching TV, 1991 limited-edition cel with matching master background print, #212/500, 11 x 15", HL/Nov 19/95 (1200-1600)   1150

Angry Jasper (10-1/2") holds bottle over Horace's head (eating can of beans, 6-1/2") as they sit on sofa, key gouache master background, SR/Spring/96 (1800-2600) 2400

Full-figure front view of angry Cruella driving car down country road, from 1993 video promotion film, color print background, 12 x 15", Disney seal, VF+, HL/Apr 28/96 (900-1200) 1093

Large-image portrait of worried Pongo, color print background of park, gold DL label, 8 x 10", F+, HL/Apr 28/96 (900-1200) 1265

Angry Cruella pulls Jasper toward her face with fist on his coat, DL printed background of snowy forest, 7-1/2", CE/Jun 20/96 (1500-2000) 2185

Nanny tries to restrain Jasper (5-5/8") & Horace from exploring house, gouache key master background with line print overlay, ct, SR/Fall/96 (1800-2600) 1820

Full figure of irritated Patch sitting & scratching near TV, 4 x 5" cel image, color print background from film, as sold at DL, F, HL/Oct 6/96 (900-1200) 1150

Near-full figure of Pongo with paws on seat cushions looking around apartment, 11 x 15", master background of apartment's bay window (tempera on background sheet), VF, HL/Oct 6/96 (1500-2000) 5720

5 attentive puppies sitting facing right & looking behind them to left, 4 x 10-1/2" cel image, non-Studio complementary background painting, VF, HL/Oct 6/96 (1200-1600) 2530

Smiling Cruella sitting reading newspaper & smoking; non-Studio background & cel of pink blanket; 7 x 8" cel image, F+, HL/Oct 6/96 (1200-1600) 2530

Full figures of carolers Goofy, Donald Duck & Minnie Mouse from *Pluto's Christmas Tree*, complementary color print background of snowy forest from *101 Dalmatians*, 4 x 4-1/2" cel image, HL/Oct 6/96 (1200-1600) 920

Full-figure long shot of Roger & Anita walking Pongo & Perdita on leashes to left thru park, 6" & smaller, watercolor pan production background, CE/Dec 12/96 (4000-6000) 7475

Full figure of Pongo (4-3/4") holding puppy (2-1/2") in mouth by collar as he listens to collie (near-full figure, 5"), key watercolor production background of snowy field, CE/Dec 12/96 (4000-6000) 5520

Very happy Pongo looks out window, 5-1/2", DL print background, S/Dec 14/96 (600-800) 1610

Pongo lying sleepily on seat in front of window, 4 x 5" (w/out tail), one tear in cel, printed DL background, S/Dec 14/96 (800-1200) 1955

Angry Cruella sitting in bed talking on phone, 7", watercolor w/Xerographic line-on-celluloid background, S/Dec 14/96 (4000-6000) 8625

Anxious Pongo sits looking over shoulder, 7 x 5", preliminary production background of room, S/Dec 14/96 (3000-5000) 2875

Full figure of confused Pongo sitting in park, 5", printed DL background, S/Dec 14/96 (800-1200) 1495

Half image of sad Perdita (night colors) sitting, color print of snowy outdoor background, 8 x 10" overall, HL/Feb 23/97 (1000-1500) 1150

Roger (standing on stairs) leans forward to lecture smiling Anita (sitting in chair), both 6-1/2" Art Props set-up with matching gouache background, SR/Spring/97 (4000-7000) 4000

Full-figure rear view of embracing couple sitting on park bench, 3 cel levels with full foreground overlay, gouache background of park, 16-field, SR/Spring/97 (1200-1600) 1400

Pongo stands in snow nudging puppy forward into wind, 6", DL background of snow & stone fence, CLA/Jun 7/97 (1000-1500) 2070

Full figures of angry Patch & Lucky, each half covered in coal dust, facing left; printed DL background of snowy outdoors; 4" each, S/Jun 21/97 (800-1200) 1610

Patch perches in doorway, 4", printed DL background, S/Jun 21/97 (700-900) 1150

Perdita (4-1/2 x 5" w/o tail) walks to left thru snow w/2 puppies (3" each), printed DL background, S/Jun 21/97 (1000-1500) 1955

Room full of sleeping puppies, some watching TV, sight 11 x 14-1/2", matching watercolor with Xerox line-on-cel overlay background,

S/Jun 21/97 (8000-10,000) 9775

Angry Cruella (6-1/2") confronts Anita (5-1/2"), printed DL background of house interior, S/Jun 21/97 (2000-3000) 2875

Full figure of eager Pongo running to right, 4-1/2 x 7", complementary color print of snow-scene background, VF+, HL/Nov 16/97 (900-1200) 1150

Dark front-view set-up of Sgt. Tibs sitting on head of Colonel as they peer thru gate, 11 x 14-1/2" overall, starry background from 1960s TV show (tempera on background sheet), VF+, HL/Nov 16/97 (700-1000) 374

Near-full figure of Pongo on hind legs at window, leash in mouth, looking back, 6-1/2 x 5-1/2", matching color print background, VG-F, HL/Nov 16/97 (900-1200) 1150

Full figure of angry Nanny sitting in attic, 4", matching production set-up with watercolor pan production background & Xerox line-on-cel overlay, S/Dec 19/97 (6000-8000) 4025

Large image of Pongo walking on leash, looking back quizzically, 6 x 6", printed background of wintery outdoors, gold DL label, S/Dec 19/97 (700-900) 1380

CELS – FULL FIGURE (also see MODEL ART)

Cruella gestures with cigarette holder, 7-1/4", S/Dec 16/93 (1200-1800) 2070

Cruella with purse & cigarette holder gestures unhappily, 7-1/2", S/Jun 17/94 (1200-1800) 1840

Cruella de Vil walking, 8-1/2 x 4-1/4", CE/Jun 18/94 (1500-2000) 1840

3 running puppies in darkened colors, 2-1/2 x 11", HL/Aug 21/94 (900-1200) 1456

Somber Pongo & Perdita stand facing right, 6-1/2" & similar, CE/Dec 16/94 (1000-1500) 805

Determined Sgt. Tibs (4-3/4") pushes puppy (3-1/2"), DL label, CE/Dec 16/94 (400-600) 1093

Roger sitting, 6", CE/Dec 16/94 (500-700) 403

Horace (4-1/2") trapped under wood plank; Nanny (2-1/2") calling for help after puppies are missing; Pongo (5") chewing fiercely on Jasper's left foot, S/Dec 17/94 (5 x 9") (800-1200) 690

Perdita looks surprised; Pongo looks a bit distressed; Roger walks to right; startled Anita looks down; S/Dec 17/94 (1000-1500) 1955

Penny (3-1/2") looking quizzical; full figure of Thunderbolt (6-1/2"); S/Dec 17/94 (600-800) 920

Roger (9") & Anita (7") dancing to "Cruella De Vil"; full figure of concerned Pongo facing right, 4 x 5", S/Dec 17/94 (1200-1500) 1495

4 cels: one each of Horace & Jasper armed & stalking puppies; Cruella; Pongo barking ferociously, S/Dec 17/94 (1200-1500) 1725

Horace & Jasper advance menacingly with club raised; Sgt. Tibs; Perdita attacks; Cruella in fur coat holding purse & cigarette holder; S/Dec 17/94 (1200-1500) 1495

Sgt. Tibs; Colonel; Captain; 2 of Lucy the goose; S/Dec 17/94 (800-1200) 690

3 puppies, 2 covered with soot; Nanny holding feather duster with paw prints on apron; 2 of Anita covered with paw prints; S/Dec 17/94 (1200-1500) 2587

Anita (5") takes Perdita (2 x 3") out for evening walk, S/Dec 17/94 (800-1200) 1035

Jasper; Horace; Sgt. Tibs; Colonel; Cruella, S/Dec 17/94 (1200-1500) 1265

Nanny (7") holding Patch (2-1/2"); Perdita, 4 x 5-1/2"; Pongo sitting up & smiling with tongue out, 4", S/Dec 17/94 (1500-2000) 3737

Sad Pongo sitting, 5 x 4-1/2", VF+, HL/Apr 23/95 (900-1200) 1456

5 cels: 3 of Colonel (1 w/Tibs); terrier; bulldog; 3 x 3-1/2" to 5-1/2 x 9", F+-VF, HL/Apr 23/95 (800-1200) 1344

Full figure of inquisitive Patch, 5-1/4"; Thunderbolt (head & neck), 4", S/Jun 10/95 (700-900) 1150

Happy Roger (7-1/2") & Pongo (4-1/2") dance together, S/Jun 10/95 (1200-1500) 2875

Anita, 6"; Roger sitting & nervously smoking pipe, 5"; Nanny down on all fours, 5-1/2"; S/Jun 10/95 (700-900) 460

Nanny in profile holding hand out to right; Horace holding stomach; Jasper w/eyes closed & hand up in 'stop' gesture; Cruella in fur coat w/eyes closed; S/Jun 10/95 (1000-1500) 920

Penny crouching; Cruella looking away; stern Sgt. Tibs sitting upright; Horace wielding club; Jasper w/fireplace poker; S/Jun 10/95 (1200-1500) 1380

Cruella w/eyes closed wearing fur coat & holding cigarette holder; Rolly sitting w/eyes closed & nose scrunched; alert Sgt. Tibs sitting upright; Jasper gripping fireplace poker; Horace w/eyes closed wielding club; S/Jun 10/95 (1500-2000) 1380

4 cels: one each of Roger, Anita, Pongo and Perdita, S/Jun 10/95 (1000-1500) 2070

Surprised Anita, 9-1/2"; Roger smiling w/eyes closed, dancing & snapping fingers, 8-1/2"; Nanny (7-1/2") picking up Patch (2"); S/Jun 10/95 (1200-1500) 1035

4 cels: one ea. of Roger, Perdita, Pongo, & Penny w/eyes closed, S/Jun 10/95 (1200-1800) 1840

Pongo w/suspenders in mouth & Baduns on fire, 3-1/2 x 8-1/2", HL/Aug 6/95 (900-1200) 840

Profile of eager Pongo running right, 3-1/2 x 7", HL/Nov 19/95 (900-1200) 1495

Coal-dusted Pongo walking, 5 x 5", VF, HL/Apr 28/96 (600-900) 863

Cruella de Vil, wearing fur coat, smiling & waving cigarette, 8", S/Jun 19/96 (2000-3000) 1840

Angry Cruella de Vil, in fur coat & w/cigarette holder, walking right, 8-1/2", CE/Jun 20/96 (1500-2000) 2990

Roger (16") walks Pongo (2-1/2") on leash to left, CE/Jun 20/96 (700-900) 1150

Front view of frowning Cruella de Vil standing in fur coat & w/cigarette holder, 10", CE/Jun 20/96 (2000-3000) 2760

Smug Cruella in fur coat & with cigarette holder walks left, 7", CE/Jun 20/96 (1000-1500) 1725

Profile of Anita walking Perdita on leash to left, 5-1/2 x 6", VF, HL/Oct 6/96 (700-900) 978

Jasper loses his pants while Horace is attacked from rear, F, 5 x 7", HL/Oct 6/96 (500-700) 633

Cruella's automobile plunging down snowy embankment after driving thru wood fence, 8 x 10", VF+, HL/Oct 6/96 (700-1000) 805

Seated Roger smoking pipe, 8"; set-up of 3 tiny images of Roger in same pose as 1st, 3/4" each; Horace Badun holding satchel of puppies, 7"; signed by Frank Thomas & Ollie Johnston, S/Dec 14/96 (600-800) 460

Apprehensive Pongo walking to right, 5-1/2 x 7-1/2", HL/Feb 23/97 (1200-1500) 1380

Rolly sits looking up to left, "Mother, I'm hungry," 4-1/4 x 4-1/4", HL/Feb 23/97 (700-1000) 1150

Happy Lucky sits looking up to left, 6-1/4 x 5-1/2", HL/Feb 23/97 (700-1000) 2300

5 surprised pups sitting looking right in same pose, 4-1/4 x 10-1/4", HL/Feb 23/97 (1000-1500) 1725

Pongo (4") attacks Jasper (6-1/2") whose pants have fallen around his ankles, gold DL label, S/Jun 21/97 (700-900) 805

Roger dances with Anita, 10-1/2 x 7-1/8", 16-field cel, SR/Fall/97 (900-1200) 600

2 cels: rear view of irritated Lucky standing up & looking back, 3-3/4"; Rolly sits facing toward left, looking up with mouth open, 4-1/4"; SR/Fall/97 (1500-2000) 1230

3 concerned puppies face left, 3-1/2 x 5-1/4", VF+, HL/Nov 16/97 (500-700) 920

Happy coal-dusted Pongo & Perdita jump on Roger (all but left foot), 9 x 8", VF+, HL/Apr 25/98 (1000-1500) 1150

Large image of worried Perdita walking, looking right, 6 x 4", VF+, HL/Apr 25/98 (500-700) 920

3 curious pups in shadow colors walking/running left, 5-1/2 x 11-1/2", VF+, HL/Apr 25/98 (1000-1500) 1265

CELS – PARTIAL FIGURE (also see MODEL ART)

Diplomatic Anita; Roger plays trombone; 7-1/2 x 4" & 7 x 5-1/2"; VF+; HL/Apr 10/94 (500-700) 420

Pongo with leash in mouth, 5-1/2 x 9", signed by Ollie Johnston, F, HL/Apr 10/94 (900-1200) 1456

Cruella in profile w/dog lighter & cigarette holder, 9", S/Jun 17/94 (1500-2500) 2070

Sitting Pongo looks apprehensively over his left shoulder, 7-3/4 x 4", CE/Jun 18/94 (800-1200) 1495

Angry Cruella sitting up in bed, holding phone & cigarette holder, 10 x 7", SR/Fall/94

(1200-1800) 1480

Eager Pongo (all but right foot) running to right, ears back, tongue out, 4 x 5", VF, HL/Nov 13/94 (700-1000) 952

Jasper & Horace Badun (9" & 6"); Nanny (6") facing right shaking soot-filled feather duster, CE/Dec 16/94 (800-1200) 633

The Colonel (head & body) looking backward, 7", CE/Dec 16/94 (600-800) 345

Determined red-eyed Cruella clutches steering wheel (facing left), 7", S/Dec 17/94 (1800-2200) 2587

Cruella de Vil sitting in bed holding newspaper & cigarette holder, 12-1/2 x 7-1/2", 16-field, SR/Spring/95 (1200-1800) 1700

Portrait of pugnacious Patch sitting, 6-1/4 x 5-1/2", VF+, HL/Apr 23/95 (500-700) 1232

Color model cel of sitting Pongo looking apprehensively over shoulder, 7", CE/Jun 9/95 (1000-1500) 920

Scheming Cruella in bed with phone, 6-3/4", CE/Jun 9/95 (1500-2000) 2300

Close-up of scheming Cruella w/cigarette holder & hair in rollers, 5-3/4", CE/Jun 9/95 (1200-1500) 1725

Cruella pulls a Badun by the coat into her face, 5-1/2 x 9", as sold at DL, VF+, HL/Aug 6/95 (1500-2000) 1568

Portraits of sad Perdita & angry Pongo conversing, 5 x 8", as sold at DL, F, HL/Aug 6/95 (1500-2000) 1680

Near-full figure of curious Perdita sitting w/head tilted to her right, 7 x 5", HL/Nov 19/95 (700-900) 1495

Near-full figure of collie walking left, looking at camera, 9-1/4 x 7-1/4", gold Art Corner label, some paint chipping, SR/Spring/96 (200-400) 200

Scheming Cruella de Vil standing wearing fur coat, w/cigarette holder; 9 x 9-1/2", VF, HL/Apr 28/96 (1400-1800) 2530

Large waist-up portrait of Cruella in profile, smiling & holding up cigarette, 9", S/Jun 19/96 (2000-3000) 2070

Large waist-up portrait of Cruella in profile, wearing fur coat, smiling & holding up cigarette holder w/pinkie in the air, 9", S/Jun 19/96 (2000-3000) 2185

Waist-up portrait of anguished Cruella holding fountain pen, 7-1/2 x 7-1/2", F, HL/Oct 6/96 (1200-1600) 1380

Roger & Anita in a loving embrace, 8-1/2 x 4-1/2", VF+, HL/Oct 6/96 (500-700) 863

Cruella (facing left) throws her hands out to her sides in disbelief, 7", S/Dec 14/96 (2000-3000) 2875

Angry Cruella in fur coat & curlers talks on phone while leaning against pillow as stockings dangle from above, 7-1/4 x 7-1/2", VF, HL/May 3/97 (1500-2000) 1955

Near-full figure of wary Pongo walking left & looking back while carrying exhausted Rolly by collar, 6", 16-field cel, SR/Fall/97 (1200-1600) 1300

Near-full figures of sneering Jasper sitting looking right & sitting Horace looking up at object [plaster?] he's holding over his head, 8 x 5" & 8-1/2 x 7-1/2", VF+, HL/Nov 16/97 (400-600) 518

Portrait of Cruella nestled in fur coat with purse & cigarette holder, 7 x 5-1/2", VF+, HL/Nov 16/97 (1000-1500) 2070

Angry Nanny faces right & speaks as she cradles bundle in her arms, 5 x 4-1/4", F+, HL/Nov 16/97 (300-400) 230

DYE-TRANSFER PRINT
Dalmatian family watching TV, 12 x 8-1/2", SR/Spring/96 (300-600) 300

LAYOUT ART
2 layout drawings of Horace holding Electric Co. bag, 4-3/4" each; layout drawing of Jasper running for door, 7-1/2"; CLA/Jun 7/97 (700-900) 230

MODEL ART
Front view of roadside conference with Cruella in roadster & Baduns in lorry truck (full figure), 15 x 8", plus 5 color key & production model drawing photocopies, SR/Fall/95 (600-1200) 1320

Knees-up color model cel of angry Cruella de Vil leaning to right, mouth open, staring at tip of pen, 7-1/2 x 6-3/8", SR/Fall/96 (1200-1800) 1340

PETER PAN (1953)
Also see TELEVISION: ANTHOLOGY SERIES, THE

MICKEY MOUSE CLUB, PETER PAN PEANUT BUTTER COMMERCIALS, UNIDENTIFIED TV; UNIDENTIFIED/MISCELLANEOUS: COMBINATIONS OF MAJOR CHARACTERS
ANIMATION DRAWINGS (also see CEL SET-UPS)
Capt. Hook with hot water bottle on head, 9", S/Dec 16/93 (900-1200) 1035

17 finished "rough" colored pencil drawings, 4 x 2" to 10 x 7-1/2", F-VF, HL/Apr 10/94 (3000-5000) 4816

Full-figure drawing of Peter Pan lying in hammock holding panpipe, 4-1/2 x 4-1/2", CE/Jun 18/94 (500-700) 805

Extreme drawing: close-up frontal of determined Capt. Hook climbing [rigging] with sword, 8 x 11-1/2", VF, HL/Aug 21/94 (700-1000) 672

Capt. Hook with crazed expression & wielding sword, 6", S/Dec 17/94 (700-900) 747

20 finished "rough" drawings, 3-1/2 x 3-1/2" to 6-1/2 x 15-1/2", F-VF, HL/Apr 23/95 (3000-5000) 7560

Head-on view of angry Capt. Hook with sword, 11 x 9", VF, HL/Apr 23/95 (600-900) 840

Large-image "rough" drawing of Tinker Bell looking behind & down, VF, 12 x 10", HL/Apr 23/95 (600-800) 2464

3 full-figure drawings of Peter: flying, in repose, as Chief Little Flying Eagle; 3 x 4", 5-1/2 x 4", 7-1/2 x 9", VF+, HL/Apr 23/95 (800-1200) 1232

3 drawings of Crocodile, 5", CE/Jun 9/95 (600-800) 1265

Smiling Tinker Bell standing, 8 x 4", VF, HL/Aug 6/95 (7000-1000) 1680

Full-figure front-view drawing of demure Tinker Bell standing on tiptoes, 7-1/2", 16-field sheet, SR/Spring/96 (700-1000) 970

Front elevated-view drawing of angry Capt. Hook [climbing rigging] w/sword drawn, VF, 7 x 9", HL/Apr 28/96 (600-900) 920

Near-full figure rough drawing of surprised Tinker Bell reaching for scissors, F+, 11 x 10", HL/Apr 28/96 (600-800) 1725

22 "rough" finished drawings, 2-3/4 x 3" to 11 x 7", F+, HL/Apr 28/96 (3000-4000) 8050

Front-view drawing of angry Hook sitting holding water bottle on head, looking left, 9-1/8" 16-field sheet, SR/Fall/96 (600-1000) 680

Knees-up front-view drawing of serious Tinker Bell, 16-field sheet, SR/Fall/96 (700-1000) 750

Front-view drawing of angry Capt. Hook with sword in hand [climbing rigging], 6 x 9-1/2", VF, HL/Oct 6/96 (600-800) 690

Miserable Capt. Hook (with cold) sitting with hand & hook pulling on sides of hat brim, 9-1/2 x 6", VF, HL/Oct 6/96 (700-1000) 978

Large-image front-view rough drawing of wide-eyed Tinker Bell (knees up), signed by Marc Davis, 9-1/2 x 13", VF, HL/Oct 6/96 (900-1200) 978

Waist-up drawing of Capt. Hook looking down to left & pointing; large drawing of Peter turning to right; 2 photostat model sheets: Wendy & Lost Boys; photostat of preliminary artwork for lobby card; S/Dec 14/96 (500-700) 1035

22 detailed rough drawings, 5 x 2-1/2" to 8 x 7", HL/May 3/97 (3000-4000) 6325

Chest-up drawing of charming Capt. Hook, 6 x 9-1/4", HL/May 31/97 (400-600) 690

Full-figure drawing of smiling Tinker Bell standing looking right, 7" w/o wings, S/Jun 21/97 (1800-2200) 1725

Front-view extreme drawing of angry, hatless Capt. Hook holding sword [climbing rigging], 11 x 8-3/4", VF, HL/Nov 16/97 (600-800) 1150

Front-view drawing of hatless angry Capt. Hook holding sword [climbing rigging], 10-3/4 x 9", VF, HL/Apr 25/98 (600-800) 690

BACKGROUNDS
Gouache master background of ship's deck, 39 x 11-1/2", SR/Fall/94 (6000-10,000) 9,000

CEL SET-UPS
Waist-up image of Wendy, hand-prepared interior background, 7-1/2 x 9-1/2", CE/Dec 15/93 (1000-1500) 862

Near-full figure of scheming Captain Hook standing on ship's deck, printed line background, 10 x 13-1/4", CE/Dec 15/93 (2500-3500) 2300

Tinker Bell flying, printed background, 6-1/4",

S/Dec 16/93 (2000-2500) 2875

Full figure of smiling Peter sitting cross-legged on chair back, photographic copy of original background, 4-1/2", S/Dec 16/93 (1000-1500) 2875

5" Peter hovers in nursery; tussle in forest among Lost Boys, Darling Boys & Indians; both with photographic copy of original background, S/Dec 16/93 (1000-1500) 1380

Peter in profile gestures in nursery, photographic copy of original background, 5-1/2" (1/2 figure), S/Dec 16/93 (1000-1500) 920

8" Wendy from waist up; 4" Michael in p.j.'s; 7" Mrs. Darling leaving house; each with photographic copy of original background, S/Dec 16/93 (2000-3000) 1725

Full figure of Tinker Bell tiptoeing across mirror trailing pixie dust, watercolor production background, 7-1/2" w/wings, S/Dec 16/93 (10,000-12,000) 14,950

Full figure of Tinker Bell over complementary water-color painting plus 2 rough colored-pencil animation drawings, 7 x 2-1/2" cel image; 9 x 8", cel F-VF, HL/Apr 10/94 (2000-3000) 2464

John (torso) in top hat & glasses holding umbrella, printed background, 7", S/Jun 17/94 (500-700) 575

Tinker Bell (eyes closed) walks cockily away, printed background, 6", S/Jun 17/94 (1800-2200) 1380

Wendy (5") sings Michael (2") to sleep, publication background, S/Jun 17/94 (1600-2000) 1955

Michael dancing w/tomahawk & teddy bear, printed background, 4-1/2", S/Jun 17/94 (500-700) 747

Happy Peter (9") sits on rock with Tinker Bell (1-1/2") on his knee, watercolor production background, inscribed "To Jim, my best, Walt Disney" on mat, S/Jun 17/94 (7000-9000) 14,950

Crocodile at edge of beach looking up hungrily, printed background, 9", S/Jun 17/94 (1500-2500) 2875

Peter, Wendy, Michael & John fly, 2-1/2" & smaller, printed background, CE/Jun 18/94 (800-1000) 2990

Mermaid in sea by rock, key watercolor production background, 2-1/2 x 3-3/4", CE/Jun 18/94 (3000-4000) 3220

Tiger Lily dances on drum, complementary non-Studio background painting, 9-1/2 x 11-1/2", VF, HL/Aug 21/94 (600-900) 840

Tinker Bell (2-1/2 x 3/4") imprisoned in lantern, framed w/newly-created, non-Studio cel of wings over modern complementary background painting, 11 x 11", VF, HL/Aug 21/94 (1000-1500) 1064

Full figure of Tinker Bell standing, watercolor production background from The Black Cauldron, 7-1/2", CE/Dec 16/94 (1500-2000) 2185

Peter (5"), Wendy (7-1/2"), Michael & John (4-3/4" ea.) in Peter's hideout, watercolor production background, CE/Dec 16/94 (28,000-35,000) 27,600

Alarmed Tinker Bell trapped in lantern, 2-1/4", watercolor production background, S/Dec 17/94 (8,000-12,000) 11,500

Tinker Bell stands cockily, hand on hip, looking over right shoulder, 6", printed background of sewing materials, S/Dec 17/94 (1800-2200) 2300

Pan production set-up from Indian ceremony scene of Tiger Lily (5") & Peter (5-1/2") sitting cross-legged, watercolor production background of Lost Boys lair, S/Dec 17/94 (20,000-25,000) 24,150

Capt. Hook points finger on his way up stairs, 9-1/2 x 11", master background of ship with Never Land in distance (tempera on background sheet), stamped, VF, HL/Apr 23/95 (6000-8000) 7280

Full figure of happy Mr. Smee standing, 8 x 10, master background (tempera on background sheet) of ship's command deck w/Never Land in background, inscribed mat, authenticity certificate, VF, HL/Apr 23/95 (5000-7000) 5376

"Peter Pan: Skull Rock" limited-edition cel of Peter dueling w/Capt. Hook, 11-1/2 x 15-1/2", #35/500, color print background, VF+, HL/Apr 23/95 (1500-2000) 1232

Full figures of Wendy (7") talking to Mermaid (7"), preliminary background, mat inscribed "...Walt Disney", CE/Jun 9/95 (2500-3500) 2185

Mr. Darling (7") in formal dress (treasure map on shirt) lectures to John (4-1/2") & Michael (4-1/2"), printed background, S/Jun 10/95 (1200-1600)   1035

Half image of Hook (7-1/2") taunting angry Tinker Bell (3") standing tied-up on tree stump, circa 1955 peanut butter commercial, DL litho background of forest, Art Corner label, chipped & lifting paint, SR/Fall/95 (500-900)   500

Full figure of Tinker Bell imprisoned in lantern, 11 x 15", w/lantern overlay over original master background of Capt. Hook's cabin interior (tempera on background sheet), HL/Nov 19/95 (9000-12,000)   9775

Full figure of Peter pulling shocked Capt. Hook's hat brim to around his waist, 10 x 10" cel image, new complementary painted background, HL/Nov 19/95 (4000-5000)   4025

Full figures of Peter bouncing off tip of Capt. Hook's sword, 1990 limited edition, #90/500, 11-1/2 x 15-1/2", color print background, HL/Nov 19/95 (700-1000)   1495

Full figure of angry Captain Hook walking ship's deck w/sword drawn, 6", 16-field, color print display background, SR/Spring/96 (1900-2600)   2420

Knees-up of Capt. Hook standing on deck squinting thru spyglass, 8-5/8", master gouache background, SR/Spring/96 (4000-7000)   4000

Publicity cel: full-figure frontals of Peter, Wendy, John, & Michael standing in group in center of nursery, 7", color print display background, cel cracking, SR/Spring/96 (2000-4000)   1500

George & Mary Darling, Wendy & Nana watch from dormer window as smiling Peter Pan flies away, matching master background (tempera on background sheet), 11 x 15", VF+, HL/Apr 28/96 (10,000-12,000)   15,525

Portrait of scheming Capt. Hook on deck, complementary color print background, 7-1/2 x 6-1/2", F+, HL/Apr 28/96 (2000-3000)   2990

Near-full figure of puzzled Peter (8") sitting cross-legged w/Tinker Bell (1-1/2") standing on knee, watercolor production background of interior of Lost Boys' lair, S/Jun 19/96 (10,000-12,000)   13,800

Key set-up of Hook (5-1/2") playing harpsichord in cabin as Tinker Bell (1/2") sits atop bottle & Smee (4-1/2") listens appreciatively, matching watercolor production background, S/Jun 19/96 (10,000-12,000)   20,700

Capt. Hook (6-1/2") anxiously watches Tinker Bell (2-1/2") walk across map, watercolor production background with applied production overlay (map), S/Jun 19/96 (10,000-12,000)   16,100

Full figure of Peter Pan sitting in air whispering to left amid ship's rigging, watercolor production background, 4-1/2", CE/Jun 20/96 (8000-10,000)   9200

Full figures of Peter (9") sitting cross-legged scratching head, Tinker Bell (2") standing on knee, watercolor production background, Courvoisier label, mat signed "Walt Disney", CE/Jun 20/96 (12,000-15,000)   21,850

Knees-up side view of scheming Capt. Hook facing right, looking down, 6-1/4", color print display background, SR/Fall/96 (2000-3000)   1700

Full figure of Tinker Bell sitting on top of bottle cork laughing, 6-1/4", airbrushed wings, display set-up, HL/Fall/96 (1200-1800)   1980

Full figures of Smee (holding shaving tray) being held off ship's deck by back of shirt by pirate brandishing sword, 12 x 9", 16-field, color print background, SR/Fall/96 (1000-1600)   1210

Near-full figure of surprised brunette mermaid kneeling facing left, arms out, looking up, 3-1/4", color print background, SR/Fall/96 (300-600)   330

Full figure of flirtatious mermaid sitting on rock under waterfall, 8 x 10", master background from *Chicken Little* (tempera & watercolor on background sheet), VF+, HL/Oct 6/96 (1200-1600)   1610

Wendy holds sleepy war-painted Michael on her lap, 7-1/2 x 6-1/2" cel image, color print of complementary background, VF+, HL/Oct 6/96 (1200-1600)   1495

Full figure of smiling Mr. Smee taking stoic tied-up Tiger Lily for rowboat ride, 3-3/4 x 7" cel image, complementary printed background,

F+, HL/Oct 6/96 (900-1200)   920

Full figure of Peter Pan overhead in sitting position, 2-1/4 x 3" cel image, printed background of scene from Mermaid Lagoon, VF, HL/Oct 6/96 (700-1000)   863

Battered Capt. Hook w/arms & legs wrapped around crocodile's jaws & staring into crocodile's eyes, 9" long, Disney Art Props background of water & rocks, CE/Dec 12/96 (3000-4000)   4370

Full figures of Peter Pan (4") & Wendy (4") flying thru forest, watercolor production background, CE/Dec 12/96 (8000-10,000)   11,500

Full figures of Tiger Lily (5"), Chief (6-3/4") and Peter (5", in headdress) sitting cross-legged in front of tepee as Chief speaks, hand-prepared background, S/Dec 14/96 (2500-3500)   4600

Full figure of Tinker Bell flying to left thru plants & water drops, 5", hand-painted background, S/Dec 14/96 (1000-1500)   1150

Full figure of angry Tinker Bell sitting atop cork in bottle, 6", printed background, S/Dec 14/96 (1000-1500)   3162

Full-figure rear view of Tinker Bell standing cockily on leaf, head turned to right, one hand on hip, holding onto vertical leaf, 6", hand-prepared background, S/Dec 14/96 (1000-1500)   2587

Full-figure overhead view of Peter & Wendy flying over Never Land holding hands, approx. 5" each, printed background, S/Dec 14/96 (1500-2000)   1380

Full figure of Crocodile lying on his back in water looking up w/jaws open, 12", hand-prepared background of water & rocks, S/Dec 14/96 (1000-1500)   2587

Full figures of Peter (3-1/2"), Wendy (2"), John (1-1/2"), & Michael (1-1/4") flying over Tower Bridge, watercolor production background, "To...Walt Disney" on mat, S/Dec 14/96 (10,000-15,000)   29,900

Full figure of smiling blonde mermaid sits on rock holding hair in right hand, starfish in left, looking down; complementary painted background; 4-1/2 x 6-1/2", VF+, HL/Feb 23/97 (500-700)   920

Full figures of worried Peter standing on ship deck facing left, looking into his hat as happy Michael tugs on his jerkin from behind, 9", master gouache background, SR/Spring/97 (4600-5200)   4510

Hips-up of angry hatless Capt. Hook standing on ship deck facing & leaning left, left hand behind back, right hand in fist at face, 5-3/4", 16-field cel, color print background, SR/Spring/97 (1500-2000)   1460

Near-full figure of Capt. Hook kneeling on deck looking to left thru spyglass, complementary color print background, 7 x 6" cel image, HL/May 3/97 (1500-2000)   2070

Full figures of Peter in headdress dancing on drum as Tiger Lily stands watching, complementary background painting of Indian village, 7-1/2 x 9-1/2" overall, HL/May 3/97 (1800-2400)   2185

Humble Capt. Hook sits at harpsichord, 5", copy of matching line background of his quarters, S/Jun 21/97 (1200-1800)   1150

Peter (full figure, 5") sitting in Lost Boys' lair as weary Wendy (5-1/2') rests, watercolor production background, "With Best Wishes, Walt Disney" below, S/Jun 21/97 (10,000-15,000)   11,500

Full figure of pleased Tinker Bell standing & looking down, 6", watercolor production background of chest interior from "Mickey & Beanstalk" in *Fun & Fancy Free*, S/Jun 21/97 (2200-3000)   3450

2 limited-edition cels: Peter standing on tip of Hook's sword, #231/500; Tinker Bell, Peter, Wendy, John & Michael fly over London, #470/500; 11-1/4 x 15-1/2" & 10-3/4 x 15-1/2"; color prints of matching backgrounds; VF+, HL/Nov 16/97 (1500-2500)   2300

Full figure of smiling Tinker Bell facing left with matching wings & effects, right arm up in "come here" gesture, 8 x 3-3/4", complementary color print background of Never Land w/pirate ship in lagoon, VF, HL/Nov 16/97 (1200-1600)   3335

Full figure of excited Mr. Smee standing on ship's deck facing right, aiming pistol upward, 6", printed background, S/Dec 19/97 (700-900)   805

Full figures of John (4") & Indian Michael (3-1/4" w/o feather) dancing in forest clearing, printed

background, S/Dec 19/97 (600-800)   575

Happy John (4") leads parade of 6 Lost Boys (3" avg.) to right as Michael struggles to keep up, printed background of outdoors, S/Dec 19/97 (900-1200)   1380

Full figures of blonde, redhead & brunette mermaids sitting, looking up & waving, each approx. 3", Disney pastel-on-black construction paper background, S/Dec 19/97 (1000-1500)   1380

Full figure of haughty Tinker Bell (eyes closed, 6-1/2") suspended vertically in front of sewing materials amid pixie dust, printed background, S/Dec 19/97 (2000-2500)   2070

Knees-up front view of Capt. Hook smiling gleefully, 7" w/o plume, hand-prepared background of forest & fake stump w/top open, paint loss & cracks, S/Dec 19/97 (2000-3000)   4600

Full figure of Tiger Lily dancing enthusiastically, 4-1/2", printed background of Indian village, S/Dec 19/97 (700-900)   575

Full figure of careful Nana walking to left balancing tray of medicine on head, 6 x 5", printed background of indoors, S/Dec 19/97 (800-1200)   1035

Full figure of smiling Wendy walking, 6", printed background of nursery, S/Dec 19/97 (800-1200)   920

Full figure of Peter Pan suspended vertically in air, bent at waist & calling down; 4-3/4"; color print background of sea & sky, SR/Spring/98 (1800-2400)   2010

Knees-up of angry hatless Capt. Hook sword fighting on deck, 7 1/4", color print background, DL Art Corner stamp & gold label, ct, SR/Spring/98 (1800-2600)   1930

Front view of confused Mr. Smee on hands & knees on ship's deck, color print of film background, 3-1/2 x 4-1/2", VF+, HL/Apr 25/98 (600-800)   978

CELS – FULL FIGURE (also see MODEL ART)

Tiger Lily in dancing pose with stern Indian Chief, 9-1/2 x 10", CE/Dec 15/93 (1200-1600)   1380

Surprised Tinker Bell facing toward right, 7 x 3-1/2", CE/Dec 15/93 (2000-3000)   2300

Pirate ship looms, 10 x 9-1/2", CE/Dec 15/93 (1000-1200)   920

Tinker Bell looks in the distance, 15-3/4 x 12-1/2", CE/Dec 15/93 (800-1000)   1035

3 cels framed together: 6" Capt. Hook; 7" Peter in profile; 3" Tinker Bell creating fireworks with wand for TV show opening sequence; S/Dec 16/93 (4000-6000)   4025

John holding umbrella & waving w/Raccoon Twins, Foxy & Cubby, 6-1/2", S/Dec 16/93 (700-900)   920

One near-sequential & 3 sequential cels of Peter flying, 5", S/Dec 16/93 (2000-2500)   4600

3-cels: displeased Tinker Bell, her wings, flutter-effects cel, 8" w/wings, S/Dec 16/93 (1000-1500)   3163

7" (length) excited Nana; 8" Mr. Darling in profile in evening clothes; S/Dec 16/93 (700-900)   1150

Lost Boy Foxy on warpath, 5 x 5", VF+, HL/Feb 26-27/94 (200-400)   330

Frowning Smee stands holding package bomb, 4-1/2 x 4", DL label, restored, VF, HL/Apr 10/94 (700-1000)   784

Kneeling John Darling in feathered top hat & nightshirt, 5-1/2 x 4", VF+, HL/Apr 10/94 (500-700)   672

Jaunty Capt. Hook, 8-1/2 x 5-1/2", restored, VF, HL/Apr 10/94 (2400-2800)   2240

Matching cels of flying Tinker Bell looking back as she trails pixie dust, 3 x 7", VF+, HL/Apr 10/94 (1500-2000)   2912

Full-figure portrait of Mr. Smee shaking out sheet, 6-1/2 x 6", F+, HL/Apr 10/94 (700-1000)   784

Flying Peter (back to camera) carries Wendy, 2-1/2 x 3", VF+, HL/Apr 10/94 (600-900)   448

Smiling Peter Pan running left, 3 x 5", restored, F, HL/Apr 10/94 (900-1200)   1232

Startled mermaid leaning against rock sees Wendy, 7", S/Jun 17/94 (500-800)   805

Cross-legged Michael w/Indian paint on face and stomach; John doing Indian dance w/paint on cheeks; both 5", S/Jun 17/94 (600-800)   1092

Tinker Bell, 7-1/2", CE/Jun 18/94 (1200-1500)   2530

Wendy standing (4-1/2") & Michael kneeling (2") in night clothes, CE/Jun 18/94 (800-1200)   748

4 Lost Boys stand together, 7" & smaller, CE/Jun 18/94 (700-900)   805

Peter Pan stands facing left & holding hat like bag,

9", CE/Jun 18/94 (1500-2000) 2185

Tinker Bell stands rubbing left shoulder, 8-1/2 x 6-1/2", CE/Jun 18/94 (1500-2000) 2530

Mermaid sitting on rock enjoys waterfall, 7-1/4 x 4-1/2" (all but tip of fin), CE/Jun 18/94 (600-800) 1035

Smee stands holding pistol, glasses akilter, 5-1/2 x 5", F+, HL/Aug 21/94 (800-1000) 896

Nana being dragged from nursery with Michael hanging onto tail, 6-1/2 x 9", VF+, HL/Aug 21/94 (1000-1500) 1456

Wendy flying, 3-1/2 x 5-1/2", F, HL/Aug 21/94 (800-1200) 1008

Peter Pan flying, 3-1/2 x 6", VF, HL/Aug 21/94 (1500-2000) 1792

Concerned Peter crouching, shadow colors, 7 x 5", VF+, HL/Aug 21/94 (1200-1800) 1904

John in top hat points to ground with umbrella, 6-1/2 x 3", F+, HL/Aug 21/94 (300-500) 252

Kneeling Capt. Hook squints thru telescope to left, 7 x 6", F+, HL/Aug 21/94 (2000-3000) 2016

Innocent Michael stands facing toward left, warpaint on face, 5-1/2", 16-field, SR/Fall/94 (500-700) 410

Nana (6-1/4", all but edge of tail) walks left with medicine tray balanced on head, 16-field, SR/Fall/94 (600-1000) 710

Smiling blond mermaid sits facing left, 7-1/4", 16-field, some dents & edge wear, SR/Fall/94 (500-800) 610

Wooden-sword-wielding Michael stands leaning almost horizontally to left, 3", SR/Fall/94 (400-700) 420

Surprised Mr. Smee (8-1/2", holding tray of shaving supplies) being picked up by back of shirt, some ink wear, SR/Fall/94 (400-700) 600

Peter flies horizontally & looks down, 3 x 6-1/2", HL/Nov 13/94 (1500-2000) 2128

Angry Capt. Hook, 6-1/2 x 5-1/2", HL/Nov 13/94 (2000-2500) 3136

Angry Capt. Hook w/hat skewered on sword, 6-1/2", CE/Dec 16/94 (1000-1500) 2990

Peter sits cross-legged wearing Indian headdress facing right, 5-1/2", CE/Dec 16/94 (2500-3500) 2300

Lost Boy Foxy, 7", CE/Dec 16/94 (400-600) 288

Jumping Peter, 5", CE/Dec 16/94 (700-900) 1840

3 cels: one each of Michael (4-1/2") & John (5") sword fighting; Tinker Bell (2") flying away leaving trail of pixie dust; S/Dec 17/94 (1200-1800) 920

Irritated Mr. Darling in his 'treasure map' bib, 7-1/2"; John in top hat, 7"; Michael looking concerned, 6"; S/Dec 17/94 (1200-1800) 1035

Peter as Little Flying Eagle (5-1/2") dances with Tiger Lily (5"), S/Dec 17/94 (1500-2000) 2587

3 cels: one ea. of Mr. & Mrs. Darling preparing to go out for evening, 8" & 9"; Wendy clasping hands, 6"; S/Dec 17/94 (1200-1500) 1380

Tiger Lily (6", eyes closed) & Chief (7-1/4") sitting cross-legged together, 16-field, ct, SR/Spring/95 (800-1400) 1130

Tiger Lily jumping up with arms out, 6-1/2", photocopy-on-cel background of original layout, SR/Spring/95 (500-900) 500

Angry Nana sits facing left, 6-1/8", 12-field, ct, SR/Spring/95 (500-1000) 680

"Hello, Peter Pan. I'm Michael." Wendy, Peter, & Michael standing together, 9 x 8-1/2", VF, HL/Apr 23/95 (3000-5000) 4256

Peter leads Wendy thru air, 8 x 9", VF+, HL/Apr 23/95 (2500-3500) 4424

Serious Peter, 5 x 4-1/2"; Lost Boys Skunk & Rabbit, 4 x 5", F, HL/Apr 23/95 (1000-1500) 1456

Happy Tiger Lily facing right, from dance number, 4-3/4 x 1-3/4", VF, HL/Apr 23/95 (500-700) 532

Peter, Wendy, Michael & John flying, 5 x 10-1/2", VF+, HL/Apr 23/95 (3500-5000) 5376

Peter (5") pulls Wendy (6") up by the hand, CE/Jun 9/95 (2000-2500) 2300

John dancing, 5", CE/Jun 9/95 (600-800) 460

Flying Tinker Bell trails pixie dust & spreads dust with wand, 3", CE/Jun 9/95 (700-900) 460

Michael waving, feather in hair, with teddy and tomahawk, 5-1/2", CE/Jun 9/95 (600-800) 920

Smiling Raccoon Twin Lost Boys standing, 5-1/4", CE/Jun 9/95 (400-600) 460

Smiling Mr. Smee walking & holding shaving tray overhead, 6", CE/Jun 9/95 (500-700) 437

Large back view of Tiger Lily dancing, 8",

CE/Jun 9/95 (500-700) 460

Curious Michael drags teddy & stands hunched close to ground, 4", CE/Jun 9/95 (500-700) 978

Publicity cel: large figure of alert Tinker Bell, 8", CE/Jun 9/95 (800-1200) 2185

Striding Tinker Bell, circa 1950s, 4", DL label, CE/Jun 9/95 (500-700) 575

3 cels: one each of Mr. Darling (8") & Mrs. Darling (5"), both in coats & formal attire with eyes closed; wide-eyed Wendy (6") with clasped hands, S/Jun 10/95 (700-900) 690

Michael holding tomahawk & dancing, 3"; Lost Boys acting up, avg. 2-1/2"; S/Jun 10/95 (700-900) 690

Wendy, 7"; Mr. Darling, 8", needs restoration; S/Jun 10/95 (700-900) 690

Michael looking up, 5"; John makes a point, 5"; Mr. Darling lectures while wearing shirt with treasure map, 7"; S/Jun 10/95 (800-1200) 805

Mermaid sits underneath waterfall, 9-1/2 x 9", VF, HL/Aug 6/95 (900-1200) 1120

Sad Nana sits facing right, looking back over shoulder, evening colors, 5-1/2 x 5-1/2", VF+, HL/Aug 6/95 (900-1200) 1008

Determined Tinker Bell facing left, pointing with both hands, with non-matching cel of wings, 8 x 4-1/2", VF, HL/Aug 6/95 (1000-1500) 2912

Front view of Wendy sitting, hands in lap, looking right, 4-1/4", SR/Fall/95 (400-800) 730

Surprised Michael as war-dancing Indian, holding tomahawk, looking left, 3-1/2", 16-field, SR/Fall/95 (500-700) 440

Dancing Tiger Lily, 5-1/4", 16-field, SR/Fall/95 (400-700) 490

Back views of Mr. & Mrs. Darling walking up [stairs] with eager Nana facing them at top, Mr. Darling holding Nala's leash, entire image 5-5/8", SR/Fall/95 (600-1000) 600

Profile of Peter bending over at waist & looking down, 3 x 4", HL/Nov 19/95 (1000-1500) 1380

Wendy, Michael & John try out "wings" as Peter watches, 6 x 10", HL/Nov 19/95 (3500-5000) 5405

Surprised Peter Pan, 7-1/2 x 5", HL/Nov 19/95 1840

Front view of scheming Crocodile looking right & up, 7 x 4-5/8", 16-field, SR/Spring/96 (800-1400) 1300

Pouting Tinker Bell sits facing left, 6-1/8", signed by Marc Davis, SR/Spring/96 (2300-2900) 2530

Michael stands facing toward right, leaning forward with hands to face, 3-3/8", 16-field, SR/Spring/96 (400-800) 520

Peter standing w/knife drawn, looking up, 6 x 3-1/2", VF, HL/Apr 28/96 (1200-1500) 1955

Peter & Wendy fly hand-in-hand, 6 x 9", VF, HL/Apr 28/96 (3000-3500) 3680

Surprised Mr. Smee standing & looking right, 6 x 3-1/2", F+, HL/Apr 28/96 (500-700) 690

Front view of stern Capt. Hook walking between two rows of smiling pirates, 6-1/2 x 10-1/2", VF, HL/Apr 28/96 (3500-4500) 3220

Scheming Capt. Hook leans left & twirls mustache, 6-1/4", CE/Jun 20/96 (1000-1500) 2300

Smiling Michael, John & Wendy stand with eager Peter, 3", CE/Jun 20/96 (1500-2000) 3450

Shocked Peter with left arm out horizontally, 7-1/2", CE/Jun 20/96 (1500-2000) 1725

2 full-figure cels: smiling Mary Darling standing facing left, looking back, 5-1/4"; front view of angry George standing wearing treasure-map shirt, 6-5/8"; 16-field cels, SR/Fall/96 (600-1000) 680

Front view of cautious Michael standing looking left, holding wooden sword (all but tip of sword), 5-3/8", some wear, SR/Fall/96 (500-900) 610

Smiling Tiger Lily bows to left with eyes closed, 6-1/2 x 4", VF, HL/Oct 6/96 (600-900) 403

Lost Boys fight in pile-up, 7-1/2 x 8", F+, HL/Oct 6/96 (700-1000) 1035

John (full figure, back turned) & Michael Darling face off with wooden swords, 7 x 5-1/2", VF+, HL/Oct 6/96 (700-900) 748

Smiling Peter pulls Wendy (near-full figure) up by right wrist, 9-1/4 x 6", VF, HL/Oct 6/96 (2000-2500) 2760

Stern Indian Chief (8-3/4") stands over & points at smiling Tiger Lily (in sitting position, 7"), CE/Dec 12/96 (1000-1500) 805

Nana (2") with Christmas tree (7-1/2"), CE/Dec 12/96 (700-900) 483

3 full-figure images of Tiger Lily dancing, average 4-1/2", S/Dec 14/96 (800-1200) 1150

Promotional cel: Tiger Lily, Chief, & Peter Pan sit cross-legged watching Wendy, John & Michael dance Indian-style around a Christmas tree, sight 9-1/2 x 12", signed "Walt Disney" in unknown hand, S/Dec 14/96 (2000-3000) 2875

Peter in Hook's garb yelling orders, 7 x 4-1/2", VF, HL/Feb 23/97 (1500-2000) 2185

Nana being pulled along on her back as Michael (near-full figure) clings to her tail, 7 x 10", F+, HL/Feb 23/97 (1000-1500) 1150

Friendly mermaid sitting & waving, VF+, 6-1/2 x 4", HL/Feb 23/97 (300-500) 546

Nana stands facing left with medicine tray on her head, 8-7/8", 16-field cel, SR/Spring/97 (600-1000) 810

2 cels: waist-up of angry squaw (papoose on back, 7-1/4") facing right gesturing; full figure of Indian Chief (7-5/8") sitting with arms folded across chest; 16-field cels, ct, SR/Spring/97 (600-1000) 610

Angry Capt. Hook (5-1/2") standing with sword drawn watching Peter (5") standing above him, feet crossed at ankles, left hand on hip, right hand out, CLA/Jun 7/97 (2500-3500) 2990

Tinker Bell turns away indignantly on her toes, 6-1/2", needs restoration, S/Jun 21/97 (800-1200) 1035

Five Lost Boys fighting, 9-1/4 x 10", VF+, HL/Nov 16/97 (600-900) 748

Mr. Smee (carrying tray) being held off ground by back of shirt by sword-wielding pirate, 8-3/4 x 12-1/4", VF+, HL/Nov 16/97 (600-900) 633

Grim Peter Pan stands with knife drawn, looking up, 6 x 3-1/2", VF, HL/Nov 16/97 (2000-3500) 2070

Indian in top hat carries open umbrella & Indian pulls teddy bear on rope, walking to right, 7-1/2 x 11-1/2", VF+, HL/Nov 16/97 (300-500) 1150

Full-figure promotional cel of smiling Peter standing facing left w/thumb cocked toward chest, 8", S/Dec 19/97 (800-1200) 1495

Smiling Tinker Bell (with matching cel of wings) stands with arms out, 6 x 3", VF, HL/Apr 25/98 (1800-2200) 4600

Capt. Hook's crew face each other in 2 parallel lines, 5-1/2 x 11", VF+, HL/Apr 25/98 (500-700) 633

Child's block on edge, 4-1/2 x 6", VF+, HL/Apr 25/98 (200-300) 288

Small front view of grinning Michael standing in sleeper, 1-1/2 x 1", VF, HL/Apr 25/98 (200-300) 403

Mr. Smee stands with hands behind, back, looking left, 5 3/4", ct, SR/Spring/98 (400-700) 810

Mr. Darling stands half-dressed facing right, left arm straight up, wearing shirt with treasure map, 7 3/4", ct, SR/Spring/98 (400-700) 400

Mermaid dives to right, 7-3/4 x 3-3/8", 12-field cel, light ink wear, SR/Spring/98 (400-700) 630

John stands in top hat & nightclothes holding furled umbrella, 5 7/8", 16-field cel, SR/Spring/98 (400-700) 400

Incandescent, smiling Tinker Bell flies vertically trailing pixie dust, 6-1/2", three cel levels, drybrushed wings, SR/Spring/98 (2500-3000) 4330

Front view of wide-eyed Michael standing in pajamas holding teddy bear, 4-5/8", SR/Spring/98 (400-700) 400

CELS – PARTIAL FIGURE

Large image of Michael with tomahawk & teddy bear, 6", S/Dec 16/93 (600-800) 920

Smiling Capt. Hook waves hook, 7" (knees up), S/Dec 16/93 (2000-3000) 2300

Peter in headdress raises arms above brown wall, gold DL label, 4", S/Dec 16/93 (2000-3000) 1150

6" Wendy singing to 5" Michael (both waist-up); 7" Wendy hailing Peter, framed together, S/Dec 16/93 (2000-2500) 1725

Father Darling in evening attire checks watch, 8-1/2 x 7", VF, Feb 26-27/94 (500-700) 880

Menacing Capt. Hook looks over left shoulder, 9-3/4 x 5", CE/Jun 18/94 (1500-2000) 2070

Delightedly surprised Capt. Hook, 9 x 4", CE/Jun 18/94 (1500-2000) 1840

Capt. Hook seated at table with map & weapons, 5-1/2 x 9-1/2", VF, HL/Aug 21/94

(2500-3000) 4928

Rapt Wendy standing, 8-1/2 x 2-1/2", VF,
HL/Aug 21/94 (800-1000) 672

Stern Indian Chief with arm raised in greeting,
9 x 9", VF, HL/Aug 21/94 (700-1000) 672

Hips-up of skeptical John facing right [examining
pixie dust], 5-3/4", SR/Fall/94 (400-700) 410

Waist-up of Mr. Smee facing left & writing with quill
pen, 6-1/4", 16-field, SR/Fall/94 (400-700) 420

Knees-up of Wendy facing right, bend forward at waist,
hand cupped to open mouth, 4-1/2", 12-field,
SR/Fall/94 (600-1000) 680

Mrs. Darling standing, right arm out, 8-1/4", 16-field,
SR/Fall/94 (300-700) 330

Torso-up of angry Mr. Darling facing left, 8-1/2", 16-
field, SR/Fall/94 (400-700) 440

Weapons raised, 8 pirates charge from right, 13 x 6",
16-field, SR/Fall/94 (700-1200) 720

Near-full figure of Wendy standing, 6-1/2 x
2-1/2", HL/Nov 13/94 (600-900) 728

Knees-up image of Surprised Peter standing wearing
Indian headdress, 7", CE/Dec 16/94
(1200-1500) 1955

Close-up of Capt. Hook, 7", CE/Dec 16/94
(800-1200) 2530

Mr. Smee thinking, 6", CE/Dec 16/94 (500-700) 863

2 cels of Croc: rubbing stomach & licking lips;
close-up with mouth open & eyes closed;
each 8", S/Dec 17/94 (1000-1500) 1725

Knees-up of hatless Capt. Hook standing facing right,
left arm above head, 10-1/4", gold Art Corner
label, ct, SR/Spring/95 (900-1500) 2030

Near-full figure of worried Mr. Smee pointing,
4-1/2 x 3", VF, HL/Apr 23/95 (900-1200) 784

Hopeful Wendy; surprised Mrs. Darling, 6 x 3" &
8 x 5", F-VF, HL/Apr 23/95 (1200-1600) 1232

Hungry Crocodile rising from water with effects
cels of water & drool, 8 x 8", VF,
HL/Apr 23/95 (1000-1500) 3808

Grinning Capt. Hook holding present, 8-1/2",
CE/Jun 9/95 (1200-1500) 1955

Knees-up image of determined Capt. Hook standing
looking right, 7", CE/Jun 9/95 (1000-1500) 1955

Near-full figure of wary Peter lying on back, looking
up, 8-1/2", S/Jun 10/95 (1000-1500) 1380

Large portrait of Nana looking up, 6-1/2"; Mr.
Darling holding rope, 8", needs restoration;
S/Jun 10/95 (600-800) 1035

Knees-up image of standing Capt. Hook lecturing,
9 x 7", VF, HL/Aug 6/95 (1800-2400) 2352

Smiling Peter Pan wearing Indian headdress, F,
8-1/2 x 6", HL/Aug 6/95 (1200-1800) 1792

Capt. Hook peers thru spyglass, as sold at DL,
5-1/2 x 6", F, HL/Aug 6/95 (1500-2000) 2016

Large waist-up image of George Darling in partial
formal dress, head turned left with eyes
closed, 8 x 7", F, HL/Aug 6/95 (300-500) 179

Waist-up of pained Captain Hook sitting with water
bottle on head & eyes closed, 5-1/4", 16-field,
some ink wear, SR/Fall/95 (500-900) 680

Thighs-up of surprised Mr. Smee standing facing left,
left arm up, 7-1/2", 12-field, SR/Fall/95
(400-700) 540

Profile portrait of Wendy gesturing, 6-1/2 x 4",
HL/Nov 19/95 (600-900) 1380

Portrait of Capt. Hook wearing gold hook, 8 x
5-1/2", HL/Nov 19/95 (2400-2800) 2530

Profile portrait of angry Capt. Hook in shadow
colors, 9 x 8", HL/Nov 19/95 (2000-3000) 1972

Near-full figure of Mr. Smee walking to right with
arms partially extended, 6-1/4 x 4-1/2",
HL/Mar 16-17/96 (600-900) 690

Thigh-up of diligent Mr. Smee standing facing right,
mixing shaving lather, 5-1/2", 12-field,
SR/Spring/96 (500-900) 1020

Near-full-figure front view of sitting Peter Pan
gesturing, 4-1/2", 16-field, SR/Spring/96
(900-1500) 1210

Torso-up front view of Cubby with mouth open, 7",
SR/Spring/96 (400-700) 440

Hips-up image of Capt. Hook studying gold hook,
6-1/2 x 4-1/2", VF, HL/Apr 28/96
(2400-2800) 2070

Near-full figure extreme pose of angry Capt.
Hook w/hook raised, 10-1/2 x 8", VF,
HL/Apr 28/96 (2000-3000) 2300

Angry Mr. Starkey grabs Mr. Smee (carrying tray
of shaving supplies) by the shirt and pulls
him nose-to-nose, 7-1/2 x 6", F+,

HL/Apr 28/96 (700-1000) 748

Near-full figure of Peter Pan standing in
commanding pose, 7-1/2 x 4-1/2",
F+, HL/Apr 28/96 (700-1000) 978

Near-full figure of Peter beating chest & crowing,
DL label, 6", S/Jun 19/96 (1000-1500) 1725

Angry Capt. Hook holding double cigar holder
& looking back at camera over right arm,
6", CE/Jun 20/96 (800-1200) 1380

Near-full figure of smiling Captain Hook holding
roped gift, 8-1/2", SR/Fall/96
(1900-2400) 2850

Profile of smiling Wendy facing left with right
arm out, palm up, 6 x 4-1/4", VF+,
HL/Oct 6/96 (700-900) 1035

Portrait of Capt. Hook admiring ruby ring set
on gold hook, 4-3/4 x 5-1/2", VF,
HL/Oct 6/96 (1800-2400) 1495

Waist-up portrait of Peter looking up & to right,
7", CE/Dec 12/96 (1500-2000) 1610

Waist-up of smiling John Darling in top hat, arms
spread, umbrella in right hand, sold at DL,
6 x 8", VF, HL/Feb 23/97 (300-400) 460

Knees-up front view of angry Capt. Hook standing,
right fist clinched, 6-1/4 x 5-1/2", F+,
HL/Feb 23/97 (2000-2500) 3220

Hips-up portrait of Capt. Hook (with gold hook)
in thinking pose, 6-1/4 x 3-3/4", VF,
HL/Feb 23/97 (2000-2500) 2415

Near-full figure of Peter brandishing sword in
fencing pose, 8-1/2 x 11", HL/May 3/97
(2000-2500) 2185

Capt. Hook struggling to get out of Crocodile's
mouth, 7", CLA/Jun 7/97 (3000-4000) 3680

Imposing hips-up view of stern war-painted Chief with
right arm raised in greeting, 9-1/4", dent on
Chief's face & 1/2" tear at bottom of headdress,
SR/Fall/97 (300-500) 460

Hips-up view of stern George Darling wearing
shirt with treasure map, 7-3/4 x 6-3/4"
VF, HL/Nov 16/97 (600-900) 546

Large image of anxious Peter rubbing bar of
soap on left shoe sole, 10-1/4 x 6-1/2",
VF+, HL/Nov 16/97 (1400-1800) 2530

Large image of Indian Chief speaking with arms
spread at head level, 9-1/4 x 10-1/2", VF,
HL/Nov 16/97 (600-900) 863

Knees-up image of happy Capt. Hook, 8-1/4
x 8", VF+, HL/Nov 16/97 (1200-1600) 2300

Waist-up large image of attentive Wendy looking
left, 8-1/2 x 5-1/2", VF, HL/Nov 16/97
(700-900) 1035

Waist-up large image of John speaking, 9-1/2
x 8", VF+, HL/Nov 16/97 (500-700) 552

Near-full figure of surprised Mrs. Darling facing right,
hopeful Wendy facing left; 8-1/2 x 5" & 5-1/2
x 3"; VG-F, HL/Nov 16/97 (700-1000) 748

Nana (6-3/4", all but tip of tail) walks to left balancing
tray on top of her head, 16-field cel,
SR/Spring/98 700-1100) 870

Close-up of pouting Tinker Bell brushing her arm, 6",
DL Art Corner stamp & gold label, restored,
SR/Spring/98 (2000-3000) 2040

Half vertical image of smug Crocodile in water, eyes
closed, 6-1/2", SR/Spring/98 (700-1200) 1040

Arms-&-shoulders-up front view of laughing Capt.
Hook holding gift package by hook, 5-1/4
x 3-3/4", VF, HL/Apr 25/98 (1000-1500) 1610

CONCEPT AND INSPIRATIONAL ART

Signed concept painting by David Hall of Wendy
offering Peter candy, 6-5/8 x 5"; watercolor,
pastel & pencil; SR/Spring/95 (600-1000) 1020

Story concept painting of Tinker Bell escaping pirate
ship, gouache & pastel, 7 x 5-3/8"; tipped onto
8-1/4 x 8-3/4" sheet, dialogue "4 Bells & all is
well!" taped beneath painting, some wear,
SR/Spring/96 (900-1400) 1010

Concept painting by Mary Blair of Lost Boys
being led as captives to Indian village on
cliff, tempera on board, 8-1/2 x 11",
VF+, HL/Apr 28/96 (1500-2000) 3680

Signed inspirational painting by David Hall of Peter
Pan & Wendy watching Peter's reclaimed shadow,
watercolor on animation board, 5-1/2 x 6-1/2"
including signature, VF, HL/Feb 23/97 (2000-
2500) 3910

Signed rendering by David Hall of near life-size
luminescent Tinker Bell standing on a
desktop, pencil & watercolor on animation

board, 6-1/2 x 8" including signature, VF,
HL/Feb 23/97 (1500-2000) 3680

Sheet of early character studies of Capt. Hook
(w/unrelated sketches), mid-1940s, conté
crayon on animation sheet, 11 x 14",
HL/May 31/97 (100-150) 69

9 rough studies of John [misidentified as Michael], 8" &
similar, graphite on trimmed paper applied to
board, CE/Dec 18/97 (600-800) 253

Inspirational painting by David Hall of Crocodile in
jungle with footprints in sand, shedding tears &
inhaling smoke from cast-off cigars; ink & watercolor on animation-punched illustration board;
signed; 8 x 10-3/4"; VF; HL/Apr 25/98
(1200-1600) 5750

DYE-TRANSFER PRINTS

Pan & Hook duel on deck as Wendy & Smee watch,
SR/Fall/94 (300-600) 330

Pirate ship with Peter's silhouette sails across moon
amid pixie dust as children wave from dormer,
11-1/2 x 8-1/4" SR/Spring/95 (300-600) 300

Full figure of smiling Tinker Bell standing on leaf
facing left, right hand out amid pixie dust
in "come here" motion, 11-1/4 x 9",
SR/Spring/95 (300-600) 350

MODEL ART (also see ANIMATION DRAWINGS)

Model sheet of Peter, 5" & smaller, trimmed paper,
CE/Dec 16/94 (600-800) 978

Partially colored model drawing of Capt. Hook,
7 x 5", VF, HL/Aug 6/95 (300-500) 1232

Unpainted animator's maquette of Michael Darling
standing & holding teddy bear, 6" high,
S/Jun 19/96 (1500-2000) 1725

Full-figure single-level color model cel of demure Tinker
Bell standing facing left & looking up, 7-1/4 x 3-
3/4", VF, HL/Oct 6/96 (1000-1500) 2990

5 original mounted drawings of Princess Tiger Lily
(pencil & conté crayon on board) likely as they
were photographed during production as a
model sheet, 11 x 19", VG, HL/Oct 6/96
(700-1000) 546

2 pages of character drawings of Lost Boy Cubby
(bonking Twins' heads together in one), 6 x
9-1/2" & 9 x 11", VF, HL/Oct 6/96
(300-500) 230

2 matching color model drawings for levels of
animation in scene showing George Darling
& treasure map the boys drew on front of
shirt, 8 x 7-1/2", 4-1/2 x 3", HL/May 31/97
(100-200) 104

Color model drawing of angry Capt. Hook
wrapped in blanket & looking down while
removing teapot from head, 8-1/2 x 9",
with notes, HL/May 31/97 (200-250) 748

Partial-figure color model drawing of sad Wendy,
5 x 3-1/2", HL/May 31/97 (150-200) 316

Full-figure color model cel of sad Nana sitting
facing left with eyes closed, 7 x 7",
HL/May 31/97 (300-400) 345

5 drawings of Tiger Lily mounted to a board [model
sheet?], pencil & conté crayon on board, 11
x 19", VG, HL/Nov 16/97 (700-1000) 403

STORY ART

Drawing of Tinker Bell flying from window of
pirate ship, 5-1/2 x 7", conté crayon on
story sheet, HL/Nov 13/94 (300-400) 728

Story painting of perplexed John sitting & staring
at monkey in Never Land, 8-1/2 x 10-1/2",
ink & watercolor on heavyweight animation
sheet, signed by David Hall, HL/Nov 13/94
(1000-1500) 1904

Early story drawing of Capt. Hook & Wendy
with caption, 7 x 7", colored pastel on
story sheet, HL/Aug 6/95 (300-400) 336

2 storyboard drawings of Nana tied up with Lost Boys
& a target for flaming arrows, 8-13/16 x 5-
13/16", 12-field sheets, some wear & discoloration, SR/Fall/96 (400-800) 540

Story drawing of angry Capt. Hook at piano looking
right w/caption "Lets try it again boys –",
colored conté crayon on story sheet, 5-1/2 x 7",
w/photocopy of storyboard photograph with
this drawing in sequence, HL/May 31/97
(200-300) 374

Early story drawing of 3 scary pirates greeting
John & Lost Boys with caption "With the
sordid details –", colored conté crayon on
story sheet, 5-1/2 x 7", with photocopy of
storyboard photograph with this drawing in

sequence, HL/May 31/97 (100-200)   345

Story drawing of Mr. Smee with bongo drum, pastel & conté crayon on story sheet, 5-1/2 x 7", F, + photocopy of storyboard showing it in place, HL/Apr 25/98 (200-300)   259

PETE'S DRAGON (1977)

CELS – FULL FIGURE

Shocked Elliott, 7-1/2 x 11", HL/Apr 23/95 (300-500)   616

Contented Elliott facing right with tail raised [warming backside], 5 x 8-1/2", HL/Apr 28/96 (200-300)   431

CELS – PARTIAL FIGURE

Near-full pose of Elliott, 7 x 12", Disney seal & WDP label, VF+, HL/Feb 26-27/94 (300-500)   413

Large-image portrait of yellow-brown Elliott, 10-1/2 x 14", Disney seal, VF+, HL/Apr 10/94 (400-500)   532

Portrait of smiling Elliott, 9 x 6", seal & label, HL/Nov 13/94 (300-400)   308

Portrait of sleepy Elliott, 10 x 9-1/2", seal & label, HL/Nov 13/94 (300-500)   392

Chest-up large-image front view of ferocious, menacing Elliot, 9-1/4", 16-field cel, Disney Art Program seal, SR/Fall/96 (300-600)   330

Portrait of perplexed Elliott looking straight down, 9 x 8-1/2", HL/Oct 6/96 (300-400)   403

Portrait of Elliott w/tongue out, 9-1/2 x 8-1/2", VF+, HL/Nov 16/97 (300-400)   403

Stomach-up front-view large image of Elliott with arms up, seal & certificate, 10-1/2 x 7", VF+, HL/Apr 25/98 (300-400)   403

DYE-TRANSFER PRINTS

Full figure of Elliot standing under tree facing right, smiling at camera, 13 x 10", SR/Fall/95 (100-300)   130

PINOCCHIO (1940)

Also see SHORTS & FEATURETTES: FIGARO AND CLEO, FIGARO AND FRANKIE; TELEVISION: ANTHOLOGY SERIES, THE MICKEY MOUSE CLUB, UNIDENTIFIED TV

ANIMATION DRAWINGS

Full drawing of Geppetto holding wet Pinocchio, 9 x 7", CE/Dec 15/93 (600-800)   1495

Full figure of Pinocchio standing, 6-1/2" square, CE/Dec 15/93 (700-900)   632

5 drawings of Figaro in various poses, each with WDP stamp, S/Dec 16/93 (1000-1500)   1495

4 drawings of Stromboli: leaning over (3); holding Pinocchio by head; full margins, 6" avg., S/Dec 16/93 (800-1200)   690

8 small drawings of Figaro, WDP stamp on each, 4 to a mat, S/Dec 16/93 (400-600)   920

15 rough drawings of Jiminy hopping, dancing & singing, 4", S/Dec 16/93 (1200-1800)   1035

Pinocchio sick from smoking, 7 x 8", studio stamps & notes, VF, HL/Feb 26-27/94 (600-900)   1430

Stromboli introduces show, 7 x 6", studio stamp & notes, VF, HL/Feb 26-27/94 (300-400)   468

2 drawings: smug Lampwick rubbing cigar on pool cue tip & full figure of worn Jiminy Cricket, 5 x 5-1/2", 2-1/2 x 2-1/2", studio stamps & notes, VF+, HL/Feb 26-27/94 (400-600)   567

6 rough drawings: 3 Stromboli, Pinocchio, Figaro, & Jiminy Cricket; 3 x 3" to 7 x 7", trimmed close to image size, F-VF, HL/Feb 26-27/94 (800-1200)   1320

Portrait of Blue Fairy looking left, 7-1/2 x 6", F+, HL/Apr 10/94 (600-900)   1008

Pinocchio sprouting donkey ears, 5-1/2 x 5-1/2", VF, HL/Apr 10/94 (600-900)   700

3 rough drawings in sequence of Stromboli, 6-1/2 x 6-1/2" to 5 x 7", VF, HL/Apr 10/94 (300-400)   392

4 drawings of Figaro, all stamped "original WDP", 2-1/2 to 4", S/Jun 17/94 (300-500)   690

3 drawings of Figaro, 4" each, S/Jun 17/94 (700-900)   1035

2 drawings of Figaro, 3-1/2" & smaller, both with "Original WDP" stamp, CE/Jun 18/94 (400-600)   633

Pinocchio (3") & Jiminy Cricket drop under water, studio stamp & notes, CE/Jun 18/94 (1500-2000)   1380

6 full-figure drawings of early Pinocchio, all approx. 5", 12-field, SR/Fall/94 (1500-2500)   1540

Surprised Stromboli, 7-1/2 x 5-1/2", HL/Nov 13/94 (600-800)   560

Key drawing of Pinocchio, 5", CE/Dec 16/94 (700-900)   633

Waist-up drawing of smiling Blue Fairy, 8-1/2", CE/Dec 16/94 (800-1200)   805

Pinocchio looks under hat, 6-3/4", CE/Dec 16/94 (600-800)   575

Pinocchio tries to dance like Russian puppets, 4-1/2", stamped, S/Dec 17/94 (600-800)   977

Waist-up drawing of Blue Fairy looking right, 7", 12-field sheet, some rippling, SR/Spring/95 (600-900)   610

Full-figure drawing of Geppetto dancing & playing fully colored hand concertina, 8-1/2", 16-field sheet, painter's notations, production stamp, SR/Spring/95 (400-800)   2120

Full-figure drawing of smiling Pinocchio sitting with hands on top of shoes, facing left, looking up, 5" 16-field sheet, production stamp, SR/Spring/95 (700-1200)   1200

4 drawings: full figure of angelic Figaro sitting toward right, wearing bib, looking up to left, 4-1/4"; shoulders-up of shocked hobo Jiminy looking left, hands down [on table top], 2-1/2"; full figure of surprised Cleo facing left, 2-1/4"; full-figure front view of Geppetto walking with lantern, 6-3/4"; all 12-field sheets, notations, some wear & discoloration, SR/Spring/95 (800-1400)   920

Full-figure front-view drawing of Stromboli standing behind footlights looking left, w/shadow, 8-7/8", 16-field sheet, production stamp, SR/Spring/95 (300-700)   510

Full-figure drawing of Blue Fairy standing facing left, 7-3/8", 16-field sheet, production stamp, SR/Spring/95 (600-900)   960

Full-figure drawing of happy Pinocchio walking straight-legged to left, 5-1/4", 12-field sheet, SR/Spring/95 (400-700)   480

Full-figure rear-view drawing of Jiminy Cricket riding seahorse, 8 x 4-1/2", HL/Apr 23/95 (600-900)   952

58 drawings of sea creatures, 2-1/2 x 3" to 7 x 10", F-VF, HL/Apr 23/95 (1000-2000)   1456

Drawing of street-level Jiminy watching Pinocchio, Honest John & Gideon walk by, notes; rough layout drawing of Jiminy; 4" & smaller; CE/Jun 9/95 (600-800)   1610

Full-figure drawing of angry Figaro walking, 2-1/2", mat inscribed "Walt Disney", CE/Jun 9/95 (300-500)   633

4 key drawings of Jiminy Cricket, 2" & similar, CE/Jun 9/95 (600-800)   1725

Full-figure illustration drawing of happy Geppetto (5-3/4") holding dripping Pinocchio (4", with donkey ears & tail), CE/Jun 9/95 (1000-1500)   1265

Pinocchio looks cross-eyed down at his nose, 5", S/Jun 10/95 (400-600)   460

6 trimmed drawings of Figaro matted together, 2" avg., S/Jun 10/95 (400-600)   1035

3 drawings framed together: 2 of fish, 3rd of Pinocchio (4") swimming in middle, S/Jun 10/95 (800-1200)   1495

3 drawings: Figaro crouching down & looking up, 2"; surprised Figaro sitting on top of large fish, 3-1/4 x 6"; colorful fish (partial), 2-1/2"; S/Jun 10/95 (300-500)   632

3 drawings: Figaro crouched, wagging tail; Figaro reaching toward Cleo's bowl as Cleo draws back in fear; Figaro diving into old shoe & peeking out; each approx. 3", S/Jun 10/95 (400-600)   1265

Full-figure front-view drawing of kneeling Jiminy Cricket as tramp, 4 x 3", VF, HL/Aug 6/95 (600-800)   1344

Waist-up drawing of dapper Lampwick holding pool cue & cigar, 5-1/2 x 6", VF, HL/Aug 6/95 (400-600)   840

Full-figure drawing of angry Jiminy Cricket w/crushed hat, 3 x 2-1/2", HL/Aug 6/95 (300-400)   672

Near-full-figure drawing of wary Figaro standing facing right, reaching out with left paw while looking back & down, 2-1/4", Courvoisier seal & debossed stamp, sheet trimmed to 4-3/8 x 4", SR/Fall/95 (200-400)   200

Full-figure drawing of sad Geppetto walking left, holding lantern at side, right hand up in fist, 7", 16-field, production stamp, SR/Fall/95 (500-1000)   610

Full-figure drawing of Pinocchio lying on stomach facing left, raising up on hands, looking straight up, 3-1/4", 12-field sheet, production notes, inker's notes, green shadow drawn on reverse, SR/Fall/95 (800-1200)   1300

2 drawings of Pinocchio in highlight carrying lamp plus 3 negatives, 5-1/2 x 9-1/2" & 5 x 8", HL/Nov 19/95 (500-800)   460

Angry Stromboli, 8-1/2 x 11", HL/Nov 19/95 (600-800)   978

Flamboyant Stromboli, 5-1/2 x 9" & 9 x 4", HL/Nov 19/95   690

2 full-figure drawings: shy Pinocchio in spotlight, Jiminy Cricket gestures w/closed umbrella, 5 x 3-1/2" & 4-1/2 x 3-1/2", HL/Nov 19/95 (600-900)   1495

Rough drawing of Stromboli holding Pinocchio's head close to his, 5-1/2 x 8-1/2", HL/Nov 19/95 (300-400)   460

2 drawings: Lampwick holding pool cue & cigar, Jiminy Cricket speaking w/arms folded & eyes closed; 3 x 2-1/2", 5 x 4-1/2", HL/Mar 16-17/96 (600-900)   633

Extreme drawing of Pinocchio lying down ill while smoking, 7 x 8", HL/Mar 16-17/96 (400-500)   748

Full-figure rough drawing of Jiminy Cricket in top hat & tails tossing closed umbrella, 5-1/2 x 5", HL/Mar 16-17/96 (150-250)   805

Full-figure drawing of Blue Fairy standing facing left, 7-3/8", 16-field sheet, production stamp, edge wear, SR/Spring/96 (800-1400)   990

Full-figure drawing of smiling Pinocchio sitting, holding up burning finger, 7", 12-field, production stamp & notes, smoke & flame by George Rowley, detailed ink & airbrush directions, SR/Spring/96 (1000-1600)   4240

Full-figure front-view drawing of serious Gideon standing with pencil & pad, 6-1/8", 16-field, inker's notations, call-outs, production stamp, SR/Spring/96 (400-800)   450

Full-figure drawing of Geppetto playing hand organ & dancing, 8-1/2", 16-field, production stamp, SR/Spring/96 (800-1400)   1520

Chest-up drawing of surprised Pinocchio looking left, 7", 12-field sheet, timer's chart, SR/Spring/96 (500-1000)   610

Full-figure drawing of charming Stromboli bowing to right, 9-1/4", 16-field sheet, production stamp, shadow & footlights at his feet, SR/Spring/96 (400-700)   920

Full-figure drawing of smiling Jiminy Cricket holding hat & umbrella, Courvoisier label, 5 x 3", HL/Apr 28/96 (500-700)   1035

Full-figure drawing of exhausted Geppetto lying on back, 4 x 12", HL/Apr 28/96 (300-400)   633

Full-figure drawing of angry Jiminy Cricket wearing collapsed hat standing looking up with arms raised, 3 x 3-1/2", HL/Apr 28/96 (300-500)   633

Expansive Stromboli, 7 x 10", HL/Apr 28/96 (500-700)   575

Full-figure drawing of puppet Pinocchio with hat raised & right arm extended [to pet Figaro], 6-1/2 x 4-1/2", HL/Apr 28/96 (600-900)   690

4 non-production drawings: Pinocchio; Gideon; full figure of Foulfellow; Foulfellow's head and hands; S/Jun 19/96 (1200-1800)   920

Full-figure drawing by Milt Kahl of Pinocchio as real boy on his knees, hands on chest, looking down; 5", CE/Jun 20/96 (700-900)   633

Full-figure drawing by Milt Kahl of worried Pinocchio as donkey, standing facing left, looking up, holding tail; 4"; shallow creases; SR/Fall/96 (400-800)   400

Full-figure front-view drawing of Geppetto walking holding lantern, left hand cupped to mouth, mouth open; 7-1/4"; 12-field sheet with timer's chart; SR/Fall/96 (400-900)   410

Near-full-figure drawing of surprised Figaro standing looking back to left, 2-1/4", Courvoisier monogram seal & debossed stamp, image back colored in green pencil to create mask to be double exposed for lighting effects, SR/Fall/96 (200-400)   600

Three full-figure drawings of early Pinocchio losing balance while walking, all 5", 12-field sheets, SR/Fall/96 (800-1400)   1000

Full-figure drawing of awed Pinocchio sitting looking up,

5-5/8", 16-field sheet, inker's notations, timer's chart, production stamp, edge wear, small light stains, SR/Fall/96 (700-1200) 1150

Two full-figure drawings: sitting Figaro with napkin around neck smiles & looks up & to left, 4-1/4", camera notations & timer's chart, some wear & discoloration; Cleo swims left, 2-1/8"; 12-field sheets; SR/Fall/96 (400-800) 610

Full-figure extreme drawing of smiling Jiminy Cricket standing looking up, 3-1/4 x 3", HL/Oct 6/96 (600-900) 978

Full-figure drawing of donkey-eared Pinocchio standing looking to right w/rock tied to tail, matching drawing of air bubbles, 3-1/2 x 2-1/2" & 7-1/2 x 5-1/2", HL/Oct 6/96 (600-900) 863

Stromboli measures stack of coins, 7 x 9", HL/Oct 6/96 (500-700) 575

Rough drawing of Lampwick w/arms outstretched, holding cigar, 9 x 6", HL/Oct 6/96 (600-900) 748

Awed puppet Pinocchio sits looking up & to right, 5-1/2 x 3-1/2", HL/Oct 6/96 (800-1000) 1955

Full-figure drawing of surprised Pinocchio on hands & knees looking down, 4 x 4-1/2", HL/Oct 6/96 (600-900) 1265

Attentive Blue Fairy looks left, holding wand, 8-1/2 x 7-1/2", HL/Oct 6/96 (600-900) 1265

Full-figure polished rough drawing of Pinocchio as real boy on knees, hands on chest, looking down, 4-3/4 x 2-1/2", HL/Oct 6/96 (300-500) 633

Rough drawing of shocked Gideon & Foulfellow being pulled to right by their coats by two [coachman's] arms, looking back & down, 7-1/2 x 10", HL/Oct 6/96 (700-900) 748

4 rough drawings of Coachman, Gideon, & Honest John, 12" long, CE/Dec 12/96 (800-1200) 1093

Portrait drawing of Blue Fairy, 7", CE/Dec 12/96 (1000-1200) 748

10 drawings: Gideon with special-effects drawing; 8 rough drawings of Figaro (3), Honest John, Honest John & Gideon, Honest John & Pinocchio, Jiminy, and Figaro & Pluto; sight 10 x 12" each, CE/Dec 12/96 (1000-1500) 1150

3 drawings: Pinocchio as real boy sitting up on knees, rough of Pinocchio examining right hand; clean-up of Stromboli holding axe & talking to left, signature of Milt Neil; 4-1/2", 4-1/2", 6-1/4"; S/Dec 14/96 (800-1200) 1265

8 items (1st 6 drawings): Pinocchio looking up as hat has fallen down over one eye; Geppetto creeping in nightclothes holding candle and pistol; Stromboli describes to Pinocchio places they'll travel; 2 consecutive drawings of Figaro walking to left & looking face forward w/tired expression; Figaro sitting looking warily to left; temporary photostat model sheet of Geppetto; photostat model sheet of Geppetto's bed; S/Dec 14/96 (1800-2200) 1495

Large-image drawing of wide-eyed Pinocchio lying with smashed cigar in teeth, 8 x 8", HL/Feb 23/97 (500-700) 633

Waist-up drawing of thoughtful Stromboli, 7-1/2 x 8", HL/Feb 23/97 (300-400) 345

3 full-figure roughs of Jiminy Cricket lecturing expressively; 2-1/2 x 2-1/2", 3-1/4 x 2-1/4", 3 x 2-1/2", HL/Feb 23/97 (900-1200) 1150

Waist-up drawing of scowling Coachman seated at table, 6-1/4 x 7-1/4", HL/Feb 23/97 (500-700) 748

Near-full-figure drawing of smiling Blue Fairy facing right, 8-1/2 x 6", HL/Feb 23/97 (700-1000) 1323

Full-figure drawing of worried Pinocchio (with donkey ears) on one knee, 5 x 4-1/2", HL/Feb 23/97 (700-1000) 978

6 rough & clean-up drawings: Geppetto, Pinocchio (2), Foulfellow, Jiminy, & Figaro; 2-1/4 x 2-1/2" to 9 x 7-1/2", F, HL/Feb 23/97 (500-1000) 805

Knees-up drawing of Gideon using whisk broom, 6-1/2 x 9", F, HL/Feb 23/97 (400-600) 460

Waist-up detailed, finished rough drawing of angry Geppetto in nightclothes facing right, wagging finger; 7 x 7"; VF; HL/Feb 23/97 (300-400) 403

Full-figure drawing of Blue Fairy holding wand, standing facing left, 7-1/8", 16-field sheet, production stamp, glow of wand detailed on back, SR/Spring/97 (800-1400) 1180

Chest-up front-view drawing of Geppetto leaning right, left hand up, looking left, 6-7/8"; 12-field sheet; SR/Spring/97 (1000-1500) 720

Full-figure drawing of sad Geppetto standing facing left, donning coat, 8-1/2" with shadow, 16-field sheet, production stamp, some wear, SR/Spring/97 (500-900) 550

Full-figure drawing of Gideon holding pencil over his head, pad of paper in outstretched left arm, 7-3/4", 16-field sheet, production stamp, SR/Spring/97 (400-800) 440

Full-figure front-view drawing w/shadow of flamboyant Stromboli standing behind footlights, 8", 16-field sheet, production & inker's stamps, SR/Spring/97 (500-900) 500

Full-figure detailed rough drawing of happy Jiminy Cricket walking left under umbrella, 5-1/4 x 4", HL/May 31/97 (200-250) 403

Full-figure rough extreme drawing of early Jiminy Cricket standing looking surprised to left, 4-1/2 x 3-1/2", HL/May 31/97 (200-300) 92

Full-figure drawing of angry Jiminy Cricket standing looking up & to left w/hands on hips, 3-1/2 x 2-1/4", HL/May 31/97 (200-300) 403

Confident Lampwick rubs tip of pool cue with cigar, matching special-effects drawing of cigar smoke, 5 x 5-1/2", HL/May 31/97 (300-400) 345

Lively hips-up drawing of Stromboli introducing puppet show, 8 x 8-1/2", HL/May 31/97 (300-400) 138

2 full-figure large-image extreme rough drawings of perplexed Figaro, 5-1/2 x 5" & 5-1/2 x 3-1/2", HL/May 31/97 (300-400) 518

34 drawings: Honest John w/cigar, 23 from waist up, 5 later signed by Shamus Culhane; 5 waist-up of Honest John & Gideon; 6 concepts of Figaro later signed by Culhane; dimensions: Gideon 5", Gideon & Honest John 6", CLA/Jun 7/97 (1000-1500) 2185

Rough portrait drawing of smiling Pinocchio looking down, 12", CLA/Jun 7/97 (1000-1500) 2530

Rough full-figure drawing of Pinocchio showing off donkey tail, 4-1/2", CLA/Jun 7/97 (1000-1500) 690

Full-figure drawing by Milt Kahl of Pinocchio as boy kneeling, 5", CLA/Jun 7/97 (500-700) 345

Full-figure drawing of smiling Pinocchio sitting & looking up to left, 6", S/Jun 21/97 (800-1200) 1495

2 thumbnail drawings matted & framed together: Gideon & Foulfellow eye pile of coins; smiling Coachman packs his pipe, each 2-1/2 x 3", S/Jun 21/97 (700-900) 805

Full-figure front-view drawing of panicked Pinocchio standing [trapped in cage], 4-5/8", 12-field sheet, SR/Fall/97 (900-1200) 875

Full-figure rough drawing of sad Pinocchio as donkey standing holding hat, looking left, 4-3/8", shallow creases around figure, SR/Fall/97 (450-700) 300

2 drawings: knees-up of Blue Fairy facing right holding wand, 9-3/16", 16-field sheet, 2 vertical folds at right edge; full figure of smiling Pinocchio sitting, looking up to left, 4 3/4", 12-field sheet, SR/Fall/97 (1800-2400) 1700

Full-figure drawing of Geppetto in nightclothes stepping left playing fully colored concertina, 8-1/2", 16-field with color call-outs, production notation & stamp, SR/Fall/97 (1200-1800) 1000

Full-figure preliminary drawing of puppet Pinocchio being walked to right, based on Freddie Moore's early model, 5-1/2", 12-field sheet, SR/Fall/97 (450-700) 390

Full-figure animation drawing of angry Jiminy Cricket standing wearing crushed hat, looking up, 3-1/4 x 2-1/2", VF, HL/Nov 16/97 (300-500) 431

Waist-up drawing of Lampwick chalking pool cue with cigar, plus matching special-effects drawing of cigar smoke, 5-1/2 x 6", VF+, HL/Nov 16/97 (500-700) 690

Stromboli speaks, 6-1/2 x 9", VF, HL/Nov 16/97 (400-600) 489

Full-figure polished rough drawing of Pinocchio as real boy on knees, hands on chest, looking down, 4-3/4 x 2-1/2", VF, HL/Nov 16/97 (300-500) 345

5 animation drawings: roughs of Jiminy Cricket & Gideon; Katharine Hepburn as Bo Peep from *Mother Goose Goes Hollywood*; Pete from *Officer Duck*; 4 x 3-1/4" to 6 x 10", F overall, HL/Nov 16/97 (600-900) 978

Close-up drawing of ill Pinocchio lying face down

with smashed cigar in mouth, 6-1/2 x 8", S/Dec 19/97 (800-1200) 805

2 drawings of Figaro matted together: sitting [in high chair] & turning around, 4"; in bed wearing night cap, looking up, 2"; Courvoisier label, S/Dec 19/97 (400-600) 1380

4 small drawings of Figaro matted together, approx. 2" each, Courvoisier label, S/Dec 19/97 (800-1200) 1265

2 drawings: Foulfellow placing flower in lapel, 7", Courvoisier label; Gideon pointing to himself smiling, 6"; S/Dec 19/97 (700-900) 690

Rough animation drawing of seated puppet Pinocchio facing left, looking up, 5-1/2"; 9 rough animation drawings of Jiminy from TV series; one full-figure rough animation drawing of Jiminy from film; Jiminy 4" & smaller, CE/Dec 18/97 (800-1200) 863

Full-figure rough animation drawing of smiling Pinocchio standing facing left, 4", CE/Dec 18/97 (700-900) 748

Full-figure rough animation drawing of smiling Pinocchio sitting looking up (matching drawing for lot #140), 6-1/2", CE/Dec 18/97 (2000-3000) 1725

Full-figure rough animation drawing of Pinocchio standing toward right, looking up, arms outstretched, apple in right hand, 5", CE/Dec 18/97 (2000-3000) 1725

Full-figure study drawing of Jiminy Cricket in rags standing facing left, mouth open, right hand out in 'stop' motion; 5"; CE/Dec 18/97 (1000-1500) 920

Full-figure front-view drawing of Gideon holding pencil & pad of paper, 6 1/8", 16-field sheet, studio production stamp & color call-outs, SR/Spring/98 (400-700) 510

Full-figure drawing of Stromboli with shadow standing in mid-introduction, 8", 12-field sheet, studio production stamp, SR/Spring/98 (500-900) 520

Chest-up front-view drawing of smiling Coachman with arms up [sitting at table], 5", 12-field sheet, inker's notation, shadow effects, SR/Spring/98 (600-900) 510

Full-figure preliminary drawing of puppet Pinocchio being walked to right, based on Freddie Moore's early model, 6-1/16", 12-field sheet, SR/Spring/98 (300-600) 375

Full-figure model drawing of Pinocchio standing facing toward right, arms spread, apple in right hand, looking up; 5"; 12-field sheet; SR/Spring/98 (1000-1500) 880

Full-figure drawing of happy Figaro standing on hind legs to right, 3-3/4", Courvoisier monogram & debossed stamps, SR/Spring/98 (400-800) 540

Full-figure drawing of Blue Fairy standing facing left holding glowing wand, 7-1/4", 16-field sheet, production stamp, SR/Spring/98 (800-1400) 880

Front-view drawing of flamboyant Stromboli as master of ceremonies, 7 x 8-1/4", VF, HL/Apr 25/98 (400-500) 431

Full-figure drawing of joyful donkey Pinocchio jumping, 7-1/2 x 8-1/2", VF, HL/Apr 25/98 (700-900) 978

Extreme drawing of ill Pinocchio lying on stomach with shredded cigar in mouth, 7-1/2 x 8", VF, HL/Apr 25/98 (500-700) 633

"I'm through!" Full-figure drawing of disgusted Jiminy Cricket in squashed hat standing facing left, 3 x 2-1/2", VF, HL/Apr 25/98 (300-400) 489

Matched pair of drawings of Lampwick chalking pool cue with cigar, 6 x 4-1/2" each, includes effects drawing of smoke & ash, VF, HL/Apr 25/98 (300-500) 288

BACKGROUNDS

Final design for master background of Geppetto's workbench area, 11 x 14-1/2", pencil on animation sheet, stamps & notes, HL/Nov 13/94 (2000-2500) 5986

Geppetto's workshop interior, preliminary watercolor pan production background by Claude Coats with notes, CE/Dec 16/94 (18,000-25,000) 20,700

Master watercolor background of Cleo's home, 13-1/2 x 9-3/4", studio stamp, name of Don DaGradi, SR/Fall/96 (1400-2600) 1500

Watercolor production background of interior of Stromboli's wagon, sight 10-1/2 x 13-3/4", CLA/Jun 7/97 (5000-7000) 8625

Background painting of interior of raft cabin w/fish bowl & stove, watercolor on background sheet, 8-1/4 x 11", VF+, HL/Nov 16/97 (5000-7000) 6095

CEL SET-UPS

Figaro chases butterfly, Courvoisier airbrush background, 7-3/4 x 9-1/2", CE/Dec 15/93 (1500-2000) 1725

Jiminy Cricket runs w/hat full of water & trips over pencil, key watercolor production background, 9-3/4 x 11-1/4", CE/Dec 15/93 (6000-8000) 5750

Jiminy rides sea horse, Courvoisier watercolor & airbrush background, 3-1/2 x 4", CE/Dec 15/93 (1000-1500) 1725

Jiminy floats underwater, Courvoisier watercolor & airbrush background, 4 x 4" diameter, CE/Dec 15/93 (800-1200) 1265

Coachman stands firm, Courvoisier airbrush background, 8 x 7-1/2", CE/Dec 15/93 (700-900) 1495

Jiminy Cricket & moth, Courvoisier airbrush background, 3-1/2 x 3-1/2", CE/Dec 15/93 (1000-1500) 1725

Figaro, Courvoisier background, 3-1/2 x 3-3/4", CE/Dec 15/93 (800-1200) 1610

Geppetto's hands hold 5-1/2" Pinocchio as he reaches to pat 2" Figaro, airbrushed background, Courvoisier label, S/Dec 16/93 (3000-4000) 5750

Cleo smiling amidst bubbles, Courvoisier background, 4", S/Dec 16/93 (2000-3000) 2185

Figaro fishes with string tied to tail inside Monstro, painted veneer background, 3", S/Dec 16/93 (1000-1500) 1495

5-1/2" Pinocchio listens to 1" Jiminy atop matchbox, airbrushed background, S/Dec 16/93 (4000-6000) 6325

Jiminy watches butterfly, airbrushed background, WDP label, 4", S/Dec 16/93 (1000-1500) 2185

Jiminy peeking from under umbrella, airbrushed background, 2-1/2", S/Dec 16/93 (1000-1500) 1610

Jiminy putting on coat on run, painted veneer background, Courvoisier label, 5", S/Dec 16/93 (2000-3000) 2588

Jiminy floating to ground w/umbrella, airbrushed background, WDP label, 3-1/2", S/Dec 16/93 (1800-2200) 2300

Cleo, 7 x 7-1/2", mounted w/bubble overlay cel on complementary background for sale by Courvoisier, VF+, HL/Apr 10/94 (2000-3000) 2128

Jiminy & medal, matching cel & watercolor master background as prepared for Courvoisier, 7-1/2 x 8-1/2", VF, HL/Apr 10/94 (15,000-20,000) 15,680

Cleo sleeping in castle with air bubbles, 6 x 7", painted background, in mat inscribed "Cleo," Courvoisier label, VF, HL/Apr 10/94 (1500-2000) 2240

Full figure of jauntily-walking Figaro from *Pinocchio* w/watercolor master background from *Figaro and Cleo*, 8 x 11", studio notes & stamps, restored, VF, HL/Apr 10/94 (2500-3500) 2548

2 full-figure cels of Pinocchio & Dutch girl marionette over complementary airbrush background, 7 x 6-1/2", Courvoisier label, VF, HL/Apr 10/94 (4000-5000) 6160

Jiminy Cricket nose-to-nose w/sea horse, 8 x 9-1/2", mounted with 2 cels of fish to Courvoisier airbrush & watercolor background, in original mat with label of authenticity, VF, HL/Apr 10/94 (3500-4500) 4032

Promotional cel: Pinocchio w/donkey ears (3-1/2") & Jiminy Cricket (1") running, publication background, S/Jun 17/94 (2500-3500) 2587

Figaro watches moth, airbrushed Courvoisier background, 4", S/Jun 17/94 (1200-1800) 1955

Jiminy's head peeks under door to Geppetto's studio, airbrushed Courvoisier background, 1", S/Jun 17/94 (800-1200) 805

Unsure Pinocchio w/dancing Dutch girl puppet, airbrushed Courvoisier background, 4-1/2" each, S/Jun 17/94 (4000-6000) 6900

Cleo swims amidst bubbles, airbrushed Courvoisier background, 3-1/2", S/Jun 17/94 (1000-1500) 1955

Jiminy stands w/umbrella, airbrushed Courvoisier background, 4-1/2", S/Jun 17/94 (1800-2200) 3162

Jiminy leans on umbrella & smiles at butterfly, airbrushed Courvoisier background, 3-1/2", S/Jun 17/94 (1800-2200) 2875

Jiminy dressed in rags, floats to ground with umbrella, airbrushed Courvoisier background, 3-1/2" (cel severed where umbrella meets handle), S/Jun 17/94 (1000-1500) 1840

Figaro sits in chair with napkin around neck, airbrushed Courvoisier background & label, 4", S/Jun 17/94 (1200-1800) 2587

Jiminy slides along violin strings, airbrushed Courvoisier background & label, 4", S/Jun 17/94 (2000-3000) 3162

Jiminy dressed in rags, tips hat to porcelain lady, airbrushed Courvoisier background, 4", S/Jun 17/94 (1800-2200) 4312

Jiminy sings, Courvoisier airbrush background and label, 3-1/2 x 3", CE/Jun 18/94 (800-1200) 2415

Pinocchio (3 x 1-1/2") dances with Dutch doll (3-1/2 x 2-1/2"), Courvoisier airbrush background, CE/Jun 18/94 (2500-3500) 4370

Jiminy Cricket (3") watches moth, Courvoisier label & airbrush background, CE/Jun 18/94 (1000-1500) 2530

Jiminy Cricket warms backside, 3-1/2 x 1-1/2", Courvoisier label & airbrush background, CE/Jun 18/94 (2000-3000) 4370

Jiminy floats on sea in bottle, 2-1/4 x 2", airbrush Courvoisier background, CE/Jun 18/94 (1000-1500) 2530

Publicity cel of Jiminy Cricket, 5 x 4-3/4", circa 1940s, DL background, CE/Jun 18/94 (700-900) 863

Puppet Pinocchio (7") walks, curious Figaro (3-1/2") follows closely, Courvoisier airbrush background, CE/Jun 18/94 (3000-4000) 5175

Full figure of Jiminy Cricket making "stop" gesture, Courvoisier airbrush background & label, inscribed, 4-1/2 x 4", HL/Aug 21/94 (2000-3000) 2912

Full figure of Figaro sneaking uneasy look back as he follows Geppetto's slipper-clad foot, complementary Courvoisier airbrush background, inscribed, labels, 4-1/2 x 6", HL/Aug 21/94 (1600-1800) 2240

Portrait of surprised Pinocchio, complementary Courvoisier airbrush background, 5 x 5", HL/Aug 21/94 (3000-5000) 5376

Figaro in chair w/bib admiring dinner, complementary modern non-Studio background, 4 x 4", HL/Aug 21/94 (3400-4000) 2912

2 expressive full-figure cels of Jiminy Cricket, 1980s, color print backgrounds, 3 x 3" & 2-1/2 x 2", HL/Aug 21/94 (700-1000) 616

Half image of irritated Figaro in bed wearing nightcap, looking left & up, 5-1/2" with quilt, watercolor Courvoisier background & label, SR/Fall/94 (2200-3200) 2200

Full figure of worried, hatless Jiminy dangling by pants from spring, 5", Courvoisier watercolor background & label, SR/Fall/94 (2800-3400) 3080

Full figure of tired Figaro creeping along window sill to left against starry sky, 1", Courvoisier watercolor background, mat & labels, SR/Fall/94 (1200-1600) 1210

Full-figure rear view of Figaro clinging to side of box, smacking fish in mouth, 3-1/2", Courvoisier watercolor-on-wood-veneer background & label, water-effects cel, SR/Fall/94 (1800-2800) 1800

Paws & head on table, Figaro stares at moth, 4 x 5", complementary Courvoisier background & label, HL/Nov 13/94 (1400-1800) 1512

Limited-edition cel of Blue Fairy addressing Pinocchio & Jiminy, 11-1/2 x 15-1/2", color print background, #55/275, seal & certificate, HL/Nov 13/94 (4000-5000) 6608

Determined Jiminy raises umbrella on sea floor to strike large fish, 7-1/2 x 9-1/2", Courvoisier airbrush background, label remnant, inscribed & signed by Walt Disney, HL/Nov 13/94 (3500-4500) 4032

"Tramp" Jiminy Cricket peers down from workshop ledge, 6-1/2 x 5", complementary Courvoisier background, HL/Nov 13/94 (1500-2000) 3024

Cleo sleeps serenely inside castle, 6-1/2 x 7", Courvoisier painted background & label,

HL/Nov 13/94 (1200-1600) 2464

Left profile of startled Figaro sitting atop fish, 4-1/2 x 5", simple Courvoisier airbrush background & label, HL/Nov 13/94 (2000-2500) 2016

Full figure of Pinocchio under water amid fish school, 7" & smaller, Courvoisier airbrush background, CE/Dec 16/94 (3000-4000) 5750

Owl clock on shelf, 4", key watercolor production background with shading added by Courvoisier, CE/Dec 16/94 (4000-6000) 4830

Geppetto in bed asleep, 6-1/2 x 10", watercolor production background, stamps & notes, CE/Dec 16/94 (5000-7000) 5175

Jiminy Cricket trips over pencil on shelf while carrying hatful of water, 3", watercolor production background, notes, CE/Dec 16/94 (4000-6000) 5750

Full figures of Figaro & butterfly, 1-1/2", Courvoisier airbrush background & label, CE/Dec 16/94 (600-800) 1725

Jiminy Cricket enters Stromboli's wagon, 1-1/4", watercolor production background, CE/Dec 16/94 (4000-6000) 9200

Pinocchio trapped by puppets, 5-1/2", Courvoisier airbrush background, CE/Dec 16/94 (3500-4500) 5175

Full figure of Jiminy Cricket riding sea horse amid fish, 1", Courvoisier airbrush & watercolor background, CE/Dec 16/94 (700-900) 2070

Full figure of French girl puppet, 6", Courvoisier airbrush background, CE/Dec 16/94 (700-900) 1035

Publicity cel of happy Geppetto holding dripping Pinocchio, 5-1/2", illustration background of workshop interior, CE/Dec 16/94 (2500-3500) 3220

Full figure of Pinocchio dancing, 4", Courvoisier airbrush background, CE/Dec 16/94 (3500-4500) 7130

Full figure of happy Figaro walking, 4", Courvoisier wood-veneer background, CE/Dec 16/94 (700-900) 690

Smiling Pinocchio (7-1/2") listens to Jiminy Cricket (1-1/2") lecture from flower, airbrushed Courvoisier background, S/Dec 17/94 (4000-6000) 8625

Cleo sleeps contentedly in castle, 2", airbrushed Courvoisier background, S/Dec 17/94 (1800-2200) 2300

Pinocchio smiles at curious seahorses underwater, 6", airbrushed Courvoisier background, S/Dec 17/94 (3500-4500) 6037

Jiminy Cricket in rags warms himself by fire, 3-1/4", airbrushed Courvoisier background, S/Dec 17/94 (1800-2200) 3450

Figaro (2 x 2") on patchwork quilt stalks flying moth (1/2"), airbrushed Courvoisier background, WDP label, S/Dec 17/94 (1500-2000) 2070

Pinocchio (6-1/2") looks at smiling Jiminy Cricket (2"), airbrushed Courvoisier background & label, needs restoration, S/Dec 17/94 (1500-2000) 6900

Jiminy Cricket in bubble eyes top hat in separate bubble, 3-1/2", airbrushed Courvoisier background & label, S/Dec 17/94 (1800-2200) 3737

Promotional cel of Pinocchio (3") skipping to school with Jiminy (1") not far behind, publication background, S/Dec 17/94 (2500-3500) 3450

Publicity cel of Pinocchio sitting (5-1/2" x 4-1/2") on table with Jiminy (1") perched on his toe, preliminary watercolor background, Courvoisier label, Walt Disney signature, S/Dec 17/94 (10,000-12,000) 18,400

"Who's da beetle?" Lampwick holds angry Jiminy up by back of coat, 6", Courvoisier watercolor background, mat & label, SR/Spring/95 (3000-6000) 3730

Bow tie-up profile portrait of Pinocchio facing right, 8-1/4", Courvoisier watercolor background in circle format, mat & label, SR/Spring/95 (3000-6000) 4000

Full figures of surprised Pinocchio (3") standing, turning left to see Dutch-girl puppet (3-1/2", strings on overlay), Courvoisier watercolor background, label & mat, SR/Spring/95 (5000-10,000) 5200

Figaro asleep in his bed under quilt, 5", shadow & dry brush work, detailed watercolor Art Props background with stamps, 12-field, SR/Spring/95 (2000-4000) 4030

Full figure of happy Pinocchio walking with apple

& notebook, 2-1/2 x 2" cel, complementary Courvoisier airbrush background, VF, HL/Apr 23/95 (2500-3500) 3584

Full figure of sitting Pinocchio looking at Jiminy on box, 8-1/2 x 10", complementary shadow airbrush background, Courvoisier label, mat inscribed by Walt Disney, VF, HL/Apr 23/95 (5000-7000) 14,560

Full figure of Jiminy Cricket (on back in sand) as he tips hat & smiles to angry fish, 8-1/2 x 11-1/2", atmospheric master background (watercolor on background sheet), overlay cel of bubbles, Courvoisier label, VF, HL/Apr 23/95 (12,000-16,000) 12,320

Unhappy Figaro at window w/stars in background, 9 x 11", complementary painted background, Courvoisier label, inscribed "...Walt Disney", F, HL/Apr 23/95 (2000-2500) 3696

Portrait of Jiminy w/automaton in Geppetto's workshop, 6-1/2 x 6", body of automaton is from Courvoisier background, w/color print background, matted w/clipped autograph of Ward Kimball, F, HL/Apr 23/95 (1500-2000) 3136

Near-full figure of smiling Jiminy Cricket pointing, 3", Courvoisier airbrush background, CE/Jun 9/95 (1500-2000) 3220

Surprised Figaro sitting up in bed, 2", Courvoisier airbrush background, mat inscribed "Walt Disney", CE/Jun 9/95 (1500-2000) 4025

Smiling Geppetto (8") holding angry Figaro (3"), wood-veneer background, CE/Jun 9/95 (2500-3500) 4025

Full figure of charming Cleo swimming, 5", overlay, Courvoisier watercolor and airbrush background, CE/Jun 9/95 (1000-1500) 2760

Monstro cruising on surface w/sea gulls, 8-1/2", Courvoisier watercolor background, mat inscribed "Sincerely, Walt Disney", CE/Jun 9/95 (2000-3000) 7475

Worried Jiminy standing in puddle looking back from under umbrella, 2-1/2", partial overlay, Courvoisier watercolor & airbrush background, CE/Jun 9/95 (1500-2500) 2760

Publicity cels of Jiminy (3"), Geppetto (10") and Pinocchio (4-1/2"), studio wood-veneer background, CE/Jun 9/95 (4000-6000) 4600

School of fish, 1-1/4" & smaller, partial overlay, Courvoisier watercolor production background, mat inscribed "Sincerely, Walt Disney", CE/Jun 9/95 (700-900) 1840

Full figure of gracious Jiminy Cricket standing on hill, 3-1/2", Courvoisier airbrush background, mat inscribed "Walt Disney", CE/Jun 9/95 (1200-1500) 3680

Figaro (7-1/4") & Cleo (2-1/2") kiss as Pinocchio (7") watches, Courvoisier airbrush background, CE/Jun 9/95 (4000-6000) 14,950

Full figure of Jiminy Cricket making a point while standing outside in snow, circa 1950s, 4-1/2", DL printed background, CE/Jun 9/95 (700-900) 403

Full figure of Jiminy Cricket on window sill, commercial cel circa 1950s/60s, 4", key watercolor production background, CE/Jun 9/95 (600-800) 575

Alarmed Figaro (11/2") peeks out from atop startled Geppetto's head (81/2"), airbrushed Courvoisier background & label, S/Jun 10/95 (2000-3000) 3450

Full figure of smiling Jiminy Cricket standing with hands behind back & eyes closed, 3", airbrushed Courvoisier background & label, S/Jun 10/95 (1800-2200) 3737

Pinocchio (6") smiles & extends hand to curious seahorses, airbrushed Courvoisier background & label, S/Jun 10/95 (3500-4500) 5462

Geppetto (4"), Pinocchio (2") & Figaro (3/4") being blown away on raft by Monstro's sneeze, airbrushed Courvoisier background & label, S/Jun 10/95 (3000-5000) 6325

Happy Figaro in bed wearing nightcap, 1-1/2", airbrushed Courvoisier background & label, S/Jun 10/95 (1000-1500) 1840

Circa 1940 promotional cel of Pinocchio (2-1/4") sitting on Geppetto's (4-1/4") lap, publication background, S/Jun 10/95 (2500-3000) 2587

Jiminy Cricket peeks inside window with stars in background, 1", airbrushed Courvoisier background & label, S/Jun 10/95 (1800-2200) 2185

Circa 1940 promotional cel: Pinocchio, Geppetto, Jiminy & Figaro on speeding raft, hand-prepared background, 2-1/2 x 6" w/o sail, S/Jun 10/95 (2000-3000) 2070

Full figure of rag-clad Jiminy warming backside by fire, 3", airbrushed Courvoisier background & label, S/Jun 10/95 (2000-3000) 3737

Full figure of Pinocchio w/donkey ears sitting on post at workbench, 10-1/2 x 14", watercolor on background sheet, probably as sold thru Courvoisier Galleries, F+, HL/Aug 6/95 (3000-5000) 7616

Jiminy Cricket removes hat (coat lies nearby) as he enters Stromboli's lock, 6-1/2 x 6-1/2", complementary airbrush background as prepared for Courvoisier, F+, HL/Aug 6/95 (2400-2800) 2912

Full figure of curious Pinocchio standing looking left & up, 3-1/2", wood-veneer background, lifting & missing paint, SR/Fall/95 (2000-5000) 3570

Full figure of Jiminy standing at attention facing toward left, hat in hand in front of chest, eyes closed, 3-1/2", Courvoisier watercolor background & labels, SR/Fall/95 (2500-3500) 2750

Limited-edition cel of Jiminy, Pinocchio & Blue Fairy, 1990, #228/275, 11-1/2 x 15-1/2", color print background, HL/Nov 19/95 (4000-5000) 4830

Blue Fairy looking at Jiminy Cricket & Pinocchio on workbench; for publicity related to initial release; 8 x 12"; airbrush, watercolor-&-conté-crayon background, HL/Nov 19/95 (4000-5000) 16,100

Tiny full figure of cheerful Jiminy Cricket sitting on pipe stem, 2-1/2 x 3-1/2", airbrush background as prepared for Courvoisier, HL/Nov 19/95 (900-1200) 2300

Monstro swimming on surface, 10 x 14", Courvoisier complementary background w/cels of waves & sea gulls, mat signed by Frank Thomas & Ollie Johnston, HL/Nov 19/95 (4000-5000) 7763

Full-figure rear view of happy Figaro (3-1/8") standing at boat rail, looking back at tuna, Courvoisier watercolor-on-wood-veneer background & label, original water effects overlay cel, SR/Spring/96 (2400-3400) 2400

Full figure of shy hobo Jiminy Cricket kneeling facing left under tip of wand, 2-3/4", Courvoisier watercolor background, circular mat, SR/Spring/96 (2400-3200) 3710

Full figure of Gideon standing, hands on hips, facing right, 4-3/4", wood-veneer Courvoisier background & label, SR/Spring/96 (1200-1600) 1200

Full-figure key images of startled Pinocchio (5-1/4") standing on stage between 2 Dutch-girl puppets, Courvoisier watercolor background & label, SR/Spring/96 (5000-10,000) 5500

Full figure of happy Figaro (eyes closed, 4-1/2") walking to left, drybrush enhanced, Courvoisier wood-veneer background, SR/Spring/96 (1200-2000) 1200

Full figure of Jiminy Cricket walking toward right (& whistling?), 3-1/2"; Courvoisier watercolor background, label & mat; SR/Spring/96 (1400-1800) 2390

Pinocchio (w/donkey ears) sinks in sea amid seaweed, 5 sea horses & bubbles, complementary painted background, Courvoisier label, 8 x 8", HL/Apr 28/96 (5000-7000) 5520

3-cel setup of background painting (airbrush on heavy-weight background paper) of full-figure fearsome Monstro swimming on top of wave, created for experimental/story purposes, 8-1/2 x 11-1/2", HL/Apr 28/96 (1000-1500) 1840

Full figures of Jiminy Cricket confronting playful fish, over complementary Disney Studio drawing of undersea scene (pastel on black animation sheet), 8 x 10", HL/Apr 28/96 (3500-4500) 4140

Full figure of Jiminy Cricket floating in top of bottle & holding inverted umbrella, facing hungry sea gull, complementary Courvoisier background painting, 6-1/2 x 8", HL/Apr 28/96 (2800-3500) 3565

Near-full figure of sitting Pinocchio looking up & smiling, blue-paper backing as prepared for Courvoisier, 5 x 4-1/4", HL/Apr 28/96 (2400-3000) 6325

Full figure of surprised Jiminy Cricket as tramp facing forward w/right hand on indignant lady figurine, complementary Courvoisier airbrush background, 6-1/2 x 8", HL/Apr 28/96 (3000-3500) 4370

Near-full figure of Cleo swimming among plants & bubbles, airbrushed Courvoisier background, 4", S/Jun 19/96 (1000-1500) 2070

Full figure of smiling Pinocchio standing on one foot holding book in left hand & apple outstretched in right, wood-veneer Courvoisier background, within apple-shaped mat, 4-1/2", S/Jun 19/96 (4000-6000) 5750

Full figures of Geppetto (7") walking puppet Pinocchio (3-1/2") across floor as Figaro (2") follows, painted-veneer Courvoisier background, S/Jun 19/96 (8000-10,000) 12,650

Full figure of Pinocchio (2-1/2" total) with rock tied to tail sinking to bottom of sea amid fish, watercolor Courvoisier background, S/Jun 19/96 (5000-7000) 4600

Full-figure production set-up of shy Pinocchio on stage looking over shoulder, 3", watercolor production background, S/Jun 19/96 (8000-12,000) 8625

Full figure of Cleo swimming amid bubbles & water plants, airbrushed Courvoisier background, 1-1/2", S/Jun 19/96 (1000-1500) 2070

Huge publicity cel of Pinocchio (9-1/2") talking to Jiminy Cricket (2") who's standing on his toe, patterned paper background, S/Jun 19/96 (7000-9000) 10,350

Full figure of ragged Jiminy Cricket holding satchel standing at door to Geppetto's workshop, airbrushed Courvoisier background, 2-1/2", S/Jun 19/96 (2000-2500) 2875

Full figure of surprised Jiminy in ragged dress hanging from puppet strings, Courvoisier watercolor background, 2-1/2", CE/Jun 20/96 (3000-5000) 3220

Donkey-eared Pinocchio sinks underwater with sea plants & sea horses, Courvoisier airbrush & watercolor background, 7-1/4" with tail, CE/Jun 20/96 (3000-5000) 5175

Full-figure portrait of smiling Figaro sitting, Courvoisier airbrush & watercolor background, 6", CE/Jun 20/96 (2000-3000) 4600

Portrait of surprised Geppetto with Figaro's head sticking out of nightcap, Courvoisier airbrush background, 10", CE/Jun 20/96 (2500-3500) 4025

Blue Fairy (4-1/2") talks to Jiminy Cricket (full figure, 1") in rags standing on box on shelf, Courvoisier airbrush background, CE/Jun 20/96 (10,000-15,000) 14,950

Full figure of smiling Jiminy Cricket (3") blindly leaning w/hand on lady figurine's derriere, Courvoisier watercolor background & original hand-lettered mat, SR/Fall/96 (2600-3600) 4460

Full figure of cautious hobo Jiminy Cricket stepping forward, 4-5/8", enhanced with airbrushing, starry watercolor Courvoisier background, SR/Fall/96 (2200-2800) 5300

Figaro & Geppetto asleep in bed, enhanced with dry-brushing, 5-1/2", Courvoisier watercolor background w/original mat & label, set-up is 7-1/2" round, SR/Fall/96 (2500-3500) 2530

Limited-edition cel of Blue Fairy talking to Pinocchio & Jiminy (on workbench), #44/275, color print background, 11-1/2 x 15-1/2", HL/Oct 6/96 (4000-5000) 4370

Full-figure profile of Jiminy Cricket walking to right, 3-1/4 x 2-1/4", airbrushed background with Courvoisier label, VF+, HL/Oct 6/96 (3000-3500) 2990

Full figure of Jiminy Cricket standing outdoors facing right & pointing w/umbrella, portion of pan master background (watercolor on background sheet), 8-1/2 x 11-1/2", HL/Oct 6/96 (5000-7000) 5463

Full figure of smiling Pinocchio walking carrying book & looking at apple in his extended right hand, 4", Courvoisier wood-veneer background, CE/Dec 12/96 (2000-2500) 3680

Smiling Figaro asleep in bed, 1-1/2", Courvoisier airbrush background & label, CE/Dec 12/96 (1000-1500) 1265

Full figure of smiling Jiminy Cricket in ragged dress holding open umbrella as if falling head-first thru air, looking down w/right hand shielding eyes, 2-1/2" length, Courvoisier airbrush background & label, CE/Dec 12/96 (1500-2000) 2875

Full figure of Pinocchio as real boy lying on bed with eyes closed, 6-1/2", key watercolor production background (key set-up), CE/Dec 12/96 (25,000-35,000)   36,800

Full figure of surprised Jiminy Cricket (3-1/2") standing on sea bottom amid seaweed and bubbles confronted by angry father fish with baby (4-1/2"), Courvoisier watercolor background, partial special-effects cel, CE/Dec 12/96 (4000-6000)   6900

Full figures of Geppetto (5") at open door of home while holding Figaro (2") by back of neck, key watercolor production background, Courvoisier label, CE/Dec 12/96 (15,000-20,000)   25,300

Full figure of happy Pinocchio high-stepping down sidewalk carrying book & looking at apple in extended right hand, 5", watercolor production background, Courvoisier label, mat inscribed "To ... Walt Disney", CE/Dec 12/96 (8000-10,000)   9775

Full figure of curious Figaro walking on quilt watching butterfly, 3" length, Courvoisier airbrush background and label, CE/Dec 12/96 (1500-2000)   2530

Full figures of Jiminy Cricket (3-1/2") underwater startled by curious seahorse (6") amid seaweed & fish, airbrushed Courvoisier background, S/Dec 14/96 (3000-3500)   3737

Full figure of Figaro standing on edge of wooden box taking swipe at fish tail, 3-1/2", airbrushed Courvoisier background & label, S/Dec 14/96 (1000-1500)   1495

Curious Pinocchio dropping in sea amid seahorses, seaweed, & bubbles, 6", airbrushed Courvoisier background & label, S/Dec 14/96 (4000-6000)   5175

Geppetto (7-1/2") holds angry Figaro (3") up by back of neck & scolds him, printed background of cottage interior, S/Dec 14/96 (2000-3000) 2875

Full figure of Lampwick leaning [on unseen railing], 2 mugs in right hand, calling out, 6", printed background of Pleasure Island, S/Dec 14/96 (2000-3000)   1840

Smiling Blue Fairy standing by shelves full of toys, 6", printed background, needs restoration, S/Dec 14/96 (8000-10,000)   8625

Full figure of sitting Figaro (4") turning to frown at coy Cleo (2-1/2"), airbrushed Courvoisier background & label, S/Dec 14/96 (3000-4000) 3162

Full figure of embarrassed Jiminy (dressed in rags) standing on workbench amid toys looking up, 3-1/3", printed background, S/Dec 14/96 (2000-3000)   3162

Geppetto (6") & Figaro (3") sleeping side-by-side in bed, airbrushed Courvoisier background, S/Dec 14/96 (1500-2000)   2070

Full figure of smiling Jiminy Cricket lifting hat and looking up as he stands on table amid junk, 6", printed background, S/Dec 14/96 (2000-3000)   3162

Full figures of J. Worthington Foulfellow (7") & Gideon (5") standing on street looking left with great interest, printed background, S/Dec 14/96 (2000-3000)   3737

Full figure of smiling Pinocchio standing, arms outstretched, apple in right hand, looking up, 5", wood-veneer Courvoisier background, S/Dec 14/96 (4000-6000)   7475

Full figure of Jiminy Cricket (1") riding seahorse (1-1/2") amid other fish & seaweed, airbrushed Courvoisier background, S/Dec 14/96 (1000-1500)   1495

Full figure of happy Jiminy facing left & tipping hat as moth flutters by above, 3-1/2", airbrushed Courvoisier background, S/Dec 14/96 (2500-3500)   3162

Full figure of "angry mother spanking baby" clock, 3-7/8", Courvoisier wood-veneer background, "WDP Original" stamp, SR/Spring/97 (1000-1600)   1210

Full figure of tattered, pensive Jiminy Cricket sitting on small shelf, 3-1/8", 12-field cel, color print background, SR/Spring/97 (2800-3800)   3080

Full figure of Cleo (2-1/8") facing right above bowl at head level with startled Figaro (clinging to bowl, near-full figure, 6-3/4") as smiling Pinocchio (partial figure, 8-7/8") watches, Courvoisier watercolor background & overlay with label, SR/Spring/97 (6000-10,000)   8500

Full-figure front view of standing Jiminy Cricket looking down to admire shiny badge on chest, 5-5/8",

1970s promotional, 16-field cel, airbrush special effects, star-dusted watercolor background, SR/Spring/97 (1400-2400)   1410

Full-figure (except tip of tail) front view of Pinocchio sinking in ocean amid fish & seaweed, 6-1/4", Courvoisier watercolor background with original bubble effects on full cel overlay, original hand-lettered Courvoisier mat & label, SR/Spring/97 (4500-6500)   5600

Full figure of curious vagabond Jiminy Cricket, holding carpetbag, leaning to right, 3", starry watercolor Courvoisier background with airbrush overlay, SR/Spring/97 (3200-5200)   3880

Chest-up front view of shocked Gideon, 8-1/2", Courvoisier wood-veneer background & label, SR/Spring/97 (2200-2800)   2420

Full figure of confident Jiminy Cricket walking to right along sea floor, elaborate painted background w/cels of 2 sea creatures as prepared by Courvoisier, 5 x 5-1/4" overall, HL/May 3/97 (2000-3000)   3680

Numerous sea creatures swimming underwater, elaborate painted background, as prepared by Courvoisier, 10 x 15-1/2", HL/May 3/97 (1000-1500)   2300

Full figure of carved owl-on-branch clock sitting on shelf, 4", key watercolor production background w/shading added by Courvoisier, CLA/Jun 7/97 (4000-6000)   4600

Geppetto holds angry Figaro up by nap of neck to introduce him to puppet Pinocchio, 7", Courvoisier airbrush background & label, CLA/Jun 7/97 (7000-9000)   7475

Pinocchio looking right in scouting pose underwater amid fish & seaweed, 6", Courvoisier watercolor background & label, CLA/Jun 7/97 (4000-6000)   6900

Full figures of surprised Pinocchio (3-1/4") turning to see Dutch girl marionette (3-1/2"), Courvoisier airbrush background & label, CLA/Jun 7/97 (4000-6000)   4600

Full figure of surprised Jiminy Cricket in ragged dress floating thru air under umbrella, 3-1/2", Courvoisier label & airbrush background of sky & grass blades, CLA/Jun 7/97 (1500-2000) 2990

Full figures of Jiminy Cricket (4") standing on sea floor being confronted by angry mother fish (5-1/2") w/baby, airbrushed Courvoisier background of sea floor & seaweed, S/Jun 21/97 (4000-6000)   6900

Full figure of smiling Pinocchio sitting looking up, 6", wood-veneer Courvoisier background, S/Jun 21/97 (4000-6000)   5462

Startled Figaro sits up in bed, 2-1/2", airbrushed Courvoisier background, S/Jun 21/97 (1000-1500)   2300

Surprised Jiminy Cricket (1-1/2") amid sea plants & creatures on ocean floor, airbrushed Courvoisier background, signed by Ward Kimball, S/Jun 21/97 (4000-6000)   3450

Full figures of surprised Pinocchio (back partly turned, 2-1/2") inspecting Dutch Girl marionette (3"), airbrushed background, S/Jun 21/97 (3000-5000)   2587

Jiminy Cricket (3-1/2") is startled by seahorse (7") amid fish & plants, airbrushed Courvoisier background & label, S/Jun 21/97 (3000-3500)   4312

Geppetto (7") in nightclothes stands holding candle high as Pinocchio (3") looks up & smiles from lying on floor amid overturned furniture & surprised Figaro (1-1/2") watches, watercolor production background, needs restoration, S/Jun 21/97 (15,000-20,000)   23,000

Close-up front view of Geppetto holding Figaro by back of neck to introduce him to puppet Pinocchio, 6-5/8 x 7-1/4", solid-color Courvoisier watercolor background, SR/Fall/97 (6000-9000)   4000

Full figure of dapper smiling Jiminy Cricket walking to right, 3-1/4 x 2", complementary background & label as prepared by Courvoisier, VF, HL/Nov 16/97 (2000-2500)   2530

Limited-edition cel of Pinocchio, Jiminy, & Blue Fairy, #81/275, 11-1/2 x 15-1/2", color print background of workshop interior, VF+, HL/Nov 16/97 (2000-3000)   4140

Surprised Jiminy Cricket (full figure, stuck on top of hat) & Gideon staring at each other, 8 x 8" cels, 9" diameter overall, complementary airbrush background & label as prepared by Courvoisier, VF,

HL/Nov 16/97 (2500-3500)   2760

Cel of cuckoo clocks mounted on walls, 3" & smaller, key watercolor production background, Courvoisier label, CE/Dec 18/97 (3000-5000)   4830

Bow-tie-up portrait of smiling Pinocchio facing forward & looking right, 8", Courvoisier airbrush background, CE/Dec 18/97 (3000-4000)   4140

Full figure of frustrated Figaro sitting in high chair with napkin around neck & paws crossed with dinner on table in front of him, 4", watercolor production background from Figaro & Cleo, stamp, CE/Dec 18/97 (4000-6000)   3680

Full figure of high-stepping smiling Pinocchio walking by stone wall carrying apple & book, 5", watercolor production background, Courvoisier label, mat inscribed "To Maria Cristina ... Walt Disney", CE/Dec 18/97 (7000-9000)   8625

Full figures of Geppetto (4-1/2") holding small jacket, Pinocchio (2-1/2") & Figaro (1" long) all standing on steps in front of open door, key preliminary watercolor background, CE/Dec 18/97 (10,000-15,000)   10,925

Full figures of smiling Pinocchio (6") sitting on work bench looking up with surprised Figaro (2-1/2") standing by his side, key watercolor production background, Courvoisier label, CE/Dec 18/97 (25,000-35,000)   28,750

Pinocchio (5-3/4") bends (as hand holds back of suit) & pets happy Figaro (full figure, eyes closed, 3-1/2" length), Courvoisier airbrush background, CE/Dec 18/97 (5000-7000)   5520

Honest John (7-1/2") reaches for apple on ground & holds up his left hand to stop Pinocchio (full figure, back turned, 5"), matching watercolor production background of stone path & wall, cels are key to background but not to each other, stamps & notes, CE/Dec 18/97 (15,000-20,000)   17,250

Full figures of Jiminy Cricket standing on ocean floor facing right, tipping hat to small fish, 4", watercolor Courvoisier background & label, CE/Dec 18/97 (2000-3000)   2760

Full-figure front view of smiling Jiminy Cricket walking toward camera, 3-1/2", Courvoisier airbrush background & label, CE/Dec 18/97 (1500-2000)   3220

Full-figure rear view of standing Figaro turning to check fishing line tied to tail, 4", airbrushed Courvoisier background & label, S/Dec 19/97 (1200-1800)   1840

Full figure of Jiminy Cricket (4") floating in bottle & confronting angry sea gull (4"), airbrushed Courvoisier background of sea & sea gulls, S/Dec 19/97 (4000-6000)   3450

Full figure of Jiminy Cricket standing holding hat in hand, eyes closed, 3", airbrushed background & Courvoisier label, S/Dec 19/97 (1500-2500)   2300

6 fish swimming right amid bubbles & sea plants, sight 3-1/2 x 5-1/2", airbrushed Courvoisier background & label, S/Dec 19/97 (400-600) 632

Neck-up of alarmed Figaro in bed looking up & right, 1-1/2", airbrushed Courvoisier background, S/Dec 19/97 (800-1200)   1150

Full figure of happy Figaro walking to right & moth, 2-1/2", airbrushed Courvoisier background & label, S/Dec 19/97 (1200-1800)   3450

Full figure of surprised Pinocchio looking back while doing Russian dance, 4-1/2", airbrushed Courvoisier background & label, S/Dec 19/97 (3000-5000)   3450

Geppetto (7", needs restoration) stands in workshop holding candle high, Pinocchio (3") kneeling on floor smiles & looks up, surprised Figaro (full figure, 1-1/2") watches from bench; partial key production set-up with watercolor production background, S/Dec 19/97 (15,000-20,000)   14,950

Full figure of dapper smiling Jiminy Cricket standing facing right, bend at waist, holding umbrella; 3"; airbrushed Courvoisier background and label, S/Dec 19/97 (2000-3000)   2587

Full figure of worried Figaro sitting in high chair w/napkin around neck, looking down, 4", airbrushed Courvoisier background, WDP label, S/Dec 19/97 (1000-1500)   2300

Promotional cel of surprised Pinocchio (5-1/2") sitting in front of wall w/smiling Jiminy Cricket (1")

perched on toe, trimmed watercolor production
background, "to Erik O. Hansson ... Walt
Disney" on mat in studio artist's hand, WDP
label, S/Dec 19/97 (8000-10,000) 7475
Jiminy Cricket (1-1/2") sinks to bottom of sea as
a fish (1") watches, airbrushed Courvoisier
background, S/Dec 19/97 (1000-1500) 1610
Full figure of Gideon standing on one leg holding
pencil in right hand & pad of paper in left,
6-1/2", wood-veneer Courvoisier background
and label, S/Dec 19/97 (1200-1800) 1265
Key production set-up of Figaro sleeping in bed next
to sandbox, 9 x 11", watercolor production
background, WDP label, S/Dec 19/97
(6000-8000) 13,800
Full figure of Pinocchio high-stepping to left holding
book & apple in outstretched hands, 3 3/4",
Courvoisier wood-veneer background, label,
hand-lettered mat, SR/Spring/98
(4500-9000) 4180
Full figures of Pinocchio (6", being held by straps
by 2 hands) bending down to see Figaro
(jumping to left) & Jiminy Cricket, Courvoisier
watercolor background, SR/Spring/98 (8000-
12,000) 7000
Full-figure front view of Jiminy Cricket sitting on shelf,
looking up with mouth open, 3-1/8", color
print background, SR/Spring/98, 1940
(2800-3800) 3240
Full figure of Jiminy Cricket leaning to left to talk to
three fish while riding seahorse away from
camera as other fish watch, 7", undersea Courvoisier watercolor background w/original
bubble effects overlay & Courvoisier hand-
lettered mat & label, SR/Spring/98
(5000-9000) 5600
Full figure of seductive Cleo, 3-1/2", watercolor
display background, SR/Spring/98
(1500-2200) 1520
"Look, Figaro, the wishing star!" Geppetto in bed under
quilt looks out as starlight glows thru window, 5
3/8", 12-field cel, Courvoisier custom watercolor
display background. ct, SR/Spring/98 (1400-
1800) 2790
Full figure of Jiminy Cricket holding collapsed umbrella
& standing in neck of bottle floating in sea as two
angry sea gulls watch, complementary background
painting by Disney for Courvoisier, label, 6-1/2
x 8", VF, HL/Apr 25/98 (2000-2500) 2990
Full figure of Jiminy Cricket in threadbare clothes standing facing left on blade of grass under open
umbrella, complementary painted background as
prepared by Disney for Courvoisier, altered label,
3-3/4 x 2-1/2" cel, VF, HL/Apr 25/98
(2000-3000) 2415
Full figures of Geppetto walking puppet Pinocchio to
left as Figaro follows, complementary background painting of workshop floor, as prepared
by Disney for Courvoisier, mat signed by Walt Disney, 7-3/4 x 8" cels, F+, HL/Apr 25/98 (3000-
5000) 16,100

CELS – FULL FIGURE (also see MODEL ART)
Gideon pulled by cane, 6 x 5-1/2", CE/Dec 15/93
(800-1200) 460
Gideon, 5-1/2 x 6", CE/Dec 15/93 (800-1200) 345
Jiminy walking with umbrella, circa 1950, 4",
S/Dec 16/93 (400-600) 575
2 cels of Pinocchio & Sorcerer Mickey Mouse
produced by New York animation studio under
Disney supervision for film promoting *Pinocchio*
on home video, 6 x 3" & 5-1/2 x 4", VF+,
HL/Feb 26-27/94 (800-1200) 1540
Cleo, 5" long, CE/Jun 18/94 (700-900) 1495
Pinocchio (4") & Dutch doll puppet (5"),
CE/Jun 18/94 (3000-4000) 6670
Geppetto (6"), Jiminy & Figaro view Pinocchio (4-1/2")
sitting against jug amid paint cans, promotional
cel circa 1940s, CE/Jun 18/94
(2500-3500) 3680
Puppet Pinocchio (6 x 3-1/2") walks, curious Figaro
(3/4 x 2-1/2") follows, CE/Jun 18/94
(800-1200) 5520
Lampwick smokes cigar, 8-1/2 x 5", HL/Aug 21/94
(1500-2000) 1904
4-cel limited-edition portfolio: Geppetto & puppet
Pinocchio; Pinocchio & Dutch puppet;
Pinocchio & Foulfellow; seated Pinocchio &
Jiminy; laminated w/seal & labels, #269/275;
7 x 6-1/2", 7 x 9-1/2", 8-1/2 x 11", 9-1/2

x 4", VF+, HL/Aug 21/94 (3000-5000) 4144
Lampwick stands in leaning pose with cigar, 7-1/2
x 3-1/2", VF, HL/Aug 21/94 (1500-2000) 1344
4 limited-edition cels: Geppetto holding puppet Pinocchio; Pinocchio & Dutch girl puppet;
Honest John & Pinocchio; smiling Pinocchio
sitting w/Jiminy (who sits on match box),
9 x 4-1/2" to 9 x 11", all #126/275, with
seals, HL/Nov 13/94 (3000-5000) 4592
Pinocchio dances with 5 Russian puppets, 3-1/2"
and similar, CE/Dec 16/94 (1500-2000) 2990
Jiminy Cricket (3") stares at fish (2"); concept
drawing of underwater scene, pastel on
black paper; CE/Dec 16/94 (1000-1500) 2530
Publicity cel: Pinocchio, Geppetto, Jiminy, Cleo &
Figaro on raft, 4-1/2", CE/Dec 16/94 (2500-
3500) 2300
Jiminy Cricket in classic pose, 4", CE/Dec 16/94
(1500-2000) 3220
Gesturing Pinocchio with key animation drawing,
5-1/2", circa 1970s educational cel,
CE/Dec 16/94 (600-800) 863
Surprised Pinocchio walking, 3-3/4", circa 1970s
education cel, CE/Dec 16/94 (300-500) 460
Proud Jiminy stands facing right, showing off medal,
1958 promotional cel, 6-1/8", 16-field, cel
rippling, ct, SR/Spring/95 (1200-2200) 1780
Smiling Pinocchio walks toward left, 7-1/2", 12-field,
some rippling & surface wear, ct, SR/Spring/95
(3000-5000) 4840
Angry Figaro stands w/paw upraised, 4-1/2 x
3-1/2", VF, HL/Apr 23/95 (1200-1600) 1680
3 marionette can-can dancers; cel of curtain
backdrop; 7-1/2 x 9", w/personal note,
VG, HL/Apr 23/95 (1000-1500) 2016
Publicity cel of Pinocchio (3-3/4") sitting with
Jiminy (on matchbox, 1-1/2") by 2 paint
cans, CE/Jun 9/95 (2500-3500) 2300
Downcast Geppetto carrying armload of firewood,
8 x 5", HL/Aug 6/95 (1800-2200) 1456
Pinocchio (with donkey ears) braying, 4 x 4-1/2",
HL/Aug 6/95 (2500-3500) 2688
Jiminy sits with hat over one eye & collar undone,
2-1/2 x 2-1/2", HL/Nov 19/95 (900-1200) 1150
Jiminy Cricket peers thru glasses, 3 x 2-1/2",
HL/Nov 19/95 (1000-1500) 1955
Pinocchio walks w/apple & book, looking over
left shoulder, 2 x 2-1/2", HL/Nov 19/95
(1000-1500) 2990
Curious Figaro in mid-step, 1-1/2 x 1-3/4",
HL/Nov 19/95 (700-1000) 1150
Donkey-eared Pinocchio hands kindling to Geppetto,
7-1/2 x 8", HL/Apr 28/96 (2500-3000) 2530
Pinocchio lying on stomach facing right with limbs
spread, 4"; from *Sleeping Beauty*: 3 happy birds
standing, 2-1/2"; CE/Jun 20/96 (600-800) 1380
Promotional cels: full figures of Pinocchio (3") and Lampwick (3-1/2") eating from pile of candy; Pinocchio (3") & Jiminy Cricket (3/4") sitting
outside Geppetto's house, CE/Jun 20/96
(1500-2000) 2070
Large image of flirtatious Cleo veiling her face with fin
amid bubbles, as prepared by Courvoisier, 4-3/4
x 5-1/2", F+, HL/Oct 6/96 (1200-1600) 2128
Figaro stands facing right & yawns, 2-1/4 x 2",
VF, HL/Oct 6/96 (750-1000) 863
Worried donkey-eared Pinocchio sits with hands
on sides of head, 6-1/2", CE/Dec 12/96
(2000-3000) 3795
Flirtatious Cleo looking left & up amid bubbles, 4",
S/Dec 14/96 (1000-1500) 1840
Figaro sits in chair, napkin around neck, looking
back to right, 4", S/Dec 14/96 (1200-1800) 1610
Surprised Jiminy Cricket walking to right, 3-1/2", Cour-
voisier label, S/Dec 14/96
(1200-1800) 2587
2 cels of Dutch girl marionette, 4-1/2" & 2"; color
model drawing of the marionette, sight 6-1/2
x 5-1/2"; cel of Figaro, 2-1/2";
CLA/Jun 7/97 (1000-1500) 1955
Jiminy Cricket stands bent forward at waist, looking
down, right hand out, 1-1/2 x 1-1/2", VF+,
HL/Nov 16/97 (900-1200) 1955
Surprised Jiminy Cricket stands looking right, 5 x 3",
VF, HL/Nov 16/97 (1800-2200) 3393
Smiling Jiminy Cricket walking to left, trimmed &
mounted inside hand-made Christmas card,
3-1/4 x 3 cel, VF, HL/Nov 16/97
(1800-2200) 2530

Jiminy Cricket stands facing left, holding umbrella
& looking up with mouth open, 3 x 2-3/4",
VF, HL/Nov 16/97 (1200-1600) 2300
Geppetto, Pinocchio & early Jiminy Cricket standing
[for color model or publication?], 6-3/4 x
6-1/2", VF, HL/Nov 16/97 (900-1200) 1093
Full figure [minus area covered by Geppetto's hand] of
puppet Pinocchio sitting facing left, 4-1/2 x 4-
1/4", VF, HL/Nov 16/97 (1000-1500) 2530
Promotional cel of smiling Pinocchio walking left,
7", S/Dec 19/97 (1500-2500) 1380
Promotional cel of smiling Pinocchio sitting looking
up & to left, 5", S/Dec 19/97 (4000-6000) 3737
Smiling Pinocchio walks left, *A Lesson In Honesty*
1978 educational film, 4-1/4", 12-field cel with
airbrush & drybrush effects, SR/Spring/98
(300-600) 300
CELS – PARTIAL FIGURE (also see MODEL ART)
Near-full-figure promotional cel of Pinocchio
walking, 10", circa 1940s, CE/Jun 18/94
(1500-2000) 2185
Smiling Blue Fairy facing right & gesturing, 8-1/2
x 5-1/2", VF, HL/Aug 21/94 (2500-3500) 9520
"Father! Here I am!" Arm raised, Pinocchio stands
amid fish, 4-1/2 x 8", VF, HL/Apr 23/95
(3000-3500) 4480
Awed Pinocchio & Figaro stand staring at each
other, 6", CE/Jun 9/95 (3000-4000) 5520
Portrait cel of Coachman whispering to his right,
right hand shielding mouth, 7-1/2 x 7-1/2",
VF, HL/Aug 6/95 (1500-2000) 1232
Foulfellow & Gideon lean to their left together &
listen, 9 x 12-1/4", VF, HL/Aug 6/95
(2500-3500) 4704
Waist-up of Lampwick facing right, holding pool
cue & cigar, 5", 12-field, some lifting paint,
SR/Spring/96 (800-1400) 970
Close-up of smiling Jiminy Cricket (3 x 4-1/2")
leaning against figure of singer from music
box (6-1/2"), S/Jun 19/96 (2000-3000) 3162
Near-full-figure large image of kneeling Pinocchio
as donkey tying tail [to rock], 6 x 5-1/2", VF,
HL/Apr 25/98 (3000-4000) 3680
Large-image portrait of smiling Figaro facing left,
1940s, unidentified indoor background,
restored, VF, HL/Apr 25/98 (800-1000) 863
CONCEPT AND INSPIRATIONAL ART
Inspirational sketch of Jiminy Cricket among
carvings, 1-1/2", CE/Jun 18/94 (500-700) 460
Watercolor character study by Joe Grant of Stromboli
standing working two puppets, 4-3/4" on 9-3/4
x 9-3/4" sheet, SR/Fall/94 (900-1500) 830
8 sheets of character studies: Lampwick, Geppetto,
Coachman, unnamed boy; 5 x 4-1/2" to
6-1/2 x 8", HL/Nov 13/94 (500-700) 392
Geppetto's storefront in winter, Gustav Tenggren
inspirational sketch, watercolor on paper,
inscribed "Tenggren", CE/Dec 16/94
(9000-12,000) 21,850
4 pieces of pre-production artwork: graphite-&-colored-
pencil drawing of children dumping medicine over
cliff, signed by Phil Eastman; graphite drawing of
boys defacing school; 2 atmospheric undersea
watercolor & oil paintings; S/Dec 17/94
(800-1200) 862
6 pages of character studies of marionettes; 5-1/2
x 4-1/2" to 9-1/2 x 11"; pencil, watercolor
& conté crayon on animation sheets; some
are stamped, HL/Apr 23/95 (600-900) 840
6 finished character studies of Cleo, 4-1/2 x 3" to
8 x 9", colored & black pencil & colored pastel
on animation sheets, F-VF, HL/Apr 23/95
(800-1200) 1344
11 sheets of drawings of sea creatures by Albert
Hurter, 2-1/2 x 9-1/2" to 7-1/2 x 10",
F-VF, HL/Apr 23/95 (1200-2000) 1904
Watercolor renderings of Pinocchio (3-1/3"), Stromboli
(4-1/2"), Geppetto (4"), & Jiminy (4") matted
together on board, S/Jun 10/95 (300-500) 345
Watercolor & ink designs of Jiminy, Geppetto, Stromboli, & Pinocchio wearing Santa hat
& bowing, unknown source, 1 to 2-1/2",
on board, S/Jun 10/95 (200-400) 575
4 sheets of polished study drawings: Gideon and Foulfellow, Pinocchio, 4 Dutch marionettes
in Stromboli's theater, 6 x 6-1/2" to 9-1/2
x 10-1/2", HL/Apr 28/96 (900-1200) 805
Colored concept sketch of happy Geppetto dancing
with broom, 6 x 5-1/4", Originally released by

Courvoisier, with monogram seal & debossed
stamp, SR/Fall/96 (400-700)   810
Concept painting of 8 seahorses (4 finished including
2 as zebra & donkey), watercolor & pencil on
15-1/2 x 12-1/2" sheet, wear & discoloration,
spotting, trace of vertical fold, SR/Fall/96
(200-500)   200
Design drawing of frog orchestra wind-up toy,
colored conté crayon on animation sheet,
10-1/2 x 8", VF, HL/Feb 23/97 (300-500)   489
Rendering of marionette Russian snow scene of snow
princess fleeing wolves by Gustav Tenggren,
watercolor on heavyweight paper, 7-1/4 x
9-1/2"; detailed color model drawings of
marionette wolf & horse, 6 x 6-1/2" & 4-1/2
x 9-1/2", HL/May 3/97 (12,000-16,000)   9775
Concept drawing of Geppetto's workshop-home
by Gustav Tenggren, sight 6-1/4 x 10-1/2",
CLA/Jun 7/97 (5000-7000)   8625
Concept drawing of village by Gustav Tenggren, sight
8-1/2 x 12", CLA/Jun 7/97 (3000-5000)   6325
Signed concept drawing of village by Gustav Tenggren,
sight 12-3/4 x 6", CLA/Jun 7/97
(3000-5000)   2875
Signed concept drawing of village by Gustav Tenggren,
sight 8 x 8", CLA/Jun 7/97 (3000-4000)   4140
2 concept drawings of village, sight 5 x 4-1/2" &
5 x 3-1/2", CLA/Jun 7/97 (1500-2000)   2070
Signed concept drawing of village by Gustav Tenggren,
sight 9 x 9", CLA/Jun 7/97 (3000-5000)   4830
Pan concept drawing of Geppetto's workshop-home
by Gustav Tenggren, sight 9-1/4 x 17",
CLA/Jun 7/97 (8000-10,000)   16,100
Humorous full-figure early character study by Albert
Hurter of Geppetto standing working on marionette, 4-1/4 x 2-1/2", VF, HL/Nov 16/97
(400-600)   345
Inspirational sketch of Pleasure Island, color graphite
on paper, 10-1/2 x 14", signed by Carl Perkins,
CE/Dec 18/97 (2000-3000)   1725
Signed painting by Gustav Tenggren of grim Geppetto
carrying lifeless Pinocchio out of sea, watercolor
& india ink on heavyweight paper, 10-1/2 x 14",
VF+, HL/Apr 25/98 (12,000-16,000)   39,100

DYE-TRANSFER PRINTS
Full figure of ebullient Jiminy standing on sea bottom
facing right, 10-1/4 x 9-1/4", SR/Fall/94
(300-600)   350
Full figure of surprised Pinocchio sitting on work table,
looking at Jiminy standing on his foot, 10-1/8
x 7-5/8", SR/Fall/95 (300-600)   300

LAYOUT ART (also see STORY ART/TITLE ART)
Publicity layout drawing: Pinocchio under sea
with Monstro, production notes, 9",
S/Dec 16/93 (2000-3000)   2070
Special-effects layout drawing of Gideon and
Foulfellow, 7-1/2 x 8-1/2", studio note,
VF, HL/Apr 10/94 (500-700)   1008
Ferry of boys arriving at Pleasure Island, colored
pencil layout drawing, 6-1/2 x 11", studio
note, VF+, HL/Apr 10/94 (700-1000)   560
Layout sketch of Geppetto & Figaro sleeping in
bed, F, HL/Apr 10/94 (200-400)   532
Background layout drawing of boat interior, 11-1/2 x
15", 2 camera fields marked, HL/Nov 13/94
(600-900)   1008
6 atmospheric layout drawings of Geppetto's
boat & interior of Monstro, 8 x 14" to
12 x 15", HL/Nov 13/94 (700-1000)   1680
Two photostat layout drawings of Geppetto's work
bench: one developmental, one final; 14 x 11",
some edge wear, SR/Spring/95 (300-600)   480
"Walt Disney Presents" title layout drawing, black
pencil on 12-field sheet, SR/Fall/96
(500-1000)   680
Layout drawing of inside of Stromboli's wagon,
sight 12-1/2 x 15-1/2", CLA/Jun 7/97
(1500-2000)   1495
Key layout drawing of Geppetto's boat [inside Monstro],
31 x 12", CLA/Jun 7/97 (2000-3000)   1955
Original production layout of Geppetto's workshop
exterior, sight 12-1/2 x 15-1/2",
CE/Dec 18/97 (3000-4000)   5520

MODEL ART (also see ANIMATION DRAWINGS, CELS - FULL FIGURE, CONCEPT & INSPIRATIONAL ART)
Full-figure large-image model cel of Geppetto,
10 x 5", HL/Aug 21/94 (1000-1500)   1680
3 photostatic model sheets: "Cricket Heads," "Ship

Models Made by Geppetto," "Geppetto's Boat,"
all 14 x 11", some wrinkling, SR/Spring/95
(300-600)   420
Large-image full-figure model cel of suave Jiminy Crick-
et, 5-1/2 x 3-1/2", HL/Aug 6/95
(1200-1600)   2688
Classic model cel of smiling Pinocchio sitting,
6 x 5", VF, HL/Aug 6/95 (3000-3500)   4144
Model cel: Figaro yawns in bed, 6 x 6", F,
HL/Aug 6/95 (1500-2000)   1008
Full-figure model cel of Cleo, 3 x 4", HL/Nov 19/95
(1000-1500)   3220
Full-figure frontal model cel of smiling Jiminy
Cricket walking, 6-1/2 x 3-1/2",
HL/Nov 19/95 (1200-1600)   3220
Full-figure model cel of coy Cleo, 3-1/2 x 3-1/4",
HL/Apr 28/96 (1000-1500)   1265
Full-figure color model cel of peeved Figaro, 3-1/2
x 3-1/2", HL/Apr 28/96 (1000-1500)   1380
Animator's maquette of smiling Figaro sitting up,
5", S/Jun 19/96 high (2000-3000)   1725
4 original photostat model sheets: Pinocchio, lobsters,
Foulfellow, Gideon, 13-7/8 x 11", some wear,
repaired edge tears, SR/Fall/96 (200-400)   430
Full-figure color model cel of smiling Pinocchio
holding apple & standing w/Geppetto
who holds book in both hands, 7 x 7",
HL/Oct 6/96 (2000-2500)   5060
Full-figure model cel of smiling Pinocchio walking
to left, 4-3/4 x 3", VF, HL/Feb 23/97
(3000-4000)   3910
Model sheet of Blue Fairy, original studio print,
12-1/2 x 10", some wear, SR/Spring/97
(200-400)   310
Full-figure model drawing of Pinocchio in blanket,
7", inscribed "model for blanket...",
CLA/Jun 7/97 (800-1200)   518
Original model sheet of Geppetto's cuckoo clocks
attributed to Albert Hurter, graphite & color
pencil on trimmed paper pasted on large post-
board, sight 16-1/2 x 18-1/2", CLA/Jun 7/97
(5000-7000)   13,800
35 photostat model sheets: 19 showing development
of Figaro, Gideon, 5 of Foulfellow, 2 of
Geppetto, Blue Fairy, 2 of Pinocchio, early
character, Gendarme, 4 of octopi,
S/Jun 21/97 (800-1200)   1725
4 vintage detailed photostatic model sheets: front stoop
of Geppetto's house; his workbench, including
Pinocchio & Cleo; various scenes of his home
inside Monstro; & several designs of brush
holders & candlesticks; approx. 13-1/2 x 11",
SR/Fall/97 (300-500)   280
Full-figure model drawing of defiant Lampwick
standing holding cigar, 7-1/4 x 5-1/2",
F+, HL/Nov 16/97 (400-600)   575
10 drawings (mostly color models): Coachman, 5 of
Jiminy Cricket, 4 of Geppetto, each 10 x 12";
file folder w/17 photostat model sheets of 'Kid
Suggestions'/Pleasure Island, each 11 x 14",
hole-punched & clipped in, 10 of which are
different, S/Dec 19/97 (1200-1800)   2185
Animator's model sheet of Jiminy Cricket, 4" &
smaller, CE/Dec 18/97 (2000-3000)   1495
Original studio stat model sheet of "Cricket Heads,"
14 x 11", SR/Spring/98 (200-400)   430

STORY ART
Dancing toy soldier, story sketch, pastel on paper,
7-3/4 x 5-3/4", CE/Dec 15/93 (500-700)   632
Pinocchio walks with Jiminy, story sketch released
by Courvoisier, 7-1/4 x 9-3/4",
CE/Dec 15/93 (800-1200)   920
Figaro swings from bucket, story sketch, 5-3/4 x
7-1/2", CE/Dec 15/93 (400-600)   552
Figaro's tail is tied, story sketch, 6 x 7-1/2",
CE/Dec 15/93 (400-600)   345
Figaro tries to wiggle off string, story sketch, 5-3/4
x 7-1/2", CE/Dec 15/93 (400-600)   345
Story sketch: 7" Honest John takes 4" Pinocchio's
pulse, graphite & white paint on paper,
©1939 "Walt Disney Prod." stamp, Courvoisier
label, S/Dec 16/93 (1800-2200)   2588
2 storyboard drawings of Pinocchio as real boy: waking
up, graphite w/red & blue crayon borders on
paper; Geppetto lifting him off bed, graphite &
yellow pencil w/red crayon borders on paper,
production information, S/Dec 16/93
(1200-1600)   1150
3 storyboard drawings: Figaro & Jiminy riding

waves on Cleo's fishbowl (2); Monstro in
surf; graphite on paper, 3rd w/red crayon
borders, S/Dec 16/93 (1500-2000)   1150
Story or character study of Jiminy Cricket, 5 x
3-1/2", VF, HL/Apr 10/94 (300-500)   896
Pinocchio & Pleasure Island pals, early story
drawing by Earl Hurd, 5-1/2 x 7", VF,
HL/Apr 10/94 (600-800)   336
Jiminy walks away in rain, 4 x 1", storyboard
sketch, CE/Jun 18/94 (500-700)   1840
2 sequential story sketches of Pinocchio and
Lampwick meeting on way to Pleasure
Island, 6 x 9", HL/Nov 13/94 (600-800)   616
Story painting of Pinocchio wandering along ocean
floor, 6 x 8", pencil & watercolor on heavyweight paper, HL/Nov 13/94 (400-600)   1344
2 story drawings: Pinocchio with rock tied to
tail amid seahorses, 6 x 5" & 7 x 6",
HL/Apr 23/95 (1000-1500)   840
Story drawing of Pinocchio meeting lobster on sea
floor, 9 x 10", HL/Apr 23/95 (600-900)   672
2 storyboards of Figaro fishing w/his tail, 3" & 4",
S/Jun 10/95 (300-500)   747
2 storyboard drawings: Coachman's wagon filled with
children, 'For Bustin A Light' across top, 4-1/2
x 6"; Lampwick (4") talking to Pinocchio (3"), 'If
You See A Fat Policeman' across top; S/Jun
10/95 (400-600)   862
2 storyboard drawings of Figaro in bucket, 4"
each, S/Jun 10/95 (300-500)   517
Story drawing of Geppetto hugging donkey-eared Pinocchio as Figaro jumps onto barrel,
5-1/2 x 7", orange & black pencil on story
sheet, HL/Nov 19/95 (500-700)   1495
Story drawing of Geppetto aboard boat [inside Monstro],
pencil on separate sheet laid into story sheet, 5-
1/2 x 7", HL/Oct 6/96 (300-400)   460
Story drawing of angry Monstro turning on top
of water, 5-1/2 x 9-1/4", HL/Oct 6/96
(800-1200)   1150
Captioned story sketch of Figaro hiding in shoe, 5-3/4
x 4-1/2" sheet taped to 12-field sheet, released
by Courvoisier, "WDP Original" & debossed
copyright stamp, SR/Spring/97 (500-900)   520
Storyboard drawing: close-up of worried donkey-eared
Pinocchio (6") & Jiminy (1-1/2") talking, stamp,
CE/Dec 18/97 (800-1200)   1495
8 story & layout drawings of Pinocchio & Geppetto;
red, blue & black pencil, brown conté crayon
on animation sheets; 5-1/2 x 4-1/2" to 9 x 9";
overall VG-F, HL/Apr 25/98 (500-1000)   3220
Story drawing of angry Jiminy Cricket (full figure)
flicking cigar out of Pinocchio's mouth, 7-1/4
x 11", VF, HL/Apr 25/98 (900-1200)   1265
2 layout or story drawings: fish being swept into angry
Monstro's mouth, fish & raft go down Monstro's
throat; pencil & conté crayon on animation
sheets; 11 x 14", 10-1/2 x 14"; F;
HL/Apr 25/98 (1000-1500)   4600
Storyboard drawing of Lampwick on knees yelling
downward, conté crayon & white tempera on
animation sheet, 4-1/2 x 6-1/4", VF, HL/Apr
25/98 (300-500)   345
2 story drawings: sad Figaro sitting in high chair, Geppetto on raft trying to hook large fish; 5 x 4",
7 x 9"; F+; HL/Apr 25/98 (600-900)   1380

POCAHONTAS (1995)
CEL SET-UPS
"Two Worlds": limited-edition cel of Pocahontas
& John Smith kneeling facing each other,
touching palms, 11 x 15-1/2", #86/500,
color print background, VF+, HL/Nov 16/97
(1000-1500)   460
All other items in this section were auctioned at
Sotheby's, February 24, 1996.
These include original art actually used in the making
of *Pocahontas*. Each set-up featured a production background (except for three noted lots) accompanied by
character and effects cels specially created by artists in
the Ink & Paint department at the Walt Disney Studios
in Burbank, California. The basis for the cels were original animation drawings rendered by Disney animators
and used in the production of the film. In many cases
set-ups also included production overlays/underlays. No
original production cels were created in the making of
Pocahontas. Each set-up was matted and framed.

Full-figure rear view of John Smith walking toward

James and the Giant Peach: Fully armatured production Spider puppet (7 x 10") w/15 faces, sheet featuring various spider designs (24 x 26-3/4"), replica of spider's web nailed onto board (9-3/4 x 18-1/2"); (4000-6000)   10,350

The Jungle Book: Studio publicity cel of Baloo holding Mowgli, jungle master tempera background, 11 x 15", studio notes, w/matching animation drawing, VF+, HL/Apr 10/94 (4000-6000)   5600

The Jungle Book: Pan watercolor concept painting of 2 monkeys carrying Mowgli (5") off, signed by Walter Peregoy, S/Dec 17/94 (2000-3000)   2875

The Jungle Book: Pan production set-up of Baloo (6") picking Mowgli (4") up from scene where Baloo 'comes back to life', with pan watercolor production background from scene where Rama examines bundle in front of den, S/Dec 17/94 (8000-10,000)   9775

The Jungle Book: Full figures of smiling Mowgli (3") sitting in leaves under tree looks up as Baloo (7") stands watching, matching watercolor production background, S/Jun 21/97 (7000-9000)   23,000

The Jungle Book: Waist-up front view of worried Baloo standing w/paws up, looking down, 8-1/2", matching gouache key master background w/filtered jungle light, 16-field, SR/Fall/95 (2500-4500)   3680

The Jungle Book: Full figure of Shere Khan (eyes closed, 5-3/4") lying on ground talking to suspended Kaa (half image, 4-5/8"), 16-field 2-cel set-up w/color print jungle background, SR/Spring/97 (1200-1600)   1430

The Jungle Book: Full figures of angry Baloo (7-3/4") sitting facing right, holding squirming Mowgli off ground around waist, photographic color print jungle background, SR/Spring/95 (1100-1600)   1340

Lady and the Tramp: Tramp (4") puts left front paw on delighted Tony (6") as Lady (4" long) & Joe (behind dutch door, 3-3/4") watch, hand-prepared background by a gallery, CLA/Jun 7/97 (4000-6000)   3680

The Jungle Book: Head of angry Bagheera amid temple ruins, 5", key watercolor production background, CE/Dec 16/94 (3000-4000)   5175

Lady and the Tramp: Pan preliminary art of Trusty's, Lady's & Jock's homes, 12 x 37", watercolor on heavy paper applied to board, S/Jun 21/97 (2000-3000) 5175

Lady and the Tramp: Tramp with book in mouth meets professor (bent at waist), master background of Lady's front yard, studio notes, 10 x 14", VF, HL/Aug 21/94 (6000-8000) 6720

Lady and the Tramp: Tempera original background of family home with two complementary cels of Lady & Tramp trimmed to outline & mounted on overlay cel, 10 x 23", restored, VF, HL/Apr 10/94 (8000-12,000) 15,120

Lady and the Tramp: Near-full figures of Lady (3") in mid-stride and Tramp (4-1/2") standing on sidewalk, watercolor production background from 1950s short, CE/Jun 9/95 (4000-6000) 6325

Lady and the Tramp: Long pan watercolor production background of zoo w/cel of Lady (3") & key cel of Tramp (4"), S/Jun 17/94 (20,000-25,000) 23,000

Lady and the Tramp: Pan production set-up of Tramp (4 x 6"), Pedro (2"), Boris (5-1/2"), Peg (6 x 7-1/2"), & shocked Lady (6-1/2") in pound, pan watercolor production background, S/Jun 21/97 (12,000-15,000) 11,500

Lady and the Tramp: Full figures of Lady sitting up w/ball in her mouth (5"), happy Tramp lying down (4 x 5"), Trusty (near-full figure rear view, 6" w/o tail) sitting; Jock (4") in sweater standing; watercolor production background of porch, S/Dec 14/96 (12,000-15,000)   23,000

Lady and the Tramp: Near-full figure of eager Lady rounding corner of house, 2-1/2", matching pan watercolor production background, S/Jun 21/97 (12,000-15,000)   11,500

Lady and the Tramp: Tramp (5") eats spaghetti as Lady (3-1/2") watches admiringly, watercolor production background, mat signed "Walt Disney", Courvoisier label, CE/Jun 20/96 (25,000-35,000) 57,500

Lady and the Tramp: Tramp & muzzled Lady look into pond at zoo, 10-1/4 x 20-1/2", matching master background (tempera on background sheet), HL/Nov 19/95 (7000-10,000)   8050

Lady and the Tramp: Full figure of Lady (3-1/2"), Tramp (5"), & Jock (3-1/2") sitting in yard, watercolor preliminary background, mat inscribed "...Walt Disney", CE/Jun 20/96 (4000-6000)   6900

Lady and the Tramp: Full figure of somber Lady standing in doorway facing left, looking up, 4-3/8", detailed gouache key master background of kitchen, set-up is 20-3/4 x 9-3/4", SR/Fall/97 (7000-11,000)   11,100

Lady and the Tramp: Hips-up of curious Lady standing on hind legs inspecting table of gifts, 6", key gouache master background, crease across lower body, ct, SR/Spring/95 (7000-12,000) 9600

Lady and the Tramp: Knees-up of Joe (eyes closed) facing right, stirring pot on stove, 8", key gouache pan master background, SR/Spring/97 (12,000-18,000)   did not sell

The Lion King: Zebras splash thru river, S/Feb 11/95 (2500-3000)   9775

The Lion King: Timon closes Pumbaa's mouth: "Not in front of the kids!", S/Feb 11/95 (3500-4500)   14,950

The Lion King: Pumbaa & Timon charge mass of fighting lions & hyenas, S/Feb 11/95 (2500-3500)   4025

The Lion King: Circle of Life Continues: Rafiki presents cub as adult Simba, Nala, Pumbaa, Timon & Zazu look on, specially created art, S/Feb 11/95 (6000-8000) 37,375

The Lion King: Close-up of Rafiki presenting infant Simba on Pride Rock, S/Feb 11/95 (3000-5000)   19,550

The Little Mermaid: 4-cel setup of Flounder tugging Ariel & barrel (2 x 2") out to Prince Eric's ship, matching watercolor background, certificate of authenticity, S/Dec 17/94 (2500-3500) 2587

The Little Mermaid: 4-cel pan set-up: Ursula ordering Flotsam & Jetsam after Eric, watercolor production background, 8", S/Dec 16/93 (7000-9000) 10,350

Make Mine Music: Inquisitive Peter holding Ivan by nap of neck and Sasha in palm, 8 x 10-1/2", w/master background (tempera on board), HL/Nov 19/95 (3500-4500) 3450

Mary Poppins: Pearly Band marching & playing, 4-1/2" x 9", pan gouache & pastel production background, S/Jun 10/95 (3000-5000) 3450

Peter Pan: Pan production set-up from Indian ceremony scene of Tiger Lily (5") & Peter (5-1/2") sitting cross-legged, water-color production background of Lost Boys lair, S/Dec 17/94 (20,000-25,000)   24,150

Peter Pan: Happy Peter (9") sits on rock with Tinker Bell (1-1/2") on his knee, watercolor production background, inscribed "To Jim, my best, Walt Disney" on mat, S/Jun 17/94 (7000-9000) 14,950

Peter Pan: Capt. Hook (6-1/2") anxiously watches Tinker Bell (2-1/2") walk across map, watercolor production background with applied production overlay (map), S/Jun 19/96 (10,000-12,000)   16,100

Peter Pan: George & Mary Darling, Wendy & Nana watch from dormer window as smiling Peter Pan flies away, matching master background (tempera on background sheet), 11 x 15", VF+, HL/Apr 28/96 (10,000-12,000)   15,525

Peter Pan: Full figures of Peter (3-1/2"), Wendy (2"), John (1-1/2"), & Michael (1-1/4") flying over Tower Bridge, watercolor production background, "To...Walt Disney" on mat, S/Dec 14/96 (10,000-15,000)   29,900

Peter Pan: Concept painting by Mary Blair of Lost Boys being led as captives to Indian village on cliff, tempera on board, 8-1/2 x 11", VF+, HL/Apr 28/96 (1500-2000)   3680

crowd & Susan Constant (2000-3000) 4312

"I've heard some amazing stories about him" Close-up of admiring Thomas (1000-1500) 2587

John Smith standing atop cannon being hoisted aboard (1500-2000) 3105

Gov. Ratcliffe strides aboard as townspeople wave & rat scurries up rope (2000-3000) 2587

John Smith swings on rope towards deck in storm (2000-3000) 1840

John Smith & Thomas struggle with loose cannon in storm (2000-3000) 1610

John Smith fights to hold onto rope as waves crash over him (1500-2000) 1380

Ben, Lon & Roy pull Thomas & John Smith out of water (1000-1500) 805

"Trouble on deck?" Front view of Gov. Ratcliffe holding Percy, Wiggins holding lantern & umbrella (2500-3500) 2415

"A stirring oration, Sir..." Wiggins holding lantern & umbrella, rigging in background (1500-2000) 1150

"Let us hope so." Wiggins holding lantern & umbrella for Gov. Ratcliffe & Percy at cabin door (2500-3500) 2300

"I'll need those witless peasants to dig up my gold..." Close-up of Gov. Ratcliffe talking to smiling Percy (2000-3000) 2070

Indians canoe thru tunnel of trees toward shafts of sunlight (2000-3000) 5750

Indians spear fish as two canoes row by (3000-4000) 6612

Child chases crow as crops are harvested (includes production overlays/underlays applied to non-production background) (2500-3500) 1955

Indians carry harvest down hill toward river & village (3000-4000) 6325

Kekata creates rabbit from campfire smoke for children (1500-2000) 1380

Excited child pulls Grandmother from village (2000-3000) 1840

Front view of Powhatan standing in first of 5 warrior canoes (1500-2000) 1610

Kekata & Powhatan: "Your return has brought much joy to the village." (1500-2000) 1150

Pocahontas stands at cliff edge watching Nakoma's canoe in river (3000-5000) 9200

Nakoma calling from canoe (1500-2000) 1610

Pocahontas turns back from forest as Meeko & Flit continue (4000-6000) 14,375

Happy Meeko dives off cliff as disbelieving Flit watches (1500-2000) 1150

Smiling Meeko in mid-dive (2000-3000) 3737

Panicked Meeko holding Flit in mid-dive (2000-3000) 1610

Pocahontas spits water into Nakoma's face (2500-3500) 4600

Close-up of sputtering Flit resurfacing (1500-2000) 2875

Close-up of happy Flit hovering [before attacking Meeko] (1500-2000) 2185

Slide view of Meeko struggling to climb onto overturned canoe (1500-2000) 1725

Flit underwater w/beak stuck in canoe (1000-1500) 805

Nakoma & Pocahontas' canoe (w/Meeko & Flit) approaches shore & village gathering (3000-4000) 7187

Powhatan praises Kocoum: "Tonight we will feast in his honor." (1500-2000) 1265

Close-up of Nakoma, Pocahontas & third Indian cheering (2500-3500) 2875

Powhatan & Pocahontas walk to longhouse: "I want to hear everything..." (2000-3000) 1610

Close-up of Happy Flit hovering inside longhouse (1500-2000) 2300

Powhatan talks to Pocahontas in longhouse w/hands on her shoulders (1500-2000) 1150

Pocahontas & Powhatan at longhouse's entrance: "But he's so serious." (2000-3000) 2875

Meeko stands in bowl on shelf imitating Kocoum as disgusted Flit watches (2500-3500) 2875

Surprised Pocahontas catches Meeko after he falls from shelf (2500-3500) 2875

Dazed Flit pops out of cracked bottom of overturned bowl (1500-2000) 1500

Close-up of Powhatan & Pocahontas walking together in forest: "It's time to take your place among our people." (2500-3500) 2300

Powhatan places necklace around Pocahontas' neck (2500-3500) 4887

Close-up of 2 otters in water (1000-2500) 1150

Pocahontas in canoe as Meeko jumps aboard from shore (2000-4000) 3105

Happy Meeko in bow of canoe as Flit flies ahead (2500-3500) 2875

Long shot of Pocahontas & Meeko in canoe (& Flit) coming to river bend (3500-4500) 10,925

Close-up of eager Pocahontas paddling w/happy Meeko & Flit (2500-3500) 20,700

Pocahontas & Meeko in canoe going thru rapids accompanied by Flit & otter (2000-3000) 1610

Animals on shore watch canoe (3000-4000) 6325

Pocahontas sings to Meeko as she touches his chin: "Can I ignore the sound of distant drumming?" (3000-4000) 3737

Beaver builds lodge w/canoe gliding behind waterfall in background (2000-3000) 1610

Frightened Meeko turns around as waterfall looms (2000-3000) 2587

Close-up of thrilled Pocahontas with canoe's stern tilted up (3000-4000) 5462

View at top of waterfall as Flit hovers excitedly (2000-3000) 2185

Pocahontas sings at bottom of waterfall as terrified Meeko clings to top of her head (3000-4000) 6900

Overhead view of Pocahontas (arms outstretched) & Meeko in canoe (3000-4000) 4312

Canoe touches rainbow as animals on shore watch (3500-4500) 6325

Front-view close-up of Pocahontas & Meeko in canoe, Flit hovering w/rainbow in background (4000-6000) 18,400

Canoe drifts to opening in Grandmother Willow's fronds (3000-4000) 6900

Close-up of Pocahontas looking up at willow fronds as Meeko smiles (2500-3500) 2185

2 owls on branch stare (1000-1500) 2185

Close-up of Grandmother Willow speaking (2000-3000) 1840

Long shot of Pocahontas & animals sitting before Grandmother Willow (2500-3500) 5750

Pocahontas describes dream as Meeko, Flit & bunny listen (3500-4500) 9775

Pocahontas stands as animals watch: "I hear the wind." (3000-4000) 4025

Long shot of Pocahontas & animals standing in front of Grandmother Willow looking outward: "...You will understand." (2000-3000) 2070

Pocahontas & animals stand before Grandmother Willow: "...Listen to your heart." (2000-3000) 2587

Pocahontas, Meeko & Flit look out over top of Grandmother Willow (2500-3500) 17,250

Susan Constant's sails above the trees (2500-3500) 3737

2 set-ups: Wiggins brushes Percy's head inside cabin; close-up of Ratcliffe (3000-4000) 2415

2 set-ups: smiling Wiggins holding gift baskets; Ratcliffe pulls map from slot (3000-4000) 3450

John Smith & Governor Ratcliffe discuss disembarking: "Give the order." (2000-3000) 1610

Close-up of Ratcliffe holding wine glass: "The men like Smith, don't they?" (1500-2000) 1840

Back of Ratcliffe as he looks into mirror at his & Wiggins' reflections (1500-2000) 1150

Wiggins attaches Ratcliffe's belt & sword (1500-2000) 1150

Long shot of John Smith, Thomas, Ben & Lon rowing dinghy to shore (1500-2500) 1840

Medium long shot of Pocahontas, Meeko & Flit running thru forest (3000-4000) 8625

Meeko runs thru forest with Flit beside him (2000-3000) 2300

Smith (standing), Thomas, Ben & Lon rowing in dinghy & inspecting forest (2000-3000) 2300

2 set-ups: Pocahontas peering over rock; Smith jumping out of dinghy (3000-4000) 2415

Smith climbs tree toward Pocahontas (behind ledge) as Thomas pulls rope (2500-3500) 6612

Worried Pocahontas pulls Meeko's tail as he walks forward w/determination (3000-4000) 3737

Close-up of horrified Flit & Pocahontas (2000-3000) 3162

Smith whirls w/knife drawn (1000-1500) 1955

Meeko (w/kneeling John Smith) triumphantly holds up biscuit (2000-3000) 3162

Close-up of frightened Pocahontas hiding (2000-2500) 3162

Medium close-up of John Smith swatting at attacking Flit (1500-2000) 1265

John Smith (on ledge) swats at Flit as Meeko (at his feet) holds biscuit (2500-3500) 3737

Close-up of Meeko happily eating biscuit on rock ledge (1500-2000) 2875

Kekata evokes smoke images (1000-1500) 1035

Kekata w/smoke image of settler aiming musket (1000-1500) 1495

Standing Powhatan addresses Council: "...Take some men to the river..." (1500-2000) 2300

Close-up of Powhatan speaking: "Let us hope they do not intend to stay." (1000-1500) 1150

Ratcliffe claims land in front of Susan Constant and rows of settlers (2000-3000) 3162

Smiling Wiggins leans out ship's window holding scrub brush: "Bravo!" (1500-2000) 1150

Front view of Meeko's distorted image in soap bubbles (1000-1500) 1035

Surprised Percy stares at Meeko's soap-bubble image (1500-2000) 1265

Shocked Percy in bath stares at smiling Meeko who holds cherry (2500-3500) 6900

Angry Percy chases Meeko out cabin door as bubbles fly (1500-2000) 1150

Percy sprawled in mud by barrels (1500-2500) 1955

Ratcliffe & Smith stand on rock & discuss settlement's location (2000-3000) 2300

Ratcliffe sings & helps Thomas hold shovel as others watch (1500-2500) 4025

Scheming Ratcliffe holds pistol upward in forest (1800-2200) 1610

Very long aerial shot of settlers circled around Ratcliffe by Susan Constant (2000-3000) 2300

Ratcliffe fantasizes standing by throne wearing crown & holding scepter amid court attendants as king bows to him (1800-2200) 1380

Singing John Smith swings around cliff on vine (1500-2000) 1725

John Smith walks across log bridging falls (1500-2000) 1265

Long shot of Smith gesturing in middle of log above falls: "...The greatest adventure is mine!" (1500-2000) 1610

Overhead shot of Ratcliffe singing amid settlers digging holes (1500-2000) 1150

Ratcliffe singing in forest: "This beauty untold." (1000-1500) 805

Ratcliffe w/torch singing atop cannon before an admiring Wiggins (2000-3000) 1610

Close-up of grinning Ratcliffe holding flag (1800-2200) 3162

"Music room": rocks above John Smith where Pocahontas remains hidden (1500-2000) 3737

Close-up front shot of Pocahontas crawling forward over rock (2000-3000) 3162

Pocahontas climbs down to rock at edge of river by waterfall (2000-3000) 4025

John Smith aims musket at Pocahontas standing on rock in mist (includes production overlays/ underlays applied to non-production background) (2500-3500) 7475

Portrait of Pocahontas standing in mist, hair flowing in wind (3000-4000) 13,225

Long shot of Pocahontas, Meeko & Flit running toward canoe under large tree (2000-3000) 4887

Close-up of fearful Pocahontas (in canoe) turning around (2500-3500) 4312

Pocahontas & Smith stand holding hands on riverbank as Meeko (in canoe) & Flit watch (2500-3500) 13,225

Ratcliffe stands at top of hole as Thomas digs: "Anything yet?" (1000-1500) 805

Close-up of horrified Percy (1000-1500) 1150

Panicked Wiggins by topiary (1800-2200) 1610

Frightened Percy tries to hide under helmet (1000-1500) 1035

Powhatan addresses Kocoum & 2 other Indians: "We will fight this enemy..." (1000-1500) 1380

Kocoum & Indian leave longhouse as wounded Indian is treated (1500-2000) 1150

Long aerial view of Meeko in tree w/compass as Pocahontas & Smith look up (1500-2000) 1150

Close-up of John Smith sprawled on grass looking up: "He can keep it." (1000-1500) 805

Curious Meeko in tree inspects compass (1500-2000) 4600

Angry Pocahontas walks away from Flit & kneeling John Smith (2000-3000) 7475

John Smith stands in river blocking Pocahontas'
canoe: "There's so much we can teach you..."
(2000-3000) 2875

Close-up of angry Pocahontas: "Savages?"
(2000-3000) 2070

Close-up of Pocahontas & Smith nose-to-nose: "Let
me explain!" "Let go." (4000-5000) 12,075

Pocahontas sits on tree branch as John Smith holds
bow of empty canoe (2000-3000) 3450

Long shot of John Smith climbing tree (
1500-2000) 2587

Pocahontas walks toward fallen John Smith sitting
under tree (2000-3000) 4887

"Listen To Your Heart" specially created art with non-
production background: landed settlers amid colored leaves & Pocahontas, John Smith, Flit,
Meeko & Percy w/Grandmother Willow
(6000-8000) 8050

Close-up of bear w/3 cubs (1000-1500) 2070

Close-up of Pocahontas looking upward & singing
(2000-3000) 3335

Pocahontas & John Smith hold hands amid colored
swirl (2000-3000) 2990

Pocahontas & John Smith hold hands underwater
with heron & otters (3000-4000) 3335

Pocahontas & Smith lie on rock in middle of river:
"In a circle, in a hoop..." (2500-3500) 4600

Pocahontas & John Smith hold eagles on their arms
(2000-3000) 2645

Eagles fly toward tree top (2500-3500) 4887

Pocahontas & Smith look up (2000-3000) 2415

Pocahontas & John Smith stand atop cliff in shaft of
sunlight w/orange leaves & purple sky (2000-
3000) 10,350

Long shot of Pocahontas & John Smith standing
hand-in-hand under tree (2000-3000) 4887

Portrait of somber John Smith (1500-2000) 2760

Meeko scrambles up settlement's log wall
(1500-2500) 1495

Percy licks chops & inspects bone-laden carrousel
(1500-2000) 4025

Eager Meeko peeks under tent (1500-2000) 1840

Close-up of Percy happily chewing beside carrousel
(1500-2000) 2645

Long overhead shot of Percy chasing Meeko thru
forest (2000-3000) 1725

Snarling Percy runs past bone-chewing Moose with
Meeko on his head (3000-4000) 3737

Angry Ratcliffe snatches fake arrow-thru-head trick
from Wiggins (1500-2000) 1150

Close-up of appeasing Pocahontas in cornfield: "Yes,
Father." (2500-3500) 4887

Determined Pocahontas fingers necklace & looks
upward (3000-4000) 3737

Close-up of terrified Nakoma (1500-2000) 1150

Pocahontas turns to see smiling John Smith who has
emerged from corn (2000-3000) 2530

Angry Flit hovers in cornfield (2000-3000) 2185

Close-up of John Smith: "I had to see you again."
(1500-2000) 1265

Pocahontas takes John Smith's hand as Nakoma
watches (2000-3000) 2530

Long overhead shot of Pocahontas leading John
Smith across root bridge to Grandmother
Willow (2500-3500) 2185

Kneeling John Smith examines corn as Pocahontas
& Meeko watch (2000-3000) 5462

Front view of Pocahontas & Smith staring ahead:
"Did you see something?" (2000-3000) 3105

"My bark is worse than my bite." Close-up of 2 owls'
reactions (1000-1500) 1150

Pocahontas & John Smith hide behind Grandmother
Willow as Ben & Lon approach
(2500-3500) 4025

Powhatan talks to fellow Indian leader in front of longhouse as warriors watch: "Now that we are
joined..." (1000-1500) 1035

Pocahontas talks with Powhatan: "We don't have to
fight them." (2000-3000) 2415

Long front shot thru trees of Ben & Lon standing
guard atop log walls (1500-2000) 1265

John Smith (Meeko around his neck) puts hands up
at sight of musket barrel (1500-2000) 1380

John Smith gives Thomas a musketry lesson by log
wall (1500-2000) 1265

Ratcliffe addresses Smith as Thomas & Wiggins
(holding scrub brush) watch (2000-3000) 1840

Ratcliffe orders Smith to kill Indians on sight as
Thomas, Ben, & Lon watch (1500-2000) 1150

Nakoma finds Pocahontas sneaking away into corn
(2000-3000) 1725

Nakoma grabs Pocahontas' arm: "He's one of them."
(2000-3000) 1955

Ratcliffe orders Thomas to follow John Smith
(1500-2000) 1150

Nakoma approaches as Kocoum kneels at campfire
(1500-2000) 1610

Pocahontas standing in front of willow fronds: "The
warriors are here." (2000-3000) 1840

Pocahontas tries to calm Percy & Meeko as Smith
stands on root bridge (2500-3500) 2185

Willow frond fishes startled Percy out of water
(1000-1500) 1725

Grandmother Willow addresses Pocahontas, Smith,
Flit, Percy & Meeko: "There's something I
want to show you." (2000-3000) 2990

Pocahontas & John Smith reach out to each other
amid willow fronds (2500-3500) 2300

Pocahontas & Smith kiss (2000-3000) 2300

Kocoum tackles John Smith as shocked Pocahontas
watches (2000-3000) 1840

Kocoum's axe just misses John Smith as Pocahontas
cries out (2000-3000) 1610

Pocahontas watches Kocoum & Smith struggle with
knife (1500-2000) 1150

Smith tells Thomas to flee as Pocahontas watches
& Flit, Percy & Meeko huddle beneath Grandmother Willow's roots (3000-4000) 2530

Meeko & Flit comfort frightened Percy hiding in
willow roots (1500-2000) 3737

Front view of Smith being led thru group of warriors
(1000-1500) 805

Elevated front view of downhearted Pocahontas
(2000-3000) 1610

Pocahontas kneels & touches John Smith who's tied
to stake in longhouse (2000-3000) 1840

Wiggins in nightclothes runs to Ratcliffe's tent holding
candle (1500-2000) 1380

Close-up of scheming Ratcliffe w/hand over Wiggins'
mouth after extinguishing candle: "I couldn't
have planned this..." (1000-1500) 805

Torch in hand, Ratcliffe incites armed settlers: "Now
it's up to you, men!" (1500-2000) 1150

2 set-ups of smoke clouds w/reflected images rising
from each camp (1500-2000) 1725

Depressed Pocahontas kneels in front of Grandmother
Willow as Percy & Meeko walk along root
(2000-3000) 2645

2 set-ups: Pocahontas stands holding compass with
Meeko & Percy at her feet; close-up of compass
face in her hands (2000-3000) 2760

Portrait of determined Pocahontas amid leaves: "You
know your path..." (2000-3000) 1610

Pocahontas stands on rock w/Flit, Meeko, Percy &
birds in front of reddish sky (3000-4000) 4025

Overhead view of Pocahontas & animals running
w/eagle shadow (2000-3000) 1610

Side view of Pocahontas racing downhill w/animals
& ghost eagle (2000-3000) 3220

Long view of Pocahontas, animals & ghost eagle
jumping chasm (2000-3000) 4025

Close-up of Ratcliffe shouting: "Kill them!"
(1000-1500) 805

Front view of determined Pocahontas running thru
forest (1500-2500) 3737

Pocahontas' image superimposed over execution
party on cliff (3000-4000) 18,400

Close-up of Pocahontas shielding John Smith: "If
you kill him..." (2000-3000) 1840

2 set-ups: close-up of shocked Powhatan & death
mallet; Pocahontas lifts head to speak as she
shields Smith: "This is the path I choose,
Father. What will yours be?" (2500-3500) 2990

Overhead close-up of Pocahontas shielding Smith:
"Look around you..." (2000-3000) 2645

2 set-ups: close-ups of somber Powhatan's face & Pocahontas' face as she shields Smith (1500-2000)
1955

Long view of Indians & settlers standing off on &
around cliff as Pocahontas shields Smith from
Powhatan w/mallet raised (2500-3500) 2415

Overhead shot of Pocahontas looking up as she
protects Smith (2000-3000) 2990

Pocahontas & Smith embrace (2500-3500) 3220

Somber Powhatan stands holding death mallet at his
side (1000-1500) 805

Front view of alarmed Pocahontas rushing forward
(2000-3000) 1840

Pocahontas kneels over grimacing John Smith laying
on rock holding side (2000-3000) 2645

Overhead view of Ratcliffe w/musket surrounded by
shadows (1500-2000) 1150

Side view of Pocahontas walking from Indians toward
settlers (1500-2500) 1610

Long view of Susan Constant's stern w/Indians &
settlers on shore (2000-3000) 1840

Determined Pocahontas runs thru trees
(2000-3000) 2990

Long view of Pocahontas running thru meadow
w/Susan Constant's sails above hilltops &
treetops (3000-4000) 2990

Pocahontas stands on cliff watching Susan Constant
sail away (3000-5000) 8050

MODEL ART

All items in this section were auctioned at Sotheby's,
February 24, 1996.

These are animation maquettes specially hand-painted for the auction by The Walt Disney Studios. All are
full figure unless noted.

Pocahontas, #36/36 (2000-3000) 3220
Powhatan, #10/16 (1000-1500) 805
Nakoma, #1/13 (1500-2000) 1265
John Smith, #19/27 (2000-3000) 1610
Governor Ratcliffe, #1/21 (1800-2200) 1380
Percy, #8/22 (1500-2000) 2185
Meeko, #11/22 (1500-2000) 4140
Flit, #8/17 (1500-2000) 5462
Pocahontas bust, #25/38 (2000-3000) 2990

THE RELUCTANT DRAGON (1941)

Segments were *Baby Weems*; *Casey, Junior*; *Old
MacDonald Duck*; *How to Ride a Horse*; and *The
Reluctant Dragon*.

ANIMATION DRAWINGS (also see CELS-FULL FIGURE)

Drawing of Dragon (eyes closed) facing left & lecturing,
8 x 6-1/2", VF, HL/Nov 16/97 (300-500) 633

Full-figure drawing of happy Dragon sitting on his tail,
looking right; 8-1/2 x 6"; VF; HL/Apr 25/98
(500-700) 1035

CEL SET-UPS

Goofy & reluctant horse, 6", Courvoisier watercolor
& airbrush background & label, WDP stamp,
CE/Jun 18/94 (1000-1500) 863

Goofy (4-3/4 x 3") & uncooperative horse,
Courvoisier watercolor & airbrush
background, CE/Jun 18/94 (1500-2000) 2415

Full figures of Goofy (9") looking at camera holding
bunch of carrots as eager Percy (9-1/2")
watches; Courvoisier watercolor background of
farm, captioned mat & label; SR/Spring/96
(1600-2200) 1760

Full figure of Goofy riding upside down on Percy's
neck to left, 6", 16-field, color print Courvoisier
background of farmyard, SR/Spring/96
(600-1000) 1320

2 color model cels: Dragon playing flute for 3 birds
sitting on branch, master background, 7-1/2
x 9-1/2", VF, HL/Apr 28/96 (3000-4000) 3795

Full figure of stretched Goofy mounting irritated horse
(w/hoof on Goofy's foot), Courvoisier watercolor
background of ranch, 6", CE/Jun 20/96
(1500-2000) 1955

Scheming Goofy rides scheming horse, Courvoisier
watercolor & airbrush background of ranch,
5-1/2", CE/Jun 20/96 (1500-2000) 2300

Goofy stands facing left, eyes closed, riding crop
extended as horse behind him puts hoof over
muzzle w/laughter; 9 x 22"; complementary
painted background; Courvoisier label,
HL/Oct 6/96 (1000-1500) 2185

Full figure of smiling Donald (dressed for *Old MacDonald Duck*, carrying bucket) walking left, looking
back & up, 6", watercolor master background of
outdoors from *Donald's Garden*, SR/Spring/97
(3000-5000) 3080

Full figures of toothy horse (6" long) standing with
surprised Goofy's (6") left arm in his mouth, Courvoisier watercolor background of ranch
& label, CLA/Jun 7/97 (1500-2000) 2185

CELS – FULL FIGURE

Eager Goofy rides smiling Percy to left, 6-1/2 x
6-1/2", S/Dec 16/93 (1200-1800) 3450

Goofy waves riding crop & rides Percy, 6" x 7",
S/Jun 17/94 (1500-2000) 1725

Percy (5" length) kneels before Goofy (4") who waves
riding crop, S/Jun 17/94 (1500-2000) 1725

*Thoughtful Goofy on horse, 5-1/2",
CE/Dec 16/94 (800-1200) — 1380

Goofy (5") smiling with eyes closed, raises hat &
gestures to Percy the horse (6-1/2"), who
laughs with hooves crossed over face,
S/Dec 17/94 (1800-2200) — 1840

Worried Goofy rides eager horse galloping to left,
7", CE/Jun 20/96 (1000-1500) — 805

Side view of Casey Jr. facing left, 6",
CE/Dec 12/96 (1000-1500) — 863

Sir Giles in horse-riding pose facing right, 6-1/2",
SR/Spring/97 (700-1100) — 720

Sad Boy stands looking right & up, 4", some rippling,
SR/Spring/97 (400-800) — 390

Confident Goofy (5") carries ladder toward
laughing Percy (3-1/2 x 3-1/2"),
S/Jun 21/97 (1800-2200) — 4600

3 full-figure cels: Dragon standing facing right, eyes
closed, throwing kiss, 6-1/4"; Sir Giles standing
facing right, left hand to mouth, mouth open,
5-1/8"; Boy sitting facing left, looking up with
mouth open while reading book, 4-7/16",
2"-piece missing from lower right edge; ct;
SR/Spring/98 (2200-3200) — 2220*

CELS – PARTIAL FIGURE

Goofy (knees up) in riding attire, 4", CE/Dec 16/94
(400-600) — 748

LAYOUT ART

2 layout drawings: cart full of wide-eyed villagers;
crowd of villagers outside inn, S/Jun 19/96
(800-1200) — 1495

STORY ART

Entire storyboard for Robert Benchley live-action
segment in original cloth-bound album, 13
photostatic sheets, 14 x 11", w/415 sequential
drawings, mounted on black paper for ledger-
post style album, SR/Spring/96 (300-700) — 510

Baby Weems: story drawing of doctors rushing to
operating room, colored litho, crayon on
animation sheet, 8-1/4 x 10-1/2",
HL/Oct 6/96 (300-400) — 259

THE RESCUERS (1977)

ANIMATION DRAWINGS (also see CELS-FULL FIGURE)

Hips-up rear-view drawing of Penny looking left, 8",
16-field, scene & sequence notations, timer's
chart, some edge wear & discoloration,
SR/Spring/96 (200-400) — 850

Hips-up drawing of suspicious Penny, left hand to chin,
holding lantern, looking back right & up, 8", 16-
field sheet, timer's charts, some rippling,
SR/Fall/96 (200-400) — 250

CEL SET-UPS

Madame Medusa seated, matching cel & master
background, 10-1/2 x 12-1/2", VF+,
HL/Apr 10/94 (3000-5000) — 2688

Madame Medusa lectures from sofa, master background of houseboat interior w/notes, 10-1/2
x 12-1/2", HL/Aug 21/94 (3000-5000) — 2800

Bianca & Bernard entering Evinrude's boat,
complementary background print, seal,
10-1/2 x 13", HL/Aug 21/94 (900-1200) — 896

Smiling Orville (all but wing tips) watches Bianca &
Bernard sit in sardine can atop him, 14-3/4 x
9-3/4", litho background of "airport," 16-field,
limited edition: #35/500, certificate,
SR/Spring/95 (800-1400) — 850

Cautious Bernard in front of leaf boat, 4", key watercolor production background w/notes; 2 background layout drawings; exposure sheet; 18
Xeroxes on original animation paper of
sequence of animation drawings,
CE/Jun 9/95 (1500-2000) — 2530

Full-figure long shot of Bernard & Bianca standing
on floor of Albatross Airlines office, 1", four
cel levels, including effects & brown & blue
line overlays, layout line background, 7-3/8 x
5-1/2" picture image, SR/Fall/97 (600-900) — 400

Excited Bianca & terrified Bernard seated in
sardine can on Orville's back during deep
dive, 10 x 13", background painting from
unknown production (tempera on background
sheet), VF, HL/Nov 16/97 (500-700) — 431

CELS – FULL FIGURE

Profile of Orville flying, 4-1/2 x 7-1/2", Disney
seal & WDP label, VF+, HL/Feb 26-27/94
(300-400) — 330

Bianca, 5 x 5", seal & Disney label, VF+,
HL/Feb 26-27/94 (300-500) — 330

Sad Penny holds teddy (partial figure); Bernard &
Bianca stand in rain gear; Evinrude pushes
Bernard & Bianca in leaf boat; Rufus sitting
(partial figure); Orville in hat, boots & sunglasses
flying Bernard & Bianca; rough pencil animation
drawing of Bernard signed by Dale Oliver; 3-1/2
x 7" to 6 x 9"; Disney seal & certificate from DL's
Disneyana Shop; VF+; HL/Apr 10/94 (1200-
1600) — 1568

Bianca in rain gear & Bernard reading map; separate
cel of Bianca under umbrella; seal, 8 x 6",
6-1/2 x 10-1/2", HL/Aug 21/94 (500-700) — 784

Large image of Evinrude holding scroll, 7 x 8",
HL/Aug 21/94 (300-500) — 672

Large full figures of Bernard & Bianca; Penny
& teddy; 7 x 7-1/2" & 7 x 8-1/2",
HL/Apr 23/95 (900-1200) — 672

Bernard & Bianca stand together, 6", WDP stamp,
CE/Aug 9/95 (500-700) — 690

Nervous Bernard & Bianca hold hands and tiptoe,
4 x 6", HL/Nov 19/95 (400-600) — 489

Bernard (side view, 6-1/2") & Bianca (front view, 6-
1/4") stand together, 16-field, SR/Spring/96
(400-700) — 440

Admiring Bianca & thoughtful Bernard standing,
5-1/2 x 9-1/2", Disney seal, WDP label,
VF+, HL/Apr 28/96 (200-300) — 748

Sitting Orville (6-3/8") adjusts goggles as standing
Bernard (2") watches, 16-field, Disney Art Program seal & label, SR/Fall/96 (400-600) — 410

Shocked Bernard (4-1/2") sitting in raincoat holds tip
of frazzled tail as Bianca (6-3/4", raincoat &
scarf) stands watching, 16-field, Disney Art Program seal & label, SR/Fall/96 (300-500) — 370

Elegant Miss Bianca standing on bend in vertical
rope, 9-1/2 x 4", Disney seal, VF+,
HL/Feb 23/97 (300-400) — 288

Thoughtful Bernard & admiring Bianca stand together,
5-5/8", 16-field cel, SR/Fall/97 (450-650) — 300

CELS – PARTIAL FIGURE

Near-full figure of seated Madame Medusa smiling,
silver WDP seal, 8" S/Dec 16/93 (500-700) — 345

Angry Madame Medusa points to right, 7 x 10",
Disney seal, VF+, HL/Feb 26-27/94
(400-600) — 440

Portrait of Madame Medusa clutching Devil's
Eye, 7 x 6-1/2", Disney seal, VF+,
HL/Feb 26-27/94 (300-400) — 440

Front view of Bernard adrift on leaf w/matching
cel of water; portrait of smiling Bianca,
9-1/2 x 14-1/2", Disney seals & 2 WDP
labels, VF+, HL/Feb 26-27/94 (600-900) — 495

Front view of wide-eyed Penny, 8 x 4", Disney seal
& label, VF+, HL/Feb 26-27/94 (300-400) — 275

Partial figures of Medusa (8-1/2") talking expansively
to unimpressed Penny (clutching teddy), 16-field,
SR/Spring/95 (400-700) — 300

Near-full figures of Bernard & Bianca in rain gear,
7 x 11", HL/Apr 23/95 (400-600) — 532

Portrait of gesturing Madame Medusa with towel
wrapped around hair, 8-1/2 x 8", VF+,
HL/Apr 23/95 (300-500) — 616

Angry Madame Medusa holds gun; seated Medusa
holds staff; 10-1/2 x 3-1/2" & 8 x 11"; VF+;
HL/Apr 23/95 (500-700) — 1008

Devilish Madame Medusa pointing down with both
hands, 8-1/2"; Brutus (12") carrying Penny
(4") by her jumper straps; both w/silver Walt
Disney Certified seal; S/Jun 10/95 (500-700) — 690

Large-image portrait of weary Bernard in rainwear,
8 x 8", WDP seal, VF+, HL/Nov 19/95
(300-400) — 345

Hips-up of Penny clutching Teddy, looking left &
down, 6-3/4", 16-field, SR/Spring/96
(200-400) — 390

Ankles-up of grinning Medusa holding Teddy away
from Penny, 8-1/2", 16-field, SR/Spring/96
(400-700) — 920

Portrait of screaming Madame Medusa clutching
Teddy, 8 x 10-1/2", VF+, HL/Apr 28/96
(300-500) — 690

Frightened Bernard and Bianca caught inside
Madame Medusa's trunk, 10 x 14", Disney
seal, VF+, HL/Apr 28/96 (500-700) — 403

Angry Mr. Snoops holds Penny (holding Teddy) by her
right wrist, 9-1/4", 16-field cel, SR/Fall/96
(500-900) — 500

Miss Bianca (full figure) tiptoes away as Madame
Medusa peers into suitcase, 8-1/2 x 10",

Disney seal, VF+, HL/Oct 6/96 (300-500) — 345

Madame Medusa, 7"; Bernard, 6"; Chairman (4")
& Bianca (3"); Disney seals; CE/Dec 12/96
(1000-1500) — 748

Madame Medusa clutches her staff & wails, 8",
S/Dec 14/96 (300-500) — 402

Smiling Bernard & Bianca seated in sardine can
under umbrella, 7-1/4 x 14", Disney seal,
VF, HL/Feb 23/97 (400-600) — 805

Front view of shy Penny standing holding Teddy, 9
x 4-1/2", VF+, HL/Feb 23/97 (200-300) — 288

Chest-up front view of Madame Medusa on phone, 8-
5/8", 16-field cel, Disney Art Program seal,
SR/Spring/97 (300-700) — 420

Knees-up of combative Penny standing facing left
holding Teddy, looking up, right hand clinched
into fist; 7", 16-field cel; SR/Spring/98
(300-600) — 390

Portrait of enraged Madame Medusa facing right
holding Teddy & gun, seal & certificate, 8
x 10-1/4", VF+, HL/Apr 25/98 (300-500) — 489

Hips-up view of Orville standing facing right, seal
& certificate, 6 x 8", VF, HL/Apr 25/98
(300-400) — 316

STORY ART

2 story drawings (one by Milt Kahl), india ink &
watercolor on animation sheet and paper,
8 x 9-1/2" & 7-1/2 x 15", F+,
HL/Apr 28/96 (700-1000) — 2070

THE RESCUERS DOWN UNDER (1990)

CEL SET-UPS

Near-full figure of Bernard (back turned, 3"), 3 large
eggs, & surprised Wilbur (9"), matching watercolor production background, S/Jun 21/97
(1500-2500) — 2300

Waist-up side views of smiling Bernard (7") facing
happy Bianca (6-1/4") as he holds her hand,
matching watercolor production background,
S/Jun 21/97 (1200-1800) — 3450

SPECIAL ART

Special full-figure drawing of Marahute flying with
Cody on his back, inscribed & signed by Glen
Keane, 10 x 14-1/2", VF+, HL/Apr 25/98
(400-600) — 161

ROBIN HOOD (1973)

ANIMATION DRAWINGS

Waist-up rough drawing of Robin Hood reacting
to arrow thru his cap, 8 x 6-1/2",
HL/Feb 23/97 (150-250) — 690

Expressive portrait drawing of smiling Sir Hiss in
plumed cap, signed "From Ollie," 9 x 8" inc.
signature, HL/May 31/97 (200-300) — 173

Full-figure drawing of determined Skippy Bunny
in Robin Hood cap standing facing right,
drawing bow & arrow; signed by Frank
Thomas; 8-1/2 x 5" including signature,
HL/May 31/97 (300-400) — 403

BACKGROUNDS

Preliminary or production background of castle
courtyard w/inscribed notes, CE/Dec 16/94
(700-900) — 3220

CEL SET-UPS

Prince John, Little John & Sir Hiss with matching
tempera master background from Tournament
at Nottingham, 8-1/2 x 11-1/2", studio notes,
VF+, HL/Apr 10/94 (4000-4500) — 3920

Full figure of grim Sheriff of Nottingham walking right,
6-1/2", gouache key master background of castle
courtyard, SR/Fall/94 (1200-1800) — 1780

Portrait of happy Prince John gesturing, 9 x 12",
matching master background, seal & notes,
HL/Nov 13/94 (2000-2500) — 2016

Near-full figure of Alligator Guard knocking Robin
backward with shield, 12-1/2 x 9-1/4", castle
courtyard master background, SR/Spring/95
(1000-1600) — 1460

Sir Hiss w/tail wrapped around Prince John's leg
& teeth clamped on bag of coins being
pulled out of bedroom by overhead rope,
matching master background, 10-1/2 x
26-1/2", F+, HL/Apr 23/95 (5000-6000) — 5152

Maid Marian (6") accepts flower from hand as she
sits w/Lady Cluck (5"), matching watercolor
background, S/Jun 10/95 (2500-3500) — 2070

Full figure of Trigger walking right in courtyard with
crossbow at ready, looking back, 3-3/4",

gouache master background is 11-5/8 x 11-1/2", SR/Fall/95 (900-1500) 1320

Little John & Skippy Bunny ride on royal coach, 10-1/2 x 17", matching master background (tempera on background sheet), VF+, HL/Nov 19/95 (3000-4000) 4600

Rhino guards charge thru hole in castle wall, 10-1/2 x 16", matching master background (tempera on background sheet), VF+, HL/Nov 19/95 (2000-3000) 2013

Full figure of Robin (4-1/3") sword fighting Crocodile (8-1/2"), watercolor production background with overlay, Disney seal, CE/Jun 20/96 (3000-4000) 3910

Half image of relaxed Robin leaning on elbow, looking up, 8-1/8", 16-field cel, pre-production background of stone room & straw pile, Disney Art Program seal, SR/Fall/96 (1200-1800) 750

Portrait of smiling Robin, head tilted to left; 10 x 14"; Studio Art Props background painting of Sherwood Forest (tempera on board), HL/Oct 6/96 (700-1000) 863

Seated Maid Marian in loving pose, 8 x 10", matching master background from tournament scene (tempera on background sheet), HL/Oct 6/96 (2000-3000) 2300

Head-&-chest front view of Robin (5-1/2") looking down & to left w/Maid Marian (4-1/2") looking over his shoulder, watercolor of landscape w/Xerographic line cel overlay, S/Dec 14/96 (1500-2500) 1380

Full figures of Robin (3-1/4") & Little John (4-3/4") as Gypsy women sitting/lying on ground by wagon amid gold coins, matching key pre-production gouache background, ct, SR/Spring/97 (2200-3200) 2200

Waist-up front view of disguised Robin Hood & Little John talking while hiding in bushes, 5" ea., matching watercolor background, CLA/Jun 7/97 (3000-4000) 2875

Full figures of Grandma & Grandpa Owl (4" each), Mother Rabbit (5-1/2", with 2 children in arms), & 4 children (2-1/2" each) rejoicing, matching watercolor production background of outdoors, CLA/Jun 7/97 (3000-5000) 6325

Waist-up of Robin Hood (6-1/2") & Maid Marian (5-1/2") talking in forest, watercolor production background from The Sword in the Stone, CLA/Jun 7/97 (2000-3000) 2530

Full figures of Robin (4") sword fighting Crocodile (7") outdoors in front of reviewing stand, preliminary watercolor background, S/Jun 21/97 (2500-3500) 2875

Robin swings on rope while carrying Maid Marian, 3-1/2" overall, printed background, S/Jun 21/97 (600-800) 805

Portrait of Prince John with mouth open, 6", watercolor production background of wall & window with Xerox line-on-cel overlay, S/Jun 21/97 (1500-2500) 1380

Robin & Marian standing together facing toward left, looking down, 7-1/2 x 13" overall, preliminary background of countryside (tempera on background sheet), F, HL/Nov 16/97 (1200-1600) 1265

Full figure of Robin as stork (7") competing against Sheriff (5-1/2") in archery contest, key production set-up w/matching watercolor production background, S/Dec 19/97 (1800-2200) 2070

Matching production set-up of Robin (4") tying bags to overhead rope as Prince John (8") sleeps, watercolor w/Xerox line-on-cel background of royal bedroom, S/Dec 19/97 (3000-5000) 4312

CELS – FULL FIGURE (also see MODEL ART)
Sister Bunny & sibling, 7 x 7-1/2", Disney seal & label, VF+, HL/Feb 26-27/94 (200-300) 468

Robin & Little John walking, 6 x 5-1/2", Disney seal, WDP label, VF+, HL/Feb 26-27/94 (600-900) 715

Sword-wielding Robin with special-effects cel, 10-1/2 x 14", Disney seal, VF+, HL/Feb 26-27/94 (500-700) 660

Vulture guard, Disney seal; Robin & Marian in wedding coach; one WDP label; 7-1/2 x 11" & 9-1/2 x 7", F, HL/Feb 26-27/94 (800-1200) 1100

Tournament archers in set of 5 cels, 8-1/2 x 15", Disney seal, VF+, HL/Feb 26-27/94 (500-700) 468

Robin & Marian leaping, 3 x 2-1/2", VF, HL/Apr 10/94 (400-600) 784

Robin & Little John as gypsy women, 5-1/2 x 8", VF+, HL/Apr 10/94 (500-700) 784

Sword fight between Robin Hood & mean-looking crocodile (all but half of tail), WDP seal & label, 8 x 12", VF+, HL/Aug 21/94 (500-700) 728

Prince John stands wearing crown, 6-3/4", SR/Fall/94 (600-900) 610

2 cels: waist-up front view of Robin disguised as stork, arms up, looking right; full figure of tail-powered Sir Hiss flying w/head inside balloon, eyes closed; both 6", 16-field, SR/Spring/95 (400-700) 410

Row of archers, 8" high, WDC seal, CE/Jun 9/95 (400-600) 345

Full figure of smiling Robin with sword, 5-1/2"; rhinoceros, 10", CE/Jun 9/95 (600-800) 1035

Robin & Maid Marian (holding bouquet) walk thru doors, 5", CE/Jun 9/95 (600-800) 805

Robin (full figure, 3") as gypsy woman carries bag & runs happily toward Little John (as woman, 7"), S/Jun 10/95 (600-800) 575

Front view of Prince John standing wearing his night-gown & crown, recoiling in fright, 6-1/4", SR/Fall/95 (500-800) 500

2 full-figure cels together: smiling Marian kneeling, looking left & up, 7-1/4"; ferocious Skippy, holding bow & wearing Robin's hat, standing facing left, 6"; 16-field, Disney Art Program seal, SR/Fall/95 (400-700) 400

Robin balancing arrow on tip of finger, 9 x 8-1/2", VF, HL/Mar 16-17/96 (300-500) 805

Relaxed Robin sits with hat over eyes, 7-1/4", 16-field, SR/Spring/96 (400-700) 440

Worried Robin hangs from horizontal rope with one hand, 5 money bags tied to rope, bag in front of him pierced by arrow, Disney seal, VF+, 7-1/2 x 13", HL/Apr 28/96 (500-700) 546

2 cels: eager Robin as gypsy woman walking left, 5-1/4"; Little John putting on bloomers, 7"; both 16-field; SR/Fall/97 (600-1000) 400

Robin balancing arrow on finger tip, 9 x 8-1/2", VF, HL/Nov 16/97 (700-900) 805

Profile of Prince John (6-1/2") & three-quarter pose of Robin Hood (4"); both with eyes open; CE/Dec 18/97 (700-900) 437

Robin & Little John as Gypsy women: Robin pushing on Little John's chest, 5-1/2", 16-field cel, some cel rippling , SR/Spring/98 (400-700) 700

CELS – PARTIAL FIGURE (also see CELS-FULL FIGURE)
9" Robin marrying 8" Maid Marian; frazzled 7" (head & shoulders) Prince John; each with WDP seal & labels, S/Dec 16/93 (800-1200) 805

Prince John holds ear & sucks thumb, partial multi-cel set-up, WDP seal, 12-1/2 x 15-1/2", CE/Dec 15/93 (800-1200) 1610

Portrait of eager Prince John rubbing paws together; matched cels of stunned Sir Hiss with hand mirror broken over his head; 7-1/2 x 9", 9-1/2 x 6-1/2", both with Disney seal and label, G-VF, HL/Apr 10/94 (600-900) 896

Cross-eyed Prince John with pleading Maid Marian, 7-1/2 x 11", Disney seal, VF, HL/Apr 10/94 (600-800) 532

Friar Tuck (8 x 6-1/2") & Skippy Bunny (3 x 4-3/4"); Little John (9 x 12") examines arrow, CE/Jun 18/94 (400-600) 978

Expressive portrait of Robin; 2-cel set of Prince John squeezing Sir Hiss as Sheriff watches, seal & labels; 8 x 11-1/2" & 6 x 7"; F-VF, HL/Aug 21/94 (1000-1500) 1456

2 portrait cels: Robin; Little John; 8 x 6" & 6-1/2 x 6", seal & 2 labels, HL/Nov 13/94 (600-900) 1232

Portrait of smirking Prince John; Sheriff squeezing taxes from Otto (foot in cast) in rocking chair; 8 x 6-1/2" & 7 x 9", seals and one label, HL/Nov 13/94 (600-900) 840

Chest-up front view of scheming, crown-wearing Prince John with paws crossed looking right, 8", 16-field, SR/Spring/95 (700-1000) 810

Chest-up of haughty Prince John (eyes closed) holding crown, 7", SR/Spring/95 (600-900) 640

2 waist-up cels: frustrated Maid Marian, Prince John in crown looking right, both 7", 16-field, Disney Art Program seals, SR/Spring/95 (700-1200) 720

Medium close-up of startled Prince John wearing crown, 6", WDP seal, CE/Jun 9/95

(400-600) 518

Portrait of puzzled Prince John, 7", WDP seal, CE/Jun 9/95 (400-600) 748

Prince John, 6-1/2", WDP seal, CE/Jun 9/95 (400-600) 552

Angry Prince John in royal robes, WDP seal, 7-1/2", CE/Jun 9/95 (400-600) 368

Hips-up of Robin Hood looking right, 11"; Sheriff of Nottingham, 10", WDP seal, CE/Jun 9/95 (600-800) 690

Portrait of alert Prince John wearing crown, 7 x 6", HL/Aug 6/95 (400-500) 616

Portrait of adoring Skippy (wearing Robin's hat) being held by embarrassed Robin, 6", 16-field, Disney Art Program seal & label, SR/Fall/95 (400-700) 490

Robin & Maid Marian converse, 5-1/2 x 5-1/2", Disney seal, WDP label, VF, HL/Nov 19/95 (600-900) 748

Large image of Robin shrugging his shoulders, 10-3/4 x 8-1/4", HL/Mar 16-17/96 (400-600) 633

Half image of frightened Robin & Marian holding each other, 8", 16-field cel, Disney Art Program seal, SR/Spring/96 (500-900) 550

Arrogant Prince John wearing crown and holding out paw w/rings on fingers, 7 x 7-1/2", VF, HL/Apr 28/96 (500-600) 575

Chest-up front view of delighted Prince John (wearing crown, rings missing stones) with paws at head level, studying crystal ball, 7-1/2", 12-field cel, SR/Fall/96 (500-900) 500

Portrait of Sir Hiss peering around loop in neck, 8 x 7-1/2", HL/Oct 6/96 (400-500) 863

Large image of gleeful [cowering?] Prince John wearing crown, 7 x 7-1/4", HL/Oct 6/96 (400-600) 633

Front view of angry Prince John (6") pointing finger at alarmed Sir Hiss (5"), WDC seal, S/Dec 14/96 (600-800) 1035

Portrait of beady-eyed Prince John wearing crown, 6 x 8", HL/Feb 23/97 (400-600) 633

Shoulders-up portrait of bored Robin Hood with iron collar secured by ropes around his neck, 9-1/4 x 12-1/4", HL/May 31/97 (300-500) 316

Sir Hiss leans thru curtain to whisper in crown-wearing Prince John's ear, 9-3/4 x 11", VF+, HL/Nov 16/97 (700-1000) 748

Front-view portrait of excited Prince John (wearing crown but rings missing jewels) in front of crystal ball, 7-1/2 x 9", F, HL/Nov 16/97 (700-1000) 748

Stomach-up portrait of triumphant Prince John, seal & certificate, 7-1/4 x 6-1/2", VF+, HL/Apr 25/98 (500-700) 575

Large-image shoulders-up portrait of somber Robin held captive with ropes & collar, seal & certificate, 9 x 12", VF+, HL/Apr 25/98 (400-600) 546

CONCEPT AND INSPIRATIONAL ART
Full-figure color studies of 6 major characters by Ken Anderson, 28 x 9-3/4", pen & markers on heavy board, SR/Spring/97 (2200-2800) 3930

Robin & Little John floating on their backs in lake, signed watercolor & gouache concept painting by Jim Coleman, 10-3/8 x 7-7/16", SR/Spring/98 (400-700) 470

MODEL ART
3 pages of character sketches by Milt Kahl: Robin & Little John disguising themselves, Robin relaxing by tree; india ink & pencil on animation sheets; 6-1/2 x 8" to 12 x 13", F+, HL/Apr 28/96 (900-1200) 2530

Full-figure color model cel of sad Allan-a-Dale (eyes closed) standing facing left, playing mandolin with chain around leg, 7-1/8", 16-field cel, SR/Fall/96 (200-400) 200

SPECIAL ART
Presentation drawing of Robin Hood about to balance arrow on fingertip, ink & gray watercolor on animation sheet, inscribed & signed by Milt Kahl, 9-1/2 x 8-1/2", VF, HL/Apr 25/98 (500-700) 805

SALUDOS AMIGOS (1943)

Also see TELEVISION: ANTHOLOGY SERIES, UNIDENTIFIED TV; UNIDENTIFIED/MISCEL-LANEOUS: COMBINATIONS OF MAJOR CHARACTERS

Segments were *Lake Titicaca*, *Pedro*, *Aquarela do Brasil*, and *El Gaucho Goofy*.

BACKGROUNDS

Master background of Chilean countryside, oil on background sheet, 9 x 11", studio notes & stamps, "OK Ken" (Ken Anderson), VF+, HL/Apr 10/94 (1500-2000) 3360

CEL SET-UPS

Full figures of Pedro meeting El Condor mounted to complementary Courvoisier airbrush background, 8-1/2 x 10-1/2", restored, F-VF, HL/Apr 10/94 (1500-2000) 896

Full figure of Pedro wearing cap, flying with mail pouch around right wing, smiling at camera, 4", some cel dents, restoration, Courvoisier background of sky, SR/Fall/94 (700-1100) 800

Excited Donald in jungle w/camera around neck, 3", watercolor Courvoisier background, Walt Disney inscription & signature, S/Dec 17/94 (800-1200) 3162

2 birds, 6" & smaller, Courvoisier watercolor background, CE/Jun 9/95 (500-700) 115

Full figures of dancing Donald Duck & José Carioca, complementary Art Props background (watercolor on heavyweight paper), 7-1/2 x 9-1/2", HL/Apr 28/96 (1800-2200) 1495

Full figure of smiling Donald Duck standing in Andean dress holding end of flute (partial figure) vertically, 6", watercolor preliminary background of outdoors, Courvoisier label, CE/Dec 12/96 (1000-1500) 1093

2 items: full-figure front view of happy José playing concertina, 5", watercolor preliminary production background of jungle; storyboard drawing of José holding Donald by his feet, 2", CE/Dec 12/96 (1000-1500) 978

Full figure of happy Donald Duck in Andean Indian dress admiring flute in his left hand, 6", watercolor preliminary production background of landscape, Courvoisier label, CE/Dec 12/96 (1000-1500) 1265

Full figure of determined Gaucho Goofy high-stepping right & swinging lasso over head, 4-1/2" w/out lasso, watercolor production background of Pampas, Courvoisier label, S/Dec 14/96 (2000-3000) 2070

Full figure of happy Donald Duck in Peruvian dress examining flute, 5-1/4" watercolor production background of landscape, Courvoisier label, S/Dec 14/96 (2500-3500) 1840

Full-figure front view of dancing José Carioca, complementary painted background as prepared by Courvoisier, 8 x 8" overall, HL/Feb 23/97 (600-900) 518

José Carioca playing concertina, 5"; Donald Duck & José dancing, 3-1/3" each; both over airbrushed Courvoisier backgrounds of outdoors, S/Jun 21/97 (1500-2000) 1725

Full figure of Donald floating in jar with jar stuck on his hand & stack of pots balanced on his head, 6-1/2", airbrushed background of water, S/Dec 19/97 (800-1200) 690

CELS – FULL FIGURE

2 full-figure mirror images of Pedro, 1950s-early 1960s (TV?), 3-1/2" times two, 16-field, SR/Fall/94 (200-500) 530

2 cels: Donald clings face down by hands & feet to 2 parallel ropes as llama (all but top of head) sits on his back, 7-1/2"; Donald dangling at end of rope, 6-1/2"; 12-field, ct, SR/Spring/95 (700-1200) 900

Front view of surprised Goofy, ears up & hat above head, standing wearing serape, 5-1/2", 12-field, ct, SR/Spring/95 (1100-1600) 1100

Shocked condor flying left, wings flapping down, 3-5/8", 12-field, ct, SR/Fall/95 (200-500) 220

Front view of stunned Goofy in gaucho garb, 4-1/2 x 4", HL/Nov 19/95 (1000-1500) 920

CONCEPT AND INSPIRATIONAL ART

Inspirational or publicity art: full figures of José & Donald dancing on floor of wavy shapes, india ink & watercolor on heavyweight paper, 7-1/4 x 11-3/4", VF+, HL/Apr 25/98 (1000-1500) 891

SLEEPING BEAUTY (1959)

Also see TELEVISION: ANTHOLOGY SERIES

ANIMATION DRAWINGS

5 drawings: 8-1/2" Maleficent holding staff; 6" King Stefan (2); 7" King Hubert (2) in orange pencil; S/Dec 16/93 (800-1200) 920

Clean-up drawing of Maleficent, 9 x 5-1/2", VF+, HL/Feb 26-27/94 (700-1000) 1540

2 rough pencil drawings: Prince Phillip on Samson & mock prince, 4-1/2 x 3-1/2", 6 x 5", F+, HL/Feb 26-27/94 (200-250) 413

2 drawings of Briar Rose (one an animator's extreme), 8 x 5-1/2", 8 x 7", F-VF, HL/Apr 10/94 (900-1200) 1120

Clean-up drawing of regal Maleficent, 9 x 5-1/2", F+, HL/Apr 10/94 (700-1000) 840

14 detailed rough drawings of Prince Phillip riding Samson by Milt Kahl, 6-1/2 x 5" to 9 x 9-1/2", F+, HL/Apr 10/94 (2000-3000) 1904

47 rough drawings in sequence of a squirrel, 5" & smaller, CE/Jun 18/94 (400-600) 288

5 drawings of Briar Rose, 5-1/2", CE/Dec 16/94 (700-900) 633

Full-figure drawing of Prince Phillip holding Briar Rose's hand, 6 x 4-1/2", HL/Aug 6/95 (400-500) 672

Full-figure drawing of elderly Prince Phillip astride an elderly horse, 7-1/2 x 8", HL/Nov 19/95 (400-500) 460

2 full-figure drawings of dashing Prince Phillip, 6-1/2 x 4-1/2" & 8-1/2 x 5", HL/Nov 19/95 (400-600) 374

Two near-full-figure drawings: side-view of Prince Phillip on Samson, notations, production & color model stamps; alert Briar Rose sitting; both 16-field sheets, SR/Spring/96 (600-1000) 760

Half-image drawing of Maleficent facing right w/head bowed, 9-1/2", 16-field, production & color model stamps, SR/Spring/96 (500-900) 500

Ankles-up drawing of sitting Briar Rose with berry basket on lap, facing left, looking over shoulder, 16-field, inker's notation & timer's chart, SR/Spring/96 (400-700) 540

Extreme drawing of Maleficent bending over with laughter, 7-1/2 x 9", HL/Apr 28/96 (500-800) 1380

2 near-full-figure drawings: Briar Rose standing with hands behind back looking up, 7-1/2"; wide-eyed Princess Aurora standing with left arm outstretched, 9"; CE/Jun 20/96 (800-1200) 805

Chest-up front-view drawing of King Hubert looking right & up with suspicious eye, 5-1/2", 16-field, timer's chart, SR/Fall/96 (150-300) 170

2 full-figure drawings keyed to each other: Samson standing facing left, 7-1/2"; Prince Phillip standing, right hand up [on saddle], looking right, 7"; 16-field sheets, timer's chart & inker's notations; SR/Fall/96 (300-700) 310

Knees-up front-view polished drawing of regal Maleficent, 8-3/4", 16-field, horizontal crease at figure's base, SR/Fall/96 (500-900) 610

Near-full figure drawing of sitting Briar Rose, berry basket in lap, 7-1/2", 16-field sheet, inker's notations, timer's chart, some wear, SR/Fall/96 (400-700) 540

2 drawings: full-figure front view of sitting King Hubert looking left, 5-1/2"; waist-up front view of King Stefan standing looking left, 7-1/2"; 16-field sheets, timer's charts, SR/Fall/96 (200-500) 430

Full-figure front-view drawing of Prince Phillip (looking right) astride Samson, F+, 9 x 3-1/2", HL/Oct 6/96 (300-400) 489

Large-image drawing of angry Maleficent pointing, 11-1/2 x 20", VF, HL/Oct 6/96 (1200-1600) 1955

102 rough drawings of King Hubert from different scenes, done by Milt Kahl, 7" & smaller, CE/Dec 12/96 (1500-2000) 2185

6 drawings: 3 of Briar Rose: sitting w/berry basket on lap; walking to left w/eyes closed, wearing shawl over head & swinging berry basket; head-&-shoulders portrait of her wearing shawl & looking inquisitively to right. 3 drawings of King Hubert: 2 sitting in profile at feasting table & gesturing; extreme close-up of face as he sleeps; S/Dec 14/96 (800-1200) 460

Front-view drawing of calm Maleficent, head turned slightly left, 9", S/Dec 14/96 (800-1200) 920

2 drawings: waist-up of King Stefan looking right, 6-5/8"; full figure of surprised King Hubert looking right, 5-1/2"; 16-field sheets, some surface wear, SR/Spring/97 (300-600) 250

Full-figure drawing of barefoot Briar Rose standing facing left, holding berry basket & waving, 5-1/4", 16-field sheet, inker's notation, some surface wear, SR/Spring/97 (300-600) 300

Drawing of sitting Prince Phillip facing right & looking up as he holds boot upside down, 7 x 5", HL/May 31/97 (200-250) 173

Hips-up drawing of Fauna (in peasant dress) holding pitcher, 10 x 8", HL/May 31/97 (100-200) 196

Final full-figure drawing of Prince Phillip wearing cape & standing facing forward, looking right, 6 x 3-1/2", with notes, HL/May 31/97 (200-300) 81

Near-full figure rough drawing of distressed Briar Rose standing facing left (faint blue pencil outline of Flora at left), 8 x 3", HL/May 31/97 (300-400) 316

Pan drawing of Dragon with sword in belly, 12-1/2 x 22", CLA/Jun 7/97 (1500-2000) 1150

4 consecutive pan drawings of Flora, 7" & smaller, CLA/Jun 7/97 (800-1200) 552

6 pan drawings: bird flying with special effects drawing; waist-up on Fauna w/cake, eyes open; waist-up of drunken Lackey taking drink, eyes open; cottage floor; half-body profile of Merryweather; Flora's back; sight 12-1/2 x 33", CLA/Jun 7/97 (800-1200) 368

Prince Phillip crosses a broken bridge, 93 rough animation drawings, 2 different scenes, sight 12 x 15-1/2", CLA/Jun 7/97 (600-800) 1150

2 drawings: waist-up of King Stefan looking right with right hand raised, 6-5/8"; ankles-up of sad Briar Rose with hands up & eyes closed, 8"; 16-field sheets; SR/Fall/97 (300-500) 330

43 assorted characters drawn by Milt Kahl, Ollie Johnston, Frank Thomas, & Marc Davis; sight 12-1/2 x 15-1/2"; CE/Dec 18/97 (3000-4000) 2990

46 rough drawings of owl & birds as prince by Marc Davis, 8-1/2" & smaller, CE/Dec 18/97 (2500-3500) 3220

55 consecutive rough drawings of fighting Prince Phillip on his horse, 15" long, CE/Dec 18/97 (2500-3500) 4370

Maleficent, 116 drawings by Marc Davis: 60 full figure, others special effects, 14" & similar, CE/Dec 18/97 (15,000-20,000) 27,600

27 consecutive drawings of Briar Rose by Marc Davis, 8" & similar, CE/Dec 18/97 (3500-4500) 3450

12 rough drawings of Briar Rose by Marc Davis: each full figure, 4 views from her back as she turns, 2 signed; 7" & similar; CE/Dec 18/97 (2500-3500) 2990

7 rough drawings by Marc Davis of Maleficent with Raven on shoulder, 10" & similar, CE/Dec 18/97 (3000-4000) 3680

200 consecutive rough drawings of Prince Phillip & Princess Aurora dancing, 4-1/2" & smaller, CE/Dec 18/97 (2000-3000) 4830

12 drawings of dragon: 5 pan, 7 by Marc Davis, 16" & smaller, CE/Dec 18/97 (2000-3000) 6900

51 rough drawings of Maleficent (12 of head only), each by Marc Davis, 10" & similar, CE/Dec 18/97 (8000-10,000) 13,800

2 drawings: full figure of Briar Rose standing looking toward camera, 5"; front view of Maleficent looking right, 9", S/Dec 19/97 (1000-1500) 920

Near-full figure drawing of Briar Rose standing facing right, bend forward at waist, hands behind back, looking up; 6-3/4", 16-field sheet, SR/Spring/98 (500-900) 570

Portrait drawing of Dragon facing left, wings spread,

leaning forward, looking down; 20-1/4" x 12"
on 30 x 12-1/2" pan sheet, signed by Marc
Davis, moderately shallow fold down center,
SR/Spring/98 (2200-2800)   2010

2 full-figure drawings: Prince Phillip stands looking
right with open arms, Prince Phillip lifts King
Hubert off ground; 6-1/2 x 4", 7-1/2 x 5";
VF; HL/Apr 25/98 (500-700)   575

BACKGROUNDS

Watercolor production background: interior
close-up, CE/Jun 18/94 (1000-1500)   1495

Production background of crowd scene inside castle,
pencil & watercolor on trimmed board,
production notes, CE/Dec 16/94
(1000-1500)   2185

Gouache master background of forest cottage interior
at night, 27-1/4 x 9-3/4", SR/Fall/95
(5000-10,000)   16,000

Waist-up of Alice (1-3/4") sitting in spoon from King
Stefan's castle as caterpillar-as-butterfly (3")
hovers against tapestry background, *Alice in Wonderland* characters from Jell-O commercial,
1955, DL Art Corner label, SR/Fall/95
(300-600)   660

Section of background painting of Woodcutter's
Cottage kitchen, tempera on background sheet,
11-1/2 x 8", VF, HL/Oct 6/96 (500-700)   1955

Production background: close-up of castle interior,
sight 13 x 4-3/4", watercolor on trimmed
board, CE/Dec 12/96 (600-800)   805

Unfinished production background of forest,
tempera on background sheet, 11 x 18",
F+, HL/Nov 16/97 (1000-1500)   3910

CEL SET-UPS

Briar Rose sings to birds, preliminary poster
background, 8 x 10", CE/Dec 15/93
(2000-2500)   2070

2-cel set-up of 8" King Stefan laughing & 5-1/2"
King Hubert holding fish, together with cel
of 7" Queen looking concerned; both with
Konica copy of original background,
S/Dec 16/93 (700-900)   460

Full figure of Maleficent in profile; Prince Phillip bound
& gagged w/eyes closed; one of Maleficent's
demons; 3rd with Konica copy of original background, S/Dec 16/93 (2500-3500)   2070

3 fairies & Briar Rose in cottage, watercolor pan
production background attributed to Eyvind
Earle, production notes, WDP stamp,
S/Dec 16/93 (15,000-20,000)   24,150

6-1/2" Merryweather flying; 5-1/2" Flora with
hand out; both w/Konica copy of original
background; S/Dec 16/93 (700-900)   690

2-cel set-up of surprised Briar Rose (6-1/2") in profile
& Merryweather (5") with wand & wings issuing
warning; 7 x 8" Prince Phillip w/eyes closed rides
thru forest on Samson; both w/appropriate print
background & gold DL label, S/Dec 16/93
(800-1200)   805

Samson; each w/appropriate print background &
gold DL label, S/Dec 16/93 (800-1200)   805

Maleficent holding staff w/Diablo perched on top,
print background, gold DL label, 8-1/2", needs
restoration, S/Dec 16/93 (800-1200)   2300

Briar Rose looks at squirrel in tree that's part of
cottage interior, watercolor production background, production notes, inscribed "To Don
DaGradi, Best Wishes, Walt Disney", WDP
stamp, 7", S/Dec 16/93 (5000-7000)   12,650

Prince Phillip awakens Aurora with kiss, matching
cel & background painting (tempera on background sheet) created for publication or
publicity use, 8-1/2 x 12", VF,
HL/Feb 26-27/94 (900-1200)   1980

Prince Phillip battles full-length dragon,
complementary color print background,
VF+, HL/Apr 10/94 (5000-6000)   9520

Flora prepares to bake, tempera master background
of cottage kitchen, 8-1/2 x 20", studio
notes, signed by Eyvind Earle, VF+, HL/Apr 10/94
(5000-7000)   6720

Portrait of Aurora, watercolor background painting of
cottage interior for scene cut from film, 11 x 20",
notes, VF, HL/Apr 10/94 (6000-8000)   5376

Fairies in castle dress: full figures of Flora & Fauna in
evening colors, color print background; Flora
dispensing magic sparkles; both sold at DL;
7-1/2 x 9", 7-1/2 x 9-1/2", VF,
HL/Apr 10/94 (1500-2000)   1568

Briar Rose dances with Prince Phillip in forest, pan
watercolor production background with
production overlays, 3" each, S/Jun 17/94
(12,000-15,000)   11,500

Briar Rose (7") walks thru forest with animals,
pan watercolor production background
with production overlay, S/Jun 17/94
(12,000-15,000)   11,500

Maleficent stands in profile (waist up) as Raven alights
upon her hand, printed background, gold DL
label, 6", S/Jun 17/94 (2000-3000)   2875

Scheming Maleficent, 9", unidentified background of
castle interior, CE/Jun 18/94 (2000-2500)   3220

Briar Rose (8-3/4 x 4-1/2") walks w/forest animals,
printed background, CE/Jun 18/94
(1500-2000)   2530

Curious Maleficent, 6 x 5-1/2", Hanna-Barbera
production background, CE/Jun 18/94
(2000-2500)   2300

Smiling Briar Rose in cottage, 5-1/2", DL printed
background, CE/Jun 18/94 (1500-2000)   1725

Prince Phillip (looking back, 6") on Samson, DL label
& printed background, CE/Jun 18/94
(600-800)   483

2 birds dress Owl in Prince's cape, unidentified background of forest, 5-1/2 x 5", CE/Jun 18/94
(500-700)   518

Briar Rose walks in forest, background unidentified,
6-1/2 x 2-1/2", CE/Jun 18/94
(1500-2000)   1955

Flora waves wand, 7", DL printed background,
CE/Jun 18/94 (500-700)   863

Briar Rose walks thru forest, 6 x 2-1/2", illustration
background, CE/Jun 18/94 (1000-1500)   1495

Triumphant Maleficent, 7-1/2", printed background,
CE/Jun 18/94 (1200-1500)   2990

Prince Phillip in forest, color print background of
forest as sold at DL, label, 7-1/2 x 9-1/2",
VG, HL/Aug 21/94 (500-700)   392

Full figure of Merryweather in castle dress in front of
cottage, color print background as sold at DL,
label, 8-1/2 x 10", VF, HL/Aug 21/94
(500-700)   700

Maleficent & bound Prince Phillip in cottage, Studio
Art Props background painting, 9-1/2 x
13-1/2", VF+, HL/Aug 21/94
(3000-5000)   5600

One cel each of Flora, Fauna & Merryweather, 2 over
color print backgrounds w/DL mats & labels;
10 x 8", 7-1/2 x 5-1/2", F-VF, HL/Aug 21/94
(1800-2400)   1456

Prince Phillip riding Samson; Aurora talks to seated
Merryweather in cottage; color print back-
grounds w/DL mats & labels, 8 x 10", VG,
HL/Aug 21/94 (1000-1500)   1232

Trussed Prince Phillip struggles against six goons,
13-1/2 x 7-3/4", master gouache background
of Maleficent's dungeon, SR/Fall/94
(4000-8000)   4070

Torso-up of Flora draping pink fabric [on Merryweather],
8-1/2", gouache master background of cottage
interior, SR/Fall/94 (5000-10,000)   6200

Briar Rose talks to Merryweather (back to camera) with
hands under her chin, 7", DL litho background of
forest & Art Corner label, some cracked paint &
color shift, SR/Fall/94 (700-1200)   1580

Full figure of Aurora in trance standing in castle passage
doorway, 7", 29-1/2 x 11-1/4" key master background, special-effects overlay, SR/Fall/94
(7000-11,000)   6500

Maleficent smiles as she pets Diablo perched on her
staff, 11 x 7-1/2", color print background, as
sold at DL, HL/Nov 13/94 (2000-2500)   3360

Briar Rose in forest with 2 birds, 8 x 10", color print
background, as sold at DL, HL/Nov 13/94
(1000-1500)   1792

Prince Phillip in profile, 8 x 10", color print background of forest, as sold at DL, HL/Nov 13/94
(800-1200)   1568

Merryweather in peasant garb carrying material &
sewing basket, 8-1/2 x 10", color print background as sold at DL, HL/Nov 13/94
(400-600)   952

2 expressive cels: King Hubert; King Stefan; 8-1/2
x 10-1/2", both over color print backgrounds
as sold at DL, HL/Nov 13/94 (600-900)   1232

Over-the-shoulder view of Maleficent as dragon
attacking Prince Phillip, DL background & label,
1-1/2" & 8", CE/Dec 16/94 (1200-1500)   2530

Briar Rose dancing with animals as mock prince,
7" & similar, DL printed background,
CE/Dec 16/94 (1500-2000)   2185

4 trumpeters on balcony, 2-1/2", key watercolor
production background, production notes,
CE/Dec 16/94 (4000-5000)   3450

Briar Rose in forest w/animals on tree branch,
5-3/4", key watercolor production background, CE/Dec 16/94 (15,000-25,000)   21,850

Prince Phillip riding Samson thru forest w/sword
& shield, 6", DL background & label,
CE/Dec 16/94 (1000-1500)   920

Briar Rose (6") walks in forest with Owl (1-1/2"), DL
background and label, CE/Dec 16/94
(1200-1500)   1840

Maleficent in castle with Raven on shoulder looks back,
7", DL background & label, CE/Dec 16/94
(1000-1500)   3220

Flora (6-1/2") talks to Briar Rose (7") in cottage, pan
gouache master background (33-1/2" wide by
8-1/4" to 10" high), SR/Spring/95
(6000-12,000)   8000

Front view of enraged Maleficent with both hands in
air, her right hand holding staff, 10-1/2", pan
gouache master background of her throne,
SR/Spring/95 (10,000-16,000)   10,700

Full-figure rear view of Flora in castle dress, holding
wand, 5", master background of castle interior,
SR/Spring/95 (1800-3000)   4360

2 DL set-ups: hips-up of Fauna with bluebird, 4-1/4";
hips-up of Merryweather with red bird, 4-1/2";
unidentified backgrounds, Gold Art Corner
labels, SR/Spring/95 (700-1200)   800

Extreme close-up of Maleficent battling Prince
Phillip, 8 x 10", color print background,
HL/Apr 23/95 (2500-3000)   2016

Frontal close-up of Prince Phillip swinging
sword, 9 x 7-1/2", color print background as
sold at DL, F+, HL/Apr 23/95 (900-1200)   840

Anxious Prince Phillip rides determined Samson,
8-1/2 x 10", color print background as sold
at DL, VF, HL/Apr 23/95 (900-1200)   1904

Briar Rose in forest with animals, 5-3/4", DL printed
background, CE/Jun 9/95 (1500-2000)   2990

Close-up of gesturing King Stefan in castle, 6", DL
background, CE/Jun 9/95 (500-700)   403

Full figure of Briar Rose walking in forest as animals
watch, 6-1/2", watercolor production background, CE/Jun 9/95 (15,000-20,000)   25,300

Alert Maleficent in castle, 7-3/4", DL printed
background & label, CE/Jun 9/95 (1500-2000)   2300

Full-figure front view of Briar Rose sitting in forest
clearing with animals, 4", printed DL background & label, CE/Jun 9/95 (1500-2000)   2185

Smiling Maleficent in castle holding candle, 7", DL
printed background & label, CE/Jun 9/95
(1500-2000)   2990

Kings Stefan (6-1/2") & Hubert (5") toasting in
castle, printed background, DL label, S/Jun
10/95 (400-600)   460

Flora (6"), Fauna (4") & Merryweather (5") plan to
save Princess Aurora while hidden in jewel
case, watercolor production background,
S/Jun 10/95 (6000-8000)   11,500

Full figures of three fairies in castle dress (Flora 6")
walking together thru Maleficent's castle,
gouache master pan background, tear in
corner of background, SR/Fall/95
(6000-12,000)   7000

Briar Rose w/basket & 19 forest friends, 9 x 11",
color print forest background, gold DL label,
VF, HL/Nov 19/95 (2000-3000)   2070

Maleficent instructs Raven, 8-1/2 x 10-3/4", w/color
print background of King Stefan's castle interior,
gold label as sold at DL, VF, HL/Nov 19/95
(2500-3500)   4025

2 full-figure cels of Flora, Fauna & Merryweather in
castle dress mounted to large cel sheet & framed
w/printed images simulating cradle scene, 7-1/2
x 11-1/2 (cels only), VF, HL/Nov 19/95
(1000-1500)   2760

Hips-up profile of Briar Rose facing right, 7-1/4", DL
litho background of forest, gold Art Corner label,
SR/Spring/96 (1200-1600)   1200

Full figures of worried Flora (9 x 7"), Fauna, & Merryweather in castle dress flying over Maleficent's castle, all key to each other, pan gouache background, SR/Spring/96
(3000-7000)   5400

Full figures of Phillip (7-3/8") & Hubert (5-3/4")
standing together talking in castle, color print
display background, SR/Spring/96
(1000-1500) 1100

Full figures of Briar Rose (4") standing on forest
promontory facing right toward Prince Phillip
on Samson (4") on promontory looking back;
3 fairies in castle dress w/wings, wands & fairy
dust, each 1/2"; 2 rabbits & 2 birds, gouache
display background, SR/Spring/96
(4500-9000) 5000

Fauna as peasant holds wand & reads cookbook in
messy cottage kitchen, master background
(tempera on background sheet), mat inscribed
"To Una Merkel, My Best Wishes, Walt Disney",
WDP label, 9-1/2 x 12-1/2", VF+, HL/Apr
28/96 (5000-7000) 7475

Near-full figure of Briar Rose w/2 forest friends over
print of forest originally issued by DAE w/limited
edition, VF+, 11 x 29-1/2", HL/Apr 28/96
(1200-1600) 2070

Large-image full-figure production set-up of Princess
Aurora (8-1/2") & Prince Phillip (10") dancing in
castle, watercolor production background, S/Jun
19/96 (15,000-25,000) 19,550

Pan production set-up of Prince Phillip on Samson
(5-1/2 x 9") battling Maleficent as Dragon (16")
outside castle, pan watercolor production background from another scene, S/Jun 19/96
(15,000-20,000) 11,500

Anxious Princess Aurora in castle, printed background,
3-1/2"; Prince Phillip holding shield, DL label,
5-1/4", S/Jun 19/96 (1000-1500) 1840

3 fairies (2") trail Maleficent (holding staff & w/raven
on shoulder, 8") in castle passageway, pan watercolor production background by Eyvind Earle,
CE/Jun 20/96 (15,000-18,000) 13,800

Aurora & Prince Phillip dancing, 6-5/8" on full 30 x
12-1/2" pan cel with full-length custom airbrush
background, SR/Fall/96 (1200-1800) 1920

Flora (8"), Fauna (7"), & Merryweather (6-3/4") together
in castle dress, glimmers of fairy dust, color print
background of castle passage, SR/Fall/96
(1200-1600) 1800

Front view of determined Prince Phillip astride Samson
fighting thru thorn forest w/sword & shield, color
print background as sold at DL, 9 x 11", VF,
HL/Oct 6/96 (800-1200) 978

Princess & fairies waving up castle circular staircase,
matching Technirama master background
(tempera on background sheet), signed by Eyvind
Earle, 11-1/4 x 29-1/2", VF+, HL/Oct 6/96
(10,000-12,000) 9775

Portrait of Merryweather & Fauna in castle dress, color
print of forest background from film as sold at
DL, 8 x 10", VF, HL/Oct 6/96 (700-900) 863

Kings Stefan & Hubert raising goblets, matching cels
over color print of castle background from film
as sold at DL, 6-3/4" x 8", F, HL/Oct 6/96
(700-900) 1380

Prince Phillip sings to startled Briar Rose in forest as
he grasps her left hand from behind, background
of forest, 6-1/2 x 9", VF, HL/Oct 6/96
(2000-2500) 3220

Full figure of Prince Phillip (background) confronting
Maleficent as Dragon (foreground, back to camera), 8-1/2 x 11-1/4", color print of background
as sold at DL, VF, HL/Oct 6/96
(1800-2200) 2990

Full figures of Merryweather (opening top half of Dutch
door) & Flora in peasant dress inside cottage, 11
x 9-1/2", complementary non-Studio painted
background, Disney seal, signed by Marc Davis,
VF, HL/Oct 6/96 (600-900) 1035

Full figures of angry Kings Hubert & Stefan standing
in castle arguing in castle, 9 x 7" cel image,
unidentified background, VF+, HL/Oct 6/96
(600-900) 575

Full-figure front view of determined Prince Phillip
riding ferocious Samson w/sword & shield at
ready, 5-1/2 x 4-1/4", complementary non-
Studio painted background, VF+,
HL/Oct 6/96 (600-900) 949

Full figure of sad Briar Rose walking to right thru forest,
head down, shrouded in blue cloak, 6 x 3-1/2",
unidentified background, VF, HL/Oct 6/96
(700-900) 575

Merryweather (3") & Fauna (6") watching Flora (6") cry,
all in castle dress standing behind castle parapet,

key watercolor production background, CE/Dec
12/96 (6000-8000) 6900

Full figure of Briar Rose coyly glancing back as she
walks thru forest, 7", Disney illustration background, CE/Dec 12/96 (1500-2000) 2875

Full figures of Briar Rose (6-1/2") in forest dancing
w/animals' mock prince, owl & squirrel in cloak,
6-1/2", rabbits in boots, 3" ea, trimmed non-
matching production background, S/Dec 14/96
(7000-9000) 16,100

Flora, Fauna, & Merryweather in castle dress standing
against castle wall, table w/covered serving dish
on red cloth in foreground, 5-1/2 x 4",
watercolor production background,
S/Dec 14/96 (12,000-15,000) 8050

Full figures of Fauna (8", w/2 bunnies at feet), Merryweather (6") & Flora (near-full figure,
8-1/2") in castle dress standing in forest
looking happily to left, printed background,
S/Dec 14/96 (1500-2500) 2587

Thoughtful Maleficent (8") w/Diablo (3") watching her
w/one leg on staff & wings spread, printed DL
background of castle, S/Dec 14/96
(2500-3500) 5750

Full figures of 8 animals perched on tree limb, matching
master background of forest (tempera on background sheet), 7-3/4 x 16", VF, HL/Feb 23/97
(2500-3500) 6038

Full-figure color model cel of Goon standing guard in
castle, color print background, 9-1/2 x 5-1/2",
F+, HL/Feb 23/97 (400-500) 345

Full figure of Prince Phillip struggling against rope &
gag in dungeon, color print background, 6-1/4
x 3-1/4", F, HL/Feb 23/97 (500-700) 403

Full-figure front view of Maleficent standing in castle
with mouth open & arms spread, robe flowing;
14-1/2 x 9-1/8", tear in upper left; color print
background; restored; SR/Spring/97
(3500-5000) 3960

Near-full figure of Princess Aurora walking thru castle
in trance, 8", 16-field cel, color print background,
Original Art Program seal, SR/Spring/97
(1000-1600) 1050

Briar Rose (5-1/2") & Prince (5-3/4") hold hands &
talk in forest, Disney illustration background,
CLA/Jun 7/97 (1500-2000) 2070

Full figure of confident Maleficent (6") standing in palace
court w/arms raised as guards converge, Xerox
line-on-cel background, S/Jun 21/97 (2000-
3000) 4600

Concerned Flora (5"), Fauna (4"), & Merryweather (4")
in peasant dress look up as they huddle in corner
of cottage interior, printed background, S/Jun
21/97 (1200-1500) 920

Excited Briar Rose (5-3/4") at cottage, printed DL
background; Prince Phillip (6") shielding himself
while astride Samson (6 x 5-1/2");
S/Jun 21/97 (1500-2500) 1495

Full figure of surprised Briar Rose standing shoeless in
forest facing right w/arms out, 7", + 2 bunnies
& bird, print background, S/Jun 21/97
(1000-1500) 1150

Briar Rose (7") looks affectionately at Merryweather
(rear view, 4"), printed DL background of outdoors, S/Jun 21/97 (1800-2200) 1725

Waist-up image of diabolical Maleficent standing in
repose in castle w/chin resting on left hand,
8", printed background, S/Jun 21/97
(2500-3500) 2587

Chef Donald (6-1/2") & birthday cake from *Sleeping
Beauty*; full figure of Daisy (5-1/2") looking over
shoulder as she stands holding mannequin; one
of Donald's nephews on skates, 5"; nephew
wearing cap holding arms out, 4"; all with
printed DL backgrounds & gold labels,
S/Jun 21/97 (1200-1800) 1150

Full figures of miniature Fauna (3-3/4") & Merryweather
(3") in castle dress flying along drawbridge past
chain, gouache master background, overall 24 x
10-1/2", SR/Fall/97 (4500-9000) 2620

Full figure of Briar Rose (6-3/4") reaching for mock
prince (6-3/8") as other animals watch, color
print background, SR/Fall/97 (2700-3700) 1800

2 cels: smiling Fauna in peasant dress holding wand &
lopsided birthday cake, 5-3/4 x 8-1/2", color
print of background of cottage interior, label as
sold at DL, VF, HL/Nov 16/97 (500-700) 1150

Phillip puts arms on & speaks to King Hubert, 6-1/2
x 7", color print of background of castle, gold

& red DL labels, VF, HL/Nov 16/97
(900-1200) 748

Matching set of cels of Dragon spewing fire, 11-1/4 x
29", original master background painting of castle
bridge & thorns (tempera on background sheet),
VF, HL/Nov 16/97 (10,000-12,000) 11,788

Portrait of wistful Briar Rose, 6 x 4-1/2", color print of
forest background & label as sold at DL, VF+,
HL/Nov 16/97 (1000-1500) 1495

Waist-up profile of Briar Rose walking to right, 7 x 5-
1/2", color print background of outdoors as sold
at DL, VF+, HL/Nov 16/97 (1000-1500) 978

Large-image profile of Flora in castle dress in forest
facing right, unidentified background, overlay
cel signed by Frank Thomas & Ollie Johnston,
10-1/2 x 9" overall including signatures, VF+,
HL/Nov 16/97 (400-600) 920

Portrait of Maleficent facing left & laughing, 6-1/4
x 5", complementary painted background of
castle wall, VF, HL/Nov 16/97 (1000-1500) 1610

Full figures of Briar Rose (facing right) & squirrel standing in forest, 4 x 1-3/4" & 1-1/4 x 1-1/4", color
print of background, VF+, HL/Nov 16/97
(700-1000) 1265

Full figures of Briar Rose (6") dancing in forest with owl
(5") as prince, DL background & gold DL label,
CE/Dec 18/97 (1500-2000) 1150

Full figures of Briar Rose (6-1/4") dancing with mock
prince (owl 4-1/2") amid animals, watercolor production background of forest, Courvoisier label,
mat signed "Walt Disney", CE/Dec 18/97
(8000-10,000) 8625

Side view of Princess Aurora & Prince Phillip dancing
in castle, 7" each, watercolor production background, CE/Dec 18/97 (7000-9000) 6900

Full figure of Briar Rose standing toward right on stone
path, 7-1/4", DL background & gold seal,
CE/Dec 18/97 (1000-1500) 1265

Full figures of mock prince (5-1/2") inviting Briar Rose
(7-1/4") to dance, printed background of forest,
S/Dec 19/97 (1800-2200) 2070

Merryweather (as model, 6-1/2") & Flora (w/scissors,
6") in peasant dress struggle with pink material,
pan watercolor production background of
cottage interior, S/Dec 19/97 (7000-9000) 5750

Full figures of 3 surprised Fairies in castle dress standing
huddled in a row, 3 x 3" overall, printed background, S/Dec 19/97 (700-900) 1380

Flora (8"), Fauna (7"), & Merryweather (6-3/4") in castle
dress conversing, master gouache background
painting of castle wall, SR/Spring/98
(4000-7000) 4800

Briar Rose sits on log amid admiring animals, 7-1/4",
four cel levels, color print background,
SR/Spring/98 (2200-2800) 2000

Prince Phillip speaks to King Hubert in castle, color
print of background from film, red & gold
DL label, 7-1/2 x 9" cels, VF, HL/Apr 25/98
(700-1000) 920

Full figures of Merryweather dancing as dripping mop
emerges from bucket, matching master background of cottage interior (tempera on
background sheet), 9-3/4 x 22", VF,
HL/Apr 25/98 (4000-6000) 10,350

Near-full figure of Fauna in castle dress standing
looking right, complementary painted
background of castle wall, 8 x 4-1/4", VF+,
HL/Apr 25/98 (400-600) 690

CELS – FULL FIGURE (also see MODEL ART)

3-1/2" Briar Rose strolls w/berry basket in profile
w/1-1/2" (length) rabbit beside her,
S/Dec 16/93 (800-1200) 575

6" Flora w/measuring tape; 5" Merryweather;
S/Dec 16/93, S/Dec 16/93 (600-900) 460

8-1/4" King Stefan; 7" King Hubert; each full figure
standing in profile, S/Dec 16/93 (400-600) 690

4 cels: Merryweather (2); Flora; Fauna; each circa 3",
S/Dec 16/93 (800-1200) 690

3 cels of fairies, each in cape w/wings & wand,
images vary from 6" to 9", S/Dec 16/93
(1200-1500) 1495

Flora in profile w/wings & wand, 8", S/Dec 16/93
(400-600) 575

3 fairies fly amid stars, 2", S/Dec 16/93
(800-1200) 575

Smiling Briar Rose, 6-3/4", S/Dec 16/93
(1000-1200) 1265

Contented King Hubert w/wine glass, 6 x 5-1/2",
laminated, Disney seal, WDP & DL labels,

VF+, HL/Feb 26-27/94 (300-400) 825
Briar Rose & Prince Phillip meet, shadow colors, 2-1/2 x 2-1/2", VF+, HL/Apr 10/94 (600-800) 616
Briar Rose walking right w/berry basket & bunny, 3 x 2-1/2", VF+, HL/Apr 10/94 (900-1200) 1008
Maleficent gloats, 8 x 5", backing board & label, distributed in 1959 promotion, restored, VF, HL/Apr 10/94 (2000-2500) 2016
Animals as mock prince, 6-1/2 x 3-1/2", VF+, HL/Apr 10/94 (500-700) 784
Briar Rose w/berry basket facing right, 6-1/2 x 3", VF+, HL/Apr 10/94 (1000-1500) 1904
Surprised Samson rears w/Prince Phillip riding, 7-1/2 x 9", VF+, HL/Apr 10/94 (900-1200) 896
Briar Rose in profile, 6", S/Jun 17/94 (1000-1200) 1150
Alarmed Flora (6"), Fauna (3-1/2") & Merryweather (4"), S/Jun 17/94 (1200-1500) 920
Briar Rose, wearing shawl & holding berry basket, turns head, 6-1/4", S/Jun 17/94 (1000-1200) 1495
Briar Rose w/shawl over head & basket sings to animals, 5-1/2", S/Jun 17/94 (700-900) 1725
Briar Rose stands holding berry basket, 6-1/2 x 3", VF+, HL/Aug 21/94 (1000-1500) 1568
3 concerned good fairies in castle garb standing looking left, night colors, 4-1/2 x 8-1/2", VF, HL/Aug 21/94 (1000-1500) 1232
Front view of Briar Rose standing holding berry basket, right arm out, eyes to right, 7-1/4", SR/Fall/94 (1000-1500) 1680
Prince Phillip (back to camera) & Aurora dancing, 2-1/2", SR/Fall/94 (100-300) 400
Aurora in pink gown facing left in dancing pose, 8-1/2", SR/Fall/94 (1400-1900) 1700
Front-view xerographed image of Briar Rose walking with head cloaked, carrying berry basket, 1-3/4", SR/Fall/94 (100-300) 170
Profile of surprised Briar Rose, 6 x 3", HL/Nov 13/94 (900-1200) 1232
Briar Rose with cape over arm, 6-1/2", CE/Dec 16/94 (1000-1500) 1380
High-stepping Briar Rose w/basket, 10", CE/Dec 16/94 (1000-1500) 1265
Merryweather in peasant disguise, 6-3/4", CE/Dec 16/94 (400-600) 403
Prince Phillip standing, 7", CE/Dec 16/94 (600-800) 575
Briar Rose (eyes closed) walks with berry basket, 6-1/2"; Prince Phillip sits dripping wet in water, 4 x 7"; Samson stands watching Phillip, 8 x 8"; S/Dec 17/94 (1200-1800) 2185
5 cels: full figure of Briar Rose; large image of Flora casting spell; two of Fauna; Merryweather; S/Dec 17/94 (1000-1500) 1955
4 cels: Briar Rose walking away with berry basket; Prince Phillip riding Samson armed with shield & sword; Maleficent's demon henchmen; Samson galloping to right; S/Dec 17/94 (600-800) 1265
6 cels: one each of good fairies in robes with wings & wands; King Stefan; King Stefan's Queen; King Hubert; S/Dec 17/94 (1000-1500) 1265
3 cels of fairies in peasant dress with wands: near-full figure of Flora facing right casting spell, 7-1/8"; full figure of smiling Fauna standing facing right, 6"; full figure of surprised Merryweather standing facing left, 6-3/4"; all 16-field, SR/Spring/95 (900-1500) 1300
Full figure of angry King Hubert standing facing left in sword-fighting pose with fish for sword, 6-1/2", SR/Spring/95 (400-700) 460
2 full standing figures: Prince Phillip with eyes closed & arms out in singing pose, Briar Rose with head turned away & eyes closed, both 5", SR/Spring/95 (900-1500) 970
Briar Rose walks with broom, 4-1/2 x 2-1/2", HL/Apr 23/95 (800-1200) 672
Prince Phillip walking, 6 x 2-1/2", HL/Apr 23/95 (600-800) 616
Good fairies in castle dress painted in shadow colors, 6-1/2 x 12-1/2", HL/Apr 23/95 (1000-1500) 1792
Prince Phillip (looking back) astride Samson, 9-1/2 x 8", HL/Apr 23/95 (1000-1500) 2016
3 full-figure cels: Flora, Fauna & Merryweather in castle dress, 7-1/2 x 5", 8-1/2 x 6-1/2", 6 x 4", VF, HL/Apr 23/95 (1500-2000) 3360

Court jester plays lute, 7 x 6", HL/Apr 23/95 (500-700) 476
Prince Phillip riding Samson w/sword & shield, 6 x 6-1/2", HL/Apr 23/95 (900-1200) 1232
Maleficent w/swirling cloak, 7 x 7", HL/Apr 23/95 (2500-3000) 3808
King Hubert standing w/goblet, 6-1/2 x 5", HL/Apr 23/95 (400-600) 504
Prince Phillip running, 3-1/2 x 3-1/2", HL/Apr 23/95 (400-600) 448
Frightened Merryweather in castle dress, 6 x 4", HL/Apr 23/95 (500-700) 476
6 cels of forest animals (most full figure), 2-1/2 x 2" to 4 x 3", VF, HL/Apr 23/95 (600-800) 560
Aurora & Prince Phillip dancing, 2-1/2", CE/Jun 9/95 (600-800) 633
Prince Phillip stands facing right, 7", CE/Jun 9/95 (500-700) 276
6 cels: one each of 3 fairies; Queen; King Hubert; Briar Rose walking with berry basket, S/Jun 10/95 (1000-1500) 920
Briar Rose reaching up, 6-1/2"; Prince Phillip waving sword & riding Samson, 4 x 5" (not including sword); wistful Fauna clasping hands, 7", S/Jun 10/95 (1000-1500) 1725
4 cels: one each of good fairies; Briar Rose making a point, S/Jun 10/95 (1000-1500) 1955
4 cels: each fairy in peasant garb; Briar Rose holding berry basket w/eyes closed; S/Jun 10/95 (800-1200) 920
Briar Rose points to right, 6-1/2"; Samson gallops to right, 4 x 10"; Prince Phillip waving sword astride Samson, 4-1/2 x 4", S/Jun 10/95 (800-1200) 1150
Tiny full figure of Briar Rose walking w/basket, owl reclining in basket, 3 x 1", HL/Aug 6/95 (200-300) 476
Surprised Flora in peasant dress, 7 x 4", HL/Aug 6/95 (500-700) 476
Fauna in castle dress holding teacup & saucer, 5-1/2 x 3", HL/Aug 6/95 (400-600) 616
Determined Prince Phillip struggling against chains, 9-1/2 x 7", HL/Aug 6/95 (900-1200) 784
Prince Phillip kneels beside Samson, 6-1/2 x 9-1/2", HL/Aug 6/95 (900-1200) 1120
Full figures of Prince Phillip & Briar Rose standing together, 3-3/4", 16-field, SR/Fall/95 (500-1000) 1430
Large full figures of Prince Phillip & Princess Aurora waltzing in the finale, VF+, HL/Nov 19/95 (2000-2500) 2070
Defiant Prince Phillip sits in chains, 6-1/2 x 6", VF, HL/Nov 19/95 (700-1000) 748
Briar Rose w/forest animals, 7-1/2 x 9", VF+, HL/Nov 19/95 (1200-1600) 1840
Lackey walking w/precariously balanced wine tray, 7-1/2 x 6", VF+, HL/Nov 19/95 (500-700) 403
Prince Phillip & Briar Rose standing together, 3-1/2 x 2-1/2", VF+, HL/Nov 19/95 (900-1200) 863
Thoughtful Fauna in castle dress, 7-1/2 x 5-1/2", VF+, HL/Nov 19/95 (600-800) 1035
Merryweather in castle dress & Flora in peasant garb; 6 x 5", 6 x 4", VF, HL/Nov 19/95 (900-1200) 863
Coy Briar Rose walks right, looking into camera, 7-3/8", 16-field, SR/Spring/96 (1000-1600) 1340
Front view of winged Fauna in castle dress looking right with wand raised, 6-7/8", 16-field, SR/Spring/96 (400-800) 300
Prince Phillip riding determined Samson to right, 3-3/4", SR/Spring/96 (500-1000) 500
Prince Phillip (back to camera) & Aurora dancing, 2-1/2", SR/Spring/96 (100-300) 270
Front view of Jester (eyes closed) standing playing lute & holding goblet, 7-1/2", SR/Spring/96 (400-700) 400
Profile of Briar Rose walking with basket, 2-1/2 x 1-1/4", HL/Apr 28/96 (400-600) 748
Prince Phillip (holding sword & shield) & Samson, both in night colors, 7-1/2 x 4" & 6-1/2 x 5", HL/Apr 28/96 (1000-1500) 920
Wistful Fauna wearing peasant garb, 7 x 4", HL/Apr 28/96 (600-900) 518
Merryweather as mannequin & Fauna as cook, 6-1/2 x 10", HL/Apr 28/96 (700-900) 633
Prince Phillip & Aurora waltzing, 6-1/2 x 5", HL/Apr 28/96 (2000-2500) 2300
Side view of regal Maleficent standing w/eyes

closed, 8 x 6-1/2", VF+, HL/Apr 28/96 (2000-2500) 2530
5 cels: Samson, Jester holding building plans (both near-full figures), owl as mock prince, red bird, Fauna in castle dress; 2-1/2 x 2" to 8-1/2 x 5-1/2", VF, HL/Apr 28/96 (1000-1500) 1092
3 full-figure cels: each good fairy standing in peasant garb holding wand; 7 x 4", 4-1/2 x 5-1/2", 7-1/2 x 3-1/2", HL/Apr 28/96 (1200-1600) 1380
Front view of Maleficent w/robes outspread, 3-1/2 x 6-1/2", HL/Apr 28/96 (1500-2000) 2300
Full figure of Briar Rose facing forward w/shawl over head & berry basket in hand, 6-1/2"; full figure of Prince Phillip w/eyes closed, 5". Plus three photostat model sheets: 2 of Briar Rose, one "Comparative Sizes", S/Jun 19/96 (1000-1500) 1092
3 cels: one each of Flora (7"), Fauna (7") & Merryweather (6") in castle dress, holding wands & flying, S/Jun 19/96 (1500-2000) 2070
3 happy birds standing, 2-1/2"; from Pinocchio: full figure of Pinocchio lying on stomach facing right w/limbs spread, 4"; CE/Jun 20/96 (600-800) 1380
Briar Rose walking w/berry basket, 6", CE/Jun 20/96 (1000-1500) 1265
3 Fairies cloaked & disguised as peasant women in night colors, Fauna (7") carrying baby Aurora, on two 14-3/4 x 12-1/2" cel levels key to each other, SR/Fall/96 (1500-3000) 1000
Barefoot, smiling Briar Rose stands holding berry basket, facing right, 7-1/8" on 32 x 12-1/2" pan cel, SR/Fall/96 (1200-1600) 1340
Phillip & Aurora walk together, 2-1/2", only heads & faces hand inked, SR/Fall/96 (100-300) 430
Front image of Prince Phillip walking forward, dark colors, 6-3/4", Disney Art Program seal, SR/Fall/96 (400-700) 420
Profile of Briar Rose walking to right w/berry basket & 2 birds, 3 x 2", VF+, HL/Oct 6/96 (600-900) 633
Anxious Fauna in castle dress stands holding wand in both hands, 8 x 3-3/4", VF+, HL/Oct 6/96 (500-700) 690
Full figures of 3 fairies in peasant dress facing right, 4 x 9-1/2", VF, HL/Oct 6/96 (800-1000) 863
Defiant Prince Phillip sits manacled, 7 x 6-1/2", F+, HL/Oct 6/96 (600-900) 805
Prince Phillip battling nine of Maleficent's goons, 9-1/2 x 14", VF, HL/Oct 6/96 (1000-1500) 1035
Combative King Stefan pointing finger at King Hubert as Hubert swings fish, 8 x 10", F, HL/Oct 6/96 (700-1000) 690
3 hand-inked & -painted limited-edition cels: Maleficent holding raven, full figures of 3 Fairies in castle dress, full figures of Aurora & Prince Phillip dancing; each #161/275; 10 x 7-1/2", 9-1/2 x 9", 7-1/2 x 10-1/2", HL/Oct 6/96 (1500-2000) 2185
Maleficent, arms upraised, staff in left hand, costume flowing, raven on shoulder, 7 x 14", CE/Dec 12/96 (3000-3500) 4370
King Stefan holding goblet of wine & gesturing w/eyes closed, 8", signed by Frank Thomas & Ollie Johnston, "drawing by Milt Kahl" in unknown hand; Maleficent's disembodied, pupil-less face, 5"; S/Dec 14/96 (800-1200) 1150
Princess Aurora (in pink) & Prince Phillip dancing (Prince's back to camera), 7 x 5-1/2", VF+, HL/Feb 23/97 (1000-1500) 920
Sad Briar Rose sits amid animals, 7-1/2 x 11", VF, HL/Feb 23/97 (2000-2500) 1840
Prince Phillip riding reluctant Samson (near-full figure) to left, 9-1/2 x 7-1/2", VF, HL/Feb 23/97 (600-900) 978
Set of 2 near-match cels of tree branches & 5 of birds, 4 x 8-1/2", VF+, HL/Feb 23/97 (400-600) 489
King Hubert runs to right, 5-1/2 x 4-1/2", VF+, HL/Feb 23/97 (300-400) 374
Lackey stands playing lute, 7-1/4 x 4", VF+, HL/Feb 23/97 (300-500) 460
Prince Phillip on Samson galloping to right, 3-1/4 x 4-1/2", VF, HL/Feb 23/97 (400-600) 345
Front view of sad King Hubert sitting, looking left, 5-1/2", 16-field cel, SR/Spring/97 (400-700) 310
Prince Phillip rides Samson to left, 4-5/8", original DL color background & gold Art Corner label, SR/Spring/97 (500-900) 550

Regal Maleficent stands facing left, 8 x 7-1/2", VF+, HL/May 3/97 (2000-2500) 1955
Maleficent walking away & to left, 9 x 8-1/2", HL/May 31/97 (800-1200) 748
Merryweather, 8-1/4"; Flora, 6"; CLA/Jun 7/97 (600-800) 1093
Prince Phillip (7") w/sword & shield at ready standing next to wall of flame, S/Jun 21/97 (800-1200) 1610
Large full figure of Dragon facing left & looking down w/mouth open, 13", S/Jun 21/97 (1500-2500) 2875
Prince Phillip astride Samson facing left, 8 x 8", S/Jun 21/97 (800-1200) 805
11 cels: Kings Hubert & Stefan toasting, forest animals in Prince Phillip's clothing; from *Cinderella*: King, Bruno, Anastasia in nightclothes, Grand Duke, orchestra leader, Lady Tremaine, 3 of Bruno as footman; S/Jun 21/97 (700-900) 1725
Barefoot Briar Rose stands facing right with arms straight out, 6-3/4", original color card background, gold DL Art Corner label, SR/Fall/97 (1000-1400) 800
Merryweather in peasant dress, facing left & looking up while carrying sewing basket & fabric, 5-1/4 x 5-1/4", VF+, HL/Nov 16/97 (400-600) 633
Demure Briar Rose walking barefoot, carrying broom, looking down [descending stairs], 4-3/4 x 2-1/2", VF+, HL/Nov 16/97 (700-900) 633
Determined Merryweather in peasant dress stands holding magic wand above her head, includes sparkles effect, 7-1/4 x 4", VF+, HL/Nov 16/97 (500-700) 431
Full-figure front view of owl (eyes closed) & squirrel wearing Prince's cape, 6 3/4", restored, SR/Spring/98 (600-1000) 650
Phillip & Aurora waltzing from finale, 7 x 6-1/2", VF+, HL/Apr 25/98 (1000-1500) 1725

CELS – PARTIAL FIGURE (also see MODEL ART)

Maleficent (waist-up) holding staff w/Diablo on shoulder, production note, 7-1/2", S/Dec 16/93 (2000-3000) 3163
Close-up of surprised Aurora as Prince Phillip joins her song, 5-1/2 x 7-1/2", VF, HL/Apr 10/94 (1000-1500) 1120
Briar Rose in peasant's garb, 5 x 3", VF+, HL/Apr 10/94 (1000-1500) 1680
Determined Flora & Fauna in castle garb & nighttime colors, 9 x 6" & 9 x 7", VF+, HL/Apr 10/94 (600-800) 1232
Maleficent holding candle high, 9 x 7-1/2" (scene animated by Marc Davis), VF+, HL/Apr 10/94 (2500-3500) 3136
Briar Rose kneeling (right side view, all but bottom of cloak), 6-1/2 x 5-1/2", CE/Jun 18/94 (1000-1500) 863
Waist-up of Maleficent gesturing, 7-1/2", DL label, CE/Jun 18/94 (1200-1500) 2300
King Stefan standing facing left, looking down, 7", DL label, CE/Jun 18/94 (400-600) 345
Waist-up of Kings Hubert & Stefan drinking together, 9-1/2 x 7", VF+, HL/Aug 21/94 (700-1000) 728
Aurora & Prince Phillip walk arm-in-arm, 7-1/2 x 8", VF, HL/Aug 21/94 (2000-3000) 2464
Maleficent looking right w/raven on shoulder, 6-1/2 x 5", VF, HL/Aug 21/94 (2000-3000) 3472
Prince Phillip & Aurora dance, 7 x 5-1/2", VF, HL/Aug 21/94 (1500-2000) 1456
Aurora sings & Merryweather dances, as sold at DL, 5-1/2 x 8-1/2", VG-F, HL/Aug 21/94 (600-900) 504
Ankles-up front view of sitting Jester cradling lute, is a 5-1/2" image, hand inked on 10 x 7-1/4" cel, SR/Fall/94 (200-500) 170
Proud King Stefan & Queen greet Princess Aurora, 11 x 9-5/8", 16-field, SR/Fall/94 (1600-2200) 2140
Upper half of Dragon (5") amid green flames, full image with flame levels 9" (effects cels not key to dragon), SR/Fall/94 (1200-1600) 1480
Ankles-up of Briar Rose sitting facing left, berry basket on lap, 6-3/4", 16-field, SR/Fall/94 (1200-1800) 1400
Knees-up view of Smiling Briar Rose, 6-1/2", CE/Dec 16/94 (1000-1500) 2070
Medium close-up of wide-eyed Briar Rose wearing cloak, 6", CE/Dec 16/94 (800-1200) 1265
Briar Rose looking up to right, 5", CE/Dec 16/94 (800-1200) 1265
2 knights & soldiers, 2 cels; together w/townspeople; 10-1/2" & smaller, CE/Dec 16/94 (1500-2000) 1150
Waist-up of King Stefan, 6-1/2", CE/Dec 16/94 (500-700) 253
Near-full horizontal figure of Maleficent as dragon, 12", S/Dec 17/94 (1000-1500) 1955
Concerned Flora holds dress fabric, 5-1/2" (waist-up), gold DL label, S/Dec 17/94 (300-500) 287
Neck-up close-up of Maleficent laughing evilly, 7-1/2", S/Dec 17/94 (1800-2200) 2875
Smiling Briar Rose with cloak over hair, 5", S/Dec 17/94 (800-1200) 1725
Head & neck of dragon facing left amid flames, 8", 16-field, SR/Spring/95 (1200-1600) 1400
Chest-up front view of Goon with eyes closed & hand over mouth, 7", 16-field, SR/Spring/95 (200-400) 200
Half images of Kings Hubert & Stefan standing facing each other toasting, 5-3/4", some cracking paint & offset ink lines, SR/Spring/95 (500-900) 500
Near-full figure of standing Briar Rose, arms outstretched & singing, 5-1/2 x 4-1/2", HL/Apr 23/95 (1000-1500) 1344
Prince Phillip & Aurora from the scene where they meet, 7 x 3", VF+, HL/Apr 23/95 (1500-1800) 2016
Jovial King Hubert entertains cautious King Stefan, 5-1/2 x 6-1/2", VF+, HL/Apr 23/95 (700-1000) 868
Left-facing profile of kneeling Prince Phillip smiling, 8 x 7-1/2", VF, HL/Apr 23/95 (600-900) 952
Front view of King Hubert; Kings Stefan & Hubert together; 5 x 6-1/2" & 6 x 7"; F; HL/Apr 23/95 (700-1000) 728
Near-full figure of Briar Rose seated w/basket in lap & animals (full figure) around, 7", CE/Jun 9/95 (1500-2000) 3220
3 cels w/DL labels: Merryweather, 5"; King Hubert, 6"; Kings Hubert & Stefan, 5" & smaller, CE/Jun 9/95 (1000-1500) 1035
Close-up of happy Briar Rose (waist up), 5-1/2", DL label, CE/Jun 9/95 (600-800) 552
Concerned King Stefan facing left & gesturing, 6-1/2"; plus Merryweather & Flora, 5"; both w/DL labels, CE/Jun 9/95 (700-900) 552
Near-full figure of laughing Maleficent with arms upraised, 8 x 9", HL/Aug 6/95 (2000-3000) 4480
Hips-up of Fauna in peasant dress facing right, bent horizontally at waist, wand up, right hand out, 5-1/2", DL Art Corner label, SR/Fall/95 (300-600) 510
Close-up of Briar Rose standing with arms folded, holding berry basket, looking up & to left, 7", 16-field, SR/Fall/95 (1200-1800) 2380
Chest-up of Maleficent facing right with Diablo (full figure) flying to left at her chin level, 5-1/2", DL Art Corner label, ct, SR/Fall/95 (1600-2400) 2600
2 cels: hips-up of curious Fauna facing toward left, looking back, 8"; chest-up portrait of Merryweather standing with both fists clinched, 7-1/4", both with gold Art Corner labels, SR/Fall/95 (700-1000) 770
Knees-up of King Hubert standing facing toward left, looking down, 5-3/4", SR/Fall/95 (400-700) 450
Flora & Merryweather in peasant clothes holding magic wands, 5 x 8-1/2", gold DL/INA sticker, VF, HL/Nov 19/95 (600-800) 690
Maleficent pets Raven, 6 x 7-1/2", gold DL/INA sticker, F+, HL/Nov 19/95 (2000-3000) 2990
Near-full figure of dancing Briar Rose in mid-twirl, 5-1/2 x 3-1/2", VF+, HL/Nov 19/95 (800-1200) 805
Portrait of stern King Stefan looking down, 6 x 6-1/2", VF+, HL/Nov 19/95 (300-500) 431
Near-full figure of smiling Maleficent, 9 x 7-1/2", VF, HL/Nov 19/95 (2000-2500) 2990
Ankles-up of Briar Rose sitting facing left with berry basket on lap, 6-5/8", 16-field, SR/Spring/96 (1200-1800) 800
Knees-up right-facing profile of Prince Phillip standing talking to Briar Rose (w/back turned), (not exact match), 6-1/2 x 8", VF+, HL/Apr 28/96 (1600-2000) 1840
Profile portrait of smiling Maleficent, 6 x 3-1/2", VF+, HL/Apr 28/96 (1800-2200) 2760
Profile of smiling Briar Rose looking up (basket handle visible), 5-1/2 x 4", VF+, HL/Apr 28/96 (1200-1600) 1035
Angry Maleficent (holding staff) turns to look over right arm into camera, DL label, 7-3/4", CE/Jun 20/96 (800-1200) 2760
Stern Maleficent (holding staff) looking left & down, DL label, 6-1/4", CE/Jun 20/96 (1500-2000) 3450
Attentive Maleficent (holding staff) looking left & down, DL label, 5-1/2", CE/Jun 20/96 (1500-2000) 2760
Maleficent (waist up) speaking w/eyes closed & left hand up, DL label, 6", CE/Jun 20/96 (1500-2000) 1265
Maleficent (w/Raven on shoulder & holding staff) looking right, 7-1/2", CE/Jun 20/96 (1500-2000) 3680
Phillip rides cantering Samson to left (all but part of left foreleg), 7-1/4", 12-field cel, some ink wear, SR/Fall/96 (400-900) 410
3 near-full-figure cels: Flora in castle dress, Fauna in castle dress, Merryweather in peasant dress; 8-1/4", 8-1/4", 6-1/2", 12-field cels; SR/Fall/96 (1500-3000) 1680
Hips-up front view of happy King Hubert looking right, 4-3/4", 16-field, SR/Fall/96 (300-600) 300
Maleficent caresses Diablo's (full figure) neck with index finger, 7 x 10", red & gold DL label, VF, HL/Oct 6/96 (2000-2500) 2990
Portrait of smiling Prince Phillip facing right, gesturing w/palms up, gold DL label, VF+, 5 x 4", HL/Oct 6/96 (900-1200) 805
Portrait of Briar Rose peeking coquettishly out from shawl to the right, gold DL label, VF, 5 x 5", HL/Oct 6/96 (1000-1500) 1380
Near-full figure of wide-eyed Briar Rose sitting facing left & looking to right, w/full figure of Owl facing right, 6-3/4 x 8-3/4", VF+, HL/Oct 6/96 (1200-1600) 1725
Large-image front view of startled Maleficent, 10 x 7", VF, HL/Oct 6/96 (2500-3500) 3220
Near-full figure of Briar Rose standing holding berry basket & facing left, 6 x 2-3/4", VF+, HL/Oct 6/96 (800-1200) 1380
Dragon with mouth open surrounded by flames, 4", partial cel overlay of flames, CE/Dec 12/96 (2000-3000) 2530
Maleficent facing right, holding candle in front of her, staff at side, 8-1/2", CE/Dec 12/96 (2000-3000) 2760
Maleficent's arm w/hand caressing smiling Raven (near-full figure), 5 x 4", VF+, HL/Feb 23/97 (300-400) 431
Knees-up of Beautiful Briar Rose w/arms crossed & holding berry basket, 6-1/2 x 4-1/2", VF, HL/Feb 23/97 (1000-1500) 2185
Smiling Prince Phillip kneeling to left in profile, 8 x 7-1/4", VF+, HL/Feb 23/97 (600-900) 863
2 near-full-figure cels: front view of Merryweather looking down, 5-1/2 x 4-1/4"; Fauna looking back & down, 4-1/2 x 4", VF, as sold at DL, HL/Feb 23/97 (400-600) 690
Near-full figure of smiling Briar Rose standing facing left, holding berry basket; 5-1/2 x 2-3/4", VF+, HL/Feb 23/97 (1200-1600) 1380
Waist-up of surprised Flora in peasant costume facing left, looking back over left shoulder, 5-3/4", original DL color background & gold Art Corner label, SR/Spring/97 (400-700) 400
Knees-up of Briar Rose facing right, hands behind back, looking up, 7", 16-field cel, SR/Spring/97 (1200-1800) 1210
Hips-up of hatless Prince Phillip standing facing right with arms out, 5-3/4", 16-field cel, Original Art Program seal, DL & Art Program labels, SR/Spring/97 (300-600) 300
Knees-up of startled Briar Rose looking behind her, 6-1/2 x 4-1/2", VF+, HL/May 3/97 (900-1200) 1265
Knees-up view of Prince Phillip & Princess Aurora walking arm-in-arm, 7-1/2 x 8", VF+, HL/May 3/97 (2000-2500) 3450
2-level cel of Dragon's head & neck w/wings spread & mouth open, 8 x 11", gold & red DL Art Corner label, VF, HL/May 3/97 (1800-2400) 1610
Princess Aurora & mother embrace, 7 x 7-1/2", VF, HL/May 3/97 (800-1200) 1380
Hips-up portrait of befuddled Fauna & bluebird

(full figure), 5 x 5-1/2", HL/May 31/97 (300-500) 316
Thighs-up view of Prince Phillip facing right w/arms outstretched, 6 x 6-1/2", HL/May 31/97 (300-500) 288
Stomach-up front view of jovial King Hubert hoisting wine goblet, 4-1/4 x 6-1/2", HL/May 31/97 (300-500) 316
Near-full figure of shocked (mouth open) Samson standing facing right, 6-1/2 x 9", HL/May 31/97 (200-300) 230
Hips-up view of bewildered Fauna in peasant garb looking at camera while pointing wand to right, 5-1/4 x 6-1/2", HL/May 31/97 (400-500) 431
Knees-up front view of Briar Rose with cloak over shoulders and owl & bird hovering, 6", CLA/Jun 7/97 (1000-1500) 2530
Waist-up images of singing Prince Phillip (6") taking Briar Rose's (5" + 5" extended arm) hand from behind, S/Jun 21/97 (2000-3000) 1955
Waist-up front view of cowering henchman, 9-1/4", 16-field cel, SR/Fall/97 (450-700) 300
Knees-up of smiling Prince Phillip looking right, adjusting hat, 8-1/8", original DL color background & gold Art Corner seal, SR/Fall/97 (600-1000) 440
Near-full-figure front view of Prince Phillip standing looking right, holding crown in both hands, 6-3/4", 16-field cel, SR/Fall/97 (900-1400) 600
Near-full figure of demure Briar Rose sitting facing left holding full berry basket, head down, eyes closed; 6-1/4", SR/Fall/97 (1200-1600) 900
Near-full figure of Phillip standing facing right, holding crown & looking down, 6-3/4 x 3", VF+, HL/Nov 16/97 (500-700) 489
Near-full figure of Flora in castle dress facing right, 8-1/2 x 4-1/4", VF+, HL/Nov 16/97 (400-600) 489
"...you're not offended, Your Excellency?" Worried Queen facing left, 7-1/2 x 4-1/2", VF+, HL/Nov 16/97 (600-800) 949
"No carrots." Angry sitting Prince Phillip speaks to Samson, w/water-effects cel, 7-1/2 x 16-1/2", VF+, HL/Nov 16/97 (1200-1600) 2185
2 cels: King Stefan holding goblet, facing right & speaking, intent King Hubert holding goblet & facing left, 6 x 3-1/2" & 5-1/4 x 5-3/4", F, HL/Nov 16/97 (700-900) 633
Close-up of Maleficent (6") conferring with Diablo; Lackey (5" w/o feather) pouring 2 goblets of wine; each w/gold DL Art Corner label, S/Dec 19/97 (2500-3500) 2587
Upright Dragon facing left, 7-3/8" on pan 30 x 12-1/2" cel, SR/Spring/98 (1200-2000) 2530
Hips-up of Briar Rose (eyes closed) facing left in forest, extending right hand to two birds, 6-1/8", litho background, gold DL Art Corner label & original mat, SR/Spring/98 (800-1200) 1300
Chest-up of Flora in castle dress & with wings showing facing right & gesturing with eyes closed, 5-1/2", SR/Spring/98 (250-450) 390
Maleficent at dungeon door holding key as Diablo (on door) watches, 9-1/2 x 7-1/2", VF+, HL/Apr 25/98 (2000-3000) 2990
Briar Rose holds basket high with sleepy Owl inside, seal, 8-1/4 x 4-3/4", VF, HL/Apr 25/98 (1000-1500) 1265
Portrait of Maleficent with arms outstretched, restored, 5-3/4 x 9-1/2", VF, HL/Apr 25/98 (1000-1500) 2070
Hips-up front view of happy King Hubert looking right & gesturing, 5 x 5-1/4", VF+, HL/Apr 25/98 (500-700) 316

CONCEPT AND INSPIRATIONAL ART

Miniature pan concept painting of Briar Rose walking in forest, believed to be by Eyvind Earle, gouache on board, SR/Fall/94 (1500-2200) 2250
6 paintings (by Eyvind Earle?) depicting development of variegated foliage, 6 x 4-1/2", tempera on background sheet, HL/Aug 6/95 (1200-1600) 1568
4 early character design paintings of Kings Hubert & Stefan & throng of courtiers, 6 x 12" & 15 x 6", tempera on board, F+, HL/Nov 19/95 (800-1000) 1179
Conceptual painting of tree amid grass & plants, watercolor on board, 6-1/2 x 7-1/2", S/Jun 19/96 (1200-1800) 1380
Two Eyvind Earle concept paintings of King Hubert, gouache on 5 x 6-1/4" boards, SR/Fall/96 (500-800) 350
Inspirational painting of gargoyle with castle spires in background by Eyvind Earle (signed), tempera on illustration board, 5 x 11", VF+, HL/Oct 6/96 (1500-2000) 4370
Signed design painting of Prince Phillip in thorn forest w/sword drawn, by Eyvind Earle, tempera on board, 6-1/4 x 15", VF, HL/Feb 23/97 (3000-4000) 8913
Atmospheric thumbnail concept of Maleficent appearing in palace court at Aurora's christening, sight 2-1/2 x 7", S/Jun 21/97 (600-800) 1495
Signed design painting by Eyvind Earle of helmeted Prince with sword upraised amid thorns, 6 x 15", tempera on board, VF, HL/Nov 16/97 (3000-5000) 4140
Painting by Eyvind Earle of forest, 12 x 30", tempera on illustration board, VF, HL/Nov 16/97 (12,000-15,000) 16,675
Limited-edition serigraph of Eyvind Earle's 1956 concept painting, #184/500, 12-1/2 x 30", signed; plus inscribed & signed copy of *The Compete Graphics of Eyvind Earle*, VF+, HL/Nov 16/97 (1400-1800) 3910
Inspirational drawing of throng in front of castle or cathedral, sight 12-1/2 x 15-1/2", charcoal on paper, CE/Dec 18/97 (700-900) 1265
Inspirational art by Eyvind Earle of carriage moving amid castle walls, tempera on board, signed, 6-1/4 x 15", VF, HL/Apr 25/98 (3000-4000) 6900

DYE-TRANSFER PRINTS

Briar Rose sits under tree in meadow amid animals as Prince Phillip & Samson watch from behind tree, castle in distance, 9 x 12", SR/Spring/95 (300-600) 500

LAYOUT ART (also see STORY ART)

Background layout drawing: stain of Maleficent's silhouette (& that of sword) on scorched canyon floor, charcoal & conté crayon on Technirama animation sheet, 11 x 28", F, HL/Oct 6/96 (1500-2000) 1610
Pan layout drawing of Fauna in cottage talking while working on collapsing birthday cake, 7-1/2", CLA/Jun 7/97 (2000-3000) 1265
2 pan layout drawings of the three good Fairies, 7" & smaller, CLA/Jun 7/97 (600-800) 748
Pan layout drawing of castle courtyard, sight 12-1/2 x 30", CLA/Jun 7/97 (1000-2000) 1150
Layout drawing or study for publicity/book illustration of Prince Phillip battling Dragon, 11 x 14-1/2", F, HL/Nov 16/97 (400-600) 920

MODEL ART (also see CELS – FULL FIGURE)

3 model cels of Briar Rose in colors different from film, 7 x 4", 8 x 4-1/2", 7-1/2 x 5-1/2", F-VF, HL/Apr 10/94 (1500-2000) 1680
Color model cel of Briar Rose being embraced by mock prince, 11 x 3-1/2", restored, notes, VF, HL/Apr 10/94 (1500-2000) 1680
Color model cel: rear view of fairies standing together watching sleeping Aurora (head only) thru curtains, 8", 16-field, SR/Fall/94 (700-1000) 720
Color model cel of Princess Aurora dancing in gown, 8-1/2", S/Dec 17/94 (1500-2000) 1725
Full-figure model cel of early Aurora, 13 x 4-1/2", HL/Apr 23/95 (700-900) 2240
Color model cel: Fauna (8"), Merryweather (6") & Flora (8-1/2") in castle dress, CE/Jun 9/95 (1000-1500) 1150
2 full-figure model cels of Kings Hubert & Stefan standing, 6 x 4-1/2" & 8 x 3", HL/Aug 6/95 (700-1000) 616
Near-full-figure front-view color model cel of terrified Samson looking left, 10-1/4" 16-field, SR/Spring/95 (400-700) 460
Near-full-figure profile color model cel of King Stefan, 10 x 5-1/2", HL/Mar 16-17/96 (200-310) 633
Full-figure front & back images of Prince Phillip (used as inkers' guide), 6 x 5-1/4", HL/Apr 28/96 (500-700) 230
Full-figure color model cel of Briar Rose standing facing right with eyes closed, holding berry basket, 6-3/4", SR/Fall/96 (700-1100) 710
3 color model drawings of singing Briar Rose & birds; 1/2 x 1-1/4", 1 x 1-1/4", 5 x 4", HL/May 31/97 (200-300) 460
Waist-up portrait model cel of King Stefan holding wine goblet & facing left, 6-1/2 x 5", HL/May 31/97 (300-400) 316
Full-figure early model cel (more brown color) of shoeless Briar Rose standing facing right with eyes closed, 6 x 3", HL/May 31/97 (400-500) 460
Model cel of suspicious Maleficent facing left, fingering orb, looking over left shoulder, labeled "Maleficent"/"9160", 9-1/2 x 6", VF, HL/Nov 16/97 (1800-2200) 2530
Full-figure front view color model cel of Maleficent w/arms raised, 9-1/4 x 15", VF, HL/Nov 16/97 (2000-3000) 3565
Model drawing of Phillip riding Samson to left, 10-1/2 x 11", F, HL/Apr 25/98 (200-400) 633

STORY ART

3 story drawings: 2 of Aurora dancing w/mock prince; pensive Prince Phillip; conté crayon on story sheets, 4 x 8", 4 x 10", VF, HL/Aug 21/94 (1000-1500) 784
3 story drawings of forest meeting of Aurora & Prince Phillip; india ink & conté crayon on story sheets; 4 x 8", 4 x 10", VF, HL/Aug 21/94 (1000-1500) 840
13 original story drawings, 4-3/4 x 7" to 4-1/2 x 10", conté crayon on paper, HL/Aug 6/95 (700-1000) 784
Story painting by Eyvind Earle: extreme long shot of Maleficent atop castle parapet amid explosion of magic, prince & thorn thicket in foreground, 7-1/4 x 9-1/2", tempera on heavyweight paper, HL/Aug 6/95 (2000-2500) 7952
7 story drawings of Prince Phillip encountering Briar Rose in forest; 4 x 7-1/2", 4-1/4 x 8-1/2"; conté crayon on paper, HL/Aug 6/95 (700-1000) 616
Eyvind Earle story painting of Prince Phillip meeting Maleficent as dragon, signed, tempera on board, 6 x 15", VF, HL/Apr 28/96 (4000-6000) 16,100
2 storyboard & layout drawings by Ken Anderson of Dragon falling off cliff, 9" long & similar, charcoal on paper, CLA/Jun 7/97 (1000-1500) 920
6 story sketches of Briar Rose & Prince meeting in forest, 4-1/4 x 8-1/4", india ink & conté crayon on story sheets, VF, HL/Nov 16/97 (800-1200) 1380

STORYBOOK ART

Sleeping Aurora in castle, Prince Phillip standing at her side, fairies hovering, storybook cover art by Eyvind Earl, 10-1/2 x 14", tempera on board, VF+, HL/Aug 6/95 (7500-10,000) 7840

TITLE ART

Title cel with matching gouache background from original release's television & theatrical trailers; plus follow-up title cel: "Walt Disney's Most Wonderful Achievement in the Art of Animation"; 16-field, SR/Spring/96 (300-600) 880

SNOW WHITE AND THE SEVEN DWARFS (1937)

Also see SHORTS & FEATURETTES: THE WINGED SCOURGE; TELEVISION: ANTHOLOGY SERIES

ANIMATION DRAWINGS (also see MODEL ART)

Knees-up of Snow White standing looking startled, 10 x 12", CE/Dec 15/93 (700-900) 1150
Happy waves a pick, 9-1/2 x 11-1/4", CE/Dec 15/93 (900-1200) 977
Doc, Bashful & Sleepy play instruments, 11-3/4 x 15", CE/Dec 15/93 (1000-1200) 977
Drawing of dwarf being dragged by animals, 4", S/Dec 16/93 (900-1200) 920
25 pencil drawings: 3 of witch; 7 of Snow White; 13 of a dwarf; 2 of birds, S/Dec 16/93 (2500-3500) 3738
4 drawings: Grumpy standing steadfast; Sleepy, Bashful & Happy leaning forward to get kiss from Snow White; layout drawing of Doc gesturing; layout drawing of happy Sneezy; production notes, S/Dec 16/93 (1800-2000) 2185
Drawing of Grumpy discovering sleeping Snow White, 4 x 5-1/2", studio notes, VF, HL/Feb 26-27/94 (300-500) 578
2 matched drawings of Happy & Dopey, studio stamps, VF, HL/Feb 26-27/94 (600-800) 605

9 rough drawings, 3 x 2" to 3 x 10", VG-F,
HL/Feb 26-27/94 (800-1200)   2530
Drawing of reclined Snow White singing, 5 x 5", F,
HL/Apr 10/94 (800-1200)   1232
Extreme drawing of Bashful announcing end of
day's work, 5-1/2 x 5", VF, HL/Apr 10/94
(600-800)   952
Drawing of Sleepy yawning, 5-1/2 x 5-1/2, studio
stamps, matted,VF+, HL/Apr 10/94
(500-700)   728
Drawing of Grumpy as kiss takes effect, 4-1/2 x 6",
scene animated by Vladimir Tytla, studio
stamps, VF+, HL/Apr 10/94 (600-900)   1036
Full-face drawing of smiling Witch peering into
kitchen window, 6 x 7-1/2", VF,
HL/Apr 10/94 (800-1200)   952
Drawing of 2 dwarves washing faces, production
notes, both 3" (chest up), S/Jun 17/94
(500-700)   575
3 drawings of forest friends, each w/"Copyright Walt
Disney Productions" stamp, S/Jun 17/94
(400-600)   690
3 drawings of rabbits in bed, 2 x 3/4",
CE/Jun 18/94 (300-500)   345
Full-figure drawing of Snow White sweeping, 6 x
2-1/2", HL/Aug 21/94 (500-700)   1064
Extreme drawing of startled Snow White dropping pie,
notes & stamps, 5-1/2 x 3", HL/Aug 21/94
(1000-1500)   2128
Frontal drawing of Witch at cottage window, stamps
& notes, 6 x 8", HL/Aug 21/94 (600-900) 1120
Drawing of Wicked Queen, Studio stamps, 7-1/2
x 8-1/2", HL/Aug 21/94 (2000-2500)   2352
3 sequential rough drawings of 6 dwarfs 6 x 10-1/2",
HL/Aug 21/94 (1000-1500)   2688
Hips-up drawing of Queen looking left w/arms raised,
7-1/2", 12-field sheet, production stamp,
inker's notations, SR/Fall/94 (900-1500)   940
Hips-up front-view drawing of Snow White looking
right, recoiling in terror, 7-1/2", 12-field sheet,
some wear & discoloration, shallow tear,
SR/Fall/94 (500-900)   1400
Half-image drawing of scheming Witch facing left,
looking back, clutching apple, 6", 12-field
sheet, production stamp, SR/Fall/94
(1200-1800)   1340
Full-figure character drawings of Sneezy (3"), Bashful,
Doc, & Sleepy, single 12-field sheet, some edge
wear & discoloration, SR/Fall/94 (300-600)   350
2 standing full-figure drawings: Sneezy plays duckette,
3-3/4"; dancing Bashful plays concertina, 4";
16-field, production stamps, SR/Fall/94
(800-1400)   1180
Half-image front-view drawing of Witch holding
up basket of apples & offering one, 6",
12-field sheet, production stamp,
SR/Fall/94 (1200-1800)   1630
Full-figure drawing of Witch polishing apple on sleeve,
7-1/2", 16-field sheet, production stamp,
SR/Fall/94 (1200-1800)   1480
Front-view drawing of regal Queen, head back, looking
left, 10", 16-field sheet, timer's chart, production
stamp, SR/Fall/94 (1200-1800)   1800
2 full-figure front-view drawings of Dopey on single
12-field sheet, 5-1/2", SR/Fall/94 (400-900) 770
Full-figure drawing of surprised Grumpy walking left
by Vladimir Tytla, 4-1/2 x 6-1/2", VF,
HL/Nov 13/94 (500-700)   616
2 matched drawings of Dopey looking under Happy's
beard, 5 x 3-1/2" & 6 x 4-1/2", VF, HL/Nov
13/94 (600-800)   840
Front-view drawing of smiling Witch as seen thru
cottage window, 6 x 8", VF, HL/Nov 13/94
(800-1200)   1064
Drawing of Queen clutching throat after drinking
potion, 8 x 8-1/2", VF, HL/Nov 13/94
(1500-2000)   2128
Portrait drawings of Sleepy & Grumpy, 3-1/2 x
3" & 4 x 3-1/2", VF+, HL/Nov 13/94
(600-800)   1120
Drawing of beaming Snow White from film's
conclusion, 7 x 5-1/2", notes, F,
HL/Nov 13/94 (900-1200)   1456
Drawing of Grumpy as face changes to adoring
expression, 5 x 7", HL/Nov 13/94
(600-800)   728
Drawing of 6 Dwarfs crowded together & carrying
picks, 2-1/2", CE/Dec 16/94 (1000-1500) 1840
Drawing of The Witch at the cottage window, 5-1/2",

production stamp, CE/Dec 16/94 (600-800) 633
Drawing of Grumpy being dragged by animals,
2-1/2", production stamp, CE/Dec 16/94
(700-900)   1150
2 rough drawings: angry Grumpy, 3-1/2"; Prince,
6-1/2", CE/Dec 16/94 (500-700)   288
Drawing of surprised Happy, 4", S/Dec 17/94
(300-500)   345
16 drawings: Snow White; 6 of various dwarfs; vulture;
8 of various forest creatures; many with studio
stamps, S/Dec 17/94 (2000-3000)   2070
Near-full-figure front-view drawing of Snow White
standing with arms out & mouth open,
7-1/4", 12-field sheet, production stamp,
SR/Spring/95 (500-900)   750
Full-figure front-view drawing of panicked Witch
standing looking down at hem of cloak, 5",
12-field sheet, production stamp & timer's
charts, SR/Spring/95 (1000-1600)   1610
Full-figure drawing of Snow White standing facing
right, bending forward at waist, extending right
hand, 5-1/4", 12-field sheet, animator's
notations, SR/Spring/95 (300-600)   320
Hips-up front-view drawing of Queen standing with
arms out spreading cloak, looking left, 8-1/2",
12-field sheet, production stamp,
SR/Spring/95 (900-1500)   1300
Knees-up drawing of smiling Snow White standing
facing toward right, 6 5/8", 12-field sheet,
production stamp, SR/Spring/95 (500-900)   830
Waist-up front-view drawing of Queen holding heart
box at waist level, 10-1/4", 16-field sheet,
timer's chart, production stamp, SR/Spring/95
(1000-1600)   1980
Knees-up drawing of determined Huntsman standing
facing toward left with knife drawn, 7", 12-field
sheet, timer's charts, production stamp,
SR/Spring/95 (500-900)   1130
Full-figure drawing of Snow White sitting facing left,
hands cupped in front, looking up, 8-1/4",
16-field sheet, painter's notations, production
stamp, SR/Spring/95 (600-1000)   1610
Full-figure drawing of Snow White, initialed "MD"
(Marc Davis), 5 x 3-1/2", HL/Apr 23/95
(500-700)   952
2 drawings of Snow White, 6-1/2 x 5" & 7-1/2 x
3-1/2", HL/Apr 23/95 (1500-2000)   1680
13 finished "rough" drawings, 4-1/2 x 4" to 5-1/2
x 2-1/2", HL/Apr 23/95 (1000-1500)   3808
2 drawings framed together: Snow White, 6-1/2";
Witch, 7"; CE/Jun 9/95 (2000-2500)   3680
Drawing of 7 Dwarfs (1 full figure), 3-3/4" & smaller,
CE/Jun 9/95 (400-600)   1610
Key full-figure drawing of 5 Dwarfs marching to right
w/picks over shoulders, 7-1/2" & smaller, copyright stamp, CE/Jun 9/95 (2500-3500)   3680
Rough drawing of haughty Snow White in profile, 4"
& smaller, CE/Jun 9/95 (500-700)   1035
Close-up drawing of Happy looking back, 6-3/4",
CE/Jun 9/95 (600-800)   1265
Front-view drawing of Witch offering apple, 5-1/2",
S/Jun 10/95 (1200-1600)   2300
Drawing of Queen holding heart box in classic pose,
10", S/Jun 10/95 (1800-2200)   2875
Matched set of 2 drawings of Happy & Dopey;
4-1/2 x 3-1/2", 3-1/2 x 3", HL/Aug 6/95
(600-800)   1008
Front-view drawing of smiling Witch, "...makin' pies?",
5-1/2 x 7-1/2", HL/Aug 6/95 (900-1200) 1568
Drawing of argumentative Grumpy, 4 x 4",
HL/Aug 6/95 (500-700)   896
Full-figure drawing of Grumpy stalking away, 4-1/2
x 6-1/2", HL/Aug 6/95 (600-900)   1064
Full-figure drawing of smiling Doc facing toward right,
bent forward at waist, 6-1/2", 12-field sheet,
SR/Fall/95 (400-800)   900
Full-figure drawing of witch polishing apple on sleeve,
7-3/4", 12-field sheet, production stamp,
SR/Fall/95 (1200-1800)   1610
Full-figure front-view drawing of panicked Snow White
with dress being pulled to right, 6", 12-field
sheet, SR/Fall/95 (500-900)   1520
Full-figure drawing of animals dragging Sleepy to right,
8-3/4 x 3-3/8", 12-field sheet, timer's chart,
production stamp, SR/Fall/95 (400-800)   1180
Front-view drawing of regal queen looking left, head
back, 10-1/2", 12-field sheet, production
stamp, SR/Fall/95 (1200-1800)   1920
Partial-figure drawing of 5 dwarfs standing together

facing right with hands behind backs & mischievous smiles, 7-3/4 x 5-3/8", 12-field sheet,
SR/Fall/95 (1300-1800)   1700
Near-full-figure drawing of sinister Queen standing,
left hand on top of heart box, looking into
camera, 10", 12-field sheet, production
stamp, SR/Fall/95 (1400-2000)   2750
Captioned partial-figure rotoscope drawing of sitting
Witch (actor Dave Brodie) facing left, 5",
12-field sheet, SR/Fall/95 (600-1200)   600
Near-full-figure drawing of Snow White facing toward
left, leaning forward, mouth open, both arms out
to side, 7", 12-field sheet, production stamp,
SR/Fall/95 (500-900)   1040
Half-figure front-view drawing of Witch with hands
resting [on window sill], 5-3/4", 12-field sheet,
SR/Fall/95 (1100-1600)   1200
Full-figure drawing of Grumpy w/hat askew, 4-1/2
x 3", HL/Nov 19/95 (500-800)   1093
Full-figure drawing of Grumpy using pick, 4-1/2 x 5",
HL/Nov 19/95 (600-900)   1093
Full-figure drawing of deer pushing Doc, 4 x 7",
HL/Nov 19/95 (600-900)   1840
Large drawing of Hag taking apple from basket,
6-1/2 x 6-1/2", HL/Nov 19/95
(1500-2000)   2760
Full-figure drawing of cackling Hag holding tree
limb as lever, 9 x 8", HL/Nov 19/95
(1200-1600)   1840
Full-figure drawing of Bashful resting pick on ground,
6-1/2 x 4-1/2", HL/Nov 19/95 (600-900) 1495
Drawing of Queen just after she's drunk potion,
6-1/2 x 7-1/2", HL/Nov 19/95
(1500-2000)   2990
Drawing of kneeling Snow White, 6 x 5",
HL/Nov 19/95 (600-900)   748
Full-figure rough drawing of Sneezy about to sneeze
w/worried Dopey balanced atop his head,
8 x 5", HL/Mar 16-17/96 (200-300)   920
Drawing of curious Happy, 4-1/2 x 4-1/2",
HL/Mar 16-17/96 (200-300)   748
Near-full figure drawing of surprised Happy, 3-1/2
x 2-1/2", HL/Mar 16-17/96 (400-500)   633
Drawing of Snow White sitting looking down w/hands
extended, comforting lightly drawn bird, 6-5/8",
12-field sheet, production stamp, SR/Spring/96
(700-1100)   1200
Full-figure drawing of smitten Grumpy sitting facing
right, 5", 12-field sheet, SR/Spring/96
(700-1000)   825
Full-figure drawing of surprised Bashful standing
looking left, 4", 12-field, SR/Spring/96
(700-1000)   800
Thighs-up front-view drawing of grim Huntsman
standing holding knife, 7-1/4", 12-field sheet,
production stamp, timer's chart,
SR/Spring/96 (800-1400)   1140
Drawing of Witch looking back & down while running
right, rain & lightning effects, 5-1/4",12-field
sheet, production stamp, SR/Spring/96
(1200-1800)   1460
8 sequential animation drawings of shy rabbit, vertical
12-field sheets, 2" to 3-3/8", SR/Spring/96
(150-300)   390
Half-image drawing of scheming Witch facing left,
looking back, clutching apple, 6-1/8", 12-field
sheet, production stamp, SR/Spring/96
(1200-1800)   1460
Near-full-figure drawing of sitting Snow White holding
bird, looking up, 8-3/8", 16-field sheet, timer's
chart, inker's notation & production stamp
SR/Spring/96 (1200-1800)   1650
Full-figure drawing of awed Sleepy, Bashful, Happy,
Sneezy & Doc standing in group, facing toward
right, looking up, 7-3/4 x 5-1/4", 12-field
sheet, production stamp, SR/Spring/96
(1500-1800)   2500
Half-image front-view drawing of regal Queen looking
up & to left, 7-3/8", 12-field sheet, production
stamp, SR/Spring/96 (1200-1800)   1920
Front-view drawing of Witch at Dwarf's window,
6 x 8", HL/Apr 28/96 (900-1200)   920
Drawing of cackling Witch using branch as lever,
9 x 8-1/2", HL/Apr 28/96 (1000-1500)   1725
Full-figure drawing of Snow White sweeping w/broom,
6 x 3", HL/Apr 28/96 (700-1000)   1150
Full-figure drawing of Grumpy stomping off in a huff,
5 x 6-1/2", HL/Apr 28/96 (600-900)   920
12 finished "rough" drawings of bashful Bashful,

5 x 2-1/2", HL/Apr 28/96 (1000-1500) 1955

Full-figure drawing of angry Grumpy sitting & making point, 4-1/2 x 3", HL/Apr 28/96 (600-800) 920

Drawing of Grumpy being dragged by animals, 7-1/2" length, CE/Jun 20/96 (700-900) 1265

Full-figure drawing of Bashful standing holding pick at side, 6", CE/Jun 20/96 (800-1200) 1610

Knees-up drawing of regal Queen standing looking left with head up, 11-5/16", 16-field sheet, production stamp, SR/Fall/96 (1200-1800) 1780

Full-figure drawing of Witch running right amid vines, 7", 16-field sheet, production stamp, SR/Fall/96 (1200-1800) 1210

Wide-eyed fawn in set of 4 drawings from same sequence, 2-5/8" to 3-1/2", 12-field sheets, SR/Fall/96 (150-300) 170

Full-figure front-view drawing of Bashful standing facing left, 4-1/4", 12-field sheet, production stamp, SR/Fall/96 (600-1000) 650

Knees-up drawing of Snow White, 6-3/4", 12-field sheet, production stamp, SR/Fall/96 (600-1000) 730

Hips-up front-view drawing of Queen standing holding heart box, 10-1/4", 16-field sheet, production stamp, SR/Fall/96 (1400-2000) 2610

Full-figure drawing of animals dragging Sleepy, 8-1/4 x 3-3/8", 12-field sheet, inker's notation, production stamp, SR/Fall/96 (1500-2000) 1320

Hips-up drawing of Doc facing toward left, 4-3/8", 12-field sheet, SR/Fall/96 (400-800) 440

Hips-up drawing of eager Witch holding out apple toward left, 7-5/8", 16-field sheet, production stamp, SR/Fall/96 (1200-1800) 1580

Waist-up portrait drawing of Snow White looking to right, 6 x 4-1/4", HL/Oct 6/96 (900-1200) 863

Full-figure drawing of animals dragging dwarf by clothes & beard, 4-1/4 x 8", HL/Oct 6/96 (600-800) 1150

Drawing of Witch admiring apple suspended by string, 6-1/2 x 4-1/2", HL/Oct 6/96 (1200-1600) 1955

Front-view drawing of grumpy Grumpy sitting looking to right, 4 x 3", HL/Oct 6/96 (600-900) 920

Full-figure drawing of angry Grumpy stomping away to left, 4-1/2 x 7", HL/Oct 6/96 (600-800) 920

Near-full-figure drawing of Happy holding pick, 5-1/2 x 5-1/4", HL/Oct 6/96 (600-800) 748

Drawing of coaxing Witch facing left, 6-1/2 x 8-1/2", HL/Oct 6/96 (1200-1600) 1380

Drawing of angry Witch holding apple, 6-1/2 x 6", HL/Oct 6/96 (1200-1600) 2760

Key drawing of kneeling Snow White, hands up, looking at right hand [baby bird was in separate drawing]: 7 x 5-1/2", HL/Oct 6/96 (1200-1500) 2070

Full-figure drawing of Grumpy bringing deer he's riding (to right) to screeching halt by pulling on left antler, 5 x 6-1/2", HL/Oct 6/96 (500-700) 518

Drawing of eager Dopey w/both arms around soup bowl & large tongue extended [from soup-eating sequence], 4 x 4-1/2", HL/Oct 6/96 (600-800) 1093

Full-figure drawing of Snow White standing & sweeping w/head thrown back & eyes closed, 6 x 2-1/2", HL/Oct 6/96 (700-900) 690

Full-figure front-view rough drawing of 7 Dwarfs standing talking among themselves, 4" & similar, CE/Dec 12/96 (1000-1500) 1610

Full-figure rough drawing of Dwarfs marching with picks on shoulders, Doc (near-full figure) in lead holding lantern, 7" to 3", CE/Dec 12/96 (1500-2000) 3220

Full-figure front-view drawing of Doc standing looking to right, 7", CE/Dec 12/96 (1000-1500) 1495

3 clean-up drawings of The Prince by Grim Natwick, 6" & similar, CE/Dec 12/96 (1000-1500) 920

Full-figure front-view drawing of startled Witch holding apple in right hand, clutching robe w/left, looking up & to right, 6", CE/Dec 12/96 (1500-2000) 1725

Near-full-figure drawing of Prince looking upward & singing, 8", CE/Dec 12/96 (1000-1500) 1955

4 items: full-figure front-view drawing of Bashful & Doc standing playing their instruments, 5-1/2" each; three model sheets of animals, CE/Dec 12/96 (800-1200) 2530

2 items: drawing of haughty Snow White pointing w/right hand, left hand on hip, 7"; rough drawing

of 5 Dwarfs sitting in admiring poses, 3-1/4" & similar, CE/Dec 12/96 (1500-2000) 1610

Drawing of Snow White watching bird perched on her finger, 6", CE/Dec 12/96 (800-1200) 1265

Front-view production drawing of Witch, 6" (approx. waist-up), S/Dec 14/96 (1000-1500) 920

2 matched drawings: concerned Happy & side view of Dopey facing left, 4-1/2 x 3-1/2" & 3 x 3", HL/Feb 23/97 (600-900) 748

Full-figure front-view drawing of grumpy Grumpy standing, 4 x 2-1/2", HL/Feb 23/97 (500-700) 633

Chest-up front-view drawing of Witch, 5 x 8", HL/Feb 23/97 (1000-1500) 1093

Waist-up animator's rough drawing of surprised Dopey, 4-1/4 x 3-1/4", HL/Feb 23/97 (600-900) 863

Waist-up rough drawing of angry Grumpy pointing left, 4 x 5-1/2", HL/Feb 23/97 (300-500) 518

Full-figure drawing of Witch standing polishing apple on sleeve, 8 x 6", HL/Feb 23/97 (1200-1600) 2185

Full-figure drawing of Grumpy standing smiling in awe, 5 x 3", HL/Feb 23/97 (600-800) 1093

Chest-up front-view drawing of sleepy Sleepy with hands resting on bed footboard, 4 x 3-3/4", HL/Feb 23/97 (250-350) 546

Portrait drawing of smiling Witch [at cottage window], 5-1/2 x 8", HL/Feb 23/97 (900-1200) 1150

Near-full-figure front-view drawing of Snow White standing with mouth open & arms out, 7-1/4", 12-field sheet, production stamp, SR/Spring/97 (600-1000) 810

Knees-up drawing of haughty Queen standing facing left with head up, 10-1/2", 16-field sheet, production stamp, SR/Spring/97 (1200-1800) 2140

Knees-up drawing of Witch standing facing right, closely examining poison apple on string, 6-3/4", 16-field sheet, production stamp, SR/Spring/97 (1200-1800) 1630

Knees-up drawing of Huntsman standing with knife drawn, 7-1/8", 12-field sheet, production stamp, SR/Spring/97 (800-1400) 1480

Hips-up drawing of Snow White standing facing toward right, 7", 12-field sheet, production stamp, inker's notation, SR/Spring/97 (600-1000) 810

Full-figure drawing of smiling Sleepy, Bashful, Happy, Sneezy, & Doc standing in group facing right, 7-1/2 x 5-3/8", 12-field sheet, SR/Spring/97 (1800-2600) 2530

Rough drawing of melee of 7 dwarfs (mostly from rear), 8 x 10", HL/May 31/97 (300-400) 518

Rough drawing of 5 dwarfs sitting with admiring expressions, 5-1/2 x 11", HL/May 31/97 (200-400) 863

Front-view drawing of smiling Witch [at window], 5-1/2", CLA/Jun 7/97 (800-1200) 920

Key full-figure drawing by Shamus Culhane of six dwarfs marching, 5 with picks on shoulders, Doc with lantern in lead, 7-1/2" & smaller, CLA/Jun 7/97 (1500-2000) 3450

Full-figure drawing of Grumpy standing w/arms folded across chest, 5-1/2", CLA/Jun 7/97 (800-1200) 460

Full-figure drawing of Doc [Happy?] standing shyly, 7", CLA/Jun 7/97 (1000-1500) 920

Full-figure drawing of Doc standing with hands up, 5-1/2", CLA/Jun 7/97 (800-1200) 2070

Full-figure drawing of Snow White (7") bending over to talk to three shy Dwarfs (5") standing w/hands behind backs, CLA/Jun 7/97 (1500-2000) 1610

Full-figure drawing of happy Sneezy, 4", CLA/Jun 7/97 (800-1200) 460

Full-figure drawing of smiling Sneezy standing holding mandolin, 5", CLA/Jun 7/97 (800-1200) 1150

Full-figure drawing of 4 Dwarfs holding fingers under Sneezy's nose, 4" ea., CLA/Jun 7/97 (1500-2000) 1495

Full-figure front-view drawing of Bashful, 6", CLA/Jun 7/97 (800-1200) 633

3 drawings of Snow White, 5" & similar, CLA/Jun 7/97 (2000-3000) 2300

Full-figure drawing of Prince riding horse to right, 7", CLA/Jun 7/97 (1000-1500) 1955

Key full-figure drawing of Snow White sweeping, 5-1/2", CLA/Jun 7/97 (1500-2000) 805

9 individual drawings of Snow White (8"), Witch (6"), & 7 Dwarfs (5" & similar) framed together,

CLA/Jun 7/97 (4000-6000) 4025

Front-view key drawing of haughty Queen holding open heart box, 9-3/4", CLA/Jun 7/97 (1500-2000) 3680

4 individual full-figure front-view open-eyed rough drawings of Sleepy, Grumpy, Sneezy & Doc; 4 rough drawings of Doc from waist up, 3", 3 later signed by Frank Thomas & Ollie Johnston, CLA/Jun 7/97 (1000-1500) 2530

Animator's sketches of Grumpy in 8 various moods & expressions, sight 9 x 11", S/Jun 21/97 (500-700) 920

Drawing of eager Dopey hunkered over soup bowl w/tongue out, 4 x 4-1/2", S/Jun 21/97 (800-1200) 1265

Full-figure drawing of stooped Witch polishing apple on sleeve, 6-1/2", S/Jun 21/97 (1500-2000) 1725

2 full-figure drawings: perky chipmunk stands facing right, 2-1/16"; mother rabbit & 2 bunnies, 4 x 1-1/2", inker's notation; both 12-field sheets, WDP copyright & Courvoisier debossed stamps; SR/Fall/97 (600-900) 525

Full-figure drawing of friendly Sleepy, Bashful, Happy, Sneezy, & Doc standing together, 7-1/2 x 5-3/8", 12-field sheet, with timer's chart, SR/Fall/97 (2500-3000) 2000

Full-figure drawing of Snow White sitting toward left, looking up, hands cupped; 8-3/8"; 16-field sheet w/inker's notations & production stamp; some edge wear; SR/Fall/97 (1200-1800) 1560

Full-figure drawing of Witch running right amid vines & water effects, 6-3/4", 16-field sheet, inker's notation, production stamp, SR/Fall/97 (1200-1800) 800

Full-figure drawing of 9 animals dragging Sleepy to right, 8-3/4 x 4-1/2", 12-field sheet, inker's notation, production stamp, SR/Fall/97 (1000-1400) 1180

Waist-up front-view drawing of grim Witch, 5-1/2 x 7-1/2", F-VF, HL/Nov 16/97 (900-1200) 1035

Waist-up drawing of argumentative Grumpy, hands down [on bed?], leaning left, 3-3/4 x 4-1/2", VF, HL/Nov 16/97 (300-500) 633

Full-figure drawing of stern Grumpy standing pointing right, "A fine bunch of water lilies ....", 4-1/2 x 3-3/4", VF, HL/Nov 16/97 (800-1200) 805

Knees-up front-view drawing of awed Prince looking up, 6-1/4 x 4-1/4", VF, initialed "MK", HL/Nov 16/97 (300-400) 1150

2 matching drawings: Happy looking back & up, Dopey lifting beard; 3-3/4 x 5" & 4-1/2 x 3-1/2"; VF; HL/Nov 16/97 (600-900) 978

Full-figure drawing of Grumpy standing facing left w/silly grin, 5 x 2-1/2", VF, HL/Nov 16/97 (500-700) 1093

Drawing of eager Witch facing left in "encouraging" pose, 6-1/2 x 7-1/4", F-VF, HL/Nov 16/97 (900-1200) 1035

Full-figure front-view drawing of Grumpy standing w/fists clinched & hat down over one eye, 4-1/2 x 3", VF, HL/Nov 16/97 (500-700) 690

3 drawings: rough of Happy by Bill Tytla, full figure of Snow White standing with arms outspread initialed by Marc Davis, full figure of shocked Happy standing holding pick facing right; 3 x 3-3/4", 4 x 3-1/2", 5 x 4"; F overall, HL/Nov 16/97 (600-900) 1610

3 rough drawings of all 7 Dwarfs framed together; 5 x 3-1/2", 6 x 11-1/4", 5 x 3-1/2", F+, HL/Nov 16/97 (700-1000) 1840

Knees-up drawing of Snow White standing, bend forward at waist, arms out, mouth open, 6-3/4 x 5-1/2", VF, HL/Nov 16/97 (1200-1600) 1265

Waist-up drawing of surprised Doc leaning forward, hands down [on table?], 6-1/2", CE/Dec 18/97 (800-1200) 633

Full-figure drawing of shy Doc standing facing left, 7", CE/Dec 18/97 (1000-1500) 1265

52 rough drawings of Dwarf hanging onto running doe, 5-1/2" & similar, CE/Dec 18/97 (600-800) 1265

Full-figure front-view drawing of smiling Snow White sitting looking left, 4", CE/Dec 18/97 (1000-1500) 978

Rough drawing of Snow White (6") bending over with arms out, facing three dwarfs standing together (full figure, 5"), CE/Dec 18/97 (1000-1500) 1380

5 drawings: full figure, eyes open Grumpy, 5-3/4";
  profile, eyes open Doc, 5"; full figure, eyes
  open Sneezy, 5-1/2"; full figure, eyes open Bashful, 5-1/2"; half figure, eyes closed
  Sleepy, 6"; CE/Dec 18/97 (1500-2000)   1955
Waist-up drawing of surprised Doc [Happy?] looking
  down & to right, 6-1/2", CE/Dec 18/97
  (800-1200)   460
Drawing of eager Dopey, tongue out, leaning forward
  [over soup bowl], 4 x 4-1/2", S/Dec 19/97
  (800-1200)   920
Rough drawing of smiling Dopey preparing to sweep
  up loose diamonds, 4-1/2", S/Dec 19/97
  (1000-1500)   1035
Full-figure drawing of Sneezy (3") being dragged to
  right by animals, S/Dec 19/97 (800-1200)   805
5 drawings: Dopey tugging on Snow White's dress;
  Snow White from back; Bashful & Doc playing
  instruments; all 7 Dwarfs; Snow White w/arm
  extended; each sheet 10 x 12", S/Dec 19/97
  (3000-5000)   3737
Full-figure front-view rough drawing of eager Dopey
  standing holding dustpan & broom, 4-1/2",
  S/Dec 19/97 (1000-1500)   1035
Full-figure drawing of Prince Charming standing
  facing right & singing, 8-1/4", S/Dec 19/97
  (800-1200)   805
3 drawings of Dopey (holding hat) matted together:
  running, standing w/tongue out & eyes closed,
  standing w/tongue out & dreamy look; avg. 4",
  S/Dec 19/97 (3000-5000)   3162
3 drawings of Dopey (holding hat) matted together:
  running, standing excitedly, & puckering up;
  approx. 4" each, Courvoisier label,
  S/Dec 19/97 (3000-5000)   5462
Waist-up front-view drawing of Queen holding heart
  box, 10 1/2", 16-field sheet, production stamp,
  SR/Spring/98 (1500-2200)   2940
Knees-up drawing of determined Huntsman standing
  holding knife, 7-1/8", 12-field sheet, studio production stamp, SR/Spring/98 (800-1400)   1700
Knees-up drawing of happy Snow White standing, 6-
  3/4", 12-field sheet, studio production stamp,
  SR/Spring/98 (600-1000)   810
Full-figure drawing of attentive bunny on hind legs
  facing right, looking up, 3-1/2", 12-field sheet,
  inker's notation, WDP copyright & Courvoisier
  debossed stamps, wear & discoloration at right-
  hand corners, SR/Spring/98 (250-450)   200
Hips-up drawing of apprehensive Sneezy standing
  facing right, 4-1/4", 12-field sheet,
  SR/Spring/98, (400-800)   520
Front-view hips-up drawing of Snow White w/mouth
  open holding broom & looking right, 6-1/2 x
  8-1/2", VF, HL/Apr 25/98 (300-400)   460
Hips-up drawing of Grumpy looking back to right
  while pointing left, 4-1/4 x 4", VF, HL/Apr
  25/98 (300-500)   805
2 matching drawings of Dopey looking under
  Happy's beard; 5-1/4 x 4", 7 x 4-1/2";
  VF; HL/Apr 25/98 (600-800)   633
Chest-up front-view drawing of Witch at window,
  5 x 8", VF, HL/Apr 25/98 (800-1200)   863
Full-figure front-view drawing of Bashful standing
  holding pick at his side, 6-1/2 x 4-1/2", VF,
  HL/Apr 25/98 (600-800)   1725
Full-figure drawing of starstruck Grumpy walking
  left, 4-3/4 x 6-1/2", VF, HL/Apr 25/98
  (600-800)   633
2 matching drawings: hips-up of Happy looking right
  with right arms raised, waist-up of Dopey facing
  left with eyes closed; 5 x 4", 4 x 3"; VF,
  HL/Apr 25/98 (600-800)   690
27 original pencil rough animation drawings: 12 full
  drawings, 3 layouts, 2 cottage scenes, early
  drawing of Dwarfs in mine, 9 of animals, trees
  & clothing drying; 2-3/4 x 3-1/2" to 9-1/2 x
  12-1/4"; overall F; HL/Apr 25/98
  (1000-1500)   3680
Full-figure drawing of angry Grumpy walking to left,
  4-1/4 x 7", VF, HL/Apr 25/98 (500-700)   1035

BACKGROUNDS (also see CONCEPT AND INSPI-
RATIONAL ART, LAYOUT ART)

Still life: table & utensils in Dwarfs' cottage, production
  background, watercolor on paper, 11-1/4 x
  15-1/2", CE/Dec 15/93 (1800-2200)   5175
Forest painting done for background development,
  9-1/2 x 12", opaque watercolor on illustration
  board, HL/Nov 13/94 (1800-2400)   4928

Master background of Dwarf's cottage, 12 x 15",
  watercolor on background sheet, stamps,
  notes, artists' signatures & initials, VF+,
  HL/Nov 13/94 (30,000-40,000)   78,400
Pan production background of Dwarf's Cottage, 34"
  wide, watercolor on background sheet, extensive
  notes, CE/Jun 9/95 (30,000-50,000)   50,600
Preliminary background of items in corner of Dwarf's
  cottage, watercolor on heavyweight paper,
  8 x 10-1/2", HL/May 3/97 (2000-2500)   4370
Preliminary watercolor background of Dwarf's sunlit
  cottage in forest, 9 x 10", signed "Flohris",
  CLA/Jun 7/97 (10,000-15,000)   27,600

CEL SET-UPS (also see MODEL ART)

Grumpy sits atop barrel, Courvoisier wood-veneer
  background, 7-1/2 x 5-1/2", CE/Dec 15/93
  (1000-1500)   2990
Deer covered with Dwarf's clothing, Courvoisier
  watercolor & airbrush background, 7-3/4 x
  8-1/2", CE/Dec 15/93 (700-900)   805
Snow White surprised by chipmunk in pie, unidentified
  background, 6-3/4 x 7-1/2", CE/Dec 15/93
  (5000-6000)   5750
Bashful, Courvoisier wood-veneer background,
  7-3/4 x 8", CE/Dec 15/93 (1000-1500)   2990
Doc, Courvoisier wood-veneer background, 7-1/2"
  square, CE/Dec 15/93 (1000-1500)   2990
Witch hovers over cauldron, Courvoisier airbrush
  background, 9-3/4 x 8-1/2", CE/Dec 15/93
  (8000-12,000)   6900
Sneezy tries not to sneeze, hand-prepared Courvoisier
  background, 5-3/4 x 5-1/2", CE/Dec 15/93
  (1000-1500)   2530
Dopey playing cymbals, wood-veneer background,
  mat inscribed "Dopey from Snow White,"
  original WDP, S/Dec 16/93 (1200-1600)   1955
Witch plans Snow White's death, airbrushed background, 5", S/Dec 16/93 (6000-8000)   4888
Prince preparing to lift Snow White onto horse as 4
  dwarfs wave goodbye, airbrushed background,
  S/Dec 16/93 (6000-8000)   8050
Full figure of Doc w/hands behind back, polka-dot
  background, 5", S/Dec 16/93 (1800-2200)   2875
4 dwarfs hide hands behind backs before dinner time,
  wood-veneer background, WDE label, avg. size
  4-1/2", S/Dec 16/93 (3000-4000)   6900
4" witch offers apple to 4" Snow White, with cel
  overlay, airbrushed background, S/Dec 16/93
  (10,000-12,000)   14,950
3" doe & 2" (length) fawn, airbrushed background,
  S/Dec 16/93 (800-1200)   575
Grumpy looks angrily over shoulder, polka dot background, WDE label, 4-1/2", S/Dec 16/93
  (1000-1500)   2588
3-1/2" Sneezy, Bashful & Doc investigate cottage
  while animals watch, airbrushed background,
  WDE label, S/Dec 16/93 (2500-3500)   4025
Dwarfs look over cliff where witch has fallen in rain,
  airbrushed background, S/Dec 16/93
  (5000-7000)   8050
2 cels of forest animals, each w/airbrushed background
  & WDE label, S/Dec 16/93 (600-800)   863
Snow White singing by well framed by vines, airbrushed
  background, WDE label & copyright stamp, 7",
  S/Dec 16/93 (5000-7000)   6900
4" Bashful & 4" Sneezy listen to 4-3/4" Doc,
  wood-veneer background, S/Dec 16/93
  (2500-3500)   4313
Happy smiling, wood-veneer background, Walt Disney
  signature, WDP stamp, 3-1/2" (waist-up), S/Dec
  16/93 (1200-1500)   3738
4-1/2" Snow White sits in forest w/animals, airbrushed
  background, S/Dec 16/93 (5000-7000)   5175
5" Snow White leans to kiss 3-1/2" Doc, wood-veneer
  background, S/Dec 16/93 (2500-3500)   5750
Snow White in Dwarf's cottage, 3 x 3-1/2", complementary modern woodgrain-style background,
  F+, HL/Apr 10/94 (3000-4000)   2912
Wicked Queen, 12-1/2 x 9-1/2", mounted to
  complementary airbrush background, in mat
  embossed "© W.D.E." for Courvoisier,
  2 contemporary authenticity labels, VF,
  HL/Apr 10/94 (8000-12,000)   12,880
Snow White, Prince & Dwarfs in finale, mounted to
  complementary airbrush background for Courvoisier, label, restored, VF,
  HL/Apr 10/94 (5000-7000)   10,080
Portrait of cheerful Doc, 6 x 6", mounted to
  complementary woodgrain background for Cour-

voisier, Disney labels, F+,
  HL/Apr 10/94 (1400-1800)   2464
Portrait of Snow White & animals peering into window,
  7-1/2 x 9", complementary painted background
  in mat embossed "© W.D.E.", Courvoisier label,
  VF, HL/Apr 10/94 (4000-6000)   8400
Dopey duels with fishes, 7-1/2 x 7", complementary
  airbrush background, 2 original labels, in mat
  inscribed & embossed "© W.D.E." for
  Courvoisier, restored, VF, HL/Apr 10/94
  (2500-3500)   3136
DAE limited-edition cel of 7 Dwarfs marching home,
  #54/275, 10-1/2 x 21-1/2", Disney seal &
  certificate, color print background, VF+,
  HL/Apr 10/94 (4000-5000)   5376
Frightened Snow White flees, atmospheric watercolor
  master background, 9 x 11-1/2", studio stamps
  & notes, restored, VF, HL/Apr 10/94
  (12,000-16,000)   10,080
Dopey walks w/pick over shoulder, airbrushed background, 5", S/Jun 17/94 (1800-2200)   3450
6 Dwarfs guiltily hide hands behind backs, wood-
  veneer Courvoisier background, avg size
  4-1/2", S/Jun 17/94 (3000-5000)   6900
Snow White in rags (eyes closed) washes steps as
  doves fly around her, airbrushed Courvoisier
  background, 6", S/Jun 17/94 (5000-7000)   5462
Dopey plays cymbals, wood-veneer background (cel
  cracked throughout), 6-1/2", S/Jun 17/94
  (1000-1500)   1955
Angry Grumpy at organ, wood-veneer background,
  Walt Disney signature, WDP stamp, 4",
  S/Jun 17/94 (1200-1500)   3450
Happy smiles, wood veneer Courvoisier background, 3-3/4" (waist up), S/Jun 17/94
  (1800-2200)   2587
Snow White sits up in bed w/2 drowsy rabbits,
  polka-dot Courvoisier background, 5",
  S/Jun 17/94 (2500-3500)   6325
Snow White & animals peer thru cottage window,
  wood-veneer Courvoisier background, 4 x
  4-1/2", S/Jun 17/94 (3000-5000)   6900
Snow White (2") waves farewell from atop Prince's
  horse as he (3") leads her out of woods, water-
  color production background w/production
  overlays, S/Jun 17/94 (20,000-25,000)   17,250
Snow White (6") ascends stairs & bids good night to 6
  dwarfs, wood-veneer Courvoisier background,
  S/Jun 17/94 (5000-7000)   6325
Sneezy (3") & Happy (3-1/2") play instruments &
  sing, Courvoisier wood-veneer background,
  S/Jun 17/94 (2500-3500)   4600
Sneezy holds pick & calls "Heigh-Ho", trimmed,
  wood-veneer Courvoisier background, 4-1/2",
  S/Jun 17/94 (1500-2000)   3162
Waist-up image of Snow White singing to bluebird
  on her finger, 2 other birds circle, airbrushed
  Courvoisier background, inscribed "To Aage Bre-
  merholm, with best wishes, Walt Disney"
  on mat, 5", S/Jun 17/94 (3000-5000)   6325
Matching set-up of scowling Grumpy with arms
  crossed at dinner table, matching watercolor
  production background, notes, 4",
  S/Jun 17/94 (12,000-15,000)   12,650
Surprised Dopey standing by a giant bubble,
  airbrushed background, 4-1/2",
  S/Jun 17/94 (1800-2200)   4312
Snow White leans over well & sings to 8 doves,
  airbrushed Courvoisier background, 3",
  S/Jun 17/94 (5000-7000)   7475
Sitting Dopey reaching for feather, Courvoisier
  airbrush background, 4 x 4", CE/Jun 18/94
  (1500-2000)   3450
Portrait of Bashful, Courvoisier wood-veneer back-
  ground, 4", CE/Jun 18/94 (1000-1500)   2300
Snow White (6 x 6") bakes pie as birds watch (1-1/2
  x 3/4" & smaller), unidentified background,
  CE/Jun 18/94 (4000-6000)   6440
Prince (8-1/2 x 2-1/4") carries Snow White away
  (5-1/2 x 4"), Courvoisier airbrush background,
  CE/Jun 18/94 (3000-5000)   5750
Dopey as giant, 8", Courvoisier airbrush background,
  CE/Jun 18/94 (2500-3500)   6325
Happy, Sneezy & Bashful (4 x 2-1/2") look up at
  animals on window sill, airbrush Courvoisier
  background, CE/Jun 18/94 (2000-3000)   5750
Snow White in cottage, 7", pan watercolor production
  background, production notes, Courvoisier label,
  "C 1937 Walt Disney Prods." stamped on cover

cel, CE/Jun 18/94 (15,000-25,000)   32,200

Double image of Queen (8-1/2") reading & Witch (5") pointing, Courvoisier airbrush background, CE/Jun 18/94 (8000-12,000)   14,950

Forest animals, 1-1/2" & smaller, airbrush Courvoisier background, CE/Jun 18/94 (800-1200)   920

Doc, Grumpy, Sleepy & Bashful in cottage, 4-1/2" & smaller, pan watercolor production background w/stamps & notes, CE/Jun 18/94 (10,000-15,000)   24,150

2 sleeping deer, 5" long, Courvoisier airbrush background, CE/Jun 18/94 (800-1200)   1380

Animals guiding Snow White (7") thru forest, airbrush Courvoisier background, CE/Jun 18/94 (3500-4500)   5980

Apprehensive Dopey sitting on bench, 3 x 2-3/4", Courvoisier airbrush background, CE/Jun 18/94 (1500-2000)   3680

Snow White standing in front of cottage waving, 7-1/2", pan watercolor production background, notes, Courvoisier label, copyright stamp, CE/Jun 18/94 (15,000-25,000)   19,550

Grumpy sits grumpily on barrel, 5", Courvoisier wood-veneer background, CE/Jun 18/94 (1500-2000)   4140

Dopey wields broom & dustpan, 4", Courvoisier airbrush background, CE/Jun 18/94 (2000-3000)   6325

Happy opens cottage window, 6-1/2 x 5-1/2", key watercolor production background, Courvoisier label, CE/Jun 18/94 (10,000-15,000)   9200

2 deer & bird, 5" & smaller, Courvoisier watercolor & airbrush background, CE/Jun 18/94 (800-1200)   748

Snow White (4-1/2 x 2-1/2") leans out window toward smiling Doc (5 x 3-1/2"), wood-veneer Courvoisier background, CE/Jun 18/94 (3000-4000)   8280

Snow White at well with pigeons, Courvoisier complementary painted background, labels, inscribed, 8-1/2 x 10", HL/Aug 21/94 (4000-6000)   7280

2 limited-edition 50th anniversary cels: Queen presents heart box; Prince carries Snow White amid happy Dwarfs; #220/500, special color print backgrounds, seals & labels; 11 x 15", HL/Aug 21/94 (2000-2500)   3584

Full figure of whistling Dopey carrying hand ax, Courvoisier airbrush background & label, sparkle overlay cel, 5 x 4-1/2", HL/Aug 21/94 (2000-3000)   3584

Full figure of Sleepy hiding dirty hands, complementary Courvoisier ink & airbrush background, original frame & labels, 6-1/2 x 4-1/2", HL/Aug 21/94 (1800-2400)   4032

Snow White sings to sad bluebird on finger, cel of vines over Courvoisier airbrush background, inscribed mat, 8-1/4 x 8", HL/Aug 21/94 (5000-7000)   8960

22 full images of animals running thru forest (key to scene), key master background as prepared Courvoisier, full set-up 22-1/2 x 11", with original oil paint-on-cel overlay of tree & mushrooms, SR/Fall/94 (12,000-20,000) 17,000

Snow White (6") sits in right corner facing left, watching 2 bluebirds, Courvoisier watercolor background of forest, restoration, SR/Fall/94 (2500-4000)   5800

Guilty Doc, Bashful & Sneezy hide their hands, airbrushed woodgrain Courvoisier background & labels, inscribed, HL/Nov 13/94 (2500-3500)   5600

3 Dwarfs looking up & 3 forest animals on window sill, 6 x 6", complementary Courvoisier airbrush background & labels, F+, HL/Nov 13/94 (3000-3500)   5376

Snow White cooking in fireplace over complementary background print created for "The Plausible Impossible" TV episode, 6 x 4-1/2", HL/Nov 13/94 (1800-2400)   2912

Full figure of Grumpy sitting at organ glaring over his shoulder, Courvoisier wood-veneer background, 3-1/2", CE/Dec 16/94 (3000-3500)   3680

Oval image of the Prince (7") carrying Snow White (5"), Courvoisier airbrush background, CE/Dec 16/94 (4000-6000)   9775

Publicity cel of love-struck Dopey sitting w/chin in hand, Courvoisier airbrush background, 6-1/2", CE/Dec 16/94 (2500-3500)   8050

Full figure of Snow White w/water bucket & 5 birds, 6", Courvoisier airbrush background, mat inscribed "Walt Disney", CE/Dec 16/94 (7000-9000)   11,500

Witch working at cauldron, 4", Courvoisier airbrush background, mat inscribed "Walt Disney", CE/Dec 16/94 (7000-9000)   12,650

Full figures of 7 Dwarfs marching & singing, 3" & smaller, Courvoisier wood-veneer background, CE/Dec 16/94 (1000-1500)   8625

Full figures of two surprised rabbits, 3" ea., Courvoisier airbrush background, CE/Dec 16/94 (400-600)   633

Full figures of 6 eager-to-please Dwarfs, Courvoisier wood-veneer background, 5" & smaller, CE/Dec 16/94 (5000-7000)   10,350

Snow White & Prince beside horse as 3 Dwarfs look on, 7" & smaller, Courvoisier airbrush background, CE/Dec 16/94 (8000-12,000)   17,250

Snow White at wishing well w/8 birds, 3", Courvoisier airbrush & watercolor background, CE/Dec 16/94 (8000-12,000)   12,650

Snow White (6") trims pie crust as 5 birds watch, patterned Courvoisier background, inscribed "To Ned from Walt Disney", S/Dec 17/94 (4000-6000)   10,925

Dopey (4") walks happily, looking over shoulder as assortment of animals (2-1/2" to 1/2") follow, airbrushed Courvoisier background, Walt Disney label, S/Dec 17/94 (2500-3000)   5750

Animals run to Snow White's rescue, 2" to 1/2", airbrushed Courvoisier background, WDE label, S/Dec 17/94 (400-600)   632

Doc smiles knowingly with hands pressed together & eyes closed, 4", airbrushed Courvoisier background, S/Dec 17/94 (1500-2000)   2875

Snow White sings to birds, 5-1/2", airbrushed Courvoisier background, Walt Disney label, S/Dec 17/94 (3000-5000)   8625

Portrait cel of Queen, 5", airbrushed background, S/Dec 17/94 (6000-8000)   10,062

Dopey happily sweeps up diamonds, 4" airbrushed Courvoisier background, WDE label, S/Dec 17/94 (1500-2500)   6037

Large image of Doc plucking duck-shaped mandolin, 7", airbrushed Courvoisier background, S/Dec 17/94 (2500-3500)   5175

Witch (4") stirs cauldron under watchful eye of raven (2-1/2"), airbrushed Courvoisier background, WDE label, S/Dec 17/94 (6000-8000)   8337

Snow White (3-1/2") is led to dwarfs' cottage by forest friends, airbrushed Courvoisier background, S/Dec 17/94 (5000-7000)   8050

Snow White & animals clear dust from cottage window to peer inside, 4", airbrushed veneer Courvoisier background, S/Dec 17/94 (3000-5000)   17,250

Snow White (5") comforts frightened baby bird; bunny with chipmunk on head (3-1/2") & turtle; both over airbrushed Courvoisier backgrounds, S/Dec 17/94 (3000-5000)   7475

Full figures of forest animals gathering on hill at mushroom-shaped house, 10 x 8" Courvoisier watercolor background w/labels, some cracking & discoloration, SR/Spring/95 (700-1200)   730

Waist-up portrait of Sneezy, leaning to left with arms out, looking right, 3-1/4", Courvoisier wood-veneer background, circle vignette w/watercolor shadow & hand lettering, mat & label, SR/Spring/95 (1600-2200)   3150

Near-full figure of laundry-covered young stag with bluebird on antlers standing in dwarf's cottage, 5 3/8", watercolor display background & overlay, ct, SR/Spring/95 (1200-1800)   1400

Full figures of surprised squirrel (3-1/8") sitting on hill & two bluebirds, Courvoisier watercolor background, label & mat, ct, SR/Spring/95 (500-800)   600

"Off To Bed" #242/350 cel painting issued by DAE, 11 x 20", color print background, HL/Apr 23/95 (4000-5000)   3472

Profile portrait of Witch, 5-1/2 x 5-1/2", woodgrain airbrushed background titled "The Old Witch," 2 labels of authenticity, as prepared by Courvoisier Galleries, HL/Apr 23/95 (4000-5000)   8400

Full figures of 6 Dwarfs with hands behind backs, 6 x 10" cel, woodgrain background, 2 labels of authenticity, as prepared by Courvoisier, HL/Apr 23/95 (4000-5000)   8400

Full figure of happy Bashful, 6-1/2 x 3", shadow airbrushed woodgrain background as prepared by Courvoisier, labels, HL/Apr 23/95 (2000-2500)   4032

Sleepy drives mine car, 7 x 9", complementary painted woodgrain background, matching cels of donkey, cart & sparkles, as prepared by Disney thru Courvoisier, HL/Apr 23/95 (2500-3500)   5264

Queen stares at glass of magic potion, 8-1/2 x 7", complementary painted background, inscribed mat, authenticity certificate, as prepared for Courvoisier, HL/Apr 23/95 (9000-12,000)   13,440

Full figures of 4 Dwarfs pulling mine car, 7 x 12-1/2", complementary painted woodgrain background w/cel of sparkles, as prepared for Courvoisier, HL/Apr 23/95 (5000-7000)   9520

Full figure of Dopey dancing on Sneezy's shoulders (hidden by coat), 6-1/2 x 10", complementary painted background, HL/Apr 23/95 (3000-4000)   4816

Full figure of enthusiastic Dopey running with key, 5-1/2 x 5-1/2", complementary shadow woodgrain background, 2 labels as prepared for sale thru Courvoisier, HL/Apr 23/95 (3000-4000)   4928

Smiling Dopey holding cymbal, 3-1/2", Courvoisier airbrush background, CE/Jun 9/95 (2500-3500)   4370

4 horrified Dwarfs staring over cliff in rain, 1-1/2", partial overlay, Courvoisier watercolor & airbrush background, CE/Jun 9/95 (4000-6000)   4830

Full figure of Grumpy lying in kettle, 4-1/2" width, Courvoisier wood-veneer background, CE/Jun 9/95 (2000-3000)   4025

Full figure of angry Grumpy walking & looking back over shoulder, 5", partial overlay & Courvoisier airbrush background, CE/Jun 9/95 (2500-3500)   3450

Full figures of 4 Dwarfs pulling mine car, 3" & similar, Courvoisier wood-veneer background, CE/Jun 9/95 (4000-6000)   7475

Full figures of Sneezy, Happy, angry Doc (holding lantern) in cottage w/animals, 4", Courvoisier airbrush background, CE/Jun 9/95 (3000-4000)   7475

Full figure of Bashful standing inside cottage holding cup, 4-3/4", Courvoisier wood-veneer background, CE/Jun 9/95 (2500-3500)   3680

Queen looking thru magic book, 7-1/2", hand-prepared background, CE/Jun 9/95 (7000-9000)   8050

Snow White speaking as she sits by hearth, 7", cardboard background, CE/Jun 9/95 (5000-7000)   6900

Full figures of Grumpy sitting on barrel outside by tree surrounded by other 6 Dwarfs, 4-1/2" & smaller, Courvoisier pastel-on-paper background, CE/Jun 9/95 (6000-8000)   10,925

Portrait of Dopey, 5", Courvoisier wood-veneer background, CE/Jun 9/95 (2000-2500)   4600

Full figure of Dopey playing cymbal, 7-1/2", Courvoisier wood-veneer background, CE/Jun 9/95 (2500-3500)   6325

Full figure of Dopey playing drum inside cottage, 5", Courvoisier wood-veneer & watercolor background, trimmed drum applied by Courvoisier, CE/Jun 9/95 (2500-3500)   4600

Full-figure Doc (Happy?) plays "swanette", 4", Courvoisier watercolor background, CE/Jun 9/95 (1500-2000)   3680

Witch at cauldron, 7-3/4", Courvoisier airbrush background, CE/Jun 9/95 (8000-10,000)   9200

Full figures of 5 Dwarfs marching to left w/picks over shoulders, 3" & smaller, Courvoisier wood-veneer background, CE/Jun 9/95 (3500-4500)   7475

Full figure of Sneezy sitting in corner w/beard tied under nose, 4", Courvoisier watercolor background, CE/Jun 9/95 (2500-3500)   6325

Near-full figure of Grumpy sitting in kettle, 4", Courvoisier airbrush background, mat inscribed "...Walt Disney", CE/Jun 9/95 (3000-4000)   5750

Full figure of Dopey walking, 4-3/4", Courvoisier watercolor background, CE/Jun 9/95 (2500-3500) 5175

Portrait of Doc, 3-1/2", Courvoisier wood-veneer background, CE/Jun 9/95 (1500-2000) 3680

Full figures of Dopey pushing Sleepy who's pushing mine car inside mine, 3", Courvoisier airbrush background, CE/Jun 9/95 (3500-4500) 5750

Full-figure publicity cel of all 7 Dwarfs, 5-1/4" ea., Courvoisier wood-veneer background, CE/Jun 9/95 (12,000-15,000) 13,800

Full figure of chastened Doc standing w/hands behind back, 5", Courvoisier wood-veneer background, CE/Jun 9/95 (2000-3000) 4370

Full figure of Doc looking back w/finger to lips as he holds lantern, 3-3/4", Courvoisier airbrush background, CE/Jun 9/95 (2000-2500) 4370

Snow White at wishing well w/doves, 3-1/2", Courvoisier watercolor background, CE/Jun 9/95 (8000-10,000) 13,800

Bashful twirls his beard, 6", wood-veneer Courvoisier background, S/Jun 10/95 (1800-2200) 3737

Frightened Dopey leans away & crosses his arms protectively, 4", airbrushed Courvoisier background, S/Jun 10/95 (1500-2000) 4312

Classic portrait of Sleepy, 3-1/4", wood-veneer Courvoisier background, S/Jun 10/95 (800-1200) 2300

Dopey (2-1/2") watches happy Doc (3-1/2") hold large gem, airbrushed Courvoisier background, S/Jun 10/95 (4000-6000) 7475

Full figure of Snow White (5") walking thru forest w/animals, wood-veneer Courvoisier background, S/Jun 10/95 (8000-10,000) 10,350

2 Courvoisier set-ups: smiling Dopey reaches out (3-1/2") w/arms hidden by sleeves while surrounded by animals; rabbit (3") & turtle look at each other; each w/airbrushed Courvoisier background, S/Jun 10/95 (2000-3000) 5175

Full figure of Dopey happily sweeping gems into dustpan, 5-1/2", airbrushed Courvoisier background; set-up of animals peering in window, each approx. 1-1/2", patterned paper Courvoisier background, S/Jun 10/95 (2000-3000) 6325

Full figure of Doc plucking duck-shaped mandolin, 6-1/2", airbrushed Courvoisier background, S/Jun 10/95 (3000-4000) 6900

Portrait of Snow White looking down in surprise, 4-1/4", wood-veneer Courvoisier background, S/Jun 10/95 (2000-3000) 8050

Full figures of Doc, Happy , Bashful & Sleepy standing & laughing w/Dopey sitting on floor in front of them, approx. 4" each, wood-veneer Courvoisier background, S/Jun 10/95 (5000-7000) 9775

Full figure of Grumpy smiling, 5", polka dot-print Courvoisier background, S/Jun 10/95 (1800-2200) 4600

Full figures of mother & baby deer, moth, & blue bird in forest, 7-1/2 x 7-1/2", woodgrain background from Disney Studio, HL/Aug 6/95 (1000-1500) 896

Full figure of admiring Dopey sitting head in hand, 7 x 11", clouds or smoke in background, as prepared for Courvoisier, F, HL/Aug 6/95 (4000-5000) 6384

Full figures of Dopey (& Sneezy) dancing w/Snow White while Doc, Sleepy, & Bashful play instruments, 10 x 13", complementary painted woodgrain background as prepared for Courvoisier, HL/Aug 6/95 (8000-10,000) 14,560

Full figures of 6 Dwarfs w/hands behind backs, 6 x 10" cel, airbrushed woodgrain background as prepared for Courvoisier, HL/Aug 6/95 (5000-7000) 8960

Full figure of Snow White kneeling in forest holding baby bird, 11-1/2 x 15-1/2", color print background, #53/500 in 1993 limited edition, HL/Aug 6/95 (2200-2800) 1456

Full figure of happy Doc sitting on bench in cottage, 7-1/2 x 5-1/2", complementary painted background for release thru Courvoisier, HL/Aug 6/95 (2500-3500) 4032

Full figure of Happy standing in cottage, 7-1/2 x 5-1/2", complementary painted background for release thru Courvoisier, HL/Aug 6/95 (2500-3500) 4032

Full figure of Dopey cavorting amid soap bubbles, 5-1/4 x 5-1/4", complementary airbrush background as prepared for Courvoisier, HL/Aug 6/95 (3000-4000) 5152

Full figure of angry Grumpy (4") standing as 5 birds descend on him, one grabbing his beard, key watercolor background prepared for sale by Courvoisier, stamps & notations, Courvoisier label, ct, SR/Fall/95 (10,000-20,000) 13,500

7 surprised dwarfs sitting/standing around dining table looking up; key watercolor matching background of cottage interior, 24-1/2 x 11-3/4", studio stamps & notations, Sam Armstrong's okay; as prepared for sale thru Courvoisier with label, SR/Fall/95 (30,000-50,000) 33,500

Full figures of 12 forest animals circling hilltop tree, Courvoisier watercolor background with labels, SR/Fall/95 (600-1000) 900

Full figure of smiling Sleepy standing, hands behind back, looking left, 4-1/2", Courvoisier dotted paper background w/airbrushing, mat & label, name at bottom, SR/Fall/95 (1600-2400) 3470

Snow White w/2 chipmunks in lap, 6-3/4 x 6-1/2", shadow woodgrain background as prepared for Courvoisier Galleries, HL/Nov 19/95 (7000-9000) 9200

Hag looks up from bubbling cauldron & points, 6-3/4 x 7-1/4", complementary airbrush background as prepared for Courvoisier, HL/Nov 19/95 (8000-10,000) 12,075

2 full-figure cel set-ups of forest friends, 6" diameter & 5 x 5-1/2", complementary airbrush backgrounds, HL/Nov 19/95 (900-1200) 1495

Full figures of angry mouse (3/4", all but tip of tail) standing at mouse hole blowing dust back as squirrel lifts rug & rabbit watches (together 4-1/4"), Courvoisier watercolor background, typewritten label, hand-lettered mat, SR/Spring/96 (1200-1600) 1200

Full figure of Snow White sitting on hillside w/mouth open amid animals, 4-7/8", Courvoisier watercolor background, original label & mat, "WDE" stamp, SR/Spring/96 (4000-6000) 6800

Full figure of anxious Dopey walking right thru grass holding key, with rabbit & bird, 4-1/4", Courvoisier watercolor background & original overlay cel, original labels & mat, "WDE" stamp. SR/Spring/96 (3500-4500) 3000

Full figure of Sleepy standing facing right, looking back, 3-1/4", Courvoisier star-studded paper background accented with airbrushing, label & mat, SR/Spring/96 (1600-2400) 2390

Full figure of whistling Dopey walking right carrying pick on shoulder, looking down, 3-3/4", Courvoisier watercolor background w/sparkling gem effects, typed label, original mat with debossed "WDE" stamp, SR/Spring/96 (3000-5000) 3630

Full figures of thoughtful Doc, Bashful & Sneezy standing w/hands behind backs, Courvoisier airbrushed woodgrain background, 6-1/2 x 8-1/2", HL/Apr 28/96 (4000-5000) 5693

Full figures of sheepish Doc, Bashful, Sneezy, Happy, Dopey & Sleepy standing w/hands behind backs, Courvoisier woodgrain background, mat signed by Walt Disney, 7-1/2 x 10-1/2", HL/Apr 28/96 (7000-9000) 10,925

Full-figure large image of apprehensive Dopey in mid-step w/pick upraised, complementary Courvoisier airbrush background w/sparkles, 7-1/2 x 7", HL/Apr 28/96 (3500-4000) 6038

Full figure of happy Happy standing & looking left, Courvoisier wood-veneer background, 6", S/Jun 19/96 (2000-3000) 4887

Snow White looks up from wishing well amid vines, Courvoisier background, 6", S/Jun 19/96 (5000-7000) 8050

Full figures of all Dwarfs huddled in bedroom, printed background, each 2-1/2", S/Jun 19/96 (8000-10,000) 12,075

Full figures of 4 dwarfs pulling mine car inside mine, 3" each, airbrushed wood-veneer Courvoisier background, S/Jun 19/96 (5000-7000) 9775

Snow White (6") trims pie crust as birds watch, patterned Courvoisier background, S/Jun 19/96 (7000-9000) 8050

Full figures of Dopey & Grumpy walking at night w/picks over shoulders as Doc leads way w/lantern, airbrushed Courvoisier background, approx. 4" each, S/Jun 19/96 (5000-7000) 9200

Large full figure of bashful Bashful standing & looking left, wood-veneer Courvoisier background, 7", S/Jun 19/96 (2000-3000) 4312

Full figure of smiling Sleepy standing with hands beneath beard & looking left, Courvoisier patterned paper background, 5", S/Jun 19/96 (2000-3000) 3737

Full figures of fawn (2 x 2-1/2") & 5 bunnies (1" each) leading Snow White (holding flower bouquet; 6") thru forest, Courvoisier background, inscribed "...Walt Disney" in Hank Porter's hand, S/Jun 19/96 (8000-10,000) 13,800

Full figure of Grumpy lying in kettle, wood-veneer Courvoisier background, 4-1/2 x 4", S/Jun 19/96 (2000-3000) 3737

Full figures of Bashful, Sleepy, Happy, & Grumpy walking w/picks over shoulders, Doc leading w/lantern, wood-veneer Courvoisier background, 1-1/2 to 3-1/2", S/Jun 19/96 (5000-7000) 6900

Key set-up of serious Dopey playing the drums, key watercolor production background, Courvoisier label, 4", S/Jun 19/96 (20,000-25,000) 24,150

Portrait of Sneezy w/finger under nose, Courvoisier wood-veneer background, labeled "Sneezy", 4", CE/Jun 20/96 (2500-3500) 2990

Near-full figure of concerned Happy standing & pointing left, Courvoisier wood-veneer background, 6", CE/Jun 20/96 (2500-3500) 3220

Full figure of eager Dopey sweeping gems into dustpan, Courvoisier airbrush background, 3-1/2", CE/Jun 20/96 (3000-4000) 5750

Full figure of Grumpy lying in kettle holding spoon, Courvoisier wood-veneer background, 5", CE/Jun 20/96 (2500-3500) 3220

Full figure of Snow White sweeping dust into shovel held by 2 chipmunks, Courvoisier airbrush background, 4-1/2", CE/Jun 20/96 (6000-8000) 5750

Doc speaking in front of large tree trunk, key watercolor production background, 5-1/2", CE/Jun 20/96 (10,000-15,000) 12,650

Full figure of happy Dopey standing looking over right shoulder, Courvoisier paper background, 3-3/4", CE/Jun 20/96 (2500-3500) 5520

Portrait of Sneezy, head up, finger under nose; Courvoisier wood-veneer background, labeled "Sneezy", 4", CE/Jun 20/96 (2500-3500) 2990

Queen, Courvoisier airbrush background, 5", CE/Jun 20/96 (7000-9000) 11,500

Portrait of Snow White sitting outdoors w/face in profile looking right, 6", Courvoisier airbrush background, CE/Jun 20/96 (6000-8000) 6900

Full figures of 4 dwarfs standing by mine car, Courvoisier wood-veneer background, 3" each, CE/Jun 20/96 (5000-7000) 5520

Full figure of Sleepy (5-1/2") waking up in tilted mine bucket w/chipmunk on beard & squirrel standing on ground (1-1/2" & smaller), Courvoisier wood-veneer background, CE/Jun 20/96 (3000-4000) 4370

Full figure of disgusted Grumpy walking toward tree while looking back over shoulder, matching watercolor production background of forest (left part of pan background, Grumpy is key w/right part), Courvoisier label, 5", CE/Jun 20/96 (12,000-18,000) 17,250

Smiling Dopey reaching toward cymbal, string of bells hanging on right, Courvoisier airbrush background, 4", severely faded, CE/Jun 20/96 (1000-1500) 3220

Worried Dopey, Happy, Sneezy & Doc confer at foot of beds, Courvoisier wood-veneer background, 4" each, CE/Jun 20/96 (6000-8000) 8050

Full figures of 2 bunnies hugging, Courvoisier paper background, 2", CE/Jun 20/96 (500-700) 518

Heads of 4 Dwarfs peer over cliff in rain, Courvoisier airbrush background, partial overlay, 1-1/2", CE/Jun 20/96 (5000-7000) 4600

46 Dwarfs confer at railing, Courvoisier wood-veneer background, 2" each, CE/Jun 20/96 (5000-7000) 5520

Grumpy standing by chair looking down, right arm out, key watercolor production background (missing overlay), 4-1/4", CE/Jun 20/96 (10,000-15,000) 10,350

Near-full figures of Snow White (7-1/2") talking to 3 shy Dwarfs (4") inside cottage, key watercolor pan production background, Courvoisier label,

CE/Jun 20/96 (30,000-40,000)   85,000

Full figure of angry Grumpy sitting on barrel, Courvoisier wood-veneer background, 4", CE/Jun 20/96 (3000-4000)   3220

Full figure of Grumpy sitting on barrel with arms folded & mouth open, looking right, 4-3/8"; watercolor display background of cottage exterior; SR/Fall/96 (2800-3800)   2810

Rear view of Grumpy looking back over right shoulder while playing organ, 4", watercolor display background, SR/Fall/96 (3200-4200)   3520

Seven dwarfs stands at foot of bed looking at each other, 6-1/8", surface wear, trimmed by Courvoisier, applied to full new cel, watercolor background, SR/Fall/96 (4000-10,000)   12,000

Full figure of cautious Dopey walking to right with candle held high, 5-1/4 x 3" cel image, star-print background airbrushed to simulate candle's glow & doorway, 2 labels as prepared at Disney for sale thru Courvoisier, HL/Oct 6/96 (3000-3500)   3795

Full figures of family of 3 happy bluebirds on tree branch, 4-1/2 x 5", complementary painted background, 2 labels as prepared by Disney for sale thru Courvoisier, HL/Oct 6/96 (1000-1500)   805

Mother deer lying w/fawn & 2 butterflies, 6-1/2 x 6-1/2", complementary painted background as prepared by Courvoisier, HL/Oct 6/96 (1000-1500)   978

Set of 2 limited-edition cels for 50th anniversary of film's release, both #175/500: Snow White being carried by Prince among Dwarfs, Queen presenting heart box; 11 x 15-1/2" overall; color print backgrounds as issued, HL/Oct 6/96 (1500-2000)   2990

Full-figure front view of smiling Bashful standing playing accordion, 5 x 3-1/4" cel image, airbrushed woodgrain background as prepared by Disney for sale thru Courvoisier, HL/Oct 6/96 (2000-2500)   3795

Smiling Sleepy resting on wood pile, 6-1/4 x 5" cel image, painted background as prepared by Disney for Courvoisier, HL/Oct 6/96 (2500-3000)   3910

Portrait of happy Bashful looking down & to left, 4", Courvoisier wood-veneer background & label, CE/Dec 12/96 (2000-3000)   2990

Witch poling boat along stream bank with apple basket at her feet, 6", water special effects, Courvoisier airbrush background, CE/Dec 12/96 (10,000-12,000)   17,250

Witch (4") offers apple to frightened Snow White (3-1/2") thru cottage window, Courvoisier airbrush & watercolor background, CE/Dec 12/96 (8000-10,000)   13,800

Full-figure long view of Prince leading white horse, w/Snow White riding, into sunset, 2-1/2", Courvoisier airbrush & watercolor background, CE/Dec 12/96 (8000-10,000)   7475

Snow White sitting on stone step, scrub brush in hand, bucket at feet, soapy water on step, looking up & to left, w/3 white doves, 4-1/2", Courvoisier airbrushed background, CE/Dec 12/96 (12,000-15,000)   14,950

Snow White sings to bird perched on her finger, 6-1/2", Courvoisier airbrush background, "To ... Walt Disney" on mat, CE/Dec 12/96 (10,000-15,000)   18,400

Terrified crow staring at candle while jumping on top of skull, 6-1/2", Courvoisier airbrush background, CE/Dec 12/96 (3000-4000)   6900

Front view of Queen holding heart box, 7-1/2", Courvoisier airbrush background, CE/Dec 12/96 (8000-10,000)   21,275

Full figures of Snow White (7-1/2") dancing w/Dopey-Sneezy (7") as Doc, Bashful & Sleepy (3-1/2" each) stand playing instruments, Courvoisier wood-veneer background, CE/Dec 12/96 (12,000-15,000)   23,000

Full figures of Doc, Bashful (partially hidden), Sneezy, Happy & Dopey standing looking up shyly w/hands behind backs, approx. 4" ea, wood-veneer Courvoisier background, S/Dec 14/96 (5000-7000)   6325

Full figure of cautious Dopey w/pick-axe in hand facing left, 3", wood-veneer Courvoisier background, S/Dec 14/96 (2000-3000)   3737

Rabbit (3") looks at mouse (1") who's out of his hole to

protest dirt being swept in, airbrush-on-textured-material Courvoisier background, S/Dec 14/96 (600-800)   632

Full figure of Bashful standing bashfully, 5-1/2", patterned paper Courvoisier background, S/Dec 14/96 (2000-3000)   3162

Full figure of bashful Bashful standing, 5-1/4", patterned paper Courvoisier background, S/Dec 14/96 (2000-2500)   3450

Near-full-figure front view of Prince lifting Snow White on horse amid leafy vines, 7 x 4", airbrushed Courvoisier background, S/Dec 14/96 (8000-10,000)   9200

6 grim Dwarfs stare at somber Dopey as he turns & looks up stairs, Doc & Dopey (full figure) 4-1/2" each, others vary; airbrushed Courvoisier background, S/Dec 14/96 (10,000-12,000)   9775

Portrait of somber Snow White facing right, holding apple in both hands, 3-1/2", wood-veneer Courvoisier background, S/Dec 14/96 (6000-8000)   6900

Profile portrait of grinning Witch facing left, right hand raised, 3", wood-veneer Courvoisier background, S/Dec 14/96 (6000-8000)   6900

Heads of Dwarfs stick over (& thru) railing [at top of stairs], approx. 2" each, airbrushed wood-veneer Courvoisier background, S/Dec 14/96 (10,000-12,000)   11,500

Front view of Queen holding heart box out with both hands, 6-1/2", airbrushed Courvoisier background of curtains, S/Dec 14/96 (10,000-15,000)   24,150

Standing full figures of Doc holding lantern and gesturing to Bashful (partly behind Doc) & Sneezy in front of window as animals watch, approx. 3-1/2" each, airbrushed & patterned paper Courvoisier background, S/Dec 14/96 (2500-3500)   4600

Full-figure promotional cel of 7 Dwarfs standing w/Dopey in middle, each averages 5", wood-veneer Courvoisier background, needs restoration, S/Dec 14/96 (8000-10,000)   8625

Full figure of Snow White (3-1/2", w/out ink lines) carrying bouquet of flowers & walking with fawn (3") & bunnies, airbrushed Courvoisier background of trees & meadow, S/Dec 14/96 (5000-7000)   4600

7 surprised Dwarfs stand at foot of their beds; Sleepy 4", others approx. 2" each; airbrushed Courvoisier background, needs restoration, S/Dec 14/96 (8000-10,000)   10,925

Full figures of 5 singing Dwarfs marching in line w/picks on shoulders as Dopey marches alongside, complementary painted woodgrain background, Courvoisier labels, 5-1/2 x 8-1/2" overall, HL/Feb 23/97 (7000-9000)   8050

Full figure of admiring Dopey sitting cross-legged, chin in right hand; painted background of dream clouds as prepared for sale thru Courvoisier; 11-1/4 x 10-3/4" overall; VF; HL/Feb 23/97 (5000-6000)   5060

Wide-eyed Sneezy standing w/one leg on bench, painted woodgrain background as prepared for Courvoisier, 8-1/2 x 10-1/2" overall, HL/Feb 23/97 (2500-3500)   3220

Snow White sitting outdoors singing to animals, complementary painted background, as prepared for Courvoisier, 7-1/2 x 7" overall, HL/Feb 23/97 (7000-9000)   12,075

Full figure of nervous Dopey climbing stairs holding candle, complementary woodgrain background as prepared for Courvoisier, 7 x 5" overall, HL/Feb 23/97 (3000-3500)   3680

Full figure of cautious Dopey taking a high step to left, plus cel of key to mine, complementary painted woodgrain background as prepared for Courvoisier, 7 x 6-1/2" overall, HL/Feb 23/97 (4000-5000)   4140

Limited-edition cel of Wicked Queen presenting heart box, #163/500, background print, 11 x 15-1/2", HL/Feb 23/97 (800-1200)   1610

Full figures of Happy (4-1/8") standing before cooking kettle with spoon in hand as panicked Grumpy (3-5/8") stands pointing warning, all-key multiplane set-up, Sam Armstrong key master watercolor background, full overlay painted in oils on cel, stamps & Armstrong's okay on rear, Courvoisier label, ct, SR/Spring/97 (12,000-18,000)   17,000

Full figure of Snow White (3-3/4") sitting on hilltop amid 8 animals, leaning down to pet bunny, some lifting paint, watercolor Courvoisier background, SR/Spring/97 (8000-12,000)   8400

Large front view of fearsome Witch holding apple at her waist, 8-5/8", Courvoisier wood-veneer background & label, SR/Spring/97 (6000-10,000)   8500

Side view of confused Sneezy standing at wash trough, 4", wood-veneer background & 2 water effects overlays, SR/Spring/97 (1800-2400)   2010

Full-figure color model cel of Grumpy standing with arms crossed, 5-1/2", wood-veneer background, restored, SR/Spring/97 (1500-2000)   1520

Three chipmunks clamber about shelves, clock, & clothing on wall in Dwarf's cottage, prepared for sale by Courvoisier, key master watercolor background by Sam Armstrong, full overlay of cobwebs, set-up is 11-1/2 x 15-1/4", Courvoisier & debossed © WDP stamps, SR/Spring/97 (25,000-35,000)   18,500

Full figure of Snow White sitting storytelling in Dwarf's cottage, 5-3/4", blush & dry brush effects, color print background, restored, SR/Spring/97 (7000-10,000)   7800

Full figures of doe nuzzling fawn, airbrushed woodgrain background, Courvoisier labels, mat signed "To Peg ... Walt Disney", 9-3/4 x 8-1/2" including signature, HL/May 3/97 (4000-5000)   2990

Full figures of Snow White sweeping with squirrel at her feet, complementary airbrushed shadow background as prepared for Courvoisier, 7-1/4 x 4-3/4" overall, HL/May 3/97 (6000-8000)   5980

"Well, if you insist..." Full figure of Snow White standing on steps turning to speak to 5 dwarfs [backs turned], complementary painted woodgrain background as prepared for Courvoisier, 10 x 13" overall, HL/May 3/97 (12,000-15,000)   10,350

Bird sits in nest, 1", Courvoisier watercolor background, CLA/Jun 7/97 (700-900)   805

Full figure of Doc standing & playing mandolin, 6-1/4", Courvoisier wood-veneer background, CLA/Jun 7/97 (3000-4000)   3680

Kneeling Snow White comforts baby bird in her hands, 5", Courvoisier airbrush background of forest, CLA/Jun 7/97 (7000-9000)   6900

Full-figure front view of cross-eyed Dopey sitting with squirrel at his feet, 3", solid Courvoisier airbrush background, CLA/Jun 7/97 (2500-3500)   3220

2 deer (3"), turtle & squirrel (1" & smaller) in forest, Courvoisier airbrush background, CLA/Jun 7/97 (700-900)   920

Snow White (5") bakes pie as animals (1-1/4" & smaller) watch, studio-prepared wood-veneer background by Marion Smith, CLA/Jun 7/97 (6000-8000)   6900

Full figures of Dopey (4") standing with skittish deer (3"), Courvoisier airbrush background, CLA/Jun 7/97 (3000-5000)   3450

Full figure of Snow White sitting on ground and singing to animals, 5", Courvoisier watercolor background of forest, CLA/Jun 7/97 (7000-9000)   8625

3 Dwarfs (4") standing looking at 3 bunnies (1" ea.) sitting on window sill looking up, Courvoisier airbrushed background, CLA/Jun 7/97 (3000-4000)   4025

Full figures of determined Dopey (holding axe), Sneezy (watching Doc), & angry Doc (holding lantern, index finger to lips in "shush" gesture) standing in cottage; 3" each; watercolor preliminary background, CLA/Jun 7/97 (15,000-20,000)   23,000

Hips-up front view of determined Dopey w/finger in mouth, blowing soap bubbles from ears, 3-1/4", Courvoisier airbrush background, CLA/Jun 7/97 (3000-4000)   4025

Full figure of curious Grumpy sitting on barrel holding beard in fingers, 4-3/4", Courvoisier wood-veneer background, mat signed by Walt Disney, CLA/Jun 7/97 (3500-4500)   4600

Full figure of Snow White holding pan at fireplace, 7", hand-prepared gallery background, CLA/Jun 7/97 (6000-8000)   4600

Full figures of worried Dopey standing on Sneezy's head with left foot around Sneezy's nose, 8", Courvoisier airbrushed background,

CLA/Jun 7/97 (4000-6000) 5520

Full figure of Witch poling boat into swamp w/castle in background, 4-1/2", trimmed celluloid on post-production overlay with airbrush special effects applied to pan watercolor production background that's separated horizontally for multiplane camera use, CLA/Jun 7/97 (40,000-60,000) 48,300

Squirrel (3"), bunny (3-1/2"), & mouse (1-1/2"), Courvoisier airbrush background & label, CLA/Jun 7/97 (700-900) 978

Snow White, chipmunk, squirrel, raccoon & faun peer thru window into dwarfs' cottage, 4 x 4-1/2", wood-veneer Courvoisier background, CLA/Jun 7/97 (10,000-15,000) 14,950

Smiling Snow White sitting w/2 sleepy bunnies sitting in lap, 5", Courvoisier watercolor pattern background, CLA/Jun 7/97 (7000-9000) 8625

Chipmunk perched on back of sad fawn (5 x 4") standing draped w/dwarfs' laundry, airbrushed Courvoisier background of grasses, S/Jun 21/97 (700-900) 1495

Full-figure front view of Bashful standing playing concertina, 5", wood-veneer Courvoisier background, S/Jun 21/97 (2000-3000) 3450

Dopey smiles at cymbal as bells dangle, 4-1/2", airbrush-on-patterned-paper Courvoisier background, S/Jun 21/97 (4000-6000) 4887

5 Dwarfs w/ore cart in mine, approx. 3" each, airbrushed wood-veneer Courvoisier background, S/Jun 21/97 (6000-8000) 6325

Snow White (5") proudly show pie to forest friends, airbrushed-on-patterned-paper Courvoisier background, S/Jun 21/97 (6000-8000) 8050

Publicity cel of 6 dwarfs in characteristic poses standing in semi-circle w/smiling Dopey in middle, avg. 5" each, airbrushed veneer background, S/Jun 21/97 (8000-10,000) 9200

Full figure of smiling Dopey standing facing right, looking back over shoulder, 5-1/2" airbrushed wood-veneer Courvoisier background, S/Jun 21/97 (4000-6000) 3737

Witch (4") stirs cauldron as Raven (full figure, 3") watches, airbrushed Courvoisier background, S/Jun 21/97 (6000-8000) 6325

Full figure of unhappy Grumpy sitting on barrel with hands folded, 4-1/2", airbrushed wood-veneer Courvoisier background, S/Jun 21/97 (2000-3000) 3162

Full figure of happy Dopey snapping fingers while atop Sneezy's shoulders (face visible) during dance, 9-1/2", airbrushed Courvoisier background, Walt Disney signature, S/Jun 21/97 (6000-8000) 7475

Full figure of angry Doc walking left w/fists clinched, 5", patterned-paper Courvoisier background, S/Jun 21/97 (2000-3000) 3737

Full-figure front view of Bashful standing in classic pose, 5-1/4", patterned-paper Courvoisier background, S/Jun 21/97 (2000-2500) 3737

Full figure of smiling Snow White (4") sitting amid animals, airbrushed Courvoisier background, S/Jun 21/97 (6000-8000) 5750

Faun (3-1/3"), squirrel (1-1/2"), & turtle (2"), airbrushed Courvoisier background of outdoors, S/Jun 21/97 (600-800) 1265

Full-figure front view of blushing Bashful standing looking coyly over beard, 5-1/2", patterned-paper Courvoisier background, S/Jun 21/97 (2000-3000) 3162

Smiling Snow White prepares pie as bird & two raccoons watch, 5-1/2", airbrush-on-patterned-paper Courvoisier background, S/Jun 21/97 (6000-8000) 5750

Full figure of Sleepy waking up in mine car as animals watch, 5-1/2", airbrushed wood-veneer Courvoisier background, S/Jun 21/97 (2500-3500) 4025

Witch (4-1/2") offers apple to Snow White (4") thru window, airbrushed Courvoisier background, S/Jun 21/97 (10,000-12,000) 13,800

Full figure of Sleepy lying on pillow as he plays fish horn, 4 x 6", airbrushed patterned-paper Courvoisier background, S/Jun 21/97 (2500-3500) 4887

Full figure of Dopey standing playing cymbal, 6-1/2", wood-veneer Courvoisier background, S/Jun 21/97 (4000-6000) 5175

Full figures of Snow White (7") dancing with Dopey (on Sneezy, 7") as Sleepy, Bashful & Doc

stand playing instruments (4" each), wood-veneer Courvoisier background, S/Jun 21/97 (10,000-12,000) 14,950

Front view of Snow White standing holding broom handle as animals watch, 7", print background of cottage interior, S/Jun 21/97 (3000-4000) 4312

Waist-up image of smiling Dopey watching dangling bells, 4-1/2", airbrush-on-patterned-paper Courvoisier background, S/Jun 21/97 (4000-6000) 5750

Apprehensive Bashful & Happy stand behind wash basin holding bars of soap, looking right, both 3-1/2", detailed Courvoisier watercolor background with original water effects & reflection on two levels, hand-lettered mat & label, ct, SR/Fall/97 (6000-9000) 4000

Full-figure front view of bewildered hatless Sneezy sitting looking left with beard tied around nose, 3-3/4", Courvoisier decorative-paper-&-watercolor background, hand-lettered mat, SR/Fall/97 (2600-3200) 2420

Waist-up of Dopey eyeing cymbal with bells hanging at right, 4-1/8", Courvoisier watercolor background & small labels, SR/Fall/97 (5000-8000) 3500

Full figure of Dopey, standing behind overlay of airbrushed bubbles, looking right; 4-1/4"; Courvoisier solid-color background; ct, SR/Fall/97 (6000-9000) 4500

Full figures of six reluctant Dwarfs standing in group with hands behind backs, 9-1/2 x 6-1/2", Courvoisier wood-veneer background. SR/Fall/97 (6000-9000) 5500

Full figure of Dopey in long coat (on Sneezy's shoulders) looking down with stricken expression, 7", Courvoisier wood-veneer background, SR/Fall/97 (4500-7000) 3050

Limited-edition cel of Snow White at wishing well, #138/275, 11-1/2 x 15-1/2", color print of special matching background, VF+, HL/Nov 16/97 (1000-1500) 2875

Limited-edition pan cel "Heigh Oh", #61/275, 10 x 21-1/2", color print of matching background painting, VF, HL/Nov 16/97 (2000-3000) 4945

Full figure of grumpy Grumpy sitting on barrel with arms folded, 4-3/4 x 2-1/2", complementary woodgrain background, as prepared by Disney for Courvoisier, VF, HL/Nov 16/97 (3000-3500) 3910

2 limited-edition cels: Queen holding heart box, #374/500; Snow White carried by Prince amid Dwarfs, #374/500; 11-1/4 x 15-1/4"; matching color print backgrounds, VF+, HL/Nov 16/97 (1000-2000) 3220

Full figures of doe & fawn standing on grass amid leaves & vines, 6-1/2 x 7-1/2", complimentary painted background as prepared by Disney for Courvoisier, F+, HL/Nov 16/97 (700-1000) 1092

Portrait of stern Huntsman, 4-1/2 x 3", woodgrain background titled "The Huntsman" as prepared by Disney for Courvoisier, VF, HL/Nov 16/97 (1500-2000) 4600

Full figure of eager Dopey sweeping up gems w/whisk broom into dustpan, 4-1/2 x 6", complementary airbrush background, as sold thru Courvoisier, VF, HL/Nov 16/97 (2000-3000) 4715

"Off To Bed": limited-edition pan cel of Snow White shooing dwarfs away, 11-1/2 x 20", Publisher's Proof #35/35, matching color print of cottage interior, VF+, HL/Nov 16/97 (1000-2000) 2760

Full figure of Bashful standing looking left, 4-1/2", Courvoisier airbrush background & label, CE/Dec 18/97 (2500-35000 3220

Full figure of Snow White (6") looking back while climbing stairs with 5 dwarfs (backs turned, 5") in foreground, Courvoisier wood-veneer background & separately framed label, CE/Dec 18/97 (8000-12,000) 6900

Full figure of Dopey walking right holding soap inside huge bubble, 4-1/2", Courvoisier airbrush solid background with bubbles, CE/Dec 18/97 (2500-3500) 3680

Full figure of Bashful holding switch, driving cart full of gems; 3-1/2"; Courvoisier watercolor background; CE/Dec 18/97 (5000-7000) 4830

Snow White (3-1/2") sings at wishing well as 8 birds (1-1/2") sit & watch, Courvoisier watercolor

background, CE/Dec 18/97 (8000-10,000) 8050

Full figure of suspicious Grumpy standing with arms crossed. looking left; 5", Courvoisier airbrush background, WDE label, CE/Dec 18/97 (2000-3000) 2990

Profile of Snow White facing left, head up, eyes closed, hands holding skirt, 6-1/2", key production background of cottage interior not used in final film, Courvoisier sticker, CE/Dec 18/97 (15,000-20,000) 10,925

Full figure of Dopey standing facing right, 4", Courvoisier star background, CE/Dec 18/97 (2000-3000) 3220

Full figure of Snow White sitting, left arm around fawn, petting rabbit as two chipmunks watch, 5", Courvoisier watercolor & airbrush background of outdoors, CE/Dec 18/97 (6000-8000) 5520

Happy (4"), Doc (3-1/4") & Sneezy (4") stand around wash basin, Courvoisier watercolor production background, CE/Dec 18/97 (7000-9000) 9775

Front view of Queen standing holding open heart box, 8-1/2", Courvoisier "star" background, CE/Dec 18/97 (12,000-15,000) 16,100

Happy Snow White sitting on hill gathering bouquet of flowers amid animals, 2", airbrushed Courvoisier background, WDP label, S/Dec 19/97 (3000-5000) 3162

Full figure of shy Doc standing looking down, 5-1/2", patterned paper Courvoisier background, Walt Disney Enterprises label, S/Dec 19/97 (2000-3000) 2875

Surprised Snow White sits up [in bed] w/2 bunnies in lap, 5-1/2", patterned paper Courvoisier background, WDE label, S/Dec 19/97 (7000-9000) 8050

Near-full-figure front view of Happy standing, looking left & gesturing, 4-1/2", patterned paper Courvoisier background, WDE label, S/Dec 19/97 (2000-3000) 2875

Matching cel & master background (watercolor on background sheet) of Snow White waking up in dwarfs' beds, stamps, restored, 8-3/4 x 11-3/4", F+, HL/Apr 25/98 (8000-10,000) 16,675

Near-full figure of Dopey holding candle & tiptoeing up stairs, complementary painted wood-grain background as prepared by Disney for Courvoisier, labels, 4-1/2 x 4" cel, F+, HL/Apr 25/98 (2000-3000) 2760

Chest-up of dreamy Dopey with head in right hand, looking up, 5" close-up, Courvoisier wood-veneer background, vignetted in airbrushed circle & accented with drop shadow & hand-lettered name, small labels, ct, SR/Spring/98 (2400-3400) 4180

Ankles-up of smiling Dopey standing facing left, looking up, extending hands for inspection; 4"; Courvoisier custom wood-veneer background; ct; SR/Spring/98 (2800-3800) 2810

CELS – FULL FIGURE (also see MODEL ART)

2 full figures of deer, 3 x 2-1/2", 3-1/2 x 1-1/2", F, HL/Apr 10/94 (700-1000) 952

Publicity cel of shy Dopey standing holding flowers behind back, 5", 1950s, CE/Jun 18/94 (600-800) 3450

Front view of Snow White standing holding broom, 5-3/4", 12-field pre-production cel, paint restoration, SR/Fall/94 (2500-4500) 4670

Full figures & heads of happy Dwarfs [crowded around foot of bed], 8-1/2 x 8", paint restoration, SR/Fall/94 (5000-9000) 10,100

Set of 4 1974 limited-edition cel paintings, made from original drawings, all #35/275: Snow White kissing Grumpy's head, sitting with bird on finger, dancing with Dopey, being offered apple by Witch (partial figures); 7 x 12" & 8 x 12"; VF+; HL/Nov 13/94 (3000-5000) 4592

Doc strains to lift sack by mine door, 7-3/8, ct, SR/Spring/95 (2200-3200) 3240

Excited Sneezy stands facing left, 5-1/2", ct, SR/Spring/95 (400-1800) 3030

2 full-figure cels: happy Dwarf celebrating w/hat in air; startled squirrel looking back; 1-1/2 x 5-1/2", 5 x 3", HL/Apr 23/95 (1000-1500) 1008

Embarrassed Sneezy & Bashful walking, 4 x 6", HL/Apr 23/95 (2500-3500) 5152

Snow White sitting, 6", CE/Jun 9/95 (4000-6000) 5750

Snow White (7") & Dopey (4") standing together,

CE/Jun 9/95 (7000-9000) 8625

Dopey (4") helping Sleepy into mining cart (2-1/2"),
S/Jun 10/95 (3000-5000) 5175

Dopey stands beside squirrel, 4-1/2 x 4-1/2", as
prepared for Courvoisier, VF, HL/Aug 6/95
(3000-4000) 4480

Determined Wicked Queen standing, 9-1/2 x 4",
VF, HL/Aug 6/95 (10,000-12,000) 12,880

Deer pushes Doc, 4 x 7", HL/Nov 19/95
(2000-3000) 3680

Set of 4 1974 limited-edition cel paintings, made
from original drawings, all #88/275: Snow
White dancing w/Dopey, sitting with bird,
kissing Grumpy, taking apple from Witch
(partial figures); #88/275; 6-1/2 x 5-1/2"
to 9 x 6-1/2"; VF; HL/Nov 19/95
(2500-3500) 4025

Smiling Snow White stands in rags & wooden
shoes facing left & looking up, 8 x 3", VF,
HL/Nov 19/95 (4000-6000) 6325

Heavily armed Happy, Grumpy, Dopey (& top of
4th head) walking cautiously, 4-1/2 x 8-1/2",
HL/Nov 19/95 (4000-5000) 7245

Snow White stands looking back in terror, 4-1/2 x 3",
HL/Nov 19/95 (3000-4000) 8050

Smiling Dopey behind large soap bubble, 4-1/2 x 4",
HL/Nov 19/95 (3000-4000) 5520

Cheerful Doc stands holding lantern, 6 x 4-1/2",
HL/Nov 19/95 (2500-3500) 3910

Surprised Dopey, 4 x 3-1/2", HL/Nov 19/95
(3000-4000) 3450

Squirrel & 2 rabbits sitting, 4 x 6", HL/Nov 19/95
(600-900) 805

Mother deer & fawn, 3-1/2 x 4", HL/Nov 19/95
(600-900) 1150

Sneezy stands with index finger of left hand raised,
5-1/2 x 4", HL/Apr 28/96 (2000-2500) 2990

Set of 4 1974 limited-edition cel paintings, made
from original drawings, all #138/275: Snow
White kissing Grumpy, sitting w/bird on her
hand, dancing w/Dopey, taking apple from
Witch (partial figures); 7 x 12", 8 x 12"; VF+;
HL/Apr 28/96 (2000-3000) 3220

2 full-figure cels: Bashful holding pick at side while
calling "Hi-Ho", 5", fawn standing, 4 x 3",
S/Jun 18/96 (1500-2500) 3335

Set of 4 1974 limited-edition cel paintings, made
from original drawings, all #270/275: Snow
White kissing Grumpy's head; sitting with bird
on finger; dancing with Dopey; being offered
apple by Witch (partial figures); 7 x 12" & 8
x 12"; VF: HL/Oct 6/96 (2000-3000) 4140

7 Dwarfs rejoice amid happy forest animals, 4-1/2"
each, CE/Dec 12/96 (4000-6000) 9200

Front view of Doc & Sneezy playing their instruments,
3-3/4" each, CE/Dec 12/96 (2500-3500) 4600

Grinning Witch walks to right, head down, holding
basket of apples with red apple on top, 5",
S/Dec 14/96 (7000-9000) 7475

Front view of kneeling Snow White looking left
w/flower bouquet in left arm, chipmunk on
skirt; plus 5 cels of forest friends; 3/4 x 3/4"
to 4 x 3", as prepared for Courvoisier, VF,
HL/May 3/97 (4000-6000) 5750

Innocent Dopey looking up w/hands behind back,
3-3/4 x 2", VF, HL/May 3/97 (3000-4000) 3680

Angry Grumpy striding away to left, 4-1/4 x 7",
HL/May 31/97 (400-600) 431

2 perched vultures look down eagerly, 4",
CLA/Jun 7/97 (2000-3000) 2300

Dopey running to left into another dwarf who's lying
down, 5-1/2", CLA/Jun 7/97 (2000-3000) 1955

Snow White dances with Dopey (& Sneezy) (6") as
Doc, Sleepy, & Bashful play instruments (3"
each), CLA/Jun 7/97 (15,000-20,000) 13,800

Bashful & Doc stand playing instruments while
looking left, 3-1/4" each, S/Jun 21/97
(4000-6000) 3737

Set of 4 limited-edition cels, all #214/275: Snow
White kissing Grumpy's head, sitting with bird
on finger, dancing with Dopey, being offered
apple by Witch (partial figures); 16-field cels;
SR/Fall/97 (3000-4500) 2810

Confused Grumpy stands on one foot, facing right,
4-1/4 x 3-3/4", VF, HL/Nov 16/97
(2000-2500) 2760

Front view of Sneezy standing, left index finger
raised, 5-1/2 x 4", F+, HL/Nov 16/97
(2800-3200) 2760

Startled Snow White dressed in rags & clogs stands
looking back toward camera, 3", S/Dec 19/97
(1000-1500) 2587

Publicity cel of 7 Dwarfs standing together, 5" &
similar, CE/Dec 18/97 (8000-10,000) 8625

CELS – PARTIAL FIGURE (also see MODEL ART)

Portrait of Dopey with diamonds in eyes, 9-3/4 x
8-3/4", CE/Dec 15/93 (1500-2000) 5750

Happy (4") & Dopey (3") from waist up, 3 cels,
CE/Jun 18/94 (2000-3000) 5750

Queen (waist-up) gesturing, 4 x 3", HL/Aug 21/94
(2000-3000) 4256

Queen reads from book of spells, 10 x 10-1/2", F+,
HL/Nov 13/94 (10,000-12,000) 11,200

Close-up of worried Dopey looking to right, 4-1/2",
CE/Jun 9/95 (1500-2000) 2530

Near-full figure of Snow White standing holding
candle & stretching, 7", CE/Jun 9/95
(4000-6000) 4600

Wicked Queen holds heart box open, 8-1/2 x 7",
F, HL/Nov 19/95 (9000-12,000) 12,075

Snow White sitting w/bouquet of flowers, 2-1/2 x 2",
VF, HL/Nov 19/95 (1000-1500) 4600

Hips-up close-up of Snow White facing right, hands
together, mouth open, eyes closed, 7", 12-field,
drybrush effects, some cracking, SR/Spring/96
(4000-6000) 5200

Portrait of Snow White singing, 5-1/2 x 3-1/2", VF,
HL/Apr 28/96 (2500-3500) 4370

Half images of Dopey leaning in from left, Grumpy
from right, both pointing to center, 6-1/2",
CE/Jun 20/96 (2500-3500) 2875

Large-image waist-up front view of terrified Snow
White, 8 x 9", HL/Oct 6/96 (6000-8000) 6613

Smiling Snow White (7") meets Bashful (5"),
CE/Dec 12/96 (7000-9000) 8625

Bashful holds bouquet in Sneezy's face, 4" ea., partial
cel overlay, CE/Dec 12/96 (4000-6000) 4600

Waist-up profile portrait of smiling Dopey facing
right & looking up, 4 x 3", HL/Feb 23/97
(2000-3000) 2760

Large image of Snow White, hands together at waist,
looking down; 6-1/2 x 4", F, HL/Feb 23/97
(6000-8000) 6900

Waist-up front view of Witch offering apple, 7-1/4 x
8-3/4", VF, HL/May 3/97 (9000-12,000) 13,225

Knees-up view of Snow White standing & stretching
flanked by deer & chipmunk (full figure); as
prepared for Courvoisier; 3 x 2-1/2", 4 x
3-1/2", 1 x 1"; VF; HL/May 3/97
(3000-5000) 2990

Sneezy in reclining position, 4-1/2", CLA/Jun 7/97
(1500-2000) 1725

Hips-up view of frowning Sleepy [Happy?] looking
down, 4-1/2", CLA/Jun 7/97 (1500-2000) 1840

Waist-up portrait of smiling Snow White, 4-1/2",
CLA/Jun 7/97 (3000-4000) 4600

Knees-up front view of worried Doc w/hands clasped
in front, 5", CLA/Jun 7/97 (1500-2000) 2530

Hips-up side view of Sleepy playing fish horn, 5"
(minor cracks), S/Jun 21/97 (2500-3500) 2875

Hips-up portrait of Snow White singing, 5-1/2",
S/Dec 19/97 (800-1200) 4025

Promotional cel featuring heads & names of all 7
dwarfs, approx. 3-1/2" each, S/Dec 19/97
(2000-3000) 4312

"She stays!" 7 Dwarfs gathered [around beds],
restored, VF, HL/Apr 25/98 (7000-9000) 9200

CONCEPT AND INSPIRATIONAL ART

Concept drawing by Al Hurter of Snow White in
forest standing picking flowers with 2 horses
& Huntsman in distance, black pencil on
12-field sheet, some wear & discoloration,
SR/Spring/95 (2500-3500) 3660

Concept drawing by Al Hurter: front view of Snow
White standing surrounded by animal friends,
black pencil on 7-3/4 x 7-1/8" sheet, small
sketch of a dwarf in upper right,
SR/Spring/95 (250-500) 830

Gag concept of Dopey collecting feathers by scaring
Owl, 11-7/8 x 9-3/8", stamp, some edge wear
& discoloration, SR/Spring/95 (800-1400) 2500

10 studies of Huntsman by Albert Hurter, 6 x 3-1/2"
to 8-1/2 x 9-1/2", w/copy of book He Drew
As He Pleased, HL/Apr 23/95
(1500-2500) 2240

Collection of drawings & sketches on 10 animation
sheets of Albert Hurter's concepts for
Huntsman, 4 x 4" to 8 x 8", HL/Apr 23/95

(1500-2500) 2128

Carl Barks 4-panel gag idea, titled in his own hand:
"Gag for Snow White in which Bashful procures
some spun cobweb sheets & pillowcases for the
bed. Submitted by Carl Barks." 12-field sheet,
SR/Fall/95 (1500-2500) 1500

Signed gag-idea drawing by artist Ambrozi Paliwoda
captioned "Daffy Directs The Way": 4 dwarfs
carry bed headboard, 5th on top steering them
using beards as reins, SR/Fall/95 (400-800) 420

2 full-figure study drawings of Dopey: standing facing
left, looking back & facing left, leaning forward
at waist, 5-1/4" & 3-3/4"; rough drawing on
reverse of Dopey holding candle & wiggling
ears, 6"; 12-field sheet, SR/Fall/95
(500-900) 500

Concept sketch by Albert Hurter of Snow White
walking thru forest, 7 x 4-5/8", 12-field sheet,
some staining, SR/Fall/95 (800-1600) 970

2 concept drawings by Al Hurter of Snow White &
animals set off by blue frame lines, smaller
trimmed & pasted on larger sheet, 9-7/8 x
8-1/4", SR/Spring/96 (600-1000) 730

Hips-up concept drawing by Milt Kahl of Prince,
6-1/2", black & colored pencil on bond,
trimmed, mounted on 12-field sheet,
SR/Spring/96 (500-1000) 500

Two matched background concept paintings by Sam
Armstrong of forest friends in dwarf's cottage,
pencil & watercolor on watercolor sheets,
SR/Spring/96 (1800-3000) 2500

Concept sketch of Witch dunking apple, 4-3/4",
12-field sheet, SR/Spring/96 (600-1000) 600

Concept drawing: raven nests on top of skull & book,
4-3/4", colored pencil, crayon, & watercolor
on 12-field sheet, SR/Fall/96 (400-700) 540

Concept layout of open book "Once Upon a Time...";
calligraphed in black, illuminated with red, blue,
& gold watercolor; 7-1/4 x 6-5/8"; SR/Fall/96
(900-1800) 1630

Concept drawing for bed-building scene: woodpecker
stitches mattress with thread from cocoon; when
lifted, top half shows thread unraveling from
long underwear; full size 9-5/8 x 12-1/4", small
faint drawing at bottom shows scene slightly
differently, SR/Fall/96 (900-1500) 1510

Early Milt Kahl character study of prince: two 4" heads
on 12-field sheet, SR/Fall/96 (300-600) 480

Concept drawing by Al Hurter of Witch standing
talking to raven on perch, 5", 12-field sheet,
SR/Fall/96 (600-1000) 660

Concept piece for unproduced dream sequence:
Snow White & Prince (1-1/2") dance in
clouds before audience of stars & moon,
by Ferdinand Horvath, signed "Horvath",
S/Dec 14/96 (3000-5000) 3450

Concept sketch of Dwarfs acting in character from
lodge-meeting portion of bed-building sequence,
10-3/8 x 10" sheet, some wear & discoloration,
SR/Spring/97 (900-1800) 1140

Concept drawing by Al Hurter of Witch walking left
with cane past clique of crows, 5-7/8", 12-field
sheet, SR/Fall/97 (700-1500) 465

2 inspirational studies from deleted dream sequence:
Swan Boat in cloud-studded sky, character/
action studies of Prince riding flying horse &
waiting Snow White; 18 x 14", 9 x 8-1/2";
pencil & conté crayon on animation sheets;
F+, HL/Nov 16/97 (700-1000) 2070

Inspirational drawing by Walt Kelly of Queen's torture
chamber from deleted sequence, captioned
"Attendant pulls curtain aside, revealing torture
chamber", signed, 8 x 10" inc. caption, F+,
HL/Apr 25/98 (1500-2000) 1955

LAYOUT ART (also see ANIMATION DRAWINGS)

Rough layout drawing of 3 nonchalant dwarfs before
grabbing Grumpy for his bath, 7-1/2 x 7", VF,
HL/Feb 26-27/94 (150-200) 660

Layout drawing of happy Dwarfs crowded around foot
of Snow White's bed, colored conté crayon on
16-field sheet, scene & sequence notations &
camera instructions, "Gooseberry pie!" written
at upper right, edge wear & some discoloration,
shallow tear, SR/Fall/94 (900-1500) 3870

Layout drawing of forest animals coming to rescue,
10 x 13", stamped, HL/Nov 13/94
(300-500) 448

Pan background layout drawing for "bed building"
sequence, 11 x 54", HL/Apr 28/96

(1000-1500) 1955

Background layout drawing of main room in Dwarf's cottage, 11 x 15", HL/Apr 28/96 (900-1200) 1955

Full-figure rough layout drawing of Dopey standing (5") in profile & Sleepy propped up holding "fish horn" w/bee on nose, CLA/Jun 7/97 (5-1/2") (1000-1500) 920

2 layout drawings of interior of Dwarfs' cottage, sight 12-1/2 x 15-1/2", CLA/Jun 7/97 (800-1200) 1495

Layout drawing of angry Grumpy running with upraised club, sight 12 x 15", notes, S/Jun 21/97 (1800-2200) 1725

2 layout prints: early photocopy of Potions book, open to poison apple recipe, 11-3/8 x 9-1/8"; Ozalid print of cobweb-draped Disguises book, 15-1/2 x 12-1/2"; SR/Fall/97 (300-600) 310

Layout drawing of Dwarfs mounting deer & riding amid frantic animals, 11 x 14-1/2", VF, HL/Nov 16/97 (1000-1500) 4370

Layout drawing of Happy [Bashful?] (lying down, 6") & Dopey (full-figure sitting, 7") looking up with loving expressions, CE/Dec 18/97 (3500-4500) 4830

Detailed pan layout drawing of dwarf's table seen when they first arrive home, sight 12 x 33", Courvoisier label, S/Dec 19/97 (3000-5000) 2300

Quick sketch for camera view of gloating Witch facing right & holding apple up, by Norm Ferguson, 6-3/4" on 7-1/4 x 12-1/2" piece of paper, right edge torn unevenly, wear & general darkening, SR/Spring/98 (600-1000) 600

Layout drawing of hungry Dwarfs around table in cottage, captioned "(O.S.) Snow White: Ah! Ah! Ah!...Just a minute!", 10 x 12", VF, HL/Apr 25/98 (1400-1800) 3220

Background layout drawing of Queen's dungeon from deleted scene, 8 x 10-1/2", F, HL/Apr 25/98 (800-1200) 805

MODEL ART (also see ANIMATION DRAWINGS, CEL SET-UPS)

Snow White's witch, model cel created in 1971 from archives, hand-prepared background, 8-3/4 x 14", CE/Dec 15/93 (2500-3500) 2300

Color model cel: Sneezy about to sneeze, 7", S/Jun 17/94 (1800-2200) 2875

12 model photostats which include at least one of each dwarf, S/Jun 17/94 (1000-1500) 4025

Full-figure color model cel: rear view of Grumpy sitting on bellows, looking back, 4", SR/Fall/94 (1500-2200) 2060

Seven print model sheets of forest animals, 12-1/2 x 10", SR/Fall/94 (300-600) 590

Doc model sheet from late 1930s-early 1940s, 8-1/2 x 10-1/2", signed by Ted Boriksen, HL/Nov 16/97 (300-400) 1120

Model sheet of Dopey, 2-1/2" & smaller, Sharpie on paper, extensive notes & inscribed "...Frank Thomas", CE/Dec 16/94 (2500-3500) 4370

Waist-up front-view color model drawing of Witch holding apple, colored in ink & pencil w/call-outs, 7-3/8 x 7-5/8" stapled to full sheet, production stamp, SR/Spring/95 (1200-1800) 1870

Model sheet for Doc, CE/Jun 9/95 (1500-2000) 2760

Full-figure color model animation drawing of animals dragging Sneezy by beard, shoes & tunic, 5 x 8", HL/Nov 19/95 (700-1000) 920

Head-only portrait drawing of angry Snow White labeled "model of 1st Snow White", 2 x 2", F+, HL/Apr 28/96 (500-700) 489

Full-figure late model cel of all Dwarfs standing individually dressed in bow ties & tails, approx. 4" ea, S/Dec 14/96 (2000-3000) 1725

Full-figure color model animation drawing of 4 dwarfs standing huddled in conference, 4-1/2 x 7", HL/Feb 23/97 (300-400) 460

Color model painting of 3 tree limbs as eerie reaching hands, pencil & watercolor on animation sheet, 5 x 6-1/2", HL/Feb 23/97 (200-300) 403

Model drawing of Grumpy, hat off, looking in mirror, 5-1/2 x 5-1/2" image, HL/May 3/97 (700-1000) 1380

Training model sheet of Sleepy by Les Clark, sight 9-1/2 x 12", CLA/Jun 7/97 (1500-2000) 1380

Original model sheet "Chart of Relative Fields to Dwarf Eyes", colored pencil & white tempera

on animation sheet, 12 x 15-1/4", plus photostat of this model sheet, G-VG, HL/Apr 25/98 (2000-2500) 3220

Waist-up front-view colored model drawing of Witch, trimmed & stapled to sheet of paper; pencil, india ink & colored crayon; 6 x 5-1/2"; F+; HL/Apr 25/98 (1500-2000) 1495

Color model drawing: waist-up front view of Witch holding apple, 6-1/2", 16-field sheet, stamps, some edge wear, folded to size of 12-field sheet, paint smear, SR/Spring/98 (1200-1600) 1210

Sheet of head studies of Snow White, 1-7/8" to 3-1/8", 12-field sheet, SR/Spring/98 (400-700) 540

STORY ART

7 early story drawings of Dwarfs including Deafy & Stubby, 6 are captioned, one signed by Harry Reeves, all cut down close to image size, 2-1/2 x 4" to 5-1/2 x 9-1/2", F+, HL/Apr 10/94 (2000-2500) 1568

Storyboard sketch of Snow White on horse w/Prince & 7 Dwarfs, each 1/2 x 1/4" & similar, CE/Jun 18/94 (1000-1500) 805

Early story drawing of Doc polishing glasses, 9 x 11", HL/Aug 21/94 (800-1200) 532

Story drawing: 12 sequential images of Dopey after swallowing soap, 8 x 11-1/2", HL/Aug 21/94 (500-700) 336

2 story sketches of bed-building scene: master shot of all Dwarfs working, 9-1/2 x 5-5/8", 12-field; Doc sets headboard w/gems, 7-1/8 x 5-1/4" on 8-1/2 x 6-5/8" sheet, studio stamp; edge wear & discoloration; SR/Fall/94 (1200-1800) 1980

15 story drawings from soup-eating sequence, 3-1/4 x 2-3/4" to 7-3/4 x 3-1/2", SR/Fall/94 (4000-8000) 5100

Detailed story sketch of Doc's shop under tree roots, 13 5/8 x 6-3/4", black pencil with red frame line, vertical fold, considerable wear & some discoloration, SR/Spring/95 (800-1400) 2270

3 story drawings of discarded fantasy tableau for "Some Day My Prince Will Come", 6 x 8" to 9 x 11", HL/Apr 23/95 (1500-2000) 1792

Storyboard drawing of Dwarfs fighting, 4" & smaller, CE/Jun 9/95 (700-900) 575

3 storyboards framed together of hand reaching out of drawer & grabbing frightened Doc, 4" avg., S/Jun 10/95 (3000-5000) 3450

Story sketch of Happy making quilt, 11 x 9-1/2" sheet, "Unit G" stamp, tape stains & mended cut, SR/Fall/95 (1200-2200) 2380

Story sketch of 4 Dwarfs pleading with Grumpy, with frame line & red caption "Well she can stay til we get our gooseberry pie", 12-field sheet, SR/Fall/95 (500-900) 550

Story drawing of 7 Dwarfs arguing at foot of beds as Snow White watches, 16-field sheet, scene & dialogue notation, vertical fold, SR/Spring/96 (1500-3000) 1200

Story drawing of Happy & Dopey, 5-1/4" & 5-3/4", 12-field sheet, scene notation, 2 small sketches of heads at top, SR/Spring/96 (400-700) 610

Captioned story drawing of blonde Snow White standing inside Dwarf's door, 5-1/2 x 6-1/2", HL/Apr 28/96 (900-1200) 805

Polished story drawing of storybook page from opening scenes, 6 x 6-1/2", HL/Apr 28/96 (600-900) 2530

Story drawing of scullery maid Snow White beside wishing well w/doves, done w/multiple images, pencil on story sheet, 7 x 9", HL/Apr 28/96 (3000-4000) 4140

11 atmosphere/story drawings mounted to 7 boards, each signed by William Wallett; pencil & conté crayon on paper; 3-1/2 x 5" to 6-1/2 x 9", HL/Apr 28/96 (2000-3000) 2530

Six-frame captioned gag idea of Dopey & Grumpy working on end panel, frames 5-3/4 x 4-1/4" on matched & punched 7-1/2 x 6-1/2" sheets, SR/Fall/96 (1000-2000) 1850

2 captioned sequential storyboard drawings of Dwarfs investigating cottage, 3" & smaller, CE/Dec 12/96 (1500-2000) 2185

2 storyboards of unused gag: mop in bucket, then dwarf's head pokes out of bucket; sight each aperture 7-1/2 x 7-1/2", S/Dec 14/96 (1500-2000) 1150

Full-figure story drawing of Dopey (profile) & 2 other Dwarfs (backs turned) looking up, 6 x 8", HL/Feb 23/97 (300-400) 546

Detailed finished story drawing of 5 dwarfs in bed-building sequence, 7 x 9-1/4", HL/Feb 23/97 (500-700) 2185

Story drawing: full figures of Doc bouncing Grumpy with his belly, 6 x 6-1/2", HL/Feb 23/97 (400-600) 920

Storyboard drawing of Grumpy whittling, captioned "Hrumph - Alright if ya' want t'spoil 'er ... Make 're a bed -", sight 7 x 7-1/2", S/Jun 21/97 (800-1200) 920

3 story sketches: Dopey bending over gem; Sneezy smiling; Doc & Bashful smiling at each other; sight 4 x 5-1/2", 5 x 6", 5-1/2 x 7-1/2", S/Jun 21/97 (1000-1500) 1610

4 drawings of bed-building gag: Dopey makes off with Doc's red flannel undershirt, 7-3/4 x 6" two-hole punched paper, SR/Fall/97 (1200-1800) 900

Captioned story sketch of Snow White sitting on hill holding bouquet of flowers, 7-1/2 x 5-3/4", SR/Fall/97 (1000-1500) 900

Storyboard drawing of Dopey, 4", CE/Dec 18/97 (800-1200) 1610

Storyboard drawing of Dopey (3-1/2") sticking finger in cup Bashful (5") is holding, then licking finger; caption: "My Cup's Been Washed -"; S/Dec 19/97 (700-900) 1380

2 captioned storyboard sketches matted together of Sneezy smelling vase of flowers, then dropping vase & starting to sneeze, 3", Courvoisier label, S/Dec 19/97 (800-1200) 1035

3 captioned storyboards matted together of Sneezy & Happy ridiculing Grumpy, avg. image size 3-1/2", S/Dec 19/97 (1500-2000) 2587

Captioned story/concept drawing of birds, animals, & Dwarf carving from bed-building sequence, 7-1/2 x 6-1/2", SR/Spring/98 (400-800) 420

Story drawing of Dopey sitting by large tree stump crunching on a nut as annoyed Doc (leaning on stump) looks on, 5-3/4 x 7", F, HL/Apr 25/98 (500-700) 518

Storyboard drawing of carved dovecote & 2 doves, 6 x 8", VF, HL/Apr 25/98 (300-500) 546

TITLE ART

Two final matched drawings for opening storybook pages, 7 x 7" image areas on 16-field vertical sheets, SR/Spring/97 (8000-10,000) 9000

SO DEAR TO MY HEART (1949)

CELS – FULL FIGURE

Surprised Danny, 4 x 3-1/2", HL/Aug 21/94 (400-600) 336

Wise Old Owl reading from book (all but book edge); eager Danny (near-full figure); 3-1/2 x 4", 4 x 2-1/2"; F; HL/Apr 28/96 (1000-1500) 1380

SONG OF THE SOUTH (1946)

ANIMATION DRAWINGS (also see MODEL ART)

3 rough drawings of Brer Rabbit, 6-1/2 x 2", CE/Jun 18/94 (400-600) 1093

Drawing of shocked Brer Fox facing right, looking back & up over shoulder by story man Bill Peet, 6 x 8", conté crayon on story sheet, HL/Oct 6/96 (700-900) 1150

BACKGROUNDS

Landscape, watercolor pan preliminary background, sight 9-1/2 x 60", CE/Jun 20/96 (3000-5000) 2875

"Music room" of Brer Rabbit's home on hill at sunset, watercolor on board, 12-1/2 x 15-1/2", S/Jun 21/97 (5000-7000) 20,700

CEL SET-UPS

Brer Fox prepares tied-up Brer Rabbit, Courvoisier airbrush background, signed "Walt Disney" on mat, 7-1/2 x 9-1/2", CE/Dec 15/93 (1500-2000) 2760

Brer Bear growls, Courvoisier airbrush background, signed "Walt Disney" on mat, 7-3/4 x 9-1/2", CE/Dec 15/93 (2000-3000) 2300

Brer Rabbit w/possessions bundled on stick, master tempera background of view from inside Brer Fox's lair, attributed to Claude Coats, 8 x 11", studio notes, F-VF, HL/Apr 10/94 (10,000-15,000) 9520

Set of 2 limited-edition cels (#325/350): Brer Rabbit

meets Tar Baby; Brer Fox, Bear & Rabbit go to Laughin' Place; 10-1/2 x 14-1/2"; 1986; seals, labels & color print backgrounds as issued; VF+, HL/Apr 10/94 (1800-2200) 2436

Full figure of awed Brer Rabbit sitting, complementary airbrush background, WDP label & mat mistakenly titled *Fun and Fancy Free*, signed "Best Wishes, Walt Disney" by a studio artist, 7-1/2 x 8", HL/Aug 21/94 (3000-4000) 3360

Eager Brer Fox listening, 5 x 5-1/2", Courvoisier airbrush background, CE/Dec 16/94 (1000-1500) 2070

Set of 2 limited-edition cels: Brer Rabbit meets Tar Baby; Brer Bear, Fox & Rabbit going to Laughin' Place; 1986; #329/350; 10-1/2 x 14-1/2"; seals, labels & color print backgrounds as issued; VF+; HL/Nov 19/95 (1800-2400) 1725

Brer Rabbit (left leg raised to head level) studies palm of left hand, watercolor production background, mat inscribed "...Walt Disney", 7", CE/Jun 20/96 (4000-6000) 5175

Full-figure front view of surprised Brer Rabbit sitting, 5", airbrushed Courvoisier background with large circle on solid field, "Best Wishes, Walt Disney" on mat in hand of Manuel Gonzales, S/Dec 14/96 (3000-5000) 4312

Large image of Brer Rabbit, left foot scratching ear, left hand under chin & left eye closed in thinking pose, 7", airbrushed Courvoisier background with falling leaves & label, S/Dec 14/96 (2500-3500) 2587

Close-up of puzzled Brer Rabbit thinking after passing Tar Baby, 7-1/2", gouache display background of Tar Baby & road, SR/Spring/98 (2400-3000) 2700

CELS – FULL FIGURE

Eager Brer Fox running left with axe, 6 x 9", VF+, HL/Apr 10/94 (1500-2000) 4032

Brer Rabbit with hammer & nails, 4-1/2 x 3", VF, HL/Apr 10/94 (1500-2000) 2240

Brer Fox holding Brer Rabbit by ears, 5 x 7-1/2", F, HL/Apr 10/94 (2000-3000) 3808

Front view of Brer Bear walking, 5 x 2-1/2", CE/Jun 18/94 (600-800) 1035

Irate Brer Frog w/pipe & smoke ring, 7 x 4-1/2", HL/Aug 21/94 (1000-1500) 1568

Brer Rabbit (4") looks happily at butterflies, S/Dec 17/94 (1800-2200) 2070

Grimacing Brer Rabbit caught in snare, 4 x 3", HL/Nov 19/95 (900-1200) 863

Brer Rabbit sits covered with tar, 4-1/2 x 5-1/2", VF+, HL/Nov 19/95 (1000-1500) 1265

Surprised Brer Rabbit looks up while sitting covered with tar, 4-1/4 x 5-1/2", VF, HL/Nov 19/95 (1500-2000) 2185

Brer Fox grabs coat of angry Brer Bear (w/bare spot on rump), 5 x 7-1/2", VF+, HL/Nov 19/95 (1500-2000) 5750

Happy Br'er Rabbit stands with hobo pouch on shoulder, looking right, 4-1/2", SR/Spring/96 (2000-3000) 2420

Publicity cel painting of Brer Rabbit (partial figure) tickling sleeping Brer Fox's nose, 9 x 6-1/2", VF, HL/Apr 28/96 (900-1200) 1380

Brer Fox holding Brer Rabbit up by ears w/one hand & shaking his hand w/other, signed by Ken Anderson, 6 x 8-1/4", VF, HL/Apr 28/96 (2000-2500) 3450

Disgusted Brer Rabbit caught in rope snare, 5-1/2 x 3", HL/Oct 6/96 (1000-1500) 2070

Pleased Brer Fox stands looking to right as he wipes his hands together, 4-1/4 x 4-1/2", HL/Oct 6/96 (1000-1500) 2070

Angry Brer Fox (5") walks to right with rope as Brer Bear (9") follows, holding Fox's tail, CLA/Jun 7/97 (1000-1500) 2185

Brer Rabbit suspended in rope snare, 5-1/4 x 3-1/4", VF, HL/Nov 16/97 (900-1200) 1150

Curious Brer Rabbit stands holding (& looking into) empty tin can, 4-1/2 x 3-3/4", VF+, HL/Nov 16/97 (1500-2000) 2300

Rear view of Brer Fox standing in middle of Brer Bear's back, 6-1/2 x 4-1/4", VF+, HL/Nov 16/97 (1500-2000) 2070

Front view of stunned Brer Rabbit sitting as stars & planets circle his head, 3-1/2 x 4", S/Dec 19/97 (2000-3000) 1840

Brer Fox stands holding blob of tar on a stick, 6 x 5-1/2", VF, HL/Apr 25/98 (1200-1600) 2300

CELS – PARTIAL FIGURE

Large-image portrait of nonchalantly curious Brer Rabbit, 8 x 3", HL/Aug 21/94 (2400-2800) 2464

Near-full figure of angry Brer Rabbit leaning to his right & rolling up sleeves, reddish paper backing w/airbrushed shadow, 5-1/2 x 5-1/2", F, HL/Apr 28/96 (1800-2400) 2300

Portrait of eager Brer Bear (mouth open) looking right, 8 x 8", VF, HL/Nov 16/97 (1000-1500) 3450

Surprised Brer Fox (ankles up, 6-1/4") holds carefree Brer Rabbit (full figure, 3-1/2" w/o ears) by ears, S/Dec 19/97 (2500-3500) 3450

CONCEPT AND INSPIRATIONAL ART (also see STORY ART)

Early "Suggested Models" for 6 characters by Campbell Grant & John P. Miller, 3" to 6", colored pencil & pastel on paper cutouts on poster board, notes, S/Jun 10/95 (800-1200) 1495

2 study drawings of Brer Rabbit: full figure & polished portrait; 3 x 2", 4 x 3-1/2", HL/Apr 28/96 (300-400) 805

7 detailed concept drawings of creature abodes, each 10 x 12", S/Jun 19/96 (2000-2500) 1495

Concept painting: Brer Bear, Brer Fox, & Brer Rabbit (rope around neck) walking (linked together by tails & rope) in silhouette along crest of hill, watercolor on board, CE/Jun 20/96 (2500-3500) 2990

DYE-TRANSFER PRINTS

Full figures of Brer Fox holding Brer Rabbit up by ears & pushing Brer Bear in chest, 11 x 8-1/2", SR/Spring/95 (300-600) 390

MODEL ART

9 items: 2 photostat model sheets of Brer Rabbit; 2 blue pencil drawings of enraged Brer Fox; practice model drawing of Brer Fox in various poses; 4 drawings of Brer Rabbit: pleading, hanging tied up, looking joyous, looking quizzically to right; S/Dec 14/96 (1000-1500) 1495

STORY ART

Story painting of Uncle Remus with long walking stick leaning on split-rail fence, 8-1/2 x 6-1/2", watercolor on paper, HL/Nov 13/94 (900-1200) 2688

4 color storyboard drawings of Tar Baby segment, 6 x 8", color conté crayon on paper mounted to story sheets, HL/Nov 19/95 (1500-2000) 5405

6 color storyboard drawings from Tar Baby scene, color conté crayon on paper mounted to black story sheets, 6 x 8", HL/Apr 28/96 (4000-6000) 3220

Knees-up front-view storyboard sketch of Br'er Rabbit, hands on suspenders, looking right, charcoal & pastel on 8-3/16 x 5-15/16" storyboard sheet stapled to black paper; Mary Blair gouache concept painting of rural South, 7-1/8 x 5-7/16" on 8-3/4 x 7 15/16" sheet; in triple-opening double mat w/color image of Br'er Rabbit, Fox, & Bear, brass plaque; SR/Spring/97 (700-1200) 920

Story drawing of angry Brer Rabbit walking to left, head down, colored conté crayon on story sheet, 4 x 8-1/4", VF, HL/Nov 16/97 (500-700) 1265

6 pastel storyboards: Brer Bear waving happily; Brer Fox smiling & tipping hat; rear view of Brer Fox peering around bushes; Brer Fox swiping angrily at Brer Bear; Brer Rabbit yelling at tar baby; Brer Rabbit stuck in tar baby; colored pastel on paper, each stapled at 4 corners to supporting piece of black construction paper; each sheet 6 x 8", S/Dec 19/97 (2500-3500) 2587

2 storyboard drawings: Brer Fox & Brer Bear argue; disgusted Brer Rabbit thinking while suspended in snare; pastel & charcoal on 7 x 5" sheets; SR/Spring/98 (1000-1500) 1090

Story drawing by Bill Peet of Brer Fox shushing Brer Bear, colored conté crayon on story sheet, 6 x 8", VF, HL/Apr 25/98 (700-1000) 1035

TITLE ART

Title card for release of "Brer Rabbit's Laughing Place" as separate short: photo reproduction of original 1946 feature title with cel overlay of hand lettering, 16-field, SR/Spring/95 (300-700) 430

Title-card painting listing supporting actors, slightly modified for Spanish version, 10 x 14", tempera & airbrush on board, HL/Aug 6/95 (500-1000) 476

Seven title cards, six final versions as photographed, two with hand-lettered title cel overlays; seventh original pen & ink artwork for main title; avg. size 14 x 11"; SR/Fall/96 (1000-2000) 1820

THE SWORD IN THE STONE (1963)

ANIMATION DRAWINGS (also see CELS – PARTIAL FIGURE)

Two drawings: full figure of Wart standing on tree branch looking right, 9-1/2"; hips-up of Merlin directing to right, 10-3/4"; 16-field sheets; SR/Fall/96 (200-500) 200

2 waist-up large-image drawings of Sir Ector; 7-1/2 x 7", 8-1/2 x 6-1/2", HL/May 31/97 (300-400) 81

CEL SET-UPS

7 cels: Merlin as blue rabbit; Wart sitting holding head; Wart holding Kay's helmet, Wart as fish (2); Wart as fish w/frog; frog; 1st two w/Konica copy of background, S/Dec 16/93 (1000-1500) 460

9 cels: mean pike; scullery maid; wolf; Wart in profile pointing; small images of Wart jumping & crawling (5); 1st two w/Konica copy of original background, S/Dec 16/93 (700-900) 575

Wart, Merlin & Archimedes; tempera preliminary background painting of British countryside; 10-1/2 x 14", studio notes, VF, HL/Apr 10/94 (2500-3500) 3136

Wart, 4-1/4 x 3-3/4", DL printed background; together w/Aristotle[?], 4 x 3-3/4", DL printed background, CE/Jun 18/94 (400-600) 345

Waist-up front view of thoughtful Merlin in Bermuda dress, looking left, 7", DL litho background, gold Art Corner label, SR/Fall/94 (300-600) 410

Full figure of Madame Mim as spotted dragon sitting throwing temper tantrum, 7-1/4", gouache production background from *Donald and the Wheel*, 16-field, SR/Fall/94 (600-1000) 610

Full figure of the Wolf, key watercolor production background, Ken Anderson's initials, 5 x 4", CE/Dec 16/94 (1500-2000) 978

Merlin (8") & Wart (4") arguing, DL background & label, CE/Dec 16/94 (600-800) 633

Half images of thoughtful Madame Mim (6-1/4") & angry Merlin (8") standing facing each other, unidentified colored background, Art Corner label, SR/Spring/95 (600-1000) 700

Full figures of Madame Mim & Merlin standing outdoors, 7" & similar, DL printed background & label, CE/Jun 9/95 (400-600) 518

Presentation cel: Merlin (5-1/2") crowns Wart (4") as Madame Mim (3-1/2"), Sir Ector (6-1/2"), Sir Kay (3"), Sir Pelinore (6") & Archimedes (on Merlin's hat, 1") watch, key watercolor production background, CE/Jun 20/96 (4000-6000) 5175

Full figure of frightened boy King Arthur walking into sunlit area of throne room, 11 x 15", master background of castle interior (tempera & ink

on background sheet), HL/Oct 6/96
(3000-4000) 4370
Full figures of giddy Mad Madam Mim & serious
Merlin (w/cane raised over her) standing in
castle, 7-1/2 x 10", color print background,
HL/Oct 6/96 (600-900) 920
Mad Madame Mim seated at table in cabin, deck of
playing cards in right hand, card in upraised
left hand, staring at table, 7", key watercolor
production background, CE/Dec 12/96
(3000-4000) 3450
Grinning Mad Madam Mim confronts scared Wart
as a bird, color print of complementary background of cottage interior, 8 x 10",
HL/Feb 23/97 (600-800) 575
Full figures of critical Merlin (6-1/4") standing, holding
cane & bag, looking back as Wart (4") walks
toward him, Art Props set-up with master pan
gouache background of cottage exterior &
forest, SR/Spring/97 (4000-8000) 4290
Full figure of Wart sitting on ground staring at girl
squirrel hugging his chest, 9", 16-field cel,
2 cel levels with color print forest background,
SR/Spring/97 (500-900) 680
Waist-up close-up front view of surprised Wart
standing in castle great hall, looking &
pointing right, 6-1/4", litho background,
gold DL Art Corner label & stamp,
SR/Spring/97 (500-700) 570
Full figures of Merlin (2-1/2") & Wart (1-1/2") as fish,
gold Art Corner label & DL color background
with bubble effects, SR/Fall/97 (600-1000) 400
Full figure of Merlin standing examining book cover,
9-1/2", key gouache background painting of
cottage interior, 16-field, SR/Spring/98
(4500-9000) 5000
Full figures of Wart as squirrel caught in tail of
flirtatious girl squirrel, 4 1/4", color print
background, SR/Spring/98 (400-700) 410

CELS – FULL FIGURE (also see CELS-PARTIAL FIGURE)

Mad Madam Mim disguised as young miss standing
facing right, 8 x 5", VF+, HL/Apr 10/94
(400-600) 336
Wart reaching up & to right, 7", SR/Fall/94
(500-900) 610
Merlin stands dressed in traditional garb, 6 x 3",
HL/Nov 13/94 (400-600) 560
Madame Mim looking over shoulder w/hands up,
6", CE/Dec 16/94 (400-600) 207
Merlin & Sir Kay stand together, 10-1/2",
CE/Dec 16/94 (500-700) 518
5 cels: Scullery Maid; Sir Pelinore (eyes closed);
Sir Ector (eyes closed); 2 of Wart sitting
(eyes closed), S/Dec 17/94 (400-600) 230
Madam Mim (facing left) makes point, 7"; Wart sits
w/eyes closed, 6"; Merlin (6-1/2" with hat)
& Sir Ector (5-1/2") chat while walking;
S/Dec 17/94 (300-500) 575
Combative Madame Mim as alligator (6-1/2", all
but tail) faces Merlin (full figure, 4") as rabbit,
16-field, SR/Spring/95 (400-700) 420
Merlin (3-1/2") & Wart as fish; Angry pike, 4-1/2";
both with bubble effects & DL Gold Art Corner
labels, SR/Spring/95 (400-700) 275
Angry Archimedes sits in water facing right w/wings
crossed, 3-1/2"; Hatless Merlin stands holding
old helmet above head, 8-1/2"; both 16-field,
SR/Spring/95 (500-900) 510
Surprised Merlin sits in overstuffed chair, 8 x 9",
HL/Apr 23/95 (500-800) 728
Madam Mim as snake & Merlin as mouse, 8-1/2
x 13", VF, HL/Apr 23/95 (1000-1500) 896
2 full figures: Wart holds Excalibur; puzzled Merlin;
7-1/2 x 4", 6-1/2 x 2-1/2", VF+,
HL/Apr 23/95 (600-900) 784
Surprised Merlin stands amid magic dust, 7-1/2",
CE/Jun 9/95 (300-500) 460
Close-up of sprightly Merlin walking, 9-1/2",
CE/Jun 9/95 (500-700) 345
Surprised Wart in profile wearing royal robe, 5-1/2";
Merlin holding satchel & wand running to right,
6-1/2"; angry Madam Mim in profile, 7";
S/Jun 10/95 (200-400) 747
Wart holding knight's helmet; Sir Ector peering into
Merlin's satchel; Madam Mim w/eyes closed; Mer-
lin lifting satchel w/staff, S/Jun 10/95
(300-500) 460
Surprised Merlin (partial figure); full figure of Madame
Mim as attractive woman; 9 x 4", 10 x 8", VF+,

HL/Aug 6/95 (600-900) 672
Wart holding fish; surprised Wart sitting & being
held by lovesick squirrel; Wart as squirrel;
3-1/2 x 4-1/2" to 10 x 10"; F-VF;
HL/Nov 19/95 (600-900) 920
2 full figures: Wart holding sword with tip dragging
ground; happy Merlin carrying bag & cane
striding to right; 7-1/2 x 6", 6 x 4-1/2",
VF+, HL/Apr 28/96 (600-900) 748
Wart walks uncertainly to left, in kingly robe, 4 x 6",
VF, HL/Apr 28/96 (500-700) 230
2 cels: full figure of Archimedes facing right & leaning
forward with mouth open, 2"; waist-up of Merlin
standing facing left, examining steam engine, 9";
16-field cels, ct, SR/Fall/96 (500-1000) 550
Large-image full figure of irritated Merlin standing
facing right, 9-1/4 x 8-1/2", HL/Oct 6/96
(500-700) 518
Gloating Mad Madame Mim sits holding Wart as
sparrow, 7 x 7-1/2", HL/Oct 6/96
(700-1000) 805
Spry Merlin, dressed for Bermuda, stepping right,
5-3/8", Art Corner label, SR/Spring/97
(400-800) 500
Wart as squirrel being cuddled by love-struck girl
squirrel, 3-1/2 x 5", HL/May 31/97
(500-700) 288
Irritated Merlin sits conferring with Archimedes
(who's staring straight ahead), 8-1/2 x
8-1/4", VF, HL/Nov 16/97 (400-600) 546
Front view of Madame Mim standing leaning forward
with fists clinched & crazed eyes, 5-1/8",
16-field cel, SR/Spring/98 (400-700) 660
Merlin stands dressed for a contemporary tropical
vacation, 10 x 5-1/4", VF+, HL/Apr 25/98
(500-700) 460

CELS – PARTIAL FIGURE (also see CELS-FULL FIGURE)

Portrait of Merlin, 5 x 4", VF+, HL/Feb 26-27/94
(300-500) 385
2 cels: waist-up of Wart looking right, holding tea cup,
hand on top of head, 5-1/2"; chest-up side view
of Merlin (8") looking straight up & pointing
cane at Archimedes (sitting on hat); both
16-field, SR/Fall/94 (700-1100) 880
Front view of Merlin (waist up) & Archimedes (full
figure) staring at each other, 5 x 4-1/2" & 2
x 2-1/2", VF+, HL/Apr 23/95 (700-1000) 560
Madame Mim as cat holds Wart as sparrow; Merlin
w/armful of books & unruly beard; 6 x 6-1/2"
& 10 x 6-1/2", VF+, HL/Apr 23/95
(600-900) 672
Coy Wart; stern Merlin (w/armload of books)
holding beard; 7 x 5" & 9-1/2 x 8",
VF+, HL/Aug 6/95 (500-900) 560
Madame Mim (w/pig head) pulls hair w/both hands,
8-1/2 x 10", VF+, HL/Nov 19/95 (600-900) 546
Wart looking back; frustrated Merlin (w/armload of
books) untangling beard; 7 x 5", 9-1/2 x
6-1/2", VF+, HL/Apr 28/96 (600-900) 748
Knees-up front view of Madame Mim in romantic
pose, 7-1/2", SR/Fall/96 (400-800) 440
Hips-up of irritated Merlin (9-1/2") facing left with
armful of books, shaking sugar away with
beard; plus similar drawing of Merlin (eyes
closed) carrying books, 9-1/4", 16-field sheet;
both signed by Frank Thomas & Ollie
Johnston, SR/Spring/97 (900-1200) 990
Knees-up front view of scheming Madame Mim,
7-3/8", 16-field cel, SR/Fall/97 (600-900) 400
Waist-up of bundled-up Wart facing forward &
looking left, 6-1/2", 16-field cel,
SR/Spring/98 (400-700) 400
Mad Madam Mim stares at Wart (as sparrow)
sitting on her fingertip, 7 x 7-1/4", VF,
HL/Apr 25/98 (600-800) 489

CONCEPT AND INSPIRATIONAL ART

Inspirational art by Bill Justice of Madam Mim reading
tarot cards in her home, 2", CE/Dec 18/97
(2000-3000) 2300

DYE-TRANSFER PRINTS

Wart & Merlin stand in front of tournament scene
w/sword in stone, SR/Spring/96 (200-400) 200

THE THREE CABALLEROS (1945)

**Also see TELEVISION: ANTHOLOGY SERIES,
UNIDENTIFIED TV; UNIDENTIFIED/MISCEL-
LANEOUS: COMBINATIONS OF MAJOR
CHARACTERS**
Segments were *The Cold-Blooded Penguin, The*

Flying Gauchito, Baia, and *La Piñata,* plus connecting
animation.

ANIMATION DRAWINGS

3 rough drawings of José & Panchito, 5" & smaller,
CE/Jun 18/94 (500-700) 483
Knees-up drawing of Panchito standing facing right,
arms up, mouth open, 6-7/8"; 12-field sheet;
moderate overall discoloration & minor wear,
SR/Fall/97 (300-600) 240
4 cleaned-up animator's rough drawings of
Panchito singing, 6 x 4" to 7 x 5", F overall,
HL/Nov 16/97 (800-1200) 1955
10 polished rough drawings of José (one with Donald),
5 x 4" to 5 x 5-1/2", F overall, HL/Nov 16/97
(1000-1500) 1150

CEL SET-UPS/MODEL ART

Panchito gestures amid confetti & streamers, watercolor background, Walt Disney signature, WDP
stamp, 5-1/2", S/Dec 16/93 (1200-1500) 1955
José Carioca strolls w/broom, watercolor background,
Walt Disney signature, WDP stamp, 4", S/Dec
16/93 (1200-1500) 1150
Full figure of Panchito over complementary
background, 7-1/2 x 12", VF+,
HL/Apr 10/94 (700-1000) 476
Background of wall painting & full-figure cel of heroic
matador Goofy from *For Whom The Bulls Toil*
mounted to single-color master background
(tempera on background sheet) from *The Three
Caballeros*, 11-1/2 x 8-1/2", Art Props Dept.
mat inscribed "Walt Disney's 'Goofy'", VF,
HL/Apr 10/94 (800-1200) 896
Full figures of Donald & José Carioca dancing,
complementary painted Courvoisier *Baia*-style
background stamped w/WDP monogram &
copyright, 7 x 9-1/2", HL/Aug 21/94
(1800-2000) 1792
Full-figure front-view color model of casual Panchito,
Jose, & Donald standing together amid streamers
& confetti, 7 x 6-1/2", 12-field, color copy
background, SR/Fall/94 (1500-2200) 2060
Full figure of Panchito posing in spotlight, 5",
Courvoisier airbrush & watercolor
background, CE/Dec 16/94 (700-900) 978
2 cels of José Carioca, 4-1/2", Courvoisier limited-
edition background, CE/Dec 16/94
(600-800) 863
Full figure of José Carioca posing in spotlight,
7 x 7-1/2", painted background, inscribed
mat, Courvoisier label, HL/Apr 23/95
(1000-1500) 2016
Full figures of two sad penguins carrying block of ice
(containing bundled Pablo reading map) between
two poles to right, 5-1/4", color print of arctic
background, ct, SR/Fall/95 (600-1400) 1180
Full figures of Amigo Panchito with arms around
Amigos Donald & José, black-paper background
w/confetti, Courvoisier label, 5-1/2 x 7-1/2",
HL/Apr 28/96 (2500-3500) 2530
Full-figure portrait of Panchito standing in spotlight
amid streamers, Courvoisier airbrush &
watercolor background, mat signed by Walt
Disney, 5-1/2", major paint loss,
CE/Jun 20/96 (500-700) 1380
Full figures of 4 Josés in identical poses as female
samba dancer amid streamers & confetti,
9-1/8 x 5-1/4", 12-field cel, color print
background, ct, SR/Fall/96 (1400-2200) 1210
Full figure of Burrito standing facing left w/Gauchito
riding backwards, both looking into camera,
4-7/8", 12-field cel, display background of
desert, ct, SR/Fall/96 (500-900) 750
Full figures of Caballeros posing on shelf: Donald (5")
in middle, José (3-1/4") & Panchito (3-5/8")
lying as bookends, custom watercolor display
background, ct, SR/Fall/96 (2000-3000) 2200
Full figures of Panchito greeting surprised José &
Donald (who are holding hands), 8-1/2 x
10-1/2", painted black paper background, Courvoisier label, HL/Oct 6/96 (1500-2000) 1150
Full figure of bundled Pablo, candle on beak, standing
on ice looking left & holding map amid snowflakes, 5", airbrushed Courvoisier background of
large circle on solid field, mat signed by Walt
Disney, S/Dec 14/96 (1800-2200) 2300
Full figure of bundled Pablo standing on ice outside
igloo looking left w/candle on beak & holding
map amid snowflakes, 5", airbrushed
Courvoisier background & label,

S/Dec 14/96 (800-1200) 1150

Full-figure front views of happy Amigos José and Panchito standing with hands & guitars in air amid streamers, both 5-1/2", color print background, SR/Spring/97 (700-1100) 720

Full figures of Donald, José, & Panchito dancing [drawn in modeled realistic style]; complementary painted solid background with streamers; 4-1/2 x 6-1/2" overall, HL/May 3/97 (1500-2000) 1610

Full figures of Donald, José, & Panchito standing in identical dancing pose in cel painted to blend w/live action, 4-1/2 x 4", complementary painted background, VF, HL/Nov 16/97 (2000-3000) 1840

Full figures of smiling Caballeros José, Panchito & Donald standing together, each holding up 3 fingers, complementary airbrushed spotlight background as prepared by Courvoisier, label, restored, 5 x 5-3/4" cel, F+, HL/Apr 25/98 (1400-1800) 1783

CELS – FULL FIGURE

José with umbrella & cigar, 4-1/2 x 5-1/2", CE/Jun 18/94 (700-900) 518

Panchito (4-1/2 x 4-1/2") forcefully hugs Donald (1-1/2 x 3-1/2") & José (2-1/2 x 3-3/4"), CE/Jun 18/94 (1500-2500) 1265

Publicity cel of Donald (4-1/2") & José (4"), circa 1960s, CE/Jun 18/94 (200-300) 345

José Carioca in welcoming pose, 6 x 3-1/2", HL/Aug 21/94 (600-800) 728

Donald energetically hugging José, 5-1/2"; plus publicity cel of José, 5-1/4", CE/Dec 16/94 (700-900) 1380

Front view of Jose Carioca standing watching spinning cane, dry-brush effects, 4", 12-field, SR/Spring/95 (800-1200) 830

Gauchito sits on surprised Burrito's back (flapping ears), facing left, 4", 12-field, dry brush & shadow effects, some rippling, SR/Spring/95 (300-600) 350

Laughing Donald Duck in arms of happy José Carioca, 5-1/2 x 5", HL/Aug 6/95 (700-1000) 896

Panchito peers intently over side of flying serape, 3-1/2 x 8-1/2", HL/Nov 19/95 (700-1000) 690

Pablo on snowshoes & two of Pablo's friends; 3 x 2" & 4 x 2-1/2", HL/Nov 19/95 (800-1200) 690

Amigos Donald & José standing side by side with tongues out & huge pupils, 3-3/4", ct, SR/Fall/96 (900-1400) 910

Panchito holds Donald & José off ground by shoulders, 6-1/8", SR/Fall/96 (1000-1500) 2180

Front view of José standing, 5", ct, SR/Fall/96 (700-1200) 610

Publicity cel: surprised José & Donald (wearing sombreros) watching Panchito (in center) gesture, 4" each, CE/Dec 12/96 (1000-1500) 978

Donald, Panchito, & José facing left in step with serapés over arms & wearing Mexican hats, 5 x 7", HL/Feb 23/97 (1200-1600) 2530

Donald, José, & Panchito ride magic serape, 3-1/2 x 3-1/2" overall, S/Jun 21/97 (600-800) 575

Donald & José standing together & harmonizing while holding sombreros, 3-1/4 x 10-3/4", F, HL/Nov 16/97 (800-1200) 690

José & Panchito stand with hands clasped in front of them in identical dancing pose, wearing sombreros, 5 x 5-1/4", VF, HL/Nov 16/97 (600-900) 748

José & Donald lay & Panchito stands on serape, 3-1/4 x 5-1/4", F+, HL/Nov 16/97 (1000-1500) 1265

CELS – PARTIAL FIGURE

José Carioca (4-1/2") w/unidentified moose (7"), DL label, CE/Dec 16/94 (600-800) 288

CONCEPT AND INSPIRATIONAL ART

Inspirational painting for sequence where Aurora Miranda sings & dances thru Baia streets, watercolor on heavyweight paper, WDP stamp, 7-1/4 x 9", VF+, HL/Apr 25/98 (700-900) 575

DYE-TRANSFER PRINT

3 casual Caballeros stand together amid streamers, contemporary colored background, SR/Fall/95 (200-400) 220

STORY ART

Story painting of Baia by Mary Blair, 7 x 6-1/2", tempera on black paper, HL/Oct 6/96 (500-700) 1840

TIM BURTON'S THE NIGHTMARE BEFORE CHRISTMAS (1993)

All items in this section were auctioned at Sotheby's, December 16, 1993.

PROP ART (SETS AND FIGURES)

Bed (prop from opening sequence) (800-1200) 2588

Man Under the Stairs set & creature (1000-1500) 1265

Group of 5 Halloweentown residents (1000-1500) 5175

Town square fountain, gates, props & puppets (2000-2500) 4313

Town hall exterior, major, hearse (2000-3000) 4313

3 musicians & their wall (1500-2000) 7475

Jack & Zero on Spiral Hill (half scale) (2000-3000) 4313

Christmastown snowmobile & Santa Jack (500-700) 6325

Town hall interior w/puppets (3500-4500) 12,650

Jack's house (800-1200) 11,500

Interior of Jack's tower (1500-2000) 17,250

Sally & her herb patch (1000-1500) 4025

Evil Scientist tower, Igor, Scientist's companion (1000-1500) 3163

Armory set w/Lock, Shock & Barrel (5 puppets) (1500-2000) 7475

Oogie Boogie & Santa Claus with props (1500-2000) 5750

Santa Jack, Zero, Reindeer & Sled (1500-2000) 8625

Santa Jack & 7 real-world puppets (1000-1500) 5463

5 tombstones & Santa Jack (700-900) 8050

Oogie Boogie exposed & 3 one-armed bandits (1000-1500) 7475

Witch & face buildings (2 total) (700-900) 3738

Cat building (400-600) 4600

TREASURE ISLAND (LIVE ACTION, 1950)

STORY ART

Story painting of Jim Hawkins setting tables in Long John Silver's tavern, 10-3/4 x 9", mixed media on a 13-1/8 x 10-5/8" board, SR/Fall/97 (300-600) 280

TRON (LIVE ACTION, 1982)

STORY ART

Six storyboard drawings of cyberspace battle sequence on game grid, colored pencil on black paper, SR/Fall/96 (200-500) 150

VICTORY THROUGH AIR POWER (1943)

ANIMATION DRAWINGS

Full-figure drawing of attacking eagle, 8-1/2 x 8-1/2", HL/Nov 19/95 (600-900) 575

BACKGROUNDS

Master background of urban area from altitude, watercolor & tempera on heavy paper, 8 x 12", studio notes & stamps, VF, HL/Apr 10/94 (500-800) 560

Watercolor production background of London from the air at dusk, sight 12-1/2 x 15-1/2", stamps, CE/Dec 18/97 (800-1200) 920

CONCEPT AND INSPIRATIONAL ART

Six concept sketches: enormous amphibious plane, itself a flying aircraft carrier, in various scenes; pastel on black & blue sheets; 9-1/8 x 6 7/8" to 12 x 10"; SR/Fall/96 (600-1000) 700

6 concept sketches of flying airports, charcoal on animation paper, 10-7/8 x 4-3/4" to 12 x 10", SR/Fall/96 (600-1000) 610

STORY ART

17 story drawings & sketches, pencil & conté crayon on paper, 3 x 5" to 9 x 11", HL/Aug 21/94 (1000-1500) 1568

4 original story drawings, 5-1/2 & 7", pencil and conté crayon on story sheets, HL/Nov 19/95 (300-400) 138

Story drawing of bombers flying westward over U.S. west coast, colored pastel on black paper, 4 x 4-1/2", HL/May 31/97 (150-250) 431

WHO FRAMED ROGER RABBIT? (1988)

Also see TELEVISION: MICKEY'S 60TH BIRTHDAY

ANIMATION DRAWINGS

Front-view extreme rough drawing of Baby Herman gesturing w/cigar in right hand, blue pencil &

india ink on animation sheet, 7 x 7-1/2", HL/Feb 23/97 (300-400) 374

CEL SET-UPS

3-cel progression: Roger bursting out to foil Judge Doom, each w/matching photographic backgrounds, white Touchstone/Amblin seal, S/Dec 16/93 (2000-2500) 1725

Jessica visits Eddie Valiant's office, photographic background, white Touchstone/Amblin seal, S/Dec 16/93 (2000-2500) 1725

Toons rejoice as Roger reads will, matching color photographic background, white Touchstone/Amblin seal, 8-1/2", S/Dec 16/93 (7000-9000) 8050

Publicity set-up: octopus bartender serves penguin waiter, photographic background, S/Dec 16/93 (1000-1500) 805

Pointing finger threatens Roger with return to science lab, airbrushed color card, white Touchstone/Amblin seal, S/Dec 16/93 (2000-2500) 1840

R.K. Maroon tells Roger his wife has been playing pattycake, photographic background, white Touchstone/Amblin seal, also black & white photostat of frame set-up w/robotic arm before animation was added, S/Dec 16/93 (2000-2500) 2300

2 cels featuring Roger & Jessica, each w/Disney seal & set over print of matching background, autographed "Here's looking at you. G.K. Wolf and Roger Rabbit too!", 8 x 13" & 10 x 15", VF, HL/Apr 10/94 (2000-2500) 2576

Jessica convincing Eddie that Maroon set her and Marvin Acme up, photographic background, white Touchstone/Amblin seal, S/Jun 17/94 (2500-3500) 2587

Roger & Eddie find Benny locked up in Toon Patrol van & set him free, photographic background, white Touchstone/Amblin seal, S/Jun 17/94 (1500-2000) 1725

2-cel progression: Baby Herman's mother threatening Roger (7-1/2"), white Touchstone/Amblin seal, [Lot 49, Art of Who Framed Roger Rabbit?, S/Jun 28/89], S/Jun 17/94 (4000-6000) 2875

Roger looks into camera as he drives Benny the Cab down street to left, color print background, as sold in 1989 auction, 8-1/2 x 12-1/2", HL/Aug 21/94 (1800-2500) 2240

6-cel progression: Baby Herman (4") happily crawling along stove as Roger (7 to 9") reacts, color photographic background, Touchstone/Amblin seal, S/Dec 17/94 (2500-3500) 6037

4-cel progression of Roger's reaction to whiskey, 6" avg., color photographic print, Touchstone/Amblin seal, S/Dec 17/94 (2000-2500) 4025

The next six items were property of Richard Williams. All have a WDC seal & are signed by Williams.

Director Raoul (7-1/2") stops scene with Roger (5-1/2") inside refrigerator & Baby Herman (5") angry, matching color photographic background & special silver frame, S/Dec 17/94 (1500-2500) 3737

Jessica gives come-hither look over shoulder, 9-1/2", matching b&w photographic background, S/Dec 17/94 (1500-2500) 2300

5-cel set-up: weasels Smart Ass, Greasy, Wheezy, Stupid & Psycho advance menacingly, 9 to 5", matching b&w photographic background, S/Dec 17/94 (1200-1800) 1035

Bewildered Eddie (8") holds singing sword (10-1/2" from 2nd bend), matching b&w photographic background, S/Dec 17/94 (1200-1800) 1035

Eddie (8-1/2") grabs Roger (9") by throat before kissing him, matching b&w photographic background, S/Dec 17/94 (1200-1800) 1380

Toons applaud reading of will (Goofy 9-1/2", others smaller), matching b&w photographic background, S/Dec 17/94 (4000-6000) 5175

Benny the Cab gestures angrily as Roger sucks thumb, 8 x 12", black & white photoprint background with Eddie Valiant, HL/Apr 23/95 (800-1200) 1568

Roger & Jessica tied up & dangling from hook, 6 x 2-1/2", black & white photoprint background, HL/Apr 23/95 (1000-1500) 1680

Startled Eddie w/Singing Sword, 8 x 12-1/2", matching color print background, HL/Apr 23/95 (800-1200) 896

Jessica talks to Eddie Valiant, 7", b&w photo

reproduction background, CE/Jun 9/95
(1000-1500) 978

Roger pinned by cutlery w/knife coming at him,
5-1/2", color photographic background,
S/Jun 10/95 (1000-1500) 1495

Pelican mail carrier (8") losing control of bike with Sorcerer's Apprentice brooms (2") in back-
ground; 4-cel set-up of Eddie (8") walking amid
"cattle call" (7-1/2" avg.); both w/matching
b&w photographic backgrounds,
S/Jun 10/95 (700-900) 805

Roger fights for balance atop rolling pin, 10",
matching color photographic background,
S/Jun 10/95 (1000-1500) 1840

Front view of Jessica Rabbit, hands on hips, with
photoprint background of Ink & Paint Club
audience, 10 x 15", HL/Aug 6/95
(1400-1800) 2128

Front view of frightened Benny & Roger, 9 x
12-1/2", b&w photoprint background of
alley, with presentation letter,
HL/Aug 6/95 (1000-1500) 2464

Roger smiles amid stars as Jessica positions arms
to lift him from bricks, 7-1/2 x 12-1/2", b&w
photoprint background, framed with patch
given to animation crew, HL/Nov 19/95
(1000-1500) 978

Benny closes eyes w/eager Roger at his wheel,
8-1/2 x 13", matching color photoprint
background, HL/Nov 19/95 (1500-2000) 1265

Roger & Eddie fight over wheel of frightened Benny,
7-1/2 x 13", b&w photoprint background,
HL/Nov 19/95 (1000-1500) 1265

Close-up portrait of seductive Jessica, 8", 16-field, Disney Art Program seal, key photographic
frame blow-up background, SR/Spring/96
(2500-3200) 2750

Angry Jessica confronts Eddie in warehouse, matching
b&w photoprint background, 8 x 12", VF+,
HL/Apr 28/96 (1000-1500) 1093

Judge Doom watches as Roger (bug-eyed, tongue out)
holds neck w/both hands, matching b&w photoprint background, 8-1/2 x 11", VF+,
HL/Apr 28/96 (1000-1500) 1265

Roger confers w/Dolores in rotgut room, matching
b&w photoprint, 10 x 14", VF+,
HL/Apr 28/96 (1000-1500) 1323

Happy Roger looks over his shoulder as he's being
held by Jessica, matching b&w photoprint
background, 9 x 12-1/2", VF+,
HL/Apr 28/96 (1500-2000) 1955

R.K. Maroon talks to Eddie Valiant at window
w/Dumbo behind blinds, airbrushed sky
background & color print of live-action
footage in lighted box frame, 9-1/4 x
11-1/4 x 2-3/4", VF+, HL/Apr 28/96
(2000-2500) 2070

Maroon raises blinds to reveal Dumbo as Eddie
watches; airbrushed sky background & color
print of live-action footage in lighted box
frame, 9-1/4 x 11-1/4 x 2-3/4", VF+,
HL/Apr 28/96 (2500-3000) 4140

Full figures of Donald & Daffy playing their dueling
pianos on stage, 11 x 16-1/2", VF+,
HL/Apr 28/96 (3000-3500) 4140

6 set-ups in sequence of effects of whiskey on Roger
despite Judge Doom's grip, 8-1/2 x 12-3/4"
each, VF+, HL/Apr 28/96 (3000-4000) 4140

Eddie Valiant & Jessica w/hands up, b&w
photoprint of warehouse, 8 x 12",
HL/Apr 28/96 (1000-1500) 978

Eddie Valiant tries to stop Judge Doom from strangling
Roger, b&w photoprint background, 8 x 12",
HL/Apr 28/96 (1000-1500) 1150

Roger uses his ears to keep from being dipped by
Judge Doom, b&w photoprint background,
8 x 11", HL/Apr 28/96 (1000-1500) 1208

Elevated rear view of Eddie Valiant, Dolores, Roger
(4") & Jessica (7-1/2") walking out of warehouse
together w/Toons gathered around, matching
color photographic background, S/Jun 19/96
(8000-12,000) 8050

Close-up of Roger's face as whiskey takes effect,
8-1/2 x 13", b&w photoprint of live-action
background, VF+, HL/Oct 6/96
(1000-1500) 920

Full figure of Roger waving as Baby Herman's mother
walks out door from *Somethin's Cooking'*
opening, 11 x 14-1/2", color print of matching

master background, mat signed by author Gary
Wolf, VF+, HL/Oct 6/96 (900-1200) 863

Full figures of all 5 weasels standing in street looking
& pointing left, 8-1/2 x 12-1/2", color print
of live-action background, VF+, HL/Oct 6/96
(1000-1500) 1150

Roger shakes Eddie's hand while watching movie
in theater balcony, 7 x 5-1/2" cel image,
matching b&w photoprint background, VF+,
HL/Oct 6/96 (800-1000) 575

Full figures of wide-eyed Roger & Jessica hanging
from crane hook in front of brick wall, 6-1/4
x 2" cel image, b&w photoprint of live-action
background, VF+, HL/Oct 6/96 (800-1200) 1093

Eddie Valiant nose-to-nose with Roger in bed, 3-1/2
x 6" cel image, b&w photoprint of matching
live action, VF+, HL/Oct 6/96 (500-700) 748

Pan set-up of over 30 characters from finale, custom
airbrushed studio-prepared background, sight
10 x 35", S/Dec 14/96 (15,000-20,000) 17,250

2-cel progression: Roger (6") asks Eddie if his days
of being sourpuss are over as Jessica (9") &
Dolores look on. He gets his answer when he
shakes Eddie's hand w/buzzer. Matching color
photographic background, S/Dec 14/96
(3000-4000) 2587

Benny (5") finds it hard to control himself around
Jessica (10"), reproduction background,
S/Dec 14/96 (1500-2000) 1150

2-cel progression: Daffy Duck (8") plays piano
unaware that devil-horned Donald Duck (2")
is looking out from his piano with cannon,
matching color photographic background,
S/Dec 14/96 (2000-3000) 1610

Eddie Valiant & agitated Roger peer thru rotgut
room peep hole, b&w photoprint of
matching live action, 8 x 12" overall,
HL/Feb 23/97 (800-1200) 633

Chest-up portrait of alluring Jessica, b&w photoprint
of matching live-action frame, 8-1/2 x 12"
overall, HL/Feb 23/97 (1000-1500) 1093

Eddie stands watching as Roger (sitting on box of
soap) points left, b&w photoprint of matching
live-action, 9-1/2 x 14" overall,
HL/Feb 23/97 (700-1000) 633

Detailed overhead view of chaotic Toontown
intersection, sight 11 x 16", trimmed
celluloid on matching color photographic
background, S/Jun 21/97 (4000-6000) 5750

Roger (6") shakes Eddie's hand with joy buzzer in
warehouse as Dolores & Jessica (9") look on,
matching color photographic background
(2-cel progression matted together),
S/Jun 21/97 (3000-4000) 4025

Full figure of Roger counting on fingers inside near
open door, 6-1/2", matching color photographic
background, S/Jun 21/97 (2000-3000) 2300

Roger vows to take care of Baby Herman, 8", color
photocopy of matching background,
S/Dec 19/97 (1000-1500) 1610

Close-up front view of blown-up Roger whizzing thru
air, 3-cel progression: each applied to color
photocopy of original background, matted &
framed together, S/Dec 19/97
(3000-4000) 3450

Calm Baby Herman sits in baby carriage holding cigar,
looking up & right; b&w photoprint of matching
live-action background; seal; 6-1/2 x 6-1/2" cel;
VF+; HL/Apr 25/98 (500-700) 575

Large chest-up side image of angry Eddie almost nose
to nose with Roger, b&w photoprint of matching
live-action film, seal, 9-1/4 x 9-1/4" cel, VF,
HL/Apr 25/98 (700-1000) 1035

CELS – FULL FIGURE
The next six items were property of Richard Williams.
All have Walt Disney Co. seals & are signed by Williams.
Innocent Baby Herman (4") sits in playpen facing right
as mother (legs & hem 9-1/2") walks by,
S/Dec 17/94 (1500-2500) 1725

Roger naming relatives with aid of fingers, 9",
S/Dec 17/94 (1000-1500) 1610

Panicked Roger runs [to aid Baby Herman], 6 x 11",
S/Dec 17/94 (1200-1800) 1955

Roger blowing up like balloon with lips stuck to
vacuum cleaner, 7-1/2 x 10", S/Dec 17/94
(1200-1800) 1725

Frightened Roger pinned to wall by cutlery, 6 x 8",
S/Dec 17/94 (1200-1800) 2587

Roger (9-1/2" length) gleefully catches Baby Herman

(4") who holds cookie w/refrigerator suspended
overhead, S/Dec 17/94 (1500-2000) 3737

Frantic Roger bunches carpet as he runs left with
arms out, 7" (image includes floor), 16-field, Disney Art Program seal, SR/Spring/96
(1400-2200) 1400

Cels of Roger, Jessica, Dumbo, Donald Duck, Mickey
Mouse, Minnie, Goofy, Baby Herman,
Pinocchio, Peter (partial), Toby Tortoise, Smart
Ass & 2 penguins trimmed & mounted to
painted board, 14-3/4 x 18-1/4", VF+,
HL/Apr 28/96 (4000-5000) 3450

MODEL ART
5 publication model sheets translating characters into
drawn characters: Roger, 13 x 10" (trimmed);
Dolores, 13-7/16 x 10"; Benny the Cab, 14
x 10-1/8"; Eddie, 14-7/16 x 10-1/4"; Baby Herman's Girlfriend; plus 14-1/2 x 7-3/8"
comparative size sheet showing Benny, Baby Herman, Roger, Eddie, Jessica, Judge Doom;
SR/Fall/96 (100-300) 300

PRINT ART
3 photo prints of posters for Roger Rabbit & Baby Herman cartoons: "The Wet Nurse,"
10-3/16 x 14-7/8"; "Babes in Arms,"
10-5/8 x 15-3/8"; "Herman's Shermans,"
10-1/2 x 15"; SR/Fall/96 (300-600) 660

SHORTS & FEATURETTES

This section is organized alphabetically by title and art
type, then chronologically by auction. For other artwork
featuring Shorts characters, see **TELEVISION:
ANTHOLOGY SERIES** and **UNIDENTIFIED/ MIS-
CELLANEOUS**

ALICE IN COMMUNICATIONLAND
(EDUCATIONAL)
CELS
Chest-up of Alice facing right, talking to frazzled
Dormouse standing in her right hand, 10-1/2",
from film strip for Walt Disney Educational
Media Company, SR/Spring/97 (500-900) 830

ALICE THE COLLEGIATE (1927)
**Also see UNIDENTIFIED/MISCELLANEOUS: ALICE
COMEDIES**
ANIMATION DRAWINGS
4 drawings of groups of animal characters, 2-1/2 x
2-1/2" to 6-1/2 x 11-1/2", HL/Apr 28/96
(1000-1500) 1093

ALL IN A NUTSHELL (1949)
STORY ART
20 storyboard drawings by Nick George of Donald
as pushcart vendor with Chip & Dale, pastel
& charcoal on 8 x 6" storyboard sheets,
SR/Fall/95 (1500-2500) 2970

ALPINE CLIMBERS (1936)
ANIMATION DRAWINGS
Drawing of Mickey, 4 x 4-1/2", CE/Jun 18/94
(1000-1500) 748

Drawing of smiling Mickey, 3-1/2", CE/Dec 16/94
(600-800) 633

3 full-figure rough drawings of Mickey stranded [on
a limb], 4-1/2 x 4", 3-1/2 x 4", 4 x 5-1/2",
HL/Mar 16-17/96 (200-400) 633

6 detailed rough drawings of Mickey w/grass around
neck fleeing [from eagle's nest], 3-1/2 x 4" to
4 x 4", HL/Feb 23/97 (600-800) 1725

Full-figure drawing of Mickey facing left squatting
by bag, holding egg up, turning to grin
nervously, 3-3/4 x 3-1/2", VF,
HL/Apr 25/98 (500-700) 460

CEL SET-UPS
Falling Donald (4-1/2") grabs Mickey (3 x 2") who
dangles from rope, veneer background,
S/Dec 17/94 (6000-7000) 6325

CELS – FULL FIGURE
Chastened Donald Duck walking & singing, 2-1/4
x 3-1/4", HL/Aug 6/95 (2000-2500) 2688

AQUAMANIA (1961)
BACKGROUNDS
Chest-up portrait of Walrus looking at left hand from

Alice in Wonderland, 6-1/2", master gouache background from *Aquamania*, SR/Spring/96 (600-1000) 600

CEL SET-UPS
Full figure of panicked Goofy skiing to left, 4-1/2", water & bubble effects, DL background & gold Art Corner label, SR/Spring/96 (500-900) 610
Full figure of terrified Goofy water-skiing to left, one ski out of water, 5", water effects, color print background of water & sky, SR/Fall/96 (500-900) 830

THE ART OF SELF DEFENSE (1941)
TITLE ART
Title card: Goofy in boxing pose, Goofy & hand lettering on three cel levels over watercolor background, 12-field, original production cover flap, SR/Fall/94 (2000-4000) 2220

THE ART OF SKIING (1941)
CEL SET-UPS
Goofy on ski lift, Courvoisier watercolor background, 7-3/4 x 8-3/4", CE/Dec 15/93 (1500-2000) 1150
Goofy hugs tree, Courvoisier watercolor background, 8-1/4 x 7-1/2", CE/Dec 15/93 (1500-2000) 1265
Airborne Goofy clings to skis, airbrushed & watercolor preliminary background, 3 x 8", S/Jun 17/94 (2000-2500) 2587
Fallen Goofy, 4 x 5", watercolor & airbrush Courvoisier background, CE/Jun 18/94 (1500-2000) 2990
Skiing Goofy carries uprooted tree, 4", airbrush Courvoisier background, CE/Jun 18/94 (1000-1500) 863
Determined Goofy in fine form skiing down mountain, 3 x 7", airbrushed Courvoisier background & label, WDP stamp, S/Dec 17/94 (1500-2000) 4025
Goofy (5") skiing while hugging tree (9"), airbrushed Courvoisier background & label, S/Dec 17/94 (1500-2000) 1495
Full figure of smiling Goofy in sitting position, looking down at skis pointed in opposite directions, 4-1/2", snow effects, Courvoisier watercolor background & mat with caption, SR/Spring/95 (1100-1400) 1980
Full figure of smiling Goofy squatting on skis and smiling into camera, airbrushed Courvoisier background, 4 x 4", S/Jun 19/96 (1000-1500) 4887
Full figure of Goofy lying in snow with waist & legs in air & skis on feet, vibration lines, Courvoisier watercolor & airbrush background, 5", CE/Jun 20/96 (1500-2000) 1495
Similar to previous: full figure of Goofy lying in snow w/waist & legs up in air & skis on feet, fewer vibration lines, Courvoisier airbrush watercolor background, 5-1/2", CE/Jun 20/96 (1500-2000) 1380
Full figure of determined Goofy skiing downhill, Courvoisier watercolor & airbrush background, 5", CE/Jun 20/96 (1500-2000) 2300
Full figure of exhausted Goofy twisted & caught in skis stuck upright in snow, Courvoisier airbrush background, 5-1/2", CE/Jun 20/96 (1500-2000) 2070
Full figure of smiling Goofy looking at camera while hanging horizontally between ski poles and skis, 6 x 6-1/4", complementary painted background as prepared by Courvoisier, VG+, HL/Nov 16/97 (1500-2000) 1840
Full figure of Goofy standing with legs twisted and one ski reversed, 4 x 6-1/2", complementary painted background & label as prepared by Courvoisier, VF, HL/Nov 16/97 (1000-1500) 2300
Full figure of shocked Goofy at top of hill in skiing position w/head between his legs, 3-3/4 x 5-1/2", complementary painted background & label as prepared by Courvoisier, VF, HL/Nov 16/97 (800-1000) 1955

CELS – FULL FIGURE
Determined Goofy in textbook skiing position, 2-1/2 x 7-1/2", VG, HL/Aug 21/94 (800-1200) 1344

THE AUTOGRAPH HOUND (1939)

ANIMATION DRAWINGS
Full-figure drawing of sitting Donald Duck, 3-1/2", CE/Dec 16/94 (500-700) 322
2 full-figure drawings: profile caricature of Mickey Rooney making stop gesture, angry Donald Duck holding violin & bow; 5 x 6" & 5 x 4"; HL/Nov 19/95 (700-1500) 690
Animation drawings of Groucho (colored as Ink & Paint model) & Harpo Marx; 7 x 7-1/2", 5-1/2 x 4", HL/Nov 19/95 (800-1200) 1265
2 full-figure drawings: Mickey Rooney standing facing right, 5-1/4"; angry Donald standing facing left, holding hat, looking up with egg on head, 3-1/4"; 12-field sheets with timer's charts; SR/Fall/96 (600-1000) 640
Front-view drawing of Charles Boyer as Napoleon standing holding book, pencil behind ear, 7-1/4 x 6-1/2", HL/Oct 6/96 (500-700) 518
Full-figure front-view drawing of Harpo Marx standing poised to honk horn, 5-1/4 x 3-1/2", HL/Oct 6/96 (600-800) 518
Full-figure drawing of Shirley Temple walking in sailor outfit, 4-1/2", 12-field sheet, some edge wear & discoloration, SR/Spring/97 (300-600) 530
3 drawings of Marx Brothers playing violins: one of Groucho framed together w/one of Chico & Harpo; one of Harpo; each approx. 4-1/2"; S/Dec 19/97 (800-1200) 690
6 celebrity caricatures: Martha Raye, Clark Gable, Roland Young, Greta Garbo (holding outline of Clark Gable), Joe E. Brown, Charles Boyer as Napoleon; each sheet 10 x 12"; S/Dec 19/97 (900-1200) 1150

BACKGROUNDS
Watercolor master background of a front room, 11 x 8-3/8", SR/Spring/95 (2000-4000) 2480
Master background of house interior, 8-1/2 x 11", watercolor on background sheet, HL/Nov 19/95 (3000-3500) 3220

STORY ART
3 storyboards of Donald Duck hauling block of ice w/Sonya Henie's autograph, then having it melt, average 4-1/2" each, matted & framed together, S/Jun 21/97 (1000-1500) 1610

BABES IN THE WOODS (1932)
ANIMATION DRAWINGS
Full-figure drawing of Witch flying on rotary-powered broom with Hansel & Gretel, 9 x 12", HL/Oct 6/96 (400-600) 345

BACKGROUNDS
Master background of dwarf's forest community, watercolor on background sheet, 8-1/2 x 11", HL/Feb 23/97 (2000-3000) 3220
Master background of dwarf's forest community with tree house doors open, watercolor on background sheet, 8-1/4 x 11", HL/Feb 23/97 (2000-3000) 4830
Master background of cages & spiderwebs, watercolor on background sheet, 8 x 11", HL/Feb 23/97 (2000-2500) 1840
Master background of cages on floor, watercolor on background sheet, 8-1/2 x 11", HL/Feb 23/97 (2000-2500) 1840
Master background of witch's house interior, watercolor on background sheet, 8-1/2 x 11", HL/Feb 23/97 (2000-3000) 2300

BAGGAGE BUSTER (1941)
CEL SET-UPS
Full figure of Goofy bent over, looking back between legs toward train (hand-inked on cel, key to background), battered tophat stuck to rump, 4"; pan watercolor background of station platform & farmland, SR/Fall/96 (4000-7000) 6400

THE BAND CONCERT (1935)
CELS – FULL FIGURE
Intense Mickey Mouse, 4-1/2 x 3-1/2", HL/Aug 6/95 (5000-6000) 8960
Donald Duck w/mischief in his eyes, 3-1/2 x 3", HL/Aug 6/95 (3500-4500) 3584

LAYOUT ART
Detailed layout drawing of bandstand, black pencil on 12-field sheet, red frame line, background notation, studio stamp, some wear & discoloration, SR/Spring/95 (1800-3000) 12,100
Layout drawing of airborne Maestro Mickey conducting amid open door & other debris, 8 x 11", HL/Nov 19/95 (1500-2000) 3220
Detailed layout drawing of Mickey conducting amid objects picked up by cyclone, 8-1/2 x 11-1/2", HL/Apr 28/96 (2000-2500) 2300
2 polished, partly colored layout drawings: door & household items suspended in air, Mickey standing on box conducting suspended in air w/music stand; 7-1/2 x 12", 4 x 3-1/4", HL/Feb 23/97 (2000-2500) 6325
5 layout drawings from cyclone sequence, circa 8 x 12" ea., VF, HL/Nov 16/97 (1000-1500) 1150

MODEL ART
Full-figure color model drawing of Mickey, 6-1/2 x 3", HL/Nov 19/95 (500-700) 1840
Model drawing of angry Mickey Mouse holding baton, shaking left hand, 5 x 7-1/2", VF, HL/Nov 16/97 (500-800) 690

STORY ART
Detailed story drawing of bewhiskered Goofy-like trombonist sitting facing right, 5-1/4 x 6-3/4", VF, HL/Apr 25/98 (350-500) 489

THE BARN DANCE (1928)
ANIMATION DRAWINGS (also see LAYOUT ART)
Mickey & Minnie dance, 3", rough drawing, CE/Jun 18/94 (800-1000) 1840
3 drawings of Horace Horsecollar, 6" & similar, CE/Jun 9/95 (400-600) 1610
Full-figure drawing of Minnie Mouse dancing w/large cat, 5 x 7-1/2", HL/Nov 19/95 (600-900) 1093
3 full-figure drawings of laughing Mickey, flirtatious Minnie, & eager cat, 3 x 3", 3 x 2", 4-1/2 x 5", HL/Nov 19/95 (1200-1600) 1265
Full-figure rear-view drawing of Mickey dancing with broom, 3 x 4", HL/Mar 16-17/96 (300-400) 633
Full-figure drawing of smiling Mickey dancing while straddling broom, 3 x 3", HL/Feb 23/97 (600-900) 1265
Rough sketch & animation drawing: full figures of Minnie dancing w/cat, 4 x 6-1/4", HL/Feb 23/97 (700-1000) 1265
Full-figure rear-view drawing of Mickey jumping in air while dancing with broom, 4-1/2 x 2-1/2", HL/May 3/97 (800-1200) 1495
Full-figure drawing of smiling Mickey "riding" broom to right, 3 x 4", F+, HL/Nov 16/97 (900-1200) 1380

CONCEPT AND INSPIRATIONAL ART
16 pages of studies of various barnyard characters, CE/Jun 18/94 (800-1000) 1725
Script w/sketch of Mickey & Minnie; 4 pages of notes, CE/Dec 16/94 (600-800) 1610

LAYOUT ART
Full-sheet pan layout drawing of animals playing music in forest, notes, CE/Dec 16/94 (600-800) 1610
2 layout drawings; animation drawing of dancing broom; 7-1/2 x 12", 8-1/2 x 12", 4 x 1-1/2", notes, HL/Apr 23/95 (1000-1500) 1904

THE BARNYARD BROADCAST (1931)
LAYOUT ART
2 background layout drawings, CE/Jun 18/94 (600-800) 1265

THE BARNYARD CONCERT (1930)
LAYOUT ART
Layout drawing of animals assembled in barnyard listening to band under "Mickey's Follies" banner, sight 9-1/2 x 12", CLA/Jun 7/97 (2000-3000) 4600

BARNYARD OLYMPICS (1932)
LAYOUT ART
Full-figure layout drawing of Mickey (3") standing looking right & waving, next to cat (5-1/2") standing flexing muscles, CE/Dec 18/97 (2000-3000) 1955

BATH DAY (1946)
CELS – PARTIAL FIGURE
Half image of Minnie reaching to pick up Figaro (on his back), 6-1/4", 12-field, ct, SR/Fall/95 (1000-2000) 1210

TITLE ART
Title card: watercolor airbrush with hand lettering

on cel overlay, with original production cover
flap, 12-field, SR/Fall/95 (1500-2200) 1500

THE BEACH PARTY (1931)
CONCEPT AND INSPIRATIONAL ART
Inspirational sketch: full figures of Mickey & Minnie
sitting on log under umbrella playing guitar &
ukulele as Clarabelle Cow dances hula, 4" &
smaller, CE/Jun 18/94 (1000-1500) 1955
Concept drawing of Pluto under umbrella with crab
pinching nose & tail, 5-1/2", CE/Dec 16/94
(200-300) 253
Fred Moore study of Mickey & Pluto; plus 1-page
storyboard study of Pluto, CE/Dec 16/94
(800-1000) 1725
STORY ART
Storyboard featuring Horace, Clarabelle & Mickey
Mouse, graphite on 4 sheets animation paper;
plus script, CE/Dec 16/94 (1500-2500) 4370
Sequence of 23 captioned drawings by Ben
Sharpsteen; 3-1/2 x 4", 3-1/4 x 8",
5 x 4", VG-F, HL/Aug 6/95 (6000-8000) 8960

BEACH PICNIC (1939)
ANIMATION DRAWINGS
11 drawings of Pluto licking captive Donald Duck,
each 10 x 12", S/Jun 21/97 (1000-1500) 805
BACKGROUNDS
2 cels of Mickey swimming from *Lonesome Ghosts*,
7" & 6" wide, 12-field cels, water effects; pan
master watercolor background from *Beach
Picnic*, set-up 40-1/4 x 9", SR/Fall/96
(3000-6000) 4460
CEL SET-UPS
Happy Donald (in old-fashioned suit, 4-5/8") & wary
Pluto frolic in water with inflatable horse, water
effects, three cel levels, color print background,
SR/Spring/97 (3000-6000) 3080
Full figures of Pluto (5-1/2") with nose to ground
stalking running ant (1"), watercolor
production background of beach,
S/Jun 21/97 (1500-2500) 1610
CELS – FULL FIGURE
Smiling Pluto pushing pile of bones to right, 4-1/2
x 8", CE/Jun 18/94 (800-1200) 1265
Angry Pluto walking to left with turtle in mouth,
4 x 8-1/2", CE/Jun 18/94 (600-800) 1093
Pluto on front paws w/nose & rump stuck to piece
of flypaper, 5 x 6", HL/Aug 6/95 (400-600) 616

BEE AT THE BEACH (1950)
STORY ART
20 storyboard drawings by Nick George, pastel &
charcoal on 8-1/2 x 6" storyboard sheets,
SR/Spring/95 (1500-2500) 2140
4 colored large-image storyboard drawings of
Donald & Spike, pastel & charcoal on
8-7/16 x 5-5/16" storyboard sheets,
SR/Spring/97 (400-800) 520

BEE ON GUARD (1951)
ANIMATION DRAWINGS
2 full-figure matching drawings: angry Donald Duck
(disguised as bee) standing in fighting pose
looking back, surprised Buzz Buzz flying
backwards; 5-1/2 x 5", 3/4 x 3/4",
HL/Oct 6/96 (300-400) 345
CELS – FULL FIGURE
Mischievous Donald stands forcing bee into glass
jar at spearpoint, 7-3/4", on four 9 x
12-1/2" cel levels, SR/Fall/96 (900-1500) 1320

BELLBOY DONALD (1942)
CEL SET-UPS
Full figure of bellhop Donald Duck standing at
attention facing right & saluting, 5",
airbrushed Courvoisier background &
label, S/Jun 21/97 (1000-1500) 1955

BEN AND ME (1953)
ANIMATION DRAWINGS/LAYOUT ART (also see CELS
- FULL FIGURE)
27 animation & layout drawings, 4 x 3-1/2" to
8-1/2 x 7-1/2", HL/Apr 23/95 (500-1000) 952
Full-figure drawing of angry Amos standing holding
charred tail, 5 x 3-1/4", HL/Oct 6/96

(300-500) 431
Full-figure detailed rough drawing of Ben Franklin
walking while whistling & twirling cane, 8 x
5-1/2", HL/May 31/97 (100-200) 196
BACKGROUNDS
Watercolor-on-paper production background of
candleholder on edge of table, inscription
& 2 illegible signatures, CE/Jun 18/94
(1500-2000) 978
Production background of 2 partial shoes w/wooden
floor between, sight 10 x 12", watercolor on
board, CLA/Jun 7/97 (700-900) 633
CEL SET-UPS
Portrait of smiling Ben Franklin looking behind
him with Amos in his hat, 7-1/2", printed
background of indoors, S/Dec 19/97
(600-800) 920
CELS – FULL FIGURE
Amos writing, 4", CE/Jun 9/95 (600-800) 253
2 cels: full figure of hatless Ben Franklin walking
away looking back over left shoulder, 7-1/2";
Amos, 4" length; CE/Jun 20/96 (700-900) 460
Smiling Amos standing looking up, pointing with
left hand, right hand behind back, 6",
S/Jun 21/97 (800-1200) 805
Ben Franklin walks toward camera, holding cane,
looking right; w/near-match animation drawing,
6-3/4 x 4", VF, HL/Apr 25/98 (600-800) 518
CELS – PARTIAL FIGURE
Chest-up close-up of ebullient Ben Franklin looking
left with Amos in hat brim, 7-1/2 x 9-1/2",
VF+, HL/Apr 23/95 (900-1200) 1232
Amos Mouse takes notes while flying in kite, 7 x
5-1/2", F, HL/Aug 6/95 (300-500) 420
CONCEPT AND INSPIRATIONAL ART
Concept drawing of Amos arriving at exterior of
Ben Franklin's print shop, S/Jun 10/95
(600-900) 747
Concept art of Ben Franklin flying kite with key
attached, gouache on paper, sight 6 x 8",
S/Jun 21/97 (600-800) 460
DYE-TRANSFER PRINTS
Full figure of Amos inside mouse-hole home, 8-1/2
x 12", VF, HL/Nov 19/95 (75-100) 374

THE BIG BAD WOLF (1934)
ANIMATION DRAWINGS
Big Bad Wolf (5"), 2 Little Pigs (3"), Little Red Riding
Hood, 2 animation drawings, CE/Jun 18/94
(1000-1500) 920
1930s drawing of Big Bad Wolf (4") snagged by
tree branch attempting to flee, S/Dec 17/94
(600-800) 575
CELS – FULL FIGURE
Stalking Wolf peers thru bushes, 4 x 7",
S/Dec 17/94 (1500-2000) 1150
Practical Pig shovels red-hot coals, 4",
S/Jun 10/95 (800-1200) 575
Fifer Pig & Fiddler Pig shake hands, 3-1/2" each,
needs restoration, S/Jun 19/96 (700-900) 747
Wolf disguised as fairy supported by ropes, 4",
S/Jun 21/97 (1000-1500) 1380
CELS – PARTIAL FIGURE
Little Red Riding Hood (approx. waist up) carries
basket & points to left, 5-1/2", S/Jun 21/97
(800-1200) 1035
Little Red Riding Hood speaking to disguised Wolf at
bedside; 2 pig derrieres peeking out from under
bed from *The Three Little Pigs*; each sheet
9-1/2 x 12"; S/Jun 21/97 (1200-1800) 1380
MODEL ART
2 model sheets of wolf; photo stat; script; 2 pages
of notes, CE/Jun 9/95 (400-600) 633

THE BIG WASH (1948)
ANIMATION DRAWINGS
Full-figure drawing of Goofy on scaffold with brush,
7-1/2 x 10", color model notes,
HL/Nov 19/95 (500-700) 575
4 drawings of Goofy: screaming on swinging scaffold
(*The Big Wash*); dressed in fur coat (*Polar Trappers*); in band (*Amateur Hour* [sic]); one from
Mickey's Service Station; each sheet 9-1/2
x 12"; S/Dec 19/97 (800-1200) 920

BILLPOSTERS (1940)
BACKGROUNDS
Master watercolor background of shack and

---

wall, 23-1/4 x 8-3/8", SR/Spring/96
(2500-5000) 2000

BLUE RHYTHM (1931)
BACKGROUNDS
Full figures of Mickey (3-1/2") chasing Minnie (3-1/4")
on stage from *The Grocery Boy*, watercolor
production background from *Blue Rhythm*,
CE/Dec 18/97 (10,000-15,000) 16,100
STORY ART
Partial preliminary storyboard of Mickey & piano,
3 pages in graphite, CE/Dec 16/94
(1000-1500) 2990

BOAT BUILDERS (1938)
ANIMATION DRAWINGS
Drawing of smiling Mickey saluting while hanging
from mast, 8 x 7", HL/Apr 23/95 (500-700) 672
Half-image drawing of Admiral Mickey climbing to
left, 4 x 2", 12-field sheet, inker's notation,
SR/Fall/96 (300-600) 370
Full-figure drawing of Mickey hanging upside down
from mast, 8 x 7", VF, HL/Nov 16/97
(500-700) 460
TITLE ART
Title card: Admiral Mickey on deck holding plans,
watercolor & gouache w/title hand-lettered
on cel overlay, 12-field, original production
cover flap signed by Walt, SR/Fall/94
(2500-4500) 4360

BONE BANDIT (1948)
CEL SET-UPS
Full figure of angry Pluto muzzled & on leash in front
of his dog house, 6", watercolor production
background, S/Jun 21/97 (1000-1500) 1610

BONE TROUBLE (1940)
ANIMATION DRAWINGS
Full-figure drawing of smiling Pluto sitting facing left
in front of his distorted image, 6-1/4", 12-field,
inker's notations, SR/Fall/95 (300-700) 460
Full-figure drawing of 2 Plutos: normal & wildly
distorted by fun house mirror, 5-1/2 x 6-1/2",
HL/Apr 28/96 (500-700) 460
BACKGROUNDS
Half image of eager Pluto looking up (one ear up)
while lying down from *Talking Dog*, 6"; master
watercolor background of Butch's barrel from
Bone Trouble, SR/Fall/96 (2000-5000) 1700
CEL SET-UPS
Pluto walks into Hall of Mirrors, pan master
background (watercolor on background sheet),
8-1/2 x 32", HL/Nov 13/94 (5000-7000) 5040
Full figure of angry Butch lying guarding bone,
matching master background (tempera
on background sheet) 8 x 10-1/2",
HL/Apr 28/96 (2000-3000) 1380

BOOTLE BEETLE (1947)
Also see UNIDENTIFIED/MISCELLANEOUS: BOO-
TLE BEETLE
CEL SET-UPS
Full figure of Donald on hands & knees looking thru
magnifying glass, 3", 12-field cel, color print
background of outdoors from *Donald's
Garden*, SR/Spring/97 (700-1000) 730
CELS – FULL FIGURE
Young Bootle Beetle standing & smiling eagerly,
5 x 3-1/4", late 1940s, VF+, HL/May 31/97
(200-300) 575

THE BRAVE ENGINEER (1950)
MODEL ART
2 stat model sheets: Casey Jones & Casey Jones Jr.
from *Dumbo*; both 14 x 11", some wrinkling
SR/Spring/95 (200-400) 240

BRAVE LITTLE TAILOR (1938)
ANIMATION DRAWINGS
3 drawings of Mickey, framed together, 5" avg.,
S/Dec 16/93 (1500-2500) 2588
Drawing of Mickey sitting chin in hands, production
notes, 4", S/Dec 16/93 (400-600) 920
2 drawings: forlorn Mickey, 4"; giant, 6";
S/Jun 17/94 (700-900) 747

Drawing of woeful Mickey sitting on rock, 4 x 4",
HL/Aug 21/94 (600-800)   1344
Full-figure drawing of Mickey walking away looking
fearfully over shoulder, 4-1/2 x 3-1/2",
HL/Nov 13/94 (600-800)   560
2 full-figure drawings: Minnie standing facing left,
leaning forward, left hand cupped to mouth,
mouth open, 3/3/4"; Mickey standing facing
right, holding scissors, reeling with lipstick on
face, 5-5/8"; 12-field sheets, some wear &
discoloration, SR/Spring/95 (800-1200)   1270
Full-figure drawing of confident Mickey standing,
4-3/4 x 3", HL/Apr 23/95 (500-700)   1120
Full-figure drawing of astonished Mickey standing
staring toward right, 5-1/8", 12-field sheet,
SR/Fall/95 (500-1000)   750
Full-figure drawing of smiling Mickey with color
notes & painter's timing chart, 4-1/2 x 3",
HL/Nov 19/95 (1000-1500)   978
Drawing of Princess Minnie & Mickey making eyes at
each other [from carousel-riding scene], 5 x 6",
HL/Nov 19/95 (800-1000)   1840
2 full-figure drawings: awed Mickey looking up, angry
Mickey walking right with hands in fists
overhead; 5" to 6", 12-field sheets; various
production, inker & camera notations, edge
wear, SR/Spring/96 (5000-10,000)   6500
5 sequential drawings: 3 of Mickey in giant's cuff,
giant reaching into sleeve for Mickey, Mickey
cutting himself out with sheers, 6-5/8" to
7-1/4", notations, SR/Spring/96
(1000-2000)   1960
Full-figure extreme drawing of sitting Giant holding
well as Mickey dangles from rope, w/notes,
7-1/2 x 6", HL/Apr 28/96 (600-800)   575
Full-figure drawing of sitting Giant flicking Mickey
aside, w/notes, 7-1/2 x 10", HL/Apr 28/96
(600-800)   575
Full-figure drawing of hatless, pleading Mickey
standing facing right, 4-1/4", 12-field,
inker's notation, Art Props stamp,
SR/Fall/96 (500-1000)   550
2 full-figure drawings: Mickey stands with scissors
raised & kisses on face, 6-1/2", camera
notation; admiring Minnie stands facing
left, 4-1/8", timer's chart; 12-field sheets;
SR/Fall/96 (800-1200)   1920
2 full-figure drawings: nervous Mickey standing
holding hat, front view of determined King
standing looking down, 5 x 2-1/2",
5 x 5-1/2", HL/Oct 6/96 (1000-1500)   978
4 drawings: Mickey walking proudly to left; Mickey's
cottage w/cart of pumpkins to left; 2 of Giant
picking up well to take drink with Mickey
attached; Mickey 5", Giant 7", S/Dec 14/96
(1200-1800)   1265
3 drawings: Mickey sitting & looking glum, 5"; color
model drawing of King, 5"; Giant sitting
contentedly, 7"; S/Dec 14/96 (800-1200)   1495
Full-figure drawing of angry Mickey facing left
w/head down & fists upraised, 4 x 4-1/2",
HL/Feb 23/97 (600-800)   1150
Full-figure rough drawing of angry Mickey stepping
left with fists clinched above head, 4-3/4",
12-field sheet, SR/Fall/97 (600-1000)   500
Near-full figure drawing of shocked hatless Mickey
standing, 4-1/2 x 3-1/2", VF, HL/Nov 16/97
(500-700)   748
Waist-up front-view drawing of Giant with arms up
looking down to see Mickey in his right sleeve,

7-3/4", 12-field sheet, SR/Spring/98
(500-900)   650

CEL SET-UPS
Minnie smiles, Courvoisier wood-veneer
background, 6-1/2" x 6-3/4",
CE/Dec 15/93 (4000-6000)   7130
Minnie smiles, Courvoisier watercolor background,
7" square, CE/Dec 15/93 (2000-2500)   3220
Mickey w/fly swatter in each hand & 7 flies,
wood-veneer Courvoisier background,
4", S/Jun 17/94 (3000-5000)   8050
Depressed Mickey sits on rock, 3-1/4 x 4",
Courvoisier wood-veneer background,
CE/Jun 18/94 (4000-6000)   6325
Smiling Princess Minnie on throne, complementary
Courvoisier watercolor & airbrush background,
label, inscribed, 7 x 6", HL/Aug 21/94
(2000-3000)   5152
Mickey peers from sleeve as giant raises hands,
6 x 8-1/2", over complementary watercolor
master background from Paul Terry cartoon,
HL/Nov 13/94 (2500-3500)   3360
Angry Mickey sits with garment on lap, looking up
at flies, reaching to left with hands, 4",
Courvoisier background of tailor shop interior
in watercolor on fruitwood veneer, ct,
SR/Spring/95 (2000-4000)   5400
Near-full figure of Giant pulling up a well, 8", wood-
veneer Courvoisier background, S/Jun 10/95
(3000-5000)   5462
Full figure of depressed Mickey sitting on rock with
head in hands, 3-1/2" (not including feather),
airbrushed wood-veneer Courvoisier
background, mat inscribed "to ... Walt
Disney", S/Jun 10/95 (600-800)   5462
Full figure of whistling Mickey sewing garment,
7-1/4 x 6-1/4" overall, complementary
background, HL/Aug 6/95 (5000-7000)   6608
Full figure of confident Mickey Mouse winking &
punching air, 8 x 8", complementary
background as prepared for Courvoisier,
mat inscribed w/Disney signature by Studio
artist, HL/Nov 19/95 (5000-7000)   7188
Full figures of Princess Minnie (5-1/2") standing in
profile next to Mickey (5") standing reeling
with lipstick all over face, contemporary
watercolor background of castle interior by
Toby Bluth, CE/Dec 18/97 (8000-12,000)   9200
Depressed Mickey sits on rock with head in hands,
3-1/2" w/o feather, inscribed "To...Walt
Disney" on mat, airbrushed wood-veneer
Courvoisier background with framed reprint
of Courvoisier certificate, S/Dec 19/97
(4000-6000)   4600

CELS – FULL FIGURE
Awed Mickey looking up, 4-1/2 x 4",
HL/Apr 23/95 (4000-6000)   11,200
Non-production cel of awed Mickey looking straight
up, 4", CE/Jun 9/95 (1000-1500)   3450
Apprehensive Mickey walking, 4-1/2",
CE/Jun 9/95 (3000-5000)   3450
Publicity cel of triumphant Mickey, arms outstretched,
5-1/2 x 5-1/2" overall, on backing board for
Courvoisier, HL/Aug 6/95 (6000-9000)   7168
Angry Mickey in boxing pose facing right, 4 x
3-3/4", HL/Oct 6/96 (3000-5000)   5520
Princess Minnie (4") stands on tiptoes facing left with
hand cupped to mouth (needs restoration); 5
pieces matted & framed together: cels of Zazu
Pitts & Mae West (4-1/4" each) blowing horns
from Mother Goose Goes Hollywood, Practical
Pig (2-1/2") (both w/paint loss); pencil drawing
of Jiminy Cricket (3") holding up umbrella; head-
only pencil drawing of alarmed Pinocchio (3");
S/Jun 21/97 (1800-2200)   1840
Depressed Mickey sitting with hands on sides of
face, 3-1/2 x 4-1/4", VF, HL/Nov 16/97
(400-600)   690

CELS – PARTIAL FIGURE
Near-full figure of anxious King sitting leaning
forward & looking down, 6-1/2", ct,
SR/Fall/96 (600-1000)   730

CONCEPT AND INSPIRATIONAL ART
4 character studies of townsfolk, 4 x 3-1/2" to
5 x 5", HL/Nov 19/95 (400-600)   345

MODEL ART (also see ANIMATION DRAWINGS)
Photostatic model sheet of Mickey, 12 x 10",
SR/Spring/95 (200-400)   140
3 model drawings: seated Giant reaching down,

triumphant Mickey, the King standing making
'stop' gesture; 4-1/2 x 4", 6 x 7", 6 x 5",
HL/Oct 6/96 (700-1000)   920

BROKEN TOYS (1935)
ANIMATION DRAWINGS/LAYOUT ART
Layout drawing & full-figure animation drawing of
Aunt Jemima doll, 8 x 10" & 5-1/2 x 3",
HL/Nov 19/95 (700-1000)   690

BUBBLE BEE (1949)
TITLE ART
Title card: full figure of happy Spike on hands &
knees riding atop pink bubble, watercolor
& airbrush on board w/title hand lettered
on cel overlay, 12-field, SR/Spring/95
(2000-5000)   2000

BUGS IN LOVE (1932)
CONCEPT AND INSPIRATIONAL ART
11 sheets of studies of bugs, accessories and
backgrounds, CE/Jun 18/94 (500-700)   1725
LAYOUT ART
4 background layout drawings, 7 x 9" & similar,
CE/Jun 18/94 (400-600)   483
2 layout drawings: junk pile, bug mob with common
items as weapons; 8 x 10", 6-1/2 x 19",
HL/Apr 28/96 (500-700)   173
STORY ART
9-page preliminary storyboard, CE/Dec 16/94
(600-800)   345

BUILDING A BUILDING (1933)
ANIMATION DRAWINGS
Full-figure drawing of Minnie running left with box
lunches, 9-1/2 x 12", CE/Dec 15/93
(300-500)   632
Full-figure drawing of Mickey & Minnie standing on
girder as flying rivets destroy it behind them,
both 2-1/2", CE/Jun 18/94 (700-900)   1495
Drawing of Minnie carrying picnic basket & lunches,
4", CE/Jun 18/94 (700-900)   690
Full-figure drawing of Mickey & Minnie on girder
that's being shot behind them by hot rivets,
6 x 10-1/2", HL/Apr 28/96 (800-1200)   834
4 drawings in sequence of Mickey pulling fish
skeleton from submarine sandwich, 3-1/2
x 3-1/2" to 3-1/2 x 4", VF, HL/Nov 16/97
(2000-2500)   3220
LAYOUT ART
Layout drawing w/4 sequential images of Minnie
(2 w/Pluto) as she drives lunch wagon, 8-1/2
x 48", on pan animation sheet, notes &
stamps, HL/Apr 23/96 (1500-2000)   4256
Detailed layout drawing of Pegleg Pete grabbing
Mickey & dropping him off building platform,
8 x 10-1/2", on background sheet,
HL/Nov 19/95 (1200-1600)   2760

THE CACTUS KID (1930)
ANIMATION DRAWINGS
2 full-figure drawings of Pete riding away with Minnie
as hostage, 5-3/4", 12-field sheets, some edge
discoloration, SR/Fall/94 (600-900)   700
35 sequential animation drawings of sitting Mickey
[playing piano], six w/o stool, 6", rest w/stool,
7-1/4", 12-field sheets, some w/inker's
notations, some w/exposure stamp, edge wear
& discoloration, SR/Fall/94 (7000-12,000)   8500
Full-figure rough drawing of Mickey playing piano,
7-1/4", CE/Jun 9/95 (600-800)   4600
Full-figure drawing of Mickey sitting on piano stool
w/arms in playing position, 7", S/Jun 10/95
(600-800)   575
Full-figure front-view drawing of Mickey dancing,
12-field sheet, SR/Fall/95 (500-1000)   1400
6 full-figure drawings of determined Mickey sitting
on stool playing piano keys, 7", 12-field
sheets, SR/Fall/95 (1800-3000)   1900
Full-figure front-view drawing of Mickey sitting
on piano stool, 5-3/4", 12-field sheet,
SR/Spring/96 (800-1600)   800
Full-figure drawing of Mickey sitting on stool playing
piano keys, 12-field sheet, SR/Spring/96
(800-1600)   1430
3 full-figure drawings of Mickey playing unseen piano,
5-1/2" ea., CE/Jun 20/96 (1000-1500)   978

Full-figure drawing of Peg Leg Pedro firing six-gun
back to left as he rides off to right with
screaming Minnie, 5-3/4", 12-field sheet,
camera notation, SR/Fall/96 (400-800) 640

Full-figure drawing of Mickey sitting on piano stool,
hands stretched above keys, 8-3/4 x 7-1/2",
12-field sheet, SR/Fall/96 (800-1600) 900

Full-figure drawing of Peg Leg Pedro riding horse to
right, holding screaming Minnie in one hand,
firing back with six-gun with other, 6-13/16",
12-field sheet, SR/Fall/97 (600-900) 540

LAYOUT ART
Layout drawing of Minnie sitting on bar talking to
mirror, 4", CLA/Jun 7/97 (2000-3000) 4830

CALIFORNY 'ER BUST (1945)
CEL SET-UPS
Full figure of bored Goofy in saddle of weary horse
stepping to left, 6 x 6-1/2", painted background
of large circle on solid field, S/Dec 14/96
(700-900) 1265

CAMP DOG (1950)
BACKGROUNDS
Master background of valley w/stream, 9 x 11-1/2",
tempera on background sheet, HL/Aug 6/95
(1000-1500) 1792

Master background of full moon rising over hill,
9 x 11-1/2", tempera on background sheet,
HL/Nov 19/95 (1000-1500) 920

CEL SET-UPS
Bent-Tail & Bent-Tail Junior prepare to dine, 5" and
smaller, key watercolor production background,
CE/Jun 18/94 (1500-2000) 1150

CAMPING OUT (1934)
ANIMATION DRAWINGS
4 drawings of Mickey & unruly campers, 10 x 12",
CE/Dec 15/93 (500-700) 690

CANINE CADDY (1941)
ANIMATION DRAWINGS
2 full-figure drawings: frustrated golfer Mickey Mouse
gripping club, surprised Pluto as caddy; 6 x 6",
5-1/2 x 6"; HL/Nov 19/95 (1000-1500) 1495

Full-figure drawing of determined Mickey swinging
club, 6-1/2 x 4-1/4", HL/Mar 16-17/96
(400-600) 863

2 full-figure drawings: Pluto caddying, golfer Mickey
swinging; drawing from *Donald's Golf Game*
(1938): Donald Duck holding golf club; each
sheet 10 x 12", S/Dec 19/97 (1000-1500) 1610

CEL SET-UPS
Full figure of smiling golfer Mickey holding driver
in right hand, looking into distance with left
hand shielding eyes, standing by hole with
flagstick on ground, 6-1/4", watercolor
production background, CE/Dec 18/97
(10,000-15,000) 9775

LAYOUT ART
3 layout drawings of Mickey Mouse golfing,
3-1/2 x 4-1/2", 5-1/2 x 6", 5 x 7",
HL/Apr 23/95 (700-1000) 1456

2 layout drawings of Pluto, 8-1/2 x 10" & 5 x
8-1/2", HL/Apr 23/95 (500-700) 2464

2 layout sketches: Mickey & Pluto, Pluto examining
ball; 6 x 8-1/2" & 5 x 10"; VF+;
HL/Nov 16/97 (400-600) 633

CANINE CASANOVA (1945)
CELS – FULL FIGURE
Large image of surprised Pluto sitting looking left
& 5 puppies, 7-1/2 x 7-1/2", restored, VF,
HL/Apr 10/94 (1000-1500) 1008

CANINE PATROL (1945)
CEL SET-UPS
Full figure of angry turtle on back, 7" diameter, master
background (watercolor on background sheet)
from *The Ugly Duckling*, Courvoisier label,
HL/Apr 23/95 (1500-2000) 2128

CELS -- FULL FIGURE
Front view of sitting turtle with shell on backwards,
3-3/8", ct, SR/Fall/96 (400-800) 510

CANVAS BACK DUCK (1953)

CELS – FULL FIGURE
Front view of Donald standing with both hands on
his vest, looking down; 3-1/2 x 2-1/4"; F+;
HL/Apr 25/98 (300-500) 173

CASEY BATS AGAIN (1954)
ANIMATION DRAWINGS
12 full-figure sequential animation drawings by
Freddie Moore of Patsy swinging bat,
SR/Fall/95 (1000-1800) 2180

Full-figure extreme drawing of scheming Casey
standing pointing to bat raised in right hand,
7-1/2 x 5-1/2", HL/May 31/97 (300-500) 690

CEL SET-UPS
6-piece band, 10-1/2 x 14-1/2", with Art Props
background painting, plus publicity still,
HL/Nov 19/95 (800-1200) 805

CELS – FULL FIGURE
Mrs. Casey holding baby, 6 x 5-1/2", VF,
HL/Apr 10/94 (400-600) 336

One of Casey's daughters prepares to batter-up with
eyes closed, 6", S/Dec 17/94 (300-500) 172

Pleading Mrs. Casey standing facing right, holding
infant in right arm, left arm out palm up,
6-1/4", 12-field, SR/Fall/95 (300-600) 300

Confident Casey stands facing right, holding bat
upright with one finger, right hand on hip,
5", 12-field, SR/Fall/95 (300-600) 580

CELS -- PARTIAL FIGURE
Triumphant Casey (eyes closed) tips hat & holds
cigar at back of "Casey's Girls Special"
trolley car as 9 daughters fill in behind him,
7", SR/Spring/96 (1000-1600) 1000

Triumphant Casey (eyes closed) tips hat & holds
cigar at back of "Casey's Girls Special"
trolley car as 9 daughters fill in behind him,
7-5/8", 16-field cel, ct, SR/Spring/97
(1000-1600) 830

TITLE ART
Title card: diamond & baseball gear painted in gouache
on background, hand lettering w/floral scrollwork
on cel overlay, 12-field, w/original production
cover flap, SR/Fall/95 (1500-2200) 1500

THE CASTAWAY (1931)
ANIMATION DRAWINGS
3 drawings: tiger cub at piano keys, sitting on tree
branch, & being held up by angry Mickey,
4 x 3-1/2", 2-1/2 x 3", 5-1/2 x 6",
HL/Nov 19/95 (900-1200) 1610

2 drawings of Mickey holding tiger cub, 6-1/4
x 6" & 2-3/4 x 2-1/2", HL/Feb 23/97
(700-1000) 633

THE CHAIN GANG (1930)
BACKGROUNDS
Original 12-field black-&-white watercolor production
background w/notes, CE/Jun 18/94
(1500-2000) 1955

LAYOUT ART
2 layout drawings of Mickey Mouse, 6-1/2" &
similar, CE/Jun 18/94 (1500-2000) 3680

CHICKEN IN THE ROUGH (1951)
CEL SET-UPS
Full figure of Dale lying on ground with hands over
eyes amid egg-shell pieces under acorn-laden
tree limb, 2-1/8", three 12-field cel levels key
to each other, color print background of
outdoors, ct, SR/Spring/98 (400-700) 400

TITLE ART
Title card: angry Chip stands watching Dale (3-3/4")
wave from inside egg shell, title on cel overlay,
airbrushed watercolor background, 12-field,
original production cover flap, ct, SR/Fall/96
(2500-4500) 2530

CHICKEN LITTLE (1943)
BACKGROUNDS
Full figure of flirtatious mermaid sitting on rock
under waterfall, 8 x 10" from *Peter Pan*;
master background from *Chicken Little*
(tempera & watercolor on background
sheet), VF+, HL/Oct 6/96 (1200-1600) 1610

CELS – FULL FIGURE
Foxey Loxey stands engrossed in book, 7-3/8 x
5-3/4", 12-field, w/transparent-painted shadow,

SR/Fall/95 (300-600) 300

THE CHINA SHOP (1934)
LAYOUT ART
2 layout drawings: fracas aftermath; shopkeeper
changing window sign; 12-field sheets;
annotated production stamps; SR/Fall/97
(1800-2400) 1460

CHIPS AHOY (1956)
CEL SET-UPS
Full figures of Dale & Chip (behind Dale) on deck
of toy boat, 4", full-frame image of boat
hand inked & painted on cel, watercolor
display background of sky, SR/Spring/96
(900-1500) 900

Full figure of mischievous Donald launching sailboat
with Chip & Dale aboard, Studio Art Props
background painting (tempera on background
board), 8 x 11", HL/Oct 6/96 (1200-1500) 920

CELS – FULL FIGURE
7" Donald, S/Dec 16/93 (1000-1200) 690

Angry Admiral Chip stands facing toward right with
puffed-up chest & hands in fists, red & gold
label as sold at DL, 4-3/4 x 3-3/4", VF,
HL/Apr 25/98 (300-400) 489

CELS – PARTIAL FIGURE
Near-full figure of Donald holding sailboat up to eye
level to inspect chipmunks on deck, 6" long,
CE/Dec 12/96 (800-1200) 1035

DYE-TRANSFER PRINTS
Chip & Dale tiptoeing sailboat on dock by Donald,
13 x 9", SR/Fall/94 (300-600) 310

CLOCK CLEANERS (1937)
ANIMATION DRAWINGS
8 drawings of staggering Goofy, 5" avg. size,
S/Jun 10/95 (600-800) 2185

CEL SET-UPS
Full figure of smiling Mickey standing holding broom
& poking his finger [at sleeping stork], 3-1/3",
trimmed watercolor production background
of city dump from *Mickey's Trailer*,
S/Jun 21/97 (6000-8000) 5750

THE CLOCK WATCHER (1945)
CELS -- FULL FIGURE
Donald stands facing left, holding fish bowl in bowling
pose, 5-1/8", 12-field cel, transparent paint in
shadow & bowl, dry-brush effects, SR/Fall/96
(800-1200) 1270

COCK O' THE WALK (1935)
CONCEPT AND INSPIRATIONAL ART
Pencil character-design drawing of Hick Rooster, 5 x
5-1/2", VF, HL/Feb 26-27/94 (300-400) 385

COLD TURKEY (1951)
CEL SET-UPS
Full figure of apprehensive Pluto sitting in front of TV,
10-1/2 x 14-1/2", master background (tempera
on background sheet), HL/Apr 23/95 (2000-
2500) 3584

CONTRARY CONDOR (1944)
CEL SET-UPS
Full figure of optimistic Donald Duck standing on
mountain ledge facing right, looking up, 3-3/4",
12-field cel; gouache background painting;
SR/Spring/97 (600-1000) 750

CELS – FULL FIGURE
Determined Donald walking vertically w/plumbing
plungers on feet, 5", 12-field, ct,
SR/Spring/95 (900-1200) 1300

Front view of angry Donald standing looking left with
fists clinched, 3-1/4", 12-field, SR/Spring/96
(800-1200) 880

THE COOKIE CARNIVAL (1935)
CONCEPT AND INSPIRATIONAL ART
2 concept drawings by Albert Hurter: rolling pin float,
ridden by cookie men in ice cream cone hats &
pulled by peppermint horses, black & colored
pencil on 7-1/2 x 5-1/4" paper; angel food
cake figure; pencil & watercolor on 3-3/4 x

5-1/2" paper, SR/Fall/95 (300-700)   330

CORN CHIPS (1951)
CELS – FULL FIGURE
Angry Donald jumping, 4 x 4-1/2", VF,
HL/Apr 10/94 (500-700)   476
Donald in winter clothes carrying fireplace roaster
& bowl, signed by Jack Hannah, 6 x 7",
HL/Aug 21/94 (700-1000)   952
Frightened Donald fleeing, DL label, 4-1/2 x 8",
HL/Aug 21/94 (600-900)   728
Combative Chip & Dale, 4 x 2-1/2" each,
HL/Nov 19/95 (800-1000)   805
Cheerful Donald standing watching bundle in his
hands, 4-1/2 x 3-1/4", HL/Oct 6/96
(500-700)   460
Devilish Donald Duck facing left holding shovel
horizontally, signed by Jack Hannah, 6-1/2
x 8" with signature, VF+, HL/Nov 16/97
(700-1000)   633
Warmly dressed Donald stands ready to swing ax,
3-1/2 x 2-3/4", VF, HL/Apr 25/98
(500-700)   489
TITLE ART
Title card: Chip & Dale with popcorn from spilled bag,
hand-lettered title, two cel levels over watercolor
background, airbrushed shading, 12-field,
original production cover flap, SR/Spring/96
(2500-4500)   2500
Matching title cel & master background (airbrush &
tempera on background board): happy Chip &
Dale sit amid spilled bag of popcorn under title,
with Studio's original titled cover sheet, 8-1/2
x 11", VF+, HL/Apr 25/98 (2400-2800)   3910

THE COUNTRY COUSIN (1936)
ANIMATION DRAWINGS
2 drawings of Abner, 5-1/2 x 7" & 5 x 4",
HL/Feb 23/97 (400-500)   460
ART – MISCELLANEOUS
Monty on match box looking thru eyeglasses at Abner,
5-1/2 x 9", pencil study for publicity illustration,
pencil & gray wash on heavyweight paper,
HL/Nov 19/95 (600-900)   1265
Two-sheet gag idea by Charles Payzant of Abner
falling into ice-cube tray, both 12 x 8-7/16",
SR/Fall/96 (400-900)   410
CEL SET-UPS
Abner cleans ear with handkerchief, airbrushed
background, Courvoisier label, 6-1/2",
S/Jun 17/94 (1200-1800)   1035
Full figure of skeptical Abner standing on hill,
5-1/2 x 5-1/2", complementary airbrush
background, Courvoisier label,
HL/Apr 23/95 (1200-1600)   1568
CELS – FULL FIGURE
Eager Abner holding furled umbrella & looking up,
3 x 4", HL/Aug 6/95 (1000-1500)   1008
Sophisticate Monty stands examining tidbit of cheese
as he tosses another bit away, 6-1/2 x 5-1/2",
HL/Oct 6/96 (700-1000)   690
MODEL ART
Model sheet of Abner, 4" each, CLA/Jun 7/97
(700-900)   863

CRAZY OVER DAISY (1950)
CELS – FULL FIGURE/MODEL ART
Color model cel of dressed-up Donald riding
high-wheel bicycle to left, holding package;
dry brush effects; 6" on 12-field cel; ct;
SR/Spring/97 (300-600)   300

CRAZY WITH THE HEAT (1947)
CELS – PARTIAL FIGURE
Hips-up view of surprised Goofy (dressed for
desert) looking left, 5-1/2 x 4-1/2", VF,
HL/Apr 10/94 (600-800)   840

CURED DUCK (1945)
ANIMATION DRAWINGS
Set of 2 rough full-figure drawings: Daisy standing
facing right, 5-1/4"; Donald, standing facing
left, holding hat & cigar, laughing with eyes
closed, 4-1/4"; 12-field sheets, camera
direction & timer's chart; some discoloration
& wear; SR/Fall/96 (600-1200)   610
CELS – FULL FIGURE

Daisy Duck, 7", CE/Dec 16/94 (600-800)   920

DADDY DUCK (1948)
BACKGROUNDS
Master background (tempera on background sheet)
of interior of Donald Duck's house wi/full-figure
cel of Pluto walking with bone from another
production (likely from same period), 8 x 11",
studio notes, HL/Apr 23/95 (1500-2000)   1456

THE DELIVERY BOY (1931)
ANIMATION DRAWINGS
3 drawings: full figure of sitting Mickey playing
trombone, 3-1/2 x 4"; full figure of sitting
Minnie playing trumpet, 4"; piano;
S/Jun 21/97 (800-1200)   1265

DER FUEHRER'S FACE (1943)
CEL SET-UPS/MODEL ART
Early promotional cel: Donald speaking angrily into
phone, airbrushed background, Walt Disney
signature, 5", S/Jun 17/94 (2500-3500)   2587
Color model cel of Donald sitting at table by wall
safe eating & reading *Mein Kampf* as bayonet
pierces book, 4-7/8", 12-field, gouache display
background, ct, SR/Spring/95 (1500-2000)   2780
Full-figure publicity cel of angry Donald Duck talking
on telephone, 5", airbrushed Courvoisier background & label, S/Jun 21/97 (2000-3000)   2875
CELS – FULL FIGURE
Nazi Donald goose-steps to right with arm upraised
at point of 2 bayonets, 6-1/4", 12-field cel,
SR/Spring/96 (1200-1800)   2580
4-man Nutzi band with irritated Donald Duck
struggling to carry bass drum, 3 x 7-1/2",
HL/Oct 6/96 (1000-1500)   2300

THE DOGNAPPER (1934)
ANIMATION DRAWINGS
Full-figure drawing of Officers Mickey on motorcycle
& Donald in sidecar with wide separation,
detailed color guide, 9 x 11", CE/Dec 15/93
(800-1000)   920
Drawing of Mickey & Donald riding motorcycle
plus 2 early drawings of Mickey Mouse;
S/Jun 17/94 (1500-2000)   1265
Drawing of Policemen Mickey (2-1/5 x 2-1/2") on
motorcycle & Donald (1-1/2 x 1") in side car,
CE/Jun 18/94 (700-900)   690
Drawing of Mickey on motorcycle & Donald in
sidecar in hot pursuit, 3-1/2 x 7-1/2",
HL/Aug 21/94 (600-800)   1008
Full-figure drawing of Officer Donald, 4",
CE/Dec 16/94 (400-600)   288
Drawing of grinning Mickey & Minnie saluting each
other wearing police headgear, 3-1/2 x 5-1/2",
HL/Apr 23/95 (700-1000)   2240
Drawing of policeman Mickey riding motorcycle
w/speed lines, 4", S/Jun 10/95 (700-900)   920
2 sequential full-figure drawings of long-billed Donald
Duck standing, 2 x 2-1/2", HL/Aug 6/95
(700-1000)   924
Full-figure drawing of Mickey looking back while
running right into Donald (bill open), 3",
12-field sheet, SR/Fall/95 (400-800)   500
Full-figure drawing of Mickey driving motorcycle to left
as Donald flies backward, speed effects, 10 x
3-1/4", 12-field sheet, SR/Fall/95 (500-900)   600
Full-figure drawing of angry Officer Mickey holding
oversize pistol as ladder falls on him, 4-1/2 x
6-1/2", HL/Nov 19/95 (600-800)   1093
Full-figure drawing of Officer Mickey speeding on
motorcycle w/Officer Donald in sidecar,
4 x 8-1/2", HL/Nov 19/95 (600-900)   805
2 full-figure drawings: determined Officer Mickey
riding motorcycle, surprised long-billed
Officer Donald standing; 5 x 6-1/2",
4 x 3", HL/Apr 28/96 (700-900)   920
3 drawings: Mickey in policeman's uniform sitting
w/legs crossed & smiling, 3"; Pluto raised on
front paws w/back legs splayed behind him,
10"; Mickey sitting face forward, 3";
S/Dec 14/96 (1000-1500)   575
Full-figure drawing of Officer Mickey riding motorcycle
to left (with speed lines) as Officer Donald falls
backward thru air, 4-1/2 x 11", VF,
HL/Nov 16/97 (500-700)   863

Drawing of Officer Mickey on motorcycle facing left,
3-1/2 x 4" overall, S/Dec 19/97 (700-900)   1150
2 full-figure drawings: Officer Mickey on one foot
reaching for handle on closed door, 3 x 4";
Officer Donald standing in low crouch facing
left, 3 x 3-1/2"; S/Dec 19/97 (800-1200)   1035
Full-figure drawing of Officer Mickey riding motorcycle
to left with Donald in sidecar, 7-1/2 x 3-3/8",
including puffs of exhaust, 12-field sheet,
SR/Spring/98 (500-900)   1090
LAYOUT ART
Pan layout drawing of Pegleg Pete in pursuit of Officers
Mickey & Donald in sawmill, 9 x 43", on pan
sheet, HL/Nov 19/95 (1200-1600)   4370

DONALD AND PLUTO (1936)
CELS – FULL FIGURE
Startled Pluto sees he's stuck to plumber's plunger,
3-1/2 x 5", HL/Nov 13/94 (600-900)   1792

DONALD AND THE WHEEL (1961)
BACKGROUNDS
Full figure of Madame Mim as spotted dragon sitting
throwing temper tantrum, 7-1/4", *The Sword
in the Stone*; gouache production background
from *Donald and the Wheel*, 16-field,
SR/Fall/94 (600-1000)   610

DONALD APPLECORE (1952)
CELS – PARTIAL FIGURE
Waist-up of Donald admiring shiny apple, 5-1/2",
12-field, ct, SR/Fall/95 (500-900)   550
Determined Farmer Donald holding handle, 4-1/2
x 3", F+, HL/Nov 19/95 (500-700)   345

DONALD DOES EASTER (UNPRO-
DUCED, 1950s)
STORY ART
11 storyboard drawings of Donald & Chipmunks
fighting over candy, charcoal & pastel on
8-7/16 x 5-15/16" storyboard sheets,
SR/Spring/96 (600-1200)   660

DONALD GETS DRAFTED (1942)
CEL SET-UPS
Angry Donald peels potatoes, airbrushed Courvoisier
background, WDP stamp & copyright, 6",
needs restoration, S/Jun 17/94 (600-800)   1840
Donald marches with rifle over shoulder & looks up,
watercolor Courvoisier background, WDP stamp,
5" (rifle 5-1/2"), S/Dec 17/94 (1800-2400)   1150
Full figure of soldier Donald Duck w/rifle tipping hat &
looking up, 7 x 8", complementary painted background, "WDP" monogram stamp, Courvoisier
label, HL/Apr 23/95 (900-1200)   2016
Full figure of angry Donald marching w/rifle on
shoulder, 5", watercolor Courvoisier back-
ground & label, HL/Nov 19/95 (900-1200)   1380
Full figure of Donald Duck marching with rifle on
shoulder, 6-1/2 x 8-1/2", painted background
as prepared by Courvoisier, HL/Nov 19/95
(1000-1500)   1610
Full figure of soldier Donald, rifle on shoulder, hand
to hat, facing toward right, looking up, 5-3/4",
Courvoisier watercolor background of army
camp, label, SR/Spring/96 (1600-2200)   1760
Large image of anxious soldier Donald with rifle on
shoulder & sweat pouring down face, airbrushed
Courvoisier background, needs restoration,
6-1/2", S/Jun 19/96 (1200-1800)   1725
Full figure of intimidated Soldier Donald with
bayonetted rifle on shoulder looking up to
right & tipping hat, 6-1/2", Courvoisier
label & watercolor background of landscape,
CLA/Jun 7/97 (1500-2000)   1265
Full-figure frontal of frightened soldier Donald
standing at attention, bayonetted rifle on
shoulder, right side of hat cut off, 7",
Courvoisier watercolor & airbrush
background, CLA/Jun 7/97 (1000-1500)   1150
Full figure of chastened Donald standing facing
right carrying bayonetted rifle on shoulder,
looking up & tipping hat, 5 1/2",
Courvoisier label & watercolor background
of desert, SR/Spring/98 (1400-2000)   1210
CELS – FULL FIGURE

Poster-like cel of soldiers marching in line over
lettering "Healthful Exercise", Courvoisier
label, 4", CE/Jun 20/96 (500-700)   230

DONALD IN MATHMAGIC LAND (1959)
CEL SET-UPS
Full figure of Donald in safari clothes holding rifle,
walking thru stylized forest to right, 4-1/2",
16-field cel, color print background,
SR/Fall/97 (600-900)   550
CELS – FULL FIGURE
Seven Greeks facing one in profile, avg. size 4",
S/Dec 16/93 (400-600)   345
4-1/4" Donald Duck bows to 6" red chess king,
gold DL label, S/Dec 16/93 (400-600)   460
Donald as Greek with lyre, 7 x 8", CE/Jun 18/94
(700-900)   1035
CELS – PARTIAL FIGURE
Near-full figure of contented Donald Duck, 5",
CE/Dec 16/94 (300-500)   173

DONALD'S BETTER SELF (1938)
CEL SET-UPS
Virtuous Donald (4-7/8", airbrushed halo) walking left,
followed by angry Donald (5") carrying books,
color print background, DAE seal, #117/500,
matted in watered silk with gold liner,
SR/Spring/96 (300-500)   880

DONALD'S CAMERA (1941)
CELS – FULL FIGURE
Angry Donald Duck, 2-1/2 x 3-1/2", restored, F+,
HL/Apr 10/94 (600-900)   672
Donald walking to right with camera & tripod,
4-1/2", CE/Jun 18/94 (1500-2000)   1150
Smiling Donald stands facing left with camera up &
right index finger in air, 5-1/8", 12-field cel,
restored, SR/Spring/98 (100-1500)   1100

DONALD'S COUSIN GUS (1939)
ANIMATION DRAWINGS
Matched pair of full-figure drawings: airborne Gus
holding umbrella & dish of fruit, Donald Duck
running w/hand cart; 4-1/2 x 3-1/2", 4 x 6";
HL/Nov 19/95 (600-900)   690
BACKGROUNDS
Original master background painting of interior
of Donald Duck's home, watercolor on
background sheet, 8-1/2 x 11",
HL/Apr 28/96 (2500-3000)   1840

DONALD'S CRIME (1945)
CELS -- FULL FIGURE
Donald & Daisy dance together with eyes closed,
4-1/4", 12-field cel, SR/Fall/96 (700-1200)   850

DONALD'S DIARY (1954)
CELS -- PARTIAL FIGURE
Hem-up figure of irritated Daisy standing in purple
bathrobe, curlers & kerchief on head, right
hand on hip, holding coffee pot, staring into
camera; 6-1/2; SR/Fall/96 (400-700)   510

DONALD'S DOG LAUNDRY (1940)
BACKGROUNDS
Panoramic watercolor master background of Donald's
backyard, SR/Spring/96 (2500-5000)   2500
Pan watercolor production background of outside
w/houses & trees, sight 8-1/2 x 41",
CE/Dec 12/96 (3000-4000)   4600
CEL SET-UPS
Full figures of surprised Pluto (4"), Butch (5-1/2"),
& 3 other dogs inspecting modified bathtub
(from another short) in backyard, watercolor
pan production background, CE/Dec 12/96
(12,000-15,000)   12,650

DONALD'S DREAM VOICE (1948)
CELS – FULL FIGURE
Dressed-up Donald with microphone, 4 x 4",
HL/Aug 21/94 (500-700)   840

DONALD'S FIRE SURVIVAL PLAN (EDUCATIONAL, 1966)

CELS – FULL FIGURE
Front view of angry fireman Donald pointing
at camera, 8-1/4 x 5-1/2", VF+,
HL/Apr 25/98 (400-500)   230

DONALD'S GARDEN (1942)
BACKGROUNDS
Full figure of Donald on hands & knees looking thru
magnifying glass, 3", 12-field cel from *Bootle
Beetle*; color print background from *Donald's
Garden*, SR/Spring/97 (700-1000)   730
Full figure of smiling Donald (dressed for *Old
MacDonald Duck*, carrying bucket) walking left,
looking back & up, 6", watercolor master back-
ground of outdoors from *Donald's Garden*,
SR/Spring/97 (3000-5000)   3080
Full figure of great bull facing right from *Farmyard
Symphony*, 5-1/4", 12-field cel, color print
background from *Donald's Garden*,
SR/Fall/97 (300-500)   200

DONALD'S GOLF GAME (1938)
ANIMATION DRAWINGS
2 full-figure drawings of Donald addressing golf ball,
4" & similar; drawing of Donald from *Modern
Inventions*, 7"; CE/Jun 20/96 (1000-1500)   1150
Drawing of Donald holding golf club; *Canine Caddy*
(1941): 2 full-figure drawings: Pluto caddying,
golfer Mickey swinging; each sheet 10 x 12";
S/Dec 19/97 (1000-1500)   1610
CEL SET-UPS
Wearing golf cap, holding golf club, standing on raft,
irritated Donald watches golf ball splash into
water, airbrushed background, inscribed
"To Dave Gearhart - my most rabid rooter -
donald duck", 4", framed, S/Dec 16/93
(2000-3000)   2875
Full figures of Donald (5-1/4") standing amid golf gear
arguing with bird perched on golf ball, Art Props
watercolor background, Courvoisier-style mat &
label, SR/Fall/94 (2000-4000)   3320
Full figures of Donald (3-1/2") readying driver as
innocent Huey (3") watches, Courvoisier
watercolor & airbrush background,
CE/Jun 9/95 (1500-2000)   3450
STORY ART
2 story drawings of Donald golfing, 5 x 5" & 6 x 4",
HL/Nov 13/94 (500-700)   1008

DONALD'S LUCKY DAY (1939)
ART – MISCELLANEOUS
4 scene drawings for publicity or magazine illustrations,
2-1/2 x 5-1/2" to 8 x 11", HL/Apr 23/95
(1000-1500)   3584
CELS – FULL FIGURE
Circa 1930s publicity cel: overhead view of delivery-
man Donald approaching black cat at corner of
13th Ave & 13th St., 2-1/2", CE/Jun 9/95
(1500-2000)   1380
CELS – PARTIAL FIGURE
Head-&-arms front view of Donald Duck sitting in
pile of fish bones, publication gouache on
celluloid, D.C. Heath Publications: *Donald
& His Friends, Donald's Lucky Day*, 1939,
4 x 8", S/Jun 19/96 (800-1200)   977
STORY ART
Full-figure colored story drawing of nervous Donald
Duck riding bike & clutching package, 5-1/2
x 7-1/2", F-VF, HL/Nov 19/95 (400-600)   1265
Full-figure story drawing of surprised Donald Duck
being hit in rump w/clothespins (one pinching
tail feathers), 5 x 7", HL/Mar 16-17/96
(300-500)   863
Story drawing by Carl Barks of panicked Donald
Duck, 6 x 7", HL/Oct 6/96 (800-1200)   805
TITLE ART
Title card: day calendar with Friday the 13th, 12-field,
original production cover flap signed by Walt,
SR/Fall/95 (500-900)   830

DONALD'S NEPHEWS (1938)
CELS – FULL FIGURE
Distressed Donald choking, notes, 3-1/2 x 5",
HL/Aug 21/94 (900-1200)   896
STORY ART
2 polished story drawings of Donald reacting to
nephews' offscreen antics, 4 x 5",

HL/Apr 28/96 (600-900)   920
2 mirror-image storyboard drawings of Donald winking,
holding book & patting himself, captioned
"Donald Pats Self on the Chest," signed by Carl
Barks, 4", CE/Dec 12/96 (1200-1500)   1150
7 polished original color story drawings, 4-1/2
x 5-3/4" to 4-1/2 x 7-1/2", F-VF overall,
HL/Nov 16/97 (1000-1500)   1495
6 story drawings, 4 x 5-1/2" to 5 x 6", VF,
HL/Nov 16/97 (1000-1500)   863
6 original color story drawings, 4 x 4-1/2" to
4-1/2 x 6", VF overall, HL/Nov 16/97
(1000-1500)   2070
7 colored story drawings, VF, HL/Nov 16/97
(1000-1500)   1265
6 story drawings plus colored illustration of nephews,
approx. 4 x 6" each, F-VF overall,
HL/Nov 16/97 (1000-1500)   1093
8 story drawings, 3 x 4-1/2" to 4 x 5-1/2", F-VF
overall, HL/Nov 16/97 (1000-1500)   1265

DONALD'S OFF DAY (1944)
BACKGROUNDS
Master background of bookshelf, 8-1/2 x 11-1/2",
watercolor on background sheet,
HL/Nov 19/95 (1500-2000)   1495
CELS – FULL FIGURE/MODEL ART
Angry Donald with golf clubs over shoulder,
3-1/2 x 6", HL/Nov 13/94 (600-900)   1064
Model cel: front view of Donald standing in nightclothes, left leg up, holding upraised golf club
in right hand, egg in left; from Basmajian
collection; 4 x 4-1/2"; F+; HL/Apr 25/98
(800-1200)   690
TITLE ART
Title card: full figures of Nephews carrying objects to
right; characters, shadows & hand lettering on 3
cel levels over watercolor background, prepared
w/production cover flap signed by Walt & Jack
Hanna, SR/Spring/95 (2000-5000)   2130
Matching production cel of Huey, Dewey, Louie over
title & master background art (airbrush on background sheet), 8 x 10-1/2", with camera instructions signed in pencil "Jack Hannah" & "Walt",
VF, HL/Nov 19/95 (2500-3500)   3910

DONALD'S OSTRICH (1937)
CEL SET-UPS
Full figures of Hortense (3-1/4") & Donald Duck
(3-3/4") stalking each other on train-station
platform, 12-field cels, watercolor pan
background painting, SR/Spring/98
(5000-9000)   4000
CELS – FULL FIGURE
Donald screams & waves right arm as ostrich picks
him up, 9-1/2 x 11-1/2", CE/Dec 15/93
(2500-3500)   2300

DONALD'S PENGUIN (1939)
ANIMATION DRAWINGS
Full-figure drawing of angry Donald standing holding
shotgun in right hand & opening door with left,
8", 12-field sheet, inker's notation,
SR/Spring/98 (300-600)   350
CEL SET-UPS
Angry Tootsie (3") sits looking away with folded arms
as Donald (7") eyes him suspiciously, airbrushed
Courvoisier background, S/Jun 17/94
(1800-2200)   2875
Angry Donald (4-1/2 x 2-3/4") holds shotgun on sad
Tootsie (2 x 1-1/2"), Courvoisier wood-veneer
background, CE/Jun 18/94 (2000-3000)   2760
Donald (5-1/4") holding Tootsie (eyes closed, 3-1/2"),
Courvoisier wood-veneer background,
CE/Dec 16/94 (2000-3000)   2760
Full figures of angry Donald w/shotgun confronting
frightened Tootsie, 7 x 8", complementary
painted woodgrain background as prepared
for Courvoisier, HL/Aug 6/95 (1500-2000)   2912
Full-figure portrait of Tootsie walking, Courvoisier
wood-veneer background, 3-1/2",
CE/Jun 20/96 (700-900)   920
Full figures of Donald standing (5"), right hand making
fist, left arm holding angry Tootsie (3") up by
neck, wood-veneer background,
CE/Dec 12/96 (1500-2000)   2185

DONALD'S SNOW FIGHT (1942)
CEL SET-UPS
Full-figure overhead view of bombs dropping on
panicked Admiral Donald (2") on top of
ice-encrusted ship, key master watercolor
background, 12-field, SR/Spring/96
(3000-7000)   3000
CELS – FULL FIGURE
Horrified Admiral Donald standing facing right
with left hand shielding eyes, 4-3/4",
12-field, SR/Spring/95 (900-1400)   1010
MODEL ART
2 original photostatic model sheets: *Dumb Bell of the
Yukon & Donald's Snow Fight*, both 13-3/4 x
11", SR/Fall/97 (300-400)   310

DONALD'S TIRE TROUBLE (1943)
TITLE ART
Title card on 4 levels: montage of original newspaper
clippings, transparent-painted shadow, Donald
& tire, title hand lettering; 12-field, w/original
production cover flap signed by Walt, newspaper
has yellowed, SR/Fall/94 (1800-2800)   1300

DONALD'S VACATION (1940)
CEL SET-UPS
Full figure of Donald (eyes closed) falling backward to
right toward half image of deck chair, 4-1/2";
8-1/4 x 15-3/4" key master watercolor back-
ground, SR/Fall/94 (2500-5000)   2530
TITLE ART
Original title with overlay cels & matching master
background (watercolor & airbrush on
background sheet), 9 x 11", VF+,
HL/Apr 28/96 (3500-4000)   3450

DON DONALD (1937)
CEL SET-UPS
Donald (3") serenades Donna Duck (4") who performs
Mexican Hat Dance, trimmed, airbrushed Courvoisier background & label, S/Jun 17/94
(1200-1800)   2875
Full figures of Donald (3") flirting with Daisy (4-3/4")
as she dances in hat, Courvoisier airbrush &
watercolor background, CE/Dec 16/94
(2000-3000)   4830
Full figure of donkey, 4", Courvoisier airbrush background & label, CE/Dec 16/94 (800-1200)   460
Full figure of Donald standing facing left by 2 small
cacti wearing oversize sombrero, peering into
distance, 4", Courvoisier background of
weathered plaster, some lifting paint, ct,
SR/Spring/96 (800-1400)   970
Full figures of haughty Donna [Daisy] Duck (eyes closed,
4-7/8") riding unicycle as Donald (in Mexican hat,
holding guitar, 5-5/8") follows
on burro, watercolor background of desert road,
SR/Spring/97 (1800-2200)   1820
CELS – FULL FIGURE
Serenading Donald sits on eager burro (standing
facing left), 5", 12-field, ct, SR/Spring/95
(1100-1600)   1630
Smiling Donald wearing sombrero & holding guitar,
rides donkey to right, 5-1/2 x 3-1/2" overall,
S/Jun 21/97 (1000-1500)   1265

DON'S FOUNTAIN OF YOUTH (1953)
TITLE ART
Title card: full figure of Donald sitting wearing baby hat
& being sprayed by fountain, both Donald & title
hand lettering on cel, fountain is watercolor &
gouache, 12-field, original production cover flap,
SR/Fall/94 (2500-4000)   2790
Matching original production cel of Donald (full figure)
sitting wearing baby hat & being sprayed by
fountain, title & master background painting
for title sequence (tempera & airbrush on
background sheet), 8 x 10", VF,
HL/Nov 19/95 (3000-3500)   3450
Title cel & matching master background (tempera
on background sheet): full figure of Donald
sitting wearing baby hat & being sprayed by
fountain, 8-1/2 x 11", VF, HL/Apr 25/98
(2500-3500)   3220
CELS
4 cels: partial figures of nephews reading comic book;
2 of single nephews; full figure of befuddled

Donald standing; 3-1/2 x 2" to 5 x 5"; VF;
HL/Nov 19/95 (1000-1500)   920

DRAGON AROUND (1954)
CEL SET-UPS
Frustrated Donald Duck in steam-shovel cab, 3-1/2
x 4", key watercolor production background,
CE/Jun 18/94 (2500-3500)   2530
Full figures of smiling Chip & Dale standing near tree
trunk facing each other, Chip in homemade
armor, Dale holding lance, watercolor
production background, mat signed "Walt
Disney", Courvoisier label, 5-1/2" & smaller,
CE/Jun 20/96 (1500-2000)   10,350
Full-figure front views of happy Chip (3") & confused
Dale (4") standing in front of debris (including
open *Fairy Tales* book), watercolor production
background, S/Jun 21/97 (1000-1500)   1840
Full figures of Chip as knight riding Dale to right,
5-5/8", 12-field cel, custom watercolor display
background, SR/Fall/97 (600-900)   610
CELS – FULL FIGURE
Chip as knight rides fierce Dale toward right, 4-3/8",
some waviness, SR/Fall/96 (400-700)   720

DRIP DIPPY DONALD (1948)
BACKGROUNDS
Watercolor master background of outdoor faucet,
12-field, SR/Fall/94 (800-1400)   1020

DUCK PIMPLES (1945)
CELS – FULL FIGURE
2 full-figure cels: man in suit with right leg in book
confronts surprised Donald (falling on backside),
6-1/4"; man standing facing right juggling two
irons, 5-1/2"; ct; SR/Fall/96 (900-1200)   900

DUDE DUCK (1951)
ANIMATION DRAWINGS
Full-figure drawing of squinting Donald in sport coat
& hat, carrying suitcase & umbrella, signed by
Jack Hannah, 6 x 6-1/2", VF, HL/Aug 21/94
(300-400)   672
Full-figure drawing of Donald in sport coat & hat,
carrying suitcase & umbrella, 6-1/2 x 6",
signed by Jack Hannah, VF, HL/Nov 13/94
(400-600)   728
CELS – FULL FIGURE
Dapper Donald standing wearing burgundy coat,
bowler hat & pink ascot, holding walking stick
under arm, 4-1/2 x 2-1/2", VF, HL/Oct 6/96
(500-700)   690
MODEL ART
Model cel of dude Donald Duck standing leaning
& whispering to left, 4-1/2 x 4-1/2", VF,
HL/Nov 16/97 (400-600)   403

DUMB BELL OF THE YUKON (1946)
CEL SET-UPS
Full figures of surprised bear cub (5") & Donald Duck
(in winter dress, 6") standing facing each other,
painted background of large circle on solid field,
S/Dec 14/96 (1000-1500)   1150
CELS – FULL FIGURE/MODEL ART
Chastened Donald Duck (in undershirt) on all fours,
2-1/2 x 3-1/2", HL/Aug 6/95 (500-700)   336
Trapper Donald Duck lifting bear cub, 6 x 7-1/2",
HL/Nov 19/95 (1000-1500)   1380
Full-figure color model cel of smiling Donald Duck
standing dressed in arctic attire, looking at his
hands, 6", S/Jun 21/97 (800-1200)   805
CELS – PARTIAL FIGURE
Near-full figure of Donald Duck in arctic gear staring
down at left index finger, 4-1/4 x 5", HL/Oct
6/96 (600-900)   518
MODEL ART
2 original photostatic model sheets: *Dumb Bell of the
Yukon & Donald's Snow Fight*, both 13-3/4 x
11", SR/Fall/97 (300-400)   310

EARLY TO BED (1941)
CEL SET-UPS
Donald Duck in nightclothes staring at imprint of clock
on his bottom, 5", watercolor production back-
ground, CE/Dec 16/94 (800-1200)   1955
MODEL ART

2 photostat model sheets: *Early to Bed & Officer
Duck*, 14 x 11", SR/Spring/95 (200-400)   300

EDUCATION FOR DEATH (1943)
CELS – FULL FIGURE
Haughty Hitler as prince with eager Germania lying
crossways on back of horse, 7", 12-field, some
lifting paint, SR/Spring/95 (1500-2000)   2830

EGYPTIAN MELODIES (1931)
BACKGROUNDS
Master production background of open sarcophagus,
(watercolor & ink on paper), 9 x 10-3/4",
CE/Dec 15/93 (2000-2500)   1725

ELMER ELEPHANT (1936)
ANIMATION DRAWINGS
2 full-figure drawings: shy Tillie Tiger standing, Elmer
standing with bouquet; 5 x 2-1/2", 4-1/2 x 4",
HL/Apr 28/96 (700-1000)   748
2 full-figure drawings: Tillie faces right & leans forward
at waist, shy Elmer looks left; 4 x 4" & 4-1/2 x
3-1/2", HL/Feb 23/97 (500-700)   518
CELS – FULL FIGURE
Large image of Elmer frowning as others ridicule
trunk, 7", S/Dec 16/93 (1000-1200)   1035
CELS – PARTIAL FIGURE
Promotional cel of Elmer peeking around tree under
title "Timid Elmer", 2", CE/Jun 18/94
(800-1000)   575

EL TERRIBLE TOREADOR (1929)
ANIMATION DRAWINGS
2 full-figure drawings: Toreador; seductive barmaid;
6 x 3-1/2" & 5 x 3"; HL/Apr 28/96
(700-1000)   690

THE EYES HAVE IT (1945)
BACKGROUNDS
Master watercolor background of barn interior with
barrel, 12-field, SR/Fall/94 (800-1400)   1460
CEL SET-UPS
Angry face-off between Pluto (2-1/2 x 5") & chicken,
watercolor production background w/inscribed
notes, CE/Dec 16/94 (3000-4000)   2530

FARMYARD SYMPHONY (1938)
BACKGROUNDS
Watercolor production background of fence & barn
with thatch roof, S/Dec 17/94 (800-1200) 1035
CEL SET-UPS
Full figure of great bull facing right, 5-1/4", 12-field
cel, color print background from *Donald's Gar-
den*, SR/Fall/97 (300-500)   200
CELS – FULL FIGURE
Strutting rooster, 6 x 6", restored, VF,
HL/Apr 10/94 (400-500)   616

FATHERS ARE PEOPLE (1951)
CEL SET-UPS
Near-full figure of wide-eyed Goofy high-stepping
thru room crowded with baby paraphernalia
while holding tray of baby bottles overhead,
key watercolor production background, 6",
CE/Dec 12/96 (5000-7000)   4600

FATHER'S LION (1952)
CELS – FULL FIGURE
Front view of casually dressed, smiling Goofy
standing with double-barrel shotgun under
right arm, looking right, 6", 12-field, ct,
SR/Fall/95 (500-900)   550

FATHER'S WEEK END (1953)
CEL SET-UPS
Matching set of pan cels & master background:
Goofy leads long line of workers from Main
Shop to time clock at 5 pm, 10 x 36",
HL/Aug 21/94 (1000-1500)   3808

FERDINAND THE BULL (1938)
ANIMATION DRAWINGS (also see CELS-FULL FIGURE)
Drawing of confrontation between Ferdinand &
matador, 7 x 10", signed by Tom Wood,

HL/Apr 23/95 (400-600) 840

Close-up drawing of sitting Ferdinand smelling flower
bouquet, 7 x 7", HL/Apr 28/96 (500-700) 518

Full-figure extreme drawing of smiling Ferdinand sitting
facing left, sold thru Courvoisier, 6-1/2 x 7",
HL/Feb 23/97 (500-600) 690

3-drawing progression matted together: full figures
of angry matador standing pulling hair out,
5-1/2" avg., Courvoisier label, S/Dec 19/97
(600-800) 575

Close-up drawing of sitting Ferdinand smelling
bouquet of flowers, 7-1/4", 12-field sheet,
inker's notation, Disney copyright stamp,
3/8" piece of upper right corner missing,
SR/Spring/98 (300-600) 650

CEL SET-UPS
Matador enters arena, Courvoisier wood-veneer
background, 7-1/2 x 9-1/4", CE/Dec 15/93
(1000-1500) 977

Ferdinand sitting among daisies, airbrushed background, 4", S/Dec 16/93 (1800-2200) 1725

4" Matador sticks tongue out at 5-1/2" long
Ferdinand, studio-prepared background,
S/Dec 16/93 (2000-3000) 2070

Full-figure cels of lazy Ferdinand & crying Matador,
9 x 10", complementary painted woodgrain
background, mat w/Courvoisier label, VF,
HL/Apr 10/94 (1800-2400) 2688

Angry Matador (5") approaches Ferdinand (5") who
sniffs bouquet of daisies dangling from tail,
wood-veneer Courvoisier background,
S/Jun 17/94 (2000-3000) 3162

Full figure of ferocious Ferdinand (2-1/2") charging
along fence as amazed scouts (3-1/4") watch,
Courvoisier watercolor background, some
cracked & lifting paint, SR/Fall/94
(1400-1800) 1580

Full-figure caricatures of Walt Disney as Matador
& Freddie Moore, 8 x 10", complementary
Courvoisier painted background, Disney
labels, HL/Nov 13/94 (1000-1500) 1232

Smiling Ferdinand sitting under tree; Courvoisier
airbrush background, cel overlay & label;
3 x 4"; CE/Dec 16/94 (800-1200) 1955

Sleepy Ferdinand sitting in meadow, 4", Courvoisier
airbrush background & label, CE/Dec 16/94
(1000-1500) 978

Full-figure front view of young Ferdinand standing
smugly in field, 6", Courvoisier watercolor
background with original production overlay,
SR/Spring/95 (1400-1800) 1810

Large-image portraits of 5 skeptical spectators,
8-1/2 x 19", complementary painted
background, Courvoisier label,
HL/Apr 23/95 (1000-1200) 2464

Portrait of gentle Ferdinand with flower, Courvoisier
background, 6 x 5", HL/Apr 28/96
(1000-1500) 1265

Man smiles at the sight of Ferdinand, Courvoisier
background & label, needs restoration, 7",
S/Jun 19/96 (700-900) 690

Bee stinger-deep in flower, 4-1/2"; full figures of alert
Mother Swan & four goslings swimming among
plants from *The Ugly Duckling*, 6 x 7"; each
w/airbrushed Courvoisier background,
S/Jun 19/96 (1000-1500) 2185

Full figures of four men walking in country, Courvoisier
wood-veneer & watercolor background, 6" each,
severe paint loss, CE/Jun 20/96 (600-800) 518

Cow (8") watching bee (1") above cactus, Courvoisier
airbrush & watercolor background,
CE/Jun 20/96 (800-1200) 1840

Upset matadors & horse grimace from behind wall,
Courvoisier airbrush & watercolor background,
5" & smaller; 2 girls, 3-1/2"; CE/Jun 20/96
(700-900) 1035

Smiling man w/eye patch in bushes, Courvoisier
watercolor background, 3", CE/Jun 20/96
(700-900) 575

Smiling Ferdinand sitting partly behind tree,
Courvoisier watercolor & airbrush
background, 5", CE/Jun 20/96 (800-1200) 1265

Angry Matador (5-1/2") gestures at contented
Ferdinand (head & neck only, 4-1/2") with
head vertical, eyes closed & flower on nose,
Courvoisier watercolor background,
CE/Jun 20/96 (1000-1500) 3220

Ferdinand w/eyes closed sitting amid flowers,
Courvoisier airbrush background, 4",

CE/Jun 20/96 (600-800) 978

3 angry matadors grimace behind wooden wall,
watercolor production background with
Courvoisier label, 1-1/2" to 5",
CE/Jun 20/96 (1500-2000) 1380

Man in hat watches from tree as Ferdinand acts fierce,
7", Courvoisier background, S/Dec 14/96
(700-900) 690

Full figures of Matador (4") making face as calm
Ferdinand (5 x 6") looks on, studio prepared
background of fence & ground, S/Dec 14/96
(2000-3000) 2875

Full figures of combative matador (4-7/8") standing as
Ferdinand (6-15/16") lays on back smelling
flower, master background of stadium, released
by Courvoisier, original hand-lettered mat
& Courvoisier labels, some color shifting,
SR/Fall/97 (3000-4000) 4050

Full figure of 2 picadors riding horses to left, 8" &
similar, Courvoisier airbrush background of
desert, Marc Davis signature on glass,
CE/Dec 18/97 (1000-1500) 575

CELS – FULL FIGURE
Complacent Ferdinand, 8 x 5"; 2 drawings: sleepy
Ferdinand (8" length), 2 bulls conferring
(5" each); S/Dec 17/94 (700-900) 1380

Ferdinand stands looking up, 8 x 6-1/2",
HL/Apr 23/95 (1500-2000) 2464

Pained Ferdinand drags himself to left, 9-1/2 x 4",
12-field, SR/Spring/96 (700-1000) 1270

Manly picador astride broken-down horse, 6-1/2
x 6", HL/Apr 28/96 (400-600) 403

CELS – PARTIAL FIGURE
Large close-up of Ferdinand in profile with eyes
opened, 9-1/2", CLA/Jun 7/97 (800-1000) 920

Miniature portrait cel of surprised Ferdinand peering
out from painted wreath (painted paper), 1",
S/Dec 19/97 (200-400) 460

CONCEPT AND INSPIRATIONAL ART
Full-figure polished study drawing of bull standing
facing left & bloodied by picadors' lances,
colored conté crayon on animation sheet,
5 x 8", HL/May 31/97 (100-200) 115

Design painting of meadow with Spanish hill town
in distance, watercolor on heavyweight
paper, 16-1/2 x 11", VF, HL/Apr 25/98
(2400-2800) 2760

LAYOUT ART
Layout drawing of Ferdinand in back of farmer's
wagon, 9-1/2 x 12", CE/Dec 15/93
(400-600) 1265

STORY ART
Story painting of Ferdinand sitting in silhouette
under tree on hill from finale, watercolor
on heavyweight paper, 8 x 11", VF+,
HL/Apr 25/98 (1500-2000) 3450

FIGARO AND CLEO (1943)
BACKGROUNDS
Master background of room corner, 14-7/8 x
11-1/4", studio stamps, SR/Spring/96
(1100-1500) 1210

2 watercolor production backgrounds: fishbowl; table
with ball of yarn; each stamped; sight 10 x 12"
& similar; CE/Dec 18/97 (1000-1500) 863

Watercolor production background: looking up at sink
with pump & scrub brush, pan & ladle on wall,
shelf, doorway; stamps; sight 12-1/2 x 15-1/2";
CE/Dec 18/97 (1000-1500) 575

CEL SET-UPS
Happy Figaro (3-1/2") stands & watches Cleo (3")
swim in bowl, watercolor production
background, S/Dec 17/94 (4000-5000) 4600

Smiling Figaro stands watching Cleo swim, 8 x
10-1/2", matching master background,
watercolor on background sheet,
HL/Aug 6/95 (4500-5500) 4816

CELS – FULL FIGURE
Cleo, 3 x 4", F, HL/Apr 10/94 (600-800) 840

Angry Figaro standing & turning to make "stop"
gesture, 4-1/2 x 3-1/4", HL/Apr 28/96
(700-1000) 575

CELS – PARTIAL FIGURE
Close-up of smiling Figaro, 5-1/2", CE/Jun 18/94
(800-1200) 1380

Close-up of smiling Figaro, 6-1/4", CE/Dec 16/94
(800-1200) 690

FIGARO AND FRANKIE (1947)
CEL SET-UPS
Full figure of annoyed Minnie Mouse with broom,
8 x 10-1/2", background of house & yard
from another cartoon (tempera on background
sheet), HL/Apr 23/95 (2000-2500) 2688

CELS – FULL FIGURE
Figaro tangled in Frankie's horizontal bird cage,
5-1/2 x 9", HL/Nov 19/95 (1000-1500) 920

CELS – PARTIAL FIGURE
Minnie Mouse lovingly holds & scolds frowning
Figaro, 7-1/2 x 6-1/2", S/Dec 14/96
(1200-1800) 1610

FIRE CHIEF (1940)
CELS – PARTIAL FIGURE
Portrait of irritated Chief Donald, hand on hip, looking
left; restored; 5-3/4 x 4"; VF; HL/Apr 25/98
(800-1200) 805

MODEL ART
Photostatic model sheet of fire engine with Donald &
Huey, 14 x 11", SR/Spring/95 (200-400) 270

THE FIRE FIGHTERS (1930)
ANIMATION DRAWINGS
3 drawings: full figure of Mickey driving fire truck
pulled by Horace Horsecollar, 9-1/2" long;
four figure fighters 2" high; fire fighter riding
ostrich, 5", CLA/Jun 7/97 (2000-3000) 5980

STORY ART
Complete hand-written script with preliminary
storyboard sketches, 3 pages, 2 illustrated on
both sides, CE/Jun 18/94 (4000-6000) 10,350

FIRST AIDERS (1944)
CEL SET-UPS
2 cels: doubtful Pluto, 6 x 8", hand-prepared background; full figure of Goofy standing straddling
fishing pole entangled in fishing line from
No Sail, 1945, 5", hand-prepared background
of large circle on solid field; S/Dec 14/96
(700-900) 1610

CELS – FULL FIGURE
Horrified Pluto walking bandaged & splinted,
6-1/2 x 9", HL/Apr 23/95 (600-800) 1904

Nurse Minnie standing & yawning, 3-1/2 x 3-1/2",
HL/Oct 6/96 (700-900) 920

MODEL ART
Original model sheet of Minnie Mouse, 12 x 14-1/2",
pencil on trimmed animation sheet mounted to
heavyweight paper, HL/Aug 6/95
(2000-2500) 3136

FISHIN' AROUND (1931)
ANIMATION DRAWINGS
Rough drawing of Mickey in window with flower pot
on head, 3", CE/Jun 9/95 (600-800) 460

Full-figure drawing of Mickey rowing boat as Pluto
sits in back, 2-1/2 x 10", HL/Nov 19/95
(400-600) 1265

Full-figure drawing of happy Mickey rowing boat
w/nervous Pluto sitting in back, 4 x 10-1/4",
HL/Apr 28/96 (600-900) 920

5 drawings: Mickey & Pluto sitting in rowboat with
fishing gear; Minnie holding shoe with worn
sole; worried Mickey struggling against unseen
force; stern Mickey looking downward; guilty
Pluto crouching down & looking up; average
3-1/2", S/Dec 14/96 (800-1200) 1035

CEL SET-UPS
Mickey walking with fishing rod, studio prepared
background, 1", S/Dec 16/93 (800-1200) 575

CONCEPT AND INSPIRATIONAL ART
7 pages of inspirational sketches of Mickey, Pluto,
other characters; 9 pages of various production
notes, CE/Jun 18/94 (800-1000) 1610

STORY ART
Annotated preliminary storyboard by Bert Gillett,
graphite on 7 full sheets of animation paper,
plus script, CE/Dec 16/94 (2000-3000) 5175

FLOWERS AND TREES (1932)
ANIMATION DRAWINGS
3 full-figure drawings: group of black-eyed Susans,
2-1/2"; Old Man Tree looking left with sinister
leer 5"; lithesome Girl Tree wearing wreath of
flowers in pompadour, 5-1/2"; 12-field sheets;

SR/Fall/95 (500-900)   810

2 full-figure drawings: female sycamore posing, scheming old oak; 5-1/2 x 6", 5 x 7"; HL/Apr 28/96 (700-900)   920

2 full-figure drawings: Girl Tree leaning to left at waist, some leaves blowing away, 4-1/4"; leering Old Man Tree facing left, 4-3/4"; 12-field sheets; SR/Fall/97 (900-1400)   750

CONCEPT AND INSPIRATIONAL ART

Partial figure of mature tree, 9 x 9-3/4", watercolor on heavyweight paper, HL/Apr 23/95 (500-700)   308

LAYOUT ART

2 layout drawings of trees, 5-1/2", CE/Dec 18/97 (1500-2000)   2300

FLYING JALOPY (1943)
CEL SET-UPS

2 set-ups: Donald flying battered plane, underside of plane w/tail feathers showing; 5-1/8" & 6" wide; 12-field; watercolor display backgrounds of jungle & mountains; corner of one cel missing, SR/Spring/95 (800-1200)   1070

THE FLYING MOUSE (1934)
CEL SET-UPS

Full figure of ready-to-fly mouse standing at edge of leafy branch, watercolor master background, 11-1/2 x 11", VF, HL/Apr 10/94 (5000-7000)   4480

Full figure of eager Mouse flying, 2-1/2", production background, CE/Jun 9/95 (2000-3000)   2760

Frightened winged mouse standing on leaves with clouds in background, watercolor production background, 2-1/4", CE/Jun 20/96 (2500-3500)   2875

CELS – FULL FIGURE/MODEL ART

2 mirror-image bats, 4 x 10-1/2", HL/Aug 21/94 (900-1200)   728

Front view of eager winged Mouse crouched, looking down, 5-3/4 x 2-1/2", 16-field, paint restoration; two 12 x 9-1/2" Ozalid model sheets; SR/Fall/94 (400-700)   710

Promotional cel of cat (7-1/2" w/o tail) swatting at Flying Mouse (2 x 4-1/2") who happily hovers out of reach, circa 1930s, S/Dec 17/94 (800-1200)   460

FOR WHOM THE BULLS TOIL (1953)
CEL SET-UPS

Background of wall painting & full-figure cel of heroic matador Goofy mounted to single-color master background (tempera on background sheet) from *The Three Caballeros*, 11-1/2 x 8-1/2", Art Props Dept. mat inscribed "Walt Disney's 'Goofy'", VF, HL/Apr 10/94 (800-1200)   896

Full-figure long rear view of Matador Goofy peeking thru door from inside bullring tunnel, 9 x 11-1/2", matching master background, tempera on background sheet, HL/Aug 6/95 (1500-2000)   2016

CELS – FULL FIGURE

Suspicious Goofy does double take, 7", S/Dec 17/94 (800-1200)   977

CONCEPT AND INSPIRATIONAL ART

Character study of 4 full-figure Matador Goofys, 12-field sheet, front view center figure 5-7/8", signed by Ed Ardell, SR/Spring/96 (300-600)   300

FOUL HUNTING (1947)
CELS – FULL FIGURE

Hunter Goofy watches duck at his feet; knees-up of Goofy on safari looking right thru binoculars from another short, late 1940s; 5 x 5-1/2", 4 x 5-1/2", F+, HL/Aug 21/94 (900-1200)   896

THE FOX HUNT (1938)
CELS – FULL FIGURE

Frustrated Donald w/lazy hounds, 7-1/2 x 10", restored, VF, HL/Apr 10/94 (600-900)   560

Panicked Goofy facing & looking left while standing on hands with legs horizontal in 'T' formation, 5 x 6-3/4", restored, VF, HL/Apr 25/98 (800-1200)   1035

CONCEPT AND INSPIRATIONAL ART

Inspirational sketch: Mickey, Minnie & Horace

Horsecollar tend horses, Donald bucked by donkey, Clara kisses horse, Goofy & dogs, at "Red Fox Tavern", partial artist's signature, signed by owner, S/Dec 16/93 (1500-2500)   1265

FREEWAYPHOBIA NO. 1 (1965)
CELS – PARTIAL FIGURE

Shoulders-up close-up of battered, shell-shocked Goofy, facing right, looking into camera, 4-1/2", 16-field, SR/Spring/95 (150-300)   300

FUNNY LITTLE BUNNIES (1934)
CELS – FULL FIGURE

Smiling bunny carries 2 chocolate rabbits on tray over his head, 5" total, S/Jun 21/97 (800-1000)   920

LAYOUT ART

Four detailed layout drawings: "Supply Room," pot of chocolate, carving chocolate rabbits, painting eggs; 12-field sheets with fully annotated production stamps; wear and discoloration; SR/Spring/97 (2000-4000)   2530

A GENTLEMAN'S GENTLEMAN (1941)
CEL SET-UPS

Smiling Mickey in bed, holding up two fingers of left hand, 6", watercolor production background of bedroom, CLA/Jun 7/97 (10,000-15,000)   14,950

CELS – FULL FIGURE

Side view of smiling Pluto walking right, looking up, 6-5/8 x 3-1/8", (color model or from *A Gentleman's Gentleman*?), restored, SR/Spring/97 (600-1000)   680

GET RICH QUICK (1951)
TITLE ART

Title card: gambling objects in gouache on background, hand lettering & special effects laid over on two cel levels, 12-field, original production cover flap, SR/Fall/94 (2000-4000)   2250

GIANTLAND (1933)
ANIMATION DRAWINGS

Full-figure drawing of Mickey standing facing right, leaning back w/hands on chest, mouth open, eyes closed, 2-1/2", SR/Fall/95 (400-700)   400

CONCEPT AND INSPIRATIONAL ART

3 gag ideas of Mickey becoming part of giant's lunch: 2 on 12-field sheets; third drawn on paper cut down into two smaller parts & mounted on 12-field sheet, SR/Fall/95 (500-1000)   500

THE GODDESS OF SPRING (1934)
ANIMATION DRAWINGS

Full-figure drawing of scheming god Pluto, w/notes, 6-1/2 x 5-1/2", HL/Apr 28/96 (500-700)   518

CELS – PARTIAL FIGURE

Knees-up figure of menacing Pluto, God of Underworld, 7 x 4-1/2", VF, HL/Aug 6/95 (1000-1500)   896

GOLDEN EGGS (1941)
BACKGROUNDS

Watercolor master background: overhead view of farmyard, 11-1/8 x 8-5/8", studio stamps & notations, SR/Spring/95 (800-1600)   850

CEL SET-UPS

Sleepy rooster sticks head thru handle of basket of eggs in henhouse window, 10 x 12", matching watercolor production background, S/Jun 21/97 (800-1200)   805

THE GOLDEN TOUCH (1935)
MODEL ART

Two vintage print model sheets: King Midas; Goldie, punched hole at top edge; 12 x 9"; also used as color models with colored central figures & call-outs; SR/Spring/97 (200-400)   460

GOLIATH II (1960)
CEL SET-UPS

2 full-figure set-ups: Goliath lays on back with threatening mouse standing on his stomach; determined mouse carrying Goliath over his

---

head to left; 7-1/2" & 6-3/4"; DL litho backgrounds (forest & desert), gold Art Corner labels, SR/Spring/95 (500-900)   730

CELS – FULL FIGURE

Raja the tiger walking to left (eyes closed) with Goliath II dangling from his mouth, 6-1/2 x 7-1/2", VF+, HL/Apr 10/94 (400-600)   476

Stalking Goliath confronts Mouse in spell-casting pose, 5-1/2 x 12", HL/Feb 23/97 (300-500)   403

Side view of Goliath II & mouse wrestling, 7 1/8", gold DL Art Corner label, SR/Fall/97 (450-700)   300

Side view of Goliath II clinging to bent flower stem, 7 x 11-1/4", VF+, HL/Apr 25/98 (400-500)   431

GOOD SCOUTS (1938)
STORY ART

Story sketch of log bridge falling into ravine after two nephews crossed, 5-1/2 x 7-1/2"; photocopy of Carl Barks' letter identifying work as his; color photocopy of sketch initialed by Barks, HL/Nov 13/94 (500-700)   896

Detailed story drawing of frightened Donald beak to nose with fierce bear, captioned "Oh! Oh!", colored pencil & conté crayon on animation sheet, 6 x 8-1/2", F+, HL/Apr 25/98 (300-400)   863

GOOFY AND WILBUR (1939)
CEL SET-UPS

Full-figure front view of Wilbur high-kicking, 3-3/4", 12-field cel, Courvoisier wood-veneer background, restored, SR/Fall/97 (1200-1800)   800

Full-figure side view of Goofy (5") tripping over tree-stump limb to left (edited out of film), 12-field cel, Courvoisier wood-veneer background, ct, SR/Fall/97 (1200-1600)   900

Goofy in rowboat facing left holding fish by tail in right hand, left hand raised over his head, 6 x 5-3/4", complementary watercolor background likely for Courvoisier (watercolor on heavyweight paper), F-VF, HL/Nov 16/97 (1200-1500)   1035

CELS – PARTIAL FIGURE

Portrait of Wilbur hugging Goofy, 6-1/4 x 6-1/2", VF, HL/Apr 28/96 (1200-1600)   1380

GOOFY'S GLIDER (1940)
LAYOUT ART

Layout drawing of determined Goofy pedaling bicycle-glider past windsock with skeptical buzzard sitting on top, 6-1/2" long, CLA/Jun 7/97 (1000-1500)   805

GRAND CANYONSCOPE (1954)
ANIMATION DRAWINGS

Full-figure drawing of smiling tourist Donald, holding camera, riding burro, 9-1/4", 16-field sheet, some wear & discoloration, vertical crease, SR/Spring/96 (600-1000)   650

CEL SET-UPS

Full figures of Ranger Woodlore being chased by angry mountain lion in Civil War cap, master background of rocks by Eyvind Earle (tempera on background sheet), 9 x 11", F, HL/Feb 23/97 (1500-2000)   1955

CELS – FULL FIGURE

Tourist Donald Duck with camera around neck (4-1/2") & Ranger Woodlore (6-3/4") stand facing each other: Ranger bending forward at waist & removing Donald's cap, SR/Spring/98 (400-700)   590

GRASSHOPPER & THE ANTS (1934)
CEL SET-UPS

Matching set-up: 3" Grasshopper playing fiddle while 1" ant dances surrounded by flowers, matching watercolor production background, S/Dec 16/93 (15,000-20,000)   13,800

CELS – FULL FIGURE

Publicity cel: Grasshopper (4") splashes in barrels & fiddles as Queen Ant (3") & ants (2-1/2" & similar) dance, CE/Jun 9/95 (1000-1500)   1380

Grasshopper plays fiddle with feet splashing in barrels as Queen & ants dance, cel done from storybook illustration, early 1940s, 8-1/2 x 6-1/2", F+, HL/Nov 19/95 (500-700)   489

MODEL ART

Peter Pan: Full figure of Tinker Bell tiptoeing across mirror trailing pixie dust, watercolor production background, 7-1/2" w/wings, S/Dec 16/93 (10,000-12,000) 14,950

Peter Pan: Alarmed Tinker Bell trapped in lantern, 2-1/4", watercolor production background, S/Dec 17/94 (8,000-12,000)   11,500

Peter Pan: Full figures of Peter Pan (4") & Wendy (4") flying thru forest, watercolor production background, CE/Dec 12/96 (8000-10,000)   11,500

Peter Pan: Incandescent, smiling Tinker Bell flies vertically trailing pixie dust, 6-1/2", three cel levels, drybrushed wings, SR/Spring/98 (2500-3000)   4330

Peter Pan: Full figure of Tinker Bell sitting on top of bottle cork laughing, 6-1/4", airbrushed wings, display set-up, SR/Fall/96 (1200-1800)   1980

Pinocchio: Publicity cel of Pinocchio sitting (5-1/2" x 4-1/2") on table with Jiminy (1") perched on his toe, preliminary watercolor background, Courvoisier label, Walt Disney signature, S/Dec 17/94 (10,000-12,000)   18,400

Pinocchio: Smiling Blue Fairy standing by shelves full of toys, 6", printed background, needs restoration, S/Dec 14/96 (8000-10,000)   8625

Pinocchio: Blue Fairy looking at Jiminy Cricket & Pinocchio on workbench; for publicity related to initial release; 8 x 12"; airbrush, watercolor-&-conté-crayon background, HL/Nov 19/95 (4000-5000)   16,100

Pinocchio: Full figures of Geppetto (5") at open door of home while holding Figaro (2") by back of neck, key watercolor production background, Courvoisier label, CE/Dec 12/96 (15,000-20,000)   25,300

Pinocchio: Full figure of Jiminy Cricket (on back in sand) as he tips hat & smiles to angry fish, 8-1/2 x 11-1/2", atmospheric master background (watercolor on background sheet), overlay cel of bubbles, Courvoisier label, VF, HL/Apr 23/95 (12,000-16,000)   12,320

Pinocchio: Monstro swimming on surface, 10 x 14", Courvoisier complementary background w/cels of waves & sea gulls, mat signed by Frank Thomas & Ollie Johnston, HL/Nov 19/95 (4000-5000)   7763

Pinocchio: Full figure of sitting Pinocchio looking at Jiminy on box, 8-1/2 x 10", complementary shadow airbrush background, Courvoisier label, mat inscribed by Walt Disney, VF, HL/Apr 23/95 (5000-7000)   14,560

Pinocchio: Full figure of Pinocchio as real boy lying on bed with eyes closed, 6-1/2", key watercolor production background (key set-up), CE/Dec 12/96 (25,000-35,000) 36,800

Pinocchio: Full figure of Pinocchio under water amid fish school, 7" & smaller, Courvoisier airbrush background, CE/Dec 16/94 (3000-4000)   5750

Pinocchio: Geppetto's storefront in winter, Gustav Tenggren inspirational sketch, watercolor on paper, inscribed "Tenggren", CE/Dec 16/94 (9000-12,000) 21,850

Pinocchio: Full figures of Geppetto (7") walking puppet Pinocchio (3-1/2") across floor as Figaro (2") follows, painted-veneer Courvoisier background, S/Jun 19/96 (8000-10,000)   12,650

Pinocchio: Rendering of marionette Russian snow scene of snow princess fleeing wolves by Gustav Tenggren, watercolor on heavyweight paper, 7-1/4 x 9-1/2"; detailed color model drawings of marionette wolf & horse, 6 x 6-1/2" & 4-1/2 x 9-1/2", HL/May 3/97 (12,000-16,000)   9775

Pinocchio: Pan concept drawing of Geppetto's workshop-home by Gustav Tenggren, sight 9-1/4 x 17", CLA/Jun 7/97 (8000-10,000) 16,100

Pocahontas: Pocahontas' image superimposed over execution party on cliff, S/Feb 24/96 (3000-4000)   18,400

Pocahontas: Pocahontas & John Smith stand atop cliff in shaft of sunlight w/orange leaves & purple sky, S/Feb 24/96 (2000-3000)   10,350

Pocahontas: Ratcliffe w/torch singing atop cannon before an admiring Wiggins, S/Feb 24/96 (2000-3000)   1610

Pocahontas: Pocahontas stands on cliff watching Susan Constant sail away, S/Feb 24/96 (3000-5000)   8050

Pocahontas: Flit maquette, #8/17, S/Feb 24/96 (1500-2000) 5462

Pocahontas: Pocahontas maquette, #36/36, S/Feb 24/96 (2000-3000) 3220

Pocahontas: Percy maquette, #8/22, S/Feb 24/96 (1500-2000) 2185

Pocahontas: Nakoma maquette, #1/13, S/Feb 24/96 (1500-2000) 1265

Pocahontas: Powhatan maquette, #10/16, S/Feb 24/96 (1000-1500) 805

The Rescuers: Smiling Orville (all but wing tips) watches Bianca & Bernard sit in sardine can atop him, 14-3/4 x 9-3/4", litho background of "airport," 16-field, limited edition: #35/500, certificate, SR/Spring/95 (800-1400) 850

Robin Hood: Prince John holds ear & sucks thumb, partial multi-cel set-up, WDP seal, 12-1/2 x 15-1/2", CE/Dec 15/93 (800-1200) 1610

Robin Hood: Near-full figure of Alligator Guard knocking Robin backward with shield, 12-1/2 x 9-1/4", castle courtyard master background, SR/Spring/95 (1000-1600) 1460

Robin Hood: Chest-up front view of delighted Prince John (wearing crown, rings missing stones) with paws at head level, studying crystal ball, 7-1/2", 12-field cel, SR/Fall/96 (500-900) 500

Sleeping Beauty: Signed design painting by Eyvind Earle of helmeted Prince w/sword upraised amid thorns, 6 x 15", tempera on board, VF, HL/Nov 16/97 (3000-5000)   4140

Sleeping Beauty: Eyvind Earle story painting of Prince Phillip meeting Maleficent as dragon, signed, tempera on board, 6 x 15", VF, HL/Apr 28/96 (4000-6000)   16,100

Sleeping Beauty: Merryweather (as model, 6-1/2") & Flora (w/scissors, 6") in peasant dress struggle with pink material, pan watercolor production background of cottage interior, S/Dec 19/97 (7000-9000)   5750

Sleeping Beauty: Pan production set-up of Prince Phillip on Samson (5-1/2 x 9") battling Maleficent as Dragon (16") outside castle, pan watercolor production background from another scene, S/Jun 19/96 (15,000-20,000)   11,500

Sleeping Beauty: Prince Phillip battles full-length dragon, complementary color-print background, VF+, HL/Apr 10/94 (5000-6000)   9520

Sleeping Beauty: Inspirational painting of gargoyle with castle spires in background by Eyvind Earle (signed), tempera on illustration board, 5 x 11", VF+, HL/Oct 6/96 (1500-2000)   4370

Sleeping Beauty: Large-image full-figure production set-up of Princess Aurora (8-1/2") & Prince Phillip (10") dancing in castle, watercolor production background, S/Jun 19/96 (15,000-25,000)   19,550

Sleeping Beauty: Sleeping Aurora in castle, Prince Phillip standing at her side, fairies hovering, storybook cover art by Eyvind Earl, 10-1/2 x 14", tempera on board (7500-10,000)   7840

Sleeping Beauty: Full figure of Briar Rose walking in forest as animals watch, 6-1/2", watercolor production background, CE/Jun 9/95 (15,000-20,000)   25,300

Sleeping Beauty: Briar Rose sits on log amid admiring animals, 7-1/4", four cel levels, color print background, SR/Spring/98 (2200-2800)   2000

Sleeping Beauty: Briar Rose in forest w/animals on tree branch, 5-3/4", key watercolor production background, CE/Dec 16/94 (15,000-25,000)   21,850

Sleeping Beauty: Full figure of Briar Rose (6-3/4") reaching for Mock Prince (6-3/8") as other animals watch, color print background, SR/Fall/97 (2700-3700)   1800

Sleeping Beauty: Maleficent & bound Prince Phillip in cottage, Studio Art Props background painting, 9-1/2 x 13-1/2", VF+, HL/Aug 21/94 (3000-5000) 5600

Sleeping Beauty: Fauna as peasant holds wand & reads cookbook in messy cottage kitchen, master background (tempera on background sheet), mat inscribed "To Una Merkel, My Best Wishes, Walt Disney", WDP label, 9-1/2 x 12-1/2", VF+, HL/Apr 28/96 (5000-7000) 7475

Sleeping Beauty: 3 fairies & Briar Rose in cottage, watercolor pan production background attributed to Eyvind Earle, production notes, WDP stamp, S/Dec 16/93 (15,000-20,000) 24,150

Sleeping Beauty: Princess & fairies walking up castle circular staircase, matching Technirama master background (tempera on background sheet), signed by Eyvind Earle, 11-1/4 x 29-1/2", VF+, HL/Oct 6/96 (10,000-12,000) 9775

Sleeping Beauty: Front view of enraged Maleficent with both hands in air, her right hand holding staff, 10-1/2", pan gouache master background of her throne, SR/Spring/95 (10,000-16,000)   10,700

Sleeping Beauty: Flora (6"), Fauna (4") & Merryweather (5") plan to save Princess Aurora while hidden in jewel case, watercolor production background, S/Jun 10/95 (6000-8000)   11,500

Snow White and the Seven Dwarfs: Master background of Dwarf's cottage, 12 x 15", watercolor on background sheet, stamps, notes, artists' signatures & initials, VF+, HL/Nov 13/94 (30,000-40,000)   78,400

Snow White and the Seven Dwarfs: Doc, Grumpy, Sleepy & Bashful in cottage, 4-1/2" & smaller, pan watercolor production background w/stamps & notes, CE/Jun 18/94 (10,000-15,000)   24,150

Snow White and the Seven Dwarfs: Double image of Queen (8-1/2") reading & Witch (5") pointing, Courvoisier airbrush background, CE/Jun 18/94 (8000-12,000) 14,950

Snow White and the Seven Dwarfs: Front view of Queen holding heart box, 7-1/2", Courvoisier airbrush background, CE/Dec 12/96 (8000-10,000) 21,275

Snow White and the Seven Dwarfs: Snow White (2") waves farewell from atop Prince's horse as he (3") leads her out of woods, watercolor production background w/production overlays, S/Jun 17/94 (20,000-25,000)   17,250

Snow White and the Seven Dwarfs: Key set-up of serious Dopey playing the drums, key watercolor production background, Courvoisier label, 4", S/Jun 19/96 (20,000-25,000)   24,150

Snow White and the Seven Dwarfs: Full figure of Witch poling boat into swamp with castle in background, 4-1/2", trimmed celluloid on post-production overlay with airbrush special effects applied to pan watercolor production background that's separated horizontally for multiplane camera use, CLA/Jun 7/97 (40,000-60,000)   48,300

Snow White and the Seven Dwarfs: Queen reads from book of spells, 10 x 10-1/2", F+, HL/Nov 13/94 (10,000-12,000) 11,200

Snow White and the Seven Dwarfs: Full figure of admiring Dopey sitting cross-legged, chin in right hand; painted background of dream clouds as prepared for sale thru Courvoisier; 11-1/4 x 10-3/4" overall; VF; HL/Feb 23/97 (5000-6000) 5060

Snow White and the Seven Dwarfs: Witch poling boat along stream bank w/apple basket at her feet, 6", water special effects, Courvoisier airbrush background, CE/Dec 12/96 (10,000-12,000) 17,250

Snow White and the Seven Dwarfs: Queen stares at glass of magic potion, 8-1/2 x 7", complementary painted background, inscribed mat, authenticity certificate, as prepared for Courvoisier, HL/Apr 23/95 (9000-12,000) 13,440

Snow White and the Seven Dwarfs: Wicked Queen, 12-1/2 x 9-1/"2, mounted to complementary airbrush background, in mat embossed "© W.D.E." for Courvoisier, 2 contemporary authenticity labels, VF, HL/Apr 10/94 (8000-12,000) 12,880

Snow White and the Seven Dwarfs: Full figures of 4 Dwarfs pulling mine car, 7 x 12-1/2", complementary painted woodgrain background w/cel of sparkles, as prepared for Courvoisier, HL/Apr 23/95 (5000-7000) 9520

Snow White and the Seven Dwarfs: Snow White sings to sad bluebird on finger, cel of vines over Courvoisier airbrush background, inscribed mat, 8-1/4 x 8", HL/Aug 21/94 (5000-7000) 8960

Snow White and the Seven Dwarfs: Waist-up front view of Witch offering apple, 7-1/4 x 8-3/4", VF, HL/May 3/97 (9000-12,000) 13,225

Snow White and the Seven Dwarfs: Witch working at cauldron, 4", Courvoisier airbrush background, mat inscribed "Walt Disney", CE/Dec 16/94 (7000-9000) 12,650

Snow White and the Seven Dwarfs: Surprised Snow White sits up [in bed] w/2 bunnies in lap, 5-1/2", patterned paper Courvoisier background, WDE label, S/Dec 19/97 (7000-9000) 8050

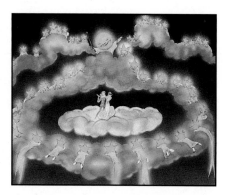

Snow White and the Seven Dwarfs: Full figures of 5 singing Dwarfs marching in line w/picks on shoulders as Dopey marches alongside, complementary painted woodgrain background, Courvoisier labels, 5-1/2 x 8-1/2" overall, HL/Feb 23/97 (7000-9000) 8050

Snow White and the Seven Dwarfs: "Well, if you insist..." Full figure of Snow White standing on steps turning to speak to five dwarfs {backs turned}, complementary painted woodgrain courvoisier background, 10 x 13 overall, HL/May 3/97 (12,000-15,000) 10,350

Snow White and the Seven Dwarfs: Concept piece for unproduced dream sequence: Snow White & Prince (1-1/2") dance in clouds before audience of stars & moon, by Ferdinand Horvath, signed "Horvath", S/Dec 14/96 (3000-5000) 3450

Snow White and the Seven Dwarfs: Snow White sitting outdoors singing to animals, complementary painted background, as prepared for Courvoisier, 7-1/2 x 7" overall, HL/Feb 23/97 (7000-9000)   12,075

Snow White and the Seven Dwarfs: Snow White at well with pigeons, Courvoisier complementary painted background, labels, inscribed, 8-1/2 x 10", HL/Aug 21/94 (4000-6000)   7280

Snow White and the Seven Dwarfs: 4" Witch offers apple to 4" Snow White, with cel overlay, airbrushed background, S/Dec 16/93 (10,000-12,000)   14,950

Snow White and the Seven Dwarfs: Full figures of Snow White (7") dancing w/Dopey (on Sneezy, 7") as Sleepy, Bashful & Doc stand playing instruments (4" each), wood-veneer Courvoisier background, S/Jun 21/97 (10,000-12,000) 14,950

Snow White and the Seven Dwarfs: Pan production background of Dwarf's Cottage, 34" wide, watercolor on background sheet, extensive notes, CE/Jun 9/95 (30,000-50,000)   50,600

The Sword in the Stone: Wart, Merlin & Archimedes; tempera preliminary background painting of British countryside; 10-1/2 x 14", studio notes, VF, HL/Apr 10/94 (2500-3500)   3136

Song of the South: 6 pastel storyboards: Brer Bear waving happily; Brer Fox smiling & tipping hat; rear view of Brer Fox peering around bushes; Brer Fox swiping angrily at Brer Bear; Brer Rabbit yelling at tar baby; Brer Rabbit stuck in tar baby; colored pastel on paper, each stapled at 4 corners to supporting piece of black construction paper; each sheet 6 x 8", S/Dec 19/97 (2500-3500)   2587

The Sword in the Stone: Full figure of frightened boy King Arthur walking into sunlit area of throne room, 11 x 15", master background of castle interior (tempera & ink on background sheet), HL/Oct 6/96 (3000-4000)   4370

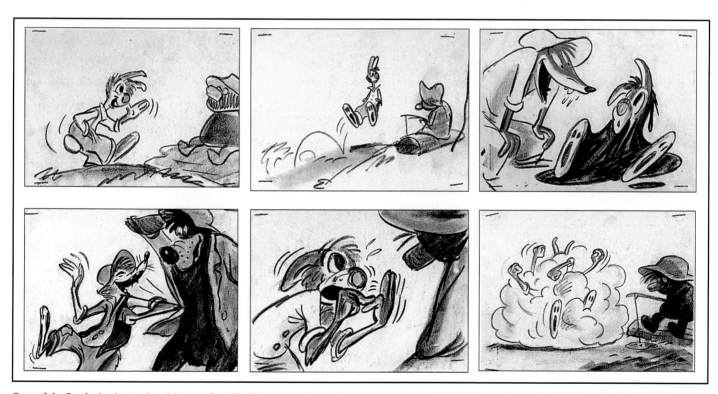

Song of the South: 6 color storyboard drawings from Tar Baby scene, color conté crayon on paper mounted to black story sheets, 6 x 8", HL/Apr 28/96 (4000-6000) 3220

Who Framed Roger Rabbit: Roger looks into camera as he drives Benny the Cab down street to left, color-print background, as sold in 1989 auction, 8-1/2 x 12-1/2", HL/Aug 21/94 (1800-2500)   2240

Who Framed Roger Rabbit: 3-cel set-up of Baby Herman (4") sitting in playpen as mother (legs & hem 9-1/2") walks by, S/Dec 17/94 (1500-2500)   1725

Who Framed Roger Rabbit: Elevated rear view of Eddie Valiant, Dolores, Roger (4") & Jessica (7-1/2") walking out of warehouse together w/Toons gathered around, matching color photographic background, S/Jun 19/96 (8000-12,000)   8050

Who Framed Roger Rabbit?: Hips-up front view of worried Roger holding love letter, 8-7/8", key photograph frame blow-up background, Disney Art Program seal & certificate, SR/Fall/96 (1200-1600)   did not sell

Who Framed Roger Rabbit?: Waist-up front view of stricken Roger in toilet, 4-1/2", 16-field, key photograph frame blow-up background, Disney Art Program seal & certificate, SR/Fall/96 (1100-1500)   did not sell

Who Framed Roger Rabbit?: Close-up portrait of seductive Jessica, 8", 16-field, Disney Art Program seal, key photographic frame blow-up background, SR/Spring/96 (2500-3200)   2750

Model sheet of all major characters, 12 x 9 1/2"
vintage Ozalid print sheet, served as color model
with key figures in colored pencil & call-outs for
paint colors, SR/Spring/98 (200-400)   310

STORY ART
Story drawing of industrious ant, 4-1/2 x 6-1/2", F,
HL/Feb 26-27/94 (300-400)   523
Detailed story/layout drawing of industrious ants
storing food, 8 x 10-1/2", HL/Feb 23/97
(200-300)   316

THE GREENER YARD (1949)
CELS – FULL FIGURE
Bootle Beetle sits on spool & reminisces; one nephew
holds hot dog & points; each 3"; S/Dec 16/93
(300-500)   345

THE GROCERY BOY (1932)
CEL SET-UPS
Full figures of Mickey (3-1/2") chasing Minnie
(3-1/4") on stage, watercolor production background from *Blue Rhythm*, CE/Dec 18/97
(10,000-15,000)   16,100

LAYOUT ART
Color layout drawing: Mickey weighs potatoes
as sitting Pluto waits, 7 x 9-1/2",
HL/Apr 28/96 (1500-2000)   2530

GULLIVER MICKEY (1934)
ANIMATION DRAWINGS
Colored-pencil drawing of Mickey motioning
for silence, 3-1/2 x 5-1/2", VF,
HL/Feb 26-27/94 (400-600)   358
Full-figure drawing of Mickey on knees talking
while holding blanket, 4 x 6",
HL/Apr 28/96 (600-800)   374
Drawing of smiling Mickey on knees with backside &
feet covered by rug, hands up in "stop" gesture,
4 x 5-1/2", HL/May 31/97 (300-500)   288
Drawing of smiling Mickey kneeling facing left with
arms up in "stop" gesture & blanket covering
rear & feet, 4 x 5-1/4", VF, HL/Apr 25/98
(300-400)   288

CONCEPT AND INSPIRATIONAL ART
One study of octopus plus 21 pages of notes &
sketches, 4-1/2", CE/Jun 9/95 (400-600)   483
Full-figure detailed study for publicity art of smiling
Mickey kneeling & shooting marble at
Lilliputian, 5-1/4 x 9", VF, HL/Nov 16/97
(700-1000)   2530

HAWAIIAN HOLIDAY (1937)
ANIMATION DRAWINGS
Full-figure drawing of suspicious Pluto standing facing
left with crab clamped to tail, 4-1/2", 12-field
sheet, timer's chart, signed by animator
Shamus Culhane, SR/Fall/95 (200-400)   410
CEL SET-UPS
Full figures of Minnie (3") & Donald w/guitar (3-1/2",
from *Don Donald*) on beach, preliminary
watercolor production background,
CE/Jun 9/95 (6000-8000)   5175
CONCEPT AND INSPIRATIONAL ART
Overhead concept drawing of Mickey & Pluto playing
with fish, CE/Jun 9/95 (400-600)   2300
Sheet of concept drawings of Goofy with surfboard,
5" long & similar, CE/Jun 9/95 (600-800)   3680
Gag suggestion on 2 animation sheets: Donald gets
eyes crossed watching flying fish while floating
on raft, 8-1/2 x 11", HL/Apr 28/96
(800-1200)   765

STORY ART
Sequence of 4 story drawings of Mickey, Minnie,
balloons & flirtatious jellyfish, 8-1/2 x
11-1/2", HL/Nov 19/95 (800-1000)   2530
4 storyboards of Mickey strumming ukulele, 3",
2 sets of 2 sheets stapled to larger supporting
sheet, S/Dec 19/97 (1200-1800)   1725

HELLO ALOHA (1952)
CELS -- FULL FIGURE
4 full-figure color model cels: Goofy as 3 natives
(chubby fellow sitting holding coconut, hibiscus
behind ears, 4"; sitting with pineapple, 5-1/2";
standing playing conch shell, 6-7/8") matted as
unit; crowd scene of Goofy being prepared as
luau guest of honor in front of grass shack,
7 x 4-3/8"; SR/Fall/96 (500-1000)   500

HELL'S BELLS (1929)
STORY ART
8-page preliminary storyboard plus study of dragon,
CE/Dec 16/94 (2000-3000)   1265

HOCKEY CHAMP (1939)
ANIMATION DRAWINGS
Full-figure drawing of smiling Donald (on skates)
pointing & holding hockey puck, 4-1/2 x 6",
HL/Nov 13/94 (500-700)   896
Full-figure drawing of smiling Donald Duck (wearing
muffler & ice skates) holding puck & gesturing,
5 x 4", HL/Nov 19/95 (500-700)   920
Full-figure drawing of happy Donald Duck on ice skates
pointing w/right hand & holding up hockey puck
in left hand, HL/Oct 6/96 (500-700)   748
2 drawings: Huey, Dewey & Louie, approx. 3-1/2"
each; Donald on skates holding puck, 5-1/2";
S/Dec 19/97 (700-900)   690
CEL SET-UPS
Full figures of angry Donald (3-1/8") & smiling Huey
(holding puck, 2") sitting/lying on ice facing
each other, Courvoisier watercolor background
of frozen pond, some lifting paint,
SR/Spring/95 (2200-3600)   2810
Full figures of Donald (3") crouching in front of
nephews (4-1/2") who are standing in identical
poses w/sticks raised, hockey puck between
them, all on skates on pond; Courvoisier
watercolor & airbrush background,
CE/Jun 20/96 (3000-4000)   6325
Full figure of determined Donald Duck winding up
for vicious slap shot, 4", airbrushed Courvoisier
background of winter scene, S/Dec 14/96
(3000-5000)   4025
3 angry nephews peer from behind snow ducks of
shaved ice, original background painting
(watercolor on background sheet), 8 x 11",
HL/Feb 23/97 (4000-5000)   4830
CELS – FULL FIGURE
3 nephews stand facing right on ice skates, hockey
sticks over shoulders in mirror poses, from
Basmajian collection, 4-1/2 x 6-1/4", VF,
HL/Apr 25/98 (1200-1600)   1265
Full figures of 2 Nephews facing right: one on all
fours, other on top of him swinging hockey
stick, 4-1/4", 12-field cel, ct, SR/Spring/98
(400-1400)   630

HOCKEY HOMICIDE (1945)
CEL SET-UPS
Full figure of angry Goofy facing left about to swing
hockey stick, complementary background of ice
rink, from Basmajian collection, 8 x 7-1/4", F,
HL/Apr 25/98 (800-1000)   1725

HOLD THAT POSE (1950)
ANIMATION DRAWINGS/LAYOUT ART
6 drawings in sequence of Goofy, one layout drawing
of Humphrey the Bear from his 1st cartoon,
5 x 6" to 6-1/2 x 9", notes, F, HL/Apr 10/94
(600-800)   448

HOME DEFENSE (1943)
CEL SET-UPS
Full figures of Donald Duck's 3 nephews in nightgowns
& caps, 2-1/2 x 3"; 2 nephews in cadet uniforms,
4-1/2 x 3"; nephew in cadet uniform looking

downcast walking to left wringing hands behind
back, 4"; each applied to printed background;
S/Dec 14/96 (700-900)   690
CELS – FULL FIGURE
Smiling Louie stands in uniform facing right holding
wooden sword, 6", 12-field, some lifting paint,
SR/Spring/95 (500-900)   520
3 full-figure cels of Huey, Dewey & Louie playing in
military costumes, 2-1/2 x 3-1/2", 4-1/2 x 2",
5 x 4", HL/Apr 28/96 (900-1200)   575

HONEY HARVESTER (1949)
CEL SET-UPS
Full figure of Donald Duck on knees in field holding
magnifying glass, satchel & honey pitcher at
his side; complementary painted Art Props
background; WDP stamp; 6-3/4 x 8-1/4";
F+; HL/Apr 25/98 (1200-1600)   1035
CELS – PARTIAL FIGURE
Waist-up horizontal of smiling Farmer Donald lining
up jars, 5-1/2", CE/Jun 9/95 (800-1200)   575

HOOK, LION AND SINKER (1950)
CELS – FULL FIGURE
Mountain Lion happily holds fish, 5 x 5",
S/Dec 17/94 (300-500)   115

HOW TO BE A SAILOR (1944)
CELS – FULL FIGURE
Front view of sailor Goofy walking carrying 2 buckets,
3 x 2", HL/Aug 6/95 (500-700)   476
Full-figure front view of dancing sailor Goofy, 6-3/4",
12-field, SR/Fall/96 (900-1500)   1610

HOW TO DANCE (1953)
CELS – PARTIAL FIGURE
Eager Goofy (thighs up) in top hat & tails facing
right, 5-1/2 x 5-1/2", VF, HL/Feb 23/97
(400-500)   403

HOW TO FISH (1942)
CELS – FULL FIGURE
Smiling Goofy pilots motorboat to left, 3-1/2 x
8-1/2", HL/Oct 6/96 (600-800)   863
CELS – PARTIAL FIGURE
Near-full figure of fisherman Goofy standing on one
foot facing right, holding fishing pole, 6",
vertical 12-field, ct, SR/Spring/95
(1100-1600)   1160

HOW TO HAVE AN ACCIDENT AT WORK (1959)
CEL SET-UPS
Full figure of cheerful worker Donald standing on step
ladder holding lit cigar, reading "No Smoking"
sign, 11 x 15", matching master background
(tempera on background sheet), VF+,
HL/Nov 16/97 (1000-1500)   1955
CELS – FULL FIGURE
2 cels: Donald reclining w/leg in cast, eyes closed,
clothes torn, 5" length; Nurse, 6";
CLA/Jun 7/97 (600-800)   173
CELS – PARTIAL FIGURE
Groggy Daisy (all but feet) in bathrobe & hair in
kerchief & rollers faces right holding coffee
pot, 6-1/4 x 2-3/4", VF, HL/Apr 25/98
(200-400)   173

HOW TO HAVE AN ACCIDENT IN THE HOME (1956)
BACKGROUNDS
Aerial view of city, tempera-on-board master background, 9-1/2 x 40", studio notes,
VF, HL/Apr 10/94 (800-1200)   1008
CELS – FULL FIGURE
Front view of Donald vibrating on clothesline next to
socks, 5" high, dry-brush effects, SR/Fall/94
(400-700)   490
CONCEPT AND INSPIRATIONAL ART
2 color styling paintings of interior of Donald Duck's
house: upstairs & stairs, tempera on board,
3-1/2 x 8-1/2", HL/Mar 16-17/96
(200-300)   1035
2 color styling paintings of interior of Donald Duck's
house: kitchen & living room; tempera on

board; 3-1/4 x 9", 5-1/4 x 12-1/2"; VF;
HL/Apr 25/98 (300-500)   633

HOW TO PLAY BASEBALL (1942)
CEL SET-UPS
Full figure of attentive Goofy in baseball uniform standing by dugout w/hands on knees & glove on left
hand amid equipment, 6", watercolor production
background, CLA/Jun 7/97 (2500-3500)   4830
Full-figure rear view of serious Goofy rounding third
with bases stuck to both feet, 5-1/8", key
watercolor background of stadium, original
dust effects, some rippling, SR/Spring/98
(3000-6000)   3110
CELS – FULL FIGURE
Goofy swings bat, 7-1/2 x 11-3/4", CE/Dec 15/93
(800-1200)   977
Determined Goofy (all but tip of right foot) facing right,
in mid-swing with huge bat, 5", dry bush effects,
paint restoration, SR/Fall/94 (700-1100) 2330
Goofy stands facing right, eyes closed, kissing baseball
bat, 5-1/4", 12-field, ct, SR/Spring/95
(1100-1600)   1610
Pitcher Goofy winds up, 5-1/2", 12-field, ct,
SR/Spring/95 (1100-1600)   1630
Determined Goofy coiled to swing, 4-3/8", 12-field,
SR/Fall/95 (1200-1800)   1200
Puzzled Goofy stands holding severely charred bat, 5",
12-field cel, ct, SR/Spring/98 (1200-1800) 1480

HOW TO PLAY FOOTBALL (1944)
CELS – FULL FIGURE
Exhausted footballer Goofy standing bent over, resting
ball on ground, transparent shadow, 2-3/4", 12-
field cel, SR/Spring/97 (600-1000)   920

HOW TO PLAY GOLF (1944)
CEL SET-UPS
Donald & Goofy walking with clubs, watercolor
production background from The Adventures
of Ichabod & Mr. Toad, 3-1/2 & 5-1/2",
inscribed "… Walt Disney", CE/Dec 16/94
(2500-3500)   6900
CELS – FULL FIGURE
Enraged Bull ready to charge to right, 3", 12-field cel,
SR/Spring/95 (200-500)   480
Front view of dancing golfer Goofy holding club
horizontally with both hands like a cane,
4-1/4 x 3-1/2", VF+, from Basmajian
Collection, HL/Apr 25/98 (900-1200)   1495

HOW TO SWIM (1942)
CELS – FULL FIGURE
Front view of Goofy with blank expression riding
end of diving board, 6-1/2 x 8-1/2", VF,
HL/Nov 13/94 (600-900)   1904
Goofy in vintage bathing suit stands facing right
holding inner tube around waist, 4-1/2",
12-field, ct, SR/Spring/95 (1100-1600)   1160

IN DUTCH (1946)
CEL SET-UPS
Full figure of Pluto hitched to milk cart holding milk
bottle in mouth, complementary color print
background, 2 x 3", HL/Aug 21/94
(800-1200)   784
CELS – FULL FIGURE
Eager Pluto ready to pull milk wagon, 1-1/2 x 2-1/2",
HL/Aug 6/95 (300-500)   476

IT'S TOUGH TO BE A BIRD (1969)
CELS – FULL FIGURE
3 production cels of a bird, 5-1/2" [listed in catalog as
"Difficult to be a Bird, 1968"], CE/Dec 16/94
(600-800)   345

JACK AND OLD MAC (1956)
CELS – FULL FIGURE
Old MacDonald & Mrs. MacDonald dancing, 6-1/2"
& similar, CE/Jun 18/94 (300-500)   81

THE JAZZ FOOL (1929)
ANIMATION DRAWINGS
Full-figure rough drawing by Ub Iwerks of Mickey
w/mallet tied to tail playing large saxophone

---

w/bucket underneath, 4", CE/Jun 20/96
(1000-1500)   1725

JUNGLE RHYTHM (1929)
BACKGROUNDS
Production background, pencil & ink on paper,
inscriptions, CE/Jun 18/94 (3000-4000)   3680
Master background of river winding thru wooded landscape, sepia & gray watercolor on background
sheet, 9-1/2 x 11", VF+, HL/Apr 25/98   3795

JUST DOGS (1932)
LAYOUT ART
Layout drawing of eager Pluto [?] sitting, 5"; 2-page
annotated production draft; CE/Jun 18/94
(300-500)   518

THE KARNIVAL KID (1929)
ANIMATION DRAWINGS
Full-figure drawing of hot dog vendor diving over
Mickey into cart, 5 x 7-1/2", HL/Nov 19/95
(600-900)   2300
Full-figure drawing of surprised Mickey being jumped
by a ferocious cat, 5-1/4 x 7", HL/Feb 23/97
(700-1000)   3220
BACKGROUNDS
3 master black & white backgrounds of outdoor
carnival scenes, ink & gouache on heavy
12-field paper, SR/Fall/94
(10,000-20,000)   7,000
2 master black-&-white backgrounds: Mickey's hot
dog cart, with carnival background; interior
of Mickey's trailer; ink & gouache on heavy
12-field sheets w/two-hole punch, inscribed
"Scene 9" & "Scene 29"; SR/Spring/97
(4000-8000)   6000
Watercolor production background of wagon interior
with bed & posters, sight 9 x 11",
S/Dec 19/97 (4000-6000)   3450

KING NEPTUNE (1932)
ANIMATION DRAWINGS
Drawing of angry Neptune hoisting pirate ship on
trident, 6-1/2 x 7", HL/Aug 6/95 (400-600) 336

THE KLONDIKE KID (1932)
ANIMATION DRAWINGS
Full-figure front-view drawing of Pegleg Pete standing
laughing, 6-1/2", 12-field sheet, shallow tear,
SR/Fall/94 (300-500)   300
2 matching drawings of Mickey (2" & similar) & Pluto
(3"); drawing of Mickey; CE/Dec 16/94
(800-1200)   1150
Full-figure front-view drawing of Pegleg Pete standing
laughing, 6-1/2", 12-field sheet, some wear &
edge discoloration, SR/Spring/96 (300-600) 330
Near-full figure drawing of laughing Pegleg Pete
lifting Mickey by nose, 6-1/2 x 7-1/2",
HL/Apr 28/96 (800-1000)   1265
Drawing of smiling Mickey (full figure) feeding soup
to Minnie, 4 x 6", HL/Oct 6/96 (700-1000) 978
2 full-figure drawings: angry Mickey stands holding
whip, Pluto leaps to pull sled; 3 x 3-1/2" &
2 x 10"; VF; HL/Nov 16/97 (600-900)   748
Full-figure drawing of angry Mickey stepping right
& wielding bullwhip, 2-1/2 x 4", VF,
HL/Apr 25/98 (400-500)   288
LAYOUT ART
Layout drawing of sad Minnie sitting on barrel as sad
Mickey stands watching, 12-field sheet, scene
direction & production stamp, shallow center
vertical fold, SR/Spring/96 (2000-4000)   3930

A KNIGHT FOR A DAY (1946)
BACKGROUNDS
Master background of castle interior, tempera on
background sheet w/stamps & notes,
8-1/2 x 11", HL/Aug 21/94 (1800-2400)   1680
LAYOUT ART
Layout drawing of page Goofy working on rear
of horse's skirt, 2", CE/Jun 20/96
(1000-1500)   1150

LAMBERT, THE SHEEPISH LION (1952)
CELS – FULL FIGURE

Eager baby Lambert, 4-1/2 x 4", HL/Aug 21/94
(600-800)   728
Front view of baby Lambert sitting looking quizzically
to right, 3 x 2-1/2", HL/Oct 6/96 (600-900) 863
Stork walking w/eyes closed & bundle over shoulder,
5-1/2 x 5-1/2", HL/Feb 23/97 (300-500)   230

LAUGH-O-GRAM FILMS (1922)
SET-UP/TITLE ART
"…the earliest art work known to survive from a
Disney animated film." Background painting
with full-figure original ink drawings of donkey
& cat mounted to it plus end-title card "And
they lived happily ---", 8 x 10", ink & gray
watercolor on medium-weight paper, VG-F,
HL/Aug 6/95 (12,000-16,000)   23,520

LEND A PAW (1941)
CEL SET-UPS
Full figure of Mickey on knees in kitchen holding
half-empty milk bottle, 4-5/8", 12-field cel,
color print background from Pantry Pirate,
SR/Spring/97 (3000-4000)   3360

LET'S STICK TOGETHER (1952)
MODEL ART
Full-figure model cel of elderly Donald Duck walking
with cane, 4 x 4-1/2", HL/Nov 19/95
(500-700)   403

LION AROUND (1950)
ANIMATION DRAWINGS
Full-figure drawing of Huey, Dewey, & Louie
standing in ranger hats looking up with
mouths open, 4 1/2", 12-field sheet,
SR/Spring/98 (400-700)   370

THE LITTERBUG (1961)
CELS – FULL FIGURE
Full image of surprised Donald & nephews sitting
in convertible, staring right, 4-3/4", 16-field,
SR/Spring/96 (400-700)   810

LITTLE HIAWATHA (1937)
ANIMATION DRAWINGS
Full-figure drawing of Hiawatha pulling up pants,
5-1/4 x 4", HL/Apr 28/96 (500-700)   690
Sheet of 3 Fred Moore character sketches of Hiawatha,
4-3/4", 12-field, SR/Fall/96 (400-700)   200
Full-figure drawing of sad Hiawatha standing holding

bow & half-drawn arrow, 7 x 4-1/2", HL/Oct 6/96 (500-700)   460

ART – MISCELLANEOUS
Full-figure gouache-on-paper art of Little Hiawatha nose-to-nose w/bear cub, each about 5", S/Jun 10/95 (100-150)   402

CEL SET-UPS
Hiawatha stands bold, Courvoisier wood-veneer background, 8-1/2 x 7", CE/Dec 15/93 (2500-3500)   2185

Hiawatha stares in disbelief, Courvoisier wood-veneer background, 6 x 5-1/4", CE/Dec 15/93 (2000-2500)   2300

Hiawatha hunts with bow & arrow, Courvoisier wood-veneer background, 4", S/Jun 17/94 (1000-1500)   1725

Hiawatha's pants fall down, airbrushed Courvoisier background, 4", S/Jun 17/94 (1000-1500)   1840

Full figure of puzzled Hiawatha standing looking down, complementary Courvoisier painted woodgrain background, 5-1/2 x 4-1/2", HL/Apr 28/96 (1500-2000)   1725

Full-figure profile of Hiawatha stalking with bow & arrow ready, Courvoisier woodgrain & painted background, 6 x 4-1/2", HL/Apr 28/96 (400-500)   546

Full figure of Hiawatha aiming bow & arrow at grasshopper, Courvoisier watercolor & airbrush background, 3-1/2", CE/Jun 20/96 (1200-1800)   1955

Full figure of grim Hiawatha standing with bow & arrow facing left, looking back, grasshopper in front of him, 4-7/8", master watercolor background, SR/Fall/96 (3500-5000)   3750

Full-figures of Hiawatha with bow drawn confronting rabbit on stump, complementary painted background as prepared for Courvoisier, 7-1/2 x 7-1/2" overall, HL/Feb 23/97 (1200-1600)   2070

Full figure of intent Hiawatha stepping left with bow & arrow ready, 4", Courvoisier wood-veneer background, restored, SR/Spring/97 (1400-1800)   1600

Full-figure profile of Hiawatha shooting at caterpillar, Courvoisier watercolor & airbrush background, 3-1/2", CLA/Jun 7/97 (1000-1500)   1495

Full figure of Hiawatha, bow & arrow in left hand, reaching down w/right hand to pull up fallen pants, 4" w/o feathers, airbrushed Courvoisier background, needs restoration, S/Jun 21/97 (800-1200)   1380

Full-figure rear view of intent Hiawatha standing facing left, drawing arrow, pants around ankles; 4" w/o feather; airbrushed Courvoisier background, mat signed by Walt Disney, S/Dec 19/97 (1800-2200)   4312

CELS – FULL FIGURE
Hiawatha stalks with bow & arrow, 7-1/2 x 4-1/2", HL/Nov 13/94 (800-1200)   1680

Full figure of fawn standing tangled in small tree, looking back left, 3", 12-field, SR/Spring/96 (300-700)   410

Serious Hiawatha stands with bow & arrow looking back, 8-1/2 x 11", HL/Apr 28/96 (900-1200)   1495

Startled Little Hiawatha looks left in mid-step, 5-1/2 x 2-1/2", HL/Oct 6/96 (700-900)   920

2 full-figure cels: sad Hiawatha aims arrow, bear cub runs; 7 x 4-1/4" & 2 x 2"; VF; HL/Nov 16/97 (700-1000)   1380

Smiling Hiawatha walks right, holding bow in one hand, arrow in other, 3-3/4 x 3-1/2", VF, HL/Nov 16/97 (400-600)   1093

MODEL ART
Model sheet by Gustav Tenggren & Albert Hurter, sight 15 x 17", graphite on trimmed paper applied to posterboard, CLA/Jun 7/97 (2000-4000)   1955

STORY ART
Signed Gustav Tenggren story painting: Hiawatha paddling canoe thru canyon, watercolor on heavyweight paper, 4-1/2 x 7", HL/Apr 28/96 (4000-6000)   8050

THE LITTLE HOUSE (1952)
CONCEPT AND INSPIRATIONAL ART
Signed concept piece by Mary Blair showing Little House on hill, tempera on board, 7-3/4 x 9-3/4" including signature, HL/Feb 23/97 (1400-1800)   6900

THE LITTLE WHIRLWIND (1941)
ANIMATION DRAWINGS
4 rough drawings of Mickey Mouse, 3-3/4 x 3-1/2" to 4-1/2 x 3-1/2", F, HL/Nov 16/97 (1000-1500)   2760

CEL SET-UPS
Pan production set-up of Minnie (5-1/2") holding cake & glaring at lovestruck Mickey (from *The Nifty Nineties*, 5"), pan watercolor production background, S/Dec 17/94 (14,000-18,000)   16,100

MODEL ART
Set of 4 "Action Models" model sheets with unofficial ransom-note-style captions, 14 x 11-1/4", edge wear & rippling, SR/Spring/95 (400-800)   650

THE LONE CHIPMUNKS (1954)
CELS -- FULL FIGURES
Chip & Dale (1") in saddle of scared horse rearing to right, full image 8-3/4", SR/Fall/96 (400-800)   420

Dale (4") standing opening Pete's tobacco pouch, 12-field cel, some rippling, ct, SR/Fall/96 (400-800)   420

LONESOME GHOSTS (1937)
ANIMATION DRAWINGS
Colored-pencil drawing of angry Donald, 4 x 3", VF, HL/Feb 26-27/94 (300-400)   770

Full-figure drawing of angry Donald standing facing left in fighting pose with net poised above head, 4-3/4", 12-field sheet, SR/Fall/95 (200-400)   250

Full-figure drawing of horizontal squawking Donald Duck, eyes closed, bill open, 2-1/4", 12-field sheet, timer's chart, inker's notation, swish effects, SR/Spring/98 (200-400)   310

CEL SET-UPS
2 cels of Mickey swimming, 7 & 6" wide, 12-field cels, water effects, pan master watercolor background from *Beach Picnic*, set-up 40-1/4 x 9", SR/Fall/96 (3000-6000)   4460

CELS – FULL FIGURE
Profile of smiling hunter Mickey tiptoeing to left with shotgun, 4 x 4", F+, HL/Apr 28/96 (5000-6000)   4025

LUCKY NUMBER (1951)
CEL SET-UPS
Nephews in new car at gas pumps, master background, notes & initials, 7-1/2 x 10-1/2", HL/Aug 21/94 (2500-3500)   2352

Full figures of Huey, Dewey & Louie standing in garage of Donald's gas station, 8 x 11", tempera on background sheet, HL/Apr 23/95 (1800-2400)   2912

Huey, Dewey, Louie identically dressed in maroon cardigans & green hats, Xerox line-on-celluloid background, 4" ea., S/Jun 19/96 (300-500)   402

CELS – FULL FIGURE
Eager Donald stands in attendant's hat reading lottery ticket, signed by Jack Hannah, 6 x 6-1/2" including signature, HL/Feb 23/97 (700-1000)   1150

STORY ART
20 storyboard drawings by Nick George of Donald Duck & nephews at gas station, pastel & charcoal on 8-1/2 x 6" storyboard sheets, SR/Fall/94 (1500-2500)   1540

THE MAD DOCTOR (1933)
ANIMATION DRAWINGS
Drawing of Mickey on knees (eyes closed) holding chained Pluto, 3", CE/Dec 16/94 (500-700)   518

Drawing of Mickey on knees (2") holding chained Pluto (2-1/2"), CE/Dec 16/94 (600-800)   518

Full-figure drawing of kneeling Mickey embracing chained Pluto (sitting), 4 x 5-1/2", HL/Mar 16-17/96 (600-900)   1035

Full-figure drawing of shocked Mickey, standing & holding onto iron ring, leaning left, 2-3/4", 12-field sheet, SR/Fall/96 (600-1200)   680

Full-figure drawing of smiling Mickey kneeling with hands on happy Pluto who's sitting chained, 3-1/2 x 5-1/2", HL/Oct 6/96 (800-1000)   863

Full-figure drawing of worried Mickey standing facing right in ready position, 2-5/16", 12-field sheet,

MAGICIAN MICKEY (1937)
ANIMATION DRAWINGS
Full-figure drawing of angry Donald, bottle in right hand, doing a one-hand stand with his left, 3-1/2 x 3-1/2", HL/Feb 23/97 (200-400)   460

Full-figure drawing of flamboyant magician Mickey with arms out, 4-5/8", 12-field sheet, inker's notation, SR/Spring/97 (500-900)   400

Full-figure drawing of angry Donald standing facing right, one eye closed, swinging bottle in right hand; 4 x 5", VF, HL/Apr 25/98 (200-400)   489

CELS – FULL FIGURE
Befuddled Donald Duck, 3-3/4 x 3-1/4", HL/Nov 19/95 (3000-3500)   2760

LAYOUT ART
Layout drawing of Mickey producing a cage full of canaries for enraptured Donald, 4-1/2 x 10", HL/Apr 23/95 (800-1200)   3360

Layout animation drawing by Les Clark: full figure of smiling Mickey Mouse standing holding magic wand inside top hat, 4", CE/Dec 12/96 (1200-1500)   1035

Full-figure layout drawing of Mickey standing twirling scarf, 5", CE/Dec 18/97 (2000-3000)   1725

MAIL DOG (1947)
TITLE ART
Title card: Pluto & sled with mail bag amid white trees is part of watercolor background, hand lettering on cel overlay, 12-field, with production cover flap signed by designer & director, SR/Fall/95 (1500-2200)   1500

THE MAIL PILOT (1933)
ANIMATION DRAWINGS
2 drawings: Mickey flies plane, 1 x 1-1/4"; Pete flies plane, 1-1/2 x 2-1/4"; framed together, CE/Jun 18/94 (1500-2000)   2415

Full-figure drawing of Mickey piloting airplane that's trailing rope, 4 x 10-1/2", HL/Aug 6/95 (600-900)   1008

Full-figure drawing of Mickey looking back as his plane flies right towing rope, 9 x 4-1/2", 12-field sheet, SR/Fall/95 (1000-1500)   1000

Full-figure drawing of smiling Mickey flying snow-covered plane, 1-1/2 x 5", HL/Nov 19/95 (500-700)   863

Full-figure drawing of Mickey piloting plane which is pulling cable & has wings sheared off, 4 x 9-1/2", HL/Oct 6/96 (800-1000)   920

Full-figure drawing of smiling Mickey looking back while flying to right as wingless plane pulls rope, 4-1/4 x 10", HL/Nov 16/97 (500-700)   1150

2 drawings: Pete flying to right w/taut rope around airplane cannon; Mickey landing damaged plane to right & pulling rope; each sheet 9-1/2 x 12", S/Dec 19/97 (800-1200)   1265

BACKGROUNDS
Pan background sketch of airport in final scene, 8 x 29", HL/Oct 6/96 (500-700)   575

THE MANY ADVENTURES OF WINNIE THE POOH (1977)
Also see WINNIE THE POOH...; TELEVISION: THE NEW ADVENTURES OF WINNIE THE POOH; UNIDENTIFIED/MISCELLANEOUS: WINNIE THE POOH
CEL SET-UPS
Full figures of Pooh (sitting holding stick, from *The Honey Tree*) & Christopher Robin (back turned) at play in Hundred Acre Wood, complementary color print background, seal, 7-1/2 x 5-1/2" cel, VF+, HL/Apr 25/98 (500-700)   863

MERBABIES (1938)
CONCEPT AND INSPIRATIONAL ART
Two concept sketches of merbaby & crab, 6-9/16 x 4-7/8", colored pencil on 8 x 6-1/4" sheets, SR/Fall/96 (300-700)   390

Watercolor concept painting of waves crashing over rock outcropping, 10-1/2 x 7-7/8" on 14 x 10-5/16" sheet of heavy artist's watercolor paper, 2-hole punched,

SR/Spring/97 (200-500) 220

Two signed concept sketches of merbabies with
jellyfish carousel & with seahorses at sponge
cafeteria by Ferdinand Horvath, 12 x 10" &
10 x 7-1/4", SR/Fall/97 (300-600) 880

MODEL ART

Color model of Merbabe on cel with MGM 2-hole
peg system, 4-1/2 x 7-1/2" including
notations, HL/Oct 6/96 (600-800) 633

STORY ART

4 polished story drawings of starfish & snail
performing balancing act; 6 x 6",
7-1/2 x 3", 8 x 3", 7 x 4-1/2",
HL/Mar 16-17/96 (300-500) 748

THE MERRY DWARFS (1929)
ANIMATION DRAWINGS

Full-figure drawing of dwarf hoisting frothy mug
of brew, 4 x 3", HL/Oct 6/96 (300-400) 259

MICKEY AND THE SEAL (1948)
CEL SET-UPS

Full figures of Mickey standing in street laughing as
bored Pluto sits on curb, master background
painting apparently from "The Wuzzles" TV
show (tempera on background sheet),
6-1/4 x 4" & 3 x 3" cel images,
HL/Oct 6/96 (1500-2000) 1380

CELS – FULL FIGURE

Mickey stands happily dangling a fish by its tail,
6-1/2", S/Jun 17/94 (1200-1500) 1840

Mickey stands happily dangling fish by its tail,
6-1/2", S/Dec 17/94 (1800-2200) 2070

Mickey in bathrobe & towel over arm whistling &
walking with eyes closed, 4-1/2", 12-field,
SR/Fall/95 (900-1600) 800

Suburban Mickey stands facing left, arms in
grasping pose, 6", 12-field, framed with
4 x 6" reproduction of original poster,
SR/Fall/95 (2000-3000) 2200

Mickey stands facing left wearing straw hat, laughing
with eyes closed, 6-1/8", 12-field frosted cel,
ct, SR/Spring/98 (800-1400) 730

CELS – PARTIAL FIGURE

Knees-up of Mickey standing facing left, holding fish
in right hand, 6-5/8", hand inked in grease
pencil on 12-field frosted cel, SR/Spring/96
(1200-1800) 1480

Thigh-up image of puzzled Mickey, towel around
waist, holding smiling seal like baby, 6-1/2",
cel overlay signed by Phil Duncan,
S/Jun 21/97 (1200-1800) 1495

TITLE ART

Title card: full figure of happy seal swimming right,
seal & hand lettering on cel over watercolor
background, original production cover flap,
SR/Spring/95 (2000-5000) 2040

MICKEY DOWN UNDER (1948)
ANIMATION DRAWINGS

2 full-figure drawings: joyously dancing in double
image; front view of surprised Master of
Ceremonies from *Mickey's Amateurs*,
1937; 5 x 2-1/2" & 5 x 7"; F-VF;
HL/Nov 13/94 (400-600) 420

TITLE ART

Title card: map of Australia, airbrushed in watercolor,
native creatures & hand lettering on cel,
original cover flap, SR/Fall/96 (1400-2000) 1430

MICKEY IN ARABIA (1932)
ANIMATION DRAWINGS

Full-figure drawing of Mickey & Minnie riding
canopied camel w/license plates,
3-1/2 x 5", HL/Oct 6/96 (800-1000) 978

MICKEY PLAYS PAPA (1934)
ANIMATION DRAWINGS

Animation drawing of Mickey, 3-3/4",
CE/Dec 16/94 (500-700) 1840

Drawing of scary Mickey sitting in bed reading book
A Cry in the Night, 2-3/8", 12-field sheet,
SR/Fall/95 (400-700) 400

2 drawings: frightened Mickey sitting reading book,
full figure of frightened Pluto crouching;
3 x 3-1/4", 2-1/4 x 3", HL/Feb 23/97
(1200-1500) 1150

MICKEY'S AMATEURS (1937)
ANIMATION DRAWINGS

Pencil drawing of smiling Mickey as master
of ceremonies, 4 x 4", VF+,
HL/Feb 26-27/94 (600-800) 715

Drawing of Goofy sitting amid elements of his
one-Goof band, 8 x 8", HL/Nov 13/94
(500-700) 420

2 full-figure drawings: front view of surprised Master
of Ceremonies; joyously dancing in double
image from *Mickey Down Under*, 1948;
5 x 2-1/2" & 5 x 7"; F-VF; HL/Nov 13/94
(400-600) 420

Near-full figure drawing of host Mickey reading list,
4-1/2 x 3", HL/Mar 16-17/96 (300-500) 805

Drawing of Goofy in band uniform with mouth
curved to side around harmonica, signed
by Frank Thomas & Ollie Johnston, 9-1/2",
CE/Jun 20/96 (600-800) 322

Full-figure drawing of Mickey in bow tie & tail coat
standing with papers in left hand, looking
straight down, 4-1/2 x 4-1/2",
HL/Feb 23/97 (500-700) 489

Full-figure drawing of emcee Mickey standing, right
arm raised, eyes closed, 5-1/2 x 3-1/2",
HL/May 31/97 (400-500) 58

4 drawings of Goofy: screaming on swinging scaffold
(*The Big Wash*); dressed in fur coat (*Polar Trappers*); in band (*Amateur Hour* [sic]); one from
Mickey's Service Station; each sheet 9-1/2
x 12"; S/Dec 19/97 (800-1200) 920

CEL SET-UPS

Full figure of surprised Mickey standing on stage
looking right, 4-1/2", watercolor production
background, stamps, CE/Dec 18/97 (8000-
12,000) 6900

MICKEY'S BIRTHDAY PARTY (1942)
TITLE ART

Title card resembling top of birthday cake,
watercolor on 12-field board, original
cover flap, annotated production stamp,
SR/Spring/98 (2000-4000) 2010

MICKEY'S CHRISTMAS CAROL (1983)
CEL SET-UPS

5" Mickey & Minnie w/turkey watch 3" children
open presents, matching black & white
Xerox cel background, silver Disney seal,
S/Dec 16/93 (600-800) 4888

Full figure of Scrooge McDuck in night clothes with
line-print background of bedroom, 9 x 12",
Disney seal, VF, HL/Apr 10/94 (500-800) 392

Jiminy Cricket as Christmas Past, matching line-print
background cel, 9-1/2 x 14", Disney seal, VF+,
HL/Apr 10/94 (600-800) 896

Mickey w/reluctant smile at desk, Xerox
line background, WDP seal & label, 5",
S/Jun 17/94 (800-1200) 1150

Mickey looks out door, line-print background, 6-3/4
x 3", WDP seal, CE/Jun 18/94 (700-900) 805

Mickey pleading case at door, line-print background,
6 x 3-1/2", WDP seal, CE/Jun 18/94
(700-900) 1035

Full figure of Scrooge in nightshirt tiptoeing thru
snow, line-print background, Disney seal &
label, 9 x 13", F+, HL/Aug 21/94 (500-700) 392

DAE set of 2 limited-edition cels over color print
backgrounds: Scrooge counting money,
Cratchit family on Christmas Eve; each
#479/500, labels, 11 x 15", VF+,
HL/Aug 21/94 (2000-2500) 3360

Near-full figure of pleading Mickey at door, matching
line-print background, Disney seal, 10 x 13",
VF+, HL/Aug 21/94 (1200-1800) 1120

Set of 2 limited-edition cels: Scrooge counting
money, Cratchit family on Christmas Eve;
each 11 x 15" & #342/500 with Disney
seals & labels over color print backgrounds;
VF+; HL/Nov 13/94 (2000-2500) 2296

Startled Scrooge kneeling in chair, 10 x 14",
matching line-print background, Disney
seal, HL/Nov 13/94 (700-900) 605

Cheerful Mickey at desk holding quill pen, 10 x 14",
line-print background, Disney seal & labels,
HL/Nov 13/94 (1000-1500) 1232

Mickey (5") & Minnie (5") with turkey happily watch

two children (3" each) play, matching b&w line
Xerox cel background, silver Disney seal,
S/Dec 17/94 (2000-3000) 2300

Full figure of happy Scrooge standing with large bag
over shoulder, 9 x 12", line-print background,
HL/Apr 23/95 (600-900) 616

Full figures of Scrooge (5-1/4") in nightclothes
standing looking back at bundle he's carrying
as Minnie & two children watch, 16-field,
line-print background, Disney Art Program
seal & labels, SR/Fall/95 (900-1400) 990

Front view of Scrooge at desk, making point into
camera while holding quill pen, 4-1/4", key
line-print background, 16-field, Disney Art
Program seal, SR/Fall/95 (600-900) 880

Full figure of Mickey Mouse sitting toward side of
bookkeeper's chair, 9-1/2 x 13", line-print
background, HL/Nov 19/95 (1000-1500) 1035

Uncle Scrooge (4") gives money to Rat (4-1/2")
& Mole (3") for poor, Xerox line-on-cel background, seal, S/Jun 19/96 (600-800) 805

Full figure of Huey standing on Dewey's shoulders to
hang ornament on christmas tree, 6-1/4",
16-field cel, Disney Art Program seal, line-print
background, SR/Fall/96 (600-1000) 600

Set of two limited-edition cels: Scrooge counting
money, Cratchit family on Christmas Eve;
each #201/500 & over color print background; 11-1/2 x 16"; seal & certificates;
VF; HL/Oct 6/96 (1200-1600) 2070

Mickey, Minnie & "Tiny Tim" gather around table
for Christmas meal, line print from matching
background in film, 8 x 13", HL/Oct 6/96
(1500-2000) 1265

Set of 2 limited-edition cels: Scrooge counting money,
Cratchit family at home; ea. #342/500
& over color print of matching background;
11-1/2 x 16"; HL/Feb 23/97 (1200-1600) 1265

Full figure of Mickey turning in his chair away from
desk, 5-1/4 x 3-1/4", print of line overlay
for matching background, VF+,
HL/Nov 16/97 (700-900) 748

Full figure of Scrooge sliding happily down outside
railing in snow, 4", Xerox line-on-cel
background, silver WDP seal, S/Dec 19/97
(800-1200) 690

Happy Mickey seated at desk holding quill pen,
looking back; cel print of matching background
line overlay; 5-1/4 x 4" cel; WDP seal and
certificate; VF+; HL/Apr 25/98 (800-1000) 805

Full figures of Uncle Scrooge in rocking chair
surrounded by kids as Mickey & Minnie
stand looking on, 3" on 16-field cel,
matching line-print background of living
room, SR/Spring/98 (1800-2600) 1740

CELS – FULL FIGURE

Scrooge in rocking chair plays with Mickey's niece
& nephews, WDP seal, 9-1/2 x 10-3/4",
CE/Dec 15/93 (1500-2500) 1150

2 cels: Goofy as Spirit of Marley confronts Scrooge;
Willie the Giant as Ghost of Christmas Present
drops Scrooge in pocket; each, 6-1/2 x
12-1/2"; VF+; HL/Aug 21/94 (1000-1500) 784

Irritated Scrooge stands with hands on hips, looking
right, 6-1/2", 16-field, w/Disney Art Program
seal, SR/Fall/94 (400-700) 600

Willie the Giant sits in mid-air, 11 x 15", Disney seal,
HL/Nov 13/94 (400-600) 476

Gracious Scrooge (9") with arm around surprised
Mickey (6"), WDP seal, CE/Dec 16/94
(700-900) 920

Hatless Scrooge points while holding wreath,
5-1/2 x 7", HL/Aug 6/95 (600-900) 1120

Scrooge sits in rocking chair entertaining three
children, sight 9-1/2 x 11", S/Dec 14/96
(1000-1500) 2587

Transformed Scrooge (7") gleefully hugs stunned
Mickey (6-1/2"), S/Dec 14/96 (800-1200) 1725

CELS – PARTIAL FIGURE

Matching cels of Scrooge & flirtatious Isabel (Daisy
Duck), 8 x 12", Disney seal, VF+,
HL/Apr 10/94 (1000-1500) 784

Large image of Willie the Giant dangling bunch
of purple grapes, 11", silver WDP seal,
S/Dec 17/94 (600-800) 575

Suspicious Willie the Giant holds up Scrooge for
inspection, 9-1/2 x 13", seal, VF+,
HL/Oct 6/96 (500-700) 633

Ankles-up view of angry Scrooge looking left &

waving arms, seal, & certificate, 6 x 5",
VF+, HL/Apr 25/98 (500-700)   403

CONCEPT AND INSPIRATIONAL ART
2 matched concept paintings of Scrooge's wingback
chair & table studying lighting effects before &
after candle is extinguished, gouache on 10 x
7-1/2" boards by Jim Coleman, signed,
SR/Spring/98 (400-800)   460

TITLE ART
4 scenes: actual final sheets shot & composited with
textured backgrounds & hand lettering to create
titles, 15 x 11", one original ink drawing, others
copies, central images trimmed & fit into
decorative wreaths, SR/Fall/97 (900-1500)   600

MICKEY'S CIRCUS (1936)
ANIMATION DRAWINGS
Drawing of triumphant Donald Duck standing on
ringmaster Mickey (squashing his hat), 5-1/2
x 4", HL/Nov 19/95 (800-1200)   2070
Full-figure drawing of Mickey balancing on high wire,
6 x 11-1/2", HL/Nov 19/95 (600-800)   805
2 full-figure drawings: smiling Mickey diving &
worried Donald falling; 4 x 4" & 3 x 2-1/2",
HL/Apr 28/96 (700-1000)   776
Full-figure drawing of flamboyant ringmaster Mickey,
4 x 6", HL/Apr 28/96 (600-900)   575
2 full-figure drawing of Mickey swaying on
tightrope, 5-1/2 x 11-1/2" & 5-1/2
x 11", HL/Oct 6/96 (1200-1600)   1035
2 drawings: Mickey in precarious position on tightrope; Mickey holding shotgun & cautiously
opening door from *Mickey's Parrot;* approx.
4" each; S/Dec 14/96 (1000-1500)   747
Full-figure drawing of angry Donald Duck (in band
hat) bent at waist facing left & gesturing with
right hand, 2-1/2 x 3-1/4", HL/May 31/97
(200-300)   288
Full-figure drawing of ringmaster Mickey pointing
forward w/cane, 4 x 6", VF, HL/Nov 16/97
(400-600)   546

MICKEY'S ELEPHANT (1936)
ANIMATION DRAWINGS
Near-full-figure drawing of smiling Mickey, arms
spread, saw in right hand; 3"; CE/Jun 20/96
(700-900)   633
2 full-figure drawings of Mickey standing facing right
& tugging on [unseen] Bobo's trunk, 3-1/4 x
3-1/2", 3 x 4", HL/May 31/97 (600-800)   633
3 near-full-figure drawings of Mickey, 6-1/2"; cel
of Mickey from "Mickey Mouse Club", circa
1950s, 3-3/4", CLA/Jun 7/97 (1200-1500) 1150
2 full-figure drawings of Mickey standing facing right
& tugging on [unseen] Bobo's trunk, 3-1/4 x
3-1/2", 3 x 4", HL/Nov 16/97 (600-800)   633
3 drawings: Mickey; Bobo; Mickey & Bobo; each
10 x 12"; S/Dec 19/97 (900-1200)   1035
Near-full figure drawing of Mickey standing facing
right with hands on hips, 5-3/4 x 5", VF,
HL/Apr 25/98 (500-700)   489
2 full-figure drawings: Mickey stands with hands
on hips facing right, 4 3/4"; Bobo stands
facing left, 3 3/4"; 12-field sheets;
SR/Spring/98 (500-1000)   600

CEL SET-UPS
Full figures of Mickey offering ball to happy Bobo,
9-1/2 x 12", Studio Art props background
painting of circus ring (tempera on background
board), VF, HL/Nov 16/97 (1000-1500)   1265

MICKEY'S FIRE BRIGADE (1935)
ANIMATION DRAWINGS
Drawing of Mickey wrapped in fire hose turning
wrench, 3-1/2", CE/Dec 16/94 (800-1200) 920
Full-figure drawing of Mickey & Donald using
Goofy as battering ram, 3-1/2 x 7-3/4",
HL/Nov 19/95 (800-1000)   1380
Full-figure drawing of determined Fireman Mickey
standing facing right, 3-1/8", 12-field sheet,
handwritten scene & production notes, "final"
written at bottom, SR/Fall/96 (500-900)   500
Full-figure drawing of firemen Mickey & Donald
grabbing foot [of reluctant Clarabelle] amid
water & bubbles, 6 x 11", HL/Oct 6/96
(700-1000)   690
3 drawings: fire chief Mickey; Mickey & Donald
using Goofy as battering ram; Mickey &

Donald retrieve Goofy from sink; 9-1/2 x
12"; S/Dec 19/97 (900-1200)   1265

CONCEPT AND INSPIRATIONAL ART
Detailed study for publicity illustration: Mickey,
Donald & Goofy on fire truck, 7 x 9",
HL/Aug 21/94 (600-800)   1232

CELS – FULL FIGURE
Fireman Mickey facing left, right hand out, left hand
behind back, 4", S/Jun 19/96 (2000-3000) 5175

STORY ART
4 story drawings: Mickey w/hose at hydrant (2);
Mickey, Donald, Goofy huddle; fire leaping
from window; colored pencil & conté crayon
on paper; 5 x 8" to 8 x 10", HL/Feb 23/97
(400-600)   748

MICKEY'S FOLLIES (1929)
ANIMATION DRAWINGS
Full-figure profile drawing of proud Mickey Mouse,
3-1/2 x 3-1/2", HL/Aug 6/95 (500-700)   1008

BACKGROUNDS/LAYOUT ART
2 background layout drawings of barn exterior area,
8 x 11-1/2" & 9 x 10-1/2", HL/Feb 23/97
(1000-1500)   920

MICKEY'S GALA PREMIERE (1933)
ANIMATION DRAWINGS
Full-figure drawing of Will Rogers with lasso
around laughing Mickey, 5 x 8-1/2",
VF, HL/Aug 21/94 (500-700)   896
Drawing of Hollywood stars congratulating Mickey,
4-1/2 x 7", HL/Aug 6/95 (1000-1500)   1792
Drawing of stars mobbing Mickey in final scene,
5 x 10", HL/Apr 28/96 (1200-1600)   1265
10 drawings of Mickey from scene 12, 3-5/8"
to 4-1/8", 12-field sheets, SR/Fall/96
(2500-5000)   2530
Drawing of five celebrities congratulating Mickey
Mouse, 5 x 8-1/2", HL/Oct 6/96
(900-1200)   1265
Full-figure drawing of smiling Mickey turning &
waving top hat as Minnie walks behind him,
4 x 4-3/4", HL/Oct 6/96 (700-1000)   978
2 drawings: Mickey being congratulated by Hollywood
elite, 9-1/2 x 12"; Mickey & Minnie climbing
tree to escape bull, from *Mickey's Rival,*
10 x 12"; S/Dec 14/96 (1200-1800)   1265
Drawing of 3 Hollywood stars kneeling to shake
Mickey's hands (& foot), 4-1/2 x 7",
HL/Feb 23/97 (700-1000)   863
Drawing of Mickey (2-3/4") being congratulated by
mob of celebrities, 10-1/2 x 6-1/8" image
w/color keys, SR/Spring/97 (1700-2500)   1510
Drawing of Stan Laurel (full figure) helping Oliver
Hardy [exit limousine], 5-1/2", 12-field sheet,
SR/Fall/97 (600-1200)   400
3 drawings: Horace Horsecollar at head of crowd,
Clarabelle Cow, small group of spectators
behind police line; 7 x 9-1/2", 4-1/4 x 3-1/4",
1-3/4 x 4"; F+; HL/Apr 25/98 (400-600)   230

CEL SET-UPS/MODEL ART
Color model: full figures of Laurel & Hardy standing
together in front of theater, ink & gouache
master background, 12-field, paint restoration,
SR/Fall/94 (4000-8000)   4070

MODEL ART
Color guide: full figures of Will Rogers (5") roping
Mickey Mouse (3"), graphite & colored pencil
on paper, S/Jun 21/97 (1000-1500)   1035

MICKEY'S GARDEN (1935)
ANIMATION DRAWINGS
Full-figure colored-pencil drawing of Mickey
Mouse with hand sprayer, 6 x 5-1/2",
VF, HL/Feb 26-27/94 (500-700)   715
3 drawings: Mickey (5-1/2") pouring solution
into sprayer; 2 of Donald Duck (4" each);
S/Jun 17/94 (1500-2000)   1035
Full-figure color key drawing of Mickey standing
facing right, shielding himself from flit gun
stuck to pumpkin on contorted Pluto's head,
8-1/2 x 5", 12-field sheet, color call-outs,
SR/Fall/95 (300-700)   630
2 full-figure drawings: irritated Mickey using sprayer,
excited Mickey holding sprayer & jumping;
3-1/2 x 4-1/2 & 3-1/2 x 3; HL/Nov 19/95
(1000-1500)   1150
2 matched drawings: full figure of Mickey running,

angry monster bug with paint notations;
5-1/2 x 8" & 5-1/2 x 3-1/2";
HL/Nov 19/95 (600-900)   2185
2 drawings: huge angry bug, full figure of frightened
Mickey running; 2-1/4 x 5", 5-1/2 x 7",
HL/Apr 28/96 (600-900)   633
Full-figure study drawing of Pluto with forelegs on
pumpkin, licking Mickey's head protruding
from top, 8" long, CE/Dec 18/97
(1500-2000)   1725
Drawing of Mickey, eyes closed, all but feet, 5-1/2",
CE/Dec 18/97 (700-900)   253
Full-figure drawing of Mickey standing facing right
looking into pump sprayer as pumpkin-headed
Pluto flies into sprayer handle, 4 x 9-1/2", VF,
HL/Apr 25/98 (400-600)   374

LAYOUT ART
Full-figure layout drawing of surprised Mickey held
horizontally in coils of large eager snake, 7",
CE/Dec 18/97 (2000-3000)   2530

STORY ART
3 colored-pencil storyboard drawings of bug-sized
Mickey & Pluto battling in garden; 4-3/4 x
5-1/2", 7-1/8 x 5 7/8", & 7 x 5-1/2";
SR/Fall/96 (500-1000)   990

MICKEY'S KANGAROO (1935)
ANIMATION DRAWINGS
3 drawings: one of Mickey, 2 of boxing kangaroos,
2 x 2" to 4-1/2 x 4", VF, HL/Apr 10/94
(700-1000)   728

MICKEY'S MAN FRIDAY (1935)
ANIMATION DRAWINGS/MODEL ART
Full-figure drawing by Bob Wickersham of Mickey
standing facing left, playing bamboo horn,
3-1/2", 12-field sheet, handwritten notations,
SR/Spring/95 (400-700)   1520
2 full-figure drawings by Bob Wickersham of Mickey
& Friday shaking hand/foot, approx. 3-1/2";
3rd drawing by Jack Kinney of shirt flag "Fort
Robinson Crusoe," 3-3/8"; all 12-field sheets,
ink & paint & production notations, some wear
& discoloration, center vertical fold on character
drawings, SR/Spring/95 (800-1400)   1580
Full-figure drawing of Mickey in island dress standing
facing left, looking up, 3-1/2", 12-field sheet,
inker's notation; model sheet of Friday; 1940
proposed remake; SR/Fall/95 (500-1000)   325
2 full-figure drawings: worried Mickey runs to right;
Friday in mid-step to right looks behind & down;
both 3-3/8", 12-field sheets, production &
camera notations; SR/Fall/96 (800-1200)   1020
Full-figure drawing of Mickey stepping to right,
twirling rope overhead, 4-1/2", 12-field
sheet, SR/Spring/97 (400-800)   900

CEL SET-UPS/MODEL ART
Full-figure color model cel of determined Mickey
swinging by rope suspended from pulley,
7-1/2", master watercolor background of
outdoors from earlier short, 12-field,
SR/Spring/96 (9000-15,000)   7000

CELS – FULL FIGURE/MODEL ART
Color model of Mickey standing facing left,
playing bamboo horn, 3-1/2", notations,
SR/Spring/95 (3500-5500)   6,400

CONCEPT AND INSPIRATIONAL ART
2 concept sketches: Mickey, 5-1/4"; Goofy, 7-1/2";
each standing in improvised island outfits;
1940, for proposed remake; both watercolor
on 12-field sheets; blue-pencil sketch of large
man on reverse of Mickey's sheet, SR/Fall/96
(400-800)   970
Study drawing for publicity picture: Mickey sends
Friday from compound in basket for coconut
bombing run as spears fly by, 7 x 7-1/4",
HL/Feb 23/97 (300-400)   230

LAYOUT ART
Detailed vertical pan background layout drawing of
tree house w/2 different perspectives, graphite
on paper w/white pastel highlights, notes,
with original layout instruction sheet, sight
35 x 10-1/4", S/Jun 21/97 (2000-3000)   1725

MICKEY'S MELLERDRAMMER (1933)
ANIMATION DRAWINGS
Drawing of musical minstrel Mickey & Minnie,
4 x 5-1/2", VF, HL/Apr 10/94 (600-900)   896

3 drawings of Mickey (4 x 2-1/2") & Minnie (3-1/4
x 2-1/2"), CE/Jun 18/94 (1200-1500)   1783
Drawing of Mickey as Uncle Tom & Minnie as Little
Eva, 5 x 6", HL/Aug 21/94 (7000-1000)   504
Full-figure drawing of Mickey & Minnie dancing, 3"
each, CE/Dec 16/94 (800-1200)   483
Drawing of Minnie as Eva & Mickey as Uncle Tom
dancing happily, 3-1/2" each, S/Dec 17/94
(400-600)   546
Profile drawing of Mickey Mouse lighting firecracker
in mouth, 5 x 4-1/2", HL/Aug 6/95
(500-700)   840
Full-figure drawing of Mickey as Topsy & Minnie as
Little Eva, 4-1/2 x 5-1/2", HL/Nov 19/95
(800-1200)   1265
21 drawings: Mickey (2-5/8") & Minnie (2-1/2")
in 10 sequential drawings each, drawing of
backstage view of cabin; 12-field sheets,
SR/Spring/96 (2000-5000)   2200
Full-figure drawing of smiling Mickey & Minnie
dancing as Topsy & Eva, 4 x 5-1/4",
HL/Oct 6/96 (700-1000)   748
10 drawings of Mickey, 6 with Mickey's face
showing, 5", CE/Dec 12/96 (3000-4000)   3450
2 full-figure drawings: smiling Minnie as Little Eva
standing facing right, 2-13/16"; Mickey as
Uncle Tom walking forward, looking left,
2-3/8"; both 2-field sheets, SR/Fall/97
(1200-1800)   800
5 drawings in sequence of Mickey preparing for his
role with aid of firecracker, 3-1/4 x 3" to
7-1/2 x 8", VF, HL/Nov 16/97 (800-1200) 1093
LAYOUT ART
Layout drawing of Minnie Mouse popping corn,
2", CE/Dec 16/94 (1000-1500)   1725
Four layout drawings: Clarabelle & Mickey in dressing
rooms, Mickey changes costume backstage, bed-
lam on stage; 12-field sheets, annotated production stamps; wear at edges, mended tear,
SR/Spring/96 (5000-10,000)   6000

MICKEY'S NIGHTMARE (1932)
ANIMATION DRAWINGS
Full-figure drawing of juvenile mouse with cat, 4",
CE/Dec 16/94 (400-600)   748
Full-figure drawing of Mickey (2-3/4") bend over
facing right as horsey as smiling young mouse
(2") stands to left waving, 2-3/4", 12-field
sheet, SR/Fall/95 (400-700)   550
2 full-figure drawings of running child mice matted
together, 2" & 2-1/4", 12-field sheets,
SR/Spring/96 (250-500)   200
LAYOUT ART
4 layout drawings: Mickey waters lawn of love nest as
stork's shadow passes, story note; Minnie in bed
with 21 progeny; free-for-all pillow fight; Mickey
wakes up; 12-field sheets, production & WDP
Limited stamps, SR/Fall/95 (5000-12,000) 9000
Polished background layout drawing of paint shop
w/children running rampant, 9 x 11-1/2",
HL/Apr 28/96 (1200-1600)   1150
STORY ART
3 storyboard drawings: two of Mickey's nephews in
pillow fight; Mickey being hit by pillow; storyboard 7 x 9"; CLA/Jun 7/97 (2500-3500) 5980

MICKEY'S PAL PLUTO (1933)
ANIMATION DRAWINGS
Full-figure drawing of Mickey running right, 3-1/2",
12-field sheet, SR/Spring/95 (400-700)   630
Full-figure drawing of Mickey standing facing right,
3-1/4", with shadow, 12-field sheet,
SR/Spring/96 (500-900)   610
Full-figure drawing of Mickey walking to right, 3-1/2",
12-field sheet, SR/Spring/97 (400-700)   1090
Full-figure drawing of excited Mickey running right,
3-1/4", 12-field sheet, SR/Spring/98
(400-700)   510
LAYOUT/MODEL/STORY ART
1 annotated script; 1 non-annotated script; 5 model
drawings of cat; 1 layout drawing; 2 photostats
of model drawing of cat; CE/Jun 9/95
(400-600)   575

MICKEY'S PARROT (1938)
ANIMATION DRAWINGS
Full-figure drawing of Mickey standing facing left
holding shotgun, swish lines around Mickey's

head, 4", 12-field sheet, SR/Spring/95
(400-800)   460
Full-figure drawing of Mickey Mouse holding shotgun
& falling into clothes basket near ironing board,
6-1/2 x 8", HL/Aug 6/95 (600-900)   672
Full-figure drawing of Mickey (holding huge shotgun)
& frightened Pluto stepping to right, 4-1/4"
on 24 x 10" pan sheet, shallow fold,
SR/Spring/96 (500-900)   500
Large near-full-figure front-view drawing of sleepy
Mickey standing holding huge shotgun, 8",
S/Dec 14/96 (800-1200)   517
2 drawings: Mickey holding shotgun & cautiously
opening door; Mickey in precarious position
on tightrope from Mickey's Circus; approx.
4" each; S/Dec 14/96 (1000-1500)   747
Large-image front-view close-up drawing of worried
Mickey holding huge shotgun, 8 x 9", VF,
HL/Nov 16/97 (400-600)   575
LAYOUT ART
Layout drawing of Mickey (4"), Pluto (3-1/2"), &
Parrot, CLA/Jun 7/97 (2000-3000)   3450
STORY ART
2 story sketches: Pluto asleep, Mickey in bed listening
to radio story; worried Mickey & Pluto search
house; 10-3/8 x 6-15/16" & 8-1/8 x 6-5/8",
some wear, SR/Spring/97 (800-1600)   2480
2 story sketches: Mickey facing left, dropping shotgun
& looking back right in surprise; angry Pluto
with chair on back confronting parrot; 12-field
sheets; SR/Spring/98 (800-1600)   800

MICKEY'S POLO TEAM (1936)
ANIMATION DRAWINGS
Full-figure drawing of polo-player Mickey & horse
at full gallop to left with speed lines, 7-1/4
x 8-1/2", HL/Oct 6/96 (600-900)   575
CELS – FULL FIGURE
Donald (3") & donkey (4-1/2") winding up to hit
each other, CE/Dec 16/94 (1500-2000) 2530
Side view of Stan Laurel with polo mallet riding
look-alike horse, 6-1/2", CE/Jun 20/96
(1000-1500)   1495
CELS – PARTIAL FIGURE
Caricature of Clark Gable sitting holding
binoculars, 7-1/2 x 5", VF,
HL/Nov 19/95 (1200-1600)   1265
Flirtatious Clarabelle Cow [watching Clark Gable],
7-1/2 x 5", VF, HL/Nov 19/95 (1000-1500) 978
Frustrated Oliver Hardy lying down [horse sitting
on him], 4-1/2 x 9", F, HL/Apr 28/96
(1000-1500)   920
MODEL ART
Model sheet with horses & riders from both teams,
vintage Ozalid print sheet, 15 x 12 1/2",
folded vertically in center, general darkening,
corner pinholes, some wear at bottom edge,
SR/Spring/98 (200-400)   310

MICKEY'S RIVAL (1936)
ANIMATION DRAWINGS (also see MODEL ART)
Full-figure drawing of determined Mickey holding
Minnie's leg as she clings to tree branch,
7-1/2 x 9-1/2", CE/Jun 18/94 (800-1200) 403
Full-figure drawing of contrite Mickey, 5 x 2",
CE/Jun 18/94 (600-800)   460
Full-figure drawing of frightened Mickey, 4-3/4",
CE/Dec 16/94 (600-800)   230
Full-figure drawing of delighted Minnie, 4-1/2 x 3",
HL/Aug 6/95 (400-600)   504
Full-figure extreme drawing of Minnie clinging to tree
branch as Mickey climbs & grabs her ankle,
w/notes, 5-1/2 x 10", HL/Apr 28/96
(800-1200)   782
Full-figure drawing of frightened Mickey grabbing
picnic blanket, 5-1/2 x 5", HL/Oct 6/96
(600-800)   575
2 drawings: Mickey & Minnie climbing tree to escape
bull, 10 x 12"; Mickey being congratulated by
Hollywood elite from Mickey's Gala Premiere,
9-1/2 x 12"; S/Dec 14/96 (1200-1800) 1265
Full-figure drawing of shy Mickey standing facing left,
5 x 4-1/4", HL/Feb 23/97 (600-900)   633
Full-figure study drawing of standing Minnie
(3-1/2") & Mortimer (5"), CE/Dec 18/97
(1500-2000)   863
MODEL ART
Full-figure drawing of Mickey waving cape, detailed

color guide, 9-3/4 x 11-1/2", CE/Dec 15/93
(800-1000)   1495

MICKEY'S SERVICE STATION (1935)
ANIMATION DRAWINGS
Drawing of Mickey putting tire on rim, 4-1/4 x 4",
CE/Jun 18/94 (500-700)   437
Drawing with background scene of Mickey & Donald
pumping up inner tube, created by publicity art
dept. as one-sheet poster design,10 x 8",
HL/Nov 13/94 (2000-2500)   2912
Full-figure drawing of Mickey, 4", CE/Dec 16/94
(1000-1500)   1610
Full-figure drawing of worried Mickey & Donald
with left hands in stop gestures, 3 x 8",
HL/Nov 19/95 (700-1000)   1265
Drawing of worried Goofy, Mickey & Donald looking
right, 6 x 11", HL/Apr 28/96 (1000-1500) 1553
Full-figure drawing of shocked Pegleg Pete holding
onto pole & watching moving automobile
engine, 6-1/4 x 10-1/2", HL/Apr 28/96
(500-700)   460
Full-figure drawing of surprised Goofy, Mickey and
Donald standing looking right, 6-1/2 x 5-1/4",
HL/Oct 6/96 (1000-1500)   1150
3 full-figure drawings of surprised Donald, determined
Goofy, & eager Mickey all standing facing right,
from same scene; 3-1/4 x 3-1/2", 5-1/4 x 3",
4-1/2 x 3", HL/Feb 23/97 (1200-1600) 1265
4 drawings of Goofy: screaming on swinging scaffold
(The Big Wash); dressed in fur coat (Polar
Trappers); in band (Amateur Hour [sic]); one
from Mickey's Service Station; each sheet
9-1/2 x 12"; S/Dec 19/97 (800-1200)   920
Near-full figure front-view drawing of smiling
long-billed Donald Duck standing, 3 x 2",
VF, HL/Apr 25/98 (300-500)   460
CONCEPT AND INSPIRATIONAL ART
Full-figure polished final design drawing for publicity
illustration of smiling Mickey holding inner
tube as Donald pumps it up, 5-1/2 x 7", VF,
HL/Nov 16/97 (700-1000)   1495
LAYOUT ART
Layout drawing of Donald Duck carrying radiator,
2-1/2", CE/Dec 16/94 (500-700)   863

MICKEY'S STEAM-ROLLER (1934)
ANIMATION DRAWINGS
Drawing of cheerful Mickey driving his steam
roller, 5-1/2 x 8-1/2", HL/Nov 13/94
(8000-1000)   2240
6 drawings: Mickey drives steamroller (Mickey's
Steam-Roller, 1934); Mickey balancing straw
hat on end of cane; model sheet of Mickey
drawn to resemble "circa 1938" for
consumer/promotional purposes; Mickey
attempting to keep unseen force at bay; Mickey
in cadet hat playing trumpet; Mickey in yachts-
man's attire running with eyes & mouth wide
open; S/Dec 14/96 (1000-1500)   1495
Near-full-figure drawing of Mickey standing facing
right, 3-1/2 x 2-1/2", VF, HL/Apr 25/98
(350-500)   431
LAYOUT ART
Full-figure layout drawing of Mickey standing with his
right hand out next to shy Minnie, 3" each,
CE/Dec 18/97 (2000-3000)   2760
Full-figure layout drawing of Ferdy & Morty (1-1/2")
in baby carriage, serious Mickey (3-1/2")
standing beside them, Minnie (2-1/2") running
into scene from right, CE/Dec 18/97
(3000-5000)   3680

MICKEY'S SURPRISE PARTY
(COMMERCIAL; 1939)
ANIMATION DRAWINGS
Drawing of Mickey bowing, 2-1/2", S/Dec 17/94
(500-700)   402
2 full-figure drawings: surprised Minnie Mouse
wearing apron, wary Fifi; 2-1/2 x 3-1/2",
4-1/2 x 4-1/2", HL/Aug 6/95 (400-600)   504
2 full-figure drawings: Mickey in straw hat whistling,
flowers behind back, leaning w/cane extended;
alert Pluto w/bone in mouth; 4 x 6-1/2" & 5
x 6-1/2", HL/Aug 6/95 (600-900)   1904
2 matching full-figure drawings: Pluto with bone in
mouth (w/ink notations), Mickey holding

bouquet with hat raised in greeting (w/model-drawing stamp); 8 x 6", 3-1/2 x 4-1/2", HL/Apr 28/96 (700-900) — 920

Drawing of Minnie mixing batter, 5 x 3-1/2", HL/Apr 28/96 (300-400) — 431

Full-figure large-image drawing of smiling Mickey walking while holding bouquet, cane over arm, reaching back for straw hat, 6-1/2 x 10", HL/Feb 23/97 (600-800) — 748

3 drawings: front view of Minnie pouring cup [into bowl]; full figure of haughty Pluto walking to left with bone in mouth; full figure of smiling Mickey walking left, holding straw hat in front of him; 6 x 7", 4-1/2 x 5-1/2", 4 x 3-1/2", VF, HL/Nov 16/97 (700-900) — 748

Stomach-up large-image front-view drawing of Mickey with kisses & cake on face, 5 x 3-1/4", VF, HL/Apr 25/98 (300-500) — 316

2 matched drawings: full figure of Mickey standing holding straw hat, proud Pluto walking with bone in mouth (eyes closed, all but front paw); 6 x 6", 4 x 5-1/2"; VF; HL/Apr 25/98 (500-700) — 575

Full-figure drawing of Minnie stepping right; 2 layout drawings of whistling Mickey walking toward camera holding flowers & twirling cane (one full figure with Pluto following); 3 x 4", 5 x 4-1/2", 5 x 6"; F-VF, HL/Apr 25/98 (600-800) — 460

CEL SET-UPS

Minnie looks over her shoulder & cries while lying on sofa, 4", matching watercolor production background, S/Dec 17/94 (2000-3000) — 5462

Minnie sits at piano happily clutching bouquet of flowers, 5", watercolor production background, S/Dec 17/94 (2000-3000) — 3162

Production set-up of Ferdy & Morty on steamroller (one driving, one riding outside), 2" & 2-1/4", graphite-&-watercolor production background from unknown production, S/Dec 19/97 (15,000-20,000) — 11,500

MICKEY'S TRAILER (1938)
ANIMATION DRAWINGS

Drawing of Mickey in chef's outfit, production notes, full margins, 5", S/Dec 16/93 (500-700) — 575

Full-figure drawing of whistling Mickey making coffee, 6-1/2 x 7", HL/Nov 19/95 (700-900) — 1610

Full-figure drawing of smiling chef Mickey standing holding coffee pot, 6 x 4-1/2", HL/Apr 28/96 (600-800) — 978

Full-figure drawing of Chef Mickey standing balancing ear of corn on foot & holding cleaver, 6", 12-field sheet, SR/Fall/96 (700-1200) — 720

2 drawings: full figure of Mickey in chef's hat and apron holding coffee can & coffeepot, 5-1/2"; layout of kitchen; S/Dec 19/97 (1000-1500) — 1150

Full-figure drawing of Chef Mickey standing facing left, holding cleaver, 5-5/8", 12-field sheet, SR/Spring/98 (600-1200) — 600

MODEL ART

Two matched vintage Ozalid print sheets showing final model for trailer & comparative sizes of characters, trailer, & car, labeled "Trailer Troubles," SR/Spring/98 (200-400) — 310

MIDNIGHT IN A TOY SHOP (1930)
CONCEPT & INSPIRATIONAL ART/STORY ART

3 pages of studies of spider, 4" & smaller; illustration of spider, 6-1/2" diameter; watercolor on paper; 2-page typewritten script, CE/Jun 18/94 (300-500) — 748

MR. DUCK STEPS OUT (1940)
Also see TOY TINKERS
ANIMATION DRAWINGS

3 full-figure drawings of Louie, eyes closed, moving with flourish: holding ear of corn & riding crop in 1st., riding crop in others; 3 1/2" each, 12-field sheets; SR/Spring/98 (300-600) — 310

BACKGROUNDS

Full figures of argumentative Huey, then Dewey & Louie standing in line facing left, "Donald's Weekend" 1958, master watercolor background of home interior from *Mr. Duck Steps Out*, each 4", SR/Fall/95 (1500-2500) — 2220

Watercolor master background of home interior with large Philco-style cabinet radio &

---

cast-iron stove, 17-3/16 x 8-1/4", SR/Spring/98 (2000-5000) — 1980

CEL SET-UPS

Full figure of angry Donald standing facing left, holding candy & cane, 4-1/4", master watercolor background of interior wall, SR/Fall/94 (1800-2800) — 1820

Full figure of angry Donald Duck standing in Daisy's kitchen holding cane & candy box, 8 x 28", pan master background (watercolor on pan background sheet), HL/Nov 19/95 (5000-7000) — 6325

Watercolor production background of interior of disheveled house with full figure of angry Donald Duck from unknown production (5") standing facing right holding rifle, S/Jun 21/97 (1200-1800) — 3450

CONCEPT AND INSPIRATIONAL ART

Sheet of practice drawings of Donald, Daisy, & nephews, 1950s, signed "O'Malley," 10-1/2 x 13", HL/May 31/97 (200-250) — 345

MODEL ART

Photostat model sheet of Donald & Daisy captioned "Donald's Date," 1938, 13-3/4 x 11", SR/Fall/94 (100-200) — 150

TITLE ART

Title card: heart with full-figure line drawing dapper Mr. Duck, Donald & title hand lettering on cel, airbrushed candy box part of watercolor background, title 12 x 10", production cover flap signed by Walt, SR/Spring/95 (2000-5000) — 2090

MODERN INVENTIONS (1937)
ANIMATION DRAWINGS

Knees-up drawing of mischievous Donald standing facing right, wearing derby, right hand on hip, left hand holding out coin-on-string, 8-3/8", 12-field sheet, SR/Fall/95 (500-900) — 500

Drawing of Donald, 7"; 2 full-figure animation drawings of Donald addressing golf ball from *Donald's Golf Game*, 4" & similar; CE/Jun 20/96 (1000-1500) — 1150

Knees-up drawing of dapper Donald in derby holding dime on a string in outstretched left arm, 8-1/2 x 9-1/4", VF, HL/Apr 25/98 (400-500) — 575

CELS – FULL FIGURE

Curious Donald Duck (wearing sailor hat) stands facing right holding bone, wire coiled around arm, 4-1/2 x 6", VF, HL/Nov 16/97 (500-700) — 1265

MONKEY MELODIES (1930)
LAYOUT/MODEL ART

Model sheet of monkeys; layout drawing; scoring set-up; all graphite on paper, CE/Jun 9/95 (200-300) — 805

MOOSE HUNTERS (1937)
ANIMATION DRAWINGS

Drawing of Goofy, Mickey & Donald paddling in canoe, 4", S/Dec 16/93 (1000-1500) — 1610

Drawing of smiling Mickey in bush on stilts, 5", CE/Jun 9/95 (600-800) — 437

Full-figure drawing of Goofy & Donald flying thru air with moose head, 4 x 8-1/2", HL/Aug 6/95 (600-900) — 896

Full-figure drawing of Goofy, Mickey & Donald frantically paddling canoe, 7 x 16", red & black pencil on animation sheet, HL/Nov 19/95 (1000-1500) — 2300

Drawing of Goofy, Mickey & Donald furiously paddling canoe, 10 x 12", S/Dec 19/97 (1000-1500) — 1955

MODEL ART

Color-guide drawing of Goofy & Donald trying to control canoe in wave, S/Jun 17/94 (1200-1600) — 1380

THE MOTH & THE FLAME (1938)
ANIMATION DRAWINGS

3 sequential drawings of villainous flame (one as Clark Gable), 4-1/2 x 4", 5-1/2 x 4-1/2", 6 x 3", HL/Nov 19/95 (1000-1500) — 2185

2 full-figure drawings: sexy moth; flame (colored as guide to Ink & Paint); 5 x 3", 4-1/2 x 3"; HL/Apr 28/96 (700-1000) — 2300

Close-up drawing of cruel flame creature leaping

---

upward, 6-1/2 x 6", HL/Feb 23/97 (200-300) — 259

MOTHER GOOSE GOES HOLLY-WOOD (1938)
ANIMATION DRAWINGS

3 Marx brothers play fiddle, 3 drawings framed together, 8" x 6-1/2" each, CE/Dec 15/93 (1400-1800) — 1725

2 matching colored-pencil drawings: W.C. Fields as Humpty Dumpty by Marc Davis (initialed "MD") & Charlie McCarthy; 3 x 3-1/2", 2-1/2 x 3", VF, HL/Feb 26-27/94 (300-400) — 440

Drawing of strutting Cab Calloway, 5 x 4", HL/Aug 21/94 (600-800) — 448

Drawing of Mickey surrounded by Hollywood actors, 2-1/2", CE/Dec 16/94 (800-1200) — 1035

2 drawings: caricatures of W.C. Fields & Charlie McCarthy from Humpty Dumpty sequence, 4 x 3-1/2" & 3-1/4 x 2", HL/Aug 6/95 (400-600) — 420

Full-figure drawing of Charlie McCarthy, 6 x 4-1/2", HL/Nov 19/95 (400-600) — 431

Drawings of W.C. Fields playing string base & Charlie McCarthy sitting, 8 x 6-1/2" & 1-1/2 x 3-1/4", HL/Nov 19/95 (400-600) — 345

Drawing of Spencer Tracy, sitting in tub, pulling Freddie Bartholomew from water, 7-5/8", 12-field sheet, SR/Spring/96 (400-700) — 440

Full-figure drawing of energetic Cab Calloway, 5-1/2 x 3-1/2", HL/Apr 28/96 (400-600) — 460

3 drawings: Groucho, Harpo & Zeppo Marx each playing a violin; 7 x 4", 6 x 3-1/2", 6-1/2 x 5-1/2", HL/Apr 28/96 (1000-1500) — 1725

Drawing of 15+ Hollywood stars, 5 x 9", HL/Apr 28/96 (600-900) — 920

2 drawings: torso-up of Oliver Hardy as Pie Man, 8"; knees-up of Stan Laurel as Simple Simon, 8-1/2"; 12-field sheets; SR/Fall/96 (500-1000) — 610

2 full-figure drawings: Stan Laurel as Simple Simon fishing & Oliver Hardy as Pie Man, 7 x 4-1/2", 7-1/2 x 8-1/2", HL/Oct 6/96 (900-1200) — 748

2 matching drawings: full figure of W.C. Fields as spinning Humpty Dumpty; attentive puppet Charlie McCarthy; 3 x 3-1/2" & 2-1/4 x 1-1/2"; HL/Feb 23/97 (300-400) — 230

2 full-figure drawings: W.C. Fields as Humpty Dumpty; puppet Charlie McCarthy in nest; 5-1/2 x 5" & 3 x 3"; HL/Feb 23/97 (400-600) — 489

2 matched drawings: W.C. Fields plays bass fiddle (initialed by Marc Davis); sitting Charlie McCarthy; 8 x 6-1/2" & 3-1/2 x 2"; HL/May 31/97 (300-400) — 138

5 animation drawings: Katharine Hepburn as Bo Peep; roughs of Jiminy Cricket & Gideon from *Pinocchio*; Pete from *Officer Duck*; 4 x 3-1/4" to 6 x 10", F overall, HL/Nov 16/97 (600-900) — 978

2 drawings: sitting Stan Laurel fishing, 7"; Oliver Hardy as chef standing facing left, 7"; S/Dec 19/97 (700-900) — 690

Matched drawing & inked, unpainted cel: hips-up of Martha Raye mugging for the camera, 6-1/2", both 12-field, SR/Spring/98 (400-800) — 420

2 drawings: Pieman Oliver Hardy (8") facing left, holding pie in both hands, reaching up [to place on shelf]; knees-up of Simple Simon Stan Laurel (8-1/2") examining pie in his hands; 12-field sheets, SR/Spring/98 (500-1000) — 510

2 full-figure drawings: Charlie McCarthy facing right, W.C. Fields as spinning Humpty Dumpty; 3-1/2 x 3-1/4", 3-1/4 x 1-1/2"; VF; HL/Apr 25/98 (300-500) — 288

Full-figure drawing of Greta Garbo & Edward G. Robinson on see-saw, 5-1/2 x 7-1/2", VF, HL/Apr 25/98 (600-800) — 633

2 full-figure drawings: front view of Stan Laurel as Simple Simon waving & holding fishing pole with fish caught by tail, Oliver Hardy as pieman standing facing left; 7-1/4 x 9", 7 x 5"; VF; HL/Apr 25/98 (800-1000) — 920

2 animation drawings: W.C. Fields playing string bass, full figure of Charlie McCarthy sitting; 8 x 6-1/2", 3-1/4 x 1-3/4"; VF; HL/Apr 25/98 (300-500) — 546

ART – MISCELLANEOUS

Publicity illustration featuring Edward G. Robinson,

Greta Garbo & Wallace Berry, india ink on
heavyweight paper, 11 x 13", signed &
inscribed by artist, HL/Aug 21/94
(1000-1500)   952

CEL SET-UPS
Hugh Herbert & Ned Sparks as Ol' King Cole &
jester, 7-1/2 x 9-1/2", complementary
airbrush background, Courvoisier labels,
VG, HL/Apr 10/94 (1200-1600)   1120
Charlie McCarthy, 6", Courvoisier wood-veneer
background, CE/Jun 18/94 (1500-2000)   1380
Katharine Hepburn as Little Bo Peep, 6-1/2 x
4-1/2", airbrush Courvoisier background,
CE/Jun 18/94 (2000-3000)   1495
Katharine Hepburn as Little Bo Peep outboarding
in tub, new complementary background,
8 x 8", HL/Aug 21/94 (1800-2200)   2128
Portrait cel of Stan Laurel playing clarinet,
complementary Courvoisier airbrush
background, inscribed, embossed "©W.D.E.",
labels, 6 x 5", HL/Aug 21/94 (1500-2000) 1456
2 cels: Stan Laurel as Simple Simon fishing; Oliver
Hardy as Pie Man; 7-1/2 x 6" & 6-1/2 x 5",
framed together over modern complementary
airbrush background, HL/Nov 13/94
(2000-2500)   3136
Close-up of Katharine Hepburn as Little Bo Peep,
4-1/2", Courvoisier airbrush background,
CE/Dec 16/94 (1000-1500)   1380
Stan Laurel focusing on stack of pies, 6",
Courvoisier airbrush background,
CE/Dec 16/94 (1000-1500)   2530
The (3) Marx Brothers, 4-1/2", Courvoisier
wood-veneer background, CE/Dec 16/94
(1500-2000)   4025
3 cels: Ollie on his trombone; Stan out fishing;
Ollie baking pies; each approx. 8", airbrushed
background & WDE label, S/Dec 17/94
(1500-2000)   3450
Full figure of Stan Laurel sitting on mushroom fishing
from tin can, 10 x 9-1/2", complementary
watercolor painting, HL/Apr 23/95
(3000-3500)   3360
Full figures of Joe E. Brown & Martha Raye
performing on stage, 4-3/8" & 4-1/8",
Courvoisier watercolor background with
labels & original hand-lettered mat,
background wear, SR/Fall/96 (1200-1800) 1210
Full figures of Groucho, Harpo & Chico Marx playing
violins, complementary airbrush background
prepared by Disney for sale thru Courvoisier,
5-1/2 x 8-1/2" cel image, HL/Oct 6/96
(5000-6000)   5175
Portrait of Greta Garbo, complementary airbrush
background prepared by Disney for
Courvoisier, 5 x 3" cel image, HL/Oct 6/96
(1500-2000)   2530
2 items: near-full figure of smiling Eddie Cantor
leaning to right eavesdropping w/hand cupped
around left ear, 4-1/2", Courvoisier airbrush
background; animation drawing of Eddie
Cantor, 4", CE/Dec 12/96 (800-1200)   1150
Full figure of Katharine Hepburn as Bo Peep
standing on hill top, newly painted
complementary airbrush background,
HL/May 3/97 (1000-1500)   1610
Full figures of Martha Raye & Joe E. Brown dancing
on stage to Brown's banjo strummings, 4" ea.,
airbrushed Courvoisier background; Pinocchio
w/donkey ears & oar, 3"; Mickey Mouse
in bucket, 3"; (latter 2 w/paint loss);
S/Jun 21/97 (1000-1500)   1380
Full figures of 3 snazzy jazzmen standing facing left,
two playing instruments, 5-1/2 x 5-5/8",
Courvoisier wood-veneer background,
SR/Fall/97 (600-1000)   490
Full figures of W.C. Fields as Humpty Dumpty on wall
threatening Charlie McCarthy (sitting in nest
in tree branch) with cane, 5 x 3" & 2-1/4 x
1-1/2", complementary painted background,
VF, HL/Nov 16/97 (2000-2500)   2760
Full figure of Katharine Hepburn as Little Bo Peep
seated in tub in scouting pose, 8 x 8", with
water-effects cel, complementary airbrush
background of ocean as prepared for Courvoisier, F+, HL/Nov 16/97 (1000-1500)   1150
Full figures of Fred Astaire & Stepin Fetchit standing
together, 5-1/2" each, airbrushed background,
S/Dec 19/97 (1000-1500)   2300

Full figures of Fred Astaire (6") & Stepin Fetchit
(5-1/8") in dancing poses, Courvoisier
watercolor background & both small labels,
original hand-lettered mat, WDE debossed
stamp, SR/Spring/98 (1400-1800)   1460
Full figure of monocled George Arliss standing
playing huge saxophone, 5-7/8", Courvoisier
background airbrushed with musical notes,
WDE debossed stamp, SR/Spring/98
(1200-1800)   970

CELS – FULL FIGURE
W.C. Fields as Humpty Dumpty, 3 x 4-1/2",
restored, VF, HL/Apr 10/94 (1200-1600)   1008
Strutting Groucho Marx w/violin & cigarette holder,
5 x 3", HL/Nov 19/95 (1500-2000)   3220
Katharine Hepburn as Little Bo Peep running right,
right hand holding lantern, left hand shielding
eyes, 5", airbrush lantern-glow effects,
SR/Spring/97 (1000-1400)   1280
5 pieces matted & framed together: cels of Zazu Pitts
& Mae West (4-1/4" each) blowing horns; cel
of Practical Pig (2-1/2") (all w/paint loss); pencil
drawing of Jiminy Cricket (3") holding up
umbrella; head-only pencil drawing of alarmed
Pinocchio (3"); full figure of Princess Minnie (4")
from *Brave Little Tailor* standing on tiptoes
facing left w/hand cupped to mouth (needs
restoration); S/Jun 21/97 (1800-2200)   1840
Dancing Fred Astaire, 5-1/2 x 5-1/2", inscribed
"...Walt Disney" by Hank Porter, F+,
HL/Nov 16/97 (1800-2200)   2185

**CELS – PARTIAL FIGURE (also see ANIMATION
DRAWINGS)**
Charlie McCarthy looking left, 5 x 2-1/2", restored,
VF, HL/Apr 10/94 (1200-1600)   1008
Near-full figure of Clark Gable sitting & holding left
hand to side of his face, 8", CE/Jun 20/96
(1000-1500)   920
Waist-up cels w/eyes closed of Stan Laurel (6-1/2")
& Katharine Hepburn (6"), CLA/Jun 7/97
(1000-1500)   1265
Portrait of Greta Garbo looking into camera, 5 x
3-1/2", F-VF, HL/Nov 16/97 (2500-3500) 1955

CONCEPT AND INSPIRATIONAL ART
2 concept drawings: waist-up of Groucho Marx
blowing smoke rings from flute; full-figure
side view of Harpo Marx standing playing
harp; 9-1/8 x 6-3/4" & 10-7/8 x 7-3/4" on
12-field sheets; SR/Spring/97 (700-1200)   800

MODEL ART
2 print model sheets: Katharine Hepburn as Little Bo
Peep; Spencer Tracy & others; 12-7/8 x 10",
some wear, SR/Spring/97 (200-400)   250

STORY ART
2 story sketches: Eddie Cantor tips hat to Cab Calloway
& band who are singing in pie; Oliver Hardy
as chef fitted into tuba; sight 6-3/4 x 8-1/2"
& 7 x 8-1/2"; S/Jun 21/97 (1200-1800)   1150

MOTHER PLUTO (1936)
CEL SET-UPS
Pluto (4 x 3") & chicks in dog house, key watercolor
production background inscribed "Fergy" with
key watercolor overlay, CE/Dec 16/94
(3000-4000)   2990
CELS – FULL FIGURE
Ferocious Pluto laying by barrel guarding chicks,
original cel art reproduced as illustration in
cartoon storybook published by D.C. Heath
in early 1940s, 4-1/2 x 6", restored, F+,
HL/Nov 19/95 (400-600)   690

MOVING DAY (1936)
ART – MISCELLANEOUS
Full-figure publicity illustration of Sheriff Pete
showing eviction notice to Mickey &
Donald, india ink on heavyweight paper,
7 x 12", HL/Oct 6/96 (1500-2000)   2070

MR. MOUSE TAKES A TRIP (1940)
ANIMATION DRAWINGS
Full-figure drawing of surprised Conductor Pete
(7-1/2") watching shape behind curtain,
12-field sheet, SR/Spring/95 (300-600)   350
Full-figure inked drawing of Mickey standing holding
suitcase & cane, speed effects, 4-1/2",
12-field sheet, SR/Fall/95 (500-900)   700
Full-figure front-view inked drawing of Mickey

whistling & dancing soft shoe, set in square
frame area, timer's chart, 4-5/8", 12-field
sheet, SR/Fall/96 (500-900)   750
CEL SET-UPS
Full figure of Pluto slinking to right, 2-3/4", 25 x 8"
master background of train sleeper car,
SR/Fall/94 (2000-4000)   2250
Mickey's monogrammed suitcase in overhead rack,
12-field set-up, key master background,
SR/Fall/96 (600-1200)   610

MUSICAL FARMER (1932)
BACKGROUNDS
Master black, white, & gray background painting
of hen house & barnyard, 9-1/2 x 11-1/2",
ink & watercolor on background sheet,
HL/Nov 19/95 (7000-9000)   6900

MUSIC LAND (1935)
CEL SET-UPS
King of Isle of Jazz (4") scowls at Queen of Land
of Symphony (5-1/2") as bride, watercolor
production background with painted paper
production overlay, 8 x 10", S/Dec 17/94
(14,000-18,000)   11,500
LAYOUT ART
2 layout drawings of Groom Tuba (4") & Bride
Violin (5") after marriage; drawing of Justice
of the Peace cello (5-1/2"); CLA/Jun 7/97
(1500-2000)   1150
Full-figure layout drawing of nervous groom
and demure bride, 5 x 5-1/2", VF,
HL/Nov 16/97 (400-600)   575

THE NEW NEIGHBOR (1953)
CELS – FULL FIGURE
Friendly Pete standing facing toward right w/arms out,
7-1/2", 16-field, SR/Spring/96 (300-600)   320
STORY ART
20 storyboard drawings by Nick George, charcoal
& pastel on 8-7/16 x 5-15/16" storyboard
sheets, SR/Spring/96 (1500-2500)   1500

THE NEW SPIRIT (1942)
**Also see UNIDENTIFIED/MISCELLANEOUS: COM-
BINATIONS OF MAJOR CHARACTERS**
ANIMATION DRAWINGS
Full-figure drawing of angry Donald standing with
left foot high in air, 5-3/4", 12-field sheet,
timer's chart, production notation,
SR/Spring/96 (400-800)   440
CEL SET-UPS
Full figures of standing Mickey Mouse (3-1/2", holding
hat) & sitting Pluto (3-1/2 x 2") admiring smiling
soldier Donald Duck (3") standing holding rifle
vertically, patterned paper Courvoisier
background, S/Dec 14/96 (1000-1500)   1955
CELS – FULL FIGURE/MODEL ART
Color model of Donald (holding cash) & thrifty
alter-ego walking arm-in-arm to right,
6-3/4 x 5", 12-field, paint restoration,
SR/Fall/94 (900-1500)   1560
Donald's Thrifty Self walking right, looking back
in coaxing pose, 4-3/8", 12-field, ct,
SR/Fall/95 (500-900)   500

THE NIFTY NINETIES (1941)
ANIMATION DRAWINGS
Drawing of Ward Kimball and Freddie Moore
caricatured as performers, 7 x 7",
HL/Nov 13/94 (300-400)   252
Full-figure drawing of worried Mickey & Minnie
riding in horseless carriage, 3 x 3",
HL/Nov 19/95 (600-900)   1265
2 full-figure drawings of Ward Kimball (caricatured as
vaudeville comedian) laughing, 4-1/2 x 3-1/2"
& 5 x 4-1/4", HL/May 31/97 (150-250)   81
Full-figure drawing: caricatures of Ward Kimball &
Fred Moore as vaudeville comedians, 7-1/4
x 7", VF, HL/Apr 25/98 (300-400)   431
CEL SET-UPS
Full figure of surprised horse & buggy, 9 x 8",
matching watercolor background w/Ridley's
Livery Stable, 12-field, originally released by
Courvoisier, ct, SR/Spring/96 (1800-3600) 3210
CELS – FULL FIGURE
Front view of smiling Mickey (eyes closed) high-

stepping forward, 4-3/4 x 3-1/4", Courvoisier
label, F+, HL/Nov 16/97 (700-1000)   1495
MODEL ART
Sheet of model drawings of Mickey Mouse by
Les Clark, 10 x 14", HL/Apr 23/95
(1000-1500)   3136

THE NIGHT BEFORE CHRISTMAS (1933)
CEL SET-UPS
Matching cel & master background (watercolor on
background sheet): toy soldiers returning to
places beneath tree, 8-1/2 x 10-1/2",
HL/Feb 23/97 (2500-3500)   5750
LAYOUT ART
3 layout drawings: "Santa Rides Away," Santa flies
over town; "Package for Junior," disobedient
child unhappy with chamber pot; "Junior Looks
Out," parlor window shows snowy night beyond;
12-field sheets, production stamps, edge wear
& discoloration; SR/Fall/96 (2400-4800)   2420

NOAH'S ARK (1959)
STORY ART
12 storyboard sketches, watercolor on paper,
CE/Jun 9/95 (800-1200)   345

NO HUNTING (1955)
CEL SET-UPS
Full figure of determined hunter Donald Duck stalking
to right thru forest with rifle at ready, color print
of background, signed by Jack Hannah, 5 x
8-1/2" cel, VF+, HL/Apr 25/98 (700-1000) 575
CELS – FULL FIGURE/ANIMATION DRAWINGS
4 worse-for-wear hunters returning; 13 miscellaneous
drawings (includes other productions);
S/Jun 17/94 (1200-1800)   2300
7 cels: upset Grandpa Duck clutching musket (*No
Hunting*, 1955); Bent-Tail with mouth & eyes
open, paw raised, looking to left; Grandpappy
Coyote lecturing Bent-Tail Jr.; 4 coyotes
howling; Bent-Tail walking to left; 2 of J.
Audubon Woodlore; S/Dec 14/96 (500-700) 575
2 full-figure cels: stern Grandpappy Duck wearing
coonskin cap in trophy pose with dead buffalo,
7-1/4"; 2 heavily armed hunters walking right,
5-7/8"; SR/Fall/97 (600-900)   400

NO SAIL (1945)
CEL SET-UPS
2 cels: full figure of Goofy standing straddling fishing
pole entangled in fishing line, 5", hand-prepared
background of large circle on solid field; doubtful
Pluto from *First Aiders*,1944, 6 x 8", hand-prepared background, S/Dec 14/96 (700-900) 1610

OFFICER DUCK (1939)
ANIMATION DRAWINGS
Waist-up drawing of frightened Donald (disguised as
baby) looking up, 6 x 2-1/2", HL/May 31/97
(200-400)   460
5 animation drawings: Pete; roughs of Jiminy Cricket
& Gideon from *Pinocchio*; Katharine Hepburn
as Bo Peep from *Mother Goose Goes
Hollywood*; 4 x 3-1/4" to 6 x 10", F overall,
HL/Nov 16/97 (600-900)   978
MODEL ART
2 photostat model sheets: *Early to Bed* & *Officer
Duck*, 14 x 11", SR/Spring/95 (200-400) 300
TITLE ART
Title card with Donald's Radio Patrol badge, watercolor on board with hand lettering on cel
overlay, SR/Fall/96 (1000-1500)   1000

OLD KING COLE (1933)
LAYOUT ART
Layout drawing of Old Woman's Shoe, 12-field
sheet, direction & paint notations, SR/Fall/97
(900-1400)   600

OLD MACDONALD DUCK (1941)
Also see FEATURES: THE RELUCTANT DRAGON
CEL SET-UPS
Full-figure back view of sow lying in barnyard with
rumps of 5 nursing piglets visible, shoulders-up
image of 6th grinning piglet in middle, 5-3/4",
key watercolor pan master background,

SR/Spring/96 (2000-4000)   2670
Full figure of surprised Donald (2-5/8"), hand on hat,
flying thru air in sitting position w/angry goat
(1-5/8") behind him, master watercolor background of farm, SR/Fall/96 (2200-3000)   2940
Full figure of Donald in straw hat feeding chickens,
5", matching key pan master watercolor
background of barnyard by Art Props Dept,
SR/Spring/98 (9000-15,000)   10,000

THE OLD MILL (1937)
CONCEPT AND INSPIRATIONAL ART
Gustav Tenggren concept painting of ducks wading
in pond beside mill, india ink & watercolor on
heavyweight paper, 4-3/4 x 6-1/2", HL/Apr
28/96 (4000-5000)   4485
Signed concept art of mill with plants & spiderweb
in foreground by Gustav Tenggren, ink &
watercolor on heavyweight paper, 4-3/4 x
6-1/2", HL/Feb 23/97 (3000-4000)   12,075
Inspirational art of bats returning to mill at sunrise,
ink & watercolor on heavyweight paper,
3-3/4 x 5", HL/Feb 23/97 (700-1000)   5520
Concept art: interior view of mill with bats flying
toward camera, ink & watercolor on
heavyweight paper, 4-3/4 x 6-1/2",
HL/Feb 23/97 (700-1000)   2530
Serene impressionistic concept painting of mill,
watercolor on heavyweight paper, 4 x
5-1/4", HL/Feb 23/97 (700-1000)   2530
Concept painting of bats flying from mill; watercolor,
india ink & pastel on heavyweight paper; 5 x
6-1/4"; VF; HL/Apr 25/98 (2000-2500)   2990
STORY ART
Story drawing of mill in storm, 8 x 10",
HL/Aug 21/94 (400-600)   784
2 polished story drawings of outside scenes, 3 x 4"
& 7 x 9", pencil, conté crayon, ink & watercolor on paper, HL/Nov 13/94 (600-800)   504
Signed Ferdinand Horvath story drawing of 4 frogs
in swamp in various stages of raising heads
captioned "Frogs pop up from time to time to
watch wind," pencil on story sheet, 5-1/2 x
6-1/2", HL/May 31/97 (400-600)   1150

THE OLYMPIC CHAMP (1942)
CEL SET-UPS/MODEL ART
Goofy holds Olympic torch, printed background,
9-1/2 x 10-1/2", CE/Dec 15/93 (800-1200) 747
Full-figure front-view color model cel of athlete Goofy
standing, 6-1/8", watercolor background with
crowd in distance, SR/Spring/97 (900-1400) 940
CELS – FULL FIGURE
Goofy with discus, 4", CE/Dec 16/94 (700-900) 920

ON ICE (1935)
ANIMATION DRAWINGS
Full-figure drawing of Mickey standing behind Minnie
who's sitting on pillow, 4-1/8", 12-field sheet,
some edge wear & discoloration, patched tear,
SR/Fall/94 (600-1200)   730
Full-figure drawing of Mickey skating, 4",
S/Jun 10/95 (700-900)   1092
Full-figure drawing of Mickey standing behind stunned
Minnie sitting on pillow, 4-1/2", 12-field sheet,
inker's notation, SR/Fall/95 (700-1200)   1180
Partially colored full-figure extreme drawing of happy
Mickey skating on ice floes, 4-1/2 x 11-1/2",
HL/Apr 28/96 (600-900)   863
Full-figure drawing of cheerful Mickey wearing ice
skates, suspended by straps from "No Swimming"
sign, 6 x 4-1/2", HL/Oct 6/96 (700-900) 1150
Full-figure drawing of Mickey holding Minnie up from
behind over pillow, 4-1/8", 12-field sheet,
inker's notation, SR/Spring/97 (600-900)   920
MODEL ART
Full-figure model cel of smiling Mickey skating, 3-1/2
x 3-1/2", HL/Aug 6/95 (3000-4000)   8064
Full-figure model cel of smiling Minnie skating,
4-1/2 x 4", HL/Aug 6/95 (2500-3500)   2912

ORPHAN'S BENEFIT (1934 & 1941)
ANIMATION DRAWINGS
Full-figure drawing of combative Donald Duck,
3 x 4", HL/Aug 6/95 (400-500)   896
Knees-up front-view drawing of long-billed Donald,
12-field sheet, 1934, SR/Fall/95 (500-900) 500

Full-figure drawing of angry Donald Duck in fighting
pose, 3 x 4", HL/Mar 16-17/96 (200-300)   863
Full-figure drawing of Donald Duck dancing jig (1934),
4-1/2 x 3", HL/Oct 6/96 (500-700)   506
Near-full figure drawing of angry Donald Duck
standing looking up with fists clinched,
3-1/2 x 3", HL/May 31/97 (300-400)   460
BACKGROUNDS
Pan watercolor master background of stage, 23 x
9-1/8", 1941, SR/Fall/95 (2000-4000)   2940
CEL SET-UPS
Balcony full of happy orphans, key watercolor
production background, CLA/Jun 7/97
(40,000-50,000)   88,300
LAYOUT/STORY ART
Mickey & Clara bowing, colored-pencil story or layout
drawing on 2-hole animation sheet, 4-1/2 x 7",
F-VF, HL/Apr 10/94 (1000-1500)   1456
MODEL ART
Ozalid print model sheet of Donald Duck, 1934,
12 x 9-1/2", SR/Fall/94 (200-400)   200

ORPHAN'S PICNIC (1936)
ANIMATION DRAWINGS
Pencil drawing of Donald in mid-tantrum, VF,
HL/Feb 26-27/94 (150-200)   495
Full-figure drawing of angry Donald standing facing
right in fighting pose, looking up; 3-1/4 x
4-1/2", VF, HL/Apr 25/98 (300-400)   414
CEL SET-UPS
Full figures of Mickey Mouse playing blind man's
bluff outside w/3 mischievous orphans,
8 x 11", master background (pencil &
watercolor on background sheet),
HL/Aug 6/95 (7000-10,000)   17,360
CELS – FULL FIGURE
Donald lying on stomach holding layer cake, 3-1/2",
CE/Jun 9/95 (1000-1500)   1150
2 orphans with feathers on heads knocking bee
from glass jar into sandwich, 3" each,
CE/Dec 18/97 (1500-2000)   2070
LAYOUT ART
Detailed pan layout drawing depicting action of
Mickey driving truck full of orphans with
Donald standing on top into picnic grounds,
S/Dec 19/97 (2000-3000)   2587

OUT OF SCALE (1951)
CEL SET-UPS
Close up of Chip & Dale waving from train cab,
8 x 10", background (tempera on background
sheet), HL/Apr 23/95 (1400-1800)   2240
Full-figure publicity pose of smiling Engineer Donald
riding miniature steam locomotive & tender to
right, 6-1/2", 16-field cel, airbrush steam
effects, watercolor background,
SR/Spring/97 (600-1000)   800

OUT OF THE FRYING PAN INTO
THE FIRING LINE (1942)
CEL SET-UPS
Full figures of smiling Minnie holding frying pan
over Pluto's dish full of bones as eager Pluto
watches, 5-1/2 x 10-1/4", complementary
painted background of home interior & label
as prepared by Courvoisier, F, HL/Nov 16/97
(1500-2000)   2588
CELS – FULL FIGURE
Minnie (5-1/2") stands holding frying pan, Pluto
sits balancing tin on head, facing each other,
12-field, cleaned & restored, some rippling,
SR/Spring/95 (1500-2500)   1640

OUT ON A LIMB (1950)
STORY ART
23 storyboard drawings, pastel & charcoal on
8-1/2 x 6" storyboard sheets, SR/Fall/94
(1800-2800)   1820

PANTRY PIRATE (1940)
BACKGROUNDS
Full figure of Mickey on knees in kitchen holding
half-empty milk bottle, 4-5/8", 12-field cel
from *Lend a Paw*, color print background
from *Pantry Pirate*, SR/Spring/97
(3000-4000)   3360

Near-full figure of eager Pluto jumping to right, early 1940s unknown production, 6-1/2", 12-field nitrate cel, master watercolor background painting of fenced backyard & dog house from *Pantry Pirate*, SR/Fall/97 (1800-2600)   1480

PAUL BUNYAN (1958)
BACKGROUNDS
Full figure of Jiminy Cricket in plaid deerstalker cap standing facing right, 4", "The Mickey Mouse Club"; gouache master background from *Paul Bunyan*, SR/Fall/94 (300-600)   330
CEL SET-UPS
Full figure of Paul Bunyan kneeling, twirling tree to make fire, 6", DL litho background, gold Art Corner label, SR/Spring/96 (400-800)   510
CELS – PARTIAL FIGURE
Train carrying logs, sight 10 x 13", CE/Jun 18/94 (300-500)   253
CONCEPT AND INSPIRATIONAL ART
Inspirational painting of seaside forest & village by Eyvind Earle, tempera on board, 6 x 14-1/2", VF+, HL/Nov 16/97 (1000-1500)   4600

THE PET STORE (1933)
ANIMATION DRAWINGS
Full-figure drawing of Mickey & Minnie being held by a gorilla, 6 x 8", HL/Nov 19/95 (700-1000)   1380
Near-full-figure drawing of excited Minnie walking forward while looking left, 4 1/8", 12-field sheet, SR/Spring/98 (300-600)   350
STORY ART
Story drawing of Mickey sitting on floor as cages fall toward him, 7 x 10-1/2", HL/Nov 19/95 (900-1200)   920

THE PICNIC (1930)
CONCEPT AND INSPIRATIONAL ART
2 Bert Gillett annotated drafts with 4 pages notes; 3 Pluto concept drawings; bird concept drawing; storyboard concept on full page, 3" & smaller, CE/Dec 16/94 (500-700)   288
Concept drawing of Horace & Clarabelle (mimicking a train?), 3-1/2", CE/Dec 16/94 (500-700) 322

THE PIED PIPER (1933)
LAYOUT ART
Detailed colored layout of Hamelin's town center for background painting, colored pencil on animation sheet, 8 x 10-1/2", F, HL/Nov 16/97 (1000-1500)   3450

PLANE CRAZY (1928)
ANIMATION DRAWINGS
Drawing of determined Mickey & frightened Minnie in airplane, 5 x 10-1/2", F+, HL/Apr 10/94 (3500-5000)   6160

Drawing of worried Mickey's arms, head & torso, & Minnie's ears [as riding in plane], 2 x 2-1/2", HL/Nov 19/95 (700-1000)   690
2 drawings: full-figure rear long shot of Mickey & Minnie in airplane; shoulders-up of smiling Mickey holding two xylophone mallets from *Steamboat Willie*, 2-3/4 x 1-3/4", 3-3/4 x 4-1/2", VF, HL/Oct 6/96 (700-1000)   920
2 drawings framed together: Minnie (1 x 2-1/2") hanging from Mickey's pants (1-1/2 x 2"); their plane; S/Dec 19/97 (800-1200)   1150
Drawing of Mickey & Minnie in plane, 9-1/2 x 12", S/Dec 19/97 (700-900)   805
Matched set of drawings: frightened Minnie hanging onto Mickey, airplane; 2-1/4 x 2-1/2", 4 x 10"; VF; HL/Apr 25/98 (1500-2000)   1725
CEL SET-UPS
Full figure of Minnie handing Mickey (waist-up, in airplane) a horseshoe, 6-3/4 x 6", watercolor display background, late 1950s-early 1960s

promotion done from original drawings, SR/Fall/94 (4000-9000)   4000

PLAYFUL PAN (1930)
CONCEPT AND INSPIRATIONAL ART
Concept drawings of Pan, 9 pages, CE/Dec 16/94 (200-300)   104

PLAYFUL PLUTO (1934)
ANIMATION DRAWINGS
Drawing of Pluto jumping on laughing Mickey, 4 x 6-1/2", VF, HL/Apr 10/94 (1000-1200)   896

THE PLOW BOY (1929)
LAYOUT ART
2 background layout drawings of countryside (2nd may be from different cartoon), 7 x 11-1/2" & 8-1/2 x 11", HL/Feb 23/97 (1000-1500) 920
STORY ART
Complete storyboard, each box inscribed with animator's name, graphite & color pencil on 5 full sheets animation paper, CE/Jun 9/95 (20,000-30,000)   101,500

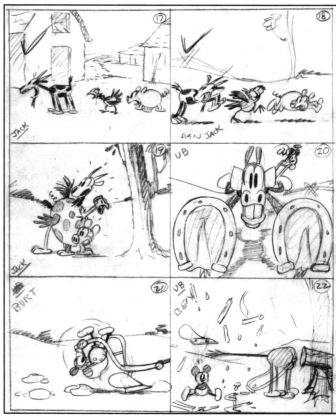

PLUTO AND THE ARMADILLO (1943)
CEL SET-UPS
Full figures of surprised Mickey (4") in pith helmet & smiling armadillo (3-1/4" long) standing amid foliage, watercolor production background from another short, Courvoisier label, CE/Jun 20/96 (1500-2000) 2530

Full-figure front view of Mickey standing holding balled-up armadillo in right hand, looking & pointing right, 4", master watercolor background, released by Courvoisier with label, ct, SR/Fall/96 (2500-5000) 2940

PLUTO, JUNIOR (1942)
CEL SET-UPS
Full-figure overhead view of surprised Pluto lying on ground looking back & up, matching master background of his & son's dog houses (watercolor on background sheet), 8-1/4 x 11", HL/May 3/97 (2500-3500) 2185

PLUTOPIA (1951)
CELS – FULL FIGURE
Smiling Mickey Mouse in casual dress standing, 4-1/2 x 3", HL/Aug 6/95 (1200-1800) 1568

Seated Mickey holding both feet & laughing, 5-1/2 x 4-1/2", HL/Oct 6/96 (900-1200) 1150

PLUTO'S CHRISTMAS TREE (1952)
ANIMATION DRAWINGS
Full-figure drawing of Mickey pointing, 5-3/4 x 4", CE/Jun 18/94 (300-400) 368

CEL SET-UPS
Full figures of carolers Goofy, Donald Duck & Minnie Mouse, complementary color print background of snowy forest from *101 Dalmatians*, 4 x 4-1/2" cel image, HL/Oct 6/96 (1200-1600) 920

CELS – FULL FIGURE
Mickey Mouse carries present, 5 x 6-1/2", HL/Aug 21/94 (1200-1600) 1680

Large image of startled Chip standing holding candy cane, 5 x 3", VF+, HL/Nov 13/94 (400-600) 616

2 full-figure cels: surprised Chip standing, Dale holding sprig; 3-1/2 x 3-1/4" & 6 x 4-1/2", HL/Apr 28/96 (500-800) 748

Smiling Dale driving toy truck, 2-1/4 x 3", HL/Feb 23/97 (200-300) 259

PLUTO'S DREAM HOUSE (1940)
CEL SET-UPS
Full figure of Pluto standing next to dog house, being covered in green paint by suspended brush, 4", matching watercolor background of backyard & building supplies, SR/Fall/94 (2500-4500) 3030

PLUTO'S HOUSEWARMING (1947)
CEL SET-UPS
Full figure of Pluto threatening turtle, 3-1/2 x 7", complementary color print background, HL/Apr 23/95 (900-1200) 1680

PLUTO'S JUDGEMENT DAY (1935)
ART – MISCELLANEOUS
Cat's eyes peer at chained & terrified Pluto, pencil on animation sheet for publicity/book illustration, 6-1/2 x 8-1/2", VF, HL/Apr 10/94 (900-1200) 672

MODEL ART
Model cel: full figure of frightened Pluto shackled to ball, 4 x 5", HL/Aug 6/95 (1500-2000) 1568

PLUTO'S KID BROTHER (1946)
CEL SET-UPS
Eager Pluto's brother, 3 x 2", printed background, CE/Jun 18/94 (500-700) 575

PLUTO'S PLAYMATE (1941)
CELS – FULL FIGURE
Smiling seal balances ball on top of head, facing left, 3 x 3", F, HL/Nov 16/97 (150-200) 230

PLUTO'S QUIN-PUPLETS (1937)
ANIMATION DRAWINGS

20 full-figure rough drawings, later signed by Shamus Culhane, 5", CLA/Jun 7/97 (800-1200) 1725

PLUTO'S SWEATER (1949)
ANIMATION DRAWINGS
Knees-up drawing of smiling Minnie Mouse standing facing right with hands folded, 5 x 3", VF+, HL/Feb 26-27/94 (500-700) 825

THE POINTER (1939)
ANIMATION DRAWINGS
Full-figure polished drawing of fearful Mickey looking up, 6-1/2 x 3-1/2", notes, HL/Apr 23/95 (800-1200) 2464

Full-figure drawing of surprised Mickey facing right, looking down with right leg raised, 4-1/2", 12-field sheet, SR/Spring/97 (500-900) 440

CEL SET-UPS
Surprised Mickey, modern complementary background, 4-1/2 x 5", VF+, HL/Apr 10/94 (5000-7000) 5040

Full figure of eager Pluto draped in greenery, bird on tail, looking back, 5", Courvoisier watercolor & airbrush background, CE/Jun 9/95 (1500-2000) 2760

Mickey (5") sitting in front of tent reading to attentive Pluto (5"), Courvoisier watercolor & airbrush background, CE/Jun 9/95 (5000-7000) 8625

Full figure of wary hunter Mickey with shotgun & small animals around him, 8 x 10", complementary Courvoisier background of forest, HL/Nov 19/95 (4000-5000) 7188

Full figure of smiling Mickey (5") sitting on log in front of tent w/closed book as Pluto (5") sits & listens, Courvoisier watercolor & airbrush background w/partial overlay, CE/Jun 20/96 (5000-7000) 8625

Full figure of surprised Mickey (5") sitting on log in front of tent holding book & looking at happy Pluto (near-full figure, 5") sitting in front of him, partial overlay of foliage, Courvoisier watercolor background, CE/Dec 12/96 (5000-7000) 6900

Full figure of surprised Pluto (3-1/2 x 3" w/o tail) standing amid grass, leaves, & baby quail, airbrushed Courvoisier background, S/Jun 21/97 (1500-2500) 3162

Full figures of hunter Mickey (3-1/2") whispering back to attentive Pluto (4-1/2"), Courvoisier watercolor background & label, SR/Fall/97 (6000-9000) 8300

Full-figure front view of startled hunter Mickey standing holding shotgun in forest amid small animals, 4-1/2", airbrushed Courvoisier background, WDP label, S/Dec 19/97 (5000-7000) 4600

Waist-up of hunter Mickey (7") talking to Pluto while holding him up by paws, Courvoisier background of outdoors, CE/Dec 18/97 (5000-7000) 5750

Full figure of surprised Mickey (4-3/4") sitting on log in front of tent holding closed book with Pluto (4 7/8", near-full figure, eyes closed) sitting in front of him, Courvoisier watercolor background of forest with full foreground overlay, SR/Spring/98 (4000-8000) 5330

CELS – FULL FIGURE
Hunter Mickey stands facing left, right arm & index finger out, looking down, 4-1/2", transparent-painted shadow, SR/Fall/94 (2500-5000) 2530

Happy Mickey as hunter, 4-1/2 x 4-1/2", signed by Frank Thomas & Ollie Johnston, HL/Apr 23/95 (5000-7000) 5880

Tearful Pluto slinking away, 3 x 7", HL/Apr 23/95 (1000-1500) 1456

Close-up of angry Mickey, 5", CE/Jun 9/95 (2500-3500) 3680

Cautious hunter Mickey standing holding shotgun, 3-1/2 x 3-3/4", HL/Nov 19/95 (3000-3500) 4370

Bewildered Pluto facing camera garlanded with flowers, 5 x 5", HL/Nov 19/95 (800-1200) 1495

Smiling hunter Mickey holding shotgun, 5-1/2 x 4-1/2", HL/Nov 19/95 (3500-5000) 4140

Smiling hunter Mickey holding shotgun at side, 5-1/2 x 4-1/2", HL/Apr 28/96 (3500-5000) 4140

Suspicious Pluto stands facing left, tail straight back, ears up; 3 x 6", HL/Oct 6/96 (800-1000) 920

Front view of worried hunter Mickey holding lit flashlight & looking down, 3-1/2 x 3", HL/Oct 6/96 (3000-5000) 3450

Hunter Mickey stands holding shotgun, facing left & smiling sheepishly, 5-1/2 x 4-1/2", HL/May 3/97 (3500-4000) 2990

Hunter Mickey stands facing left & holding shotgun at his side, restored, 5-1/2 x 4-3/4", VF, HL/Apr 25/98 (3500-4000) 2760

Front-view close-up of Pluto lying down staring into camera, 6 3/8", 12-field cel, general rippling, ct, SR/Spring/98 (600-1000) 680

CELS – PARTIAL FIGURE
Near-full figure of angry bear standing, 8 x 7-1/2", HL/Nov 19/95 (500-800) 748

Near-full figure of enraged, drooling bear, 7 x 6-1/2", HL/Apr 28/96 (500-800) 920

DYE-TRANSFER PRINTS
Mickey reading book to Pluto in camp, both sitting, 10-1/4 x 8" print, SR/Fall/94 (300-600) 310

Mickey reading book to Pluto in camp, both sitting, 10 x 8", original studio mat, Disney label, SR/Spring/96 (300-600) 300

MODEL ART
Photostat model sheet featuring Mickey, bear, & quail, 15-1/2 x 12-1/2", SR/Fall/95 (200-400) 310

POLAR TRAPPERS (1938)
ANIMATION DRAWINGS
Large-image drawing of Goofy pinning coat closed, 8 x 6", HL/Nov 19/95 (500-700) 1265

Full-figure drawing of surprised Goofy standing with arms up, hat above head, looking into camera, 7", 12-field sheet, SR/Fall/96 (300-600) 310

2 detailed rough drawings: full figure of Donald Duck standing in tuxedo imitating a penguin, 4 x 3-1/4", HL/May 31/97 (200-300) 58

4 drawings of Goofy: screaming on swinging scaffold (*The Big Wash*); dressed in fur coat (*Polar Trappers*); in band (*Amateur Hour* [sic]); one from *Mickey's Service Station*; each sheet 9-1/2 x 12"; S/Dec 19/97 (800-1200) 920

CEL SET-UPS
Full-figure publicity cel of exhausted Goofy hauling sled full of supplies as smiling Donald (barely) helps from behind, 3-3/4 x 9-1/2", pan watercolor production background of snow scene from *Donald's Snow Fight*, 1942, S/Dec 14/96 (5000-7000) 4600

CONCEPT AND INSPIRATIONAL ART
Design drawing for establishing shot of Goofy & Donald's base camp, colored conté crayon, 8-1/2 x 11-1/2", HL/Feb 23/97 (300-500) 518

MODEL ART
Original model sheet of cartoon's characters, 8 x 10-1/2", signed "Horvath", HL/Nov 13/94 (1800-2200) 4256

THE PRACTICAL PIG (1939)
ANIMATION DRAWINGS
2 full-figure drawings by Freddie Moore: scared Fiddler & Fifer running right together; angry Practical, holding plans & hammer, standing looking left; both 4-1/4", 12-field sheets, camera notation; SR/Fall/96 (400-800) 420

2 full-figure drawings: Practical standing facing right & talking sternly; swimsuit-clad Fifer & Fiddler standing facing left & leaning back in surprise; 5 x 3-1/2" & 4-1/2 x 4"; HL/Feb 23/97 (200-250) 316

CEL SET-UPS
3 large images, one of each pig, studio prepared background, WDE label, S/Dec 16/93 (2000-3000) 2588

Fifer Pig (4") bends over laughing as Fiddler Pig (5") laughs & runs, airbrushed Courvoisier background, S/Jun 17/94 (1500-2000) 1725

Practical Pig lectures brothers in front of house, 5" & smaller, Courvoisier watercolor & airbrush background, CE/Jun 18/94 (2500-3500) 2990

Full figure of Fiddler Pig laughing, 5", Courvoisier airbrush background, CE/Dec 16/94 (700-900) 633

Full figures of Wolf as postal worker delivering false message to Practical Pig, 8-1/2 x 11", comple-mentary painted background, inscribed mat, HL/Apr 23/95 (2400-2800) 2912

Full figures of Practical lecturing Fiddler & Fifer,

8-1/2 x 11", complementary airbrush background, Courvoisier labels, HL/Apr 23/95 (2000-2500)   3136

Fiddler & Fifer Pig (2-1/2" ea) lean over lumber pile to laugh at irritated Practical (full figure, 4") standing holding hammer & plans, airbrushed Courvoisier background, S/Dec 14/96 (2000-3000)   3162

Full figure of Practical tiptoeing away from brick home carrying satchel, 4", watercolor production background, S/Jun 21/97 (5000-7000)   6325

Full figures of three young wolves (7-1/2") jumping & brandishing cutlery in kitchen as tied-up Fiddler & Fifer (4-1/4") cower, Courvoisier publication master watercolor background, both small labels, SR/Fall/97 (3000-4000)   3240

Full figure of Practical tiptoeing away (to left) from brick home carrying satchel, 4", watercolor production background, S/Dec 19/97 (5000-7000)   5175

CELS – FULL FIGURE

Full standing figures: disguised Practical Pig examines tomato, 4-1/2"; happy Fifer & Fiddler hold instruments, 3-3/4"; some missing paint, SR/Fall/94 (400-800)   400

3 trimmed vignettes together: 2 full figures of two little wolves capturing Fiddler, 4-3/4 x 2-1/2"; hips-up of Big Bad Wolf sticking apples into mouths of Fiddler & Fifer (heads only), 8 x 5-1/4"; some missing paint, SR/Fall/94 (700-1200)   720

CELS – PARTIAL FIGURE (also see CELS-FULL FIGURE)

Grinning Wolf w/quill pen & paper, 5-1/2 x 7", VF, HL/Apr 21/94 (1500-2000)   1568

STORY ART

5 storyboard drawings, CE/Jun 20/96 (600-800) 1150

THE PRINCE & THE PAUPER (1990)
CEL SET-UPS

4-1/2" Pauper Mickey w/bucket on head, 5" Goofy behind him, 4-1/2" Pluto w/stick, laser background, Disney seal, certificate of authenticity, framed, S/Dec 16/93 (5000-7000)   2875

3 matching cels of Mickey, bishop & 4 couriers with color print background, 9-1/2 x 14-1/2", Disney seal, VF, HL/Apr 10/94 (1000-1600)   1120

Mickey (3 x 1-1/2") & Donald (2 x 3") in jail, laughing Goofy (5-1/2 x 5") w/keys, Disney printed background, CE/Jun 18/94 (1000-1500)   978

Full figures of smug Prince & bewildered Pauper, color print background & seal, 10 x 15", HL/Aug 21/94 (1200-1600)   1232

Pauper Mickey (2-1/2") sitting on throne about to be crowned by Cardinal (9"), printed background, Disney Co. seal, S/Dec 17/94 (1000-1500) 1150

Long shot of Mickey (11/2") approaching Cardinal (4") & throne, color print of matching background, S/Jun 10/95 (800-1200)   1840

Prince (4-1/2") smiles at his tutor (8"), copy of original background, S/Jun 10/95 (800-1200)   920

Full figure of Pauper Mickey picking up ham & loaf of bread, 9-1/2 x 15-1/2", matching color print background of village street scene, HL/Nov 19/95 (800-1000)   690

Full figures of Pauper Mickey comforting sitting Pluto, 7-3/4 x 4-1/2", DAE seal, color print display background, SR/Spring/96 (300-600)   540

Full figures of Mickey Mouse standing by throne as both prince & pauper, matching color print background, 10 x 13", HL/Apr 28/96 (1200-1600)   833

Smiling Pauper Mickey tries on crown, matching color print background, 7-1/2 x 9", HL/Apr 28/96 (900-1200)   633

Full figures of happy Mickey (5"), dramatic Goofy (5"), & happy Pluto (3") standing in village street, Walt Disney key reproduction background, CE/Dec 12/96 (2000-2500)   1380

2 cels: Pauper Mickey wearing Goofy's bucket as hat, 5" (head & shoulders only); full figure of Prince Mickey disguised as Pauper attempting to distribute King's food amidst poor, 2", printed background; S/Dec 14/96 (800-1200)   1150

Full-figure front view of shocked Pauper Mickey looking into camera & Prince Mickey looking up & licking lips, 4-1/4 x 6-1/2", matching color print background, VF+, HL/Nov 16/97 (800-1000)   1265

Waist-up front view of Mickey & Donald harmonizing, 8", unidentified background; Mickey in space

suit from Epcot Center, 4-1/2", watercolor production background, CE/Dec 18/97 (800-1200)   1495

Front view of Prince Mickey as pauper sitting in street holding loaf of bread & ham hock, 3 x 4-1/2", printed background of street & cart, silver Walt Disney Co. seal, S/Dec 19/97 (500-700)   747

CELS – FULL FIGURE

Prince & Pauper stand together, 5-1/2 x 6-1/2", HL/Apr 23/95 (1200-1600)   1344

Overhead view of wide-eyed pauper Mickey, 5 x 6", HL/Aug 6/95 (700-900)   1232

Pauper Mickey, Goofy & Pluto stand talking, 3-1/2 x 5-1/2", HL/Apr 28/96 (700-1000)   460

Pauper Mickey comforts Pluto, 5-1/2 x 8", HL/Apr 28/96 (800-1200)   690

Full figures of worried pauper Mickey (right leg raised) & pained Prince Mickey (eyes closed) standing together, facing camera, 4-3/8" & 5", Disney Art Program seal & certificate. SR/Fall/96 (600-1000)   680

Proud Mickey standing to receive crown from Archbishop, 4-1/2 x 6", HL/Oct 6/96 (500-700)   633

Stunned Pauper Mickey standing, 7 x 4-1/2", HL/Feb 23/97 (500-700)   633

CELS – PARTIAL FIGURE

Portrait cel of brooding Prince Mickey, seal, 5 x 4", VF+, HL/Aug 21/94 (800-1200)   672

Knees-up medium close-up of Prince Mickey, seal, 6 x 6-1/2", VF+, HL/Apr 23/95 (700-900)   840

Knees-up large image of worried Prince Mickey, seal, 5-1/2 x 3-1/2, VF+, HL/Nov 19/95 (800-1200)   748

Waist-up front view of Mickey adjusting crown, 6", 12-field cel, Disney Art Program seal, SR/Spring/96 (300-600)   460

Near-full figure front view of worried Prince Mickey, 5-1/2 x 3-1/2", VF+, plus letter from Feature Animation president, HL/Nov 16/97 (500-700)   403

Knees-up front view of awed Pauper Mickey holding hat & looking straight up, 6 x 4-1/2", seal, VF+, HL/Apr 25/98 (500-700)   633

PRIVATE PLUTO (1943)
CELS – FULL FIGURE

Helmeted Pluto marches proudly to right with eyes closed, 3-1/2 x 4-1/2" (without tail), S/Jun 10/95 (400-600)   747

PUPPY LOVE (1933)
ANIMATION DRAWINGS

Mickey carries candy & flowers, 2 drawings, 4 x 2-3/4", CE/Jun 18/94 (1000-1500)   748

2 matching full-figure drawings: Mickey & Minnie standing, 3-1/2" each, 12-field sheets, SR/Fall/94 (800-1200)   830

Full-figure drawing of upset Minnie walking left, 4-1/4", 12-field, SR/Fall/94 (600-900)   300

Full-figure drawing of jaunty Mickey Mouse walking with flowers & candy, 4-1/2 x 4", HL/Apr 23/95 (600-900)   1008

Full-figure drawing of Minnie standing facing left, holding parasol, 4-1/4", 12-field sheet, scene & animator's notes, SR/Spring/96 (400-700)   540

Full-figure drawing of smiling Mickey (flowers behind back, 3-1/4") & Minnie (holding heart-shaped box, 3") standing facing each other, 12-field sheet, SR/Spring/97 (600-1200)   1090

PUSS-CAFÉ (1950)
CELS – PARTIAL FIGURE

Angry Pluto attacks 2 cats in hammock, 5-1/2 x 8-1/2", restored, VF, HL/Apr 10/94 (600-800)   560

PUT-PUT TROUBLES (1940)
CEL SET-UPS

Donald sits in small run-away motorboat going right, 7-1/16 x 4-1/2", Courvoisier watercolor background of water & shore, cel fissured at boat prow, restored, SR/Fall/97 (2500-3200)   1800

RESCUE DOG (1947)
CEL SET-UPS

Full figures of alarmed Pluto (4 x 3") standing & watch-

ing Salty (4" total) balance barrel on nose, production background of frozen lake & lighthouse from unknown production, inscribed "...Walt Disney" on mat, S/Jun 19/96 (3500-4000) 3450

RIVAL ROMEOS (1928)
Also see UNIDENTIFIED/MISCELLANEOUS: OSWALD THE LUCKY RABBIT
ANIMATION DRAWINGS

Full-figure drawing of determined Oswald throwing pin, 3 x 3-1/2", CE/Jun 18/94 (1000-1500) 978

Full-figure front-view drawing of Oswald standing singing & playing one-string guitar, 4-1/4", 12-field sheet, SR/Fall/97 (1500-2000)   1450

LAYOUT ART

Full-figure layout drawing of Oswald playing banjo, looking right, 4", CE/Dec 18/97 (1000-1500)   920

THE RIVETER (1940)
CEL SET-UPS

Hatless Donald Duck stands near shack with arms full, 4", pan watercolor production background, S/Dec 19/97 (1500-2500)   3737

THE ROBBER KITTEN (1935)
ANIMATION DRAWINGS

2 drawings: full figure of smiling Ambrose standing looking up; smiling Dirty Bill; 5-1/2 x 4", 7 x 6-1/2"; HL/Apr 28/96 (700-1000)   920

CELS – FULL FIGURE

Action pose of Ambrose Kitten holding pistol & bag, 5 x 6-1/2", HL/Aug 6/95 (2400-2800)   1792

ROLLER COASTER RABBIT (1990)
CEL SET-UPS

Frightened Roger Rabbit holds equally frightened Baby Herman as they slide out of coaster tunnel, 8-1/2 x 10", matching black-&-white photoprint background, HL/Nov 13/94 (900-1200)   952

Full figure of trussed Jessica lying across coaster tracks, color print of matching background, 15 x 11-1/2" overall, seal, VF+, HL/Feb 23/97 (1500-2000)   2530

CELS – FULL FIGURE

Horizontal trussed Jessica, eyes & mouth closed; 5 x 11", seal, VF+, HL/Aug 21/94 (2000-3000)   2016

Frantic Roger Rabbit dodges 2 darts, 8 x 10", VF+, HL/Nov 19/95 (700-1000)   633

Horizontal trussed Jessica, eyes & mouth open; 5-3/4 x 11", seal, VF+, HL/Apr 28/96 (2000-2500)   3680

CELS – PARTIAL FIGURE

Wide-eyed Roger holding wide-eyed Baby Herman holding balloon in wind, both looking right; seal & presentation letter; 4 x 4-1/2"; VF+; HL/Aug 21/94 (1000-1500)   840

Grimacing Roger Rabbit nose-to-nose with fierce bull, 8 x 11", seal, VF+, HL/Apr 23/95 (800-1200)   1680

LAYOUT/STORY ART

Story/layout drawing of Baby Herman crawling toward Ferris wheel, 10 x 15", HL/Apr 28/96 (500-700)   230

2 consecutive story/layout drawings of Roger caught in Ferris Wheel gears & emerging as tractor tread; 4 x 7-1/2", 5-1/4 x 10", HL/Oct 6/96 (300-400)   1093

RUGGED BEAR (1953)
CEL SET-UPS

Full figure of Donald the hunter cleaning rifle in cabin, 4-1/2", watercolor production background, inscribed "...Walt Disney", S/Jun 10/95 (2500-3500)   3737

THE SAGA OF WINDWAGON SMITH (1961)
CEL SET-UPS

Looking thru saloon window at Conestoga wagon, 14-1/2 x 10-5/8", key watercolor master background, saloon overlay painted on cel, SR/Fall/97 (1800-2400)   1780

SANTA'S WORKSHOP (1932)
BACKGROUNDS
Original master background of Santa's castle-
workshop as seen from stables, watercolor
on background sheet, 8-1/2 x 11", VF,
HL/Feb 23/97 (3000-4000)   12,650
Master background of rocking horse assembly area,
watercolor on background sheet, 8-1/2 x 11",
VF, HL/Feb 23/97 (2000-3000)   2760
Master background of shelf work area with bucket
of "checkered paint", watercolor on
background sheet, 8-1/2 x 11", VF,
HL/Feb 23/97 (2500-3500)   20,700
Master background of work station where Santa
approves toys, watercolor on background
sheet, 8-1/2 x 11", VF, HL/Feb 23/97
(3000-4000)   10,638
Master background of workshop shelving, watercolor on background sheet, 8-1/2 x 11",
VF, HL/Feb 23/97 (2000-3000)   2990
Master background of Santa's castle exterior with
reindeer & sleigh outside door, watercolor
on background sheet, 8-1/2 x 11", F-VF,
HL/Feb 23/97 (3000-4000)   7763
Master background: close-up of Santa's sleigh
loaded w/full toy bag, watercolor on
background sheet, 8-1/4 x 11", VF,
HL/Feb 23/97 (2500-3500)   3910
LAYOUT ART
Detailed layout drawing of Santa's castle-workshop
as seen from stables, 8 x 10-1/2", F,
HL/Feb 23/97 (500-700)   1725
Detailed layout drawing of elf work area with
bucket of "checkered paint," 7 x 9-1/2",
F+, HL/Feb 23/97 (500-700)   2990

SCROOGE MCDUCK & MONEY (1967)
Also see TELEVISION: DUCKTALES
CELS – FULL FIGURE
Scrooge in professorial pose, 4 x 4", HL/Apr 23/95
(700-1000)   672
One nephew playfully choking another, 4 x 4",
HL/Feb 23/95 (200-300)   374
Hatless Scrooge standing on tiptoes w/arms out-
stretched at side as 3 nephews cheer, 5-1/2
x 11" overall, HL/May 31/97 (800-1000)   316
CELS – PARTIAL FIGURE
Waist-up of 2 scolding nephews, 5 x 4-1/2", VF+,
HL/Feb 26-27/94 (200-400)   303
Hips-up view of Scrooge facing left holding piggy
bank, 5-1/4 x 4-1/4", VF+, HL/Apr 25/98
(600-900)   546

SEA SALTS (1949)
TITLE ART
Title card: full figure of Bootle Beetle lighting
Donald's (head & neck) pipe, hand lettering,
pipe smoke over watercolor background,
12-field, original production cover flap,
SR/Spring/95 (2000-5000)   2250
Matching original title cel & master background
(airbrush on background sheet) with elderly
Donald & Bootle Beetle, 8-1/2 x 11", VF,
HL/Nov 19/95 (3000-3500)   3220

SEA SCOUTS (1939)
ANIMATION DRAWINGS
Full-figure drawing of angry Admiral Donald
hanging by foot from rope, 5 x 3",
HL/Feb 23/97 (300-400)   495
CEL SET-UPS
Matching full-figure cel & master background
(watercolor on background sheet) of Admiral
Donald standing on ship's deck, bending at
waist to inspect rope entangling right foot,
stamps, restored in part, 8-1/4 x 10-3/4",
VF, HL/Apr 25/98 (4000-6000)   3910
MODEL ART
Photostatic model sheet of Donald, nephews, boat,
& equipment; 14-3/4 x 12-1/2", some edge
wear, center vertical fold, SR/Spring/95
(100-200)   240

SELF CONTROL (1938)
CELS – FULL FIGURE
2 cels of Donald in hammock (all but end of
hammock): sitting up holding drink,

fidgeting with eyes closed; 9" wide, 12-field,
paint restoration, SR/Fall/94 (1200-1800)   1340
Angry Donald sitting in hammock looking down,
2 x 11", VF, HL/Apr 23/95 (900-1200)   1344

SHANGHAIED (1934)
ANIMATION DRAWINGS
Full-figure drawing of Mickey Mouse & Pete
swordfighting, 9 x 5-1/2", 12-field sheet,
edge discoloration, SR/Fall/94 (400-700)   800
Full-figure drawing of Pete & Mickey sword fighting,
9-1/4 x 5-5/8", 12-field sheet, SR/Fall/95
(500-1000)   1250
Full-figure drawing: rear view of Mickey holds swordfish
over his head as angry Pete with piano stool for
peg-leg stands holding sword, 9-3/4 x 6-1/4",
12-field sheet, SR/Fall/97 (900-1400)   660
LAYOUT/MODEL ART
Mickey (3") fights Pete, layout drawing; two model
drawings of Pete by Bert Gillett, 7" & smaller;
2-page typewritten script, CE/Jun 18/94
(1000-1500)   1265
Layout drawing of Peg Leg Pete climbing thru
window w/Minnie, 6-1/2", CE/Jun 9/95
(1200-1500)   1150
Layout drawing of drooling Peg Leg Pete (5")
reaching out of piano to grab unsuspecting
Minnie (4-1/2"), CE/Jun 9/95 (1200-1500)   1610
MODEL ART
Full-figure color model drawing of scruffy Peg Leg
Pete standing facing left, 6", 12-field sheet,
some edge darkening, SR/Spring/98
(300-600)   300

THE SIMPLE THINGS (1953)
CELS – FULL FIGURE
Whistling Mickey holds fish in right hand, fishing
pole in left; 5-3/4 x 8"; CE/Jun 18/94
(1500-2000)   1840
Mickey sits fishing, 4-1/2", CE/Dec 16/94
(800-1200)   1265
Sitting Mickey opens lunch pail, 4-1/2 x 5",
HL/Apr 23/95 (1000-1500)   1792
CELS – PARTIAL FIGURE
Near-full figure of casually dressed Mickey sitting
eating sandwich, 5 x 5-1/2", HL/Apr 28/96
(900-1000)   1265
Mickey Mouse looking up with arms outspread &
contented Pluto sits looking right, 4-1/2 x 4"
& 5 x 7", VF+, HL/Nov 16/97 (1200-1600)   1150

THE SKELETON DANCE (1929)
BACKGROUNDS
12-field master background of graveyard, 4th in
film, india ink & gray wash on background
sheet, 9-1/2 x 11-1/2", HL/Aug 6/95
(7000-9000)   11,760

SKY TROOPER (1942)
BACKGROUNDS
Master background of office interior, 8 x 11",
watercolor on background sheet,
HL/Nov 19/95 (900-1200)   1035

SLEEPY TIME DONALD (1947)
CEL SET-UPS
2 matching cels: full figures of stunned Daisy &
sleeping Donald w/boot on head standing
in elevator (Donald on ceiling), background
unidentified, 7-1/2 x 7", F+, HL/Nov 16/97
(900-1200)   690
CELS – PARTIAL FIGURE
Daisy holds flower & reacts to fragrance, 5-1/2
x 4", F, HL/Nov 16/97 (400-600)   546

SLIDE, DONALD, SLIDE (1949)
MODEL ART
Pencil color model drawing of Donald sprinting for
1st base, 7 x 7-1/2", F+, HL/Feb 26-27/94
(200-400)   468
TITLE ART
Title card of Donald sliding, 4-1/2 x 7", production
background, CE/Jun 18/94 (1000-1500)   5175

THE SMALL ONE (1978)
CELS – PARTIAL FIGURE/MODEL ART

Boy & Small One share smiles & a hug, 9 x 10", seal
& label, VF, HL/Nov 13/94 (300-400)   476
Boy with arm around neck of Small One, 8 x 9-1/2",
WDP seal, VF, HL/Aug 6/95 (400-600)   504
Auctioneer anticipates bids with hands cupped
around ears, 6 x 10", seal, WDP label, VF+,
HL/Apr 28/96 (105-200)   127
Somber Father w/arms on shoulders of Boy, who
looks up w/arms around neck of sad Small
One, 9 x 7", WDP seal, VF, HL/May 31/97 (300-400)   288
Color model cel: knees-up of smiling Boy (7") &
happy, sitting Small One (9-1/8") facing each
other, 16-field cel, SR/Fall/97 (450-700)   300
Hips-up color model cel of Boy w/arms around head
of & talking to attentive Small One, 9-1/2",
16-field cel, ct, SR/Spring/98 (300-600)   310

SOCIETY DOG SHOW (1939)
ANIMATION DRAWINGS
30 full-figure near-sequential animation drawings:
Mickey w/Pluto (21), Mickey alone (9); 4" to 5",
12-field sheets, SR/Fall/94 (5000-10,000)   7200
Drawing of Mickey with perfume & sprayer, 5-1/2
x 7", notes, HL/Nov 13/94 (500-700)   952
57 sequential animation drawings of Mickey emerging
from beneath viewing stand & running away,
12-field sheets, full notations, 1st sheet has edge
wear, SR/Spring/95 (10,000-15,000)   11,000
Drawing of fearful Pluto & menacing dog-show judge,
7 x 11", F+, HL/Apr 23/95 (400-600)   840
Drawing of Pluto & Mickey in mouse-powered cycle,
4-1/2 x 6", ink on celluloid, red & black pencil
on animation sheet, VF, HL/Apr 23/95
(600-900)   1344
2 full-figure expressive drawings of Mickey & Pluto,
4-1/2 x 6", F+, HL/Apr 23/95 (600-900)   2688
Full-figure rough drawing of Mickey (4") helping
Pluto (5") stand, CE/Jun 9/95 (600-800)   978
Drawing of Mickey readying Pluto, 4" x 6",
S/Jun 10/95 (600-800)   920
Full-figure drawing: smiling Mickey leads dignified
Pluto on leash, 5-1/2 x 7-1/2",
HL/Aug 6/95 (600-900)   1456
Drawing of worried Mickey emerging on hands
& knees from under bunting, 4-1/2 x 7",
HL/Aug 6/95 (600-900)   1120
20 sequential animation drawings featuring Mickey
& Pluto, 4" to 4-1/2", 12-field sheets,
SR/Fall/95 (6000-10,000)   5,200
20 sequential drawings of Pluto [entering dog show]
5-5/8 x 3" to 6-1/2 x 3-1/8", 12-field sheets,
SR/Fall/95 (2000-5000)   2000
2 full-figure matched drawings of jaunty Mickey
& Pluto going to show, 4 x 4", 3 x 6",
HL/Nov 19/95 (1000-1500)   1374
Drawing of judge presenting hero's medallion to
surprised Pluto as happy Mickey watches,
6-1/2 x 8-1/2", HL/Nov 19/95 (600-1000)   1380
4 full-figure rough drawings: 3 of Mickey comforting
Pluto; Mickey & Pluto turn to discover fire;
4 x 3" to 4 x 6-1/2"; HL/Nov 19/95
(600-800)   2070
Near-full figure drawing of Mickey pouring perfume
into sprayer, 6 x 5-1/2", HL/Apr 28/96
(600-800)   863
2 full-figure drawings: Mickey (wearing hat) walking
with suitcase, walking Pluto looking back
admiringly; 4-1/2 x 3-1/2", 3 x 6",
HL/Apr 28/96 (900-1200)   805
Drawing of smiling Mickey (3"), surprised Pluto
(2-1/2"), & judge poised to place medal
around Pluto's neck (5-1/2");
CE/Jun 20/96 (800-1200)   2300
All-key matching set of 3 animation drawings: full
figures of Mickey (4-1/8") & shy Pluto (3-1/4")

walking right, looking back & up, 12-field sheets; chest-down of bellmen & guests in lobby, 18-11/16 x 8-5/8" sheet with ink & camera notations; SR/Fall/96 (1000-1800)   800

Full-figure drawing of Mickey restraining angry Pluto jumping to right, 8-1/2 x 5-1/2", 12-field sheet, inker's notation, SR/Fall/96 (600-1000)   610

Full-figure drawing of smiling Mickey walking confident Pluto on leash to right, 4-1/2 x 8-1/2", HL/Feb 23/97 (600-900)   920

Full-figure drawing of concerned Mickey walking right, 5", 12-field sheet, camera notation, SR/Spring/97 (500-900)   400

Full-figure drawing of smiling Mickey (6-1/2") hanging onto snarling Pluto (7-1/4") by collar, S/Jun 21/97 (1000-1500)   1150

3 full-figure drawings: smiling Pluto standing facing right, 3 x 5" w/o tail; smiling Mickey walking right w/suitcase, 4"; snooty doorman standing facing left w/mouth open, 6", S/Jun 21/97 (1500-2500)   1380

Full-figure drawing of Mickey standing facing toward right with legs apart, 4-5/8", 12-field sheet, inker's notation, SR/Fall/97 (600-1000)   400

Full-figure drawing of Mickey standing over open valise, 5 3/8", 12-field sheet, SR/Fall/97 (600-1000)   400

Full-figure drawing of happy Mickey walking & carrying suitcase, 4-1/2 x 4-1/4", VF, HL/Nov 16/97 (400-600)   690

Extreme drawing of Mickey peeking out from under drapes, 4-1/2 x 5-1/2", VF, HL/Nov 16/97 (400-600)   460

Full-figure drawing of Mickey leading proud Pluto to right, 6 x 8", VF, HL/Apr 25/98 (600-800)   978

Full-figure drawing of eager Pluto standing facing right, wagging tail in Judge's (waist-up) face, 7 x 8-1/2", VF, HL/Apr 25/98 (300-400)   403

Ankles-up drawing of Mickey standing facing right, pouring liquid into hand sprayer; 6 x 5-1/2", VF, HL/Apr 25/98 (400-600)   489

ART – MISCELLANEOUS

Pluto with 1st prize as Mickey readies camera & admirer looks on, preliminary colored-pencil drawing for publicity or book illustration, 6 x 10", VF, HL/Apr 10/94 (600-900)   448

CEL SET-UPS

Full figure of haughty society dame with trophy in bosom leading haughty dachshund, 7 x 8", painted woodgrain background as prepared for Courvoisier, HL/Nov 19/95 (700-1200)   575

Full figures of sitting Pluto leaning lovingly against smiling Fifi, overall 3-3/4 x 6", unidentified background of room, S/Dec 14/96 (500-700)   345

CELS – FULL FIGURE

3 cels framed together: 4 dog-show attendees; Pluto looking at Mickey's hand holding hair dryer; Pluto carrying Fifi thru fire; S/Dec 16/93 (1200-1800)   1150

Pluto saves Fifi from burning building, 3" overall, S/Dec 16/93 (600-800)   575

CONCEPT AND INSPIRATIONAL ART

Full-figure study drawing of Mickey Mouse giving uncooperative Pluto (sitting on box) spray of perfume, 8-1/4 x 9", HL/May 31/97 (300-500)   1036

SOUP'S ON (1948)
CELS – FULL FIGURE

Livid red Donald as devil running left & looking up, 4-1/4", 12-field cel, ct, SR/Spring/98 (500-900)   510

SPRINGTIME FOR PLUTO (1944)
BACKGROUNDS

Gouache master background of worm's underground home, 10-5/8 x 8-1/4", SR/Fall/95 (800-1400)   800

SQUATTER'S RIGHTS (1946)
CEL SET-UPS

Full figures of Mickey Mouse (in hat w/pom-pom, 5") & Chip (2-1/2") standing talking expressively to each other, printed background of large circle on solid field, S/Dec 14/96 (1000-1500)   1725

CELS – FULL FIGURE

Smiling Mickey Mouse holds backpack, 4-1/2 x 4",

HL/Nov 19/95 (2000-2500)   3853

STEAMBOAT WILLIE (1928)
ANIMATION DRAWINGS

*Production drawing of Mickey (4") hopping; plus drawings of Goofy (8") stretched-out and Donald Duck (5-1/2") proudly thumping chest; S/Jun 17/94 (500-700)   1725

Drawing of Mickey reaching with xylophone strikers, 5-1/2 x 4-1/2", HL/Aug 21/94 (1000-1500)   1568

2 drawings: Mickey with xylophone strikers; scowling Pete; 4 x 5", 4 x 6", HL/Aug 21/94 (1500-2000)   3584

Drawing of smiling Mickey w/xylophone strikers, 3-1/2 x 6", HL/Nov 13/94 (1000-1500)   1344

4 drawings: Mickey with xylophone strikers; Pete; head of steer; steamboat; 3 x 6-1/2" to 7 x 10"; HL/Nov 13/94 (3000-4000)   3248

Drawing of Mickey walking away, 4-1/2", CE/Dec 16/94 (800-1200)   1495

Close-up drawing of Mickey with xylophone strikers, 2-1/2 x 4", HL/Apr 23/95 (900-1200)   952

Drawing of smiling Mickey with xylophone strikers, 2-1/2" x 4", S/Jun 10/95 (400-600)   920

Chest-up drawing of Mickey facing left, wielding xylophone strikers, 3-3/4", 12-field sheet, SR/Spring/96 (1000-1500)   1100

Shoulders-up drawing of smiling Mickey holding two drum mallets, 2", CE/Jun 20/96 (1500-2000)   1035

2 drawings: shoulders-up of smiling Mickey holding two xylophone strikers; full-figure rear long shot of Mickey & Minnie in airplane from *Plane Crazy*; 2-3/4 x 1-3/4", 3-3/4 x 4-1/2"; VF; HL/Oct 6/96 (700-1000)   920

Hips-up drawing of Mickey facing left holding two xylophone strikers over his head, 4-7/8", SR/Spring/97 (1100-1500)   2270

Close-up drawing of smiling Mickey facing left & swinging xylophone strikers, 3-1/2 x 3-3/4", HL/May 3/97 (1000-1500)   2300

Torso-up drawing of smiling Mickey facing left swinging xylophone strikers, 3 x 5", VF, HL/Nov 16/97 (1000-1500)   2185

Chest-up drawing of smiling Mickey swinging xylophone strikers, 6-7/8 x 2-1/4", 12-field sheet, SR/Spring/98 (1500-2500)   1520

CEL SET-UPS

"Mickey at the Wheel" limited-edition cel, #214/275, print background, Disney seal & authenticity certificate, 9-1/2 x 11-1/2", VF+, HL/Apr 28/96 (1000-1500)   2070

"Mickey at the Wheel" limited-edition cel, #189/275, 9-1/4 x 12", color print background, Disney seal, VF+, HL/Nov 16/97 (1000-1500)   2300

CONCEPT AND INSPIRATIONAL ART

2 full-figure character studies: *Steamboat Willie's* Pete at boat wheel; Horace Horsecollar galloping right, for unknown production; circa 1929-30, 6-1/2 x 8" & 2-1/2 x 5-1/2"; F; HL/Nov 19/95 (700-1000)   1093

LAYOUT ART

2 full-figure layout drawings: whistling Mickey standing with eyes closed holding steamboat wheel, 3"; surprised Pete standing looking up, 5-1/2"; CE/Dec 18/97 (3000-5000)   10,925

STEEL AND AMERICA (1965)
CELS – FULL FIGURE

Donald Duck as blacksmith holds pick out in front of him, 3 x 4", DL label, restored, VF, HL/May 31/97 (150-250)   58

Donald Duck in period costume stands facing right using hand-held bellows, backing board with red & gold label as sold at DL, 5 x 4", VF, HL/Apr 25/98 (300-400)   230

THE STEEPLE CHASE (1933)
ANIMATION DRAWINGS

Full-figure drawing of Mickey Mouse riding patchwork "horse" as it breaks apart, 4 x 6-1/2", HL/Nov 19/95 (700-900)   1150

CONCEPT AND INSPIRATIONAL ART

2 character studies: Mickey as jockey & porcine jockey, 7 x 11" & 4 x 9", HL/Nov 19/95 (1000-1500)   1495

LAYOUT ART

4 layout drawings: broadside poster, fairgrounds, impatient jockey Mickey, view thru stable doorway; 12-field sheets, wear & some discoloration, two have missing corners; SR/Spring/95 (1600-2600)   7800

2 polished layout drawings: full figure of smiling jockey Mickey facing right, elderly fellow in wheelchair holding pocket watch as horse looks on; 3 x 3", 4-1/2 x 7"; HL/Apr 28/96 (1000-1500)   920

THE STORY OF OIL
CELS – FULL FIGURE

Relaxed caveman with club lying on head of wooly mammoth walking right, 5-3/8", Richfield promotional film, with copy of DL ad in which it appeared, some lifting paint, SR/Spring/95 (200-500)   210

STRAIGHT SHOOTERS (1947)
TITLE ART

Title card: uniformed nephews shoot at two duck silhouettes, watercolor w/hand lettering on cel overlay, 16-field, SR/Fall/95 (2000-4000)   2000

SUSIE, THE LITTLE BLUE COUP (1952)
CEL SET-UPS

Susie wrapped in blankets rolls down street, publication background, 6", S/Dec 16/93 (900-1200)   1035

Full figure of distraught Susie sitting in junkyard, 11 x 15", matching cels (including rain) & original master background (tempera on background sheet), VF, HL/Nov 16/97 (2000-3000)   2990

CELS – FULL FIGURE

Full-figure portrait of smiling Susie, 3-1/2 x 4", HL/Aug 6/95 (800-1200)   1344

SYMPHONY HOUR (1942)
ANIMATION DRAWINGS

Drawing of determined Mickey carrying Donald away, 5-1/2 x 4-1/4", CE/Jun 18/94 (500-700)   437

Full-figure drawing of Donald standing holding flute vertically, looking down at feet, 4 5/8", 12-field sheet, SR/Spring/96 (300-600)   310

Near-full figure drawing of angry Mickey grabbing Donald (reading newspaper Help Wanted) by coat collar from behind, 4 x 6", HL/Aug 6/95 (600-900)   2464

CEL SET-UPS

Near-full figure of Horace Horsecollar rising from chair & blowing trumpet, matching master background (airbrush on background sheet), 8 x 11", HL/Oct 6/96 (1800-2200)   1610

CELS – PARTIAL FIGURE

Near-full figure of determined Mickey standing looking down, 4 x 3", HL/May 31/97 (200-300)   345

TALKING DOG (NEVER RELEASED)
CEL SET-UPS

Half image of eager Pluto looking up (one ear up) while lying down, 6"; master watercolor background of Butch's barrel from *Bone Trouble*, SR/Fall/96 (2000-5000)   1700

T-BONE FOR TWO (1942)
CEL SET-UPS

Skeptical Pluto looking thru fence boards, 4-1/2 x 4", key watercolor production background, inscribed & stamped, CE/Dec 16/94 (2500-3500)   2760

TITLE ART

Title card with full figures of Pluto & Butch in red, both dogs & hand-lettered title inked on cel

& laid over watercolor airbrush background, 12-field, with original cover flap signed with Walt's OK, SR/Fall/97 (1500-2000) 1100

TEST PILOT DONALD (1951)
ANIMATION DRAWINGS
Full-figure drawing of sad Donald (wearing baseball cap) on knees, signed by Jack Hannah, 5 x 6" with signature, HL/Oct 6/96 (300-400) 460

THREE BLIND MOUSEKETEERS (1936)
LAYOUT ART
Watercolor layout painting of bottles, barrels & flickering candle, 9 x 11-1/2", CE/Dec 15/93 (800-1000) 977
Three layout drawings: master shot of tavern, 27 x 9" sheet; tavern floor thick with traps, 12 x 9-7/8", with original exposure sheet; action of Mouseketeer tapping way to trap, 19-1/8 x 9" sheet; all with camera markings & notations; wear & discoloration, some vertical creasing; SR/Fall/96 (3000-6000) 2250
MODEL ART
4 model drawings for each of the mice & Capt. Katt, 2 x 6-1/2" to 5-1/2 x 10", HL/Nov 19/95 (400-600) 633
Three vintage ozalid print model sheets: Mouseketeers, comparative sizes of all characters, Captain Katt; all 15-1/2 x 12-1/2", SR/Fall/96 (200-400) 200
STORY ART
Colored drawing of gag idea: mouse spears grape on sword, peels & eats it, 10-1/4 x 8-3/8", some discoloration & glue stains, SR/Spring/98 (400-800) 420

THREE FOR BREAKFAST (1948)
CELS – FULL FIGURE
3 full-figure cels: 2 of Chip, 1 of Dale, 3 x 2-1/2" to 4 x 6", F-VF, HL/Apr 10/94 (600-800) 840
Chip & Dale stand laughing & shaking hands, 3-3/4 x 4-1/4", VF, HL/Nov 16/97 (600-800) 805

THREE LITTLE PIGS (1933)
Also see UNIDENTIFIED/MISCELLANEOUS: THREE LITTLE PIGS
ANIMATION DRAWINGS
2 drawings: Fifer Pig & Wolf, 4 x 7" & 3 x 2", scene animated by Fred Moore, VF, HL/Apr 10/94 (300-400) 504
Drawing of Wolf pushing against straw house, 6 x 9-1/2", scene animated by Freddie Moore, VF, HL/Apr 10/94 (700-1000) 840
Full-figure drawing of 3 pigs laughing & dancing as wolf hungrily watches from behind tree, possibly for publication purposes, sight 6-1/2 x 10-1/2", S/Dec 14/96 (500-1000) 805
CEL SET-UPS
Leering Wolf squeezing down chimney, matching master background, notes & stamps, 8 x 10-3/4", HL/Aug 21/94 (12,000-16,000) 11,200
CELS – FULL FIGURE (also see MODEL ART)
Prowling Wolf, 5-1/2 x 4-1/2", HL/Apr 23/95 (2000-2500) 2240
Smug Fiddler & Fifer, 3-1/2 x 5", HL/Apr 23/95 (1000-1500) 896
CELS – PARTIAL FIGURE
2 pig derrieres peeking out from under bed; Little Red Riding Hood speaking to disguised Wolf at bedside from *The Big Bad Wolf*; each sheet 9-1/2 x 12", S/Jun 21/97 (1200-1800) 1380
MODEL ART
Color model cel: full figures of Fiddler & Fifer dancing; smiling Practical w/brick & trowel, 3 x 9", HL/Aug 21/94 (1500-2000) 1568

THREE LITTLE WOLVES (1936)
ANIMATION DRAWINGS
4 drawings: Big Bad Wolf blowing horn with two pigs in roasting pan; Big Bad Wolf getting dose of wolf pacifier; Practical Pig pointing finger at brothers; menacing wolf in zoot suit; S/Jun 10/95 (500-700) 402
2 full-figure drawings (rough & clean-up) of Practical Pig lecturing Fiddler & Fifer, 5 x 6", attributed to Grim Natwick, HL/Aug 6/95 (500-700) 952
Full-figure drawing of Fifer & Fiddler Pig playing instruments, signed by Frank Thomas,

4-1/2 x 6", HL/Apr 28/96 (500-700) 518
Full-figure drawing of worried Fiddler & Fifer (holding horn) Pigs standing holding hands, looking left, 3-3/8", 12-field sheet, notations, faint vertical folds, SR/Fall/96 (200-400) 280
Full-figure drawings of Fiddler Pig (rear view) & Fifer Pig (front view) standing playing instruments, initialed & signed by Frank Thomas, 4-1/2 x 6" including signature, VF, HL/Nov 16/97 (300-500) 431
CEL SET-UPS
Full figure of little wolf standing dressed as chef, 5", presentation background, CE/Jun 9/95 (600-800) 460
CELS – FULL FIGURE
Fiddler Pig & Fifer Pig (3-1/2" & smaller) & Wolf as Bo Peep (5-1/2"), CE/Dec 16/94 (1000-1500) 978
2 grinning wolves standing with hands on hips, 3 x 4", HL/Aug 6/95 (1000-1500) 896
Fiddler & Fifer Pig dancing & playing, 4 x 3", HL/Aug 6/95 (1000-1500) 952
2 cels: waist-up of angry Practical Pig facing left with right hand out, 4"; full figures of attentive Fiddler & Fifer (holding horn) standing facing right & leaning forward, 3"; ct, SR/Fall/95 (700-1200) 850
Big Bad Wolf (3") tiptoes to left holding carpet bag as three identical little wolves (2-1/4") follow in same pose, 12-field, SR/Fall/95 (900-1400) 900
2 cels: scared Fidler (pointing) & Fifer (holding horn) Pigs standing facing right in identical poses, 2-3/4"; hips-up of Wolf in chef's hat looking back while working bellows, body illuminated by fire, 4-1/4"; 12-field cels; SR/Fall/97 (1200-1800) 1180
Wolf in Bo Peep's clothing about to swallow key, 7-3/16", ct, SR/Fall/97 (900-1500) 730
LAYOUT ART
Detailed layout drawing of Wolves' home, 12-field sheet, with original production form, some wear & discoloration, shallow tears, scattered staining, SR/Spring/95 (800-1600) 2340
2 layout drawings: finished layout for Practical Pig's Wolf Pacifier; petticoated Big Bad Wolf sitting in chair being pacified by automatic boot, 7 1/2"; some edge wear & general darkening, SR/Spring/98 (1200-1800) 1630

THREE ORPHAN KITTENS (1935)
ANIMATION DRAWINGS/MODEL ART
Full-figure color model drawing of 3 kittens standing looking right, 2-3/4", colored ink call-outs, 12-field sheet, SR/Fall/97 (300-500) 400
CELS – FULL FIGURE
Mammy Twoshoes (arm only, 6-1/2") holds Fluffy & Muffy (3-1/2 x 2") by scruff of necks, S/Dec 17/94 (800-1200) 2875

THRU THE MIRROR (1936)
ANIMATION DRAWINGS
Full-figure drawing of surprised Mickey being hit by hearts, 5-1/2 x 8", HL/Nov 19/95 (600-900) 1093
CELS – FULL FIGURE
Mickey Mouse dances in top hat holding cane, 3 x 4-1/2", HL/Aug 6/95 (3000-4000) 7168
STORY ART
Detailed color story drawing of Mickey standing on mantel looking into mirror, 6 x 8", HL/Apr 23/95 (6000-8000) 9520

TIMBER (1941)
ANIMATION DRAWINGS
Full-figure drawing of angry Donald standing facing left, 4-3/4", 12-field sheet, SR/Spring/98 (300-600) 430
CELS – FULL FIGURE
Pete steps to right with ax raised, 6 x 5-3/4", restored, VF, HL/Apr 25/98 (800-1200) 1035

TOBY TORTOISE RETURNS (1936)
ANIMATION DRAWINGS
Drawing of Max Hare taunting Toby, 4-1/2 x 9-1/2", HL/Aug 21/94 (500-700) 420
MODEL ART
Model drawing of grinning Max Hare wearing boxing

gloves, standing facing right in boxer's pose, 6 x 4-1/4", HL/May 31/97 (200-250) 92

TOMORROW WE DIET (1951)
CELS – FULL FIGURE
Confused overweight Goofy stands looking left, restored, 6-1/4 x 4", VF, HL/Apr 25/98 (300-500) 230

TOOT, WHISTLE, PLUNK AND BOOM (1953)
CELS – FULL FIGURE
Front view of 3 Canary Sisters, 4-1/2 x 9", studio notes, F+, HL/Apr 10/94 (400-600) 336
4 [3?] front-view cels: 3 Canary Sisters, 6-1/4"; rumba dancer, 8"; 2 minstrels, 5-1/2"; SR/Spring/96 (1000-2000) 1200
Front view of Professor Owl with wings outstretched, 3-1/2 x 3-1/2", HL/Oct 6/96 (500-700) 230
Front view of Professor Owl standing, 'arms' out, looking left; 5-1/4"; SR/Spring/97 (300-500) 300
3 standing strings players, 4 x 9", VF+, HL/Apr 25/98 (200-300) 316
3 front-view cels: standing Professor Owl holding chalk & gesturing, 5"; sitting Bertie Birdbrain plays triangle, 5 3/4"; sitting bird plays washboard, 4 7/8"; SR/Spring/98 (600-1000) 750

THE TORTOISE & THE HARE (1935)
BACKGROUNDS
Master production background, watercolor on paper, 7-3/4 x 11", CE/Dec 15/93 (800-1000) 805
CELS – FULL FIGURE
Eager Max Hare poised to start, 6 x 3-1/2", HL/Aug 6/95 (1800-2500) 2912
Toby Tortoise running upright, HL/Aug 6/95 (1800-2500) 4032
MODEL ART
4 Ozalid print model sheets: 2 of tortoise, 2 of hare; 12-1/4 x 9-3/4", SR/Fall/94 (300-600) 300

TOUCHDOWN MICKEY (1932)
ANIMATION DRAWINGS
Drawing: Mickey (2-1/2") dodging tacklers, S/Jun 17/94 (900-1200) 1150
3 drawings in sequence of Mickey eluding tackler, 3-1/2 x 8-1/2", 3 x 5", 5-1/2 x 6-1/2", HL/Aug 21/94 (1500-2000) 1680
3 sequential drawings of Mickey running left with football with burly Pete-like cat in pursuit, 3 x 6-1/2" to 3-1/2 x 8-1/2", HL/Oct 6/96 (1500-2000) 1610

TOY TINKERS (1949)
CEL SET-UPS
Donald Duck plays Santa, 4", studio-prepared watercolor background of room & Christmas tree, CE/Dec 16/94 (1500-2000) 2070
Full figure of Donald standing facing toward left, looking down, armed with popgun, toy grenade, & lethal expression, 4-3/4", master watercolor background from *Mr. Duck Steps Out*, SR/Fall/97 (1200-1600) 1090
CELS
Full figure (all but tip of right foot) of Donald standing holding vintage telephone in left hand & receiver in right, display overlay of 2 gifts at his feet, SR/Spring/95 (700-1100) 810
Donald, 5-1/4"; plus Donald (full figure, 4") holding Dolores' trunk (7") from unknown production [*Working For Peanuts*?], CE/Dec 12/96 (1000-1500) 1093

TRADER MICKEY (1932)
ANIMATION DRAWINGS
Drawing of Mickey Mouse playing mouth organ the cannibal chief has swallowed by tickling chief's belly, 5 x 6", HL/Apr 28/96 (600-900) 748
LAYOUT ART
2 color layout drawings: Mickey Mouse playing saxophone full of instruments while standing on Pluto's back, 2 natives strumming banjos with mouths; 8 x 10 & 7 x 9-1/2; colored pencil & conté crayon on animation sheets, HL/Nov 19/95 (2000-3000) 5865

Detailed layout drawing of cannibal village, 5 x 12",
HL/Apr 28/96 (600-800)   1093

TRAFFIC TROUBLES (1931)
ANIMATION DRAWINGS
Full-figure study drawing of Mickey driving taxi to left,
4-1/2" long, CE/Dec 18/97 (2000-3000)   2070
CEL SET-UPS
Full figure of worried Mickey driving cab thru city,
complementary non-Studio painted
background, 3-1/4 x 4-1/2" cel image,
HL/Oct 6/96 (5000-7000)   5520
STORY ART
Mickey (1") in gag sheet of three scenes, graphite
on paper, sight 12 x 9-1/2", CLA/Jun 7/97
(2500-3500)   4025

TRICK OR TREAT (1952)
CEL SET-UPS
Humble costumed Huey, Dewey & Louie stand
inside doorway facing angry Donald (from
circa 1950s unknown production); key
watercolor production background, 4" &
smaller, CE/Jun 18/94 (2500-3500)   1495
Happy Witch Hazel astride broom, color
print background, DL label, 8 x 10",
HL/Aug 21/94 (700-1000)   616
Full figure of Witch Hazel in greeting pose, color
print background, mat & label as sold at DL,
8 x 10", HL/Aug 21/94 (400-600)   616
Full figures of Nephews standing in living room
dressed as witch, ghost, & devil; 3-1/4 x 3-1/2"; 12-field
cel; color print background, SR/Spring/97 (300-
500)   460
Witch Hazel holding hand sprayer & flying on broom
outside house w/Donald's costumed nephews;
Witch Hazel & Donald from different production;
Donald looking out window; Donald & nephews
walking gaily to right; backgrounds unidentified;
S/Jun 21/97 (1200-1800)   805
CELS – FULL FIGURE
Witch Hazel holding hand sprayer & costumed
nephews on broom, 5 x 7-1/2", F,
HL/Apr 10/94 (1000-1500)   840
Smiling Witch Hazel standing holding hand sprayer at
ready, 5-1/2 x 3", HL/Oct 6/96 (500-700) 690

TROMBONE TROUBLE (1944)
CELS – FULL FIGURE
Front view of grinning Donald standing holding
trombone, 5-1/4", ct, SR/Fall/96 (700-1100) 830

TUGBOAT MICKEY (1940)
ANIMATION DRAWINGS
Full-figure drawing of surprised Mickey swinging from
boatswain's chair confronting drunken pelican,
7 x 7-1/2", HL/Apr 23/95 (600-900)   1232
Near-full figure drawing of frightened Mickey Mouse,
4-1/2 x 4", HL/Nov 19/95 (600-900)   863
Full-figure extreme drawing of frightened Mickey,
both feet on boatswain's chair, both arms
around pelican's neck; with animator's chart;
9 x 6"; HL/Oct 6/96 (600-900)   748
MODEL ART
Photostatic model sheet with tugboat, Mickey,
Goofy & tools, 14 x 11", some wrinkling,
SR/Spring/95 (200-400)   200

TUMMY TROUBLE (1989)
CELS – FULL FIGURE
Grinning Baby Herman sits with rattle, 5-1/2 x 4",
HL/Aug 21/94 (900-1200)   784
Roger rides Hare Splitter & gleeful Baby Herman
flies ahead, 5 x 6-1/2", HL/Apr 23/95
(1000-1500)   1344
CELS – PARTIAL FIGURE
Delighted Roger Rabbit catches Baby Herman,
7-1/2 x 6-1/2", seal, VF+, HL/Nov 19/95
(900-1200)   805

TWO CHIPS AND A MISS (1952)
CELS – FULL FIGURE
Dressed-up Chip holding bouquet, framed with
1970s signed drawing of Chip by Bill
Justice, 5-1/2 x 4" & 6-1/2 x 4-1/2", F,
HL/Nov 19/95 (600-900)   690

STORY ART
20 storyboard drawings for proposed sequel, pastel
& charcoal on 8-1/2 x 6" storyboard sheets,
SR/Spring/95 (1500-2500)   1700
10 storyboard drawings of Clarice flirting with Chip
& Dale, CE/Jun 20/96 (1800-2200)   1725

TWO GUN GOOFY (1952)
CELS – FULL FIGURE
Grinning Pete carrying lighted dynamite keg, 5 x 5",
F+, HL/Apr 10/94 (500-700)   560

TWO-GUN MICKEY (1934)
ANIMATION DRAWINGS
Drawing of Mickey & Minnie from cartoon finale
w/2nd drawing of their horse, 4 x 4", 8-1/2
x 4-1/2", VF, HL/Feb 26-27/94 (700-1000) 990
Production drawing of fierce Mickey w/2 guns, 3",
S/Jun 17/94 (500-700)   690
Full-figure drawing of Mickey as cowboy, 3-1/2",
CE/Dec 16/94 (500-700)   460
2 full-figure drawings of Mickey & Minnie as
cowboys, 3-1/4 x 2" & 4 x 2-1/2",
HL/Apr 23/95 (800-1200)   1232
Full-figure drawing of Mickey raising gun, 4",
CE/Jun 9/95 (400-600)   230
Drawing of Mickey & Minnie on horseback leading
Pegleg Pete encased in cactus, 7 x 7",
HL/Nov 19/95 (700-1000)   1495
Full-figure drawing of Mickey & Minnie riding away
in distance while pulling cactus (foreground)
with Peg Leg Pete inside, 7-1/2 x 6-1/2",
HL/Oct 6/96 (600-900)   604
Full-figure rough drawing of smiling Mickey & haughty
Minnie in cowboy dress (both 4") as horse (head
only) watches, CLA/Jun 7/97 (1000-1500) 1150
3 full-figure drawings: Mickey, Minnie, laughing horse;
3-3/4 x 2", 3-3/4 x 2", 3-1/2 x 10-1/2", VF,
HL/Nov 16/97 (600-900)   690
Full-figure drawing of Mickey & Minnie in Western
dress, 3-3/4 x 2", VF, HL/Nov 16/97
(500-700)   518
Full-figure drawing of determined cowboy Mickey
holding gun behind him & riding horse at
gallop to left, 5-1/2", CE/Dec 18/97
(1500-2000)   1150
CEL SET-UPS/MODEL ART
Full-figure color model cel of Cowboy Mickey standing
facing left holding six-guns, rope dangling from
his left gun, 6"; watercolor background from
circa 1930 Mickey Mouse short, some general
tanning; 12-field, SR/Fall/96 (7000-11,000) 7000
LAYOUT ART
Full-figure layout drawing of Minnie driving buckboard
pulled by 2 horses to right, 9-1/2" long,
CE/Dec 18/97 (2000-3000)   1840
MODEL ART
Ozalid model sheets of Mickey, Minnie, Pete, &
horses, 12 x 9-1/2", some discoloration,
SR/Fall/94 (400-700)   610
2 model-sheet guides: Mickey, Minnie & horses;
bandits; colored pencil on photocopy model
sheets w/notes, matted & framed together,
sight each opening 9 x 12", S/Jun 21/97
(600-800)   690

THE UGLY DUCKLING (1931 & 1939)
ANIMATION DRAWINGS
Drawing of Duckling being held by swan mother,
8 x 8-1/2", HL/Aug 6/95 (500-700)   1064
CEL SET-UPS
Ducking & siblings swim with mother, partial multi-cel
set-up, Courvoisier airbrush background, 8-3/4
x 11-1/4", CE/Dec 15/93 (1000-1500)   1265
Duckling begs for food as bird feeds its children,
trimmed multi-cel set-up, Courvoisier
watercolor background, 8 x 9-3/4",
CE/Dec 15/93 (1200-1600)   1380
Despondent Duckling talks with frog, partial
multi-cel set-up, Courvoisier watercolor
background, 6-3/4 x 8-1/2",
CE/Dec 15/93 (1000-1200)   1380
Duckling quacks, airbrushed background, WDP
label, 5", S/Dec 16/93 (800-1200)   1265
Surprised Duckling greeted warmly by swans,
airbrushed Courvoisier background, Duckling
2", Swan 5", S/Jun 17/94 (1000-1500)   1265
Drake (4-1/2") & duck (3") watch 4 ducklings

(1-1/2") frolic, airbrushed Courvoisier
background, S/Jun 17/94 (1500-2000)   1265
Happy Duckling smiles into camera & swims,
airbrushed Courvoisier background, 2-1/2",
S/Jun 17/94 (1000-1500)   1495
2 cels: drake (4") gestures to duck as 4 ducklings
waddle about; Ugly Duckling (5-1/2") sitting
in water; both w/airbrushed Courvoisier
backgrounds, S/Jun 17/94 (1800-2200)   2875
Ugly Duckling (3" long) fights over worm with mother
on branch as frightened siblings in nest watch,
Courvoisier label & airbrushed background,
CE/Jun 18/94 (2000-3000)   2415
Happy Duckling swims to join swan family, water
effects cel, Courvoisier painted background,
10-1/2 x 12-1/2", HL/Aug 21/94
(1800-2400)   1680
Full figures of Duckling & frog, Courvoisier airbrush
background, inscribed mat, 6-1/2 x 8",
HL/Aug 21/94 (1800-2200)   1344
Full figure of smiling Duckling sitting on log, 9 x 10",
complementary airbrush background, Courvoisier
label, HL/Apr 23/95 (1500-1800)   1904
Full figure of perplexed Duckling (3") studying frog
(1-1/2"), Courvoisier watercolor & airbrush
background, CE/Jun 9/95 (800-1200)   1495
Ugly Duckling paddles happily & smiles at butterfly,
5", airbrushed Courvoisier background & label,
S/Jun 10/95 (1000-1500)   1725
Full figure of Duckling sitting at water's edge &
shedding tear while looking at reflection, 4",
airbrushed Courvoisier background & label,
S/Jun 10/95 (1000-1500)   1495
Full figure of smiling Duckling sitting on bank facing
right, looking into camera, 5", Courvoisier
watercolor & airbrush background & label,
SR/Fall/95 (1500-2200)   1600
Full figure of smiling Ugly Duckling walking right,
3-1/2", Courvoisier watercolor background,
mat & label, cracking paint, SR/Spring/96
(1200-1800)   1780
Full figures of Mama (all but feet), Papa (3-3/4"), & 4
ducklings; Courvoisier background of nest at
base of tree, label & mat; some cracking paint &
discoloration, SR/Spring/96 (2500-3500) 2750
Full figures of alert Mother Swan & four goslings
swimming among plants, 6 x 7"; bee from
Ferdinand the Bull stinger-deep in flower,
4-1/2"; each w/airbrushed Courvoisier background, S/Jun 19/96 (1000-1500)   2185
Near-full figure of smiling Duckling (4") facing right &
looking at angry grasshopper (1-1/2"), airbrushed
Courvoisier label & background of water &
water plants, S/Dec 14/96 (1200-1800)   1610
Full figures of smiling Duckling (3-1/4") walking up
to cricket (1-3/4") stretching on water lily,
Courvoisier watercolor & airbrush background
& label, mat signed by Walt Disney,
CLA/Jun 7/97 (2000-2500)   3220
Full-figure front view of smiling Duckling standing
breaking out of shell, 4", airbrushed
Courvoisier background, WDP label,
S/Dec 19/97 (1200-1800)   1380
Full figure of Duckling looking down & behind him
as he stands out of his shell in front of tree,
4", airbrushed Courvoisier background, WDP
label, S/Dec 19/97 (1200-1800)   2875
CELS – FULL FIGURE
Father Duck, 4-1/2", CE/Dec 16/94 (700-900)   288
2 promotional cels: full-figure profile of mother duck
swimming w/ducklings on her back, 5"; full
figures of Donald (2-1/2") tying balloon to
Pluto's tail (w/balloon tied to collar, 2") from
another short, CE/Jun 20/96 (2000-3000) 1265
MODEL ART
4 print model sheets: two of duckling, mother swan,
wooden decoy duckling & baby ducks, all 12-1/2
x 10", one vertical, SR/Fall/94 (200-400) 530
STORY ART
Fully colored story drawing of angry mother duck
staring at forlorn duckling, captioned "Duckling
mumbles in self-defense", 1930s, proposed version?, 4-1/2 x 6", HL/Oct 6/96 (300-400) 288
Fully colored story drawing of angry Mother Duck
confronting Duckling, captioned "Duckling
mumbles something in self defense," picture
area 5-7/8 x 4-7/16", general discoloration,
glue stains, SR/Fall/97 (800-1200)   600

Victory Through Air Power: Six concept sketches: enormous amphibious plane, itself a flying aircraft carrier, in various scenes; pastel on black & blue sheets; 9-1/8 x 6 7/8" to 12 x 10"; SR/Fall/96 (600-1000)   700

Der Fuehrer's Face: Color model cel of Donald sitting at table by wall safe eating & reading *Mein Kampf* as bayonet pierces book, 4-7/8", 12-field, gouache display background, ct, SR/Spring/95 (1500-2000)   2780

Donald Gets Drafted: Full figure of soldier Donald, rifle on shoulder, hand to hat, facing toward right, looking up, 5-3/4", Courvoisier watercolor background of army camp, label, SR/Spring/96 (1600-2200)   1760

The Three Caballeros: Full figures of two sad penguins carrying block of ice (containing bundled Pablo reading map) between two poles to right, 5-1/4", color print of arctic background, ct, SR/Fall/95 (800-1400) 1180

Fun and Fancy Free: Worried Goofy (4-1/2"), Donald (3-1/2"), & Mickey (3-1/2") tread cautiously in castle, watercolor production background, CE/Jun 18/94 (10,000-15,000)   21,850

Ben and Me: Ben Franklin walks toward camera, holding cane, looking right, 6-1/4", 12-field, SR/Spring/98 (600-1200) did not sell

Brave Little Tailor: Near-full figure of Giant pulling up a well, 8", wood-veneer Courvoisier background, S/Jun 10/95 (3000-5000)   5462

Brave Little Tailor: Mickey w/fly swatter in each hand & 7 flies, wood-veneer Courvoisier background, 4", S/Jun 17/94 (3000-5000)   8050

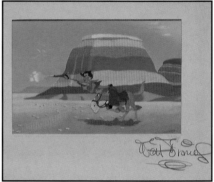

Brave Little Tailor: Full figure of depressed Mickey sitting on rock w/head in hands, 3-1/2" (not including feather), airbrushed wood-veneer Courvoisier background, mat inscribed "to ... Walt Disney", S/Jun 10/95 (4000-6000)   5462

Melody Time: Full figure of Slue Foot Sue riding Widowmaker, 9-1/2 x 10-1/2", background of desert (tempera on background sheet), inscribed mat, stamped, HL/Apr 23/95 (2000-2500) 2240

Melody Time: Full figure of Pecos Bill firing six-guns as he rides determined Widowmaker to left, 3-7/8", matching brightly colored gouache background painting of West enhanced with special effects as prepared by Art Props Department, original Disney label, mat signed by Walt Disney, SR/Spring/98 (5000-9000)   5600

Donald's Dog Laundry: Full figures of surprised Pluto (4"), Butch (5-1/2"), & 3 other dogs inspecting modified bathtub (from another short) in backyard, watercolor pan production background, CE/Dec 12/96 (12,000-15,000)   12,650

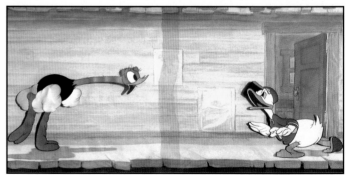

Don Donald: Full figures of haughty Donna [Daisy] Duck (eyes closed, 4-7/8") riding unicycle as Donald (in Mexican hat, holding guitar, waving to camera, 5-5/8") follows on burro, watercolor background of desert road, SR/Spring/97 (1800-2200)   1820

Donald's Ostrich: Full figures of Hortense (3-1/4") & Donald Duck (3-3/4") stalking each other on train-station platform, 12-field cels, watercolor pan background painting, SR/Spring/98 (5000-9000)   4000

Mr. Duck Steps Out: Full figure of angry Donald Duck standing in Daisy's kitchen holding cane & candy box, 8 x 28", pan master background (watercolor on pan background sheet), HL/Nov 19/95 (5000-7000)   6325

Donald's Penguin: Angry Tootsie (3") sits looking away with folded arms as Donald (7") eyes him suspiciously, airbrushed Courvoisier background, S/Jun 17/94 (1800-2200)   2875

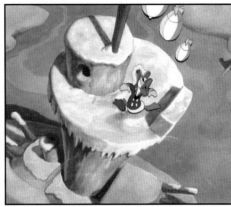

Donald's Snow Fight: Full-figure overhead view of bombs dropping on panicked Admiral Donald (2") on top of ice-encrusted ship, key master watercolor background, 12-field, SR/Spring/96 (3000-7000)   3000

Dragon Around: Full figures of Chip as knight on Dale facing left, gouache background, 12 x 10", original production cover flap, SR/Spring 1995 (2500-5000) did not sell

The Eyes Have It: Angry face-off between Pluto (2-1/2 x 5") & chicken, watercolor production background with inscribed notes, CE/Dec 16/94 (3000-4000)   2530

Ferdinand the Bull: Full-figure front view of young Ferdinand standing smugly in field, 6", Courvoisier watercolor background with original production overlay, SR/Spring/95 (1400-1800)   1810

Little Hiawatha: Full figure of grim Hiawatha standing with bow & arrow facing left, looking back, grasshopper in front of him, 4-7/8", master watercolor background, SR/Fall/96 (3500-5000)   3750

The Little Whirlwind: Pan production set-up of Minnie (5-1/2") holding cake & glaring at lovestruck Mickey (from *The Nifty Nineties*, 5"), pan watercolor production background, S/Dec 17/94 (14,000-18,000)   16,100

Lonesome Ghosts & Beach Picnic: 2 cels of Mickey swimming from *Lonesome Ghosts*, 7" & 6" wide, 12-field cels, water effects; pan master watercolor background from *Beach Picnic*, set-up 40-1/4 x 9", SR/Fall/96 (3000-6000)   4460

Ferdinand the Bull: Full figures of combative matador (4-7/8") standing as Ferdinand (6-15/16") lays on back smelling flower,   master background of stadium, released by Courvoisier, original hand-lettered mat & Courvoisier labels, some color shifting, SR/Fall/97 (3000-4000)   4050

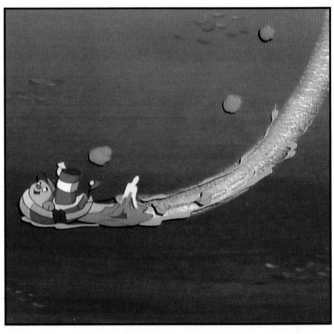

Melody Time: Full-figure overhead view of happy Little Toot (1") looking up while towing paper boats, water & smoke effects, watercolor display background, SR/Spring/96 (400-800)   990

The Mickey Mouse Club: Full figure of Mickey standing on stage smiling into camera & adjusting bow tie from "Guest Star Day" intro, 11 x 22-1/2", matching original master pan background (tempera on pan background sheet), F-VF, HL/Nov 16/97 (6000-9000)   4600

The Mickey Mouse Club: Row of 3 Mouseketrumpeters, 9-3/4 x 6", two levels, key master watercolor background, 16-field conservation treatment, SR/Fall/96 (1100-2000)   1000

Anthology Series: Full figure of Ludwig von Drake walking right with hands behind back & eyes closed, 4-1/4", 1960s, SR/Fall/95 (300-600)   did not sell

Title cards: All from SR Auctions: **Mickey & the Seal:** Spring/95 (2000-5000) 2040; **Sea Salts:** Spring/95 (2000-5000) 2250; **Donald's Tire Trouble:** Fall/94 (1800-2800) 1300

The Pointer: Full figure of wary hunter Mickey w/shotgun & small animals around him, 8 x 10", complementary Courvoisier background of forest, HL/Nov 19/95 (4000-5000)   7188

The Pointer: Full figure of surprised Mickey (4-3/4") sitting on log in front of tent holding closed book with Pluto (4 7/8", near-full figure, eyes closed) sitting in front of him, Courvoisier watercolor background of forest with full foreground overlay, SR/Spring/98 (4000-8000)   5330

Mother Goose Goes Hollywood: Full figures of W.C. Fields as Humpty Dumpty on wall threatening Charlie McCarthy (sitting in nest in tree branch) with cane, 5 x 3" & 2-1/4 x 1-1/2", complementary painted background, VF, HL/Nov 16/97 (2000-2500)   2760

The Mickey Mouse Club: Front view of happy Donald (3-1/2") tossed in air by 8 characters standing around trampoline (waist-up, looking down), 16-field cels, SR/Fall/96 (700-1200)   1120

Plane Crazy: Full figure of coy Minnie (4-5/8") standing by plane holding horseshoe for delighted Mickey (2-9/16"), 12-field, watercolor background, late 1950s-early 1960s promotional from original drawings, SR/Spring/97 (2000-4000)   did not sell

Orphan's Picnic: Full figures of Mickey Mouse playing blind man's bluff outside w/3 mischievous orphans, 8 x 11", master background (pencil & watercolor on background sheet), HL/Aug 6/95 (7000-10,000)   17,360

Mother Goose Goes Hollywood: Full figures of Fred Astaire (6") & Stepin Fetchit (5-1/8") in dancing poses, Courvoisier watercolor background & both small labels, original hand-lettered mat, WDE debossed stamp, SR/Spring/98 (1400-1800)   1460

The Night Before Christmas: Matching cel & master background (watercolor on background sheet): toy soldiers returning to places beneath tree, 8-1/2 x 10-1/2", HL/Feb 23/97 (2500-3500)   5750

The Old Mill: Gustav Tenggren concept painting of ducks wading in pond beside mill, india ink & watercolor on heavyweight paper, 4-3/4 x 6-1/2", HL/Apr 28/96 (4000-5000)   4485

Out of Scale: Close up of Chip & Dale waving from train cab, 8 x 10", background (tempera on background sheet), HL/Apr 23/95 (1400-1800)   2240

The Practical Pig: Practical Pig lectures brothers in front of house, 5" & smaller, Courvoisier watercolor & airbrush background, CE/Jun 18/94 (2500-3500) 2990

Hockey Champ: Full figures of angry Donald (3-1/8") & smiling Huey (holding puck, 2") sitting/lying on ice facing each other, Courvoisier watercolor background of frozen pond, some lifting paint, SR/Spring/95 (2200-3600)   2810

The Adventures of Ichabod and Mr. Toad: Full figure of panicked, reclined Toad, head raised to stare at ball & chain on foot, 7-1/4 x 3-1/2", master background of dirt road & sky, SR/Fall/97 (3000-5000)   2200

The Riveter: Hatless Donald Duck stands near shack with arms full, 4", pan watercolor production background, S/Dec 19/97 (1500-2500)   3737

Pluto and the Armadillo: Full-figure front view of Mickey standing holding balled-up armadillo in right hand, looking & pointing right, 4", master watercolor background, released by Courvoisier with label, ct, SR/Fall/96 (2500-5000)   2940

Susie, the Little Blue Coupe: Full figure of distraught Susie sitting in junkyard, 11 x 15", matching cels (including rain) & original master background (tempera on background sheet), VF, HL/Nov 16/97 (2000-3000)   2990

Chicken in the Rough: Title card: angry Chip stands watching Dale (3-3/4") wave from inside egg shell, title on cel overlay, airbrushed watercolor background, 12-field, original production cover flap, conservation treatment, SR/Fall/96 (2500-4500)   2530

Trick or Treat: Full figures of Nephews standing in living room dressed as witch, ghost, & devil; 3-1/4 x 3-1/2"; 12-field cel; color print background, SR/Spring/97 (300-500)   460

Toy Tinkers: Donald Duck plays Santa, 4", studio-prepared watercolor background of room & Christmas tree, CE/Dec 16/94 (1500-2000)   2070

The Ugly Duckling: Full figure of smiling Ugly Duckling walking right, 3-1/2", Courvoisier watercolor background, mat & label, cracking paint, SR/Spring/96 (1200-1800)   1780

Winnie the Pooh and the Honey Tree: Pooh skipping over words "Pooh Bears Howse" from opening, 2-5/16", color print background with Owl's House in tree, SR/Fall/96 (400-800)   650

The New Adventures of Winnie the Pooh: Full figures of thoughtful Pooh, happy Tigger, & scared Rabbit in woods; 3-1/2", 3-3/8", & 3" on three 12-field cels; key color print pan background; Disney Art Program seals & certificates, overall 43-3/4 x 8"; SR/Fall/97 (900-1400)   625

Winnie the Pooh and the Honey Tree: Full figures of Christopher Robin sitting on log (4-1/2"), Pooh (3-5/8") & Eeyore standing, & frightened Rabbit jumping, Art Props master pan watercolor background of outdoors, SR/Spring/97 (4000-8000)   4720

UP A TREE (1955)
CEL SET-UPS
Full figure of determined Donald Duck sawing thru tree
while held in place by belt, matching master
background (tempera on background sheet),
11-1/2 x 15", HL/Aug 6/95 (2000-2500) 1904
Full figure of smiling lumberjack Donald sawing tree
in mid-trunk, 4", key watercolor production
background, CLA/Jun 7/97 (2000-3000) 2070

THE VANISHING PRIVATE (1942)
BACKGROUNDS
Master background of paint laboratory interior,
8 x 10-1/2", oil on background sheet,
HL/Nov 19/95 (900-1200) 805

VICTORY VEHICLES (1943)
CELS – FULL FIGURE
Sitting Goofy points to one of the roller skates he's
wearing, 7-1/4", SR/Spring/97 (800-1200) 970

THE VILLAGE SMITHY (1942)
ANIMATION DRAWINGS
Full-figure drawing of determined Donald Duck
standing, holding mallet & horse shoe in
tongs; 4 x 5-1/2", HL/Aug 6/95 (500-700) 560

WATER BABIES (1935)
ANIMATION DRAWINGS
Pan drawing: float of swans & cygnets with flower
garlands & water babies, S/Dec 17/94
(600-800) 977
Full-figure drawing of water baby band leader,
3-1/4 x 2-1/4", HL/Feb 23/97 (100-200) 230
CEL SET-UPS
Full figure of water baby with acorn hat waving
red towel by lake, watercolor production
background, 4", S/Dec 17/94 (2500-3000) 2875
CELS – FULL FIGURE
Toreador baby tips his acorn cap, 4 x 3",
HL/Aug 6/95 (1000-1500) 560
CONCEPT AND INSPIRATIONAL ART
4 concept watercolors: over 24 babies in master
scene, two 12-field sheets joined into 23 x 10"
pan; cowboy rides tiger fish; two perform hula;
float pulled by angel fish carries hula
performers, 15 x 9-3/4" sheet; rippling,
edge wear, small tears, vertical crease;
SR/Spring/96 (800-1600) 1070
STORY ART
Story drawing of starfish clowns capturing a seahorse
as startled worm looks on, colored/black pencil
& white tempera on animation sheet, 8-1/2
x 10-1/2", VF, HL/Apr 25/98 (300-400) 374

THE WAYWARD CANARY (1932)
LAYOUT ART/BACKGROUNDS
Layout drawing of Mickey playing xylophone
& Minnie playing piano, both 3",
CE/Jun 18/94 (1000-1500) 3680
6 layout drawings (4 of Mickey), 3-1/2" & similar,
CE/Dec 16/94 (1000-1500) 2990
4 corresponding layout drawings & one background
drawing of Mickey; plus script; 2-1/2" &
similar, CE/Dec 16/94 (2000-3000) 5520

WET PAINT (1946)
CELS – PARTIAL FIGURE
Close-up of Donald Duck with Johnnie standing
on his bill, 5", CE/Dec 16/94 (400-600) 253

THE WHALERS (1938)
ANIMATION DRAWINGS
Drawing of Captain Mickey upside down in air holding
onto bell pull, 6", S/Dec 17/94 (700-900) 690
2 full-figure drawings of Mickey: standing facing right
holding plans & looking up, 4-1/4"; carrying
figurehead on his back to right, 5-1/4"; both
12-field sheets, SR/Fall/95 (1000-1500) 1100
Full-figure drawing of eager Mickey standing facing
right, ready to throw bucket of water, 4",
12-field, SR/Fall/95 (500-900) 830
2 matching full-figure drawings: boat winch, Capt.
Mickey turning handle; 4 x 4", 3-1/2 x 5",
HL/Mar 16-17/96 (300-500) 690
2 drawings duplicated from other drawings: Capt.

Mickey as look-out, close-up of ship's stern;
both w/notes; 3 x 3", 7-1/2 x 8",
HL/Mar 16-17/96 (300-500) 633
Near-full figure drawing of Capt. Mickey teetering
on edge [of ship], 4-1/2 x 3-1/4",
HL/Apr 28/96 (600-800) 431
Full-figure drawing of Capt. Mickey standing
with bucket of water, 4-1/4 x 2-1/2",
HL/Apr 28/96 (600-900) 633
Full-figure drawing of Captain Mickey standing
throwing bucket of water to right, 4-1/4",
12-field sheet, SR/Fall/96 (500-800) 610
Full-figure drawing of angry Donald Duck standing
gesturing left, 4-1/2 x 3", HL/Feb 23/97
(200-300) 489
2 matching drawings: full figure of Capt. Mickey
cranking winch handle, the winch; 3-1/2 x
4-1/2", 3-1/2 x 5", HL/Feb 23/97 (400-500) 546
Full-figure drawing of Capt. Mickey running left,
3-1/2 x 3-1/2", HL/Feb 23/97 (400-600) 403
Near-full-figure drawing w/speed lines of Mickey
(eyes closed) losing his balance, 4-1/2 x
4-1/4", HL/May 31/97 (300-500) 230
10 sequential drawings of panicked Donald Duck
running to left, 2 x 2-1/2" to 2-1/4 x 4",
HL/May 31/97 (600-800) 518
8 sketchy rough drawings of partial-figure Mickey
Mouse as ship capt. running from left to right,
2-1/2 x 2" to 3-1/2 x 3", HL/May 31/97
(300-400) 196
2 matched drawings: winch, Mickey struggling to
turn handle; 4-1/2 x 4-1/2" & 5 x 3-1/2";
VF; HL/Nov 16/97 (400-600) 633
2 drawings: waist-up of horrified Capt. Mickey
looking right with arms out, full figure of
Capt. Mickey running left; 4 x 3-1/2",
3 x 4-1/2"; VF, HL/Apr 25/98 (500-700) 546
2 drawings (full & near-full figures) of angry Donald
Duck facing left; 4 x 3-1/2", 4-1/4 x 3-1/2";
VF; HL/Apr 25/98 (400-500) 690

WHEN THE CAT'S AWAY (1929)
STORY ART
Rare complete storyboard featuring Mickey & Minnie,
drawn by Bert Gillett, 4 full sheets of animation
paper, CE/Jun 18/94 (8000-12,000) 55,200

WHO KILLED COCK ROBIN? (1935)
ART – MISCELLANEOUS
Drawing for publicity illustration: Harpo Marx-like
sparrow sits in nest for outraged parrot
prosecutor & owl judge, 8-1/2 x 12",
HL/Feb 23/97 (700-1000) 690

THE WHOOPEE PARTY (1932)
ANIMATION DRAWINGS
Full-figure drawing of smiling Mickey standing facing
left, looking back at camera, 2-3/4 x 1-3/4",
CE/Jun 18/94 (500-700) 368
Full-figure drawing of smiling Mickey standing facing
left, head turned toward front, 3 x 2-1/2",
CE/Jun 18/94 (500-700) 345
Full-figure drawing of Mickey with coffee pot on head,
standing facing right, blowing horn, 4-3/8",
12-field sheet, cameraman's stamp, edge
discoloration, SR/Spring/95 (400-800) 570
Full-figure drawing of Mickey standing with coffee
pot on head facing right, blowing horn, 4-3/4",
12-field sheet, SR/Spring/96 (400-800) 300
Full-figure front-view drawing of Mickey standing
wearing coffee pot as shako, playing
elongated trumpet to right, 4-3/8",
12-field sheet, SR/Spring/97 (300-600) 310
CEL SET-UPS
Near-full figures of Mickey (4") & Minnie (3") sitting
happily at piano, hand-prepared background
of room, S/Dec 14/96 (10,000-15,000) 19,550
LAYOUT ART
Layout drawing of Minnie Mouse playing piano
as Clarabelle fiddles, 7 x 9-1/2",
HL/Nov 19/95 (1200-1600) 2760

WILD WAVES (1929)
ANIMATION DRAWINGS
Full-figure front-view study drawing of Mickey
in dancing pose, 4", CE/Dec 18/97
(1500-2000) 1150

WINDOW CLEANERS (1940)
BACKGROUNDS
Pastel-colored painting of sunlit street, watercolor
on background sheet, 8-1/4 x 19-1/2",
HL/Oct 6/96 (5000-6000) 4370
Watercolor production background of castle on hill in
distance; 2 watercolor production backgrounds
from *The Art of Self Defense*: city street &
mountain landscape; sight 10 x 12" each;
stamps; CE/Dec 18/97 (1000-1500) 1840

THE WINGED SCOURGE (1943)
BACKGROUNDS
Mine bags labeled "Sleepy", "Grumpy" & "Sneezy"
hang open from table edge, small pile of gems
on table, watercolor-on-paper production background, CE/Jun 20/96 (2000-3000) 1725
CEL SET-UPS
Full figure of Sleepy pushing wheelbarrow filled
with empty cans & bottles to right, 5 x 5"
overall, hand-prepared background of
outdoors, S/Dec 19/97 (800-1200) 747
Full figure of Dopey bending horizontally to floor
level to use bug sprayer, 2 x 3", hand-
prepared background of indoors,
S/Dec 19/97 (1000-1500) 1495
STORY ART
Rendering of Dwarf [Sneezy?] carrying basket of plants
thru door, charcoal & conté crayon on story
sheet, 6 x 8", F+, HL/Apr 28/96 (400-600) 345

WINNIE THE POOH AND A DAY FOR EEYORE (1983)
CEL SET-UPS/ANIMATION DRAWINGS/LAYOUT ART
Half image of concerned Pooh leaning forward with
hands [on table], 6 x 8-1/2", color print background; w/matching animation drawing; VF+;
HL/May 31/97 (300-400) 328
Full figure of sad Eeyore sitting by tree, color print
background, w/matching animation drawing,
4 x 7" & 3-1/2 x 3", VF+, HL/May 31/97
(300-400) 546
Full-figure front view of happy Pooh standing in
house, 6-1/2", watercolor production
background, plus matching drawings of
head & body, S/Jun 21/97 (1000-1500) 1495
Full-figure front view of Pooh standing, 6-1/2",
watercolor production background: inside
Pooh's house; 2 matching layout drawings;
CE/Dec 18/97 (1000-1500) 1495
Large images of Christopher Robin (on knees, 8"),
Piglet (4") & Pooh (arm around Piglet, 7")
talking, printed background, gold Walt Disney
Co. stamp, S/Dec 19/97 (800-1200) 2875
Pooh stands at bridge railing holding stick, color
print of matching background, 6 x 4" cel,
VF+, HL/Apr 25/98 (600-800) 1610
CELS – FULL FIGURE
Full standing figures of friendly Eeyore facing right
(3-1/4", all but tip of one foot) & front view
of surprised Tigger looking left (4-1/2");
12-field, Disney Art Program seal,
SR/Spring/95 (600-1000) 920
Eeyore standing toward right, looking back left,
4", 12-field, Disney Art Program seal,
SR/Fall/95 (500-900) 500
Half figure of surprised Eeyore lying down facing
full figure of downcast Piglet,
4-1/2 x 9", HL/Feb 23/97 (400-500) 546
Owl, 7", WDC seal, CLA/Jun 7/97 (300-500) 276
CELS – PARTIAL FIGURE
Hips-up portrait of Pooh holding empty honey pot,
7", 12-field cel, Disney Art Program seal,
SR/Fall/96 (500-900) 680
Chest-up profile of smiling Pooh facing left with
right arm raised, 5-1/2 x 6", HL/Feb 23/97
(400-500) 374

WINNIE THE POOH AND THE BLUSTERY DAY (1968)
Also see TELEVISION: THE NEW ADVENTURES
OF WINNIE THE POOH; UNIDENTIFIED/
MISCELLANEOUS: WINNIE THE POOH
CEL SET-UPS
Full figures of Pooh & Christopher Robin, 8 x 10",

color print background, DL mat & label, VF, HL/Feb 26-27/94 (1000-1400) 1870

Limited-edition cel (#475/500) of Pooh in party hat & Piglet standing together & Christopher Robin on knees, color print background, Disney seal & label, 10-1/2 x 13-1/2", VF+, HL/Apr 10/94 (900-1200) 1344

Thoughtful Tigger, color print background, DL label, 8 x 10", VF, HL/Aug 21/94 (900-1200) 1568

Owl & Pooh marching, 8 x 10", color print background, as sold at DL, VF, HL/Nov 13/94 (600-800) 672

Limited edition cel of Christopher Robin, Piglet & Pooh in party hat, 1988, #476/500, 10-1/2 x 13-1/2", color print of original master background, HL/Nov 19/94 (1000-1500) 1495

Full figure of Eeyore sitting facing right, colored paper background, 3-1/2 x 4-1/2", HL/Feb 23/97 (600-800) 748

Full-figure front view of Piglet standing by open cupboard, looking left with eyes closed, 4-1/4", color print background, SR/Spring/97 (500-900) 920

Full figure of Tigger dancing to left, 4-1/2", litho background, gold DL Art Corner seal, SR/Spring/97 (600-1000) 1250

Owl stands on log w/wings spread (near-full figure, 4-7/8"), as Christopher Robin (waist-up, 5") in rain gear looks left, DL litho background, gold Art Corner label, SR/Spring/97 (400-800) 520

Chest-up close-up of smiling Owl looking left, 5-1/4", original DL color background & gold Art Corner label, SR/Spring/97 (300-600) 320

Full figures of Piglet standing on chair turning to call for help & Owl flying away as chair floats in flood, complementary color print background, seal & certificate, signed "John Fiedler 'Piglet'", 6-1/2 x 4" inc. signature, VF, HL/Apr 25/98 (300-500) 518

Half image of surprised Owl, wings resting on log, looking right; 5"; DL litho background & gold Art Corner label; SR/Spring/98 (300-600) 300

CELS – FULL FIGURE

3 cels: Rabbit, Tigger & Pooh; from both *Blustery Day & Honey Tree*; 2 x 2", 5 x 2-1/2", 6 x 3"; VF+; HL/Feb 26-27/94 (300-500) 330

4 cels: full figures of Pooh in party hat, Piglet adrift on chair, Heffalump; half figure of eager Gopher; 2-1/2 x 2-1/2" to 6 x 6"; VF+; HL/Aug 21/94 (1000-1500) 805

4 cels: full figures of Pooh in party hat, Eeyore, green Heffalump; half figure of Gopher; 2 x 3" to 7-1/2 x 7-1/2"; F-VF; HL/Aug 21/94 (1000-1500) 1904

Pooh in party hat bending down to right; Pooh & Gopher (partial figures); happy Heffalump; 3 x 2-1/2" to 8 x 5-1/2"; VF; HL/Nov 13/94 (1000-1500) 1344

Christopher Robin on knees (all but top of head); Pooh standing in party hat facing left with Piglet standing next to (partially behind) Pooh; 9 x 11"; VF; HL/Nov 13/94 (1200-1600) 1512

Christopher grabs Winnie's foot as he floats away with balloon, 6-1/2", CE/Dec 16/94 (400-600) 1840

Pooh (4-1/2"), Rabbit, Piglet, Eeyore & Tigger all looking sad, CE/Jun 9/95 (800-1200) 1955

Side view of Pooh in nightclothes holding pop gun, 5 x 3", HL/Aug 6/95 (600-800) 1344

Stern Pooh in nightclothes marching with pop gun on shoulder, 4-1/2 x 3-1/2", HL/Nov 19/95 (600-800) 863

Winnie in nightgown & cap facing right with left arm out, 3-1/2 x 4-1/4", HL/Oct 6/96 (500-800) 316

2 full-figure cels: Pooh leaning backwards with arms out, Piglet kneeling horizontally with arms out & eyes closed; 2-1/2 x 2-1/4", 2-3/4 x 2", HL/Feb 23/97 (400-600) 460

Full-figure front view of happy Tigger standing on one foot with arms out, 8-1/8", 16-field cel, SR/Fall/97 (1200-1800) 1200

Pooh being confronted by 4 giant honey jars, 9-1/2 x 8" overall, VF, HL/Nov 16/97 (500-700) 575

Tigger helps himself to Pooh's honey, 6-1/2", S/Dec 19/97 (600-800) 575

Pooh stands & Piglet sits on stool, both facing right; 3-1/4 x 2", 4-1/2 x 2-1/2"; VF+; HL/Apr 25/98 (700-1000) 920

CELS – PARTIAL FIGURE

Portrait of shy Tigger (eyes closed), 5-1/2 x 6-1/2", VF+, HL/Feb 26-27/94 (300-400) 495

Sitting Tigger facing right & looking down; waist-up front view of Tigger holding ears; 5 x 8" & 5-1/2 x 5-1/2"; seals; VG; HL/Nov 13/94 840

Portrait of smiling Tigger, 6 x 5-1/2", seal, VF+, HL/Nov 19/95 (700-900) 978

Near-full-figure large image of Tigger facing toward right & looking down, 6 x 8", HL/Oct 6/96 (600-900) 1150

Stomach-up front view of sad Tigger, WDP seal & certificate, 7 x 4", VF+, HL/Apr 25/98 (500-700) 978

WINNIE THE POOH AND THE HONEY TREE (1966)
Also see THE MANY ADVENTURES OF WINNIE THE POOH
CEL SET-UPS

Rabbit fixes a sign, hand-prepared background, 13-1/2 x 16-1/2", CE/Dec 15/93 (400-600) 345

Cel & background (pastel & pencil on green background sheet): map of Hundred Acre Wood, probably for publicity or publication, 15-1/2 x 20", VF, HL/Aug 21/94 (1000-1500) 3136

Pooh skipping over words "Pooh Bears Howse" from opening, 2-5/16", color print background with Owl's House in tree, SR/Fall/96 (400-800) 650

2 full-figure cels of Christopher Robin walking with drum (one w/Kanga), color prints of backgrounds, both 8 x 10" overall, HL/Feb 23/97 (400-600) 748

Full figures of Christopher Robin sitting on log (4-1/2"), Pooh (3-5/8") & Eeyore standing, & frightened Rabbit jumping, Art Props master pan watercolor background of outdoors, SR/Spring/97 (4000-8000) 4720

Full figure of Pooh sitting on log, putting stick on fire in front of "Mr. Sanders" entrance from opening scene, 3-3/8", 16-field cel, watercolor background, smoke effects, SR/Spring/97 (1800-2200) 2840

Full figure of Gopher (4") holding honey pot up to Pooh (3-1/4") whose head & arms are protruding from Rabbit's House, preliminary key watercolor background, CLA/Jun 7/97 (1500-2000) 1840

Gopher stands in front of log with eyes closed, 4-3/4", litho background, gold Art Corner seal, SR/Fall/97 (2800-3600) 200

Waist-up of smiling Winnie the Pooh looking out open window, 3-3/8", matching ink-and-watercolor Art Props background, SR/Spring/98 (2800-3600) 2810

CELS – FULL FIGURE (also see MODEL ART)

Muddy Pooh floating & holding balloon string, facing right; 10 x 5"; VF+; HL/Aug 21/94 (1000-1500) 1232

Full-figure portraits of frazzled Rabbit in robe; Gopher; Pooh; Owl w/wings spread; 4 x 3" to 6-1/2 x 7"; VF+; HL/Apr 23/95 (700-1000) 1568

4 cels: profile of Pooh pointing; pompous Owl (all but feet); Gopher grimacing; frazzled Rabbit in robe; 2-1/2 x 2-1/2" to 5 x 5-1/2"; VF+; HL/Aug 6/95 (700-1000) 1568

Pooh's bottom adorned w/painted face & tree branches, 6 x 8, VF+, HL/Nov 19/95 (200-300) 489

Concerned Winnie kneels down as two bees buzz around him, gold DL label, 3-1/2", S/Jun 19/96 (600-800) 575

Pooh, dripping mud & holding string, facing right in sitting position, 6-7/8" w/o string, 16-field cel, Disney Art Program seal, SR/Fall/96 (1200-1800) 1630

Muddy but happy Pooh hanging from balloon string, 9-1/2 x 4", HL/Oct 6/96 (800-1000) 805

Rear view of sad Eeyore with head turned back [toward camera], looking down, 4-1/2 x 5", HL/Oct 6/96 (500-700) 920

Worried Rabbit stands facing left, 6-1/4 x 5", HL/Feb 23/97 (200-250) 259

Happy Pooh dripping mud, holding onto balloon string, munching honey; 9-1/2 x 3-3/4", HL/Feb 23/97 (800-1000) 748

Sad Eeyore standing facing left, 4 x 6", seal, VF+, HL/May 31/97 (700-900) 489

Sitting Rabbit cringing [as he tests echo in hunny jar], 5-1/2 x 3-1/2", VF+, HL/May 31/97 (150-250) 173

Muddy Pooh [sneezing?] as he hangs by balloon string, 7", CLA/Jun 7/97 (700-900) 920

Kanga stands facing left with Roo in her pouch, 3-1/4 x 3", VF+, HL/Apr 25/98 (300-400) 345

CELS – PARTIAL FIGURE

Chest-up of Pooh with face stuck in jar, 7-1/2 x 6", VF+, HL/Feb 26-27/94 (100-150) 358

Rabbit serves honey to Winnie (seated, napkin around neck, holding spoon), 6 x 8", VF+, HL/Apr 23/95 (1000-1500) 1064

Near-full-figure large image of Winnie standing & reaching down [into honey jar], 5-1/2 x 3-1/2", VF, HL/Apr 28/96 (600-800) 518

Waist-up of Pooh with honey jar stuck on face, 7-1/2 x 6", VF+, HL/May 31/97 (150-200) 259

Near-full figure of smiling Gopher looking right, 4-1/2 x 4-1/2", VF+, HL/May 31/97 (150-200) 173

Standing Pooh with napkin tied around neck reaches down [into honey jar], 5-1/4 x 3-1/2", VF+, HL/Apr 25/98 (500-700) 633

DYE-TRANSFER PRINTS

Waist-up of happy Pooh looking out open window, 10 x 7-1/2", SR/Fall/94 (300-600) 330

MODEL ART

2 original photostat model sheets of Pooh, 13-3/8 x 9-15/16" & 12-9/16 x 10-1/16", SR/Fall/96 (100-300) 630

Full-figure color model cel of Eeyore looking back while chewing thistle, 4-1/4 x 4", HL/Oct 6/96 (600-900) 1035

Full-figure color model cel of Pooh standing facing right & looking up, 6-1/4 x 3", HL/Feb 23/97 (500-700) 546

WINNIE THE POOH AND TIGGER, TOO (1974)
ANIMATION DRAWINGS

25 sequential images of Tigger on 2 sheets, with dialogue, 11-1/2 x 11-1/"2 & 11 x 14-1/2", ink on animation sheets, VF+, HL/Aug 6/95 (600-800) 952

6 drawings: front view of sitting Tigger, 6"; three 4" Rabbits; 4-3/8" Roo; 1-1/4" of Roo languishing on his mailbox; 16-field sheets, some wear, SR/Spring/97 (250-500) 1150

CEL SET-UPS

Matching cel & master background of Tigger & Rabbit dancing in snow, 10-1/2 x 15", VF+, HL/Nov 13/94 (3000-3500) 2912

Portrait of Tigger facing toward left, 6-1/2", 16-field cel, Disney Art Program seal & label, color print background of Hundred Acre Wood, SR/Spring/97 (500-900) 750

Full standing figures of happy Tigger (eyes closed) holding Rabbit's hand, complementary color print background of outdoors, seal & certificate, 5-1/4 x 6", VF+, HL/Apr 25/98 (500-700) 748

Full figure of Roo sitting outdoors, facing toward right w/hands to mouth & mouth open; complementary color print background: seal & certificate; 5 x 5-1/2" cel; VF+; HL/Apr 25/98 (300-400) 748

CELS – FULL FIGURE (unless noted)/MODEL ART

Large image of Roo facing right & looking back & up, Disney seal, VF+, HL/Feb 26-27/94 (200-300) 495

Tigger bounces Rabbit, 1974, 4-1/2 x 6-1/2", Disney seal, VF+, HL/Apr 10/94 (600-900) 896

2 cels: hips-up of Kanga in apron standing facing

right, holding scarf ends, eyes closed, 7"; full figure of Roo facing right in sitting position with scarf trailing, 4-1/4"; 16-field, Disney Art Program seals, DL label, SR/Fall/94 (600-1200) — 610

Piglet in coat; Tigger dancing; 5" & smaller; WDC seal; CE/Dec 16/94 (300-400) — 322

Apologetic Rabbit standing facing right with both hands out, 6-1/2", 16-field, Disney Art Program seal, SR/Spring/95 (300-600) — 300

Happy Tigger walking; happy Rabbit standing facing left & looking back; 6 x 7-1/2"; VF+; HL/Apr 23/95 (500-700) — 952

Tigger happily bounces w/eyes closed, 5", WDP label; smiling Roo w/eyes closed, 3-1/2"; both with silver WDP stamp; S/Jun 10/95 (400-600) — 517

Panicked Pooh runs right with Piglet (mostly hidden) behind him, 4-1/2 x 5", HL/Feb 23/97 (600-900) — 460

Color model cel of nervous Rabbit (4-1/2") standing facing right with left leg up, confident Tigger (5") standing with left hand on hip, pointing with right hand; 16-field sheet; plus matching photocopy of original Color Model Dept. drawing; SR/Fall/97 (900-1200) — 600

WINNIE THE POOH DISCOVERS THE SEASONS (1981)
ANIMATION DRAWINGS/CELS – FULL FIGURE
2 cels: Pooh in sweater & stocking cap & Owl standing & talking; Pooh in sweater & stocking cap standing facing left & waving; each with matching clean-up animation drawing; 3-1/2 x 6", 5-1/2 x 3-1/2"; VF+; HL/May 31/97 (400-600) — 546

WINNIE THE POOH EDUCATIONAL SERIES
ANIMATION DRAWINGS
2 full-figure drawings: Christopher Robin lectures group by school bus, 12 x 10"; front view of Christopher & 4 characters walking toward camera, 7-1/8"; 16-field sheets; some wear; SR/Fall/96 (150-300) — 370
CEL SET-UPS/ANIMATION DRAWINGS/LAYOUT ART
Pooh & Piglet, matching master watercolor background for educational filmstrip, VF+, HL/Feb 26-27/94 (400-600) — 825

Set of matching cels & master watercolor background of Pooh as happy homemaker, likely for educational film, VF+, HL/Feb 26-27/94 (600-900) — 825

Pooh (3"), Rabbit (3-1/2") & Roo (1-1/2") view garden, circa 1980s, key watercolor production background, CE/Jun 18/94 (800-1200) — 575

Pooh with honey pot sits against tree, 3-1/2", 1980s, key watercolor production background, CE/Jun 18/94 (800-1200) — 633

Winnie (3"), Tigger (3-1/2"), Piglet (2"), Friend Owl (5" wide) outdoors, 1980s, key production background, CE/Jun 18/94 (800-1200) — 920

Pooh & Tigger on picnic, each 6-1/2", 1980s, key watercolor production background, CE/Jun 18/94 (800-1200) — 1093

Pooh (6-3/4 x 3-3/4") & Roo (4-1/2 x 3-1/2") on sailboat, 1980s, preliminary watercolor background, CE/Jun 18/94 (500-700) — 633

Pooh (7-1/2") & Piglet (5"), 1980s, key watercolor production background, CE/Jun 18/94 (1000-1500) — 805

Tigger juggling ice cubes, 7-1/2", 1980s, key watercolor production background, CE/Jun 18/94 (700-900) — 920

Pooh imagines diving into dry stream, 5-1/2", 1980s, key watercolor production background, CE/Jun 18/94 (600-800) — 368

Winnie & friends, circa 1980s, key watercolor production background 3-1/2" & smaller, CE/Dec 16/94 (600-800) — 1955

Winnie (waist up) holding fruit, 8-1/2", circa 1980s, watercolor production background, CE/Dec 16/94 (600-800) — 978

Full figures of Winnie & Rabbit w/basket of carrots, 6-1/2" & similar, 1980s, key watercolor production background, CE/Dec 16/94 (500-700) — 1725

Winnie talking to bird on his arm, 7-1/2", 1980s,

watercolor production background, CE/Dec 16/94 (600-800) — 1955

Full figures of Rabbit, Tigger, & Owl with book, 4" & similar, 1980s, key watercolor production background, CE/Dec 16/94 (500-700) — 1093

Winnie (4-1/4") & Piglet (2-1/2") carry basket thru forest, 1980s, key watercolor background, CE/Dec 16/94 (500-700) — 1265

Full figures of Winnie, Rabbit, mother duck & five babies, 3" & similar, 1980s, key watercolor background, CE/Dec 16/94 (500-700) — 1093

Full figure of happy Winnie the Pooh sitting under tree eating honey from jar, 1980s, watercolor production background, 6-1/2", CE/Jun 20/96 (500-700) — 1725

Happy Tigger (5-1/2") stands by frozen pond holding berries in left hand & thinking of Roo (2-1/2") snow sledding, 1980s, watercolor production background, CE/Jun 20/96 (500-700) — 1035

Smiling Pooh (8") & Rabbit (8-1/2") hold up vegetables outdoors, 1980s, watercolor production background, CE/Jun 20/96 (600-800) — 1150

Full figures of Owl (5") & Piglet (4") standing in forest holding numbers as Pooh (5") watches, basket of numbers on ground, 1980s, studio-prepared watercolor background, CE/Jun 20/96 (600-800) — 1840

Winter scene: close-up of Christopher Robin whispering to Pooh (eyes closed), 7-3/8", key color print background, SR/Fall/96 (150-300) — 210

Full figures of Pooh (2-3/16"), Eeyore, & Roo walking right thru farmland, key watercolor background & line-print overlay, SR/Fall/96 (300-700) — 1150

3 items: happy Winnie the Pooh in house pouring honey over cake, circa 1980s, 4-1/2", key watercolor production background; two matching animation drawings, CE/Dec 12/96 (600-800) — 1093

Tigger (4") walking into house to join Pooh (4-1/2") who holds picnic basket as he admires table of food, circa 1980s, key watercolor production background; plus matching animation drawing, CE/Dec 12/96 (600-800) — 1150

Full-figure front view of smiling Winnie the Pooh standing in forest w/right hand behind ear in listening pose, 4-1/2", key watercolor production background; 2 matching animation drawings; circa 1980s, CE/Dec 12/96 (600-800) — 978

Winnie the Pooh & friends behind table holding plates, glasses, pitcher & Eeyore's birthday cake, approx. 2" each, key watercolor production background; matching animation drawing; circa 1980s, CE/Dec 12/96 (600-800) — 2530

Near-full figure of smiling Winnie the Pooh carrying pitcher to table (holding basket, box, cups, etc.) inside cottage, 5", key watercolor production background; 2 matching animation drawings; circa 1980s, CE/Dec 12/96 (600-800) — 978

Full figure of happy Pooh walking in forest w/arms spread, circa 1980s, watercolor production background, 3"; matching animation drawing; CLA/Jun 7/97 (600-800) — 1093

Full figures of Winnie the Pooh (4") standing by tree petting sitting Eeyore (3"), 1980s, watercolor background; matching animation drawing; CLA/Jun 7/97 (600-800) — 1093

Close-up of Tigger tossing a balloon, 1980s, 9", watercolor production background of outdoors, CLA/Jun 7/97 (600-800) — 748

Full figures of Tigger (7") standing w/balloon tied to tail pointing to basket as puzzled Pooh (5") watches, circa 1980s, watercolor production background of outdoors, CLA/Jun 7/97 (600-800) — 1265

Full figures of Pooh (4"), Tigger (5"), & Piglet (3-1/2") cheering smiling Eeyore (6-1/2"), circa 1980s, watercolor production background of outdoors, CLA/Jun 7/97 (600-800) — 1380

Full figures of Pooh (standing) & Eeyore under tree, 4" each, watercolor production background; 2 key matching layout drawings, CE/Dec 18/97 (700-900) — 1380

Half figure of Tigger juggling 3 green fruit, 8-1/2", watercolor production background of outdoors, CE/Dec 18/97 (600-800) — 552

Happy Pooh stands behind table mixing ingredients in bowl with spoon, 5", watercolor production background of kitchen; 2 matching animation drawings; CE/Dec 18/97 (700-900) — 1265

Full figures of Christopher Robin (on knees, 4-1/4"), Pooh (3"), Eeyore (3"), & Piglet (2") picking wildflowers by tree; key watercolor production background; CE/Dec 18/97 (600-800) — 1955

Full standing figures of Rabbit in garden holding basket of carrots & facing Pooh, 6-1/2" each, watercolor production background, CE/Dec 18/97 (600-800) — 863

Full standing figures of Pooh with hunny pot marked "Happy Birthday," Piglet holding balloon, Owl with wings spread, Tigger, Christopher Robin, Kanga in party hat (all partly behind Owl), Roo in party hat, Eeyore in distance; 12 x 8" key watercolor background of outdoors, SR/Spring/98 (800-1200) — 820

Party-hatted Pooh cast sits around table laden with birthday treats, 10-1/2 x 8-1/2", matching watercolor background, SR/Spring/98 (600-1200) — 830
CELS – FULL FIGURE
Publicity cel of Pooh (7-3/4") & Tigger (6-1/2"), CE/Dec 18/97 (700-900) — 920

WISE LITTLE HEN, THE (1934)
MODEL ART
Vintage photostatic model sheet of Donald Duck, 14 x 11", SR/Fall/96 (200-400) — 650

WONDER DOG (1950)
CEL SET-UPS
Full figure of eager Pluto lying outside dog house, 5" long, watercolor production background, CLA/Jun 7/97 (2000-3000) — 1495

WOODLAND CAFE (1937)
ANIMATION DRAWINGS
Full-figure drawing of 2 pairs of bug dancers bumping, 4-1/2 x 9-1/4", HL/Apr 28/96 (600-800) — 633

MODEL ART
2 animation sheets of model drawings of Apache dancer; 4 x 3", 7 x 10-1/2", HL/May 31/97 (200-300) — 127
TITLE ART
Title card: watercolor airbrush with hand lettering on cel overlay, 12-field, original production cover flap, SR/Fall/95 (1500-2000) — 1650

WORKING FOR PEANUTS (1953)
STORY ART
6 storyboard drawings by story artist Nick George in pastel & charcoal on 8-1/4 x 6-7/8" storyboard sheets, SR/Spring/98 (300-600 — 570

WYNKEN, BLYNKEN & NOD (1938)
CEL SET-UPS
Wynken & Nod fish from boat, boys 1/2 x 1/4", Courvoisier label & airbrush background, CE/Jun 18/94 (600-800) — 978

Wide-eyed Wynken, Blynken & Nod sailing in shoe boat, 8-1/2 x 10", complementary airbrush background & inscribed as prepared for Courvoisier, HL/Apr 23/95 (2400-2800) — 2912

Full figure of wooden shoe under sail with three boys fishing from it, 4 x 3-1/2", airbrushed Courvoisier background of sea & clouds, S/Dec 14/96 (800-1200) — 805
CELS – FULL FIGURE
Front (chest up) & back (full figure) views of standing little boy fishing, 5 x 6-1/2" & 4 x 3-1/2", F+, HL/Nov 19/95 (900-1200) — 690

Full figure of shoe w/worried Wynken at rudder, Blynken & Nod clinging to furled sail, 8 x 6", HL/Apr 28/96 (1000-1500) — 1265
SILKSCREEN ART

Multiplane painting of Wynken, Blynken & Nod
fishing in clouds from clog boat, 3-3/4",
silkscreen on 2 pieces of glass, Courvoisier
label, CE/Dec 16/94 (700-900)   575

Multiplane shadow box of 3 boys fishing from sailing
shoe amid stars & clouds, 5-3/8 x 5", silkscreen
on 2 pieces of glass, Courvoisier frame & label,
SR/Spring/95 (600-1000)   650

Multiplane painting of Wynken, Blynken & Nod in
shoe & on clouds, silkscreen on 2 pieces of
glass, Courvoisier label, 4", CE/Jun 20/96
(700-900)   1495

Multiplane painting of Wynken, Blynken & Nod
fishing from shoe boat amid clouds, moon
& stars, 4", silkscreen on 2 pieces of glass,
Courvoisier label, CE/Dec 12/96 (700-900) 748

YE OLDEN DAYS (1933)
ANIMATION DRAWINGS
Full-figure drawing of Princess Minnie faint
in Mickey's arms, 3 x 3-1/2",
HL/Nov 19/95 (600-800)   575

Full-figure drawing of Mickey & Minnie dancing,
4-1/4 x 3-3/4", VF, HL/Nov 16/97
(600-900)   633

LAYOUT ART
3 layout drawings: scroll unfurls across turreted castle
listing Ye Caste; "Love at First Sight": Mickey,
serenading Minnie from back of horse; "Mickey
Starts Down Rope with Minnie": tower window
w/Mickey & Minnie at ledge; 1st two 12-field;
3rd 2 12-field sheets glued together; all with
production stamp, SR/Fall/95
(4000-10,000)   5900

Layout drawing of King on throne ringing gong,
7 x 9", HL/Nov 19/95 (800-1200)   1380

Three full-figure character layout drawings: Prince
Dippy Dawg (6") standing with Princess Minnie;
King sitting on throne, 5-5/8"; Mickey standing
with hands on stove (4"), mule lightly indicated
at right; 12-field sheets; copious inker, animator,
background, & color notations; some overall
wear & discoloration (were folded in thirds);
SR/Fall/97 (2400-3400)   1800

TELEVISION

This section is organized alphabetically by production,
then chronologically by auction. Show episodes (when
identified) are given in quotes.

ACADEMY AWARDS
CEL SET-UPS
4-1/2" Sorcerer Mickey at podium, w/photographic
background (w/Tom Selleck), 1988,
S/Dec 16/93 (1000-1500)   1150

Mickey Mouse in red bow tie & tails standing facing
left, 4", printed background, silver Walt Disney
Co. seal, S/Dec 19/97 (800-1200)   920

CELS – FULL FIGURE
Mickey Mouse as 1988 Show host, Disney seal &
label, VF+, HL/Feb 26-27/94 (1200-1600)   1430

Sorcerer Mickey & Donald, to celebrate Mickey's
60th birthday, 6 x 9", Disney seal, VF+,
HL/Apr 10/94 (1500-2000)   1120

3 full-figure cels of Mickey Mouse, 1988, 4" & similar,
WDC seal, CE/Dec 16/94 (4000-6000)   4600

Smiling tuxedo-clad Mickey standing & gesturing,
4-1/2", 1988, S/Jun 10/95 (700-900)   920

Donald Duck (dressed in tails) bowing to left with

left arm extended, 1988, 3-3/4 x 4-1/2",
HL/Apr 10/94 (600-800)   460

Full standing figures of Sorcerer Mickey (6") facing
right, leaning back to cast spell & Donald
Duck (5") in tails facing left, 1988,
CE/Dec 12/96 (1500-2000)   1150

Mickey, Minnie, Daisy, & tied-up Donald sitting on
bench; 60th Academy Awards, 1988; signed
by Wayne Allwine & Russi Taylor; 6-1/2 x
11-1/2" inc. signatures; VF+; HL/Apr 25/98
(1000-1500)   978

CELS – PARTIAL FIGURE/ANIMATION DRAWING
Knees-up front view of modest Mickey shrugging with
eyes closed, w/matching animation drawing,
6-1/2 x 5", HL/Feb 23/97 (600-800)   575

ALADDIN
Also see FEATURE FILMS: ALADDIN
CEL SET-UPS
2 cels of Aladdin walking thru city w/wide-eyed Abu
clinging to his neck, color prints of matching
pan master background, 10-1/2 x 46" overall,
HL/Oct 6/96 (600-800)   920

Angry Princess Jasmine chained to wall by wrists
above her head as smiling Abis Mal watches,
6-1/2 x 7", color copy of matching
background, HL/May 31/97 (200-400)   207

Aladdin & Jasmine embrace in the marketplace,
7-1/4 x 9-1/2", matching master background
(acrylics on background sheet), VF+, HL/Nov
16/97 (600-900)   575

ANTHOLOGY SERIES
This covers the series of one-hour shows run continu-
ously from 1954 to 1983 on all three major commercial
networks under various titles: "Disneyland," "Walt Disney Presents," "Walt Disney's Wonderful World of
Color," "The Wonderful World of Disney," "Disney's
Wonderful World," and "Walt Disney." Walt Disney was
the host until his death in 1966. It returned in 1986
with Michael Eisner as host as "The Disney Sunday
Movie," then "The Magical World of Disney." The show
moved to The Disney Channel on September 23, 1990,
and has reappeared on commercial television for the
1997-98 season. Episodes are identified when known.

CEL SET-UPS/LAYOUT ART
Full figure of Ludwig playing guitar w/foot on chair,
tempera master background, 10-1/2 x 15-1/2",
studio notes, VF, "Von Drake in Spain,"
HL/Apr 10/94 (1000-1500)   1008

Determined Goofy (4-1/2") carries Olympic Torch as
Caesar reads scroll, pan watercolor production
background, WDP label, "Goofy Sports Story,"
CE/Jun 18/94 (3000-4000)   4370

Full figure of smiling Bambi standing in 'O' of Noel,
watercolor key production background, with
production notes, 5-1/2", From All of Us to
All of You, CE/Dec 16/94 (600-800)   2300

Full figure of excited José standing looking left, "Two
Happy Amigos" 1960, 4-1/2", DL litho background of park, gold Art Corner label, some
cracking paint, SR/Spring/95 (300-600)   310

Head-&-neck close-up portrait of wide-eyed Goofy,
"A Salute To Father", 1961, 9-1/2", DL litho
background of stream, Art Corner label,
SR/Spring/95 (600-1000)   610

Full figures of space monster grabbing screaming
secretary, 9-1/2 x 12-1/2", complementary
painted background, signed & titled by Ward
Kimball, VF, "Mars and Beyond,"
HL/Apr 23/95 (700-900)   896

Cinderella in coach (TV cel created from feature's
original animation drawing), 1960, 8-1/2 x 12",
color print background of forest, VF+, "This is
Your Life, Donald Duck," HL/Apr 23/95
(1500-2000)   2240

Full figures of Tinker Bell ("Disneyland" TV series)
leaving pixie-dust trail by one of Donald Duck's
nephews (facing left) from a cartoon of same
period; color print background of forest as
sold at DL, 7 x 8-1/2", 1950s, VF,
HL/Apr 23/95 (600-800)   896

Full figure of Tinker Bell in scouting pose, 1950s,
8 x 10", color print of background from
Sleeping Beauty, as sold at DL,
HL/Aug 6/95 (700-1000)   672

Full figure of smiling Donald in party hat standing

before movie screen holding 4 film cans, "At
Home With Donald Duck," 6-1/4", gouache
master background, 16-field, SR/Fall/95
(900-1400)   1460

Full figures of argumentative Huey, then Dewey &
Louie standing in line facing left, "Donald's
Weekend" 1958, master watercolor back-
ground of home interior from Mr. Duck Steps
Out, each 4", SR/Fall/95 (1500-2500)   2220

Ludwig sleeps in chair w/feet on desk as Walt Disney
watches, 1960s publicity set-up, color picture
as background, 12-1/2 x 9-1/2",
HL/Apr 28/96 (1200-1600)   920

Multi-layered set-up of Magic Mirror, "Disney's
Greatest Villains," gouache painting with six
special effects levels, matching pencil layout
drawing plus inter-office memo with shooting
directions for final scene, SR/Fall/96
(2000-4000)   2730

Rear view of Donald Duck in pith helmet, holding
binoculars, sitting on "Lake Titicaca" sign,
3-1/4", 1950s for "Disneyland" TV show,
16-field cel, matching watercolor display
background, SR/Fall/96 (700-1100)   1070

Large-image full figures of smiling Donald Duck
watching gesturing José Carioca, 1960s, color
print of background from Disney film, 6-1/2 x
8-1/2" cel images, HL/Oct 6/96 (500-700)   489

Full-figure front view of Mickey Mouse in park, cane
in right hand, holding hat high in left; 1960s;
complementary 101 Dalmatians color print
background; 6 x 5-1/4" cel image,
HL/Oct 6/96 (700-1000)   978

Full figure of smiling Tinker Bell with wings fluttering
flying amid swirl of pixie dust, 1950s, colored
paper background, 6-1/4 x 6",
HL/Feb 23/97 (700-1000)   1150

Full figures of happy José & Donald (eyes closed)
shaking hands amid confetti, "Two Happy
Amigos," 5" on 16-field cel, color print
background, SR/Spring/97 (400-700)   460

Full figure of Donald Duck driving car to right thru
forest, from another Disney short, 1965[?],
7" length, watercolor production background,
"Kids is Kids," CLA/Jun 7/97 (2000-3000) 1725

Full figure of Pluto standing facing left, imitating a
chicken; April 27, 1957 "Disneyland"; 5";
original mat, color card background, DL gold
Art Corner label; SR/Fall/97 (450-700)   300

Front view of Alice looking right, beginning to curtsy;
"From All of Us to All of You," Dec. 19, 1958;
5-3/4"; DL set-up with litho background of
outdoors, SR/Fall/97 (9000-1200)   600

Full figure of young Bambi poking head thru 'O' in
Noel on Christmas card, 5-3/4", "From All of
Us to All of You," snowflake effects, key master
watercolor background of stack of cards against
decorated tree branches, small lamination
separation, SR/Fall/97 (4000-7000)   2850

Full figure of Mickey standing in spotlight playing
trumpet, 5", watercolor production background,
"From All Of Us To All Of You," S/Dec 19/97
(1500-2500)   1495

Full figures of Sleepy & Bashful walking left thru forest
with picks on shoulders, color print background
as sold at DL, "Tricks of Our Trade," 4-1/2 x
6-1/4" cel, F, HL/Apr 25/98 (600-900)   518

CELS – FULL FIGURE
Tinker Bell as host, 1970s, 4 x 4", VF+,
HL/Feb 26-27/94 (300-500)   825

Tinker Bell standing, knees bend, gesturing to right;
3 x 2"; VF+; HL/Apr 10/94 (400-600)   476

Mickey as baseball pitcher, 6-1/2 x 4", in mat with
DL label, Art Corner info sheet & illustrated
paper bag, F, "The Plausible Impossible,"
HL/Apr 10/94 (1000-1500)   1008

Procession of Peter and the Wolf stars created from
original animation from Make Mine Music,
7 x 29", VF, "This is Your Life, Donald Duck,"
HL/Apr 10/94 (1000-1500)   1232

Mary Mary Quite Contrary facing left, "The Truth
About Mother Goose," 7", CE/Jun 18/94
(400-600)   207

Panchito, 5 x 4", "A Present For Donald,"
HL/Aug 21/94 (400-600)   476

Hunter Mickey stands facing right, holding shotgun,
looking down, "Four Tales On A Mouse,"
5-1/2", SR/Fall/94 (1000-1600)   1280

Tinker Bell jumping, 1950s, 3" with wings, 16-field,

SR/Fall/94 (250-500) 430

Ludwig von Drake in opera costume, lying on back, holding sword to chest in 'death' pose, "Music For Everybody" 1966, 6 x 4-1/2", 16-field, SR/Fall/94 (200-500) 200

2 cels: front view of Ludwig von Drake speaking while holding book on floor, 6"; strutting peacock with multi-colored tail walking left with eyes closed, 4"; both 16-field, SR/Fall/94 (300-700) 310

Procession of *Peter & the Wolf* characters walking left, "This Is Your Life, Donald Duck," 31-1/2 x 12-1/2" full pan cel, SR/Fall/94 (900-1500) 1150

5 unpainted cels of Mickey sitting facing right [playing piano], "From All Of Us to All of You," 4-1/2", each hand inked in two colors on 16-field cel, SR/Fall/94 (1200-2200) 2400

Goofy dressed as Peter Pan sitting & playing lute, 1961, 4-1/2", "Holiday For Henpecked Husbands," CE/Dec 16/94 (500-700) 805

Front view of three Jesters standing together singing, 4-3/4", "The Truth About Mother Goose" 1963, SR/Spring/95 (250-500) 300

Chip & Dale stand facing each other hand to hand & nose to nose, "The Adventures of Chip 'N Dale" 1959, 5", 16-field, SR/Spring/95 (400-700) 710

2 front-view cels of Chip (6-3/4") & Dale (6-1/4") dancing in top hats & holding canes, "The Adventures of Chip 'N Dale" 1959, matted as set, SR/Spring/95 (700-1100) 720

Front view of Mickey in overalls & straw hat, holding his tail, looking right & up, 4-3/4", "Tricks of Our Trade" 1957, 12-field, SR/Spring/95 (1200-1800) 1210

Mickey as baseball pitcher, "Tricks of Our Trade" 1957, 4-1/4", 16-field, SR/Spring/95 (1200-1800) 1800

Angry dressed-up Donald walking right with box of candy & cane, "Wonderful World of Disney" 1960s, 6-1/2", SR/Spring/95 (500-900) 500

Cyril prancing to left with Toad hanging onto collar, "This Is Your Life, Donald Duck" 1960, 5-7/8", 16-field, SR/Spring/95 (300-600) 350

Mr. Toad rides on collar of prancing Cyril, 1960, 6 x 6", "This is Your Life, Donald Duck," HL/Aug 6/95 (600-900) 448

Mad Hatter (holding tea pot) & March Hare (mouth open) running to left, each 4-1/2", "This is Your Life, Donald Duck" 1960, 16-field, SR/Fall/95 (500-900) 500

Happy Huey, Dewey, & Louie stand together admiring their new uniforms, 4-1/2", "Duck For Hire" 1957, SR/Fall/95 (500-1000) 500

Front view of angry Donald standing pointing double-barrel shotgun, "The Hunting Instinct" 1961, 16-field, SR/Fall/95 (500-900) 750

2 full-figure cels: happy José stands holding photo of Mickey Mouse, 5", "Two Happy Amigos" 1960; Panchito stands in modeling pose, 5-1/2", 12-field, "A Present For Donald" 1956; SR/Fall/95 (500-800) 600

2 full-figure cels of Jiminy Cricket gesturing, 1960s, 5 x 6-1/2", 5-1/2 x 3-1/2", HL/Nov 19/95 (600-800) 1035

Mickey playing trumpet, 1958, 7 x 6", "From All of Us to All of You," HL/Nov 19/95 (900-1200) 1150

Determined Goofy as Greek running with Olympic torch, 1956, 5 x 7", "The Goofy Sports Story," HL/Nov 19/95 (600-900) 978

Worried Goofy as Peter Pan giving stop gesture with both hands, 1961, 7-1/2 x 4-1/2", "Holiday For Henpecked Husbands," HL/Nov 19/95 (300-500) 690

Hunter Mickey stands facing right, holding shotgun, 5-1/2", 12-field, "Four Tales on a Mouse" 1958, SR/Spring/96 (1000-1600) 1300

Donald walking right, looking up, wearing mouse ears, 2-1/8", "Kids is Kids," SR/Spring/96 (175-375) 150

Tinker Bell bathing screen in pixie dust [TV show opening], 9 x 9-1/2", HL/Mar 16-17/96 (400-600) 1495

Half-figure front view of mother rabbit with full figures of four bunnies lined up in front of her, 4-1/8", "From All of Us to All of You" 1958, SR/Spring/96 (300-600) 330

Mickey in straw hat walks right with fishing pole over shoulder, 1", "The Tricks of Our Trade" 1957, SR/Spring/96 (100-200) 100

Sultry Briar Rose standing w/hands on hips, 1955, 6 x 2-1/2", "The Story of the Silly Symphony," HL/Apr 28/96 (400-600) 518

Large full figure of jaunty Mickey Mouse wearing hat, whistling & walking with fishing pole, 1957, 4-1/2 x 6", HL/Apr 28/96 (1200-1600) 1150

Smiling Tinker Bell with wand, 1950s, 4-1/2 x 4", HL/Apr 28/96 (600-900) 690

Ludwig von Drake walks right, hands behind back, eyes closed, 4-1/4", SR/Fall/96 (200-400) 200

Haughty Donald as movie producer walks left, trailing cord; "Your Host, Donald Duck"; 5 7/8"; SR/Fall/96 (500-900) 400

Front view of surprised Jiminy Cricket standing, holding blackboard eraser, looking up & to right, 4-5/8", 16-field, 1960s TV, SR/Fall/96 (300-600) 300

Tinker Bell in coonskin cap shouldering rifle & looking left in scouting pose, 4 x 4", 1954-55, HL/Oct 6/96 (600-800) 1265

Seated Mickey playing piano keys, 1958, 4-1/2 x 4", "From All of Us to All of You," HL/Oct 6/96 (1000-1500) 1380

Tinker Bell (2-1/2 x 6") flying to right thru pixie dust, 8 x 9" overall, 1950s, HL/Feb 23/97 (900-1200) 805

Rear view of Tinker Bell & splash of pixie dust from title sequence, 1954, 8-1/2 x 8-1/2" including pixie dust, HL/Feb 23/97 (700-1000) 805

Mickey in white tie & tails stands playing trumpet, "From All of Us to All of You," 5-1/2", 16-field cel, SR/Spring/97 (700-1100) 730

3 full-figure cels of Martian creatures: 3-1/2 x 4", 3 x 5", 7-1/2 x 9-1/2", 1957, "Mars and Beyond," HL/May 3/97 (600-900) 1265

José Carioca & Donald Duck, 1960, 4 x 6", "Donald's Silver Anniversary," HL/May 31/97 (400-600) 115

Donald Duck stands facing left wearing beekeeper's hat & net, early 1960s, 7-1/2 x 5", HL/May 31/97 (300-400) 316

Large full-figure image of irritated Chip standing looking up, 1960s, 5 x 4", HL/May 31/97 (200-300) 288

3 full-figure cels of Ludwig Von Drake; 1960s; 6 x 4-1/2", 7-1/4 x 4-1/2", 6-1/2 x 3-1/4", VF, HL/Nov 16/97 (300-500) 460

2 cels of overconfident NBC peacock walking left, 3-3/4 x 7-3/4" & 3-1/2 x 2 x 6-1/4", F-VF, HL/Nov 16/97 (300-500) 518

Angry Donald in party hat standing faces left with arms out, 1956, VF+, "At Home With Donald Duck," HL/Nov 16/97 (500-700) 345

2 cels of bizarre creatures, 1957, 7-1/2 x 10" & 5-1/2 x 4-1/2", F, "Mars and Beyond," HL/Nov 16/97 (500-700) 690

Dressed-up Donald Duck angrily holds up & points to nephews' piggy bank, 1958 "Donald's Weekend," 7", ct, SR/Spring/98 (600-1200) 550

Procession of *Peter and the Wolf* stars created from original animation from *Make Mine Music* with drybrush effects, 29-1/2 x 7-1/4", "This is Your Life, Donald Duck," ct, SR/Spring/98 (500-900) 630

Smiling Chip & Dale step right in identical poses with hobo bundles over their shoulders, each 3-7/8", 16-field cel, SR/Spring/98 (600-1200) 600

Front view of sitting Jiminy Cricket, 1950s "Disneyland," 6 x 5-1/4", VF, HL/Apr 25/98 (400-600) 920

CELS – PARTIAL FIGURE

Half image of shocked tree (8") standing by sheet of music, "An Adventure in Art" 1958, SR/Fall/94 (100-300) 150

Near-full figure of Snow White standing with arms out, being pulled to left by her cape by birds, "This Is Your Life, Donald Duck," 7", SR/Fall/95 (2000-3000) 2000

Knees-up of happy Goofy standing with hands on hips facing toward left, 10", "On Vacation with Mickey Mouse & Friends" 1956, color print background, SR/Fall/96 (300-600) 680

Near-full figures of frightened Chip & Dale facing left, 1960s, 1-1/4 x 1-3/4", VF+, HL/May 31/97 (100-150) 259

Waist-up image of Mickey in golfing garb standing behind a bush, 1956, 3", "On Vacation,"

S/Jun 21/97 (1000-1500) 1150

Shoulders-up front view of smiling Goofy wearing fez, holding book *How To Fish*, 5-1/4", DL mat, color card background, gold Art Corner label, SR/Apr 27/97 (600-900) 400

Chest-up close-up of Mickey facing right holding two drumsticks, "Walt Disney's Wonderful World of Color": 1960s showing of "From All of Us to All of You," 3-1/4 x 4-3/4", VF+, HL/Apr 25/98 (500-900) 489

Hem-up front view of Mary, Mary Quite Contrary standing holding sprinkling can, "The Truth About Mother Goose," 6-1/4 x 6", F, HL/Apr 25/98 (300-400) 316

LAYOUT ART

Original layout drawing of hand lettering of "Disneyland" likely used to paint cel for show opening, 3-1/4 x 10", 1954-55, HL/Oct 6/96 (300-400) 403

MODEL ART

Ozalid print of five head drawings of Lady speaking, heads 5", sheet 23-3/4 x 7-7/8", "A Story of Dogs" 1954, fissured, conservation mounted, SR/Fall/95 (200-400) 310

Color model drawing of Donald Duck introducing himself to Spike the bee; "The Mad Hermit of Chimney Butte," 1960; 11 x 14"; VF, HL/Apr 25/98 (300-500) 345

STORY ART

Story drawing of Tinker Bell adding pixie dust to American Motors Corp. logo for opening credits, 5 x 7", 1954-55, HL/Oct 6/96 (600-800) 805

TITLE ART

Title card: silhouette of Headless Horseman galloping across landscape in front of full moon, *The Adventures of Ichabod & Mr. Toad*; with original hand-lettered overlay "Ichabod" from Oct. 26, 1955 "Disneyland" TV show, 11 x 8", SR/Spring/95 (1200-1800) 1540

Full figure of smiling Tinker Bell (3-5/8") hovering on "n" in "Adventureland" amid pixie dust, hand-lettered title cel (10" wide) from "Disneyland" TV, 16-field, SR/Spring/95 (600-1200) 710

Title from trailer with Mickey & Donald on carousel horses, "Disney on Parade," 8-3/4" on two 16-field cels, color print background, SR/Fall/96 (200-500) 250

2-cel set-up from opening title sequence: title & opening curtain, 11-1/2 x 15", 1954-55, HL/Oct 6/96 (1000-1500) 1380

DISNEYLAND (SEE ANTHOLOGY SERIES)

DUCKTALES

CEL SET-UPS/ANIMATION DRAWINGS/LAYOUT ART

Scrooge & Donald in money bin, printed publication background, 8 x 10", CE/Dec 15/93 (400-600) 977

Nephews play in money bin, watercolor production background, matching animation drawings & layout, Walt Disney Company seal, 10 x 14-1/2" & smaller, CE/Dec 15/93 (450-600) 747

Scrooge McDuck raises arms, print background, 7", S/Dec 16/93 (500-700) 575

Matching cels & master tempera background of Uncle Scrooge, 2 nephews, Webbigail & Mrs. Beakley in library, 8-1/2 x 10", Disney label, VF, HL/Feb 26-27/94 (500-700) 715

Nephews stand atop Scrooge's money inside derelict building, master tempera background, 8 x 20", VF, HL/Apr 10/94 (800-1200) 672

Scrooge on hands & knees as Mrs. Beakley, Webby & 3 nephews watch, over master background, 7-1/2 x 10", with 2 matching animation drawings, Disney seal & certificate, HL/Nov 13/94 (1000-1500) 896

Matching cels & master background of Scrooge, Nephews & Webbigail plus 2 layouts & 4 animation drawings, 7 total, 8 x 10-1/2", circa 1988, VF, HL/Apr 23/95 (600-900) 728

Happy Uncle Scrooge admires golden harp, matching master background (tempera on background sheet) 9-1/2 x 10", circa 1988, HL/Mar 16-17/96 (400-500) 1495

Scrooge in cowboy hat & string tie holding cooking spoon close to mouth, watercolor production

background of ranch, 8", CE/Jun 20/96
(700-900) 920

2 cels from "Don't Give Up The Ship": full figure of
sailor Donald Duck throwing duffel bag off pier,
chest-up of worried sailor Donald wearing radio
headphones; 5-1/2 x 4-1/2", 4-1/2 x 6"; each
w/matching animation drawing & color-copy
background, HL/May 31/97 (400-600) 207

Full figures of hatless Uncle Scrooge standing looking
left as 3 nephews stand watching him, original
background of outdoors, with three matching
animation drawings plus 4th showing color
details for nephews' eyes, 8 x 10" & smaller,
HL/May 31/97 (400-600) 633

CELS – FULL FIGURE/ANIMATION DRAWINGS
4 cels & matching animation drawings of Scrooge
McDuck, thoughtful Launchpad McQuack &
two nephews in arctic gear, VF,
HL/Feb 26-27/94 (300-500) 440

Huey, Dewey, & Louie standing, with matching
drawings, 4-1/2 x 7-1/2", circa 1988,
HL/Mar 16-17/96 (150-250) 633

CELS – PARTIAL FIGURE/ANIMATION DRAWINGS
Matching portrait cel & animation drawing of smiling
Scrooge McDuck looking right, 6 x 4", F+,
HL/Feb 26-27/94 (150-200) 303

Donald reading *Monster Tales* book, 7-1/4", circa
1980s, CE/Dec 16/94 (600-800) 115

Waist-up portrait of Uncle Scrooge w/right arm raised,
index finger up, with matching animation
drawing, 6 x 4", HL/Feb 23/97 (100-200) 288

FUNNY, YOU DON'T LOOK 200
(SPECIAL, 1987)
CELS – PARTIAL FIGURE
Angry Donald Duck holding rope, looking left &
up; 6-1/2 x 6" cel image; inscribed by
animator/voice Tony Anselmo; VF+;
HL/Aug 6/95 (500-700) 952

GARGOYLES
Each lot in the Sotheby's June 10, 1995 auction contained an original hand-painted production background,
in most cases with its matching original hand-painted cel
or cels. Each set-up was actually used in production.
Each lot also came with a certificate of authenticity.
Unless otherwise noted, cels are vinyl acrylic on celluloid. A book is a paint-on-paper overlay that's the top-
most element on a cel set-up.

BACKGROUNDS/LAYOUT ART
Production background of New York City's skyline
w/stone gargoyles in foreground, watercolor
on paper w/3 overlays & one book, plus 2
matching background layouts, "Awakening
Part I," S/Jun 10/95 (1200-1800) 2875

Gouache production background of Museum of
Modern Art sculpture garden at night plus
2 matching background layouts, "The Edge,"
S/Jun 10/95 (800-1200) 920

Gouache pan production background of stone Goliath
against daytime sky plus matching background
layout, "The Thrill of The Hunt," S/Jun 10/95
(1000-1500) 1265

CEL SET-UPS/PRODUCTION DRAWINGS/LAYOUT ART
Day scene with Captain of guard in foreground &
castle tower w/gargoyles behind him, 3-cel
set-up w/matching gouache production background plus matching production drawing &
2 layouts, "Awakening Part I," S/Jun 10/95
(1000-1500) 920

"Goliath, we owe you our lives." Close-up of
Lexington, Broadway, Brooklyn, Demona,
Goliath & Captain on castle wall, 6-cel set-up
on matching gouache production background
plus matching layout, "Awakening Part I,"
S/Jun 10/95 (1800-2200) 1955

"We're too late!" Full figures of Goliath & Hudson
caught on ground in daylight, 4-cel set-up on
matching gouache production background,
plus 4 production drawings, "Awakening
Part I," S/Jun 10/95 (1500-2000) 1495

"I've been denied everything, even my revenge!"
Full figures of Goliath & Princess Katherine
on cliff, 2-cel set-up on matching gouache
production background plus matching
production drawing, "Awakening Part II,"
S/Jun 10/95 (1200-1800) 2300

David Xanatos in castle ruins, matching gouache

production background plus production
drawing & layout, "Awakening Part II,"
S/Jun 10/95 (800-1200) 690

Goliath disarms Elisa Maza, matching gouache
production background plus production
drawing & layout, "Awakening Part III,"
S/Jun 10/95 (800-1200) 1035

Near-full-figure closeup of Goliath standing on ledge,
2-cel set-up on matching gouache production
background plus 2 matching production
drawings & 2 layouts, "Awakening Part III,"
S/Jun 10/95 (1500-2000) 2070

"I've never seen so many wonders!" Brooklyn,
Lexington & Broadway inspect city from atop
skyscraper, 3-cel set-up on matching gouache
production background, plus layout & 3
matching production drawings, "Awakening
Part III," S/Jun 10/95 (1500-2000) 2185

Brooklyn, Broadway, Lexington & Hudson awaken
atop skyscraper, 6-cel set-up on matching
gouache pan production background plus 6
matching production drawings & 3 layouts,
"Awakening Part IV," S/Jun 10/95
(1200-1800) 1610

"Goliath, my love!" Demona appears in castle,
matching gouache production background
plus matching production drawing & 2
layouts, "Awakening Part IV,"
S/Jun 10/95 (800-1200) 920

"I have promised to meet a friend." Close-up of
Goliath behind Demona w/right hand on her
shoulder, 2-cel set-up on matching gouache
production background plus 2 matching
production drawings & 3 layouts, "Awakening
Part V," S/Jun 10/95 (1000-1500) 1265

Demona looks back w/hand on shrouded robot
gargoyle, 4-cel set-up on matching gouache
production background plus layout & 4
matching production drawings, "Awakening
Part V," S/Jun 10/95 (1000-1500) 920

"...I think I'm going to like this century." Brooklyn,
Lexington & Broadway atop skyscraper trying
computer & Chinese food, 5-cel set-up on
matching production background plus layout
& 4 production drawings, "Awakening
Part V," S/Jun 10/95 (1200-1800) 1150

Extreme close-up of stunned Goliath, matching
gouache production background, plus matching
production drawing & layout, "Awakening
Part V," S/Jun 10/95 (800-1200) 690

Goliath, Brooklyn, Broadway & Lexington crouching
together, 4-cel set-up on matching gouache
production background plus layout,
"The Edge," S/Jun 10/95 (1200-1800) 1035

Long shot of Broadway, Brooklyn, Goliath &
Lexington gliding toward Statue of Liberty,
matching gouache production background plus
matching production drawing & 2 layouts,
"The Edge," S/Jun 10/95 (1200-1800) 2300

Broadway[?] glides upward with Statue of Liberty
in background, matching gouache pan
production background plus matching
production drawing & layout, "The Edge,"
S/Jun 10/95 (1200-1800) 1840

Broadway[?] gliding in front of Statue of Liberty,
large matching gouache pan production
background w/book, plus matching
production drawing & layout, "The Edge,"
S/Jun 10/95 (1000-1500) 920

Demona talks to Brooklyn, 2-cel set-up on matching
gouache production background plus layout
and 2 matching production drawings,
"Temptation," S/Jun 10/95 (800-1200) 805

Brooklyn brings Grimorum (book of spells) to
Demona, 2-cel set-up on matching gouache
production background plus layout & 2
matching production drawings, "Temptation,"
S/Jun 10/95 (1000-1500) 805

Long shot of Demona & Goliath standing in hall,
2-cel set-up on matching gouache production
background plus layout & 2 matching
production drawings, "Temptation,"
S/Jun 10/95 (1200-1800) 2185

Full figure of Demona gliding thru castle, matching
gouache production background plus layout &
matching production drawing, "Temptation,"
S/Jun 10/95 (1000-1500) 805

Owen Burnett escorts Elisa to castle tower & stone
Goliath, matching gouache production

back-ground w/book plus matching
production drawing & layout, "The Thrill
of The Hunt," S/Jun 10/95 (800-1200) 1495

Owen & Elisa walk atop tower amid "sleeping"
gargoyles, matching gouache production
background w/book, plus layout & 3
matching production drawings, "The Thrill
of The Hunt," S/Jun 10/95 (1000-1500) 1380

Close-up of stone Goliath cracking awake, 2-cel
set-up on matching gouache production
background w/book of Goliath in stone plus
2 matching production drawings, "The Thrill
of The Hunt," S/Jun 10/95 (800-1200) 805

Lexington, Brooklyn & Broadway atop tower wall
ready to explore, 3-cel set-up on matching
gouache production background plus layout
& 4 matching production drawings, "The Thrill
of The Hunt," S/Jun 10/95 (1000-1500) 805

Hudson & Bronx watching TV & using remote, 4-cel
set-up on matching gouache production background plus layout, "The Thrill of The Hunt,"
S/Jun 10/95 (800-1200) 690

Angry Lexington & Goliath realize they've been
trapped, 2-cel set-up on matching gouache
production background plus 2 matching
production drawings & 2 layouts, "The Thrill
of The Hunt," S/Jun 10/95 (1000-1500) 805

Close-up of Goliath in alert pose, 3-cel set-up on
matching gouache production background,
plus layout & 2 matching production
drawings, "The Thrill of The Hunt,"
S/Jun 10/95 (1000-1500) 805

Fox hunts Lexington & Goliath amid rooftop statuary
gargoyles, matching gouache production background plus layout & matching production
drawing, "The Thrill of The Hunt,"
S/Jun 10/95 (1000-1500) 2070

Overhead view of rooftop as The Pack convenes,
matching gouache production background plus
matching production drawing, "The Thrill
of The Hunt," S/Jun 10/95 (800-1200) 1265

Full figure of Goliath flying thru park carrying Elisa
Maza, 5-1/2 x 8-1/2", gouache on celluloid,
color reproduction of original background,
seal & certificate, VF+, "Awakening Part IV,"
HL/May 31/97 (200-400) 58

GUMMI BEARS
CELS/ANIMATION DRAWINGS
Waist-up of smiling Tummi holding melon with bird
looking over shoulder; full figure of happy
Toadwort walking to left carrying keg; one
matching animation drawing; 6-1/2 x 4-1/2",
5-1/2 x 6-1/2"; VF+; HL/Apr 23/95
(300-400) 252

Waist-up of Tummi holding Gruffi's arm; full figure
of happy Toadwort walking to left carrying
keg; both w/matching original animation
drawings; late 1980s; 7 x 4-1/2" & 8 x 9";
VF; HL/Nov 19/95 (300-400) 345

THE LITTLE MERMAID
(1989 MCDONALD'S COMMERCIAL)
CEL SET-UPS
Ariel, Flounder, Sebastian watch people eat,
5-1/4 x 8", 3 cels matched to black-&-white
photoprint of live-action footage, VF+,
HL/Apr 23/95 (500-700) 784

CELS – FULL FIGURE
Ariel (on her back) & Flounder face each other,
3 x 7", VF, HL/Aug 21/94 (600-900) 560

Ariel & Flounder face each other, with bubbles,
5-1/2 x 9", VF+, HL/Nov 19/95 (600-800) 633

THE MICKEY MOUSE CLUB
ANIMATION DRAWINGS
Full-figure drawing of smiling Mickey as cowboy,
4-1/2 x 3-1/2", HL/Nov 19/95 (300-500) 460

Full-figure drawing of happy Bandleader Mickey
(eyes closed) marching to right, 4-1/2 x 3
-1/2", HL/Oct 6/96 (300-400) 575

Full-figure front-view drawing of bandleader Mickey
marching, 8 x 3-1/2", VF, HL/Apr 25/98
(200-400) 863

CEL SET-UPS
Jiminy pointing with umbrella, lithographic
background, S/Dec 16/93 (500-700) 690

Full figure of Jiminy Cricket in plaid deerstalker cap standing facing right, 4", gouache master background from *Paul Bunyan*, SR/Fall/94 (300-600) 330

Full figure of smiling Jiminy Cricket standing facing left, looking into camera, holding umbrella vertically at both ends, 5-5/8", DL litho background of castle wall, gold Art Corner label, some paint discoloration, SR/Fall/94 (300-600) 480

Bandleader Mickey with trombone from Circus Day, 4-1/2 x 4", complementary background painting, HL/Nov 13/94 (1800-2400) 1624

Full figure of Jiminy Cricket, 4-3/4", DL background & label, CE/Dec 16/94 (600-800) 460

Full-figure front view of Jiminy Cricket standing holding stack of cards, 7", DL line-drawing background of teapot, gold Art Corner label, ct, SR/Spring/95 (400-700) 410

Daisy, Minnie, & Clarabelle hold trampoline for Bandleader Mickey (full-figure front view sitting, 5"), solid-color master background from "You, the Human Animal" 1956, ct, SR/Spring/95 (2600-3400) 3080

Full-figure front view of smiling Jiminy Cricket pointing at himself with left thumb, at camera with umbrella, 5-1/2", DL litho background of outdoors, SR/Fall/95 (400-700) 550

Full figure of happy Sorcerer Mickey standing on stage, 5", 12-field, color print background, SR/Fall/95 (1500-2500) 1760

Full figures of Huey & Dewey riding on flying Dumbo's back holding cards, Louie hanging onto tail, 6-7/8", gouache display background of sky, SR/Fall/95 (600-1200) 990

Row of 3 Mouseketrumpeters, 9-3/4 x 6", two levels, key master watercolor background, 16-field, ct, SR/Fall/96 (1100-2000) 1000

Full figure of smiling Jiminy Cricket standing outdoors holding furled umbrella, 5-1/2 x 3-3/4" cel image, color print background, HL/Oct 6/96 (500-700) 805

Full-figure front view of Bandleader Mickey standing on stage pointing w/baton, 3-1/2", presentation background, S/Jun 21/97 (1000-1500) 920

Full figure of Mickey standing on stage smiling into camera & adjusting bow tie from Guest Star Day intro, 11 x 22-1/2", matching original master background pan (tempera on pan background sheet), F-VF, HL/Nov 16/97 (6000-9000) 4600

Full figure of Bandleader Mickey standing on stage for Circus Day, Studio Art props background, 4-1/4 x 4-3/4" cel, VF, HL/Apr 25/98 (1000-1500) 1725

CELS – FULL FIGURE/ANIMATION ART

Jiminy Cricket, 4-1/2 x 2-1/2", VF+, HL/Apr 10/94 (500-700) 560

Smiling standing Mickey gestures to right, from Tuesday opening, 6 x 6", VF+, HL/Apr 10/94 (1400-1800) 2016

Large image of smiling Jiminy Cricket standing playing with yo-yo, 7 x 5-1/2", backing board w/label as sold at DL's Art Corner, F, HL/Apr 10/94 (600-800) 1232

Bandleader Mickey twirls baton, 5-1/2", circa 1950, S/Jun 17/94 (2000-3000) 1610

Mickey in bandleader uniform holds film reel, 5", CE/Jun 18/94 (1500-2000) 1955

Rear view of Goofy (6") walking away with clipboard, CE/Jun 18/94 (600-800) 460

2-level full figure of Jiminy Cricket, DL label, 6 x 4", VF, HL/Aug 21/94 (600-800) 476

Bandleader Mickey (back turned) sitting on trampoline held by friends (partial figures), backing board & label as sold at DL, 8-1/2 x 11-1/2", F+, HL/Aug 21/94 (1200-1600) 1792

2 cels of Jiminy Cricket: full figure strutting to right; ankle-up front view tipping hat; mats & labels as sold at DL; 4 x 6", 4 x 3"; VG-VF; HL/Aug 21/94 (500-700) 784

Smiling Bandleader Mickey in air w/hats & confetti, w/label & stamp as sold at DL's Art Corner, 6 x 8", F, HL/Aug 21/94 (1500-2000) 1568

Surprised Donald stands facing right, holding mallet, looking straight up with mouth open, 4-3/4", 16-field, SR/Fall/94 (400-700) 520

Front view of Jiminy Cricket standing with right hand up showing four fingers, 4" in top hat,

gold Art Corner label, original Carefree Corner envelope, SR/Fall/94 (300-600) 420

Mickey in dancing pose with spats, striped coat, straw hat, & cane, 6", SR/Fall/94 (1400-1800) 1400

Mickey as cowboy, 4-1/2 x 3-1/2", as sold at DL with associated papers, HL/Nov 13/94 (1000-1500) 1568

2 cels of Jiminy Cricket, 5" & similar, DL sticker & stamp, CE/Dec 16/94 (800-1000) 978

Full-figure frontal of Jiminy Cricket, 6-1/2", CE/Dec 16/94 (500-700) 805

Full-figure frontal of smiling Jiminy Cricket pointing, 6", DL label, CE/Dec 16/94 (600-800) 575

Smiling Jiminy Cricket floating down under umbrella, holding match, 3", 16-field, crease in corner, SR/Spring/95 (200-400) 310

Jiminy Cricket stands wearing mittens, 5-1/2 x 4", HL/Apr 23/95 (400-600) 532

Jiminy Cricket faces left & holds yo-yo, 6 x 4-1/2", HL/Apr 23/95 (400-600) 476

Jiminy Cricket standing, 5", DL label, CE/Jun 9/95 (600-800) 460

Front view of happy Jiminy Cricket w/head back, mouth open, left hand up (in greeting?), 3-3/4", 16-field, SR/Fall/95 (400-800) 425

Stunned Donald Duck holds gong mallet, 5 x 3", VF+, HL/Nov 19/95 (800-1200) 805

Mickey being bounced on trampoline by friends (partial figures), 8 x 10", VF+, HL/Nov 19/95 (3000-4000) 3220

Whistling Jiminy Cricket walking right, looking back, 7-3/8", gold DL Art Corner label & stamp, SR/Spring/96 (400-600) 490

Donald Duck holds mallet & stands by gong with crazed eyes, 6 x 7", HL/Apr 28/96 (1200-1600) 1150

Jiminy Cricket floats thru air under umbrella, 4 x 2-1/2", HL/Apr 28/96 (400-600) 546

Full figure of smiling Dumbo as Jiminy Cricket & Timothy Mouse hold signs spelling "MICKEY" in his hat, 8", CE/Jun 20/96 (1000-1500) 2070

Jiminy Cricket stands facing left, "I'm No Fool" series, 6", SR/Fall/96 (400-700) 540

Front view of happy Donald (3-1/2") tossed in air by 8 characters standing around trampoline (waist-up, looking down), 16-field cels, SR/Fall/96 (700-1200) 1120

Confused Jiminy Cricket pivoting at waist to look back [toward camera], holding umbrella & glasses, 5 x 3", HL/Oct 6/96 (500-700) 546

Eager Jiminy Cricket in deerstalker cap atop ox pulling hay cart to left, 4-1/4 x 7-1/2", HL/Oct 6/96 (300-500) 489

Tinker Bell, circa 1950s, 4", CE/Dec 12/96 (700-900) 690

2 items: full-figure production cel of Mickey playing piano in spotlight from "Music Day" opening, 4-3/4 x 4"; photo of publicity still from series; S/Dec 14/96 (800-1200) 1380

Front view of grinning Jiminy Cricket standing, 4-3/8", gold DL Art Corner label, SR/Spring/97 (400-700) 410

Mickey, 3-3/4"; 3 near-full-figure animation drawings of Mickey from *Mickey's Elephant*, 1936, 6-1/2"; CLA/Jun 7/97 (1200-1500) 1150

Jiminy Cricket in coonskin cap stands facing left, looking into camera, 4-3/4", gold DL Art Corner label, ct, SR/Fall/97 (600-800) 400

Full-figure front view of Jiminy Cricket standing holding hat; 4-1/4"; DL mat, color card background, gold Art Corner label; signed by Ward Kimball; small chip in his foot; SR/Fall/97 (900-1200) 725

Front view of smiling Jiminy Cricket standing with arms spread, 3-3/4 x 4", VF, HL/Nov 16/97 (400-600) 518

Front view of smiling Bandleader Mickey falling thru air in sitting position, 6-1/2 x 3", as sold at DL, VG+, HL/Nov 16/97 (800-1000) 1035

Front view of standing Jiminy Cricket looking & pointing left, 4-1/16", SR/Spring/98 (300-600) 350

CELS – PARTIAL FIGURE

Near-full figure of Jiminy Cricket lifting sheet with closed umbrella, 1950s, 4", CE/Jun 9/95 (700-900) 805

2 cels of Jiminy Cricket: knees-up front view bowing; unidentified; 5-3/4" & smaller; CE/Jun 9/95 (1000-1500) 978

Near-full figure of bandleader Mickey lifting baton [standing in water?], 3-1/2", S/Jun 19/96 (800-1200) 805

Large-image portrait of serious Jiminy Cricket in deerstalker hat looking left & up, backing board with label as sold at DL, signed by Ward Kimball, 7-1/4 x 6-1/2", F+, HL/Feb 23/97 (300-400) 460

Near-full figure of confident Jiminy Cricket standing w/eyes closed & hands on jacket lapels, 4 x 2-1/2", HL/May 31/97 (200-300) 104

TITLE ART

3 original drawings for opening titles: flashing neon "Walt Disney" & "and Mickey Mouse", layout for background of billboard set atop skyscrapers against starry sky; 1955; 3 x 4-1/2", 3 x 4", 11-1/2 x 14-1/2"; HL/Oct 6/96 (1000-1500) 834

MICKEY'S 60TH BIRTHDAY (SPECIAL, 1988)
CELS/ANIMATION DRAWINGS

Full figure of panicked Roger Rabbit tangled in rope; near-full figure of smiling Mickey on knees facing left & pointing; both with matching animation drawings, 5 x 5", 7-1/2 x 5", HL/May 31/97 (600-900) 518

THE NEW ADVENTURES OF WINNIE THE POOH
Also see SHORTS & FEATURETTES: multiple WINNIE THE POOH titles; UNIDENTIFIED/MISCELLANEOUS: WINNIE THE POOH
CEL SET-UPS

Full figures of Piglet standing & watching Tigger who's just bounced Pooh, 9 x 12-1/4, color print of master background, HL/Aug 6/95 (800-1000) 896

Full figures of thoughtful Pooh, happy Tigger, & scared Rabbit in woods; 3-1/2", 3-3/8", & 3" on three 12-field cels; key color print pan background; Disney Art Program seals & certificates, overall 43-3/4 x 8"; SR/Fall/97 (900-1400) 625

PETER PAN PEANUT BUTTER COMMERCIALS (1950S)
CELS – FULL FIGURE

Smiling Tinker Bell flying to right, 5-3/4" long, with wings, circa 1955, SR/Spring/96 (300-600) 510

Smiling Tinker Bell holding knife; in black, white & grey; 3-1/4 x 2-1/2", HL/Apr 28/96 (400-600) 403

Smiling Tinker Bell diving amid pixie dust, 2-1/2", DL mat, color card background, & gold Art Corner label, SR/Fall/97 (450-600) 300

UNIDENTIFIED TV
CEL SET-UPS/ANIMATION DRAWINGS

4" Tinker Bell & 3" Jiminy Cricket; 5" Donald swinging mallet w/2-1/2" Jiminy in chef's hat; each w/print background, each w/gold DL label, circa 1955, S/Dec 16/93 (800-1200) 805

Donald Duck cowering, 7-1/2 x 9", color print background, DL label, restored, VF, HL/Apr 10/94 (300-500) 336

2 cels: full figure of startled Donald Duck, dressed in suit & hat & walking with lunch pail, color print background; Ludwig Von Drake singing from music, guitar slung over shoulder; 8 x 10" & 6 x 7-1/2", both with labels & as sold at DL, HL/Nov 13/94 (500-700) 504

Full figure of worried Goofy water skiing to left, 8 x 10", color print background, in mat with DL label, VF, HL/Feb 26-27/94 (500-700) 715

Mickey in formal dress gesturing, 1960s, color print background, DL label, 10-1/2 x 8-1/2", HL/Aug 21/94 (1200-1600) 1120

Mickey Mouse & Donald Duck in 5 cels from early 1980s TV commercials, 4-1/2 x 4" to 5-1/2 x 5-1/2", one w/animation drawing, one w/background print, HL/Apr 23/95 (1000-1200) 1008

Four circa 1960s TV production cels of Jiminy Cricket: wearing Sherlock Holmes-style hat & talking to cattail, 4", printed DL background. Other 3: standing & smiling, approx. 2" ea.;

S/Dec 14/96 (300-500) 805
Full figure of José Carioca walking to right in country, looking & pointing up with umbrella; 1960s; color print background; 5-1/2 x 6", HL/Feb 23/97 (100-150) 178
2 full-figure cels of Jiminy Cricket, circa 1950s, 5" & 7", printed DL Art Corner backgrounds, S/Jun 21/97 (600-800) 920

CELS – FULL FIGURE
Jiminy Cricket waving to flying Tinker Bell; Tinker Bell waving wand; Donald swinging mallet as Jiminy looks on; each with gold DL label; circa 1955, S/Dec 16/93 (1000-1500) 1840
Jiminy Cricket as Sherlock Holmes, gold DL label, 4-1/2", S/Dec 16/93 (400-600) 575
Donald laughing as he holds Chip & Dale, 5 x 5", VF+, HL/Apr 10/94 (500-700) 952
Pluto jumping & licking Ludwig Von Drake, 5-1/2 x 8", VF+, HL/Apr 10/94 (500-800) 476
Jiminy Cricket brandishing umbrella, 1960, 5", S/Jun 17/94 (300-500) 230
Donald Duck & nephew, 1950s, probably TV, 4-1/2 x 4-1/2", HL/Aug 21/94 (500-700) 616
Jiminy Cricket, 1950s, 4 x 4", HL/Nov 13/94 (400-500) 420
Matched pair of full-figure cels of Chip & Dale, 1960s, 5 x 3" & 4-1/2 x 4", HL/Nov 13/94 (500-700) 840
Large-image full figure of Jiminy Cricket as friendly TV host, 1960s, 6 x 5", HL/Nov 13/94 (400-500) 728
Production cel of dwarf Happy (eyes closed) walking merrily along to right, 6", circa 1955, gold DL label, S/Dec 17/94 (200-400) 143
Donald Duck as beekeeper, 7 x 7", 1960s, HL/Apr 23/95 (300-500) 616
2 expressive full-figure cels of Jiminy Cricket, 6 x 4" & 5-1/2 x 5", 1960s, HL/Apr 23/95 (600-800) 1344
Donald Duck & José Carioca, 3 x 6", 1960, HL/Apr 23/95 (600-800) 532
Production cel of Sorcerer Mickey waving as he floats on carpet, 4-1/2", silver Walt Disney Television Production stamp, S/Jun 10/95 (800-1200) 920
Angry Donald Duck as admiral, 1960s, 5 x 3", HL/Aug 6/95 (500-700) 728
Eager Pluto jumps on Ludwig Von Drake, 1960s, 5-1/2 x 8-1/2", HL/Aug 6/95 (300-400) 532
Front view of determined Donald Duck in fireman's coat & hat pointing at camera, 1960s, 8 x 5-1/2", HL/Nov 19/95 (300-500) 575
Smiling Jiminy Cricket, 1950s, 5 x 4-1/4", HL/Mar 16-17/96 (400-600) 748
Front view of smiling Jiminy Cricket walking, 1950s, WDP art program seal, 6 x 3-1/2", HL/Apr 28/96 (500-800) 920
Determined Sorcerer Mickey gestures to right with both hands as he stands inside a jagged flash on a dark background, 4-1/2", S/Jun 19/96 (800-1200) 747
Exuberant Tinker Bell with arms up, 1960s, 5-1/4 x 3-1/2", HL/Oct 6/96 (400-600) 805
Confident Dumbo flies holding feather in trunk with Timothy riding in cap, 1950s, 3-3/4 x 5-3/4", HL/Oct 6/96 (700-1000) 1035
3 TV commercial cels of Mickey Mouse: as Sorcerer's Apprentice clutching wand; as conductor in red tie & tux; on knees smiling w/hand to ear; circa 1980s, approx. 4" each, S/Dec 14/96 (700-900) 805
Smiling Jiminy Cricket facing right, 1950s, 5 x 4-1/4", VF, HL/Nov 16/97 (600-900) 805

CELS – PARTIAL FIGURE
Donald Duck in Lake Titicaca outfit looking thru binoculars, 3 x 5", VF+, HL/Feb 26-27/94 (400-600) 220
Large image of Donald as beekeeper on tiptoes facing left, looking down, right hand up, left hand not shown, 8 x 6", VF+, HL/Feb 26-27/94 (300-400) 330
3 cels of Mickey: hips-up front view smiling with arms out; 2 unidentified; circa 1970s; probably from commercial; 7" & similar; CE/Jun 9/95 (800-1200) 1610
Large image of Donald Duck reading *Monster Tales* book, 1960s, 7-1/4 x 6-1/2", VF+, HL/Oct 6/96 (400-600) 460
2 torso-up large images of Donald Duck: front view

of puzzled Donald shrugging, nervous Donald looking into camera; 1980s; both w/matching animation drawings; 7-1/2 x 8" & 8-1/2 x 5", HL/May 31/97 (400-600) 288
Hips-up image of eager Professor Owl, circa 1959, 5 x 5", HL/May 31/97 (125-200) 127

WALT DISNEY PRESENTS (SEE ANTHOLOGY SERIES)

WALT DISNEY'S WONDERFUL WORLD OF COLOR (SEE ANTHOLOGY SERIES)

THE WUZZLES
CEL SET-UPS/ANIMATION DRAWINGS/LAYOUT ART
Close-up of scheming Bumblelion looking over shoulder, matching master background (tempera on background sheet), w/matching animation drawing & background layout, 8 x 10", seal, HL/Nov 13/94 (500-700) 448
Over-the-hood front view of Croc, Flizard, & Brat driving car, 9-3/4 x 6" on 5 cel levels, key master background; plus animation drawing of trio from same sequence, SR/Fall/97 (225-400) 150

THEME PARK
This section is organized alphabetically by production, then chronologically by auction.

BACK TO NEVERLAND (DISNEY-MGM STUDIOS)
CELS – PARTIAL FIGURE
Matching cels of Robin Williams as Lost Boy on head of angry crocodile, 5 x 8", Disney seal, VF+, HL/Apr 10/94 (1000-1500) 1680

CRANIUM COMMAND (EPCOT)
CELS – FULL FIGURE
Imposing General Knowledge, 6-1/2 x 5-1/2", VF+, HL/Feb 26-27/94 (500-700) 715
Buzzy & Gen. Knowledge, 5 x 7", Disney seal, HL/Nov 13/94 (500-700) 1008
CELS – PARTIAL FIGURE
Large waist-up image of Gen. Knowledge holding pad of paper, 1989, 6 x 9", with Disney seal & presentation letter, VF+, HL/Aug 6/95 (600-900) 1120

EPCOT MISCELLANEOUS
CEL SET-UPS
Mickey in spacesuit floats on moon with Earth in background, watercolor production background, 9-1/4 x 13-3/4", CE/Dec 15/93 (500-900) 1035

Space-suited Mickey Mouse on Moon, 1980s, complementary background from another studio, 4-1/2 x 4-1/2", HL/Aug 21/94 (500-700) 784
Full-figure front view of smiling astronaut Mickey Mouse floating in space, circa 1980 "likely created for an in-studio or theme park film.", complementary painted background, 4-1/4 x 4-1/2", VF, HL/Feb 23/97 (400-600) 633
Mickey in space suit, 4-1/2", watercolor production background; waist-up front view of Mickey & Donald harmonizing from *Prince & The*

Pauper, 8", unidentified background; CE/Dec 18/97 (800-1200) 1495
CELS – FULL FIGURE
Front view of smiling Mickey Mouse floating in space suit, 5", circa 1980s, CE/Jun 18/94 (600-800) 288
Mickey Mouse in space suit, circa 1980s, 4", CE/Dec 16/94 (300-400) 253

UNIDENTIFIED/MISCELLANEOUS
Also see UNIDENTIFIED TV
This section is organized alphabetically by character or category, then chronologically. Art with more than one major character is under "Combinations."

ALICE COMEDIES
MODEL ART
Sheet of model drawings of Julius the Cat, mid-1920s, 8-1/2 x 10-1/2", VF, HL/Apr 23/95 (1500-2000) 2688

BOOTLE BEETLE
CELS – FULL FIGURE
Elderly Bootle Beetle stands on leaf and opens casserole, late 1940s, 5-1/2", CE/Jun 18/94 (500-700) 690
Elderly Bootle Beetle stands holding casserole & lecturing, 1940s, 6", CE/Dec 16/94 (600-800) 403

CHIP 'N' DALE
Also see TELEVISION: ANTHOLOGY SERIES
ANIMATION DRAWINGS
18 pencil drawings from Christmas film, 1950s or 1960s, 4 x 3-1/2" to 7-1/2 x 11", VF, HL/Apr 10/94 (800-1200) 1344
CEL SET-UPS
Happy Chip standing on tree branch, 3", non-studio hand-prepared background, S/Dec 17/94 (400-600) 460
CELS – FULL FIGURE
Confused Chip {Dale?} looking right, 1950s, 3-1/2 x 2-1/2", F+, HL/Feb 26-27/94 (150-200) 248
Chip & Dale dance cheek-to-cheek in mirror image, 1950s, 3 x 4", VF+, HL/Aug 21/94 (300-400) 728
Full standing figures of happy Chip & Dale, 1950s, gold DL label, 3-1/2 x 5-1/2", VF, HL/Apr 23/95 (400-600) 840
5 cels of Chip & Dale, 4-1/2", CE/Jun 9/95 (1500-2000) 1495
Chip & Dale in nightclothes with "Now!" above them in script, circa 1950s, 5" & similar, cel applied to blue construction paper, CE/Jun 9/95 (400-600) 253
Chip (all but left foot) runs left with upset Dale hanging on around his neck, circa 1960s, 7" long, CE/Jun 9/95 (300-500) 230
Chip yelling at Dale, 1950s, 4 x 5-1/2", as sold at DL, VF, HL/Aug 6/95 (600-800) 560
Chip (4-1/4") running up to sleeping Dale, 1950s?, SR/Fall/95 (600-1200) 600
Jaggedly drawn Dale in sitting position with arms out, 1950s, 3 x 3", VF+, HL/Feb 23/97 (200-300) 345
Eager Dale sits facing right, 3-1/2", 16-field cel, SR/Fall/97 (300-500) 220
Panicked Chip running right with arms up, Dale looking left in leaning pose; 3-7/8" & 3"; original color card background, gold DL Art Corner label; SR/Fall/97 (900-1400) 725
MODEL ART
Two Chip & Dale model sheets, 13-7/8 x 11" original studio prints, one sheet touched up with pencil & white paint, SR/Fall/96 (100-300) 570

CLARA CLUCK
CELS – FULL FIGURE
Full-figure portrait of Clara Cluck, 5", circa 1950s, CE/Jun 18/94 (400-600) 219
CONCEPT AND INSPIRATIONAL ART
2 sheets of head studies of Clara Cluck, from estate of Les Clark, mid-1930s, 5 x 10" & 5 x 9", F+, HL/Nov 16/97 (300-400) 345

COMBINATIONS OF MAJOR CHARACTERS

ANIMATION DRAWINGS

17 rough drawings of Mickey riding magic carpet, 3" & similar; 11 rough drawings of Pluto, 3" & similar; 1930s; all full figure, eyes open except one, extremely fragile; CE/Dec 18/97 (2000-3000) 2300

ART – MISCELLANEOUS

Full-figure drawing of Donald, Daisy & three nephews relaxing on beach, 16-7/8 x 8-3/4" vellum sheet signed by Mike Royer, for consumer products, center vertical fold, SR/Spring/96 (150-300) 150

CEL SET-UPS

Full figures of Mickey (4-1/2") as farmer petting Pluto (4 x 3-1/2"), circa 1950s, watercolor production background, CE/Jun 18/94 (6000-8000) 4600

Full figures of standing Mickey (holding hat) & sitting Pluto admiring smiling soldier Donald standing holding rifle vertically, 3 x 6" & similar, circa 1940s, watercolor background, CE/Jun 18/94 [also see *The New Spirit* & Cels - Full Figure] (1500-2000) 2990

Full figures of Donald (4-1/2 x 3") & 3 nephews (2-1/2 x 1") in winter getting snow skis off car, circa 1980s, key watercolor production background, CE/Jun 18/94 (1000-1500) 2185

Donald plays duet with girl on upright piano as Minnie [Mickey?] watches over top, 2 cels over black & white phone print of corresponding live action from Coca-Cola film, 1988, seal, 8-1/2" x 14, VF+, HL/Aug 21/94 (700-1000) 672

Full-figure promotional cel of Mickey, Minnie, Donald & Pluto walking happily together, each approx. 2-1/2", unidentified background of outdoors, S/Dec 17/94 (2500-3000) 1495

Full figures of Tinker Bell (from *Disneyland* TV series) leaving pixie-dust trail by one of Donald Duck's nephews (facing left) from a cartoon of the same period; color print background of forest as sold at DL 7 x 8-1/2", 1950s, VF, HL/Apr 23/95 (600-800) 896

Circa 1930s promotional cel of Donald (2-1/2") tying red balloon to Pluto (3") who has purple balloon tied to collar, printed background, S/Jun 10/95 (1500-2000) 805

2 full-figure cels: front view of shocked Donald Duck amid flying debris (debris circa 1940 complementary Disney animation drawing); sleepy Goofy in night clothes sitting on *edge* of bed; both 1960s; 7-1/2 x 8" & 5-1/2 x 7"; F; HL/Oct 6/96 (400-600) 518

Crowd of eager Disney characters hurrying left with luggage, 1979 Eastern Airlines commercial, 12 x 8-1/8", 12-field cel, color print background of castle from same commercial, SR/Spring/97 (300-600) 770

Full figures of standing Mickey (holding hat) & sitting Pluto admiring smiling soldier Donald standing holding rifle upright, circa 1943 for war bonds, original patterned background & backing board, 3-1/4 x 6-1/2", HL/May 3/97 [also see *The New Spirit* & Cels - Full Figure] (1500-2000) 1495

José Carioca (5") dancing as Donald Duck (in blue shirt & cap, 5-1/2") reaches behind him; José (5-1/2") standing w/cigar in hand, arms crossed, eyes closed; each w/printed DL background & gold label; S/Jun 21/97 (600-800) 575

Chef Donald (6-1/2") & birthday cake from *Sleeping Beauty*; full figure of Daisy (5-1/2") looking over shoulder as she stands holding mannequin; one of Donald's nephews on skates, 5"; nephew wearing cap holding arms out, 4"; all with printed DL backgrounds & gold labels, S/Jun 21/97 (1200-1800) 1150

2 cels: full figures of Dale holding Chip like baby, 4-1/2"; Pluto yawning, 3"; both on printed backgrounds, S/Jun 21/97 (800-1200) 1150

CELS – FULL FIGURE

Giant cel of smiling & waving Mickey, Minnie, Donald, Goofy & Pluto (partly behind others), probably for publicity, 1950s, lithograph on celluloid, 60-1/4 x 30", CE/Dec 15/93 (600-800) 5980

4" Mickey & 3-1/3" Donald underneath station sign stand waving to Minnie (waist up) in passenger-car window, S/Dec 16/93 (3000-4000) 2875

Mickey talking to wary Pluto, both 4", 1940s, CE/Jun 18/94 (2500-3500) 2530

2 cels: full figure of Ludwig Von Drake lecturing; waist-up front view of deliriously happy average-man Goofy [gazing into auto showroom]; 1960s; 6-1/2 x 4", 7-1/2 x 7"; VF+; HL/Aug 21/94 (900-1200) 1232

J. Audubon Woodlore as civilian walking to left with & talking to Donald Duck, 1950s, 6 x 5-1/2", F+, HL/Aug 21/94 (500-700) 728

Ludwig Von Drake holding pink umbrella, 6"; full-figure profile of Humphrey the Bear, 7"; Huey, Dewey & Louie with identical red shirts & expressions, 3-1/2" each; S/Dec 17/94 (300-500) 287

Pluto barking angrily, 8"; Chip & Dale, each 2-1/2"; S/Dec 17/94 (800-1200) 690

2 cels: Donald stands facing toward right with hands on hips, smiling into camera; excited Daisy standing with hands out, facing left; 1940s, both 6-1/4", 12-field, ct, SR/Spring/95 (600-1000) 1380

2 cels: excited Pluto walking right, looking left in mid-stride, 4-1/4"; demure Dinah stands facing right, looking up, 3-1/2"; 1940s, 12-field, ct, SR/Spring/95 (800-1200) 800

Standing Mickey (holding hat) & sitting Pluto admire smiling soldier Donald standing holding rifle vertically, 3 x 6", circa 1943, special cel for purchasers of war bonds, VF, HL/Apr 23/95 [also see *The New Spirit* & Cel Set-ups] (1000-1500) 1792

Mickey, Goofy, Minnie, Donald & Pluto in overlapping classic poses, circa 1950, sight: 40-1/2 x 11-1/2", lithograph on celluloid, CE/Jun 9/95 (800-1200) 552

Promotional cel: full figures of excited Minnie standing talking to attentive Mickey outdoors, both 4-1/2", 1930s, S/Jun 10/95 (2500-3000) 2185

3 commercial production cels: full figure of Donald's nephews riding jet-ski on wave, each nephew 2-1/2"; close-up portrait of Uncle Scrooge w/dollar signs in eyes, 7-1/2"; near-full figure of Uncle Scrooge driving car thru gold coins, 9"; circa 1970; S/Jun 10/95 (400-600) 1495

Promotional cel of Mickey (1"), Donald (1-1/2") & Goofy (2") sailing to left on steam-powered tugboat, S/Jun 10/95 (700-900) 920

Front view of Jiminy Cricket standing looking right in presentation pose, 5-3/4"; front views of Jiminy (2") in dancing pose & Boss (left hand raised, 4-3/4") standing side by side; Jiminy from "Mickey Mouse Club," Boss (J. Audubon Woodlore) from "Duck For Hire"?; both with gold DL Art Corner labels, some lifting paint, SR/Fall/95 (300-600) 630

7 cels: Bent-Tail with mouth & eyes open, paw raised, looking to left; Grandpappy Coyote lecturing Bent-Tail Jr.; 4 coyotes howling; Bent-Tail walking to left; 2 of J. Audubon Woodlore; upset Grandpa Duck clutching musket (*No Hunting*, 1955); S/Dec 14/96 (500-700) 575

3 cels: Mickey & Minnie holding balloons, being blown away, 4-3/4"; tree, grass, & flowers being blown by fierce wind, 4-1/2"; Pluto & Donald w/balloons, airborne in wind, 4-3/4"; 1940, for Heath book *Here They Are*; ct; SR/Spring/97 (500-900) 1250

Pluto enthusiastically licks face of struggling Ludwig Von Drake, 1960s, 5-1/4 x 7", VF+, HL/May 31/97 (300-400) 288

Standing Mickey (holding hat) & sitting Pluto admire smiling soldier Donald standing holding rifle vertically, circa 1940s publicity cel, 3" each; rough drawing of Mickey & Donald; CLA/Jun 7/97 [also see *The New Spirit* & Cel Set-ups] (1000-1500) 1725

Mickey (4-1/4") in formal coat stands watching Donald Duck (3-3/4") rub ball on his right arm, circa 1930s, CLA/Jun 7/97 (5000-7000) 4025

CELS – PARTIAL FIGURE

Smiling Mickey & Donald hold water hose facing right, 1930s, 4 x 8-1/2", CE/Dec 15/93 (2500-3500) 2530

Donald, Goofy & Mickey eat ice cream, 1930s, 4-3/4 x 8-1/2", CE/Dec 15/93 (2500-3500) 2760

2 large-image commercial production cels: smiling & waving Mickey, 8-1/2"; smiling Donald,

---

6-1/2"; circa 1970, S/Jun 10/95 (400-600) 920

J. Audubon Woodlore as accountant squeezing Donald Duck's cheek & pointing upward, 1950s, Disney/INA promotional, restored, 6-1/2 x 8", VF, HL/Nov 19/95 (500-800) 403

2 items: Goofy, 9"; waist-up of smiling Donald looking up w/right hand up, palm out, 9-1/2"; circa 1950s, CE/Dec 12/96 (1000-1500) 690

ILLUSTRATION ARTWORK

Full figures of Pluto (3") pulling milk cart, Mickey (2") in wooden shoes pushing, on elevated path next to waterway with windmills & farmland in background, circa 1936, watercolor on paper, CE/Dec 18/97 (2000-3000) 3450

MODEL ART

2 rough model drawings of Mickey Mouse, 2 key drawings of Minnie Mouse, early 1930s, 4-1/2" & similar, CE/Jun 18/94 (800-1200) 633

Four studio print model sheets of Donald Duck, (Mickey, Pluto, & Goofy also appear), 1936, SR/Fall/94 (400-700) 790

4 full-figure standing portrait model cels: Mickey reading envelope, 6"; Donald, 6-1/2"; Goofy, 8"; Pluto running left, 4"; 16-field, SR/Fall/94 (1800-2600) 2700

4 print model sheets: three of Mickey, one of Minnie, 1937, SR/Fall/94 (600-1000) 750

Matched pair of print model sheets: Horace Horsecollar, 11-1/4 x 13"; Clarabelle Cow, titled "Model No. 1," 11-1/2 x 14-1/4", some repaired tearing; SR/Fall/94 (200-400) 200

3 Ozalid-print model sheets of Mickey, Donald, Goofy & animals: *Mickey's Circus*, 14 x 11"; *Grand Opera*, 12-1/2 x 9-1/2"; *Magician Mickey*, 12-1/8 x 9-3/4", SR/Spring/95 (500-900) 750

20 original photostatic print model sheets from 13 Disney features & shorts, 14-1/2 x 11" to 20 x 16", wear & rippling, SR/Fall/95 (600-1000) 850

63 photostat model sheets from 1930s shorts, S/Dec 14/96 (800-1200) 1840

2 matching print model sheets: Mickey & Minnie, WDC copyright, reprinted in 1980s from 1930s originals, 14-3/4 x 11-1/4", SR/Spring/97 (300-600) 300

STORY ART

8 story sketches: Pluto, Goofy, Mickey Mouse, Donald Duck (2), Donald & José Carioca (2), José Carioca, crayon & pastel on paper, S/Dec 16/93 (800-1200) 1380

14 rough storyboard drawings of Mickey (4-1/2") & Pluto (3-1/2"), late 1930s, CE/Dec 16/94 (1000-1500) 1610

Sheet of storyboard drawings of Mickey (3" & smaller) & Pluto (2" & smaller), circa 1930s, CE/Jun 9/95 (1000-1500) 1150

21 storyboard drawings by Nick George of Mickey & Pluto at beach, late 1940s-early 1950s unproduced short, pastel & charcoal on 8 x 6" storyboard sheets, SR/Fall/95 (2000-3000) 2670

5 storyboard drawings by Nick George of Mickey dressing in beach costume to fool Pluto, 1950s unproduced short, charcoal & pastel on 8-7/16 x 5-15/16" storyboard sheets, SR/Spring/96 (500-1000) 810

30 concept storyboard drawings of Mickey, Pluto & Minnie attending ball from never-released short, 1940s, 5-1/2 x 8", CE/Jun 20/96 (5000-7000) 5520

10 colored storyboard drawings of Donald walking Pluto for proposed cartoon, pastel & charcoal on 8-7/16 x 5-15/16" storyboard sheets by Nick George, SR/Fall/96 (500-1000) 920

20 color storyboard drawings by Nick George: Donald Duck as St. Peter admits Chip & Dale into Paradise, then puts them to work as gardeners; unproduced 1950s short; charcoal & pastel on 8-7/16 x 5-15/16" storyboard sheets; SR/Spring/97 (1500-2500) 1540

DAISY DUCK

CELS – FULL FIGURE

Front view of surprised Daisy Duck in bathrobe & hair rollers, holding coffee pot, 1950s, 7 x 3-1/2", VF, HL/Aug 21/94 (400-600) 672

CELS – PARTIAL FIGURE

Waist-up of angry Daisy Duck, 8 x 10", DL label, restored, VF, HL/Apr 10/94 (600-900) 728

Worried Daisy's head peering up from under

covers, 1940s, restored, 4-1/4 x 6", F+, HL/Nov 19/95 (400-600) — 431

DONALD DUCK
Also see TELEVISION: ANTHOLOGY SERIES

ANIMATION DRAWINGS (also see CELS - PARTIAL FIGURE)/MODEL ART

13 rough drawings of Donald: 10 fighting, 3 scared & running; avg. image size 4"; S/Dec 16/93 (700-900) — 690

3 rough drawings from *Put-Put Troubles, The Village Smithy, Clown of the Jungle*; photostat model sheet for *Donald's Lucky Day*; 4-1/2 x 5" to 10 x 12-1/2"; F; HL/Apr 10/94 (300-400) — 504

3 full-figure rough drawings of expressive Donald Duck, 5" & smaller, circa 1950s, CE/Jun 18/94 (600-800) — 460

Full-figure drawing of dapper Donald standing facing right, 4-1/2", 1940s, CE/Jun 18/94 (400-600) — 345

3 expressive rough head-and-shoulders drawings of Donald Duck matted & framed together, 4" & smaller, circa 1940s, CE/Jun 18/94 (500-700) — 368

Full-figure front-view drawing of long-bill Donald stepping carefully, 1934-35, 4 x 3", VF, HL/Aug 21/94 (500-700) — 840

1940s drawing of Donald Duck dressed elegantly, 4-1/2", S/Dec 17/94 (300-500) — 230

Full-figure drawing of dapper Donald standing looking right, 1940s, 4-1/2", CE/Jun 9/95 (600-800) — 460

Full-figure drawing of Donald in derby hat holding bucket & standing next to water pump, circa 1940 cartoon, 5-1/2 x 7-1/2", VF, HL/Apr 28/96 (300-400) — 546

Full-figure drawing of angry Donald Duck standing facing left, late 1930s cartoon, 4-1/2 x 4-1/2", VF, HL/Apr 28/96 (500-700) — 546

Full-figure drawing of Donald Duck singing passionately to cap perched on end of upright broom, late 1930s/early 1940s, G, HL/May 31/97 (100-200) — 230

12 drawings for Donald Duck cartoons, circa 1939, 4-1/4 x 2-3/4" to 9 x 11", F-VF overall, HL/Nov 16/97 (1000-1500) — 1495

9 polished & one sketchy drawings of Donald Duck likely by publicity dept. as studies for illustrations, 1940s-50s, 4-1/4 x 2-1/2" to 8 x 11", F+, HL/Apr 25/98 (1000-1500) — 2070

ART - MISCELLANEOUS

In-studio drawing of desperado Donald standing, left hand on holster, right hand twirling mustache; likely early 1940s; ink & colored conté crayon on animation sheet; 10 x 7"; F; HL/Apr 10/94 (400-600) — 392

Pen, ink & watercolor illustration of 3 Donalds walking in succession carrying apples on board, 5-1/2 x 7", S/Jun 17/94 (400-600) — 632

5 Donald Duck drawings: story drawing; *Disney Dispatch* sketch; 2 character studies; cowboy portrait signed by Hank Porter; 6 x 8" to 14 x 10", F, HL/Aug 21/94 (800-1200) — 1568

2 expressive portrait cels of Donald Duck (one hand-inked, other Xerox), 1950s/1960s, colored paper backings, gold DL labels, 6 x 8" & 4-1/4 x 7", F, HL/Feb 23/97 (300-400) — 345

Large-image portrait of hatless Donald Duck looking right, 1960s, Disney label for 1959 "INA Spotlight",5-1/2 x 6-1/2", F, HL/May 31/97 (250-350) — 259

CEL SET-UPS

Donald, hand-prepared background, 6" x 7", CE/Dec 15/93 (1500-2000) — 460

Donald wearing hat & holding cook book, print background, circa 1955, gold DL label, 6", S/Dec 16/93 (800-1200) — 805

Donald stands with mallet in hand after explosion, hand-painted background, 4", S/Dec 16/93 (800-1200) — 575

2 sets of hand-inked cels of Donald (as Scarlet Pimpernel? & in sailor suit) & one of nephews from 1950s animated films, 8 x 10", each over color print background, DL label, VF, HL/Apr 10/94 (1000-1500) — 1232

2 full-figure cels of Donald: one hand-inked from cartoon, other Xerox-outline from TV, 1950s/60s, 8 x 10", color print backgrounds, DL labels & papers, VF, HL/Apr 10/94

(800-1200) — 952

2 cels of Donald as Scarlet Pimpernel?, one with nephew, 1950s, 8 x 10", color print backgrounds w/DL gold labels, F-VF, HL/Apr 10/94 (1000-1500) — 1008

Donald jumps angrily at bee, hand-painted background, partial Courvoisier label, 1940s, 4", S/Jun 17/94 (1200-1800) — 1035

Full figure of Donald holding match & cigar, 1950s, DL printed background of yard, 5-1/4 x 3-1/4", CE/Jun 18/94 (700-900) — 575

Waist-up of worried Donald lost in wilderness facing right, 5-3/4 x 2-3/4", multiple cels on watercolor production background, CE/Jun 18/94 (1000-1500) — 633

Full figure of Donald standing holding flash camera, 6 x 4-1/2", 1940s, studio-prepared background, CE/Jun 18/94 (2500-3500) — 1725

Full figure of happy soldier Donald (eyes closed) walking right w/bayoneted rifle horizontally on shoulder, 3-1/2", 1940s, airbrush Courvoisier background, CE/Jun 18/94 (800-1200) — 920

Full figures of Donald Duck as baseball umpire walking with nephews, 1950s, color print background as sold as DL, 8 x 10", VF, HL/Aug 21/94 (700-1000) — 1232

Close-up of Donald Duck[?] driving stagecoach to right with arrows in hat, circa 1950s, DL background & label, 4-3/4", CE/Dec 16/94 (600-800) — 978

Chest-up front view of upset Donald Duck on jungle boat holding pith helmet in his left hand, 4", 1946, hand-painted background, S/Dec 17/94 (900-1100) — 1035

Full figure of irritated Donald standing brushing left sleeve, 3-1/2", early 1940s, dry-brush effects, Courvoisier wood-veneer background, ct, SR/Spring/95 (900-1500) — 1150

Full figure of angry Donald Duck standing on path loading pop gun, 8 x 10", early 1950s, forest background (tempera on background sheet), VF+, HL/Apr 23/95 (2000-2500) — 2464

Waist-up of irritated Donald pointing to his picture on futuristic TV & looking back, 6-1/2", 1970s educational, key master background of suburban home interior, 12-field, two overlays, SR/Fall/95 (500-900) — 500

Full figures of cowboy Donald Duck standing talking to nephew (holding ax), 1950s (TV?), color print background of desert as sold at DL, 8 x 11", VF+, HL/Apr 28/96 (600-900) — 748

Full figure of cocky Donald Duck walking left outdoors, early 1950s, studio-prepared background, 3", CE/Jun 20/96 (1000-1500) — 1150

Full figure of anxious Donald running from butterfly in jungle, studio-prepared watercolor background, 3", CE/Jun 20/96 (600-800) — 863

Full figure of Donald Duck standing squawking into old-fashioned phone, 1940s, 4-1/2 x 4-1/4", complementary painted background, Courvoisier label, inscribed "...Walt Disney", F+, HL/Nov 16/97 (2000-3000) — 2645

Full figure of angry Donald Duck standing facing right in front of door & holding key, 4-1/2", hand-prepared background of house interior, S/Dec 19/97 (600-800) — 1150

CELS - FULL FIGURE

Smiling Donald stands facing left, circa 1970s, 8-1/2 x 11-1/2", CE/Dec 15/93 (1000-1500) — 920

Set of 10 sequential & 3 near-sequential cels of Donald, wearing pink shirt & blue overalls, in fighting position; image sizes and expressions vary; circa 1955; S/Dec 16/93 (3000-5000) — 2875

2 cels: Donald in red hat carrying 2 water buckets; Donald in red cap & jacket launching spear; circa 1950; each with gold DL label; both 5", S/Dec 16/93 (800-1200) — 460

Donald out of control with arrows in hat & barely holding reins [to unseen horse], gold DL label, 5", S/Dec 16/93 (800-1200) — 345

Donald stands with mallet in hand, gold DL label, 4-1/2", needs restoration, S/Jun 17/94 (600-800) — 575

Frowning Donald Duck stands opening envelope, 6-3/4 x 4-1/4", CE/Jun 18/94 (800-1200) — 690

Dapper Donald Duck stands wearing straw hat & bow tie, holding cane; 4-1/2"; 1940s; CE/Jun 18/94 (1000-1500) — 978

Front view of Donald standing holding fruit, 5 x 3-1/2", circa 1950s, CE/Jun 18/94 (1000-1500) — 748

Donald in baseball cap stands looking left, 5-1/4 x 2-1/2", circa 1950s, CE/Jun 18/94 (800-1200) — 552

Smiling Donald stands facing right holding piece of paper, 1950s, seal & WDP label, 6 x 6", VF+, HL/Aug 21/94 (500-800) — 952

Donald receives sheriff's badge from J. Audubon Woodlore? (ankles up), 7", circa 1950s, CE/Dec 16/94 (1000-1500) — 575

Donald Duck as railroad engineer standing with hands on hips, facing right; 4-1/2"; 1960s; CE/Dec 16/94 (500-700) — 575

Donald Duck runs to left wearing mouse ears & counting on fingers, 6", CE/Dec 16/94 (600-800) — 518

Combative Donald Duck facing left & rolling up sleeve, 5", circa 1950s, CE/Dec 16/94 (700-900) — 460

Smiling dressed-up Donald Duck standing holding cane, 5", 1940s, CE/Dec 16/94 (800-1000) — 690

Front view of movie director Donald Duck standing, 5", 1960s, CE/Dec 16/94 (800-1000) — 345

Donald Duck flies (with aid of rope) & waves magic wand, 6", gold DL label, S/Dec 17/94 (800-1200) — 460

2 cels of Donald Duck: waist-up as chef sifting flour, 6-1/2 x 4-1/2"; full figure as ancient Greek standing looking right, 3-1/2 x 4"; 1950s; VF; HL/Apr 23/95 (500-700) — 840

Front view of Donald falling in standing position, 1950s, 5-1/2", CE/Jun 9/95 (800-1200) — 690

Sad long-billed Donald Duck stands holding tummy, circa 1930s, 3", CE/Jun 9/95 (1500-2000) — 5175

Smiling Donald Duck walking forward, circa 1950s, 4-1/2", CE/Jun 9/95 (500-700) — 288

Flamboyant doctor Donald standing looking at upraised left hand [as if admiring object], 1950s, 7-1/2", CE/Jun 9/95 (500-700) — 460

2 cels: partial figure of irritated Donald standing holding paper, looking right; full figure of cranky Donald sitting in nightclothes; Art Corner labels, SR/Fall/95 (400-800) — 490

Donald Duck 50th Anniv. Cel Portfolio: 4 limited-edition hand-inked & -painted cels from *Magician Mickey, Hockey Champ, Bill Posters, & Donald's Crime*; #254/275; 1984; 5-1/2 x 5-1/2" to 7-1/2 x 13"; VF+; HL/Nov 19/95 — 2760

2 full-figure cels of Donald Duck: waving cheerfully & angrily walking under raised umbrella, 1940s, 4-1/2 x 2" & 5 x 3-1/2", restored, VF, HL/Nov 19/95 (800-1000) — 1610

Angry Donald Duck in shower cap & towel running right carrying framed picture of 3 bears over his head, 1950s, gold Disney/INA Spotlight label, 7 x 6", restored, VF, HL/Nov 19/95 (500-700) — 460

2 cels of Donald Duck: hips-up facing left, right index finger to head, eyes closed, 6-1/2; full figure standing holding paper with worried look, 4-3/4"; both 12-field, 1980s educational, SR/Spring/96 (300-600) — 330

Large umpire Donald Duck standing holding baseball, looking down, smiling wickedly & signaling "out", 1950s, 7 x 5-1/2", VF, HL/Apr 28/96 (600-900) — 1265

Happy Donald Duck stands smoking huge cigar, 1960s, gold DL label, 5-1/2 x 4", VF, HL/Apr 28/96 (400-600) — 518

3 cels: Donald (6") waving hands triumphantly; Donald (6") as pirate with parrot puppet on hand; Huey, Dewey, Louie (3" each) in identical scarlet shirts & caps; all need restoration; S/Jun 19/96 (300-500) — 517

Donald Duck 50th Anniv. Cel Portfolio: 4 limited-edition hand-inked & -painted cels from *Magician Mickey, Hockey Champ, Bill Posters, & Donald's Crime*; #267/275; 1984; 5-1/2 x 5-1/2" to 7-1/2 x 13"; VF+; HL/Oct 6/96 (2000-3000) — 2070

Frightened Donald Duck (helmet flying) riding uncontrolled rocket-powered roller skates, *Journey to Tomorrow* (TV or park film), 1980s?, 6 x 8-1/4", VF, HL/Oct 6/96 (300-400) — 259

Publicity cel of smiling Donald Duck standing, circa 1940, 4", CE/Dec 12/96 (700-900) — 748

Hatless anxious Donald Duck running to right,

1950s, 2-1/4 x 3-1/2", VF, HL/Feb 23/97
(200-300)   230

Excited Donald stands holding bubbling test tube, 5-
1/2", 12-field cel, SR/Spring/97 (400-900)   610

Donald Duck in beret & scarf examines script,
circa 1950s, 6-1/4", gold DL label, needs
restoration, S/Jun 21/97 (200-400)   460

Front view of sleepy Donald with arms up, 6-7/8",
original color card background, gold DL Art
Corner label, SR/Fall/97 (300-500)   300

Donald, squatting facing left, holds ax in front of him
w/blade on ground; from Heath book *Donald
Duck & His Friends*, 4-3/4", 12-field 5-hole-
punch cel, SR/Fall/97 (600-900)   401

Smiling Donald Duck driving convertible coupe to
right with golf bag in right seat, 1950s (TV?),
8-1/2 x 4", SR/Fall/97 (600-900)   1090

Journey To Tomorrow[?]: Donald Duck jumping in air;
3-cel progression of Donald skating gracefully;
each approx. 3"; S/Dec 19/97 (600-800)   460

Publication cel of angry Donald Duck hanging from
balloon caught in tree, circa 1940 for D.C.
Heath book, restored, VF, HL/Apr 25/98
(900-1200)   633

Smiling Donald Duck stands facing left, 1950s, 6-5/8",
16-field cel, SR/Spring/98 (600-900)   660

CELS – PARTIAL FIGURE (also see CELS-FULL FIGURE)

Hips-up of angry Donald as western sheriff, 8",
circa 1940s, CE/Jun 18/94 (1000-1500)   1035

Hips-up of Donald Duck wearing fedora & looking
down, 4-1/2", circa 1950s, DL sticker,
CE/Dec 16/94 (500-700)   322

Close-up portrait of happy Donald Duck, circa 1970s,
8-1/2 x 12-1/2"; matching animation drawing,
CE/Jun 9/95 (300-500)   805

Large portrait of happy Donald; matching animation
drawing; 1980s, 7", CE/Jun 9/95 (300-500) 288

Waist-up image of Donald Duck singing with
handkerchief in right hand; Nephew Duck
with Pete (holding trombone); 1950s-1960s;
gold DL/INA stickers; 7 x 3-1/2" &
3-1/2 x 8"; F; HL/Nov 19/95 (800-1000)   690

Large-image portrait of irritated Donald Duck looking
right, 1950s, 7-1/2 x 6-1/2", as released thru
DL, restored, VF, HL/Nov 19/95 (400-600) 748

CONCEPT & INSPIRATIONAL ART/STORY ART

Full-figure polished story/study drawing of Donald
standing looking back & up to right, late
1930s, 3-1/2 x 3-1/2", VF, HL/May 31/97
(150-200)   207

DYE-TRANSFER PRINTS

Angry Donald talks on phone, red & black geometric
background, mat erroneously titled "Donald's
Dilemma," 10 x 8-1/2", SR/Fall/94
(300-600)   275

MODEL ART

3 original photostat model sheets of Donald
Duck, late 1930s, 10 x 12", VG,
HL/Mar 16-17/96 (75-100)   748

DONALD DUCK'S NEPHEWS

CEL SET-UPS

Full figure of smiling Huey sitting outside holding 2
coconut halves apart, circa 1930s/1940s, 7",
Courvoisier airbrush & watercolor
background, CE/Jun 9/95 (1000-1500)   1093

Nephews put finishing touches on sailboat, 12-13/16",
publication set-up with key watercolor
background, SR/Fall/97 (900-1200)   770

CELS – FULL FIGURE

3 cels, each showing 2 nephews in hats & sweaters,
one w/band member's hat & coat, each with
gold DL label & Art Corner stamp, avg. size
4-1/2", S/Dec 16/93 (500-700)   460

Golfer Louie stands on Huey's shoulders ready to
swing club at ball on prostrate Dewey's
head, 9-1/4", 1938, ct, SR/Spring/95
(800-1200)   1680

Happy Huey, Dewey, & Louie ride ocean wave
on sled [jet-ski?], circa 1970s, all 2-1/2",
CE/Jun 9/95 (300-500)   403

Surprised Huey, Dewey & Louie look up to left
while reading comics, circa 1980s,
5-1/2" ea., CE/Jun 9/95 (600-800)   460

Nephew stands on shoulders of 2nd, about to hit
golf ball off head of 3rd; 1938, likely for
publication; 9-1/4"; midline horizontal
crease; ct; SR/Fall/96 (800-1200)   1610

GOOFY

Also see TELEVISION: ANTHOLOGY SERIES

ANIMATION DRAWINGS

Full-figure animation drawing of Goofy in profile,
4-1/2", CLA/Jun 7/97 (500-700)   253

CEL SET-UPS

Frustrated Goofy seated at desk in living room
scratching head while trying to write, 4-1/4
x 2-1/4", watercolor production background,
CE/Jun 18/94 (800-1200)   1380

Full figure of irritated Golfer Goofy standing w/one
hand on hip, holding golf club w/other, circa
1950, 4-1/2", printed DL background of outdoors & gold label, S/Jun 21/97 (700-900) 1035

CELS – FULL FIGURE

Goofy in jester's cap reclines & sips martini, circa
1960, gold DL label, 6", S/Dec 16/93
(400-600)   1840

Goofy walking left & playing flute, 7 x 4-1/2",
CE/Jun 18/94 (800-1200)   460

4 production cels of Goofy (one full figure holding
golf bag), 5" & similar, circa 1960s,
CE/Jun 18/94 (1500-2000)   1840

2 cels of Goofy as big-game hunter from mid-1940s
shorts: standing looking shocked to right;
holding rifle riding on back of elephant
crawling to right; 5-1/2 x 5" & 4-1/2 x 8";
VF; HL/Apr 23/95 (1200-1600)   1456

3 full-figure cels of Goofy from early 1940s: riding
backwards on Percy from *The Reluctant
Dragon*; carrying armload of weapons from
safari film; as cop; 3 x 2-1/2", 6 x 4-1/2",
6-1/2 x 6-1/2"; VF; HL/Apr 23/95
(1200-1600)   1120

Determined Goofy as matador standing waving cape,
looking down; circa 1940s; 6"; CE/Jun 9/95
(600-800)   460

Publicity cel of Goofy as discus thrower, 4",
CE/Jun 9/95 (600-800)   253

CELS – PARTIAL FIGURE

Waist-up of Goofy standing facing left with arms
spread & head back, circa 1950s, 9 x 9-1/2",
CE/Jun 18/94 (800-1200)   978

Knees-up of scared Goofy looking down, circa
1950s, 8", CE/Dec 16/94 (500-700)   518

Hips-up front view of dressed-up, smiling Goofy, 7",
circa 1940s, CE/Dec 16/94 (1500-2000) 1495

Hips-up of debonair Goofy in evening clothes tipping
top hat to right, circa 1940s, 5", CE/Jun 9/95
(600-800)   460

Ankles-up image of serious Goofy standing wearing
safari hat & looking to right thru binoculars,
circa 1945, 5 x 5-1/2", F, HL/May 31/97
(300-500)   288

MODEL ART

Model sheet of Goofy & unidentified character, 1930s,
5" & smaller, graphite on trimmed paper
applied to board, CE/Jun 9/95 (600-800) 230

HOME MOVIES, WALT DISNEY

TITLE ART

5 title cards from Walt Disney Home Movies, hand
lettering on cels over gouache backgrounds,
b&w, 16-field, SR/Fall/94 (2000-5000)   2700

HORACE HORSECOLLAR

MODEL ART

Vintage print model sheet of Horace Horsecollar,
1931, 16-1/2 x 9-5/8", edge wear &
discoloration, SR/Spring/97 (200-400)   200

HUMPHREY THE BEAR

CELS – FULL FIGURE

Smiling Humphrey sleeping on pillow, 7-1/8 x
4-1/4", 1950s, SR/Spring/95 (200-400)   250

Humphrey the Bear (near-full figure) sits & throws
tantrum as Ranger Woodlore watches, 1950s
Disney-INA promotion with gold label, 6-1/2
x 8", F, HL/Aug 6/95 (300-400)   308

Bear in bassinet (Humphrey?) being carried by another
bear, 1950s cartoon, 5-1/2 x 5-1/2", as sold at
DL, F+, HL/Aug 6/95 (200-400)   476

CELS – PARTIAL FIGURE

2 cels: glum Humphrey chest-deep in water;
unidentified; 4" & similar; DL label;
CE/Jun 9/95 (500-700)   978

STORY ART

4 storyboard drawings by Nick George of Humphrey,

1950s, pastel & charcoal on 8 x 6" storyboard
sheets, SR/Fall/95 (200-400)   280

J. AUDUBON WOODLORE

CELS – PARTIAL FIGURE

Hips-up front view of stern Ranger Woodlore looking
down & pointing left, 1950s, 7-1/2 x 9-1/2",
restored, F+, HL/May 31/97 (200-400)   316

JOSÉ CARIOCA

CELS – FULL FIGURE

Smiling José Carioca stands holding cigar & leaning
on umbrella, mid-1940s publicity cel, 6 x 5",
restored, VF, HL/Feb 23/97 (400-600)   431

CELS – PARTIAL FIGURE

Ankles-up of José Carioca doffing hat to right, 6",
circa 1960s, DL sticker, CE/Dec 16/94
(300-500)   173

LUDWIG VON DRAKE

CEL SET-UPS

Full figure of Ludwig as artist standing in forest,
print background, 1960s, DL label, VF+,
HL/Feb 26-27/94 (200-400)   413

Ludwig sits on floor in front of TV & gestures while
leaning on *Mother Goose* book, 1960s, color
print of *101 Dalmatians* background, as sold
at DL, 7-1/2 x 9-1/2", F, HL/Feb 23/97
(200-250)   219

Full figure of Ludwig Von Drake as classic football
player leaning & running right, looking back
& up, arms out; 7-1/4 x 6-3/8"; gold DL
Art Corner label; litho background of
outdoors; SR/Spring/98 (200-400)   200

CELS – FULL FIGURE

5 cels: 4 of Ludwig, 6 to 3-1/2"; cel of small bluebird,
1"; circa 1960; S/Dec 14/96 (400-600)   632

CELS – PARTIAL FIGURE

Waist-up front view of serious Ludwig; plus
unidentified cel; 5-1/2" & similar;
CE/Dec 16/94 (600-800)   207

Portrait of Ludwig wearing patriotic hat & gesturing
with left index finger, relaxing with drink in
hand & feet up; 1960s; gold DL labels; 6 x 6"
& 5-1/2 x 8"; F; HL/Feb 23/97 (200-300) 196

MICKEY MOUSE

**Also see FEATURE FILMS: FANTASIA; TELEVI-
SION: ANTHOLOGY SERIES, MICKEY
MOUSE CLUB**

ANIMATION DRAWINGS/LAYOUT ART

Drawing of smiling Mickey standing facing left holding
rope, circa 1930s, 10 x 12", CE/Dec 15/93
(600-800)   920

16 miscellaneous drawings, mostly from various
shorts, S/Jun 17/94 (1800-2200)   2587

Full-figure drawing of whistling Mickey standing wearing
straw hat, holding cane & flower bouquet,
4", early 1940s, CE/Jun 18/94 (500-700) 345

Full-figure rough drawing of seated Mickey facing
right [playing piano], 7", early 1930s,
CE/Jun 18/94 (400-600)   483

Haughty Mickey [Minnie?] (2-3/4 x 2-3/4") driving
carriage with two haughty horses, circa 1930s,
CE/Jun 18/94 (400-600)   575

Background layout drawing of piano & 7 rough
animation drawings of Mickey, circa 1930s,
4" & similar, CE/Dec 16/94 (800-1200)   978

3 drawings of Mickey & one of car, 4" & smaller,
circa 1930, CE/Dec 16/94 (1000-1500)   3450

2 rough drawings of Mickey Mouse: full-figure standing
& speaking with eyes closed, right hand pointing
upward; unidentified; 1950s; 6" & similar;
CE/Dec 16/94 (700-900)   460

Full-figure drawing of Mickey dancing & twirling cane,
4", circa 1930s, CE/Dec 16/94 (600-800) 322

4 drawings of Mickey Mouse, 1930s, 5" & similar,
CE/Dec 16/94 (600-800)   1610

2 rough drawings of Mickey Mouse: standing facing
right & looking back frightened; unidentified;
6" & smaller; circa 1930s; CE/Dec 16/94
(1200-1500)   1150

Drawing of irritated Mickey sitting facing right,
looking back & down; 3 x 4-1/2"; circa
1930s; CE/Dec 16/94 (500-700)   690

13 consecutive drawings of Mickey, 2-1/2" & similar,
circa 1930s, CE/Dec 16/94 (1500-2000) 2530

Drawing of Mickey Mouse saluting, 3-1/2", 1930s, S/Dec 17/94 (500-700) — 546

3 drawings of Mickey Mouse: full-figure front view of smiling Mickey standing holding film reel; others unidentified; circa 1942; 4-1/2" & similar; CE/Jun 9/95 (1000-1500) — 978

Drawing of smiling Mickey standing facing right & pulling rope, 1930s, 3", CE/Jun 9/95 (400-600) — 368

Full-figure rough drawing of startled Mickey standing facing left, 1930s, 2-1/2", CE/Jun 9/95 (400-600) — 483

Full-figure profile drawing of smiling Mickey Mouse walking left on 2-hole animation sheet, early 1930s, 4 x 5", VF, HL/Aug 6/95 (500-700) — 840

Full-figure front-view drawing of standing Mickey, for Douglas Fairbanks Sr. feature *Around the World in 80 Minutes*, 3-1/4", 12-field sheet, 2-hole punch, SR/Spring/96 (400-800) — 200

4 full-figure drawings of Mickey, 1930s, 4" & smaller, CE/Jun 20/96 (800-1200) — 460

3 items: 2 Mickey drawings, circa 1930s, 3" & 4"; dye transfer of Jaq (5") & Gus (4-1/2") with mat signed "Walt Disney", CE/Dec 12/96 (1000-1500) — 2300

Near-full-figure drawing of excited Mickey sitting on cushion partly behind railing, 1952, unfinished short *Pluto Plays Football*, 5-3/4", 12-field sheet, SR/Spring/97 (300-500) — 210

7 early 1940s animation drawings trimmed & mounted on 100% rag board: *Pluto's Dream House*, 1940; *Little Whirlwind*, 1941; *Nifty Nineties*, 1941; *Mickey's Birthday Party*, 1942; largest 7-1/4"; SR/Spring/97 (700-1200) — 700

5 full-figure drawings of Mickey Mouse including two studies of Sorcerer's Apprentice, 4 x 3-1/4" to 4-1/2 x 9-1/4", VF overall, HL/Nov 16/97 (1000-2000) — 1725

4 final drawings of Mickey Mouse (one from *Magician Mickey*) plus sheet of 5 study drawings, circa 1937, 4-1/4 x 4" to 8 x 11", F-VF overall, HL/Nov 16/97 (1000-2000) — 1955

Full-figure front-view drawing of Mickey standing looking right, holding guitar vertically, early 1930s, 3-3/16", 12-field sheet, animator's notation, SR/Spring/98 (500-900) — 510

ART – MISCELLANEOUS

Mickey head, pencil sketch signed "Walt Disney", back of gelatin print, 10 x 7-3/4", CE/Dec 15/93 (2500-3500) — 4830

Circa 1935 drawing by Walt Disney, signed by Walt "To Christina and Fiona" "With Apologies to Mickey Mouse", 6", S/Dec 16/93 (4000-6000) — 8050

Mickey & Minnie stand beside baby cradle, ink & watercolor on paper by Dick Lundy, 8-1/2 x 9", inscribed & signed "To My Friends–Kenny and Eileen Stewart–Dick Lundy 7-9-30", VF, HL/Apr 10/94 (1000-2000) — 1680

Drawing of Mickey Mouse by Grim Natwick at age 92; pencil, blue conté crayon & red ink on orange paper; signed & dated; 12 x 9", VF, HL/Nov 13/94 (400-600) — 952

Design drawing of Mickey for 50th anniversary portrait by John Hench, charcoal & black ink on paper, 18-1/2 x 14-1/2", signed, notes, VF, HL/Nov 13/94 (700-1000) — 616

Drawing of Mickey's head signed by Walt Disney, red pencil on paper, 4-1/2 x 7", S/Jun 19/96 (7000-9000) — 8050

CEL SET-UPS

Mickey publicity cel, studio prepared watercolor background, WDP label, Walt Disney signature on mat, 5", S/Dec 16/93 (1800-2200) — 4025

Full figure of happy Mickey Mouse walking outdoors to right with hands in pockets, 3-1/2 x 2", circa 1950s, watercolor production background, "To Dave My Best Walt Disney" on mat, CE/Jun 18/94 (3000-4000) — 4025

Full-figure 8"-diameter frontal of smiling Mickey Mouse running movie camera, 5" image, studio-prepared background, circa 1950s, CE/Dec 16/94 (800-1200) — 2760

Full figure of Mickey standing in yard wearing apron & holding scrub brush, facing right, looking & pointing down, 5", 1980s, watercolor production background, CE/Dec 16/94 (1200-1500) — 1093

Full figure of Mickey Mouse on stage gesturing, 5", print background, S/Dec 17/94 (2000-3000) — 2300

Full figures of Mickey (4-1/2") as hunter leading Pluto (4", bone in mouth) on leash to right, circa 1950s, wood-veneer & watercolor background, CE/Jun 9/95 (2500-3500) — 4830

Full-figure publicity cel of Mickey as Mexican cowboy twirling lasso around himself, 1940s, Courvoisier airbrush background, 6", CE/Jun 20/96 (3000-5000) — 3450

Full-figure publicity cel of smiling Mickey walking to right in forest w/hands in pockets, production watercolor background, Courvoisier label, 3-1/2", CE/Jun 20/96 (2500-3500) — 2780

Full-figure publicity cel of smiling Mickey standing facing right w/hands on hips, 1950s, Courvoisier airbrush background, mat signed by Walt Disney, 6", CE/Jun 20/96 (3000-5000) — 10,350

Front elevated view of casually dressed, happy Mickey w/arms out forming half circle, 6-1/8" color print background, ct, SR/Spring/97 (1200-1800) — 1210

Mickey twirls lasso, circa 1940s publicity cel, 6", Courvoisier airbrush background, CLA/Jun 7/97 (2500-3500) — 2760

Full-figure publicity cel of smiling Mickey, hands in pockets, stepping right, 3-1/2"; production background of outdoors; prepared by Art Props Dept. as employee gift, Courvoisier mat & label, some paint cracking; SR/Fall/97 (5500-9500) — 3685

Full-figure promotional cel of smiling Mickey Mouse dressed as gaucho standing twirling lasso around him, circa 1940s, 5-1/2", airbrushed Courvoisier background & label; plus personal letter from Gunther Lessing to original owner; S/Dec 19/97 (1500-2500) — 3450

CELS – FULL FIGURE

Front view of Mickey in tuxedo on logo with arms out, looking down, Mickey's 60th Anniversary, 1988, 10-1/2 x 13-1/2", CE/Dec 15/93 (2500-3500) — 2760

3-1/2" determined Mickey standing holding open jaws of 6" bear, circa 1930, S/Dec 16/93 (2500-3500) — 2300

Front view of Mickey in top hat & tails holding bow tie with both hands, looking left; 6-3/4 x 4-3/4"; circa 1960s; CE/Jun 18/94 (800-1200) — 552

Mickey in tails holds top hat upside down in dancing pose, 4-3/4 x 4", 1960s, CE/Jun 18/94 (1000-1500) — 920

Mickey as mountain climber walks right, 4 x 2", circa 1950s, CE/Jun 18/94 (800-1200) — 1265

Front view of Mickey standing & yawning, 3-1/2", circa 1940s, CE/Dec 16/94 (400-600) — 368

Front view of dressed-up Mickey adjusting bow tie, 6-1/2", 1960s, CE/Dec 16/94 (600-800) — 748

Smiling Mickey Mouse sitting w/guitar in lap looking right, 1970s, 6", CE/Jun 9/95 (300-500) — 403

Smiling Mickey in top hat standing facing right, looking at camera, 7-1/2", CE/Jun 9/95 (600-800) — 920

2 commercial production cels of Mickey Mouse: waist-up front view with arms spread in welcoming pose, dressed in colorful tuxedo; full figure sitting & playing guitar; both 6"; Circa 1970; S/Jun 10/95 (400-600) — 920

Publicity cel of Mickey walking purposefully to left, 1950s, 5-1/2", CE/Jun 20/96 (700-900) — 1150

Mickey in seated position running left index finger along piano keys, 4-1/2", CE/Dec 12/96 (800-1200) — 920

Mickey's 50th Birthday limited-edition portfolio: Mickey & Pete, "Steamboat Willie"; Mickey & Donald, "The Band Concert"; Mickey, Minnie & huge present, "Mickey's Birthday Party"; Mickey & Pluto, "The Simple Things"; Disney Art Program seal, portfolio inset, commemorative logo, SR/Spring/98 (2500-3500) — 2750

CELS – PARTIAL FIGURE

Portrait of smiling Mickey, left arm raised, circa 1980s, 8-1/4", CE/Jun 9/95 (300-500) — 460

CONCEPT AND INSPIRATIONAL ART

3 sheets by Carl Barks from uncompleted Mickey Mouse cartoon *Northwest Mounted*, 1936, 4-1/2 x 8", 9 x 9", 9-1/2 x 10", each signed, F overall, HL/Nov 13/94 (1000-2000) — 1344

8 sketches of Mickey Mouse, early 1930s, 2 x 2" to 6-1/2 x 6-1/2", pencil on two-hole animation sheets, 1930-32?, F overall, HL/Nov 19/95 (1000-1500) — 1380

MODEL ART

Stat model sheet of pie-eyed Mickey from Hyperion Studio, 13-3/4 x 11", SR/Fall/94 (300-600) — 430

1930s stat model sheet of Mickey, titled "Model No. 1," 13-3/4 x 11", SR/Fall/94 (300-600) — 310

2 model sheets of Mickey Mouse, 1930s, 5-1/2" & similar, CE/Dec 16/94 (1500-2000) — 1150

2 model sheets of Mickey Mouse, 1930s, 5-1/2", CE/Jun 9/95 (1000-1500) — 1380

Original model studies of Mickey Mouse for publicity/publication purposes, 10 x 15", ink on Strathmore paper, F, HL/Nov 19/95 (1500-2000) — 1380

Model sheet of Mickey Mouse by David Rose, 1930s, sight 9-1/2 x 12", CE/Dec 12/96 (2500-3500) — 2530

2 model drawings of Mickey Mouse for publicity, 9", 1930s, CE/Dec 18/97 (1500-2000) — 1725

Two matched vintage studio stat model sheets, dated 10/18/38, titled "Latest models of Mickey," 14 x 11", SR/Spring/98 (200-400) — 480

SERICELS

Sericel of Mickey as animator, "Walt Disney Animation Florida Grand Opening May 1, 1989," 6-1/2 x 5", seal, VF+, HL/Nov 13/94 (400-600) — 616

STORY ART

Preliminary storyboard with Mickey Mouse, circa 1930s, 3/4", CE/Jun 9/95 (400-600) — 1150

TITLE ART

Original design drawing of pie-cut-eyed Mickey's smiling face from cartoon opening shots, early 1930s, 6-1/2 x 7", F, HL/Oct 6/96 (1200-1600) — 1035

Promotional title: full figure of Sorcerer Mickey (2") holding wand standing on top of word "Television," SR/Fall/97 (300-500) — 200

MINNIE MOUSE

ANIMATION DRAWINGS/LAYOUT ART

6 drawings of Minnie, 3/4"; 2 layout drawings; 3" & similar; early 1930s; CE/Jun 18/94 (500-700) — 748

3 full-figure drawings of Minnie Mouse, 1928-30, paper has 2 peg holes at left, 3-1/2 x 2" to 6-1/2 x 5", F, HL/Nov 19/95 (900-1200) — 748

3 drawings (2 full figure) of Minnie Mouse for early Mickey Mouse cartoons, likely rough animation or stock poses, 1928-30, 3 x 2" to 5 x 6", F, HL/Apr 28/96 (900-1200) — 748

CEL SET-UPS

Full-figure publicity cel of smiling Minnie standing facing left, 1950s, Courvoisier airbrush background, mat signed by Walt Disney, 6", CE/Jun 20/96 (3000-5000) — 9200

CELS – FULL FIGURE

Coquettish Minnie stands facing right, full-figure, 1970s, WDP seal, 10-1/2 x 13-1/2", CE/Dec 15/93 (1200-1500) — 1150

Front view of smiling Minnie, 7", 1980s, CE/Jun 18/94 (600-800) — 518

Large image of smiling Minnie facing toward left (all but shoe bottoms), 6", early 1940s, CE/Jun 18/94 (1500-2000) — 1380

OSWALD THE LUCKY RABBIT

ANIMATION DRAWINGS

Full-figure drawing of Oswald walking to right, mid-1920s, 2-1/2 x 2-1/2", F+, HL/Aug 21/94 (700-1000) — 1064

Full-figure drawing of puzzled Oswald standing looking left, circa 1927-28, 2-1/2 x 2-3/4", VF, HL/Nov 16/97 (500-700) — 1093

BACKGROUNDS

Original background layout for short, circa 1920s, graphite on paper, CE/Jun 18/94 (800-1200) — 690

PETE

CELS – FULL FIGURE

Determined Peg Leg Pete driving car to left, early 1930s, 3-1/2 x 5", CE/Dec 16/94 (2000-3000) — 1725

MODEL ART

Model sheet of Pegleg Pete for 4 cartoons, early

1930s, 15-1/2 x 12-1/2", SR/Spring/96
(300-700)   330

PLUTO
ANIMATION DRAWINGS (also see CELS-FULL FIGURE)
4 drawings of Pluto in typical dog pose, early 1940s,
3 x 4", F+, HL/Nov 19/95 (400-600)   575
CEL SET-UPS
Pluto hitched to cart of milk jugs, carries jug in
mouth; publication background; 3" length;
S/Dec 16/93 (600-800)   805
Near-full figure of eager Pluto jumping to right, early
1940s unknown production, 6-1/2", 12-field
nitrate cel, master watercolor background
painting of fenced backyard & dog house from
Pantry Pirate, SR/Fall/97 (1800-2600)   1480
Full-figure cel of smiling Pluto sitting with eyes
closed by door (blue pencil & graphite
drawing) marked "Beware of Dog",
3-1/2", S/Dec 19/97 (600-800)   575
CELS – FULL FIGURE
Pluto, 1970s, 6-1/2 x 8", CE/Dec 15/93
(1000-1200)   460
Pluto smiling with ears & tail up, 4" length,
S/Dec 16/93 (600-800)   805
Smiling Pluto sits with back turned, looking back into
camera; from 1950s cartoon; 4-1/2 x 3-1/2";
DL label; HL/Nov 26-27/94 (300-500)   715
Large frontal image of indignant Pluto sitting &
pointing to ground with right front paw,
1950s, Disney Art Program seal, 6-1/2 x
6-1/2", VF+, HL/Aug 21/94 (400-600)   616
Pluto & Dinah walking to right, 1940s, 3-1/2 x
3-1/2" & 3 x 3-1/2", restored VF,
HL/Apr 23/95 (700-1000)   1344
Worried Pluto slinking away with picnic basket
upside down on head, circa 1940s, 7" long,
CE/Jun 9/95 (700-900)   805
Sheepish Pluto sits looking left, circa 1930s, 4",
CE/Jun 9/95 (700-900)   1150
Smiling Pluto walking left, 1950s, 4 x 5", VF+,
HL/Nov 19/95 (500-700)   748
Chastened Pluto crawling left, circa 1940, 1-1/2 x
5", restored, VF, HL/Nov 19/95 (600-800)   575
Startled Pluto lunging to right, 1940s, 4-1/2 x 7",
restored, F, HL/Nov 19/95 (700-1200)   748
Color model cel of happy Pluto sitting looking into
camera, late 1930s-early 1940s, 5-1/4 x
3-1/2", VF, HL/Apr 28/96 (600-800)   863
Side view of happy Pluto standing facing left &
looking back, 1950s, 4-1/2 x 5", VF,
HL/Apr 28/96 (500-700)   863
Exuberant Pluto (on leash) sitting up to right, late
1940s, 5-1/2 x 6-1/2", VF, HL/Apr 28/96
(600-800)   805
Determined Pluto walking sneakingly to right, late
1930s, 2-3/4 x 8", F+, HL/Oct 6/96
(600-800)   518
4 items: cel of Pluto sitting beside Bent-Tail; cel of
Dinah sitting up on hind legs; drawing of Pluto
attempting to crawl away from Bent-Tail Jr.
who has Pluto's tail in his mouth; drawing
of Pluto with hind legs acrobatically up in air,
S/Dec 14/96 (700-900)   460
Terrified Pluto fleeing to right, circa 1940, 3-1/2 x
7-1/2", VF, HL/Feb 23/97 (600-800)   518
Surprised Pluto standing looking left, early 1940s,
5-1/4 x 8", VF, HL/Nov 16/97 (500-700)   805
Eager Pluto standing facing left, looking back & down,
4-1/2 x 5", VF, HL/Nov 16/97 (700-900)   920
Snarling Pluto facing left in half crouch, late1930s-
early 1940s, 3-1/4 x 7", F, HL/Nov 16/97
(400-600)   345
CELS – PARTIAL FIGURE
Sitting Pluto (eyes closed) holding shredded paper in
teeth, 8-3/8", 1950s, DL Art Corner label &
stamp, SR/Spring/96 (300-700)   300
Large-image portrait of suspicious Pluto facing left,
signed by Frank Thomas & Ollie Johnston,
late 1940s-early 1950s, 7", CE/Jun 20/96
(700-900)   1150
Portrait of worried Pluto in sailor hat, paws on
counter top, likely from 1940s cartoon,
4-1/2 x 4-3/4", VF, HL/Oct 6/96 (500-700)   489
2 matched cels from late 1930s-early 1940s Pluto
cartoon: close-up of eager Pluto drooling
profusely (drool on 2nd cel), restored, 6-1/4
x 7-1/2", HL/Apr 25/98 (700-900)   690
MODEL ART (also see CELS – FULL FIGURE)

Ozalid print model sheet of Pluto by Norm Ferguson,
14-1/2 x 11", some edge wear & discoloration,
SR/Fall/94 (125-250)   200
Model sheet "Model No. 1 Pluto The Pup" with one
drawing of Mickey,1931, original studio print,
12-1/4 x 15-1/2", SR/Spring/97 (200-400)   310
STORY ART
Close-up of Pluto with nose to ground, 3-1/2 x 6",
1940s storyboard drawing, CE/Jun 18/94
(200-300)   207

THREE LITTLE PIGS
CEL SET-UPS
Front view of regal Pig on throne, 3-1/3", key water-
color production background w/notes; pigs
hugging, 7-1/2"; from *We Give The United
Way*, CE/Dec 16/94 (300-500)   161
CELS – FULL FIGURE
2 Pigs in Mexican dress playing maracas & bongo,
looking left; 5" & similar; circa 1940s;
CE/Jun 18/94 (400-600)   403
Publicity cel of 3 Little Pigs standing facing left,
1950s, 3-1/2", CE/Jun 20/96 (700-900)   978

UNIDENTIFIED PRODUCTIONS
BACKGROUNDS
Watercolor pre-production background painting of
typical living room from unknown production,
12 x 8-1/2" on punched 12-field board,
signed on rear by Betty Nissen, SR/Fall/97
(500-900)   410

WINNIE THE POOH
**Also see THE NEW ADVENTURES OF WINNIE
THE POOH; SHORTS & FEATURETTES: mul-
tiple WINNIE THE POOH titles**
CEL SET-UPS
Full figures of Christopher & Winnie playing in snow,
watercolor production background, 1980s,
10 x 13", CE/Dec 15/93 (600-800)   1610
Waist-up of Winnie, Tigger & Rabbit going camping,
watercolor production background, 1980s,
10-1/2 x 12-1/2", CE/Dec 15/93 (700-900)   920
Pooh talks to wet Tigger, watercolor production
background, 1980s, 10-1/2 x 12-1/2",
CE/Dec 15/93 (600-800)   805
Ankles-up of confused Pooh & Rabbit standing
together, watercolor production background,
1980s, 10" x 12-1/2", CE/Dec 15/93
(600-800)   690
Winnie & Eeyore play in snow, watercolor production
background, 1980s, 10-1/4 x 13",
CE/Dec 15/93 (600-800)   1955
Pooh, Eeyore, Rabbit & Christopher stand together
watching Tigger dance with inner tube around
waist, watercolor production background,
1970s, 10-1/2 x 12-1/2", CE/Dec 15/93
(600-800)   1840
Winnie, Tigger (holding apple) & Rabbit stand in
orchard looking & pointing up, watercolor
production background, 1980s, 11" x 14",
CE/Dec 15/93 (600-800)   1150
Smiling Winnie dips paw into honey pot, watercolor
production background, 1980s, 10-1/2 x 13",
CE/Dec 15/93 (600-800)   1840
3 cels: full figures of Pooh dancing to Christopher
Robin's drumming; Pooh talking to Gopher;
Kanga smiling; each with lithographic
background; S/Dec 16/93 (2500-3500)   2588
3 cels: Pooh & Gopher; Pooh & Rabbit; large full
figure of Kanga; each with lithographic background; S/Dec 16/93 (2500-3500)   1265
Full figures of worried Winnie the Pooh (2-1/2 x
2-1/2") & Piglet (1-3/4 x 1") sitting in field
looking up, 1970s, watercolor production
background, CE/Jun 18/94 (700-900)   805
Full figure of Winnie the Pooh pulling Tigger out
of water, circa 1970s, key watercolor
production background, 4-1/2",
CE/Dec 16/94 (800-1200)   2185
Piglet (holding wagon, 8-1/2") talks to Pooh (9"),
1980s, watercolor production background,
CE/Dec 16/94 (600-800)   2760
Close-up of smiling Winnie the Pooh in profile looking up, circa 1980s, 6-1/2", watercolor studio-prepared background, CE/Jun 9/95 (700-900)   288
Full figures of Eeyore (4") sitting under tree painting
as Piglet (2") helps, circa 1980s, watercolor

production background, CE/Jun 9/95
(600-800)   1265
Full figures of Pooh (5") & Tigger (5-1/2") crossing
stream while hiking, circa 1980s, watercolor
production background, CE/Jun 9/95
(700-900)   1150
Full figures of Pooh (3-1/2") sitting in tree as Owl
(3-1/2") flies down, circa 1980s, watercolor
production background, CE/Jun 9/95
(700-900)   633
Eeyore & Tigger help Pooh over rock while hiking,
circa 1980s, 11", key watercolor production
background, CE/Jun 9/95 (700-900)   1150
Happy Tigger (full figure, 4-1/2") & surprised Rabbit
(5") outdoors with overturned basket of
vegetables, circa 1980s, watercolor production
background, CE/Jun 9/95 (700-900)   633
Full figure of happy Pooh outdoors with 2 beetles,
circa 1980s, 5", watercolor production background, CE/Jun 9/95 (700-900)   633
Knees-up of smiling Pooh outside amid bees, circa
1980s, 6-1/2", watercolor production
background, CE/Jun 9/95 (700-900)   1265
Full figures of Pooh (5"), Owl (5") & Piglet (3-3/4")
standing outside on boardwalk, circa 1980s,
watercolor production background,
CE/Jun 9/95 (700-900)   633
2 limited-edition cels: "Tug of War", #463/500,
full-color background print; "Hero Party",
#118/500, color print of matching background;
10-1/2 x 15", 11 x 15-1/2"; 1990/1995;
VF+, HL/Nov 16/97 (1000-2000)   2760
CELS – FULL FIGURE
Christopher standing, left profile of Pooh holding
honey jar, Piglet walking, Kanga crouching;
WDP seal; 1980s; 5-1/2 x 12";
CE/Dec 15/93 (1000-1500)   862
2 cels: Rabbit standing facing right holding rope; left
rear view of Eeyore standing; late 1960s; 5 x
8-1/2", VF, HL/Feb 26-27/94 (300-400)   303
Pensive Christopher Robin faces right holding Eeyore's
tail, 6", 1960s, CE/Jun 18/94 (300-400)   518
Tigger about to bounce on Pooh, 7-1/2 x 4-1/2", seal
& label, VF+, HL/Nov 13/94 (700-1000)   560
Surprised Piglet sits on stool facing left, 3", WDP
seal, 1980s, CE/Dec 16/94 (400-600)   230
2 full-figure images of Pooh: walking head down to
left, & sitting frustrated, circa 1960s, 5" &
smaller, CE/Jun 9/95 (400-600)   748
Serious Pooh bending down, paw up to face, talking
to Piglet; "What were we supposed to say?" on
cel; 5 x 7-1/2", VG, HL/Apr 28/96
(600-900)   575
5 cels from assorted features: 2 Poohs (3" & 5"
from neck up); Tigger, 7-1/2"; Rabbit, 4"; Roo,
4"; 1970s; CE/Jun 20/96 (1500-2000)   1380
Winnie the Pooh looks alarmed, 4", S/Dec 14/96
(400-600)   460
Tigger, Winnie, Kanga (each approx. 4") &
Roo (2") wheel a shopping cart thru
store, S/Dec 19/97 (800-1200)   805
CELS – PARTIAL FIGURE
Waist-up of Pooh (5 x 4-3/4") in front of image
of Eeyore (2-1/2 x 4-1/4") in windstorm,
1980s, CE/Jun 18/94 (500-700)   1035
Two 1960s production cels: Winnie (waist up)
ready to dine, 6-1/2"; Owl, 7";
CE/Jun 18/94 (700-900)   805

OTHER COLLECTIBLE ART

CHARLES BOYER
   Charles Boyer joined Disneyland's Marketing Art
Department in 1960. Since 1976 he has done a series
of paintings which have become signed and numbered
lithographs and/or special-use posters. His work is of
interest to Disneyana collectors because of the emotions
they capture. In recent years some of his original paintings have been offered for sale at Official Disneyana
Convention auctions. Here is the history of those sales.

1994 Convention, Walt Disney World, Sep 9, 1994
Mickey Mouse Self Portrait (Mickey drawing Walt),
30 x 40" (12,000-15,000)   44,000
Special Edition Convention, Anaheim, CA, Feb 17, 1995
Disney Characters on Main Street USA Bus illustration
for 1992 Disneyland Teddy Bear Convention,

acrylic on illustration board, 34-1/2 x 22"
(12,000-15,000)   6500
Family Dinner, 21 x 27-1/2"
(22,000 - 25000)   no bids at 15,000
1995 Convention, Walt Disney World, Sep 8, 1995
Barber Shop Quartet, acrylic on canvas, 30 x 40"
(16,000-18,000)   16,000

FLOYD GOTTFREDSON

Floyd Gottfredson joined Disney as an animation in-betweener in 1929. Soon he was asked by Walt Disney to take over the Mickey Mouse comic strip. Floyd did so in April, 1930 and continued until his retirement in 1975. Besides drawing the daily strip, Floyd wrote it from 1930 to 1932, drew the Sunday page from 1932 to 1938, did comic books and picture books, and headed the Comic Strip Department from 1930 to 1946. Floyd Gottfredson died in 1986.

From July 1978 to July 1983, Floyd completed twenty-four paintings based on his classic Mickey Mouse adventures. Commissioned by Malcolm Willits, the series has been offered at auction by Howard Lowery periodically beginning in March, 1993. The works have also begun appearing at other auctions.

The listings include all 24 paintings by title, date completed, and all known information if they have been offered for sale. Prices include the buyer's premium.

Mickey Mouse Outwits the Phantom Blot, Jul 1978
Mickey Mouse and the Sacred Jewel, Sep 1978, watercolor on board, 21 x 16"; plus receipt signed by artist dated Sep 7, 1978 acknowledging payment of commission; 8 x 10" color photo of Gottfredson holding painting; invitations to 1982 party at home of Malcolm Willits honoring Gottfredson & Carl Barks & exhibition of paintings held in 1993; signed & framed, mint, HL/Nov 13/94 (25,000-35,000)   20,160
Mickey Mouse and Pluto the Racer, Oct 1978
Mickey Mouse on Cave-Man Island, Nov 1978
Mickey Mouse the Detective, Mar 1979, watercolor on board, 21 x 16"; plus receipt signed by artist dated March 1, 1979 acknowledging payment of commission; 8 x 10" color photo of Gottfredson

holding painting; invitation to 1982 party at home of Malcolm Willits honoring Floyd Gottfredson & Carl Barks; signed & framed, VF+, HL/Jul 9/94 (20,000-25,000)   24,640
Mickey Mouse and the Magic Lamp, May 1979, watercolor on board, 21 x 16"; plus receipt signed by artist dated May 1, 1979 acknowledging payment of commission; 8 x 10" color photo of Gottfredson holding painting; invitation to 1982 party at home of Malcolm Willits honoring Gottfredson & Carl Barks; copy of 1942 Better Little Book; signed & framed, VF+, HL/Apr 10/94 (20,000-30,000)   16,240
Mickey Mouse as His Royal Highness, Jul 1979, HL/Oct/93 (private sale?)   41,800
Mickey Mouse on Sky Island, Sep 1979
Mickey Mouse Runs His Own Newspaper, Oct 1979, watercolor on board, framed and signed, CE/Dec 18/97 (20,000-30,000)   19,550
Mickey Mouse Adventures With Robin Hood, Feb 1980, watercolor on board, 21 x 16"; plus receipt signed by artist dated Feb 5, 1980 acknowledging payment of commission; 8 x 10" color photo of Gottfredson holding painting; invitations to 1982 party at home of Malcolm Willits honoring Gottfredson & Carl Barks and exhibition of Gottfredson paintings in Burbank in 1993; framed, VF+, HL/Aug 21/94 (20,000-25,000)   did not sell
Mickey Mouse Sails For Treasure Island, Apr 1980, watercolor on board, 16 x 21"; plus receipt signed by artist dated Apr 23, 1980 acknowledging payment of commission; 8 x 10" b&w photo of Gottfredson & others with painting; invitation to 1982 party at home of Malcolm Willits honoring Gottfredson & Carl Barks; letter from Willits to Gottfredson discussing ideas for the painting; signed & framed, mint, HL/Apr 23/95 (25,000-35,000)   did not sell
Mickey Mouse and the Seven Ghosts, Jun 1980
Mickey Mouse in the Race For Riches, July 1980
Mickey Mouse in the World of Tomorrow, Nov 1980
Mickey Mouse in Love Trouble, March 1981
Mickey Mouse Outwits the Phantom Blot, Jun 1981,

HL/Jul/94 (private sale) 42,000
Mickey Mouse in the Foreign Legion, Sep 1981, watercolor on board, 16 x 20-1/2"; plus receipt signed by artist dated Sep 30, 1981 acknowledging payment of commission; invitation to 1982 party at home of Malcolm Willits honoring Gottfredson & Carl Barks; letter from Willits to Gottfredson discussing ideas for painting; copy of Better Little Book reprinting the story; signed & framed, mint, HL/Apr 28/96 (18,000-22,000)   did not sell
Mickey Mouse in the Frozen North, March 1982, watercolor on board, framed & signed, excellent, CE/Dec 18/97 (20,000-30,000)   17,250
Mickey Mouse the Mail Pilot, May 1982
Mickey Mouse and the Pirate Submarine, Jul 1982
Mickey Mouse and the Bat Bandit, Oct 1982
Mickey Mouse in Blaggard Castle, Mar 1983
Mickey Mouse and His Horse Tanglefoot, May 1983
Mickey Mouse and Clarabelle, Jul 1983

OTHER ABBREVIATIONS USED IN ART LISTINGS

anniv. – anniversary
approx. – approximately
avg. – average
b&w – black and white
CE – Christie's East
CLA – Christie's Los Angeles
ct – conservation treatment by S/R Laboratories
DAE – Disney Art Editions
dept. – department
DL – Disneyland
ea. – each
HL – Howard Lowery
S – Sotheby's
SR – S/R Laboratories
w/ – with
WDC – Walt Disney Company
WDP – Walt Disney Productions
WDE – Walt Disney Enterprises